PUBLISHED by PARABLES
Earthly Stories with a Heavenly Meaning

Linda L. Linn

Everywhere There's a Sunrise, Let's Tell The Good News!
By
Linda L. Linn

PUBLISHED by PARABLES
Earthly Stories with a Heavenly Meaning

Linda L. Linn

Everywhere There's a Sunrise, Let's Tell The Good News!
Linda L. Linn
Published By Parables
May, 2020

All Rights Reserved. No part of this book may be reproduced or utilized in any form or by any means, electronic or mechanical, including photocopying, recording, or by any information storage and retrieval system, without permission in writing from the author.

    ISBN 9781951497675
    Printed in the United States of America

Readers should be aware that Internet Web sites offered as citations and/or sources for further information may have been changed or disappeared between the time this was written and the time it is read.

Everywhere There's a Sunrise, Let's Tell The Good News
By
Linda L. Linn

PUBLISHED by PARABLES
Earthly Stories with a Heavenly Meaning

Linda L. Linn

Everywhere There's a Sunrise, Let's Tell The Good News!

Introduction:

This is a work of fiction, except for the Bible Scriptures, which are God's Word and are therefore true. No person in this novel exists in real life except for God the Father, God the Son, (also known as Jesus, the Messiah), and God the Holy Spirit. All the characters, places and events in this novel are fictitious. Any resemblance to actual persons, living or dead, or to actual events is purely coincidental. It is realistic fiction because many of the things and especially the miracles and gifts of the Holy Spirit can really happen.

This novel is meant for adults, not children, although with parental guidance, it has parts that children might learn from or enjoy.

Scriptures are shown by italics, and are this author's paraphrase of the King James Version of the Holy Bible. I chose the KJV because it has no copyright. Basically, what I do is to change words like "thee" and "ye" to "you", "thy" to "your", take the "eth," etc. off verbs, and sometimes use synonyms, to make it sound like more modern English. You can do the same thing as you read the suggested old hymns in a hymnal.

The author encourages you to look up these scriptures in your preferred Bible translation and read them there also. The Psalms, hymns and spiritual songs chosen for this novel really do have meaningful words and teachings. I encourage you to look up the Psalms in your Bible and each hymn and spiritual song in a hymnal or songbook.

There is a list of the characters in the story in the addendum at the end of this novel. It might help you keep track of who is who as you go along.

Please tell your friends where they can buy a printed copy of this book. If they prefer to read ebooks, this novel is available from Google Play Books and free-ebooks.net.

As you read this novel be aware that the five asterisks signal a change of scenarios.

*****

Linda L. Linn

About the Author

The author, Linda L. Linn, has lived in Colorado all her life. She has believed in, and loved Jesus since she was a young child. When not doing housework, cooking or baking, she likes to play the piano, sew, and read. She also enjoys photography and travel. Before she retired, she enjoyed teaching first, second, and third graders in the public school system for 27 years. Her husband, Richard, and she have traveled to see much of God's beautiful creation in the western United States. They are presently living near Montrose, Colorado. This is the first novel she has written but there may be others. Thank you for reading this novel.

*****

Everywhere There's a Sunrise, Let's Tell The Good News!

Dedication:

This novel is dedicated with gratitude to God:
the Father, Son, and Holy Spirit
for creation and the Gospel,
and for guidance and power to serve him.

****

Linda L. Linn

Preview

    This novel is an inspirational romance. Bad news comes to Pine City, and halts a courtship that is just getting a good start. Can these two young people trust God for the outcome? How long will they be separated and what questions might result?
    Both of them agree to pray and leave it in God's hands, but they both feel very close to tears. How could two bad things happen so close together and spoil things for them? They say a very sorrowful good-bye and God bless you. Life goes on for Matt almost as it had before they had met, but now he has a big hole in his heart. Fiona has that same hole in her heart.
    You might be surprised, but some of the events in this story <u>could</u> be happening right in your city or in one near you! Jesus still works through believers to heal, do miracles, save people, change lives, and guide decisions.
    Come spend some time in Pine City, and watch the believers who attend the Grace 'n' Faith Church. They function in unity as Jesus body to show his love and bring the good results of the Good News to their city and other places. As believers, they desire to live for Jesus because they love him and appreciate what he did for them, and because lost people need him. Their lifestyle is a ministry that is accomplished by the power of God. It is by grace, through faith, and is done with love.

*****

Everywhere There's a Sunrise, Let's Tell The Good News!

Prologue

Late winter

Fiona O'Connor was shivering by the time she walked into The Garden Store on this cold winter day. "Good morning, Ernest and Connie," she greeted her bosses. "How are you and your kids?

"We're all fine. Ben and Amy like their new classes in high school. They even like this cold weather," said Ernest Clay as he waved and went back to work.

Fiona laughed, "This is the coldest winter I can remember in a long time. It's a good thing this place is heated. Otherwise the plants I take care of would all be frozen."

"You're right about that, but you look extra happy this morning in spite of the cold," Connie replied.

"Yes, I was thinking about a young man in the church small group that just started this January. I've been observing him for a couple weeks now and I'm very impressed," Fiona responded.

Connie asked, "Is he good looking?" They were talking as they walked into the break room where Fiona put her lunch in the refrigerator and hung up her coat.

"Extremely! He's tall, blond and very muscular. His smile lights up the whole room. But looks aren't everything. I'm also impressed with his comments and the way he acts. I'll keep you posted as I learn more. Right now I want to show you an idea I've been working on for the store." Fiona handed a stack of cards to Connie. "Would you please read these and see if you think they would be good to hand out to the people who buy potted plants? If you like them, would you proofread them and tell me if there are any mistakes that need to be fixed?"

"Sure. But here come some customers. It looks like I'll be too busy right now," said Connie. "I'll keep them with me and read them while I eat lunch. I'll let you know later today."

After lunch she found Fiona and told her, "These cards are fantastic! It's such a good idea to tell people how to take care of the plants they buy. It looks to me like you did a lot of research to be able to write such accurate information. You even made them plant specific and put the plant name at the top. I only found a couple errors that need to be fixed, and I would suggest that you put the plant name in bold. When you have that finished, bring them to the store on your thumb drive and we'll download them to the store computer and print them on some heavy paper. We can use the paper cutter to cut them into cards to hand out with the plants people buy."

"Thank you, Connie, for all your kind words. I'm glad you like this suggestion. I had fun doing the research. I feel like I know the plants even better now. Besides that, you are the one who gave me such good on-the-job training all the time I've been working here ever since I graduated from high school. I appreciate that very much," replied Fiona.

"It's been a pleasure for me. Wow, you've been working here for four years! Time flies," Connie exclaimed.

*****

Matthew (Matt) Anderson hurried from his pick-up into the house the Evans Construction Company was building. "Walt, I sure am thankful that we got this house closed in and can use the heaters in here while we're working!" Matt exclaimed.

"I agree with you. It's been such a cold winter that we would not have been able to work at all otherwise," commented his boss and friend, Walt Evans.

"What's the plan for today?" Matt asked.

"Before I tell you that, I want to know when you are going to find yourself the perfect girl and get married so I can have some 'grandkids' to spoil. You're so much like a son to me, Matt. I wish I could legally adopt you, but I guess that at 24 years old, you are too old for that. But my dear wife, Betty, and I still claim you as our son in our hearts. You definitely take the place of the children we could never have," stated Walt.

Matt responded, "Thank you, and I hope that you know the feeling is mutual. You and Betty have become like parents to me, and that has helped me a lot after losing my own parents in that accident a little over two years ago. I miss them a lot, but my pastor, Don Ross, counseled me, and reminded me that I'll see them again in heaven when I die because all of us believe in Jesus. I hope that someday soon you and Betty will believe in Jesus also. But, back to your question about that perfect girl. I have one in my sights."

"Tell me all about her!" Walt exclaimed. "Is she pretty? What does she look like? How old is she?"

"Whoa! How much time do we have? I don't want to talk away all our work time," answered Matt.

Walt replied, "We have enough time. You got here plenty early today and the other workers aren't here yet, so tell me as much as you can before they come!"

"Okay, I would say that she is more than pretty. She is beautiful. She's tall, slender, and has auburn, shoulder length hair. I would make a guess that she's a couple years younger than I am. She carries herself like a princess, and when she smiles, I just melt inside," responded Matt.

"Sounds to me like you are already smitten!" Walt exclaimed.

Matt answered, "I think I must be. I've only known of her for a couple weeks, but everything I've seen and learned about her tells me that her beauty is more than just skin deep. We met in the new small group that our church organized the first week of January. When I listen to her voice as she shares what she's thankful for, or when she prays out loud, it sounds like music. Her laughter is even better than music."

"Please keep me informed. I think I'm a romantic at heart, and I'll look forward to everything you can tell me. Here come the rest of the workers. The plan for today is to just carry on from where we left off yesterday," said Walt.

*****

Fiona observed Matt at the small group meeting the next week and was even more impressed this time. After that meeting she was talking to her mother, Glenda. "Matt is the nicest young man I've ever met. I'll get to spend some time watching him in another setting because we'll be in a group of four doing a project next Saturday."

That weekend, all four of them in the group enjoyed working together to help an older couple repaint a couple rooms in their house. Lots of talk and laughter made the work go quickly. Afterwards, they all went to eat supper at a quiet restaurant where they had a chance to talk some more and get better acquainted. It was easy to see how they had paired off by the end of the meal.

At that time, Matt suggested, "Maybe we could do some more things together as a foursome, since this has been so much fun. I would like to get to know you better, Fiona."

She replied, "I think that's a very good plan. I would like that also, Matt. I can see our friends nodding so it looks like we all agree."

Consequently for the next four weeks they went together with the other couple to do something one day of every weekend. They did fun things like hiking on snowshoes, playing ping-pong, ice skating, and eating out. They made sure to have time to discuss things as separate couples. They were learning what the other one believed and why certain things were important, plus plans and goals. Fiona was amazed at how often they agreed.

Fiona enjoyed telling her mother and her boss the new things she was learning and admiring about Matt. Likewise, Matt had something new to tell Walt every Monday after his time with Fiona and the other couple on one day of the weekend.

"In the early spring, Matt commented, "Fiona, I would like to be able to date you. What do you think about doing that?"

"I would like to go with you on dates," she answered. "My father, Patrick, is very old fashioned and he would want you to come and ask for his permission to court me. I think he would expect you to promise certain things, and he will tell you what they are."

"I'll be willing to do that. When would be a good time?" Matt inquired.

"I don't know, since I've never done this before," she explained. "I think I need to ask my mother if I could have you over for supper. Then you can talk to my father after supper while Mother and I clean up the dishes."

"Okay. You can let me know at the small group meeting this coming week," said Matt.

So, instead of going with the other couple as a foursome, Matt had supper with her parents and got to know them a little bit. He was very nervous about asking for permission to court Fiona, because she was already 22, but he would do it so that they could continue their relationship.

Patrick O'Connor was very nice about it and made it easy for Matt to ask and make the promise to take good care of Fiona and keep her pure. Permission was granted and the family visited for a while afterward.

For the next several weeks, Matt and Fiona enjoyed dating. It even warmed up enough to play tennis. Matt told her about the house he was planning to build. He had the blueprints ready and showed them to her. She was very interested and told him she really liked the plans for the house. He wanted to tell her it would be <u>their</u> house but he knew it was too soon to mention that. He didn't want to scare her away. He had even decided to keep living in his studio apartment instead of moving to a larger one-bedroom apartment, so he could use the savings to help build the house.

He was taking note of things she liked and wrote some of them down so he wouldn't forget them.

*****

    Just when things seemed to be going so well, and they liked each other more and more each time they went anywhere together, the O'Connor family got some bad news one morning about Fiona's great aunt and her younger brother, Riley. Both reports came within minutes of each other.

    "Glenda and Fiona," said her father, "that was my Aunt Cara on the phone. She is your great aunt, Fiona. She's gotten to the point that she cannot do her daily care because her arthritis has twisted her fingers so much and the pain is very bad. She needs someone to be there 24 hours a day, seven days a week to help with her care, and her son does not seem to be concerned about what happens to her. She's asked him several times for assistance, but all he wants to do is put her in a nursing home. She asked if one of us could come and help her."

    Just then the phone rang again. It was the doctor at the hospital in the city where Riley was attending a university. Patrick turned on the phone's speaker so everyone could hear. "Your son, Riley, went on the last skiing trip of the season today and had an accident. Both of his legs are fractured, and so is his right arm. He needs to have you come pick him up at the hospital when we release him to go home in three days. He will need a lot of extra care until he recovers. If someone in your home could also help him with his studies, he might be able to finish the semester at the university using the computer and the web. In two weeks he will need to start physical therapy to keep his muscles from atrophying. The therapists will tell you how to continue the therapy."

    When that phone conversation was over Patrick suggested, "Let's pray about these problems together and get the Lord's guidance about what to do. Everything has changed so suddenly and unexpectedly and we really need God's help."

    When they finished praying Glenda said, "I feel that we, his parents, need to be here to care for Riley. Patrick needs to keep working, but he can come home from work whenever Riley needs a man's strength to do something. I can quit my job for as long as it takes Riley to recover, and I can help him with his studies."

Linda L. Linn

Patrick asked Fiona, "Would you be willing to quit your job and go take care of your great aunt, so we can both be here for your brother? I know it's an awful lot to ask, especially since you just started dating Matt. But she really desires to stay in her home, and I can't say that I blame her."

Fiona answered, "I can understand that. Many of those nursing homes are not very clean, and some don't do a good job of caring for people. I also know that Riley would not like <u>me</u> to be the one to take care of him here at home and help him with his studies. Mother can do that best. So we really have no other choice. I <u>am</u> very disappointed that I'll have to stop dating Matt. We were making good progress in our relationship. But our Christian responsibility is to take care of our family, so I will quit my job and go take care of my great aunt."

"Thank you for being so unselfish and accepting, Fiona," her dad said. "You can call Matt and set up a time when you can talk to him and explain all that has happened. There's no way of knowing how long Aunt Cara will need your help. I guess we'll have to take it one day at a time."

"You're right. I'll call Matt and have him come over here so we can talk in the living room. Then I'll call Connie and tell her I have to quit my job without giving the customary two weeks notice. After that I'll start packing. I assume that I need to leave tomorrow and drive to her home, so she can get the care she needs as soon as possible," said Fiona.

Patrick said, "Yes, that would be best. I'll call her immediately and tell her you will be there tomorrow evening. I'm sure she'll be relieved."

Connie was very understanding and told Fiona that she hoped there would be a way they could rehire her when she returned to Pine City after taking care of her aunt.

Matt came over within the hour and listened carefully as Fiona told the happenings of the morning. When he remained speechless because of the shock, she added, "I'm very disappointed that we cannot continue dating."

He was able to reply, "I am too. Would you like for us to use the telephone and write letters so we can continue our relationship long distance?"

She answered, "I don't think that would be fair to either one of us. We have no idea how long I'll be needed at my great aunt's house. You might meet someone else and then not feel free to get to know her."

Everywhere There's a Sunrise, Let's Tell The Good News!

"And the same thing could happen for you there in the city where your aunt lives," he added.

So they both agreed to not write or call each other, or continue the relationship they had started. Neither of them would ask the other to wait for, or even <u>hope</u> for the other one, but to pray and leave it in God's hands to see what would happen. But they both felt very close to tears, and wondered how two bad things could happen so close together and spoil things for them.

They said a very sorrowful good-bye and God bless you, before he left. Life went on for Matt in Pine City almost as it had before they had met, but now he had a big hole in his heart. Fiona had that same hole in her heart. Her life was going to change radically in the city where her great aunt lived.

*****

Chapter One

One year and nine months later in some city in the USA, late winter

Matthew 7: 7,8, *Ask, and it shall be given to you; seek and you shall find; knock, and it shall be opened to you. For every one who asks receives; and he who seeks finds; and to him that knocks it shall be opened.*

Ted and Julie Blake came home from church one Sunday and just sat for a while in the car. Both of them looked discouraged and frustrated.

Ted said " Honey, we've tried every church in this city and haven't found what we're looking for."

Julie answered, "I know, and the Bible shows so clearly how Jesus wanted his church on earth to function, but it just isn't happening anywhere in this city."

Several weeks passed with Ted going to work at an auto body shop, and Julie working as a receptionist in a dental office. It just seemed so empty and useless.

Finally one evening, they sat down in the living room after supper to talk and pray about it. Then Julie suggested, "Maybe we could start a search for a city with a church that's doing it right."

Ted replied, "Good idea! We can look on the web, in newspapers, and call our friends in other cities. Surely, there must be one somewhere."

"Yes, I agree. Some people might think we're crazy, because we have our jobs and we're settled here, but they just would not understand how important this is to us. We might want to start a family sometime soon since we're both 24 years old. Of course it would have to be by adopting children, since I'm not able to have any, but this city and its churches would not be where we want to raise our kids, let alone where we want to continue to live," she said.

"You're so right. And it doesn't matter what other people think," Ted stated.

So they prayed and searched, and searched and prayed, and prayed and searched some more. Each one called people he or she knew in other cities and asked if they knew of churches in their city that were more like the church in Acts. Whenever they got a lead or suggestion, they would take off work if needed, and travel to that city to visit the church and see what they thought of it.

A couple months later, they had just returned home from visiting two cities and three churches. Ted asked, "What did you think about Pine City and the Grace 'n' Faith Church that we visited while we were there?"

"Pine City seemed nice, and I liked the church a lot. It was good to see my friend, Maria, and listen to her enthusiasm while she told us how that church really functions like the body of Christ, as the Bible explains in 1 Corinthians. I think it's just what we're looking for!" Julie said excitedly.

"I agree." So Ted questioned, "How soon do you think we could get moved there?"

Julie answered, "Well, we have to give two weeks notice at work, and for our rent here, plus find a place to live there, plus jobs. Wow! It seems almost insurmountable - but oh, so worth it!"

Ted had the same opinion and said, "Let's pray about it and get started looking for new jobs and a place to live. The web will be very helpful to get ideas and then we can make another trip to Pine City for interviews and to look at apartments.

All that didn't take nearly as long as their search for the church had taken. They were happily moved and settled by the end of March in Pine City with new jobs and a nice apartment not very far from the church. Ted would be working at Superior Auto Body Shop, and Julie got a job as a receptionist in a dental office.

*****

Everywhere There's a Sunrise, Let's Tell The Good News!

Last Sunday in March

John 4:24, God is a Spirit: and those who worship him must worship him in spirit and in truth.

After they had moved, the first Sunday at Grace 'n' Faith Church in Pine City was such a pleasant change from all the other churches Ted and Julie Blake had tried. The people were open and friendly. The singing was filled with worship. They sang the words of Psalm 57:10,11 set to music: *Be exalted, O God, above the heavens; let your glory be above all the earth. For your mercy is great unto the heavens, and your truth unto the clouds.* They also sang the hymn: "O the Deep, Deep Love of Jesus," Ephesians 3:18,19; and a Spiritual Song: "God So loved the World" based on John 3:16,17. The sermon contained a Gospel message and later gave solid teaching on how to live the way Jesus told his followers to live.

Pastor Don Ross began, "Today I would like to begin with a story I heard somewhere, but I don't remember where. There was a boy who carved a boat, painted it, and played with it in his pond. One day, he took his boat to a little stream and raced it with some of his friends' boats. During the race, the little boat went faster than all the others, but it got further and further from the stream bank and the boy could not get it back. Eventually the little stream joined a big river and the boy sadly watched, as the rushing water carried his boat far away.

"Months later, the boy was in town, window-shopping. He saw his little boat in a pawnshop, so he hurried in and told the owner that the little boat was his and how he had lost it. 'Well,' said the storeowner, 'some other boy sold it to me and so, if you really want it, you'll have to pay the price to buy it.'

"The boy looked at the price and went home to count all his money. It took every penny he owned, but he went and paid the price. Soon the little boat was in his hands. On the way out of the store, the owner heard him say, 'Now you are <u>twice</u> mine. First I made you and second I bought you back.' The boy took the boat home, cleaned, repaired, and repainted it. Even though it had a few scars from what it had been through, the boy loved it anyway. (Source unknown)

"God did that for us. We call it the Good News or the Gospel. The big difference is the price God paid. Turn to John 3:16 and read it aloud with me: *God so loved the world that he gave his only Son, so that whoever believes in him should not perish, but have everlasting life.* He sent his Son, Jesus, to earth as a baby to grow up and live a perfect life, so that he could pay the penalty for people's sins by dying in their place on the cross. Only a perfect blood sacrifice could pay the penalty. But God raised him from the dead and now he lives in heaven.

"Another big difference is that God wants each sinful person to confess his or her sins and ask God to forgive them, and believe, as it says in Romans 10: 9 & 10: *If you shall confess with your mouth the Lord Jesus, and shall believe in your heart that God has raised him from the dead, you shall be saved. For with the heart man believes unto righteousness and with the mouth confession is made unto salvation.*

"Maybe you are here today and you are like that little boat, lost from your maker and needing to be bought back by the one who created you and loves you so much. I would like everyone to bow your head and close your eyes while I pray a prayer that you can repeat in your heart with me if you want to be saved. I'll say it slowly so you can think about it and keep up. God, I realize that I am a sinner. ... ... I confess these sins to you. ... ... **Name silently, the ones you think of.** ... ... Please forgive me. ... ... Thank you that you already paid the price to buy me back. ... ... I believe in Jesus. ... ... I want you to save me, clean me and repair me. ... ... Amen. My friend if you prayed that prayer with me, you are a new believer and a member of God's forever family because you have believed God's Good News. Be sure to tell someone right after this service about your decision, and please come and tell me also, so I can give you a little booklet that explains more about your new life and has a lot of verses from the Bible that will help you.

"Now, Let's look at John 15: 9-17, and consider how we can do what Jesus said to do there. Everybody follow along with me. *As the Father has loved me, (Jesus), so have I loved you; continue in my love. If you keep my commandments, you shall abide in my love, even as I have kept my Father's commandments, and abide in his love. These things have I spoken to you, that my joy might remain in you, and that your joy might be full. This is my commandment, that you love one another, as I have loved you. Greater love has no man than this; that a man lay down his life for his friends. You are my friends, if you do what I command you. From now on, I do not call you servants; because a servant does not know what his master does; but I have called you friends; for all things that I have heard of my Father I have made known to you. You did not choose me but I chose you, and ordained you to go and bring forth fruit that will remain: that what ever you shall ask of the Father in my name, he may give it to you. This is what I commanded you: Love one another."*

Pastor Don continued, "Jesus said to love each other as he had loved them. That same week, Jesus died on the cross. Think about what God's love is like and how different it is from our own human ways of loving. Talk this over in your small group this week and practice it with each other. Next Sunday, we'll study love more in depth.

"Here is an announcement especially for parents of young children. Resurrection Sunday, which many people call Easter, will be in two weeks. Your children will be seeing and hearing a lot of things about the Easter Bunny. Be sure that you teach them the difference between make believe and reality so they won't be confused.

"Oh, and remember that <u>next</u> Sunday our church service time moves to 2 PM on Sunday. Call and remind your friends about that if, they aren't here today. Now, if any of you prayed that prayer with me, grab someone and tell him or her about it. He or she will be thrilled, and so will all the angels in heaven. I will be also, and I'll give you that booklet I talked about if you'll come see me. Now lets sing 'Love One Another' and then you are dismissed."

A couple of people went to tell the pastor they had prayed that prayer with him. He <u>was</u> thrilled and gave them a little booklet to read that would tell them more about being a new believer in Jesus.

After the service, many people greeted Ted and Julie like they had the other Sunday they had visited, so they felt welcome. Later, Pastor Don sought them out and asked it they would like to come over for lunch. They were glad to be asked. It was a wonderful meal and a nice time of getting to know Pastor Don, his wife, Anita, and their two children, Timmy, soon to be 5 years old, and Mary, soon to be 4 years old.

When they all had finished dessert, they went into the living room for more conversation while Timmy and Mary entertained themselves in the corner with some quiet activities.

"Ted, would you be comfortable telling us your story of salvation? We always enjoy hearing how others came to Jesus," said Pastor Don.

Ted replied, "I'd be glad to. I was a teenager, feeling rebellious about a lot of things. My parents were fit to be tied, because nothing they said or did made any difference. They finally grounded me except for going to a youth group they had heard about at a church in town. The youth pastor was very patient, and helped me to see that I was headed down a very destructive path. Then he told me what would eventually happen to me if I continued on that path. It says in Romans 6:23a, *For the wages of sin is death*, not just physical death sometime, but eternal separation from God and from all the members of my family who were saved. Then he taught me about how Jesus had lived a perfect life so that he could die as the sacrifice for all men's sins, and offer forgiveness to all who believe in him. I needed that, so I repented of my sins, asked God for his forgiveness and for him to change me. He turned my life around!"

"Thank you, Ted. The angels in Heaven were rejoicing that day for sure!" said Anita. "Julie, will you tell us your story?"

"Of course. Mine is somewhat similar to Ted's except that I was not in rebellion. I always thought that I was a good girl, and it wasn't until I was a teenager in that same youth group that I realized I was indeed a sinner in need of a Savior. The youth pastor was a good teacher. Ted and I both came to Christ at the same meeting. We were both baptized in water that same month. It wasn't too long after that, that we started dating, and you know how that part of the story ended," laughed Julie, joined by the others. "I think our salvation is what has made our marriage so special."

"I certainly agree with that. Only a marriage with God and love at the center can ever be special. What made you decide to move to Pine City?" asked Pastor Don.

Ted answered, "After we got married, we moved away from the city that had the youth group, which we had outgrown anyway. For years, we've been studying about the church in Acts, and have attended many churches looking for one that was close to that model."

Julie continued by telling them about their web, phone, and traveling search. "I was so glad when I called Maria Gomez, my former college roommate, and she told us about this church. We visited here about three weeks ago and were very impressed. I noticed that she wasn't here today."

"No, sometimes business takes Maria out of town for a while. It is usually on a weekend, but it can't be helped and it's confidential, so I can't tell you about it," said Anita.

Ted asked, "Would you please tell us more about the small groups you mentioned in the sermon?"

Pastor Don said, "Of course! They are really the church in action – where the real 'life of the church' happens.. Without them we would not be all that different from many other churches. "

"That's what Maria said on the phone," interrupted Julie. "Oh, I'm sorry, I shouldn't interrupt."

"It's okay. ... Anyway, the groups meet at least once a week and have time for singing, praise reports, teaching on some topic related to living for Jesus, and a 'conversational' prayer time instead of prayer requests. Some people take notes during that time, so they can continue praying at home. Often during the prayer time someone will ask the Lord a question or for guidance and another person will have a prophecy or a word of knowledge or wisdom that answers it. After the prayer time, there's usually time for fellowship and refreshments."

Anita added, "The meeting typically lasts about two hours and is usually after supper on a week night in the home of one of the members, as it says in Acts 2:46. People take turns being the host, and there's a facilitator for each group. If no home is available, the group meets in the lunchroom of the church annex building. Some members only have studio or very small one bedroom apartments that aren't large enough for a group of 10 to 16 people, but they want to take a turn as host so they bring refreshments and set the lunchroom up for a small group meeting."

"Each group is made up of the same people for the calendar year. This gives people time to get to know each other, learn to work together, and become comfortable using their spiritual gifts and other talents. Don't worry. We don't give people a 'spiritual gifts' test, because it says in 1 Corinthians 12:4 and 11, *there are different gifts, but the same Lord, and The Holy Spirit himself, distributes to every person as he wills*." Don said.

"Wow!" said Julie, "I wish I'd been taking notes! It all sounds wonderful, but it's a lot to take in."

Anita replied, "It's not a problem, we have a little booklet with all that information and more in it, and we'll be sure to give you one before you go home."

"Where do we sign up? Ted asked enthusiastically.

"We'll check with the facilitators and find one that has room for a couple of new members and let you know just as soon as we can. Do you have a phone number where we can reach you?" asked the pastor.

"Yes." Ted gave his cell phone number. "Just leave a message if I'm at work and/or can't answer. Your children have sure been good over there while we've been talking. If you need to get ready for an evening service, we had better leave so you'll have time."

"Thank you for the compliment. They really _are_ good children," agreed Anita. "Actually, we only have the one service on Sunday because other churches share our building. Do you remember that Don reminded the people that we would meet at 2 PM, starting next week? We'll explain the reason for that to you at another time so you won't feel so overwhelmed."

"Okay! We'll look forward to it. Thank you so much for the delicious lunch, wonderful fellowship and all the information. I'm feeling excited about this new adventure we're about to embark on," Julie said and smiled.

Handing Julie a booklet, Anita nodded. "Yes, with the Holy Spirit leading the way, it's bound to be an adventure!' We'll be in touch soon."

Good-byes were said, and Ted and Julie went out into a gorgeous spring afternoon. Pine City was in a beautiful part of the country, and signs of spring were already starting to appear. Not too far in the distance, snow-capped mountains made a majestic backdrop, and the sky was exceptionally blue.

When they parked at their apartment, Julie suggested, "Let's take a walk around the neighborhood since it's still early in the afternoon and not too cool. Besides, we've been sitting for a long time and I need some exercise."

"Great idea. Let's put our Bibles and the new booklet in the house and get some warmer coats and comfortable shoes before we leave."

As they were walking, Julie exclaimed, "Oh! Look, here is a crocus blooming already, and I'm pretty sure these will be daffodils and tulips soon. Spring is a good time to relocate and start on this new adventure. I'll have to admit though, that I'm a little bit nervous."

"Me too, but remember _who_ is really in charge. There might be some difficult things, but the Lord will guide and help us," returned Ted.

"You're right, of course. No sense borrowing trouble. This is a nice neighborhood. There's even a little park right over there. What's more, our apartment isn't very far from our jobs," said Julie.

Ted replied, "For sure. I can even walk to my job from here, so you can drive to the dental office since it's further away. That way, we can make-do with just one car, and it will save some money."

"Yes, and <u>maybe</u> I'll be able to find a teaching job at one of the elementary schools in the area. I miss teaching," sighed Julie.

"I know. It's too bad that they had to lay off so many teachers last year," Ted concurred. "But maybe this city won't be as financially strapped. Spring might be a good time of the year to start your search. You're a good teacher, Jewel."

She warmed and smiled at his use of the nickname he had given her and which <u>only</u> he used. She felt very blessed and well loved. "Thank you, Ted."

They walked some more, so they could enjoy and get better acquainted with the area. Then they tuned to go home along another street since it was beginning to cool off.

"Look over there, Ted! There's an elementary school right there and its only about two blocks from our apartment! Let's pray that I can get a teaching position there, if it's the Lord's will," bubbled Julie.

"Yes, let's! Just as soon as we get inside where it's warmer!" Ted said.

*****

Maria Gomez got home that Sunday evening, very tired from what seemed like an <u>extra</u> long weekend working out of town, taking care of some business that her employer would entrust to nobody else but her.

"I'm not sure it's a compliment to me that my boss, Mr. Jason Beckett, will let <u>only</u> me to do this particular job for him. I simply know that it really tires me out, and besides that, I missed church and seeing Julie on her first Sunday there this morning. Phooey!" Maria said all this to her cat upon entering her studio apartment. "Did you miss me? I see you didn't make too big a mess out of the place while I was gone. I'm happy about that." She picked up the cat and stroked her soft fur. Her calico cat answered with a contented purr.

She continued her one sided conversation with her cat saying, "Oh well, the overtime pays well, and I can give the extra money to the helps fund which can help people in need at church. Now that I'm on that committee at the church, I've found out that they carefully screen the applicants so that only needy believers, like it says in Acts 2:45, are given money. Then they are assisted to find jobs so they can be independent as soon as possible, as it says in 2Thessalonians 3:10 and 12.

"Maybe Julie will call tomorrow and I can ask her over for a visit after work sometime. We have a lot of catching up to do. Well, I'd better unpack, then fix and eat supper so I can get to bed early and maybe catch up on some of that lost sleep before I go to work tomorrow."

Suddenly she realized her bad attitude. "Lord, forgive me please, for complaining and help me to be content. Thank you for safety going and coming, and also for my home. It really is just the right size for just one person, easy to keep clean, and a good reminder to not purchase things that I don't really need." She remembered that Colossians 3: 23 says: *Whatever you do, do it heartily, as to the Lord, and not as to men.*

Maria spent the rest of the evening at peace and thankful. She even remembered that she could listen to the church service she had missed by going to the church web site on her computer. It was very good to listen while she unpacked and put her things away. She did get to bed early and had a restful sleep.

*****

Monday

The next morning after breakfast, Ted and Julie went to their new jobs and they were very much like the ones they had had in the other city. That helped with the transition and they started learning the names of their co-workers and finding out more about their schedules and what was expected of them.

*****

Maria woke feeling rested and went to work after breakfast. She was an accountant at Beckett CPA's, in a large office building downtown. Her boss, Mr. Jason Beckett, was the son of the founder of the company. He called Maria into his office shortly after she arrived. She gave him a full report about the weekend, and he seemed pleased. "You're doing a great job there, and I want you to know that I appreciate your willingness to do this on the weekends that I can't go myself, " he said.

"You're very welcome, Sir. I'm thankful I can be of assistance, and it's good to know that you think I'm doing a good job. I'll go back to work at my desk now," Maria said. When she sat down at her own desk, the first thing she did was to pray silently for patience to continue going when he asked her to and she gave thanks that he was pleased with her efforts.

*****

  Since Matt was the foreman now, he arrived 30 minutes early for the second shift of Evans Construction Company so he could talk to his boss. He needed to find out the plan for the afternoon, before Walt went home. At 60 years old now, Walt was ready for a rest. They were presently building a new home for the mayor of Pine City, and it was coming along nicely.
  By having two shifts, the hours of daylight during daylight savings time, were used to full advantage without either crew getting too tired. Since breakfast and a late lunch, <u>or</u> lunch and a late supper were eaten before or after work, no time had to be taken off to eat a meal during the time at work. They did have a "coffee" break half way through, and most of the workers ate an energy bar and had a nutritious protein drink along with it. First shift workers started at 7 AM and left at 2 PM. Second shift workers started at 2 PM, and left at 9 PM. The foreman had one half hour extra on the beginning of his work time so he could listen to the boss' plan and prepare for the day's work.
  When Walt saw Matt arrive, he hurried over and greeted him with a smile and a slap on the back. "Hi, Matt! It seems like it's been long time since I've seen and visited with you. I liked it better when we were both working all day together. But I'll have to admit that this two-shifts idea of yours is a good one, especially when people are in a hurry for completion."
  "And who isn't?" inserted Matt. "But, I agree with you. I miss our times of working together also. You've taught me <u>so</u> much about contracting and building! It's way more than I could have learned by going to a special school. Besides, you've become like a dad to me, and that means the world to me. I really appreciate you."
  "The feeling is mutual!" Walt said and they both smiled. "Now here is the plan for the second shift crew," and Walt went on to explain the next phase of the project.
  "Thanks Walt. Now, I do hope you are headed home to get some rest. You look tired. Maybe this coming Saturday we could take some time to visit since we don't work on weekends," Matt suggested. He had been looking for a chance to question Walt about the discussion they had had about a month ago.

"That sounds good," answered Walt. "And yes, I intend to go home and rest. I <u>am</u> tired. See you tomorrow."

*****

The Blakes got home within minutes of each other after their first day at their new jobs. Each one shared how they day had gone while they both helped getting supper on the table. Ted prayed before their meal, "Father, thank you that Julie's and my jobs are off to a good start, and for your provision of this good food, nice apartment and a good church. Please continue to guide all our decisions and help us to do your will. I pray in Jesus precious name, Amen."

After supper and cleanup, Julie said, "I've been thinking about Maria Gomez. Would it be okay to ask her to come over here for supper tomorrow?"

Ted nodded. "That would be fine."

"Okay, then, I'll call her right now," she said. Julie dialed and waited for Maria to answer. "Hi, Maria this is Julie. ... ... I was disappointed that I didn't get to see you at church yesterday, but Anita explained that sometimes you have to be out of town on business. ... ... I'd like to see you soon. Could you come to our apartment tomorrow evening for supper at about 6 PM? ... ... Well, maybe you could bring a few of your famous sopapillas for dessert. ... ... Great, we'll see you then. Bye and God bless you. ... ..."

"Sounds like a go," Ted said. I think I'll go to bed early tonight."

"Me too, Julie agreed. "I think the move and all the new things are catching up with me. Even though they're good things, they can tire us out, since we're not used to them." Ted nodded and they both went to get ready for bed.

*****

Tuesday

At breakfast, Ted remembered to look at his cell phone. "Oh, here's a message from Pastor Don! I forgot to check yesterday!"

"Oh, well. Let's listen to it now while we eat, okay?" asked Julie.

"Yes, here it goes with the speaker on. "Hello, Ted and Julie. This is Pastor Don. Anita and I talked with the other facilitators and decided that we would like to start a new small group. It will meet on Saturday mornings, from 9:30 to 11:30 and will accommodate some people who work evenings and can't get to an evening group. Do you think that time would work for the two of you? Talk about it and let us know. You have our phone number in that little booklet we gave you. Good bye."

"What do you think, Ted?" Julie asked.

He answered, "As far as I can tell, it sounds like it should work. Plus, it might be better to get into a group that's just starting up rather than one that has already been going for three months."

"I agree. Will you call him back and tell him that it sounds good to us?" After Ted nodded, she continued, "Thanks! I can hardly wait to see what it will be like. I wonder if they'll start this coming Saturday? Maybe you could ask that when you call."

"I'll do that now, and turn on the speaker so you can hear." They heard the dial tones and the rings.

"Hello, Don Ross speaking."

"Hi, Pastor Don, this is Ted Blake. Julie and I think that time will work out well for us," said Ted.

"Great!" Don said. "We'd like to get started this coming Saturday, but have a few details to work out about a place to meet and some more people to call who might want to join the group. We like to have at least ten but not more than 15 or 16 people in a group. I'll call you later this week and let you know the location." Ted thanked him and they both said goodbye and God bless you.

"Wow! You didn't even have to ask! They seem like such nice people. Well, we better hurry and get ready, or we'll be late getting to work. I love you, Ted!" Julie finished.

"And I love you too, Jewel, my precious jewel." ... (Hugs and kisses) ... "Now, let's go get ready for work," laughed Ted, and they both went to do just that.

*****

It was his usual time to arrive for work on Tuesday, but Matt was a little preoccupied, thinking about the phone call he had received from Pastor Don that morning. He had been hoping and praying for a way to get back into a small group since a couple weeks before, when Walt had agreed that two shifts would be a good idea. If only Walt had wanted the second shift, he would still be in his group. But of course, the older man needed to take the first shift so that he could go home and rest in the afternoon. It wasn't easy to make time for rest in the morning when you didn't feel tired yet. So it had been the best decision.

Therefore Matt had left the small group desire with the Lord, because _he_ knows best how to work it out anyway. When Matt got the phone call about a Saturday morning small group starting this week asking if he would be interested, Matt almost jumped up and down for joy like a kid, in spite of his "mature" 26 years of age. "You did it, Lord! I had no idea how you would, but you did, and I thank you very much!" he had prayed.

Now he was still thinking about it and smiling, so when Walt spoke to him saying, "You look mighty pleased about something, Matt!"

"Oh! My mind was somewhere else. Did you say something before?" asked Matt.

"Noooooooo, I just watched you smiling for a while and wondered why," said Walt.

Matt answered, "Well, I _am_ very happy about something the Lord did for me. Do you want me to tell you about it?"

"Sure! Did he bring you a girlfriend? That would sure be nice," Walt kind of teased.

"No, I'm not really sure I want one. Unless it could be Fiona, but no, I'm not allowed to even think that. But this is very nice for me. I haven't been able to attend my church small group for a couple weeks, and Pastor Don called this morning to tell me about a Saturday morning small group that's just starting this week. He asked if I'd like to join it and I told him of course. Our church small group meetings are very special. I'll tell you more about it some time if you like, but right now I better have you tell me about the work plans for second shift!" stated Matt.

"Okay, but I'm a little disappointed because I _would_ like to see you happily married, with some little ones that I could treat as grandkids," returned Walt

"I understand, and I'll tell you what!" said Matt, "I'll pray about that very thing and keep you posted."

"Maybe I'll pray about that too," said Walt.

"Please do! Perhaps I need all the help I can get," replied Matt.

Then they got down to the business of plans for the second shift in time to be ready when the workers arrived and they were usually all on time.

Later that day when Matt and Jeff Spencer had a chance to talk at break time, Matt asked, "Jeff, did Pastor Don call you ---"

"Yes," interrupted Jeff, "about a new small group starting this Saturday morning and I've been so excited about it that I could hardly keep from asking you while we were working, if he had called you also!"

"Yes, he did, and I felt like jumping up and down for joy like a little kid. I didn't realize how much I would miss going to a small group until it happened. This is very good news for us." replied Matt.

"For sure," said Jeff. "This is an answer to prayer! Karen is overjoyed as well. She had gotten her hours changed at Subway so we could have some morning time together, and therefore she hasn't been able to attend a small group either. Besides it's much nicer to be able to go together!"

"I'm sure you are right about that, since you're an 'old' married man!" teased Matt.

Jeff laughed. "Do I hear a little longing there?"

"You know it!" exclaimed Matt.

"Yes, I do, and you know that Karen and I continue to pray for you about that issue. Don't give up, Matt. Keep being patient. Remember, God is in control and his timing is best," encouraged Jeff.

"You're right of course," agreed Matt. "Thanks, I needed that reminder."

*****

After work, Maria hurried home and took a batch of dessert sopapillas out of the freezer and put them in the oven to reheat, humming as she worked. They would be ready to take over to Julie and Ted's apartment when it was time to go. She was glad that she had helped them get unpacked after the moved to Pine City, so she knew right where it was, not very far from her own apartment. While the sopapillas were in the oven, she changed into something more casual than her work suit and wrapped the house-warming gift she was going to take to them. Having Julie back in her life was like a balm to her soul. They had been as close as sisters in college, and even though Julie was married now, Maria hoped they would get to spend time together often, now that they lived in the same city.

When she arrived on time at Ted and Julie's apartment, Julie was right there to greet her with a warm embrace. "Yummy, those smell <u>so</u> good! Maybe we'll eat dessert first! Welcome, Maria we're very glad you could come over tonight - and not just for the sopapillas either. I've been thanking God that I can have such a special friend living in this city!"

Maria smiled, "And <u>I've</u> been thanking God that you moved here because I have never yet found another friend as good you've been!"

"You're going to have me in tears and then Ted will laugh at us. Come on into the kitchen and we'll put this dessert where it can stay warm while we 'clean up our plates' first. Oh, what's this?" Julie asked, seeing the package.

"Just a little welcome to Pine City gift," answered Maria. "Let's wait until after dessert for you to open it. I'm starved and it all smells so good! Here, put the honey in there where it can stay warm also."

The meal was delicious, and they all got a good laugh when Ted tried to eat his sopapilla after declining a lesson on how to do it. He had powdered sugar all over, and honey running down his chin and dripping from his fingers, but he declared, "Those are the very best dessert ever!"

Fellowship and fun continued in the living room and when Julie opened the present, she exclaimed, "Maria! This is just perfect. You always did know how to pick out just the right thing to give someone. That's really a special talent. I'll enjoy putting this picture in my kitchen and will think of you every time I see it. Now this place seems more like home. Thank you very much Maria!" And Ted agreed.

"You're very welcome, Julie and Ted. This has been a fun evening, and now I had better hurry home. Morning comes incredibly soon on week days," replied Maria.

*****

Meanwhile during the day, Anita had been making more phone calls to people who might be interested in joining the small group and maybe even hosting the first meeting. When Anita called the Suehiro home about 9 AM, they were thrilled with the news of a group they could attend and offered their home for the first meeting without being asked.

"What a blessing to have such generous people in our church," Anita told her husband when he got home. "Now we can tell the rest as we call them, when and <u>where</u> the meeting will be."

Everywhere There's a Sunrise, Let's Tell The Good News!

"Yes, and since we only know about a few other people who work evenings, our first meeting may be rather small. But that might be good because then the Blakes won't have so many new people to meet all at once. I can announce the group at our new 2 PM Sunday service time, and maybe we'll have some others who want to come to the next meeting," concurred the pastor.

Then they called the other people they knew about. Pastor Don had called Matt, and then Jeff and Karen Spencer before he went to work. They were overjoyed about the group and said they would be there. A single woman said she would plan to come on Saturday. Of course, by the time they called Ted, he wasn't available, so they left a message telling them of the location for the Saturday meeting and giving directions to the house.

*****

After Maria had left the Blakes, Ted and Julie listened to the message from Pastor Don, looked at a map of Pine City and figured out that it was only a few blocks from their apartment. It would be easy to find. Julie called and thanked the pastor for leaving the message. With great anticipation they sat down and started to read the little booklet the pastor's wife had given them about small groups so that they would feel more prepared for Saturday morning.

*****

Wednesday

After work and supper on Wednesday, Julie told Ted that she would like to understand why the church time was changing from 12:00 to 2:00 PM.

Ted replied, "So would I. Noon seemed like an odd time anyway, so I'm glad the time is going to be at 2 PM instead. I'll call Pastor Don and see if we could meet with him or them so it can be explained."

"Thank you, Ted. I'm so glad you listen to me and understand how I feel, " said Julie.

"You're welcome, and the feeling is mutual." Ted smiled and squeezed her hand.

Then Ted called the pastor and they set up a meeting for 7 PM the next evening. "He said we would have time for other questions also if we have any, so this gives us a day to think about it."

"Oh, before I forget, Maria called me on our lunch break today and asked if I would be able to come over for a "girls only" chat on Friday after supper. I told her I would check with you and let her know, " Julie explained.

"Sure," Ted answered.

Julie said, "Okay, I'll call her and say that I can be there at about 6:30. I'll plan to stay only a couple hours so I can get back home and have time with you before an early bedtime so we can be fresh for our first small group meeting on Saturday. Did you have any questions about what we read in the little booklet?"

"Yeah, I had a couple, I'll mark them in the booklet and we can ask Pastor Don about them tomorrow. How about you?" Ted asked.

Julie answered, "I did also, and I'll mark mine when you are finished with yours. Perhaps it will all be a lot clearer when we've been to a few meetings."

"Yes, this is all so new and different for us, since we've never attended a small group before. But even if we had, it would probably have been very different from what this one sounds like," added Ted.

Julie agreed, and asked, "How was your day, Ted? Is your new job going well?"

"It was a good day. I'm getting better acquainted with my co-workers and have learned my way around the shop, so to speak, so I know where the tools and materials can be found, and what is expected of me, so I'm not quite as tired as I was the first two days after work. How about your job, Julie?" he asked.

"I was pretty overwhelmed and lost on Monday, but the lady who trained me was very helpful and thorough. I'm thankful that she agreed to come back to the office on Monday morning for an hour to train me, even though the Friday before was her last day. Her baby is due in about two weeks, and she wants time to arrange things in the nursery and finish the baby clothes she's been making. She is very excited, and I'm glad for her. Somehow I don't think we are ready to be parents yet. Maybe after we feel more settled in Pine City and in the Grace 'n' Faith Church and in the small group, we can pray and think more about it.

"Anyway, back to the original topic, I had a good day too. Since this is a dental office for children instead of adults, it's fun to see the kids come in with their mom and/or dad and watch how the hygienists and dental assistants and dentists help them to relax and have fun, in spite of whatever procedure they're having. I'm glad to be working in such a nice place," Julie stated enthusiastically.

"I'm happy to hear that, Jewel. Even though you aren't teaching, you'll still have opportunities to help, interact with, and enjoy some children," encouraged Ted. She smiled and nodded and he said, "I think I'll go get ready for bed."

"Okay, Honey. I'll be there just as soon as I finish calling Maria," responded Julie.

*****

Thursday

When Matt got to the work site on Thursday, Walt hurried over. "Matt, would you be able to come to lunch with us on Saturday at about 1:00? The other day you mentioned wanting to get together on Saturday. My wife came up with this idea, since she hasn't seen you in a long time. Betty would love to have you come to eat and stay to visit as long as you can."

"That's a great idea, Walt. I'd love to see Betty also, and that solves the problem of us leaving her alone while we go some place else. This way we can *all* visit. I'll bring some of her and your favorite candy," suggested Matt.

"Yum! I'm glad you can come, Matt. Now here's what's planned for the second shift ..."

*****

That evening after supper, the Blakes went over to see Pastor Don and Anita. Julie walked over to the corner of the living room where Anita was setting up some games for Timmy and Mary. Julie talked to them about the games they were going to play. "Those are fun games. I remember playing those as I was growing up." Then she and Anita went over to join the men.

Pastor Don started right in about the church time. "We have 12 churches who share the same building in this central part of the city. The auditorium can seat 300 people, but no church has that many yet. The congregations for each church come from wedge shaped neighborhoods, radiating out from the church building to the edge of the city. Sometimes people might join one church from another part of town, so there is some overlap. All the churches have the same Grace 'n' Faith name with a number for its wedge. We are # 4. Each one has a separate pastor who can shepherd up to 275 people leaving room, for 25 visitors. Mega churches lose that ability. There are six services each on Saturday and Sunday, at 8, 10, 12, 2, 4, and 6, for one and one half hours each, to allow time to fill and clear the church and parking lot each time. The churches all rotate through the time slots, a year at a time starting on the first Sunday in April. The idea of having one church per wedge is to try to pray and reach out mostly to that area so the whole city is being covered. Any questions so far?"

"Yes, what happens if a church has more than 275 people?" Julie asked.

"I'm not sure what we'll do when a church grows to more than 275. I think we will pray and ask God for a creative solution," answered Don.

"It sounds like a well thought out plan and is a very good use of the building. I've never heard of a place doing that before. I think it's extraordinary and amazing! How many years have you been doing this?" asked Ted.

"This is our fifth year. It started out pretty small, and then when the pastor of the church in this building reached three services on each weekend, he realized that he could not really be a pastor to that many people. So he and the associate pastors met to pray and plan.

"At that time, there were about 1200 people attending from all over town. We felt that the Holy Spirit was telling us to split them into 12 groups of 50 to 150 each. Some had more and others less because of the wedge idea, and where the people lived. We had four pastors at the time and needed to find eight more who would also be willing to work at a separate job to help support himself and his family while being the pastor of his church and who would agree to the beliefs of Grace 'n' Faith Church."

"I like that name," inserted Julie.

Anita agreed, "Yes, it comes from Ephesians 2: 8&9. *For by grace you are saved through faith, not of yourselves. It is the gift of God: not of works, lest any man should boast.*"

"What are the beliefs of this church?" asked Ted.

"I'm glad you asked that," said Pastor Don. "Grace 'n' Faith Church, like many other churches believes in the trinity, the Bible as God's inspired Word, God's plan of salvation, and all that includes, that Jesus is alive and in Heaven interceding for us, and has sent the Holy Spirit to believers to empower them to serve, and that Jesus will return some day and take believers to be with him.

"Unlike many other churches, we believe that the church is made up of Holy Spirit filled believers who live like Jesus as a lifestyle, not just go to church on Sunday. Jesus works through them by the Holy Spirit, giving power and guidance to do his will in evangelism, solving problems, and edifying each other. The Holy Spirit distributes his gifts according to his will to do his work.

"We believe that the church is Jesus' Body functioning on earth to do what Jesus himself did and would do, but not just in one time and place but also through many churches around the world. That doesn't all happen in just one service on the weekend. It needs small groups and pairs of believers who are sent out to minister by Jesus through the Holy Spirit"

"Like they did in the Gospels and in Acts," said Julie.

"Yes," agreed Anita. We try to do the effective things they did in the New Testament."

Pastor Don continued, "At the weekend service and small groups we teach a concept to be practiced in daily life. If you or anyone else brings or knows of an unbeliever in the weekend meeting, get a note to me about it, and I'll include a gospel message before or just after the teaching time. Then I'll give them an opportunity to pray silently the words I say first, leading in repentance, accepting God's forgiveness, and stating their belief in Jesus, like I did Sunday. And, praise the Lord, two people came up to me after the service to tell of their decisions and ask for a booklet."

The others all joined in praise and thanks to God, and then Ted said excitedly, "This is wonderful! It makes 'church' a place where we can bring someone who is seeking, who might listen to you, even if he hasn't wanted to hear it from me!"

"Right," agreed Pastor Don. "It's always wonderful when a believer gets to lead a friend or co-worker to Jesus for salvation, but when _that_ fails, sometimes an invitation to church works. Very seldom, a person might invite someone who is an unbeliever to a small group meeting, and gives the leader a note so he can present the gospel as I did in church. If that is the case, the format of the group will change for that meeting so that the invitee won't be confused by gifts of the Spirit in action."

"That was one question Julie and I both had about what the booklet said. I assume from what you've said that you'll be the leader, and will teach us about those things very soon," surmised Ted.

"Correct, and the Suehiros will also want that kind of teaching since they haven't been in a small group before. I think that the first meeting this Saturday will probably answer most of the questions you have about the small groups. If not, you can ask me later," said Don.

"Good," said Julie. "It looks like the children have almost had enough of those games. They are so sweet. It's nice of you to share your time and all this information with us. I think we should head home. Thank you very much."

"You're very welcome. It is good to meet new people who are as interested as you are. We'll see you at the Suehiro house on Saturday morning," the pastor said.

Ted replied, "Right, we'll be there at 9:30. We're looking forward to it. Bye." They all waved and then the door closed.

*****

Friday

Maria's boss, Jason Beckett, called her into his office on Friday morning, and she worried all the way there that he was going to ask her to go out of town again this weekend. "Your will be done, Lord, but I was hoping to have a nice visit with Julie this evening and be able to go to church on Sunday," she prayed on the way to his office.

"Have a seat, Maria. I just wanted to tell you that I'm headed out of town this weekend. In the event that I don't get back in time to open the office on Monday morning, I would like to leave this key with you so you can open the door. Then you and all the other employees can carry on as usual. All you need to do is be here ten minutes early, unlock the door and start the coffee. Then you can leave ten minutes early in the evening. Will that work for you?" Jason asked.

"Of course," Maria answered. I'll be glad to do that, Sir. I hope the weekend goes well for you."

"Thank you," he said, and Maria went back to work at her desk with a lighter, thankful heart, counting the hours until she could see Julie, and glad that she could go to church on Sunday. The day went well and fast. Maria had already put the key into her purse so that she would have it to use on Monday. She put everything in order on her desk, and was ready to leave at 5:05 PM.

She had shopped for groceries on the way home from work on Wednesday, so she had an easy supper planned, and only needed to straighten a few things up in her apartment. She was ready when Julie arrived about 6:30.

They greeted one another with smiles and hugs, and sat down in two comfortable chairs facing each other so they could talk. For a couple moments, it felt awkward, and they were silent, but then the years fell away, and they carried on just like they had, back in their dorm room at college.

"I was just thinking about your wedding. It was almost two years ago, just after we graduated, Julie. You were the prettiest bride I've ever seen! And you still are muy linda, and always have been, with all that shiny brunette hair, blue eyes, and shapely figure. It's no wonder that Ted couldn't keep his eyes off you. He's a blessed man," stated Maria.

Julie replied, "Muchas gracias, mi amiga." Then they conversed in Spanish for a while about college memories and Julie thanked Maria for all the practice that had helped her to become fluent in Spanish. Maria thanked Julie for the practice in English, since her parents had only spoken Spanish in their home.

Then Julie said, "I like the way you encourage me with compliments and nice things to say. Now I get to compliment you, reminding you that I've always considered you to be a beautiful woman. You're tall, with glossy black hair and warm eyes the color of coffee. Plus, I've always been amazed by the way you can eat whatever and as much as you want, and still keep your fantastic figure! What's your secret?"

"Well, I'll have to admit that I have to be more careful now that I have a sit down job, and am not running across campus to get to my next class on time. I need to start an exercise routine to stay in better physical shape. I wonder if we could set up a time three days a week to walk together right after work, or before work in hot weather," suggested Maria.

"It sounds like a good idea!" replied Julie. "I'm not sure what Ted will say, he might even want to go with us. We all work from 8 to 5. It might take about an hour if we include changing our clothes and shoes before we head out the door. Our apartments are close enough that we could walk and meet half way in about five minutes. Do you have a city map here? I have one at home. We could set up a route starting with a short walk and add to it as we build up our endurance. I really like this idea! I've been sitting way too much especially since we moved here."

"Okay, run it by Ted and let me know. And that reminds me; I wanted to ask you a question. How do you like married life?" Maria asked.

Julie was enthused, "It's wonderful! Being married to a man like Ted is a real blessing. He's a good listener, understands me, and he's caring and loving. PLUS he is a very good Christian. We worked together very well on our search for a good church and this move. It hasn't all been easy, but it's so helpful to be unified on a goal and to pray and receive God's help in it all. How are you doing, Maria? Are you still wishing for a man of your own, like you did in college?"

Maria replied, "Not nearly as much, and I'm truly glad for <u>you</u>, Julie. I've done a lot of praying about it and can accept it either way just so long as I know I'm doing God's will. In some ways, right now it's easier not having a spouse, because I'm free to help my boss with some business, involving a number of weekends out of town. It's confidential, so I can't tell you about it. Anyway I'm content now and I enjoy this little apartment and my cat, though I do feel lonely sometimes. Not nearly as much now that I can see or talk to you once in a while."

"Are you in a small group, Maria?" asked Julie.

"Yes, and it's wonderful. I go on Tuesday nights from 7 to 9, and I'm hoping maybe they'll let you and Ted join our group," answered Maria.

"Oh, Maria, that would have been grand, but Pastor Don called and asked us if we would be able to join a new group starting up this Saturday from 9:30 to 11:30, and we said yes." Seeing Maria's face sadden Julie added, "Maybe next year, or some other year, we'll get to be in the same group. We'll need to leave that up to the Lord."

"You're right of course," inserted Maria.

"Before I forget, Pastor Don told us Sunday to call our friends and remind them about the change in Sunday service time from 12:00 to 2:00," remembered Julie.

"Oh, thank you, Julie. I might have forgotten that it happens on the first Sunday in April and would have felt silly going at the wrong church time. I would have been at the wrong church, even if it <u>is</u> in the same building!"

They both laughed, and then Maria continued, "But I'll have to admit that even though I missed going to church this week, I <u>was</u> able to listen to the service of church #1 when I got home on Sunday night by going to the church web site. I'm so glad they have that available. Isn't the concept of 12 churches using the same building amazing?" asked Maria.

"Extremely!" Julie agreed. "Yesterday evening Ted and I went over to ask Pastor Don and Anita why the service changed times, and they explained it to us. What an idea! It's fantastic to think of that many people working so well together. Sometimes I feel overwhelmed with so many new ideas, but I'm excited about this new adventure. Oh, my! Look at the time! It sure flew, and it's been so fun talking with you, but I better get going home. Thank you my dear friend for asking me over. I'll see you on Sunday! It feels good to be able to say that."

"For sure!" agreed Maria. "I can't begin to tell you how much I've missed you. I love you like a sister, and will forever.

"I feel the same way, and that's what we are in God's family, so it will be forever," laughed Julie. They hugged, and then she left. Julie hurried home and had a nice time telling Ted about her visit with Maria, and then hearing about his day. After that they went to bed early as they had planned.

*****

Chapter 2

Ecclesiastes 4:9,10a, *Two are better than one, because they have a good reward for their labor.*
If they fall, the one can help the other up.
Matthew 18:20, *Where two or three are gathered together in my name, there am I (Jesus) in the midst of them.*

Saturday

Ted and Julie woke with anticipation on Saturday morning, the day to attend their first small group. Knowing that there would be a lot to learn, Julie had found a small notebook and pen to take along. They ate a nourishing breakfast, containing complex carbohydrates and having no sugar or heavy protein so they could stay alert. Then dressing comfortably, they left a little early, taking the map and directions with them. They found the Suehiro house with no problem. It looked like a nice, modest house in a quiet neighborhood with a well cared for yard.

After waiting a few minutes in the car, they went to the door and rang the doorbell. They were greeted by a very small, older Japanese lady who welcomed them graciously. She showed them into the living room where Pastor Don and Anita, plus two other men were seated. The smaller, older man was obviously also Japanese. The other man was tall, blond, and muscular. He appeared to be in his mid 20's, and looked to be very at ease. There was also another couple sitting there. The Blakes were invited to sit in chairs that were forming a circle.

Before anyone had a chance to say anything, the doorbell rang again, and a tall, beautiful, young woman with auburn hair and a happy smile was shown into the room. The blond man stifled a gasp and then smiled a welcome. She blushed as she sat down.

Pastor Don saw their reactions, but chose to not say anything about it. He started the meeting by saying, "Welcome everyone! Since all the members are already here, we can start a few minutes early. We'll begin with introductions. Include your first and last names, where you work, and how long you've been living in Pine City. I would like the Blakes to introduce themselves first."

"Hi, I'm Julie Blake. I work at Happy Smiles for Kids dental office as a receptionist, Monday through Friday, from 8 AM to 5 PM. I've been living in Pine City for a little more than a week."

They all smiled and Ted began, "And I'm Ted Blake. I work at Superior Auto Body Shop, Monday through Friday, from 8 AM to 5 PM, and have also lived in this fine city for a little over a week."

"My turn," said Pastor Don. "Julie can take notes if she wants to since they don't know any of you yet. I'm Don Ross and I'm the Pastor of Grace 'n' Faith Church #4. My wife and I are the facilitators of this small group, I help Anita with our children and housework, and for exercise and wages I work at the Local Grocers, stocking shelves 8-5, Monday - Friday. Now, my wonderful wife," he motioned toward her.

"I'm Anita Ross. We've lived in Pine City for seven years. I help Don as he pastors the church and facilitates groups. I stay home to care for our two children, Timmy and Mary, plus I do day care for five other preschoolers from 7:30 AM to 5:30 PM, Monday - Friday. Our young friend, Mindy, who is 12 years old, comes daily after school and on vacations. She helps me a lot with the children, and in return, I'm mentoring her. She is earning a little spending money this morning by babysitting with our two children. The rest of you know her situation. Ted and Julie, Mindy is an only child whose mother died four years ago. Her dad is Vernon (Vern) Jones who is a pediatric dentist at Happy Smiles for Kids. (Julie smiled and nodded since she had just met him that week.) She and her dad are in our church, and he does a good job with her,

Everywhere There's a Sunrise, Let's Tell The Good News!

but he wants a mom-like influence for her, so I volunteered, and she pays her way by helping me with the day care children. She does NOT want anyone to think she's in my day care. It would be too embarrassing! There, I talked for too long, but I wanted the Blakes to understand her situation," she said, and the Blakes thanked her.

"Now it's time for you to meet our hosts," said Pastor Don.

"Hello, I'm Tomo Suehiro. My first name in Japanese means twin, and yes, I do have a twin brother, Afta Suehiro. His name means he's younger or born after me. My wife and I own Ami's Japanese Restaurant and work from 11 AM to 9 PM, Monday through Friday. We've lived in Pine City for 25 years," said Mr. Suehiro. "We hope you'll come and visit our restaurant sometime."

Anita inserted, "Oh, you'll love it! The food is delicious, and the ambiance is so peaceful. Go ahead, Ami."

"Hi, I'm Ami Suehiro. Ami means friend, and so we call our restaurant by my name. We have two grown children and they've moved away from Pine City. Their names are Aneko, meaning older sister, and Yoshi, meaning quiet or shy. Neither is married yet. We miss them, but they do come to visit once in a while," she said and motioned for the next person to take her turn.

"Hi, I'm Fiona O'Connor. I'm a florist and will be caring for potted plants at The Garden Store from 12:30 to 8 PM, Monday through Friday. I've lived in Pine City all my life except for the last two years while I was taking care of an elderly great aunt in another state. She just recently went home to be with the Lord, so I'm back in Pine City."

Anita said, "We are sorry for your loss. It's good to have you back with us, though. Let's have a special time of prayer for the O'Connor family right now." Several people prayed for comfort for the grieving family and others gave thanks that the aunt had been a Christian and was now with the Lord.

"Your turn, Matt," said Anita.

"Okay. I'm Matthew (Matt) Anderson, and I work as the foreman of the second shift of Evan's Construction Company from 1:30 to 9 PM, Monday through Friday. I've lived in Pine City all my life."

"Hi, I'm Jeff Spencer. I work with Matt at the Evan's construction company job site from 2 to 9 PM Monday through Friday as an electrician and whatever else is needed. This is my dear wife, Karen."

She smiled at her husband and said, "I'm Karen Spencer, and I work at Subway from 12 to 8 PM, Monday through Friday. We've lived in Pine City for about ten years."

Pastor Don said, "Thank you all for your introductions. Now that we've all been introduced, is it okay with everyone to use first names and skip the titles of Mr., Mrs., Miss, and Pastor?" They all nodded. "We have a smaller group today, but tomorrow I'll announce our new group at our new 2:00 PM service time, and maybe next Saturday, we'll have some more members. Let's open this part of our meeting with prayer."...

"We keep the singing part of our meeting simple like we do at church and use recorded music on an SD card in this little stereo boom box. None of the 12 churches has a live worship band. It would take too long for each church's band to practice during the week and set everything up in the building for each church service.

"You notice that we brought hymnals today like we use at church. I would like to encourage you all to reread the words of the Psalms, hymns, and spiritual songs that we sing on Sundays and in these small groups, because many of them have meaningful teachings in them and they can also be a way for you to have praise times at home. If any of you would like to buy a hymnal we have used ones for sale here, or you can buy new ones at either of the Christian bookstores in town. Let's sing Psalm 103:1, *Bless the LORD O my soul, and all that is within me, bless his holy name!*" Then they sang "Holy God, We Praise Your Name," Psalm 145:1; and "Come Holy Spirit," Acts 1:8. It sounded beautiful with them all singing together with the prerecorded instrumental music and singers.

Next Pastor Don said, "Since we have two couples who have never been in one of our small groups before, our teaching today will be longer. It is about the Holy Spirit and his role in our lives and in the life of the church. Julie, you don't need to take notes on this since all of it and more is in a little booklet that we'll give to you and Ami.

"While Jesus was on earth, right after his baptism in water by John the Baptist, he was filled with the Holy Spirit who, as you know is one of the 3 persons of the Trinity. Do you all know about the Trinity?" Nods all around. "Good. We sang about it in the hymn, 'Holy God, We Praise Your Name,' just a few minutes ago. The Holy Spirit, also called the Spirit of God the Father, was <u>in</u> Jesus and gave him power to do all the miracles he did on earth, and the wisdom and words to speak and teach as it says in John

14:24b, the *words I speak to you are not my own, but the Father's who sent me.* When Jesus sent the disciples out two by two, he gave them power to teach and do his miracles, but they were not yet filled with the Holy Spirit.

"Open your Bibles to these scriptures and follow along as I read them. John 14:15-17, *If you love me, keep my commandments, and I will ask the Father and he shall give you another Comforter, to be with you forever, the Spirit of truth. The world cannot receive him ... but you know him because he dwells with you and shall be in you.* Now, verse 26 says, *The Comforter, who is the Holy Spirit, whom the Father shall send in my name, shall teach you all things, and bring all things to your remembrance that I have said to you.*

"Matthew 3:11, says that *Jesus will baptize with the Holy Spirit.* In John 15:26 Jesus says, When *the Comforter has come, whom I will send to you from the Father, the Spirit of truth, he shall testify about me.* In Luke 24:49, *Jesus told the disciples to stay in the city of Jerusalem until they were empowered from on high.* That would happen 50 days after Jesus' resurrection, on the day of Pentecost.

"Turn to Acts 1:8. On the day that Jesus ascended to Heaven after his resurrection, he told them, *you shall receive power, after the Holy Spirit fills you, and you shall be my witnesses.* Acts chapter 2 tells how this happened for the disciples, and about Peter's sermon. Let's read Acts 2: 38,39. *Then Peter said to them, repent, and be baptized every one of you in the name of Jesus, and you shall receive the gift of the Holy Spirit. For the promise is to you and to your children and to all that are afar off, even as many as the Lord our God shall call.* About 3,000 people believed that day!

"From that moment the disciples had the Holy Spirit, also called the Spirit of Jesus, living in them, like he told them in John 14:20, *I am in you.* Matthew 28:20 says, *I am with you always, even to the end of the world.* They were sent out to preach and teach in His power as in Mark 16:15 and 20, *Go into all the world, and preach the gospel to everyone... And they went and preached everywhere. The Lord worked with them, and confirmed the word with signs following.*

"Jesus, by his Spirit, does his will and work through believers who are filled with the Holy Spirit and are willing to serve Jesus in his church, the body of Christ. All believers all over the world are what Paul calls the body of Christ. In 1 Co 12:12,13a it says, *for as the body is one, and has many members, and all the members of that one body, being many, are one body: so also is Christ. For by one Spirit we are all baptized into one body, whether we be Jews or Gentiles.* All believers are doing Jesus work all over the world because he *is not willing that any should perish, but that all should come to repentance* as it says in 2 Peter 3:9b. But it's up to each person to repent and believe. It is a wonderful privilege and responsibility to serve Jesus!"

Pastor Don continued, "Not all people will speak in tongues or prophesy as they did in Acts. Being filled with the Holy Spirit is <u>not</u> about experiences or feelings. Those are not the important things. When we are filled with the Holy Spirit, his fruit is the result, as it says in Galatians 5:22,23, *The fruit of the Spirit is love, joy, peace, long suffering or patience, gentleness, goodness, faith, meekness, and self-control; against these things there is no law.* His power can work through us as we all yield to him to do as he wills.

"In the church, the Holy Spirit distributes graces or gifts to people as he determines." Let's find Ephesians 4:11-13. Jesus by the Holy Spirit *gave apostles, prophets, evangelists, pastors and teachers for the perfection of the saints and for the work of the ministry, for the edifying of the body of Christ until we all come in the unity of the faith, and of the knowledge of the Son of God, to a perfect man, and the measure of the stature of the fullness of Christ.*

"Then look at 1 Corinthians 12:4-11. *There is a variety of gifts, but the same Spirit, and there are differences of administrations, but the same Lord. And there are varieties of operations, but the same God who works all in all. But the manifestation of the Spirit is given to everyone for the profit of all. To one is given by the Spirit the word of wisdom, to another the word of knowledge, to another, faith, to another the gifts of healing, to another the working of miracles, to another prophesy, to another discerning of spirits, to another varied tongues, and to another the interpretation of tongues. But all these are the work of the one and very same Spirit, giving individually to each one as he wills.*

"Turn to 1 Corinthians 12:27-31. *Now you are the Body of Christ, and members in particular. And God has placed some in the church, first, apostles, second, prophets, third, teachers, after that miracles, then gifts of healing, helps, governments, diversities of tongues. (Not all have the same gifts) ... Desire earnestly the best gifts...* All the gifts listed in these scriptures plus others listed elsewhere are <u>useless</u>, unless they are done with love, God's kind of love, described in 1 Corinthians 13: 4-8a. *Love is patient, love* is kind; it does not envy or boast and is not proud. It does not behave rudely, is not selfish, is not easily angered, and does not think evil. It rejoices in the truth, not in iniquity. It bears and believes and hopes and endures all things, and it never fails.

"We <u>usually</u> don't see gifts of the Spirit in action in the Saturday/Sunday services because of so many people and so little time. That's the reason we need small groups where there is more time and fewer people so we can follow Paul's teaching in 1 Corinthians 14:26-33,40, ... *when you come together, one or another has a psalm, a doctrine, a tongue, an interpretation, a revelation; let all things be done for edification. If any one speaks in an unknown tongue, let it be only two or at the most three, by turn, and let one interpret. If there is no interpreter, then keep silence in the group. ... Let two or three prophets speak, and let the others judge. If anything is revealed to another, let the first be quiet, for you all may prophesy one by one, in order that all may learn, and all may be comforted. The spirits of the prophets are subject to the prophets. For God is not the author of confusion, but of peace ... let all things be done decently and in order.* We often see some of these gifts operating during the conversational prayer time of a small group.

"Since this teaching has been so long, we won't take time for praise reports or conversational prayer time today. I don't want to overwhelm you, and would like to leave time for fellowship and those delicious smelling refreshments Tomo and Ami have prepared for us," finished Don. Everyone smiled, rose and stretched. Ami led the way to the dining room where it looked like a feast had been laid out. It felt good to stand around the table to talk and eat after sitting for so long. They all enjoyed the delicious Japanese finger foods that Tomo and Ami had made.

After a while, Pastor Don said, "We need to decide where to meet next week."

Ted looked at Julie and she nodded and said, "We would like everyone to come to our apartment next Saturday. It might be a little crowded if very many more come, and I'm <u>sure</u> the refreshments won't be as good as these have been!"

"Actually what Tomo and I planned here is like an appetizer to get you to want to come and eat at our restaurant sometime soon, during the week, since we're only open Monday - Friday 11AM - 9PM for lunch and supper," said Ami.

Anita said, "There, you see? It's not a contest, just a chance to show hospitality and have fellowship."

"That's a relief," replied Julie. "I've enjoyed getting to know all of you, and look forward to seeing you in church tomorrow at the 2PM service time and next Saturday at our home." Julie then gave them the address and phone number.

"Thanks for the reminder about the time change, Julie," said Don. "It <u>would</u> be embarrassing to go to the 'wrong' church tomorrow, especially if I did it!" Everybody chuckled.

*****

After the small group meeting, Jeff and Karen Spencer went to their modest little home and discussed the group while Karen put a light lunch on the table. "What did you think of the group, Jeff?"

"Well, it was a bit small, but next Saturday might be different. Other than that, it was wonderful. It's really great to be back in a small group," said Jeff.

"I agree," Karen said. Did you see the look on Matt's face when Fiona walked in? I didn't even know that she was back home!"

"I didn't either!" agreed Jeff. "I'll bet Matt didn't either from his reaction, and I saw Fiona blush as she sat down. I hope to get to talk to him tomorrow at church, or else I'll have to wait until break time on Monday and that will be hard because I'm very curious."

"Same here! Oh well, we might just have to wait. The new couple who've just moved here seemed nice, and it will be good to get better acquainted with the Suehiros. The refreshments <u>were</u> delicious. Too bad we can't go to their restaurant, but I have to be at work by noon and it would really be a rush to eat and try to get to work on time," said Karen.

"Maybe some evening I could get off work at 8 PM we could hurry over there for supper. They're open 'til 9PM," suggested Jeff. "Let's ask if that would work for them."

"Okay," agreed Karen. "That sounds good. The part of the group I liked best was the teaching about the Holy Spirit. What an amazing God we have! Only <u>he</u> could come up with the plan of salvation and filling believers with the Holy Spirit so they could do Jesus' work after his ascension. I can anticipate good things happening with this group."

"Yes, please God, let that be true! Work through us also, and thank you for the new small group. In Jesus name, Amen," prayed Jeff.

Everywhere There's a Sunrise, Let's Tell The Good News!

"And thank you for this food that is now ready to be eaten, Amen," added Karen.

*****

As people were leaving the small group meeting, Matt caught up with Fiona and said playfully, "May I have the pleasure of walking you home Miss O'Connor?"

"Yes, kind sir. I would be honored," she replied, going along with his playfulness.

They fell into step together, and walked in silence for a little way. Then, all playacting gone, Matt said, "I was startled <u>and</u> pleasantly surprised to see you walk into the group. I had no idea you were back home. It's so good to see you. Welcome home! I'm very sorry about your great aunt."

Fiona was glad for that last statement, because she didn't know how to respond to the rest. So she said, "Thank you. It's very good to be back. I've only been home a couple of days. My great aunt was so grateful to have me be there with her, and we got to know each other much better than ever before. She was a very kind woman, and I learned many things from her. It helps the sorrow a lot to know that she's in heaven. The last two months were very painful for her. Now she has no more pain!" said Fiona.

"Thank you for telling me about her and some of your time there." Then Matt asked, "Could we go over there and sit in the park for awhile, Fiona? I'd really like to ask you some questions."

"Okay," said Fiona, feeling a little anxious and wondering what the questions might be.

After they were seated on a park bench, Matt turned toward Fiona and began, "When you had to leave two years ago, we both agreed to not write or call each other, or continue the relationship we had started back then, neither of us asking the other to wait for or even hope for the other, but to pray and leave it in God's hands to see what would happen. Now that you are home again, I'm wondering. What <u>did</u> happen for you, Fiona?"

She didn't answer right away, and he could see several emotions chase across her face, so he said, "Is it fair of me to ask you to tell me first? Would you like for me to tell you what happened for me first?"

Fiona looked hesitant after the first question, but relieved after the second one. She nodded and asked, "<u>Would</u> you please tell me first, Matt? What did happen for you?" Then she sat forward praying for the desire of her heart, but hardly daring to hope.

Matt smiled and started, "I prayed, and prayed, and told God I wanted only HIS will in our situation, after admitting my frustration about you having to leave just when we were starting to get close. I spent several months asking him if he wanted me to remain single all my life or if it would be his will to be married and have a family. I felt that his answer was for me to be married and have a family, but not yet. Then I felt at peace and chose to be content and wait as patiently as I could.

"But I'll have to admit that I've missed you more than words can say, and I kept praying that if it would be God's will, he would give me the desire of my heart, to be able to continue our relationship and see where he would lead us in it. ... " He trailed off as he looked at Fiona in wonder, because tears were streaming down her face, while she was smiling!

"Oh, Matt, ... "She wiped the tears away with a tissue and said, "I didn't want to tell you first because I wanted it to come from you first. I did exactly the same thing you did, and now I'm overwhelmed with joy that I _can_ hope for the desire of my heart."

"Wow! I'm so glad. I didn't see or date anybody while you were gone," Matt stated.

"I didn't either," she inserted.

"Nobody can compare to you, Fiona. So my next question for you is: May I ask your father again for permission to court you?" asked Matt.

"Yes, please do! I'm glad you are still gentlemanly enough to ask him again. He will be impressed," she laughed, and he was pleased to hear her melodious laugh again after so long.

"Thank you, Lord, and thank you, Fiona! Now I'll finish walking you home with such a happy heart that it will feel like my feet are not touching the ground!" he said as he took her hand and walked her home.

Fiona's parents were home, and Matt asked her father right away for permission. It was happily granted, and Matt then told Fiona that he would be in touch _soon_, but that he had been invited to the home of his boss for lunch today, so he would call her later in the afternoon.

*****

When Matt arrived at the Evan's home a few minutes later, he was smiling from ear to ear. They wouldn't even let him sit down

Everywhere There's a Sunrise, Let's Tell The Good News!

until after he had told them the good news about Fiona being back home and also wanting to continue their relationship.

"It appears that my prayers were answered with a 'yes'," said Walt, "and I'm so glad for you, Matt."

"Me too," said Betty. "I haven't seen you this happy since before Fiona had to leave. Now come on into the dining room and we'll eat before the food gets cold."

"I'm sorry I was a little late, but I just couldn't wait to talk to Fiona and then ask her father for permission again to court her. I feel like I'm walking on air," confessed Matt as they went into the dining room.

"Don't worry about it," replied Walt. "Under these circumstances, I'm surprised you got here at all! Would you like to pray before we eat, Matt?"

"Yes. Father in Heaven, I'm so thankful to you that Fiona is back home and wants to continue our relationship, and that I can be here with Walt and Betty to share my good news, and visit with them. Thank you for this food and the hands that prepared it. I pray Jesus name, Amen," prayed Matt. Then he continued praying silently about the other Good News he wanted to bring up later and that they would be open to discuss it.

The serving dishes were passed, and the food was still hot and delicious. Betty was a very good cook. It all smelled and tasted so good. Matt realized he had not eaten very much at the Suehiro home. He'd been too distracted by Fiona's presence.

They discussed various topics as they ate, and then after all hands had helped with the clean up, they went into the living room to talk some more. Finally Matt brought up the topic that he and Walt had discussed a month ago. "Did you tell Betty about the discussion you and I had about a month ago?"

"Yes," answered Walt, "and we have some questions for you." Walt motioned and said, "You ask the first one, Betty."

"All right. Here goes. Do you really think God would keep good people out of Heaven just because they don't believe like you do?" asked Betty. "Aren't there many ways to get there? All the teachings I've ever heard, state that there are."

"This is a very good question, Betty, I'm glad you asked it," Matt said kindly. "The answer depends very much upon what your view is of the Bible. What do you believe about the Bible, Betty?"

"I don't really know," she answered. "I've heard so many conflicting statements about it over the years. My teachers in college said it was just a collection of fables and myths handed down through the years. My parents never even owned a Bible, so I assumed they didn't think it was worth much. It is all very confusing."

Matt said, "I can see why you would be confused with that kind of a background. Would you be willing to ask God, who wrote the Bible, to show you the truth about his Book?"

"Yes, I would," answered Betty slowly, and then proceeded to do just that, out loud.

"Good," Matt continued, "and would you be willing to read a book that I have out in my pick-up that was written by a person who used to be as confused as you are, but who did a lot of research and became convinced that God's Book, the Bible, is true and can be trusted?" If you can believe that the Bible is true and can be trusted, then I'll be able to show you in the Bible the answer to your question about 'God keeping good people out of heaven.' "

"Yes, I'll read that book," both Betty and Walt said together at the same time. Then they laughed and explained that it was a question that both of them had, and wanted answered.

"Great!" exclaimed Matt. "I'll go right out and bring the book inside," which he did, along with a Bible, assuming that they might not have one. "Here's the book, and also a Bible in case you don't have one." He put them on the coffee table. "Keep them as long as you need to."

Then Matt asked, "What about the other questions you have? Would you like to ask them now?"

"Well," answered Walt, I think we need to read this book and get clarity on this point before we proceed with the other questions. Do you agree, Betty?"

"Yes, I do," she stated. "Now can we just visit for a while?"

"Of course," answered Matt. "That would be very pleasant. What have you been doing lately, Betty?" He felt very thankful for the progress they had made.

"I've been sewing a lot. Our curtains had gotten old and faded, so I bought new material and made new ones. Then Walt helped to get the old ones down and put the new ones up," she said.

"Wow, that sounds like a lot of work, but these and the ones in the kitchen and dining room look very nice. You did a very good job on them. I like the colors also. I knew something was different when I came in today, but being a man, I wasn't perceptive enough to figure it out. The rooms look brighter and more cheery," Matt stated.

Everywhere There's a Sunrise, Let's Tell The Good News!

"Thank you, Matt," said Betty. "Your compliments help me feel even happier that I finally got finished with that project. I'm not sure what I'll do next, probably the mending that piled up while I wasn't looking."

"I really like the new curtains too. Now that they're finished, and you might do some mending, I'll appreciate having some of my old favorite, comfortable work shirts fixed so I can wear them again. You do great work with a needle and thread, Dear!" said Walt.

"Thank you, Walt. Now let's hear about you, Matt. How's your house coming along?" Betty asked.

"Very slowly, since I only work on it a couple hours a day a few days a week. I don't want to get too tired before I go over the job site," explained Matt.

"That's good," said Walt. "You're always telling me to go home and rest, so you better take the same advice!"

Matt laughed, and then they ate some of the candy Matt had brought to them. They visited awhile longer, and then Matt thanked them for the delicious lunch and their time together. He hurried home to get ready to call Fiona.

*****

After their first small group meeting that Saturday, Ted and Julie drove home, put on comfortable walking shoes and went for a walk. They talked about the meeting and other things.

"The meeting went so fast!" said Julie. Did you notice how the blond man reacted when the pretty lady came in?"

Ted answered, "I did, and I noticed that she blushed. They were obviously surprised to see each other."

Julie mentioned, "For sure, it would be fun to know their story, but I guess it's not our business. I liked the songs we sang. They went along with the teaching, and the first one had verses from a Psalm I've read before."

"Yes," agreed Ted. "The introductions were a good way to start getting acquainted with the people. I'm glad there weren't as many as there could have been. I didn't feel so overwhelmed."

Julie replied, "I agree, and it helped me to be able to take notes on the names. We can go over them before church tomorrow, and again before the next meeting."

"Good idea," said Ted. "The teaching time was pretty long, but Don made it all very clear. Since I know that we are filled with the Holy Spirit, I feel like my understanding has increased. Salvation was wonderful and still is, but it's great to know that we have Jesus and his power working through us!"

"Yes, that is awesome! It's hard to put into words, but <u>knowing</u> now that the Holy Spirit is <u>in</u> us is a great comfort and help. As I was growing up, I never did understand how Jesus, a grown man, could live in my heart. But this makes sense. The Holy Spirit is also called the Spirit of God and The Spirit of Jesus, so Jesus lives in believers by his Holy Spirit," said Julie.

"Right!" agreed Ted. "I'm looking forward to learning more. Don said that was just an overview. The booklet he gave us will teach us some more. We can get started reading it this afternoon and evening."

Julie responded, "Okay, let's do. What shall we have for refreshments next Saturday, and where will we get chairs for up to 16 people?"

Ted answered, "I don't know. Maybe Don and Anita can give us some ideas."

"Good thinking!" said Julie. "Now to a different subject. On Friday, Maria suggested that she and I, and you, if you would like to, could plan to meet half way between her apartment and ours and go for walks three days a week, since we both have sit-down jobs and need to get some exercise. We'd start out with short walks and work up to at least 45 minutes each time. She mentioned doing it after work now, and then before work when the weather gets hot. What do you think?"

"It sounds good, and even though I don't have a sit-down job, walking would be good for me also." (Ted didn't mention that he would like to tag along as a bodyguard. He'd hate for anything bad to happen to either one of those two ladies.) "I can walk along behind you and pray. That will give you two a chance to visit and keep your friendship alive while getting your exercise - three good things for one amount of time: prayer, visiting, and exercise," concluded Ted.

Julie said, "Do I tell you enough how much I appreciate you, Ted? You're such a good encourager and friend, not to mention a wonderful Christian husband and lover. You <u>are</u> my treasure! I truly am a blessed woman!"

Ted answered, "Yes, Dear, you tell me in many ways, and I hope you know that the feeling is mutual. I should tell you more often! I know how much I enjoy hearing you tell <u>me</u>, so you must also. The same goes for God and our praises and gratitude to <u>him</u>. He is such a great creator, savior, provider, friend, guide, ..."

Everywhere There's a Sunrise, Let's Tell The Good News!

  Julie began humming, and then started singing the Doxology. Ted joined her and they walked back home praising the LORD for as many things as they could think of. She loved to hear Ted singing. He had such a full, low, bass voice. They went inside and fixed a light lunch, which was all they wanted after all those delicious refreshments at the group meeting. They also decided they would enjoy going to Ami's Japanese Restaurant for supper some evening soon.

  Julie said, "The Suehiros are very nice people. I'm glad Ami said what she did about the refreshments and that Anita clarified it even more when she said it wasn't a contest. It took a big load off my mind."

  Ted replied, "Yes. It <u>is</u> nice to know that we don't need to compete."

*****

  As soon as Matt got home from his time with Walt and Betty, he changed and went for a run for about 45 minutes to clear his mind and pray for direction, as he started courting Fiona again. Then he felt at peace, so he called her on the phone as soon as he got home. "Hi, Fiona, this is Matt. How's your afternoon going? ... ... Is it too soon after your aunt's passing for us to start going places and doing things together? I want to be considerate of you and your family, so please be candidly honest with me and tell me if, or how long we need to wait. ... ... Okay, then, would you like to go with me to lunch tomorrow before the 2 PM church service and then go to church together? ... ... We can sit with your parents if you like. ... ... Then after church, if it's nice out, we could go for a walk. If it's too cold or is raining, we could visit with your parents at your house. ... ... Good. I'll pick you up at 11:30, and we can go to our favorite restaurant and have plenty of time to eat and get caught up <u>a little</u> on the events of the last two years. ... ... I'll look forward to it. Bring or wear some walking shoes and a warm jacket. ... ... Bye ... ... "Matt smiled as he hung up, relieved that they would not have to wait to start seeing each other. It seemed that he had already done enough waiting.

  Next, because he wanted to share his joy with someone else, he called Jeff and Karen Spencer to see if he could come over and visit with them for a little while. They said that would be fine. When he arrived they were both extremely curious, but waited patiently for him to share whatever he wanted to.

"Come right into our living room and sit down. Would you like to have anything to drink?" asked Karen as she walked ahead of him.

"Yes, please, just a glass of cool water. I forgot to drink anything after my 45 minute run. I'm so excited, I feel like flying!' exclaimed Matt.

"At least wait until you drink the water," she giggled. "I'll bring it right out to you. Please come help me a minute, Jeff. ... Please carry your water and his, and I'll bring mine. I don't want to miss anything," she told Jeff.

"Thank you, Karen. This is just what I needed," Matt said after drinking most of his water. I have such good news that I didn't want to wait until later to tell you both. Fiona and I were able to have a long enough talk that I could tell her how I felt and find out how she feels. She agreed to continue our relationship and I asked her father again for permission to court her. He granted it happily. Our first 'date' will be lunch tomorrow before church, and then church together. After church maybe we'll take a walk if the weather permits. If not we'll visit with her parents at her house."

"Wow! That's fantastic news!" said Jeff. "I'll have to admit, we were really curious after we saw both of your reactions at the small group meeting. Thank you for coming over to share it with us."

"You're welcome, and thank you both for being so encouraging, caring, and helpful to me these past two years. I don't know if I would have stood up very well without knowing you were praying for me. Plus, you've listened to my ramblings and understood. You have both taught me a lot."

"You're very welcome. We're glad we could be here for you," replied Jeff. "You've grown in the Lord a lot over the last few years and it's been our pleasure to have a small part in that."

"Looking back on it, now, I think I can see some of that progress. But I still have a long way to go, so I would like to ask if I could continue to count on you both to help keep me accountable and pray for me to be patient and not rush this relationship. I might be tempted to do just that because of having to wait for so long, but the Lord must have had his reasons for the delay." Matt sighed.

"Of course we'll continue, Matt. How else can we expect to keep being informed of the developments in your life, especially concerning Fiona?" Karen laughed.

Matt laughed too, and it was just what he needed to relieve some of the tension that had built up.

Everywhere There's a Sunrise, Let's Tell The Good News!

*****

Fiona was relieved, too, and happy as she put the phone back. It was very good to be home again, and even better to know that Matt still cared and wanted to court her. She could hardly wait until Sunday! It had been two long years to wait and wonder, but she felt God had planned it all for a reason, or for <u>many</u> reasons. She didn't <u>know</u> the reasons, but thought part of it <u>might</u> have been that she was too immature even at 22 years old then, and that she had learned a lot by conversing with and caring for her elderly Great Aunt Cara.

That lady was as devout a Christian as she could imagine, constantly displaying the fruit of the Spirit as it says in Galatians 5:22,23, *The fruit of the Spirit is love, joy, peace, long suffering/patience, gentleness, goodness, faith, meekness, and self-control; against these things there is no law.* Her aunt always loved the way Jesus did. Fiona was glad to have her as a model. Her own mother, Glenda, was also a good model, but Fiona had not realized that until she had spent time with Cara and could now appreciate her mother better.

Fiona's dad, Patrick, was a very good Christian man. Fiona hoped that as she got to know Matt better, she would find him to be <u>as</u> good. She realized now that if he had asked her before she had left to promise to wait for him and marry when she returned, she would have said, "Yes," but now she recognized that this way was better, because they would have a chance to discuss some more important issues and learn enough about the other person to make the right decision. Plus, she had been able to pray and feel sure of God's leading about marriage and family being in his will for her.

She went into the living room and both her parents looked up at her and smiled. She sat down and told them about the phone call and her date for tomorrow. Then she shared most of the thoughts she had just had with them.

Glenda said, "You've matured into a very intelligent young woman, and I can also see that many of your great Aunt Cara's good qualities have now become yours. You've grown in the Lord, and we can see the fruit of the Spirit in your life. I know it was a long, hard time for you to be away from home and from Matt, but as you've said, it's for the best. We missed you terribly while you were gone, even though we drove there and visited off and on. We're so glad to have you back home!"

"Thank you, Mother," responded Fiona. "I missed both of you also, and I'm extremely glad to be back home."

Patrick added, "This house was just not the same without you here, and we had no idea how long you might have to be away. We miss your Aunt Cara, also, but since we know she's with the Lord, we don't have to sorrow like people who have no hope, as it says in 1 Thessalonians 4:13. You really helped us out by going to take care of her."

"Your younger brother, Riley, was grateful to you also. Since you went to be Aunt Cara's caregiver, we could both be here for him, and not have to worry about your great aunt. He's come through his trials a stronger Christian young man. He did decide that he would never ski again, however. The risk is just too great. I was able to help him with his studies so he could complete his work for that semester. He recovered pretty quickly from his injuries and went back to the university for the next semester. He will graduate this coming May. We're proud of both of you. God is so good," Glenda added.

*****

After lunch and cleanup, Ted and Julie went into the living room to read the booklet about the Holy Spirit. Everything the pastor had said was in there and it was a good review. Then there was a list of other names for the Holy Spirit including the ones Julie had already mentioned plus Comforter, Helper, Counselor, Teacher, and Guide.

Following that part of the booklet was a description of each of the gifts of the Spirit mentioned, and some examples of how, when, and where they might be observed or experienced. Most important was an admonition that <u>all</u> the gifts should be done with <u>love and to bring glory to God</u>, not to the person or to the church. Many times one or more people might come to Christ for salvation because of a gift being used.

"I'm glad we got to read about this before seeing or experiencing any of it ourselves. It could be confusing and the gifts could be misused otherwise," commented Ted.

"Yes," agreed Julie and pointed to the next section in the booklet. "It's the next topic in the booklet. Pastor Don talked about and read those verses in 1 Corinthians 14. The Bible is a good life textbook, teaching about so many things. We're blessed to have our own. Oh, what do you think about buying a hymnal?"

"It's a very good idea. I also noticed, like you did, that many of the songs go along with the teaching, and I found myself singing the last one on the way home. It reminded me of what was taught. Sometime, I would like to find out how they prepare the music for the church services and small groups. It's very well done and so beautiful. It's only 4 PM, so we could probably get over to the nearby Bible Book Store in time to buy a hymnal," suggested Ted. "I'd like to have a new one. The used ones are looking a bit tattered."

"I agree. The church music is beautiful, and I'd rather have a new hymnal too. I can be ready to leave in ten minutes," replied Julie. "Maybe there will be enough time to look around the store and see what else is for sale."

"Sure," said Ted, and soon they were on their way.

*****

"Walt and Betty sat in the dining room talking about their afternoon with Matt. Walt mentioned how pleased he was that Fiona is home again, and still wants a relationship with Matt. "I told Matt the other day that I'd pray for him to get a wife so that maybe we can treat his children like grandkids since he's like a son to us, and helps take the place of the one we could never have. Fiona would be a great 'daughter' also."

Betty said, "That would be wonderful. I don't know Fiona very well, but if Matt loves her, she must be very special. Matt is such a nice young man. He is thoughtful and considerate, and he doesn't get impatient or upset when we don't agree with what he says about his beliefs. I wonder if his patience, and other good qualities come from what he believes."

"That could be," agreed Walt. "We've known Matt for years, and watched how he handled losing his parents in that car wreck. Many people fall apart when something like that happens, but he told me that he knew they were in heaven, and that when he died someday, he would see them again. Even though he was sad and missed them, it wasn't like when other people grieve who don't have a hope like that."

"That's for sure. I'm impressed. Shall we start reading that book he left here? We could sit on the sofa and read silently since we both read at about the same rate, and we can interrupt each other with questions and comments as we go along," suggested Betty.

"Sounds like a good plan," agreed Walt. So, they went into the living room and made good progress through the first couple of chapters before they got up to stretch their legs and walk around. "So far, it makes good sense," he said, and she agreed with him.

*****

Maria Gomez spent her Saturday cleaning her apartment and doing laundry at the onsite Laundromat, thankful that it was so handy. Since she was an early riser, she was able to have her clothes in and out of the washers and into the dryers before anybody else even got there. She visited with the people who came in. After her clothes were dry, she took them back to her apartment to fold and put them away.

Then she looked at the map to plan where she and Julie might walk for their three-days-a-week exercise, wondering if that was really going to happen. She desired to be able to visit with Julie, but didn't want to intrude into Ted and Julie's lives, so she decided to just wait and see if Julie would follow through on the idea.

*****

Pastor Don and Anita had hurried home to see how Mindy was doing with their two children. They need not have hurried. She told them that all went well and that the children had been great. Then her father, Vern, arrived to pick her up and they went home to eat lunch.

Anita put a simple lunch on the table and they sat down with the children to eat. It was Timmy's turn to pray and he said, "Jesus, thank you for this good food and the fun time we had with Mindy. Amen."

While the family enjoyed the mealtime together, Anita asked, "What did you children do this morning?"

Mary's face lit up with a smile and she said, "Mindy helped me dress Dolly. We had a tea party with real tea and cookies." That was a good narrative for an almost four-year-old! Her parents smiled at her.

Then Timmy continued by telling about some of the games they had played that morning. It <u>did</u> sound like fun.

After lunch and cleanup, the children ran off to play where their parents could keep an eye on them. "I think the small group is off to a very good start," Anita mentioned.

Everywhere There's a Sunrise, Let's Tell The Good News!

    Don concurred. "For sure. All the people there were so appreciative of us starting a new group to accommodate their work schedules, or being new to town and church. And they all listened attentively and nodded in agreement at many points during the teaching. It looks like we're all on the same page and can work together in unity."

    "I agree. Unity is a wonderful thing. It adds such freedom to everything that is said and done. Without it, big problems can arise. I look forward to how God is going to use this group to further his kingdom," Anita replied.

    "Same here. Did you see the shock on Matt's face when Fiona walked in?" Anita nodded and he said, "I didn't call either one to alert them. Maybe I should have, but it <u>was</u> fun to see their reactions!"

    "I think they were both very pleased to see each other again after so long," Anita added.

    "Yes, we can be certain of that. It will be fun to learn about how things go for them. I must remember to announce the new group at church tomorrow. I guess I had better go add that to my 'sermon' notes and practice what I'm teaching for tomorrow. It helps that the main pastor gives us notes to use for the teaching times but also gives us leeway to change or add, as might be necessary for our particular congregation," responded Don and added, "Like on Sunday when I had to add a Gospel message and shorten the teaching 'sermon.' Starting the new small group followed his ideas for introductions and people who needed more teaching about the Holy Spirit. The main pastor does a good job. I'm glad he started the church and now has one church of his own, plus he oversees all the rest of us."

    "For sure," agreed Anita. "Well, Dear, you go ahead and prepare for tomorrow and I'll look after the children and get some housework done. It's nice that Mindy didn't leave things in a mess. I think she's learning a lot about how to be a woman, wife, and mother. And it certainly is a big help to me, also."

    "I'm glad, Honey. But I wish her father, Vern, would be more open to finding a wife for himself and a mother for Mindy. I'll see you later," said Don as he gave her a hug and a kiss before going into his office.

    Anita was surprised about what Don had said about Vern, and wanted to ask him about it. Instead, she decided to pray that God would work out all the details for that little family.

*****

The Suehiros put the refreshment leftovers away and cleaned up the dishes after they ate as much as they wanted for their lunch. Then they went and sat in their recliners so they could put their feet up while they talked about the small group and the people in it.

Tomo started by saying, "I like the concept of a small group meeting every week. I think we'll get to know the people much better this way than at church where there's a large number of people and so little time to visit."

"I agree! Even though we've lived in this city for so long, we don't have very many close friends. Maybe we'll develop a connection with some couple in this group. They all seem like nice people. I hope Julie believed what I said about wanting our refreshments to be like appetizers to encourage some of them to come to our restaurant. We really weren't trying to show off," worried Ami.

Tomo cautioned, "Don't worry about it, my dear. You explained it very well and Anita did also. Julie said she was relieved, and looked at peace. Don't borrow trouble; it will all work out fine, ... you'll see."

"Thank you my wonderful husband. You're right. What would I ever do without you to steer me back on the right path and away from being anxious? I enjoyed Pastor Don's teaching about the Holy Spirit. After going to that church for the past three years, it's a delight to finally understand the Holy Spirit better and even to know that we have him right inside us to guide and help us do Jesus' work in our little worlds," said Ami.

"Yes," agreed Tomo, "we've had salvation for about three years, and it's a fabulous gift, but knowing that we are filled with the Holy Spirit compliments it. I know we have a lot more to learn, but the booklet Anita gave us will surely help us there. Shall we get started reviewing it now?"

Ami agreed and they took turns reading it out loud and discussing it as they went along."

*****
Chapter 3

Hebrews 10:25, *Do not forsake the assembling of yourselves together, as the manner of some is, but exhort one another, and so much more as you see the day approaching.*

Everywhere There's a Sunrise, Let's Tell The Good News!

First Sunday in April

    The Blakes got up at their usual time on Sunday morning, even knowing that the service didn't start until 2 PM. Julie felt like she needed to plan a whole new routine for the weekend, since much of Saturday morning was small group, and the middle of Sunday afternoon was the church service. She was used to doing most of her house work on Saturday, going to church on Sunday morning and either resting or having some couple over for lunch after church. She could still grocery shop on the way home from work on an evening when she and Maria didn't walk. That reminded her that she needed to talk to Maria at church about what Ted and she had discussed concerning the walks. It was going to be a nice addition to her week, also. Maybe she could do some housework on one of the other evenings and Saturday afternoons. That would leave Sunday morning to bake, fix and have lunch, and maybe start supper preparations for having a couple over.
    All of a sudden, Julie remembered how things had been while she was teaching. Many evenings were spent grading papers, and doing lesson plans. Weekends before report card time were full of preparing the cards four times a year and getting ready for parent-teacher conferences two times a year. Right now she was very glad she had an 8 to 5 job that she didn't have to bring home to finish. She would pray for guidance. Maybe it would be better to NOT apply for a teaching position after all. She also decided to discuss that issue with Ted. Then she spent some time praying for God to show her his will about teaching, and also about a routine, or patience plus help to just play it by ear for a while and wait for a routine to develop on its own.
    When she finished, she realized how good it was to be able to pray for guidance about big and small things, knowing that God was concerned about ALL of her life. She went to find Ted and told him all about it. He prayed with her concerning it also and then they each went to do a few things that were left over from Saturday.
    It would have relieved her mind if she had known that many of the other women in the new small group were also trying to rearrange their schedules and routines. The time change of the service and the new small group on Saturday made that necessary. But the were all very grateful and happy about the new group, so they were glad to be able to plan their lives around it.

Later, Ted and Julie sat down to lunch with the list of names and tried to remember the faces that went with them. After lunch and cleanup, they changed clothes and headed out the door to go to church.

*****

Matt spent part of his morning catching up with things he didn't get done Saturday afternoon. There had been no time to work on his house this weekend, but somehow that didn't really bother him, since he was so grateful that Fiona was finally back home. The rest of the morning, he concentrated on getting ready for his lunch date with Fiona. He was a little rusty after two years of not dating. But he was as excited as a teenager! He left his apartment with just enough time to get to her house right at 11:30.

*****

In the meantime, Fiona had helped her mother with their lunch preparations and even baked some cookies for the afternoon, if Matt did come inside to visit. The weather outside looked a little questionable, and by 3:30 after the service, it just might be raining.

She was suddenly very nervous when she went to her room to get dressed for lunch and church with Matt. She didn't see anything in her closet that seemed appropriate for that, plus a walk afterward. She almost called for her mother to come in and help her decide, but then she remembered to sit down, relax, and pray for guidance, not only about what to wear, but also for how to act and what to say, knowing that <u>all</u> that <u>really</u> mattered was to be pleasing to the Lord. Then she got up from the chair, dressed in a pretty blue pantsuit that would look good with walking shoes. She spent a little extra time styling her hair, and was ready to go with five minutes to spare. She never liked to keep <u>anyone</u> waiting, especially Matt. She could not agree with society dictating that a girl should spend a little more time getting ready, so that her date would have to wait for her.

When Matt arrived right on time, he came inside and greeted her and her parents. Then they were on their way to their favorite Italian restaurant. On the short drive, they exchanged pleasantries, and soon they were seated and looking around at the decor, and then at the menus. Not much had changed in the two years she had been gone. It felt good to be in a familiar place with a familiar person. Suddenly they both relaxed and started talking like the good friends they were.

"I think I'll order the lasagna, although, the ravioli is also tempting," Matt pondered.

Fiona agreed, "I was thinking the same thing. Let's do like we used to. You order the lasagna, and I'll order the ravioli and when it comes we can each give the other person half, so we'll have both to enjoy."

"Great idea! I'd forgotten about doing that. This will be fun, and delicious!" Matt exclaimed. "It's so good to have you back here with your spontaneity and fun ideas."

The waitress came to take their orders right then, and remembered them from before. "Where have you two been? I've missed seeing you."

Fiona explained about her aunt and how good it was to be able to come back here again. Then they gave her their orders. When the waitress left, they laughed together. "I had no idea she would still be here or would remember us," said Fiona.

"Same here. She was always nice to us. I'm glad she's still here. It makes it seem like it hasn't been so long after all. I'd like to hear about what you did at your aunt's house, and what the city was like," said Matt.

"You're right Matt, it's like we just had an intermission, and now the show goes on," agreed Fiona. "My aunt's city was a lot like Pine City only larger. I didn't go out much, because she needed me to be there all the time to help her do what she was still able to do, and do for her what she could not do any longer. Her personal care got harder and harder for her to do since her arthritis had twisted her fingers and gave her a lot of pain.

"I felt so sorry for her, but she never complained, and was always kind and appreciated everything I did. Her first name was Cara, which means loving, and she was a very loving person! We prayed a lot about her pain, but that was one of those enigmatic situations were it didn't seem to help. She said that maybe she needed to learn to let God's grace be sufficient, like Paul did with his thorn in the flesh.

"Besides personal care, I cleaned house, cooked meals, washed dishes, etc. Then we'd have time to visit, or sing, read the Bible, listen to the Grace 'n' Faith Church #1 service on the web using my laptop, watch other church programs on TV, or make shopping lists. The grocery market lets people call or e-mail their shopping lists to them. So we did. Then employees take a cart around and pick it all up. They would check it out and call me.

Then I would give my credit card number to pay for it. They delivered it all right to our door. I never even used my car, so on one of their visits to see us, my parents drove it home so they could keep it in use and maintained for me."

"Wow! That was a completely different way of life for you. I'll bet it took some getting used to. Did you get bored, or wish you could get out and go places?" asked Matt.

Just then, their lunch orders came and Matt gave thanks for the food. They cooperated to split the orders in half, and then enjoyed the delicious tastes of both the lasagna and the ravioli.

Fiona commented, "It tastes just as good as it always did! ... Now I'll answer your question. Yes, at first I got bored and wished to go places, but I asked God to help me be content and learn all he wanted me to in this experience. After that, I started a journal to write down what I was learning. I wrote in it almost every day, because I was learning new things all the time. Great Aunt Cara, herself, was a wonderful teacher and mentor. It was like a four year college course in care-giving, home making, contentment and godly living all squeezed into two years of being on duty 24 hours a day. God helped me be content, and I did get used to that way of life. Now, after two years of living like that, this other lifestyle will take some getting used to again!" She laughed. "But God is faithful, and I know he will help me do it. Now, it seems like I've been doing all the talking. Please tell me some things about yourself and what you've been doing the last two years."

"Okay. But first, I want to thank you for telling me more about your experience with your aunt. I've been curious and wondered how you were doing. I can tell by what you've said, that you've grown in the Lord and gained a lot from what you learned during your time there," said Matt.

"You're welcome, and thank you for your kind words," Fiona replied.

"You're welcome, too," laughed Matt, and they both smiled. "For the past two years, I've been very busy, also. My boss, Walt, the founder of the Evans Construction Company has taught me a lot about building, contracting, and even how to be a foreman. It was on the job training, and better than any schooling could have been, plus, I even got paid for it!

"A couple months ago, I suggested to him that we could utilize the daytime hours during daylight savings time better from March 15 to October 15, if we had two crews working without a meal break. Walt thought that over for about a month and decided to try it. He now oversees the first crew from 7 AM to 2 PM, and I oversee the second, from 2 to 9 PM. I get there at 1:30 so Walt can explain the plan for the second shift. Each crew works seven hours with a 15-minute break midway through. We've been getting almost twice as much work done as before without tiring out the workers as much."

"Wow! Matt, that sounds fantastic!" exclaimed Fiona.

"It really is helping us to get caught up," Matt agreed, "except that Walt and I miss working together, and that by overseeing the second shift, I had to stop going to the small group I was in."

"Oh! That's why Pastor Don started a new group for 'late shift' people. I'm sure glad, because those are the only hours The Garden Store needed an employee when I got home. At first I was disappointed, but when I told Pastor about it, he invited me to join the new group just getting started. He didn't tell me that you would be in it. Was I ever surprised! Isn't God amazing? He took care of that need before I even knew it existed. Thank you Father!"

"Indeed! I thank you, Father, too, because you answered my prayer for a small group so quickly, and then as a special bonus brought Fiona home and put her in the same group! I thank you and praise you for all the blessings!!" prayed Matt. "Oh, Fiona, I feel so blessed!"

She answered, "Me too! We could have a praise service right here in this restaurant."

He agreed, and then with his usual practicality, he asked, "What would you like for dessert?"

"Oh, ... I don't think I could eat another bite right now," Fiona stated. "But, I baked cookies this morning. If you'd like to come in after our walk--"

He interrupted, "Yum. That sounds better than dessert here!"

Fiona laughed and said, "Thank you for the delicious lunch, and for telling me about your job."

"My pleasure," Matt replied.

"Maybe on our walk you can tell me some more about your last two years. I'm going to stop in the restroom, now, before we go over to the church. I'm looking forward to being in church again. Hearing the service on the web and TV church is okay, but nothing compares with the real thing!" she said.

"You are so right!" He replied, "I'll meet you in the entry way of the restaurant when you're ready."

Fiona thanked him and when they were both ready, they drove to the church, parked and walked inside. They had time to greet a few people before sitting down. Many people noticed that Fiona was back and smiled and waved a welcome and she smiled and waved back. Their smiles got even bigger when they saw Matt sit beside her and her parents.

*****

Ted and Julie were in the church entryway 'practicing' name/face recognition of people in their small group, and waiting for Maria to arrive so she could sit with them if she wanted to. While they were standing there, they were able to see the composition of the congregation. There were people from many walks of life and ethnic backgrounds. It looked to be a real melting pot.

When the three of them were all seated near the front, Julie took time to really look at the sanctuary. She'd been too distracted the other two times. It was simple, but beautiful, decorated in blues, greens, and browns, with a lovely scenic photomural of a lake, trees and snow capped mountains. Comfortable, stack-able tan chairs had shelves under the seats to hold the Bibles and hymnals that were used in every weekend service. There were enough chairs to seat 300 people, and they were set up in rows with four sections and isles separating them. About half the chairs were filled up when the service started.

Julie could see that during the week, the room could be multipurpose, with baskets that would drop down for a basketball court. It made her wonder what else the room was used for during the week. The windows were high enough that the sun would give good light, but never get in people's eyes. That was good planning.

Then Julie looked at the large display board up front. It had the songs for the services listed in big enough letters that they could be seen clear in the back of the sanctuary. She took a hymnal to look them up before the service started. Most of the other people were doing the same thing. It was a good way to get prepared for the service. They would be singing the hymns: "All Glory Laud and Honor," John 12:13; and, "Hosanna, Loud Hosanna," Mathew 21:9; "Tell Me the Stories of Jesus," Mark 11:9; and the songs "Hosanna in the Highest," John 12:13; and "Love One Another," based on 1 John 4:7,8, "*Beloved, let us love one another; for love is of God, and everyone who loves is born of God and knows God. He who does not love does not know God, for*

God is love," and on 1 Corinthians 13:7 *"(Love) bears all things, believes all things, hopes all things, and endures all things."*

Pastor Don went up on the small stage and led the singing with the recorded music. Ted thought again that someday he would like to know how they prepared the music. It <u>was</u> beautifully done.

After the singing, the pastor began the teaching time. He spoke as a teacher, not like some strident, sometimes almost yelling preachers often do. "As you know, today is Palm Sunday, and we remember that Jesus, on the Sunday prior to his crucifixion and resurrection, rode humbly into Jerusalem on the foal of a donkey, not on a great white steed as a conquering king. The people could not understand who he was, or why he had come. Later in the week just before the Last Supper, Jesus humbly took the role of one of the lesser servants and washed the disciples' feet. The next day he willingly laid down his life as the perfect sacrifice to pay the penalty for man's sins. He was buried and his followers were very sorrowful. They could not understand what was happening. But on Resurrection Sunday, or Easter as many people say, God raised Jesus from the dead, and he appeared to many of his followers during the following 40 days.

"As we think about all Jesus did during his life and especially during the week following Palm Sunday, we can see that everything he did was done with God's perfect love. Let's all turn to 1 Corinthians 13 and read verses 4-8a together: *Love is patient, love is kind; it does not envy or boast and is not proud. It does not behave rudely, is not selfish, is not easily angered, and does not think evil. It rejoices in the truth, not in iniquity. It bears and believes and hopes and endures all things, and it never fails.*

"Keep your Bibles open. Last week, I talked a little bit about the Father's love and Jesus' love, and said we would study it in more detail this week. The verses we just read say it **all**, but here is a handout, which has synonyms for the positive terms, and antonyms for the negative ones. The 'ushers' (teenagers) are handing them out right now. As they do that, I'd like to mention that a good dictionary and thesaurus are often very helpful in your own personal Bible study times. Also, keeping a journal of things you are learning during those times can be invaluable.

"Now that everyone has a handout, I'd like you to read through it and think about it."

Synonyms

Love **is**:

patient: long suffering, tolerant, yielding, calm, showing self-control;
kind: compassionate, tenderhearted, attentive, considerate, thoughtful;
bears: holds up under, is understanding, is forgiving;
believes: trusts, depends, is confident;
hopes: expects, relies, looks forward to;
endures: perseveres, persists in spite of difficulties, continues.

Antonyms

Love does not or is not:
envy, but is content and happy for others gain;
boast, but is quiet about achievements;
proud, but is humble, modest, unassuming, meek;
rude, but is careful, courteous, thoughtful, gracious;
selfish, but seeks the good of others, is generous;
easily angered, but is self-disciplined, peaceful;
think evil, but thinks good or excellent things;
fail, but continues, remains, always functions.

"Go through the list again and this time circle one synonym/antonym for each term that strikes you as very important. ... Listen as I read the verses again with the words I circled when I prepared this. 1 Corinthians 13: 4-8a: *Love is long suffering, love is thoughtful; it is happy for others gain, is quiet about achievements, and is unassuming. It is courteous, seeks the good of others, is self-disciplined, and thinks good things. It rejoices in the truth. It is forgiving, is confident, and looks forward to ... and persists in spite of difficulties, and it continues.*

"The context for these verses is a discussion about the gifts of the Holy Spirit. Verses 1-3 basically say that whatever gift you have and use, if it's done without love, it's not worth anything. Look at verse 12:31b, which says, *now I show you a more excellent way*, a more excellent way than just having gifts. So I would say that love – the kind of love in verses 4-8a is the key to excellence in whatever we do. Think about it. ... Let's try to make this our goal: a lifestyle of **love**, in everything we do at all times, to all people, in all places, for the rest of our lives. I realize it's a big goal, but Philippians 4:13 says, *I can do all things through Christ who strengthens me.* Jesus, thank you for your help to live worthwhile lives in a loving way that's characterized by the love defined in 1 Corinthians 13: 4-8a.

"Before we leave, I have an announcement to make. We've started a new small group, which meets on Saturdays from 9:30 to 11:30 AM, to accommodate people who cannot attend an evening group during the week. If you are interested, please come and talk to me before you leave today, or call me early in the week."

"Now let's sing "Love One Another" again before we leave."

There were about 15 minutes to visit before having to leave in order that the parking lot would be empty for the next service, so Maria, Julie, and Ted stood and moved to a spot where they could talk. Ted said, "I like your idea of walking three times a week, like Monday, Wednesday, and Friday. I'd like to join in the project. If it's okay with you, I'll follow about ten paces behind you two so I can walk and pray while you two walk and visit."

Maria replied, "That sounds good. Shall we go now and figure out where to meet? I looked at the map, and have an idea for our first walk of about 20 minutes. We'll start out slowly and only do short walks for the first week."

"This is going to be great," said Julie. "I really need to start exercising and I've heard that walking is one of the best overall exercises. And besides that, it's easy and free, and it will give us a chance to visit at the same time. If it's too windy or rains, we'll just call and cancel."

Then Ted asked, "How about meeting in front of your apartment building, Maria? Julie and I can drive over, then if we ever want to walk in a different area, we can all go in our car."

Maria agreed, and they all left saying, "See you tomorrow at about 5:30 PM."

*****

Pastor Don saw several people waiting to talk to him and assumed it was about the new small group. They came up to him one or two at a time. The first was Clara Morgan, who had just changed to a 1 to 9 PM job when the new semester started, so that she could start nurses training. She gratefully accepted the paper with Ted and Julie's name and address, and the 9:30, Saturday morning time written on it. She left with thanks and a smile.

Next, Roy and Sherry Foster came up to him, and Roy said, "You know that we've just decided to put our twin girls in kindergarten next year in the church school. In order to pay for

Linda L. Linn

that, Sherry had to go back to work. Home Depot changed my hours to 6:00 AM to 2:00 PM and Wal-Mart is letting Sherry work from 2:30 to 10:30 PM, so that we can take turns being home with the girls during the workweek. But that meant we had to stop going to our other small group. We were thrilled when you announced the new group starting up on Saturday mornings, and would really like to be in it!"

"Of course, Roy, that will be fine. Here is the address for the meeting next Saturday. The couple are new to town and their names are Ted and Julie Blake," said Pastor Don handing him a paper.

"Thank you so much," said Sherry. "After the girls start kindergarten I'll be able to work while they're in school, so we can be in this group until all the groups change in January."

Pastor Don replied, "That sounds very good, Sherry. I'll see you both on Saturday morning, then."

They left and young man in his mid-twenties hurried up to the pastor and said, "I haven't had a chance to tell you, but about a month ago, I was promoted to assistant manager at the Fiesta Espanola Restaurante, and now I'm in charge of lunch, supper and closing, so I work from 12 to 9 PM. I'm so happy that a new group is starting which meets at a time when I can go to it. I hope there will be room for me in it."

Pastor Don smiled and said, "I'm happy to say that there's room and we'll be glad to have you in our group, Antonito. Congratulations on your promotion! I know what a good worker you are. This paper has the address of Ted and Julie Blake who are new to town. We're meeting at their apartment this coming Saturday. See you there." Antonito smiled, thanked the pastor and then went out to walk home.

After he left, the pastor saw one other couple waiting, and they were looking a bit worried so he hurried over to them and greeted them, "Larry and Jane Kelsey, it's good to see you. How have you been? It's good to have you back home, Jane. We've missed you. How did your time go with your daughter? Let's go into that little conference room, so we will be out of the way when the next congregation comes into the sanctuary."

They followed him into the little room and everybody sat down. After all those questions and comments, they didn't know where to begin. Jane started by saying, "We're doing well, thank you, and it's very good to be back home. I missed everybody here too, <u>especially</u> Larry! My daughter, Lucy, is doing very well and so is her new son, Jonathan. She was very grateful to have me stay on the extra time after his birth, which went very well. We had a special time of sharing and working together for the last two months. Plus, I really enjoyed the milder winter there. The part I didn't like was that there weren't any good churches to attend." (Pastor Don kept those last two statements in mind, because the overall church was preparing to start planting churches in other cities.)

    Larry continued by saying, "As you know, I didn't attend a small group while Jane was gone since we didn't know how long she would stay there. We thought it would be better to start together in one when she got back. A brand new group would be even better, unless there is no room. When we saw so many people talking to you about the new group we were worried that there would not be room for us in it. But, we'll understand if this is the case."

    Pastor Don smiled and said, "I'm happy to say that there <u>is</u> room and we'll be glad to have you both in our group. In fact, this will be <u>perfect</u>. Ted and Julie Blake are a new couple in town. They both have 8 to 5 jobs, but I asked them to be in the new group because I thought a new group would not be so overwhelming to them. With both of you in this group, <u>they</u> will have some early evening people to do things with when we have projects to work on later. Since you know about those kinds of projects, you can help teach them what to do. Here's a paper with their address and the time on it. We're meeting at their apartment this week. I look forward to seeing you both this Saturday."

    Both of them relaxed after he had said his first sentence and were smiling broadly when he handed them the address. After thanking him profusely, they exited using the outside door of the little room and happily went to their car. Pastor Don went and found Anita and the children patiently waiting for him in the little room set aside for mothers with crying babies or noisy children next to the sanctuary. When they were all seated in the car, he told Anita that they had six new members for the new small group.

    "I'm impressed," Anita said. "Maybe you can tell me all about them after we get these patiently waiting children home where they can run around and get rid of some of their pent-up energy. They've been very good today, by the way."

    "I'm glad to hear that. Thank you children. If everybody is buckled in and ready, we'll head right home," said Don. As soon as they arrived, Anita helped Mary change clothes. Timmy could do that by himself. Then the children were allowed to go outside and run and play to their hearts content. Their parents sat in the porch swing and watched them as Don told Anita all about the new members.

*****

Matt and Fiona drove to a nice park that had a walking path beside the river that ran through Pine City. The afternoon was warm and not very windy, just right for a slow walk and more conversation.

"It was so good to be back in church again and have it be very much like I remembered it. The congregation has grown, though. I wonder how many people are coming regularly now. I saw many new faces," Fiona mentioned.

"Yes, I'll bet it was <u>very</u> noticeable to you after two years away. It's been growing slowly all the while and I haven't noticed it. I wonder who keeps track of that kind of thing. Maybe we could ask Pastor Don about it," Matt replied.

"I like your idea. After talking about it, I'm really curious. Now, would you like to tell me more about your last two years and get me up to date there?" asked Fiona.

"Sure," answered Matt. "Let's see, I had just finished telling you about my job, so now I'll tell you about the house I'm building."

"Oh," she interrupted. You <u>did</u> get started on it! You had told me some things about it before I left. Sorry I interrupted. Please go ahead."

"Don't worry about it," he responded. "The blueprints are finished and I started construction shortly after you left. At first I was able to go work on it for several hours every day, after working with Walt, but since we have gone on two shifts, I'm being careful to only work a couple hours in the morning so I'm not too tired to do a good job as foreman. Therefore the progress has slowed down a lot. The foundation and floor are finished and some of the outside walls are framed and up."

"I'd like to see it sometime. Are you using the same floor plan you showed to me two years ago? I liked it. You had some very good ideas," said Fiona.

"Thank you, Fiona. Yes, it's the same floor plan. I'd be happy to take you to see it any time. Walt has helped me a lot by answering questions and with planning as I go along. He and Betty have become very good friends and I've even had a chance to talk to them about the Lord and the plan of salvation. Progress on that has been slow up until yesterday when I went to lunch at their house." Matt proceeded to tell her about their discussion after lunch and being able to leave that book and a Bible with them to read. "I'm praying that they'll read with an open mind and that the Holy Spirit will draw them to Jesus for salvation."

"That's marvelous! I'm so glad you haven't given up on them. Sometimes it gets very discouraging when people won't listen or harden their hearts and turn Jesus away. I'll be sure and remember them in my prayers, also. Thank you for sharing that with me. It's gotten rather chilly. Do you mind if we turn back and walk quickly to the pick-up?" Fiona asked. "Then we can go to my home, warm up and have some cookies while we visit with my parents. They mentioned that they would like to see you for a longer time than just for you to ask permission to court me. I explained to them that your boss had asked you over for lunch before you knew anything about my being back home and then they understood."

They hurried back to the car and drove to Fiona's house. When they went inside it felt nice and warm. Patrick and Glenda greeted them warmly. They didn't even tease him about how fast he had left yesterday. Fiona asked him, "Would you like coffee or milk or something else with the cookies?"

"I'm going to surprise you, Fiona. I still don't like coffee, but a hot cup of that cherry tea with honey would be delicious, and it would help warm me up after our chilly walk. I'm glad you noticed that it was cooling off and told me about it," answered Matt.

"Me too. Yes, you did surprise me, one hot cup of cherry tea with honey coming up. How about you, Mom and Dad, what would you like with your cookies?"

"Tea for me," said Dad and her mother chose the same thing.

"Good," said Fiona, "that makes it easy for me to remember. I don't know how waitresses do such a good job of remembering without even writing it down." Then she left to get it all ready.

Matt was left alone with her parents and he wondered what they would want to talk about, or if he should have offered to go and help Fiona prepare and bring it all out. He decided to relax and ask them some questions, "Mr. O'Connor how is your job going."

"Just fine, and I think you can leave the formal Mr. O'Connor out and just call me Patrick and that goes for Glenda, also," Patrick answered. "I'm still working at The Garden Store, managing all the outside work there in the spring, summer and fall. In the winter, I get to be indoors doing odd jobs. I was glad that they had a place for Fiona when she returned, even though it's a late shift. At first she wasn't very happy about the work hours, but she was extra pleased when she walked into the new small group and saw you sitting there." They all had a good laugh about that, and then heard Fiona call for her dad to come help with the tray of hot tea. She followed with a tray of mouth-watering, oatmeal-raisin cookies.

When everybody was served, the conversation continued. Matt asked, "Glenda, are you still working?"

"No," she answered. I decided to take a few months off and enjoy having Fiona back home. Plus, I would like to get some sewing done and maybe change some things around here in the house."

"What a wonderful plan, Mother." Fiona stated. "Maybe you can come with us when Matt shows me the house he's started." Then she looked questioningly at Matt.

He quickly responded, "Great idea, I only wish Patrick could come also. Hey! I know what! Let's go as soon as we finish these delicious cookies and tea. Since it is still light out, we can see the progress right out of the vehicle's windows so we won't even have to get out in the cold."

Everyone agreed and they were off, as soon as they had finished the goodies. When they got there, Fiona exclaimed, "Oh! I really like this part of town, and the view from here is spectacular! The mountains are so majestic off there in the distance. There will never be a building to block the view, because of the beautiful park on this side."

Matt was so pleased with her reaction that all her could do was smile and smile. He had picked this location with her in mind, knowing how she liked the mountains. He was finally able to speak, "I'm glad you like it, Fiona." There was so much more he could add, but it wasn't time yet. After looking at the partly constructed house for a little while and answering some questions, he drove them back to their house and promised to bring the house plans in for them to see sometime. Before leaving, he asked Fiona, "May I take you to breakfast on Wednesday morning at about 8 AM?"

She answered, "I would like that a lot. I'll be ready. Thank you for lunch and the nice walk and for showing us your house!"

"My pleasure!" Matt replied. I'll see you on Wednesday morning." Then he 'floated' out to his pick-up and went home to clean up his apartment and get his laundry ready to take to the Laundromat the next morning. Afterwards, if it would be nice out he'd get a couple hours of work in on the house tomorrow. He had a lot more incentive now that Fiona was back home!

*****

Jeff and Karen Spencer decided to go for a walk after they got home from church, so they changed clothes and shoes and walked to the park near their house. "I think spring has finally decided to come to our fine city," commented Karen as they started down the path in the park. "The grass is getting green and I think I see some flowers blooming over there. Let's go see them. I wonder how many other people are taking walks today; ... it's just the right weather for it." They walked quickly over and admired the flowers and Karen continued, "I'm glad we didn't have to wait until tomorrow to hear about Matt and Fiona. I saw them get in Matt's pick-up after church to go somewhere. I think they'll have a lovely afternoon."

"Me too," agreed Jeff. "I'm happy for them. What did you think about the teaching time today?"

"I thought that hand out was very helpful and such a good idea. It really brought those terms to life and made them more meaningful. I especially liked the antonyms because I've never enjoyed reading about all those negative things that love is not. I'm going to keep a dictionary and thesaurus on my desk where I do my Bible study and next time we go to Wal-Mart, I'm going to buy a small notebook to use for a journal," stated Karen.

"You always amaze me, the way you can remember what Pastor Don says and then do the practical things to start doing what he has suggested. I'll do the same things you just said and I thank you for mentioning them. I'm blessed to have such an extraordinary wife," declared Jeff.

She blushed and responded, "You're welcome, Jeff, and thank you for the compliments. I'm blessed to have such a godly husband who loves the Lord and wants to do his will. It's wonderful that we can be in unity about the most important thing in life. I know of too many people in this city who cannot even share these kinds of things with their spouse. It must be very hard to live that way."

"You're right." Then he prayed, "Father in heaven, you heard what Karen just said, and we ask that you will please help all those people who are in that situation. Please bring about the changes necessary to wake up the unbelieving spouse to his or her need of salvation. Show us what specific thing we can do to help any couple we know of in that situation. I think Karen may have someone in mind."

"Yes, Father, I do, and you know their names. Give me very clear guidance and then help me to do whatever you tell me to do," said Karen. Then they sprinted back to their house thinking about the song and the scripture verse that talks about how good and pleasant it is when people live in unity.

*****

When Larry and Jane Kelsey left the church, they were smiling. He said, "We have a wonderful pastor, don't we, Honey?"

She answered, "We sure do. He could tell that we were worried about asking, but he put us right at ease. It's like God had it all planned for us to get into a new group, just starting up, rather than trying to fit into one already up and running."

"Yes," Larry agreed, "and it really will help the new couple to have another couple who can do projects with them in the evenings since all the rest of the group members are on evening shifts. Wow! What a God we have, who can orchestrate even those kind of details. I'm amazed!" He started singing the chorus about how awesome our God is, and Jane joined him.

When they finished singing, Jane responded, "I'm amazed too. I'll enjoy getting to know the new couple, Ted and Julie; I think that's what he said. Oh, yes, it's here on the paper. Let's drive past their apartment so we'll know where to go Saturday."

"Okay," Larry agreed. "And I'll enjoy watching to see whatever else God has planned for us to do. I have a feeling there might be some big changes coming for us in the future."

"Why do you think that," she asked, curious to know what could have prompted a statement like that right out of the blue.

"I don't really know, but the way all these details worked out, it seems like God might have an even bigger plan in mind, besides giving us a new group to join, -- for which I am grateful, -- or even helping the pastor out with the new couple, ... he trailed off.

"I think I can see what you mean. Yes, all of these details were amazing, but they might also be like road signs to alert us that we need to be ready for something even bigger coming later," Jane agreed. "Let's stop and park here next to this nice park and pray that God will help us to watch and be ready for all the steps along the way."

Everywhere There's a Sunrise, Let's Tell The Good News!

So they did just that, and then drove past the Blake's apartment complex before heading home.

*****

Antonito (Tony) Valdez was elated that there was a new group starting that would meet when he could attend <u>and</u> that there was room in it so that he could join. He had been very pleased with his promotion at work, except that when he realized he'd have to quit going to the small group he was in, it spoiled some of his pleasure. But he had prayed about it and already God had worked it all out.

He thanked and praised God all the way, as he walked home to his studio apartment, only about 4 blocks away from the church. He also thanked God that the restaurant was even closer, along with all the shopping he needed, so he didn't have the expense of owning a vehicle or the bother of trying to find parking places. The bus service in this city was also very good. He did have a bicycle for pleasure, exercise, and errands. Pine City had good bike lanes and paths, and so he felt very well provided for. By the time he had thanked God for all those things, he had arrived home.

*****

Roy and Sherry Foster picked up their soon to be 5-year-old twin girls, Hope and Joy, from the Sunday school class they were in, and headed for their car. When the girls were buckled in, they headed to the nearest park that had playground equipment so the girls could play and work off some of their energy while their parents talked about the church service and new small group they would go to on Saturday.

"My biggest concern," mentioned Sherry, is what we'll do with the twins while we're there. We had a good baby sitter when we went to the evening group, but she might not want to do it on Saturday mornings."

"True, but we can call her and if she can't or won't do it, we'll ask Anita if she has any ideas," replied Roy. "I don't think it will be a problem. The good Lord has worked out all the other fine points of this plan to put to girls into this Christian school, so I'm sure he will fix this, too."

Sherry replied, "You're right. God is the one in control of our lives, of course! It isn't my problem and he will do a much better job of putting everything in place than I could anyway."

"You've got it!" said Roy. "I thought the handout the pastor gave us today was a unique idea. It will help me to focus on the meanings of those terms instead of just reading them."

"Yes," she answered. "You know that desk we have set up for our personal Bible study times while the other one is at work and the twins are playing quietly? I would like to put a dictionary and thesaurus on it and get us each a notebook to write in like he suggested. What do you think?"

"My thoughts exactly!" he agreed. "Let's buy us each a little notebook the next time we're at Wal-Mart. Now let's go play with the girls for a while."

*****

When Clara Morgan got home to her little studio apartment, after church that Sunday, the first thing she did was thank God for the new small group starting on Saturday mornings and that the time would work out fine for her busy schedule. Then she went to her bookcase and removed the dictionary and thesaurus from the shelf and took them over to the desk where she did her daily Bible study. She already had a little notebook that would work well to write down things she would be learning. She was grateful that she had a pastor who gave them good practical suggestions that could improve their lives <u>and</u> that it didn't cost very much to implement them.

Next, she called one of her single girl friends from church and invited her over for supper. When she said yes, Clara got busy straightening up her apartment and then cooking what they would eat for supper. It was nice to have friends who could come visit on short notice.

*****

Chapter 4

Isaiah 55: 8,9, *For my thoughts are not your thoughts, neither are your ways my ways, says the LORD. For as the heavens are higher than the earth, so are my ways higher than your ways, and my thoughts than your thoughts.*

Monday

Everywhere There's a Sunrise, Let's Tell The Good News!

Early Monday morning, Matt ate a hurried breakfast and went to the Laundromat to get his laundry into the washers before the crowd arrived. Doing laundry wasn't his favorite chore, but it surely needed to be done, especially with a job like construction. His work clothes got dirty so quickly. He was just taking his clothes out of the washers and putting them in the dryers when the first of the other people arrived. He greeted them and they talked for a while. Then he got his clothes out of the dryers, folded them, and rushed home to put them away. He changed clothes and still had time to get a couple hours of work done on his house before resting a while, eating lunch and going to the work site by 1:30 so Walt could tell him what the plan was for the afternoon.

He was so pleased that Fiona liked the site he had picked out for the house and now that she was back home, he could hardly wait to get more work done on it. Maybe someday soon they could talk about plans for the future, <u>their future</u>. But he knew he would have to be patient and not push her. They needed time to get reacquainted, and he knew both of them had changed somewhat during the past two years. Although he felt so sure that she was the one for him, it was harder to be patient.

Before he left to work on the house, he spent some time in prayer and Bible reading. When he went shopping tomorrow for groceries and other things, he would buy a good dictionary, thesaurus and a little notebook to write down what he would be learning. This made him think of Fiona and what she had said about keeping a journal of the things she was learning while taking care of her aunt. So, she was way ahead of him on doing that sort of thing.

*****

Maria and the Blakes had both gone to work as usual on Monday, and hurried home so they could go together for their first exercise walk. They changed into comfortable clothes and walking shoes and met in front of Maria's apartment building at 5:30 PM. They started off slowly to get warmed up since that is what all the books say to do. After about five minutes like that, they went a little faster. It felt good to be out in the fresh air after being inside all day.

"How was your day today, Maria?" Julie asked.

"It went very well. I went there, about ten minutes early to open up the office, because Mr. Beckett said he didn't know if he would be back from being out of town in time to do it as he usually does. Then I made the coffee, and it turned out all right since I looked up how to do it on the web yesterday afternoon. You know I don't drink coffee myself, so I didn't have a clue. He did get back about three hours late, so it was good planning to have me open up so all the employees could get to work as usual. I went to his office before I came home and gave him back the key and he told me he would like to talk to me tomorrow, at 4 PM. But he didn't say what it would be about. I sure am curious, but I'll just have to wait and see."

"That sounds intriguing!" Julie responded. "Let's pray about it right now. Somehow I get the feeling it might be something momentous. Is your boss a Christian?"

Maria answered, "I don't think so, and he does not want to talk about it. Every time I've brought up the topic, he has changed the subject hastily."

Julie prayed, "Father in heaven, we come to you in Jesus name, asking you to give Maria the wisdom she'll need to listen to and respond correctly to her boss. Give her peace as she waits for her scheduled time to see him tomorrow."

Maria continued, "Yes, please, Father, you said in James 1:5, *if anyone needs wisdom, we are to ask you for it and you will give it.* Thank you for that promise. I claim it now for myself in all my dealings with Mr. Beckett. He can seem rather intimidating at times, so I thank you for the peace I'll need also. We pray in Jesus name, Amen." Then she asked, "How was your day today, and how are you liking your job?"

"My day went well and very fast. I like this job a lot. It's fun to see the children come in with worried faces and be able to help them relax. All the employees in this dental office do a great job with the children. By the time they leave, most of them have smiles on their faces, unless their mouths have been deadened for some procedure and then they can't smile.

"But I do have a prayer request for you to pray about. You know that my major was elementary education in college, and I was able to teach for two years before the city I was in, cut back on funds and I wasn't rehired. That's why I was working at a dental office this year before we moved. They gave me a good recommendation for the job here.

"Anyway, the other day, I was remembering how much work I had to take home every evening and on weekends, and even though I like teaching, I'm glad I now have a job that I can leave at 5PM and not think about it again until the next morning. That has been especially helpful with this move and all the changes taking place to go along with it. Please pray with me about whether to try to find a job teaching sometime, or to just keep the job I have. Of course, the lady I replaced might decide to come back to work, after she has her baby and stays home with it for a while. Things are kind of up in the air, and I need direction," finished Julie.

"Father, you heard everything Julie just told me and I claim the same wisdom for her that you so freely give when we ask. Make it very plain to her what your will is in this matter, so she'll be at peace knowing she's in the center of your will. Thank you, Father. Wow, we're almost back to my home, but I'll continue to pray for you about this issue and I ask you to continue praying for me, also," said Maria.

"I'll be sure to do that and if it's okay with you, I'll explain it to Ted and have him pray about it also," she responded.

"Sure, that would be a good idea," concurred Maria.

"Look, we're back already! As I look at my watch, it took us exactly 20 minutes. That was very well planned out, Maria. You did a very good job, and here comes Ted ten steps behind us, looking mighty pleased about something," said Julie. As he approached, she asked, "How did it go for you?"

"It was a wonderful time of praying, and the 20 minutes went so fast. This is great," he answered. "It looked like the two of you were having a good time of talking together."

"We were, and I'll look forward to this coming Wednesday. See you then," Maria said and started to go inside, but Ted stopped her by asking: "Would you and Julie like to go out to eat tonight, or do you have other plans? I didn't think about this in time to even ask Julie whether she would like to, so either of you feel free to decline if you want to."

Both of them were a little shocked and then Julie answered, "For myself anyway, I would really like that, especially if we could go to the Suehiros' restaurant. I'd like to try it out and talk to Ami for a minute."

Maria jumped right in enthusiastically, "That would be fantastic! You'll both really like their food and the ambiance is also very nice. We should change into something a little nicer than our walking clothes and shoes. I can be ready in fifteen minutes."

"<u>Super</u>, we'll be back in about fifteen minutes and go to <u>supper</u>," laughed Ted and so did they.

They hurried home and changed. Then they picked Maria up and drove to Ami's Japanese Restaurant. With the directions given by Maria as they went along, it was easy to find. When they got inside, they were seated near a window giving a view of a beautiful Japanese garden. Sometime, when the weather warmed up it might be fun to sit outside at one of those tables in the midst of the garden. Ami came over to welcome them to the restaurant and even called them by name, "Welcome, Ted and Julie and Maria. It is so nice to see you."

Julie said, "See, your appetizers worked, and here we are! I'm glad you had this as a plan. What a delicious way to advertise. Your restaurant is beautiful, so welcoming and peaceful!"

Ami looked relieved and replied, "Thank you. I'm glad you like it and that our idea worked so well that it brought you here. Look over the menus, and I'll be back soon to take your orders."

After she had gone, Maria asked, "How do you know Ami and about this restaurant?"

Ted answered, "They're in the new small group with us, and the first meeting was at their house. They provided the refreshments by making finger foods of some of their restaurant items. They were all delicious."

The three of them looked at the menus, and each chose a different entree. When Ami came back, they were ready to order. Then they enjoyed the tea she had brought with her and visited while they waited. Julie noticed a booklet on the table with a pretty spring picture on the front. The title was "Our Daily Bread." Inside were scriptures and related devotionals for each day of the spring season. On the back a note said: "Take me home and finish reading me."

Later, when their orders arrived, and they had said grace, Julie stopped them from digging in by saying, "Wait! Before we taste anything, could each of us put two spoonful's of our entrée on the other two plates so that we can all see what the others taste like?"

"Superb idea," answered Maria, and Ted nodded. After the sharing was completed, they all started eating, with many sounds like "yum," expressing appreciation for each taste treat. "Now that I know the names to go with these three entrees, I'm better prepared to choose next time. They're all delicious," Maria declared.

"Right, and your eating partner can choose something new to share so you'll know of another good choice," Julie responded.

"Actually, I think no matter what I would choose, I'd like it because they're all good," added Ted.

"That's for sure!" both ladies agreed.

"Unless it is something with very hot spices in it," Julie tacked on. And the others laughed with her, remembering that she didn't care for hot food.

Just then Tomo came with the little tray of 'fortune' cookies and said, "We're so glad you all came to try out our restaurant and we hope you'll come again."

Ted answered, "I'm sure we will. This will now be one of our <u>favorite</u> places to come for special, delicious meals." Tomo nodded, smiled and went on his way.

When they opened each 'fortune' cookie they were all surprised and pleased to find a scripture verse inside instead of a silly 'fortune'.

It had been a pleasant evening for all of them, including the Suehiros. Ami hugged Tomo in the kitchen when they had a free minute and said, "You were right, Dear, everything did work out fine, and I was <u>very</u> glad to see it." Tomo smiled and hugged her again.

*****

Fiona's first evening working at The Garden Store that Monday, was almost like coming home, except that she had worked days there before she left. She enjoyed the flowers, and working with all the plants. They were pleasing to care for and it was fun to watch them grow, flourish and bloom. She would be in charge of watering, feeding, pruning, and culling dead leaves so they would stay looking beautiful while they waited for someone to buy and take them home.

She would also do anything else that needed to be done. She would be arranging flowers and answering questions or giving advice when Connie was busy or not there. When she was working there before, she had made up little cards with printed information to help the new owners continue to care for the plants they bought. She was pleased to see that it was still being done. In her opinion, it was more sensible to buy blooming plants than cut flower arrangements. But she liked arranging flowers also.

Connie was delighted to have her back, and even changed her shift on Tuesdays and Thursdays, so they could work together. On Wednesdays, she and her husband, Ernest, could still go to their small group in the evening. "I'm really sorry about your hours, Fiona," said Connie, "because I know how important small groups are to you."

They kept right on working while they talked. "Oh, don't worry about it at all!" exclaimed Fiona. The good Lord already worked that all out for me. I'm just so glad you could rehire me! Did you hear the announcement on Sunday about the new small group? Pastor Don told me about it last week when I told them about my new working hours. I already went to the first meeting on Saturday morning."

"That's _so_ good! What a caring, awesome God we have! Plus, I noticed that Matt sat with you and your parents on Sunday," she said with a gleam in her eyes.

Fiona blushed and smiled and waited just a few moments to build suspense. Connie looked at her with that expectant stare, and finally Fiona told her all about Matt being in the same group, their talk on Saturday, and how he had asked her dad again if he could court her. She also told about the lunch at their favorite restaurant before church, their walk afterward, and even about him showing her parents and her the house he had started.

"It sounds like he's _serious_, Connie said.

"I think he is, and I'm glad, but I want to take this slowly, enjoy it, and get to know him better. I want a man who is as good as my dad. I know that's a big order, but it's important to me!" Fiona stated emphatically.

"Good for you, Fiona! Lord please help Fiona to keep her eyes on her goal and be patient to see what your perfect will is in this relationship," prayed Connie.

"And thank you, Lord, for the way you have worked things out so far. Please give me wisdom and insight along with that patience. Guide me please, because now I have a lot of questions about him. Also, please help me to become the woman you want me to be," Fiona added.

They kept working and talking, and Connie asked, "What was it like while you were taking care of your great aunt? I'm sorry about your loss." Fiona thanked her and told her all about that time too. Then Connie said, "It sounds like an intense time of learning and growing for you."

Fiona agreed, "Yes, it was, and now I'm thankful for it, although it was hard at times. At first I was very homesick, but the Lord and Aunt Cara helped me get over it, and I learned to be content. Now it's your turn, Connie. What have the past two years been like for you?"

"Well, let's see." Connie answered. "It all kind of runs together, since no big thing happened like your move to set anything apart.

We've had several employees come and go, plus our oldest son, Ben, will be graduating from high school at the end of the year. I'm glad he's planning to attend the local trade school to study carpentry, plumbing, and electrician work plus anything else related to building. He isn't sure which branch he wants to major in, maybe a little of each so he can be a contractor. He's been talking a lot to Matt the last few months and that has been very helpful to him. He can still live at home and his classes won't interfere with the youth group he attends. His sister, Amy, who now wants to be called by her full name, Amelia, will be a senior next year, and wants to start dating. You can bet her parents don't like that!"

"I can just imagine, but as I remember, Amelia, she's a very intelligent, level headed girl, and has had very good training growing up, so she should do well," said Fiona. "Shall we pray for her, now?" Connie nodded, so Fiona began, "Father, you know everything, and you are in control of all our lives. Thank you for Amelia, and her wonderful parents, Ernest and Connie, who have raised her so carefully. Please give them wisdom and peace as they begin this new era in their lives. Help Amelia to stay submissive to her parents, and keep her from temptation, and from evil. Give her the desire to do your will."

"Yes, Heavenly Father, I agree with all that Fiona just prayed, and thank you in advance for your answer. I especially need your peace and wisdom," Connie finished. "Thank you Fiona. You've grown in the Lord, and he just used you to encourage me."

"I'm glad," Fiona replied and then started singing the chorus of a song she had heard many times at her great Aunt Cara's house on her old fashioned turntable. The vinyl records were still in good shape and that's what they played since her aunt didn't have anything more modern. The chorus was about the person wanting to be used by God.

When she had finished, Connie said, with misty eyes, "That was lovely, and you have a beautiful voice. Those words are so meaningful." They worked for a while in silence and then she said, "I just had an idea. Would you be willing to be a friend to Amelia? She has so few friends, and I know she would like to have a part-time job. If she could work here on part of this shift, you two could get better acquainted and maybe she would be willing to talk and listen to you, since you're closer to her age than her parents are. She's become rather silent at home, and frankly, I'm worried about her."

"Certainly, Connie, that sounds like a good idea. I could use a girl friend too, since most of my classmates have moved away or have gotten married. When could she get started? Maybe just for a third of the shift or so a couple times a week. That would still give her time to study. It sounds to me like an undertaking that needs to get started ASAP," suggested Fiona.

"I agree, and I'll talk to Amelia about it. I need to make it sound like a job for her with pay of course, and that you need the extra help. Then we'll pray that friendship will result and grow naturally. I don't want her to feel like we're manipulating her," Connie said.

"For sure! That would be counterproductive. Thank you, Lord, that you are right here with the two of us as we're discussing this important matter, and that you know all about it. You also know the best way to implement and carry out, or change our plans. So we ask for wisdom and guidance to help Amelia, and bring glory to you in the process," Fiona prayed.

"I agree, Lord. Amen. Well, this has been a very productive evening. Just look at all the plants we've nurtured, and all the while we've been able to talk and pray and become reacquainted. I'm so glad you're home, and are working here again!" exclaimed Connie.

"The feeling is mutual for sure," returned Fiona. "I'm glad that you needed an employee when I came back home. It's nice to be working in a familiar place with a good Christian boss, and not have to job hunt all over town. I'm feeling very blessed, indeed."

*****

When Matt got to the work site at his usual time, Monday, Walt came over quickly and told him, "Both of us are very impressed with the book you loaned us. We've been sitting side by side on the sofa at various times during the day, reading silently and interrupting each other when we have a comment or question or need to look up a verse in the Bible you also loaned us. We keep telling each other that so far, it makes good sense."

"I'm glad to hear that," Matt responded. "Will you let me know when you both are ready to discuss it with me?" Walt nodded, and Matt continued, "You're looking more tired today, Walt, and I'm worried about you. I really think you should go see a doctor."

"Betty said the same thing yesterday," he answered. "I'll call and make an appointment today when I get home. Now here's what's planned for the second shift ..."

Everywhere There's a Sunrise, Let's Tell The Good News!

When he finished explaining what needed to be done, Matt watched him leave and spent a few minutes in silent prayer before he organized the materials they would be using the rest of the day. Second shift went well, and they got a lot accomplished.

*****

Tuesday

On Tuesday morning, right after Ben and Amelia had left for school, Connie said, "Ernest, Fiona and I had a very nice time working together yesterday evening." Then she filled him in on parts of the conversation. "What do you think about the idea of offering an evening job to Amelia just part-time, but starting it off slowly with two 3-hour shifts a week. She could go in from 5 to 8PM on Wednesdays, and Fridays. That would still give her a couple hours to study when she gets home from school, and on the weekends, and she could still attend her youth group on Tuesdays."

Ernest considered the idea for a few minutes and then asked, "Do we <u>really</u> need another employee for that evening shift, since you changed your hours in order to work with Fiona?"

"I thought about that, but I only changed them for Tuesdays and Thursdays, and I'm willing to just work with Fiona on the days Amelia isn't there. If it works out, and she wants another day, she could add Monday, and I could still work with Fiona Tuesdays and Thursdays. My hours are flexible and I can work wherever and whenever I'm needed. Besides, perhaps I might even take a part of a day off myself, in addition to Sunday of course," she teased.

"Now <u>that</u> sounds good to me. I wonder if we could take the same part of a day sometime and go do something fun together. 'All work and no play,' you know. We don't want to become dull," he suggested.

"I <u>really</u> like that idea. Let's plan on it, but what do you think about the other proposal?" she inquired.

"I do think your idea is a good one for Amelia. I've noticed some of the same things you mentioned, and hope that this will help her. Father, I know they prayed about this last night, but I want to add my agreement and request for your help and guidance, and that your will be done for our Amelia, " he prayed. "Now I guess I had better get ready for work. Would you like me to ask Amelia if she would like the job?"

"That sounds good. It might be more appealing coming from you since you do most of the hiring. Yes, please do that when you get home today. I'd like her to get started as soon as possible but don't want to seem pushy," she answered. "I have a lot of things I want to get done here this morning before I eat lunch and go to work. Thank you for listening, and for thinking about it <u>before</u> you agreed, and for your help in praying and in being the one to ask Amelia."

"My pleasure, my dear wife. It is good to have time to talk and pray about these important things. I'll see you when you get to work, Honey." Then he left to get ready, after a hug and a kiss.

*****

Tuesday morning, Maria went to her office and got right to work. She was curious, and a little concerned about the upcoming appointment her boss made to talk with her. But that would not be until 4 PM, and before then she had a lot of work to do, so she put it out of her mind and got busy. She remembered off and on to pray that Julie would have wisdom about whether to teach again. The time went rapidly and she actually finished most of what she had to do for the day with enough time to spare, that she was able to get a quick drink of water and freshen up in the restroom before going to Mr. Beckett's office.

He was at the door to open it when she knocked. (That seemed strange to her. He must have been waiting.) He welcomed her in, and instead of sitting behind his desk the way he usually did, he had two comfortable chairs facing each other and invited her to sit in one of them. He sat in the other one and although he looked a little nervous (which was <u>very</u> unusual for him), he plunged right in. "I have very good news for you. Over the weekend while I was out of town, I was able to finish up the audit we've been doing on that company. With your expert help these past months, it went a lot faster than I expected, and I thank you very much for your willingness and hard work there."

Maria was pleased. She smiled and replied, "I'm glad I was able to help, and I'm delighted to hear that you were able to finish with the audit."

"That's not all," Mr. Beckett said, "Since you agreed to open the office for me, I was able to stay later on Monday morning, and I sold that company for a very good price. It will no longer be a bother to either of us."

"Amazing! That's wonderful," She exclaimed.

He added, "The most wonderful thing is that now I'll have time to do something I have wanted to do for a very long time."

There was a long pause and Maria had no idea what to say. She used the time to pray silently for the Holy Spirit to fill her mouth with just the right words to say at the right time.

Then he continued, "Please listen, without comment, all the way to the end of what I'm going to say." After she nodded, he went on, "Maria, you've been working for me now for about two years. I have observed you in many situations, and I've been very pleased with what I've seen. For the last year you went and helped with the audit of that company keeping everything in complete confidence as I asked you to do, and I never heard a word of complaint as you did it.

(Maria almost gulped as she remembered her attitude the last time she had returned from out of town, but she remained inscrutable.)

"We have another office in this city, and there's a vacancy there doing work much like what you do here. I would like to transfer you to that office starting tomorrow." He handed her a card with the name, address and phone number of the other office on it. "Obviously, my reason for doing this is NOT because I'm unhappy to have you working here, but because I have another rationale." After a short pause he continued, "Maria, I have fallen in love with you, and I would like to be able to court you without the stigma of us both working in the same building. My ultimate goal is to be able to ask you to be my wife, because you are everything I have been looking for, for many years, and I would like to spend the rest of my life with you." He hurried on to say, "Please don't say 'No' yet. Please give us a chance. I promise you that I only want to cherish and take good care of you," he finished.

Now he <u>was</u> waiting for an answer from Maria, so she opened her mouth in faith that the Lord would fill it with his words. "You've honored me greatly by your proposal. To say the least, I admit that I'm very surprised. I had no idea that you had any feelings for me. You've hidden them very well. First, let me say that I'll be happy to take the vacancy in the other office across town. I'll empty my things out of my desk after we finish here and go there tomorrow. Next, I must ask you a question. What do you believe about Jesus Christ?"

"In the past, when you brought up the subject of religion, I was quick to change the subject, I know. It wasn't something I wanted to discuss, especially during work hours, and since we're at work, I request that we talk about that subject when we are on our first date," he stated.

She nodded, and he went on, "I know this must seem very strange to you, and I don't plan to rush you, because I realize that all the while you were working for me, you kept yourself distant from me, not trying to get my attention or learn things about me like many of the other females in this office have done from time to time, with no effect I might add. None of them holds a candle to you, Maria," he said warmly.

She blushed and looked down at her hands, but could think of nothing to say.

So he went on, "I would like to take you out to dinner some night this week. What day would be best for you?"

"I think Thursday would be best this week," she answered, and was surprised that her voice sounded normal instead of squeaking.

"Fine, that day is a good day for me, also. I'll pick you up at the entryway of your apartment at 6:00, then. I'll be looking forward to it. It's about 4:30 now, so you should have enough time to get your things out of your office downstairs and you can leave early today. There is <u>one</u> thing I don't like about this plan, I won't be able to see your smiling face every day at work," he stated, and smiled at her.

She was really blushing now, and felt very confused and ill at ease, but she managed to thank him, agree to the time for their date and gracefully left the room without stumbling because of her shaking knees.

When Maria reached her office, she had to sit down and breathe deeply to try and relax. It had all been such a surprise that she felt like she was in shock. After a few minutes, she realized she had work to do: clean her desk and pack up all the little things she had in this office that made it seem hers. There really wasn't that much to gather up and pack. Her desk wasn't dirty, because she had always kept it spotless.

She was finished and doubled checked the room, and was out the door in just fifteen minutes. It was tempting to look up at the window of his office to see if he was watching for her, but she held herself in check and didn't even give into the urge to run to her car and peel out of the parking lot. She buckled up, did deep breathing again and drove sedately out of the lot and onto the street toward home. But instead of going home, she drove straight to Pastor Don and Anita's house. She was very much in need of their counsel.

Since she was early, she sat in her car for a while praying and thinking over all the things Mr. Beckett had said to her. She blushed again when she thought about calling him Jason. Maybe it would not be so awkward since he would no longer be her boss. It was beginning to sink in. She had not been fired, just transferred to another office. Of course, if he owned that office also, technically he would still be her boss. This was just getting more confusing, and the biggest problem was that she didn't have a clear answer about his beliefs.

Well, she would just go inside the pastor's house and play with all the children until Pastor Don and Anita both had time to listen to her "crazy" story and maybe help her make sense out of it.

*****

Jason Beckett <u>was</u> at the window watching as Maria left. She only had a little plastic grocery bag full of personal items from her office, and she looked poised as she walked across the parking lot to her little compact car. She sat for a time before starting the car, though, as if trying to get her bearings.

He wondered if he had been too abrupt, or if he should have waited for a while, or if he should not have bared his heart to her yet, or, or, or. But wondering did no good. What was done was done, and there was no possible way to fix it now, if he <u>had</u> done it wrong.

He had never felt so uncertain or nervous in his life. Usually everything was planned the way he thought was best and it worked out the way he wanted it to work. But this was different, and it was more important to him than anything else had ever been. When she had driven away, he went back to his desk, sat down, and put his head down on his arms, hoping nobody would need him before they went home.

*****

As soon as Ted and Julie got home from work Tuesday, she asked him if he had remembered to call Don or Anita about refreshments and chairs. She knew <u>she</u> had forgotten. Ted answered, "Let's wait until after supper to call them. Maybe by then they will be finished with supper also. And in the meantime, maybe we can think up some ideas of our own, and not have to bother them. They've been so helpful and willing to talk to us, but I don't want to take advantage."

"I understand what you mean," responded Julie. "So I'll go start supper and think about what we could do on our own."

During supper Julie commented, "I wonder how Maria's talk with her boss went. I prayed for her off and on throughout the day. I guess we'll find out on our walk tomorrow."

"Right; it did sound rather intriguing. That was a delicious supper, Honey," said Ted when they had finished. "I had an idea about the chairs. We have four at this kitchen table, one each at our desks, two in the bedroom, and one at your sewing machine. The couch will seat three people and our recliners two more how many is that altogether? I haven't kept track as I was talking."

"I did," she smiled. "We already have seating for 14 people and only need two more chairs if there are 16. I didn't realize that we had that many places for people to sit in this apartment. Do you think we can squeeze them all into the living room, plus two more from some place?"

"Let's go try it after we clean up these dishes, so the food doesn't get all dried and stuck on." He suggested.

"Thank you for that thoughtful suggestion. It will be much easier to wash them now rather than later. I was so interested in trying out the chairs, that I didn't remember the dishes!" she giggled.

They made short work of the dishes and other cleanup. Ted offered to bring the heavier chairs while Julie brought the more lightweight ones. All the chairs fit with plenty of room left over. So Ted asked, "What do you think about us buying some nice padded folding chairs that we can keep in the entryway closet?"

"We'll probably have small groups here on a regular basis, since that's such an important part of the way this church works. So, I agree, and I think maybe we should buy four of them just in case somebody brings visitors. Then nobody would have to sit on the floor," she answered.

"Good thinking. Let's put the chairs back in their places now, and after that we'll brainstorm ideas for refreshments," he said.

"That was good exercise," she laughed when they both got back to the living room and sat down on the couch to cuddle before brainstorming.

Later she said, "Okay, I have a piece of paper and a pen. Do you have any ideas? I thought of one so I'll write it down. We could buy ready made cookies, and have hot water with instant coffee, teas, and cocoa mix available so they could choose their favorite beverage. We could even have a pitcher of ice water for the ones who don't want something hot," she said.

"That all sounds very good to me. We don't need to brainstorm. I'd rather cuddle," he laughed.

"Me too!" They enjoyed that for a while and then Julie said, "Look, I already have a shopping list started here. I'll add the chairs and groceries and other things we need to buy, and maybe we can go shopping after supper on Thursday. We'll need to go together so you can get the chairs since they're too heavy for me. I'll get the rest and we can meet up front to pay for it all. There, I even added two little notebooks, so that we can follow the pastor's idea to write down things we're learning. We already have a good dictionary and thesaurus. I wonder if we need another set."

"I don't think so," he replied. "If we just leave them on the shelf where they are, we can get up to get them when we need to and it will give us a chance to stretch and walk around a little."

She agreed, "Good plan. I do too much sitting as it is. That wasn't a problem at all while I was teaching. My mind keeps going around in circles about the best job to have. Then I put it back in God's hands again, until the next thought comes. I guess that's normal, so I won't worry about it."

"Good for you! God will work it all out in <u>his</u> own best time and way," Ted concurred.

*****

Maria locked her car and walked up to the door and knocked. Mindy answered the door and said, "Oh, hi, Maria. It's so good to see you. Come on in and I'll tell Anita you're here."

"Hi, Mindy. I'm glad to see you also. I'll just go with you and play with the children until their parents come and pick them up." When she saw Anita, she said, "I got off work a little early today. I need to talk to Pastor and you, but not until these sweet children go home. So how can I help you best for the next half hour?"

"Welcome, Maria. I'm glad you came today. I think they all need a little rest. Would you like to read them a story before playing a quiet game with them?"

"Sure," she said. "I'll enjoy that. I get to pick the story." So she went to the bookcase and chose a calm short story with lots of pretty pictures. It was the very best way to help her relax, and she was so glad she had decided to come over here. Then they played "Button, Button, Who Has the Button?" until the parents came to pick up their little ones. Then, Maria took Timmy and Mary over to their quiet play area and got them started on some quiet activities so that she could have both Don and Anita listen to her dilemma at the same time.

Pastor Don and Anita were wise to her since she had done this before, so they both came and sat down to be ready when she came back from being with the children. "What's going on?" asked Anita.

Maria said, "You're not going to believe this. In fact I don't believe it myself, although it just happened to me a little over an hour ago." Then she told them the whole story leaving nothing out, (except the confidential part about the audit of the other company) from start to finish. "I was so surprised, shocked, and confused. AND I do not know what to do about his proposal," she finished.

"Oh, my!" Anita whispered. She didn't want to alert the children or get their attention.

Pastor Don started talking in his calm, practical way, and Maria listened carefully. "First of all, Maria, you've done nothing wrong. You've just been your sweet, caring, Christian self, and obviously, he's very impressed. At least he's told you up front how he feels, so you don't have to guess about that. You were very wise to try and find out his beliefs, but since he won't talk about it at work, I guess the only way to find out is to go on that first date. From what I know about Jason Beckett, he's a good, moral man, and his intentions sound honorable."

"I agree," said Maria. She had relaxed visibly and even smiled. "I've never gone out with a man who had told me he had feelings for me before the first date, and it is unusual and a bit awkward. I barely know him and always call him Mr. Beckett and Sir. I'll feel uncomfortable calling him Jason. I even blushed in the car when I parked here and tried it, just before I came in here."

"Then, possibly it would be a good idea to practice it off and on before Thursday night, so that you can do it more naturally," suggested Anita. "You have a lot to learn about him and need to be relaxed and alert so you can listen to him and then ask the right questions. Since you had decided last year that you would probably remain single, this is a total change of direction for you. Of course there would be no question about that if he's totally rejected Jesus, this would be your first and last date with him.

"But, if he's unsure and possibly searching, then, you still should not go out with him again until he believes in Jesus as his own personal Savior. It never works to date a person with the idea of winning them over to Christianity. I realize that you already know all these things and agree with them. I just felt I wanted to remind you because I know emotions can get involved and you would like to please him, but I do not want you to get hurt."

"Thank you, Anita," she replied. "I do understand all of that and am glad for the reminder. No way do I even want to date a man who does not share my faith. That command in 2 Corinthians 6:14 is one I memorized as a young teen. It says, *Do not be unequally yoked together with unbelievers, for what fellowship has righteousness with unrighteousness? And what communion has light with darkness?* It would only make for a miserable life and I would not be able to do the things God has planned for me.

"There's the remote possibility that Jason is a believer, and if that is the case, I would need to continue dating him and pray for guidance and the Lord's will for the outcome. Either way, I'm very glad he transferred me to an office on the other side of town. In a way, he would still be my boss if he owns that office, but I won't feel uncomfortable about being in the same building with him every day."

"Good thinking, both of you. Do you know how to get to the other office, or should you drive over that way so you'll know where to go tomorrow morning?" asked Don.

"Yes, I ran an errand over there for Mr., I mean, Jason, a week or two ago, so I'm all set. I even have all my personal belongings in the car so I can take them into my new office when I get there tomorrow. I'll have a lot of new people to meet, but at least the job will be almost the same," she responded.

"Very good, now I think I'll make you stay for supper so that I can be sure you'll eat something tonight. If it were me, I would not want to cook anything, but you need to keep your strength up and stay healthy," insisted Anita.

"I accept, and thank you very much, both of you, for listening and for your good advice. May I play with your children while you cook? You're right; I don't want to cook. I just want to get my mind off this bizarre issue for a time." When Anita nodded, Maria said, "We'll put coats on and go outside for a while. I need some exercise and they do also. I'm glad they're always so well behaved when I come over and need your full attention."

So they went outside and played tag until Anita called them in to get ready for supper. Maria actually felt hungry by then and ate quite a bit, to Anita's satisfaction.

Maria commented, "I didn't get to tell you. Ted and Julie came walking with me for exercise after work yesterday, and afterwards Ted took us all out to supper at Ami's Japanese Restaurant. It was such fun and so delicious. Julie had the idea to have each one of us put two big spoonfuls of our entree on the other two plates, so we all got to enjoy three different taste treats."

"So, Tomo and Ami's idea of appetizers to entice the small group members is starting to work already! I'm glad," stated Anita. "Ted and Julie and the Suehiros are nice people and I'm looking forward to getting to know them better now that the small group has gotten started."

They visited a little bit longer and Maria helped with the cleanup. Then, since it was almost 7 PM she drove right to the home where <u>her</u> small group was meeting this week. The praise she shared was that her boss had completed the work she had been doing out of town some weekends, so she would not have to be gone and miss church any longer. Then during the conversational prayer time she asked God for direction, guidance and wisdom in a matter that her boss had brought up today at work. She didn't go into detail, but remained discreet about the situation. After refreshments and visiting, she went home, took a nice long shower and went to bed early so she would be fresh for her job in the morning at a <u>different</u> office building. She turned her brain off as much as she could, and actually got a good night's sleep.

*****

When Connie got to work Tuesday, she greeted her husband and Fiona and they all got back to work. Patrick O'Connor was on the 8 to 4:30 shift also, with Ernest and they enjoyed working together on odd jobs, with Ernest taking care of any sales that their one sales clerk could not keep up with until Connie arrived.

The Garden Store was extra busy in the springtime. Lots of people came in, to browse, or with questions wanting advice about this or that. Connie enjoyed answering questions and giving advice so she always had the clerk call her when someone wanted that.

Ernest and Patrick took their half hour lunch breaks separately, so that one of them was always available if he was needed, and Connie and Fiona did the same for their supper breaks. Fiona had become very proficient in giving answers and advice also before she had left, and had not forgotten any of that valuable information.

When there was a lull after their suppers, Connie had a chance to tell Fiona about her talk with Ernest that morning. "I almost wish I could have been there when he asked Amelia, but maybe it's just as well. She might have noticed that I was too interested and thought we were plotting against her. I hope she'll like the idea of working at our store. One can never tell with teenagers. She might prefer to work some other place instead of a mom and pop business."

"I know what you mean. It's hard to wait and not know what's happening over at your house this evening. We'll stay extra busy and then closing time will come sooner and you can go home and see," suggested Fiona. "Of course you <u>could</u> go home early if you want to. It's not very busy tonight, and you showed me how to close up last night."

"No, that's fine. It will be good for me to have to wait and learn some more patience," she said. So they did work hard and were able to visit some more. Before they knew it, it was almost closing time. Connie and Fiona prayed together before they closed the store and went home.

Amelia was waiting for her mother to come home and was very excited. She started talking before the door was even shut. "Guess what, Mom! Dad hired me to begin working at The Garden Shop, starting tomorrow evening from 5 to 8. I'll work on Wednesdays and Fridays like that until we see whether I can keep up with my studies at school. The condition is that I have to keep my grades up. If I can, and want to work another day also, I'll work three days a week, Mondays, Wednesdays and Fridays. On Tuesdays, I can still go to my small group. And Thursdays right after school I can stop at the stores and do your grocery shopping on the way home. The best part is that Fiona is back from taking care of her great aunt, and she works that same shift. Dad said she needs help with all the plants she feeds, waters, and trims. I've always thought she was the prettiest girl in the church, and now I'll get to work with her!"

"Wow!" her mom exclaimed for more than just one reason. Amelia was back to her bubbly self and had talked more than ever before. "That sounds fantastic. Did I hear you say you were going to do my grocery shopping on Thursdays?"

"Yes, if you would like me to, that is. That way I can also shop for things that I have needed. I'll even be able to pay for them myself." Amelia sounded a little uncertain.

"That sounds good to me. You've done the shopping for me before and you do a good job of it," Connie praised.

Amelia smiled and asked, "Did you hear the new name for the store? The Garden Shop! Dad likes it, what do you think, Mom?"

"I like it too!" Connie said. "It sounds more modern and like a fun place to shop and work."

"I thought about spelling it S-h-o-p-p-e, but since I don't like fads, I'd rather have just the simple word Shop. Dad said he'd have the sign changed before I get to work tomorrow. How's that for quick?" Then Amelia ran over, gave her mom a quick hug and hurried to her room to finish her homework.

Connie went into the living room. Ernest stood up and she rushed into his arms and said, "That was amazing! Thank you, Dear, for being the one to talk with her. She is truly excited. Thank you Father in heaven for working out that part so well and now I'll relax and let you work out the rest."

*****

Chapter 5

Romans 8:28, *We know that all things work together for good to those who love God, and are called according to his purpose.*

Wednesday

On Wednesday morning, Maria had forgotten how long it had taken her to get to the other office across town, so she left half an hour earlier than usual so she would be sure to not be late. As it turned out, it only took her ten extra minutes to get there, so she had 20 minutes to spare. She drove over to a pretty little park and used the time to listen to praise music on the car stereo and pray.

By the time she got back to the office building and parked, it was the right time. So she gathered up her belongings and went inside. There was a nice lady waiting at the entrance, who introduced herself and took her to her new office, where she was told to just put her things down on the desk so she could take her on a tour of the building and introduce her to the boss. The building was much like the other one she had worked in, so that would be easy enough to get used to. Maria was a bit nervous about meeting the boss, but told herself to relax and act businesslike.

"Mr. Beckett, this is Maria Gomez. Maria this is Mr. William Beckett, Jason's father," said the lady. "I'll leave you two to get acquainted and talk about what your duties will be."

"Maria, it's a pleasure to meet you. Jason has told me so much about you," he said.

That almost took her breath away. She had no idea she would be working for his father or that Jason would have told him about her, but she gained her composure and said, "I'm pleased to meet you Mr. Beckett."

"William," he corrected her. "All the employees in this office call me by my first name, and I would like you to do the same. I think it makes for a friendlier atmosphere. Jason won't allow that in his office, because he's a bachelor. He wants to keep a professional distance from his employees, and not give any of them the idea that he's available for a relationship."

"I see. Thank you for telling me that, William. It will be hard for me to get used to a first name basis, but I'll try, and I agree it does seem more friendly," she said.

"Very good. I believe Jason told you that your job here would be very much like what you were doing there, although I think you'll have to do income taxes until April 15th. The prior employee fell pretty far behind on getting those done, so I've parceled out some of her work among the others and left you with as much as I think you'll have time to finish. If it looks like you won't be able to do it all, tell me and I'll take some of them also. With a deadline as important as this, we'll have to hurry. Therefore, I'll take you around for quick introductions to the other employees and don't worry about remembering all their names. We all wear name tags and this one is yours. Let's go now," he finished as he handed her a name tag.

After meeting all the others, Maria quickly set up her workspace just leaving her belongings in the bag, which she put into an empty bottom drawer. She was glad that she was good at doing income taxes and just hoped the people had left complete information so she would not be slowed down by having to call a client for more information. By lunchtime she had accomplished a lot and she took her sack lunch to the employee lunchroom to eat with anyone that may have brought their lunch. She was surprised that nobody was there. Well, she would just eat and then go for a short walk. It would not hurt to go back to work before the lunch hour was over either.

*****

It seemed to Matt that Wednesday would never come, but it was finally here and he would get to take Fiona out to breakfast. She was ready when he arrived, and he greeted her mother who said that Patrick had already left for work. "It is pretty chilly out there this morning. I'm glad to see that you have a warm jacket, Fiona. How does the Pancake House sound for breakfast this brisk morning?" he asked.

"It sounds just right. I haven't had pancakes in a long time," she answered. "We'll see you later, Mother. Don't work too hard while I'm gone. I can help you with some of that when I get home."

Glenda laughed and said, "Don't you worry about me, just go and have fun."

They went quickly out to Matt's pick-up, which was still warm inside, and drove to the Pancake House to have breakfast. Once inside, they were seated across from one another in a comfortable booth. A waitress came over quickly with menus and a glass of water for each of them. They thanked her and looked over the menus. "I think I'll order a two-egg American omelet with just one piece of toast, since it also comes with hash browns," Fiona said.

Matt pondered a while longer and stated, "Since I'm a growing 'boy,' I'll order big: a three-egg Spanish omelet with two pieces of toast plus an extra order of hash browns and a cup of their raspberry tea with honey. I really am hungry this morning, and I want enough food to eat that it will take me a while to finish. That will give us more time to visit. How's that for good planning?"

The waitress returned right then, took their orders and left.

Fiona laughed and said, "I think it's great, and it's not even sneaky since you told me about it. What did you want to visit about that's going to take such a long time?"

"Well, I remembered while you were talking to your mother, that she had said she had stopped working right now to be able to spend time with you. I don't want to interfere with that time, but I do desire to spend time with you also. I'm just not sure how we can balance those two things and go to our jobs also. Do you have any ideas?"

"Thank you for being so thoughtful about Mother, but she really did mean what she said this morning: for me to go and have fun and not worry about her. She does not want to monopolize my time and is delighted that you still want to court me. So I believe she'll share me generously," Fiona replied.

"Okay, in that case, how many times a week, and for how long each time, would qualify as generously? The same question goes for you, since I don't wish to monopolize your time either. I'm trying to be very considerate of both of you, so please tell me what you think would be best," he said.

"Again, I thank you. Well, I think two times a week for three or four hours each would be good for us right now, and we do not always need to eat out, either. If we continue to eat all this delicious food I'll lose my girlish figure, and you'll go broke." She laughed, and so did he, so she continued, "Once in a while you could eat a Saturday or Sunday lunch or supper with my folks and me, and then we could do something together as a family, like a board game or croquette on the lawn."

Their breakfast orders came at that point and he asked her to give thanks. They ate in silence while each one was thinking of ways to balance her time with him and with her parents.

Matt said, "This food is delicious. Let me see if I understood what you said before our food arrived. We can see each other two times a week for 3 or 4 hours each time, not always eating out, and once in a while do something together with your parents." She nodded, and he went on, "That sounds like a good plan. When the weather warms up some more, we can plan more things like hikes, picnics, a trip to the zoo, ..."

"Sounds like fun and some good exercise too. I would like to add walking to that list, because I need the exercise, and it would give us a chance to visit, get fresh air, and see the beautiful scenery this city has to offer in its lovely parks. There are a couple of museums here also, that are interesting." Then she added, "And maybe there could be something my parents and I could do to help you on the house you're building."

"Thanks for that offer, and for all the good ideas, Fiona! Is there anything I could do to help you or your parents? Working together is a good way to get to know people, and I would like to get to know your parents better," Matt replied.

"I know Mother would appreciate some help spading the vegetable garden this spring. And I heard Dad mention something about the back porch needing some repair work."

"This is brilliant. I can help them and we'll all get better acquainted at the same time. I was hoping for some ways we could do things together, and some of these will even be constructive!" He was enthusiastic and looking forward to this relationship. She was even better than he remembered, so easy to converse with and full of good ideas. "What other kinds of activities or things would you like to do during our times together?"

She answered, "Well, let me think. What have we not included? It seems like we have a pretty good list. If you still like to play tennis we could try that. I'm pretty rusty after two years. I used to want to try Frisbee golf. I have no idea how that might go."

"I haven't played tennis since our last match, so we'll both be rusty, but it sounds like fun. Frisbee golf is harder than it looks. I tried it once and enjoyed it. Maybe we could practice together someplace before we go out on the course. I know I could use some practice, but like you, I would like to try it. Those are both good ideas. We can add to our list as we go along, so be sure and tell me if you think of anything else you would like to do, and I'll do the same," he replied.

By that time they were both finished eating and were tired of sitting, so Matt called for the check and after paying for their meal, they went outside where it was still chilly. He looked at his watch and they still had about two hours before they needed to get ready for their jobs. "How would you like to go to one of those museums you mentioned earlier? I think we might have enough time."

"I would like that a lot," she responded. So they went and enjoyed it.

*****

Maria worked on more tax returns after lunch and it went well. When she had finished her first day at the new office she realized it wasn't very different from the other one. There wasn't much interaction with the other employees, but that might change after the tax rush was over on the 15th. Before she left, she ran upstairs to her new boss' office to ask, "Is it the custom to just leave at 5 PM, or am I supposed to check out someplace? Do you need me to work overtime?"

"No, that's fine, Maria. You may just leave at 5 PM, finished or not. We don't check in or out, just like the other office, it's all on the honor system. And if I <u>do</u> need you to work overtime, I'll let you know the day before so you can make any plans you might need to," he finished.

"Thank you, Mr., I mean William. Have a pleasant evening. I'll see you tomorrow," she said.

Then she hurried back to her office, picked up her things and drove home to get ready for her walk with Julie. She had so much to tell her.

"Hi, Maria!" Julie said as soon as they had arrived. "I can hardly wait to hear how your talk went with your boss on Tuesday. Looks like you're ready, so let's go."

Just as soon as they were walking, Maria started, "I can't believe how much has changed just since we walked together on Monday. You were so right, it <u>was</u> something momentous, maybe even life changing. Mr. Beckett had some good news that I was very glad to hear. But before I go on, would it be all right with you and Ted, if I ask him to come here and walk with us so he can hear about it also. I'm going to need <u>both</u> of you praying with me about this."

Julie stopped walking and said that <u>of course</u> it was all right. She called for Ted to come and join them. When he got there, Julie quickly explained, and then Maria said, "His good news was that while he was out of town over the weekend, he was able to finish up the business I've been helping with, so I'll no longer have to go there and miss church on those weekends. I'm thrilled about that, but then he shocked me by what he said next." She went on to explain and give a summary of what he had said.

"Today, I worked at the other office. At first it was awkward, but the work is much like what I had been doing. My new boss was also a surprise to me. It's Jason's father, William, and he looks a lot like Jason except with gray hair. He is friendly and insists that I call him by his first name. It's hard for me after working for his son who is only called Mr. Beckett. William explained that Jason does that because he's a bachelor and does not want his employees to think he's available for a relationship. I'm trying to get used to saying 'Jason' before our date tomorrow.

"What I need prayer for is the fact that about a year ago I had accepted the reality that I would probably stay single the rest of my life and haven't dated anybody for that long. On Monday I told you that I'm not sure if he's a Christian. I'll find out about <u>that</u> on the date, because he won't discuss it at the work place. So, I need wisdom and the right words to say, plus peace about going on a date with my former boss who has bared his heart to me already. I do <u>not</u> know how to handle this or how to act with that knowledge. There's so much I don't know about him. I feel like a fish out of water," she finished.

"Do you know what I think?" Julie asked. "I think you better come home with us this evening and we'll take all the time you need to talk and pray. We'll feed you supper too," Julie insisted.

Ted said, "I agree. We haven't had time to pray yet, and here we are back at your apartment."

"That's what Pastor and Anita did for me yesterday, and I appreciated it so much," Maria responded. "It's wonderful to have such good friends. Thank you both. Yes, I would really like to come with you and then if you'll bring me back here later, I won't even need to go up to my apartment. I don't feel like driving this evening."

"Okay, then let's get in the car and go to our home. We'll do our best to take good care of you this evening," Julie promised. "I'm so glad you got to talk to Pastor and Anita. They're such caring people." They talked some more on the short drive, and then took her inside where they all prayed before doing anything else. "At least after tomorrow's date you'll know whether or not he's a Christian and what your options are at that point. It is hard to be up in the air, but we'll continue to pray for you and you can trust your loving heavenly Father to guide you and give you the right words to say."

Maria felt more at peace after the prayer time and enjoyed a good supper with her friends. They even played a fun Bible board game for a while before it was time for them to take her back to her home.

*****

As soon as Fiona arrived at work Wednesday afternoon, Connie hurried over and told her the good news about Ernest hiring Amelia, and that she was very excited about having the job, and especially about being able to work with Fiona. "It's working out better than I could have imagined. She'll be working from 5-8 on Wednesdays and Fridays until she is sure she can keep her grades up at school. If she can, then she might add working on Mondays. She even volunteered to grocery shop for me on Thursdays. That will give her a chance to shop for things she wants and even pay for them herself. She was back to her old, bubbly self. I'm so pleased. She even came up with an idea to change the name of the store to The Garden Shop and we all like it. She'll start working today and you get to train her. Who knows, maybe she'll like working with God's beautiful creations as much as you and her parents do."

Fiona was smiling all the way through that long speech, enjoying the enthusiasm and relief that she saw and heard in Connie. "I'm so glad to hear all of that fantastic news, Connie. I'll enjoy training Amelia how to care for all these gorgeous plants, and I pray that we'll become good friends in the process. Matt said that working together with people is a good way to get to know them, so this should be good for both of us."

"True, and we worked out the hours and days so that I'll still get to work with you on Tuesdays and Thursdays, plus a few hours on the other days. Consequently we can continue to grow our friendship, also," Connie said.

"Wonderful! I'm very glad about that. I missed you while I was gone. I didn't realize how important friendships were until I had to leave them behind," finished Fiona.

They worked together until 5 PM when Amelia arrived and Connie needed to go home and fix supper for Patrick and herself, along with getting ready to go to their small group meeting. Fiona hurried over to greet Amelia as soon as she saw her come in. "Hi, Amelia! It's so good to see you again. You've grown into a beautiful young woman, and I like your name change from Amy to Amelia. It means industrious, doesn't it? It sounds much more grown up, and it fits you well. I like the new name for this store also. Did you see the sign when you arrived? The Garden Shop sounds cheerful."

Amelia had been a little nervous when she got there, but Fiona's greeting and comments helped her to relax and she replied, "Yes, I saw it, and I'm glad my parents both like it too. How are you, Miss O'Connor?"

"I'm very well, and hope you are too, because we're going to work hard. But please call me Fiona. The other name sounds too sophisticated and like I'm a schoolteacher or your boss, which I'm not. I'll just be training you on ways to cultivate plants, and if you have any thoughts of other ways to do it, please share them with me. I'm always learning," she responded.

"Okay. I like your name also, Fiona; it's beautiful just like you are," Amelia said.

"Thank you. Now shall we go over and meet some of the plants you'll be working with? They're going to enjoy having you help take care of them, and I'm glad you're here to lend a hand to me, since there are so many of them, and they all need a lot of nurturing. But they thrive when they get it. This is a very rewarding job for me because I get to see the results of my labors," explained Fiona.

Amelia was a good listener and learned quickly. She was even learning the names of the plants and that many had special needs or different ways of being cultivated, or different foods, or methods of watering. Plus she learned what would happen to them if things were done the wrong way. She exclaimed, "I had no idea that there was such a science to growing plants especially if you want them to look healthy and beautiful." By the end of the second hour, they were working well together and were able to visit while they worked. Amelia decided she was going to enjoy working here.

*****

Thursday

In the morning on Thursday before breakfast, Pastor Don and Anita were discussing their own small group that had met on Monday evening. It was for all the pastors and their wives, and was facilitated by the pastor who had started the church in the first place. There were 24 people present. Their children, if they had any, were cared for by two volunteer babysitters who played Bible games with them, read Bible stories to them, and spent time singing Christian children's songs together.

Every week, the lead pastor would tell what songs would be used, and what would be taught in the Saturday and Sunday services. He also explained the songs and teachings for the small groups. That information was sent each Tuesday morning by e-mail to the small group facilitators. They could call their pastors if they had any questions. Therefore, the churches all stayed on the same page, so to speak. He also gave each of them SD cards with the music and singing on them for the weekend services. It would be Resurrection Sunday this coming Sunday, so the songs and teachings would focus on that.

Praise time had included Don telling about the successful start of the new small group for people who worked evening shifts, and that after announcing it on Sunday they had enough members to fill it up. The lead pastor had liked the idea and had suggested that he and the rest of the pastors find out if they had enough people in their congregations who worked late or swing shifts, to start a small group for them.

Everywhere There's a Sunrise, Let's Tell The Good News!

    During the announcement time, the lead pastor had talked about an idea to plant some churches in other cities, and some of the others joined in with ideas, questions and concerns. Conversational prayer time had included a need that the church's Christian school had, some personal problems, and many prayers for members of their congregations.
    Just before Don left for work that morning, he and Anita prayed for Maria to have peace and the right words to say on her date this evening. They hoped she would call them afterwards and let them know how it went.

*****

    Roy and Sherry had called their prior babysitters, but none of them wanted to work on Saturday mornings. Roy said, "Maybe we'll have to take turns going to the small group. But you could call Anita to see if she has any ideas."
    She did call, and Anita told her, "I'll talk to Mindy when she gets here after school today and ask if she thinks that she could have the twins join Timmy and Mary on Saturday mornings. Mindy is used to working with an even larger group with the day care children and might agree if she were offered some extra pay. I'll call Roy and tell him what I find out since you'll be at work by then." At least it sounded hopeful to Sherry.
    While the children were napping in the afternoon, Mindy had a chance to talk to Anita. She had been trying to bolster her courage and figure out how to say something important for several days. Now was her chance. "Anita, I hope you know how much I enjoy and value being able to come here after school. It's almost like I have a big family of my own to come home to, that is, until I have to leave at 5:30. Sometimes I pretend that you and Don are my parents and all the kids are my little brothers and sisters. I'm not saying anything against my dad. He's wonderful, but he's still so sad and it's been four years since my mom died. I still miss her, but I wish he would meet and marry a wonderful Christian woman and be happy again. However if he does, it might mean that I would have to stop coming here after school and I do NOT want that to happen," she finished with tears in her eyes.
    Anita had tears in her own eyes by this point. She opened her arms for Mindy to come for a hug. They both cried for a little while and then dried their tears and blew their noses. Anita replied, "Yes, I do know how you feel, and I feel the same way. You've been a very big blessing and help to me, and I selfishly would like

that to continue. On the other hand, I often pray that God would send a kind, loving believer to be the wife and mother in your family."

"I pray the same thing too, and then I think I take it back when I realize it might mean that I can't come here any longer," said Mindy.

Anita replied, "I can understand how you could feel that way. Do you think we could both tell Jesus how we feel and choose to let <u>him</u> decide what would be best for both of us?"

"What do you mean?" Mindy asked.

"I mean that each of us could tell him what we just told each other and then say like Jesus did in the garden, 'Not my will, but yours be done,'" explained Anita.

"When Jesus said that, I know it was a much harder situation for him than this is for us! Yes, I think we could do that. I'll be first." Mindy proceeded to tell Jesus what she had told Anita and then added, "But if that isn't your will for me, then please do what you know will be best."

Anita followed Mindy's prayer with a very similar one for herself. They smiled at each other and said together, "May God's perfect will be done."

Anita asked, "Would it be okay with you if I share what we've discussed today with Don so he can agree with us in prayer?"

"I like your good idea, because when two or more agree, it's more effective," answered Mindy. "In addition I'll try to find a time when I can tell Dad how I feel."

"That would be good. Parents need to know about their children's feelings and thoughts," Anita agreed.

Later as soon as Don got home from work, Anita discussed Roy and Sherry's dilemma with him, and he said it would be good to ask Mindy. So then Anita asked Mindy what she thought about the idea. Mindy agreed to take care of the twins also on Saturday mornings for half again as much money, as a result, Anita called Roy to let him know. He said he would call Sherry on her break at work and inform her also.

After supper Don called Jeff and Karen to ask them if they would be willing to be trained to take over the guidance of the new small group. He made it clear that they would do a good job and it would be a good experience for them. Plus it would free up two spaces for new members later since there would be 16 in the group on Saturday. The training would take about a month of watching what Don and Anita did as facilitators. They would need to read a booklet and meet with Don and Anita for teaching and questions. He asked them to think and pray about it and to call him later to tell him what they decided.

After Timmy and Mary were in bed, Anita told Don in detail about her conversation with Mindy. Don responded, "I understand how both of you feel and I'm pleased that you were able to surrender your feelings to Jesus. Father in heaven, we pray in Jesus name that you'll do your will in this situation and help all of us to accept it. Please heal Vern's emotions so that he will be open to the idea of a wife again. If it's your will, bring Vern and Mindy and the right woman together. We pray in agreement and are thankful for your answer in advance."

*****

Following a good night sleep, Maria ate a good breakfast Thursday morning, packed her lunch and went to work at the other office. It still seemed strange, but she got right to work and accomplished a lot by lunchtime. Again she ate alone in the lunchroom and wondered what the other employees did for their lunch hour. She took a short walk and then went back to work in her office.

William came past her office and told her not to work during her lunch hour. "You need a break. I don't want to wear you out. The others all go out to lunch at different restaurants or in the park to eat a sack lunch. Tomorrow, see if you can find someone to go with at lunchtime or at least take a long walk or read a book after you eat. I can see that you're making good progress on that stack of tax returns. Don't worry about it so much." Then he left and she went on another short, fast walk. It helped relieve some of her anxiety about the pile of work and the coming evening.

She worked hard all afternoon and left at 5:00, went home, took a quick shower so she would feel fresh and clean, dressed, fixed her hair, and was down in the entry way at 5:58, hoping to be there before he was, but he was already there. She greeted him and remembered to say 'Jason'.

"You look beautiful this evening, Maria, and as usual you're a little early. I appreciate that about you," he told her. She thanked him and returned the compliments, even though she felt like it might sound a little bit unnatural. She tried hard to relax as he opened the door, and led the way to his car, which was a newer model BMW. He opened the car door, helped her in and then closed it. Then he went around and got in the drivers seat. "I'm glad you're wearing such a pretty dress. I failed to mention that I was planning to take you to Mountain View Restaurant at the golf course for supper, but you're dressed just right for it."

She almost gasped when she heard the name of that fancy restaurant, but managed to smile and thank him for another compliment. It might prove to be a very long evening if she couldn't think of a thing to say. He was totally out of her league financially and way ahead of her in his feelings for her.

He had a classical CD in the stereo and the leather seats were heated to be very comfortable on this chilly evening, so she relaxed and enjoyed the ride. Upon arrival, he got out, went around and opened her door, waited for her to get out and then closed it. She thanked him, and he offered his arm to her. She took it and he escorted her to the door which was opened for them by a porter.

This was a totally new experience for her and she decided to take pleasure in it as such. There was no waiting for a seat since he had reservations. They were taken directly to a window seat with a spectacular view of the mountains. Jason pulled out her chair and seated her at the table. "Thank you, Jason. I'm not used to being with such a gentleman. It is nice. The view of the mountains from here is magnificent. I'm glad it's still light enough to be able to enjoy them," she managed to say quite a bit finally.

"You're welcome, and it's nice to have a lady who appreciates it, and knows how to act. I agree, the view from here is spectacular. That was part of the reason I chose this restaurant," he responded. The waiter came with water and menus, and they opened them to decide what to have for their meals. "Also, all the food here is delicious."

Maria decided to not even look at the prices. If he chose to treat her to an expensive meal in an exclusive restaurant, it was his choice and his billfold. She would not dispute his right to do as he pleased. Instead she looked for something that she knew she would like and that would not upset her stressed-out stomach. She found it quickly and looked up to find him studying her. She smiled at him then and asked, "Have you already decided about what you're going to eat?"

He answered, "Yes, how about you?"

"Yes I have, and you're right, it all does look and sound delicious." The waiter returned at that moment and took their orders. He left a plate of appetizers for their pleasure while they waited for their meals. After she had tried several kinds she said appreciatively, "These are all superb."

Jason agreed and then said, "I would like to keep our conversation light like it has been so far, during this meal, and then after dessert I would like to have you ask me any questions you have, and I'll do my best to answer them. What do you think of the ambiance in this restaurant?"

She looked all around in her discerning way before answering and stated, "I like it a lot. The decor goes well with the Mountain View theme by means of bringing some of the natural colors from outdoors inside. I noticed that they have a well-placed photo mural of some of those same mountains for people to look at when it gets dark outside. I'm impressed. It seems peaceful in here too, with the classical music playing at just the right level in the background. The furnishings are real wood with comfortable upholstery and the colors match the overall theme. What do <u>you</u> think?"

He had listened actively, politely nodding and making agreeing sounds as she spoke. When she finished he replied, "I totally agree, and I think you did a very thorough job of describing it. I cannot think of a single thing to insert, except that you add to the ambiance with your natural beauty and enthusiasm while you are speaking."

Of course she blushed and looked down at the tablecloth before saying, "Thank you," another time. When she looked up she said, "Oh, look outside. There's a brilliant rainbow. I like to watch real light shows. Rainbows, sunsets and sunrises are some of my favorite things."

He looked and concurred. "For sure! I like to just sit or stand and watch the whole scene from start to finish. There are so many colors and subtle changes. It always amazes me."

Maria nodded and they just sat enjoying the show. She realized that she had just learned something about him that she liked and was glad for that along with the rainbow. Then she also realized that she needed to guard her heart, since she didn't know about his beliefs.

*****

Connie and Fiona had the whole evening Thursday, to work together. They were extra glad about that because there was so much to talk about. Connie asked, "How did it go to have Amelia work with you last night? She told me that she really enjoyed it and learned a lot."

Fiona answered, "It was great. She did learn a lot because she listens well and is a very intelligent girl. I think she was nervous at first, but that didn't last long. I enjoyed training her, and after a couple hours, we were even able to visit while we worked."

"I'm relieved to hear that. I didn't want to put extra work on you, but I really appreciate your willingness to train her for this job and be a friend to her," Connie said.

"You're very welcome. Besides, I think she'll become a big help and it will give me a chance to teach her about flower arranging later. I thought about asking her if she had eaten before she came to work but then I didn't do it because she might think I was babying her. Sometimes it's hard to know the right thing to do," Fiona commented.

"It certainly is, especially with teenagers. They want to be grown up, but at times they would rather be a child again and be taken care of. She didn't mention anything about eating. I figure if she got hungry last night that might be the best way to learn to eat before going. I think I'll see what happens on Friday. Until then, I think we can let her figure it out on her own, unless she asks, then I could suggest taking a sack lunch the way you and I do for supper," suggested Connie.

"That's a good idea," Fiona agreed. "We might have to play a lot of this by ear as we go. No, better yet, we can pray about it all as we go, and our heavenly Father will give us the guidance and words to say as we need them."

"Right you are. Let's pray about it now as we work," Connie said.

*****

Throughout Thursday, Ted and Julie had prayed for Maria that she would continue to have peace and that God would give her the wisdom and words she would need during her date with Jason. But as soon as they got home from work, Julie told Ted that she was worried about Maria's safety. "Maybe we should have talked her out of going. If Jason isn't a believer there's no telling what might happen. I remember Maria commenting that sometimes he seemed intimidating. Would it be okay with you, if we take a picnic supper and follow them to the restaurant? After we eat it in the car, we can go inside and sit in a place where we can watch. We can buy some dessert so it will look natural. That way, we can be close by if she needs help of any kind."

"Yes, that sounds like a smart plan. I haven't felt good about that date either," Ted concurred. So, Julie fixed a quick picnic type supper and they were out the door by 5:40. Ted parked where they could see the car that Jason and Maria would leave in and could follow them. While they waited, Julie called Pastor Don and Anita to tell them of the plan. Jason arrived in a BMW, ushered Maria to it and like a gentleman, opened and closed the door for her before going to the driver's side to get seated. Then they drove away, and Ted and Julie followed them at a substantial distance to the Mountain View Restaurant. Ted and Julie ate their supper in the car and then went inside. They were seated where they could see Maria and Jason, but could not be seen by them.

Pastor Don and Anita had also prayed for Maria during the day, and they wished they had told her to call them when she got home. They had both been very relieved when Julie called, and Anita told Julie that if Maria needed to leave, or have a ride home, they could tell Jason that there was an emergency, and that Anita needed Maria to come right away and help her with little Mary, since she was so good with her.

*****

While Maria and Jason were enjoying the rainbow, their meals were delivered to the table. Jason just started right in to eat, so Maria said a silent prayer as she put her napkin in her lap. This wasn't the time to say anything, so she started eating also. The food was delicious, as he had said it would be, and she enjoyed it. They kept the conversation light, but actually it seemed meaningless. They looked at the rainbow off and on while they ate, and that helped Maria. During a lull in the conversation, Maria thought about the meaning of the rainbow. It was God's promise to not send a flood on the earth again. It made her think about other promises God had made. He always keeps his promises. It filled her with peace and she knew that the Spirit of Jesus was in her heart and would guide everything that she might need to say.

The waiter was right there as they were finishing their meal, to give them dessert menus, and take away their empty dishes. As it turned out they both chose the same thing for dessert and they both chuckled about it after the waiter had left. He quickly brought their choices out to them and after the first bite, Maria exclaimed, "This is better than any other ice cream I've ever eaten!"

"That's because it's gelato and it's made just like the Italians make it in Italy," Jason explained.

When they had finished that taste treat, the waiter refilled Jason's coffee cup and Maria's Sprite, and left them to visit as Jason had requested over the phone when he made the reservations.

"Maria, please feel free to ask me any questions you would like to ask now that we're finished with dessert," Jason said as he leaned back to relax with his coffee.

"Okay, my first question is the same one I asked in your office on Tuesday afternoon: What do you believe about Jesus Christ?" she asked.

"You have a very good memory," he laughed nervously and then continued, "I believe that Jesus Christ was a good man and an excellent teacher."

Next she asked, "What church do you attend?" He told her the name, and that he attended about once a month. She recognized the name of the church as one of the high society churches in the city. Then she asked, "Where will you go when you die?"

He answered, "To Heaven of course. Good people go to Heaven when they die, and I am a good person, since I live a moral life and treat people fairly." He continued talking, telling her that he donates money to charity and to the church every month and that he tries to do good deeds often.

Maria was now aware of his beliefs, and with Holy Spirit boldness and his help, she responded, "Thank you for answering my questions. Now I would like to tell you what I believe about Jesus Christ and the way the Bible says that people can go to Heaven when they die. I agree with you that Jesus Christ was a good man and an excellent teacher, but if that is all he was, then he failed to do what God, his Father, sent him to earth to do.

"The Bible states in Romans 3:10, *there is none righteous, no not one,* that means that no person on earth is good enough to go to heaven when he dies, because when Adam and Eve sinned, every person born of human parents inherited their sin nature and is guilty. Romans 3:23 says, *All have sinned and come short of the glory of God.* And Romans 6:23 says, *the wages of sin is death.* That means eternal separation from God. That fact would leave people hopeless, but John 3:16 states, *God so loved the world that he gave his only begotten Son, that whoever believes in him should not perish, but have everlasting life.*

Everywhere There's a Sunrise, Let's Tell The Good News!

"Jesus Christ was born to the virgin Mary. He had no earthly father, but was conceived of the Holy Spirit, as it says in Mathew 1:21b, 22, *that which is conceived in [Mary] is of the Holy Spirit. She shall have a son, and you shall call him Jesus, for he shall save his people from their sins.* God's purpose in sending his Son, Jesus, to the earth as a baby, was to provide a perfect sacrifice that could pay the price of the penalty of all the sins of all the people for all time. That penalty had to be paid for with the blood of a perfect man. While Jesus lived on earth, he never sinned, and because he had no earthly father, he didn't have the sinful nature, wasn't guilty and didn't deserve death.

"He came to earth willingly as it says in Philippians 2:7,8, *Jesus, made himself of no reputation and took on himself the form of a servant, and was made in the likeness of men. Being found in the form of a man, he humbled himself, and became obedient unto death, even the death of the cross.* In John 1:29, John the Baptist called him *the Lamb of God who takes away the sins of the world.* In the Old Testament, the people of Israel had to offer lambs and other animals as blood sacrifices for their sins, but it had to be done over and over at that time. This was no longer necessary after Jesus Christ came and offered himself as a perfect sacrifice, once for all time, as it says in Hebrews 10:12 &14, *But Jesus, after he had offered one sacrifice for sins, forever, sat down on the right hand of God ... for by one offering he has made perfect forever those who are sanctified.*

"I think that what Jesus did is amazing, and since I've done what it says in Acts 16:31, *Believe in the Lord Jesus Christ, and you shall be saved,* and Romans 10: 9,10, *If you shall confess with your mouth the Lord Jesus and shall believe in your heart that God has raised him from the dead, you shall be saved. For with the heart man believes unto righteousness, and with the mouth confession is made unto salvation,* I know that when I die, I will go to Heaven. It will not be that I was a good person. It will be because of God's grace as it says in Ephesians 2: 8,9, *For by grace you are saved, through faith; and not of yourselves; it is the gift of God: not of works, lest any man should boast.*

"If what I've just told you about Jesus Christ and the way the Bible says that people can go to Heaven when they die is true, and I believe that it is true, because I believe the Bible tells the truth, then, I have one more question for you, Jason. What will you do to make sure that you'll go to Heaven when you die?"

"Don't you think I will?" he asked. He was beginning to look angry. "I told you about all the good things I've done." His voice had elevated and his face got red. "I'm a good person, and good people go to heaven!" He hit the table with his fist and said too loudly, "How can you say that I won't?"

She answered, trying to stay calm, "<u>Please</u>, just think about the things I said, and if you have any questions, my pastor, Don Ross, would be glad to talk with you about them." Her face had become quite pale and she bit her lip. She looked around the room just then and said, "Oh, I just noticed a couple over there who is beckoning me to come see them. Please excuse me. I'll be right back." She rose and quickly walked over to the table where Ted and Julie were sitting. "I'm surprised, but very glad to see you here. Jason is becoming angry about what I said, and I'm afraid to stay here any longer."

Julie quickly told her to tell Jason what Anita had said, and to bring her purse and coat right back to their table. They would be ready to leave immediately, since they had already paid for and finished their dessert.

Maria walked back over to Jason, picked up her purse and coat and said, "Jason, I thank you very much for the delicious meal and dessert. That couple over there told me that there's an emergency, and that a woman needs me to come right now and help her with her little girl. That couple will take me to them. Again, I thank you." She quickly left, and he had nothing to say, as the couple and Maria rapidly departed from the restaurant.

*****

As they were driving to the Ross home, Maria asked them how they happened to be at the same restaurant where she and Jason were. They explained to her their concern about her date, and what they had done.

Maria exclaimed, "Wow! This <u>is</u> amazing! I know now, that I should never have consented to even go on one date with Jason, even though I've worked for him for over 2 years. I barely knew him, and my first clues should have been that he would never answer my questions about Jesus, but we all gave him the benefit of the doubt. I'll wait till we get to the pastor's house to tell you all the details, but I'm <u>so</u> relieved that you two came and rescued me. Thank you very, very much, and I thank you very, very much, Lord, also. Please forgive me for going with Jason in the first place."

Don and Anita were relieved to see them, and rushed them into the living room where they could talk. "First, let me help you with Mary, so there will be no deceit about me leaving in a hurry. I know I was the emergency, so that part was true also." Maria said as she went over to the children's play area to talk and play with them for a few minutes.

By the time she returned, Ted and Julie had told their part of the story, so Maria continued by giving a summary of the events of her date. She finished by saying, "Everything seemed to be going well, until I asked him that last question after explaining the gospel to him. His face got red and his responses were definitely angry. I realized then, that I had made a mistake by going on a date with him at all. At that point, I didn't feel safe, and wondered how I could get myself out of the mess I had made. Then I looked around the room and saw Julie and Ted, and knew God had sent a rescue for me. Since Jason isn't a believer, there's no telling what he would have done. I'm just so relieved and happy that it's over and I'm safe. I've learned an important lesson and plan to not ever do anything so foolish again!"

Pastor Don said, "I agree with you, and all of the rest of us have learned the same lesson. We had the same clues, because you had told us, but we let you go anyway. Anita and I were worried, until Julie called and told us their plan. I'm glad it ended well. For tonight, I think it would be best if you would turn off your cell phone and spend the night in our guest room. I'll call in the morning and tell my boss I need to be late, so I can drive you to get your car to drive to work, and then I'll follow you to the office and go with you to talk to your new boss. You can borrow some of Anita's clothes to wear to work, and she'll fix you a lunch to take."

"Thank you all so much. I gladly accept your offer. If you don't mind, I would like to go play some active game with Timmy and Mary before they're put to bed. Maybe that will help me to relax. I've never been so stressed out in my life, but I'm totally amazed and grateful to God and all of you for taking such good care of me," Maria said. Then she gave Julie a hug and thanked them again, before going over to play with the children and then read them a bedtime story, which was quiet and peaceful and helped her to relax.

Later, when the children were in bed, Maria became aware of something and said, "I just realized that Jason is going to want an explanation, and needs to know that I won't go out with him again or say yes to his proposal. I would rather not talk to him face to face or on the phone. How would it be if I write a note to him and give it to his father to give to him?"

"That's an excellent idea. He needs to understand those things, and it will give you closure on the situation," Anita answered. "If Don and I can be of help please ask. The desk there has paper and pens."

Maria went right over there and started writing: Tomorrow's date, (next line) Jason, I am sorry I had to leave so abruptly last night. Thank you for understanding. I was able to help with the little girl, and the emergency was taken care of, also. (New paragraph) I must decline being courted by you, and also, your proposal. My father will not allow me to do it. I am very sorry to have to tell you that, because I don't want you to feel hurt. (New paragraph) Please think about the Bible verses I shared with you and ask God to help you believe what they say. They are listed here, so you can look them up in this Bible, which is my gift to you. (Then she listed the verses she had shared.) (New paragraph) Thank you again for the delicious meal and dessert. (New line) Sincerely, Maria

She read it to Pastor Don and Anita, and asked if they had a new Bible she could buy from them, and if it would be appropriate to copy her note to him on the page that says, "Given To: _____ By: _____."

Pastor Don agreed, "That's another excellent idea. Yes, we keep several new ones to give to people who visit us and express a desire to have one. I think it would be very suitable to copy your note onto that page in the Bible. I'll just go and get one for you." When he returned, she paid him for the Bible and then copied the note carefully onto that page after she had had Anita proofread the original. With a sigh of satisfaction and a feeling of closure, she closed it gently and thanked them again before going to bed where she was glad to get a good night's sleep.

About 9:30 PM the pastor's phone rang. It was Jeff and Karen who had talked and prayed about training for the small group guidance. They thought that Pastor Don should bring up the possibility to the group on Saturday, and they should all pray about it. If the group agreed to have them as facilitators, then they would be happy to train and do it.

*****

Ted and Julie went home, feeling amazed and grateful and relieved, but also very tired. It had been a very nerve-racking time for all of them. Ted said, "I'm so glad we followed your plan to help Maria if she would need it. It turned out that she did, and I wonder what will happen next. Father in heaven, thank you for your help and leading, and that so far things have turned out all right, and Maria is safe. Please help us all to use better common sense and to recognize your wisdom when you give it. Guide all decisions and actions in the future, in Jesus holy name, Amen."

"Amen," Julie added. "I'm going to walk some laps around our apartment to get the kinks out after so much sitting and help get rid of this case of nerves. Would you like to join me?"

"Sure," he laughed. "Maybe I'll end up chasing you and catch you!"

As they were walking Julie suddenly stopped and said, "We forgot to go shopping for groceries, refreshments, and chairs!"

"Don't worry, can go tomorrow after supper. That way the cookies will be even fresher for Saturday morning, and we can each have one for dessert tomorrow, too," suggested Ted.

"Great idea! Now come on and chase me," teased Julie as she took off.

*****

Friday

On Friday morning at 7:50 AM, Pastor Don and Maria entered the office building and headed upstairs to talk with William Beckett. He was surprised to see Maria there with another man and wondered what was up. He asked them into his office and offered them chairs while he closed the door. Don introduced himself and explained why he was there. William said sadly, "Maria, I'm so sorry that you had to go through that. Jason told me none of his plans when he transferred you to this office, and I didn't think it would be polite to ask you. Now I wish I had."

"Thank you, William. I have two questions. First, do I still have a job, and second, is Jason angry enough that he might harm me?" asked Maria.

He answered, "Yes, you still have a job. Jason isn't a well man. He has bi-polar disorder, and sometimes forgets to take his medication. At those times, I don't know what he might do. Therefore, since he displayed anger, for whatever reason, I'm going to transfer you to another of my offices in another part of town. It's actually closer to your apartment building than this one and has an access where you have to enter your employee number to gain admission. Jason has no number for that office and never goes there anyway because he does not like the boss in charge. You'll be safe there, and in your apartment building, since it has the same kind of entrance protection. Just don't go walking in the evenings by yourself. Day-times are probably all right, because he stays at my third office. Eventually this will blow over, and we can all pray together that your presentation of the gospel will get through to him and he will turn his life over to Christ and Jesus might heal him. His mother and I have been praying for him for so many years. At least he listened all the way through your explanation, which is a first. He must have thought you are very special, because he's never proposed to anyone and tried to work out a way to court her before."

Maria handed William the Bible and asked him to open to the page where she had written the note. "We decided last night that Jason needs an explanation from me about my abrupt departure and well, the note says the rest. Please read it and tell us whether you think it will be helpful to him. I don't desire to make his disorder any worse by what it says."

William read the note carefully and smiled, telling her that it would be just right.

"Maria _is_ very special, and we want to keep her out of harms way. Will you lead the way now, to that other office, so we can all get to work?" Don asked.

"Of course," said William. "Just let me get that stack of tax returns you were working on yesterday so you can continue on it over there." Then they all made a train of vehicles on the way to the other office. Once there, William keyed in his number and all three went inside. He called for the boss to meet them in Maria's new office, and she came right away.

"Ruth, this is Maria Gomez. Maria this is my eldest daughter, Ruth Beckett, and by the way, this office also goes by first names." The two women greeted each other and smiled. "Maria will be finishing up these tax returns for me here, and you can send them over to my office via your special courier as they are completed. After she finishes these, you, of course can have her do whatever you need to have done. She's a very hard worker. Just try to keep her from working overtime," he laughed. "I found her working on her lunch hour just yesterday." Then he held out his hand to her and said, "Maria, it's been a pleasure." He turned to Don and said, "Don, I'm glad I got to meet you. Maria will be fine here."

He put his arm around Ruth's shoulders and they left the office, so he could explain the situation to her in her office. He ended with, "Please introduce her to her co-workers and find someone who brought a lunch so they can eat together in the park and then take a walk. She's been through a lot, and I hope we can make this easier for her."

In the meantime, Maria thanked Pastor Don again. He left for his job, and she sat down at the second new desk in a week so she could get to work. Sometime she would get word to William that she had left a plastic grocery bag of her belongings in the bottom drawer of the desk in his other office building, and ask him to have them sent over to her. She was very grateful that she still had a job, and that everything possible was being done to keep her safe. Consequently, the first thing she did was say a brief prayer of thanksgiving, followed by a request for God to help her do a good job for her new boss.

*****

Tomo and Ami Suehiro sat at the table after they had finished eating breakfast on Friday morning, and looked lonely. She admitted, "I'm missing Aneko and Yoshi, more than usual. I sure wish they would move back to Pine City and go with us to this good church. They missed out on so much growing up here while we weren't attending any church at all. We really failed them."

"Very true, I was reading in the Bible the other day, I don't remember where, but it stated that God would restore the years the locust had eaten. Let's pray that it will happen that way for our dear children. If he wills to bring them back to Pine City, it would make me very happy too," he agreed.

*****

Matt woke early on Friday morning and tried to remember some of the things Fiona had mentioned that they could do. His brain was foggy this morning, so he got ready and went for a quick run to try and wake up his memory. If he remembered any of them, he would write them down when he returned. It worked! He ate breakfast and then called her phone number, turning on the speaker so that his hands could be free to check the list he had just finished. "Hi, Fiona, this is Matt. How are you this morning?"

She answered, "Good morning, Matt. I'm just fine."

"Good, I'm looking at a list of things we talked about doing together. Which day, Saturday or Sunday afternoon would be better for you this weekend, and which of the things would you like to do with your parents?" Matt asked.

"Well, if it's nice outside, this would be a good Saturday to help Mother with spading her garden," she replied.

"That sounds like a good idea. I'll plan to come over after lunch, at about 2 PM, and we'll see how much digging we can accomplish in a few hours," he said.

"Thank you for wanting to help. I'll look forward to seeing you at the group and then here after lunch. Bye until then," she said,

"Bye and God bless you." He smiled as he put the phone down, and then hurried over to the house he was building to see how much he could get done in a couple hours.

*****

At about 9AM, Jason entered his dad's office building planning to see and talk to Maria about the evening before, but when he got to her office, nobody was there. He quickly took the stairs up to his dad's office. Since the door was open, he went right in and asked, "Where's Maria?"

William answered, "Please sit down and I'll tell you about it. Maria came to my office this morning just before 8 AM, and told me what had happened last night. She handed me this Bible and had me read the note she had written to you inside it. She asked me to give you the Bible and have you read the note. Then she asked if she still had a job, and I said yes. We decided that it would be best to transfer her to my second office, so I introduced her over there and just got back here a few minutes ago."

"But, now I won't be able to see her here or talk to her! How could that be best?" he said angrily getting up and stomping to the window.

"I think you'll understand that after you read the note," his dad said quietly, and handed him the Bible.

Jason took the Bible, sat down again, opened it, and was surprised to see handwriting on the first page. He had expected a piece of paper to be there instead. He read the note, and then read it a second time, not believing what it said. Inside, he screamed NO! Then he put his face in his hands and sobbed, not caring that he was a grown man, and his dad was watching him.

William let him cry until he was all cried out and then handed him some tissues. "I know it hurts, and I'm very sorry you have to go through this, Jason."

Everywhere There's a Sunrise, Let's Tell The Good News!

"Is there <u>nothing</u> I can do? What kind of father would not allow her to be courted by me? It does not make any sense to me," he stated, looking ready to cry again.

"I know it doesn't make sense to you. I think the only thing you <u>can</u> do is what she asked you to do in her note," William replied gently.

"What did she ask me to do?" Jason almost snapped.

"Read the note again and you'll know," his dad responded gently. So Jason read it again.

"Oh, yes, she wants me to think about the verses she shared with me and ask God to help me believe what they say. She listed them in her note and gave me this Bible. Well, I don't see how <u>that</u> will help me ever get to see her again. But I'll do it since Maria asked me to do it. She's such a special person, Dad. I have never known anybody like her. I wish I hadn't gotten angry about what she said. Thank you for listening and talking to me. I think I'll take a walk and then go back to my office and get to work," he finished.

"You're very welcome. That sounds like a good plan. Feel free to call or come see me any time," William replied wanting to add aloud that he would be praying for him, but that would be counterproductive. He did pray for him fervently after he left the office, glad to see that he had settled down and had decided to do what Maria had asked.

*****

After her father left, Ruth, knocked and entered Maria's office. She started by saying, "Excuse me for interrupting your work, Maria, but I wanted to remember to give this to you. Here is your employee number, which you'll use to enter this building. Please memorize it and then destroy the paper so nobody else can get access to it and enter the building. Also, I wondered if maybe it would be better to wait until Monday to introduce you to your co-workers. I would like to be your first new friend in this office, you see. I'm sure you'll become friends with all of them given time, but I thought that we could go to lunch in the park, and a short walk afterwards. Then just as soon as we get back here, I can give you a tour of this building. It <u>is</u> a little different than my dad's office."

"I like that idea very much because I don't really feel up to meeting a lot of new people today. Thank you for the offer of eating lunch with me in the park, plus the walk and tour afterwards. That will be very nice. I assume that your father told you about what happened," said Maria.

Ruth replied, "Yes, he told me everything that Don and you had told him. It's too bad that you had to go through that. It must have been very stressful for you. We can talk more about it at noon if you feel like it. I'll go now so you can get back to your work."

"Okay. Is there a refrigerator where I can put my lunch until noon?" Maria asked.

"Oh, of course. Come with me and I'll show you where it is right now," she answered and led the way.

Then Maria went right back to her office and worked rapidly until noon, at which time Ruth showed up at her office with both of their lunches and said, "It is a little chilly outside. I'm glad to see that you brought a coat with you today. The park isn't very far from here so we can just walk."

The walk was just far enough to get them warmed up. They found a bench to sit on in a warmer, sheltered place to eat their lunches. They both bowed their heads and said a silent prayer of thanks. Maria looked up with a smile and commented, "I think the Lord has blessed me with a boss who is thoughtful, friendly, <u>and</u> is a Christian. Where do you go to church?"

"I attend Grace 'n' Faith Church #4, and I've seen you there off and on. I was so pleased when I saw you come in with Dad. It will be nice to have a fellow Christian working in the building with me. I try to talk with my employees, but it's awkward for them to be friends with their boss. My little sister, Esther, works here, and she also is a Christian, but until now she and I were the only ones. I hope you and I can be friends and that you'll have a chance to talk to some of them when you go to lunch with them," Ruth said hopefully.

"That would be wonderful! I would enjoy having you for a friend, Ruth, and I would be thrilled if God would use me to witness to my co-workers. It was lonely working in Jason's office building. I don't know how it would have been in your father's, although he did seem friendlier. I was only there for two days."

Then she asked, "Do you think Jason will be all right? I didn't want to hurt his feelings or make him angry, but I had to know his beliefs before I could even consider letting him court me. When he told me what he does believe, it was as if there was a fire burning inside me to tell him the right way to get to Heaven. He listened politely until I pushed the point, and then it looked like he was getting very angry. If I had it to do over, I would not have consented to go on a date even once without knowing his beliefs. I could have avoided the whole scenario."

"Well, maybe God will use it all for good. Dad said the note you had written was very gentle, and the Scripture verses in the Bible you gave to him were just what he needs. Let's pray together. Father in Heaven, you know the whole situation and all that transpired. Please use the words and scriptures that Maria shared with Jason to open his mind and heart to Jesus and the salvation and healing He wants so much to give. Please do what you always do best: work all things together for good to us who love you and are called by you, as it says in Romans 8:28. Thank you for the good that has already happened by keeping Maria safe, and started here by bringing her to my office building to be a friend and co-witness to the others who work here," Ruth prayed.

"Yes, Father, I agree with all that Ruth has asked, and I thank you for forgiving me for the things I did wrong in the situation. Please don't let anything I did make Jason more depressed and upset than he usually is because of being bipolar. We pray in Jesus name, Amen," Maria finished and looked at her watch. "I don't think we'll have time for a walk before we go back, if you want to have time to give me a tour of the building."

"You're right," she agreed. "We'll just walk quickly back there and use the stairs on the tour. That will give us some good exercise."

They did that, and then Maria hurried back to work in her new office with a lighter, more relaxed feeling than she had had all week. At 5:00 she ran up the stairs and told her new boss good bye and that she would look for her at church on Sunday and/or see her on Monday.

When she arrived at her apartment, she changed and called Julie. "Hi, Julie this is Maria. ... ... Yes I do. I just changed and I'll wait for you and Ted clear inside the building. One of you will need to come in the entrance where I can see you and then we can go. ... ... Okay, see you soon, bye."

Ted came inside so Maria could see him, and they went out and got in the car. He explained, "We'll drive to a nice park on the other side of town to have our walk today, <u>and</u> until we're sure it's safe enough around here. After our walk, would it be okay with you to stop at Wal-Mart? We need to buy some things for the small group that's meeting at our apartment tomorrow."

"That would be fine with me," she answered. "I could even do the shopping that I usually get done on Thursdays on the way home from work ... except that I don't have my purse with me."

"No problema mi amiga, we'll just loan you some cash, ... and so that neither of us has to cook tonight, let's go eat at some nice quiet place before we shop," Julie suggested.

"On one condition," Maria laughed. "You also loan me enough cash to pay for all our suppers! You took me out on Monday, and had me over to supper on Wednesday. I would like to do my share. Do you realize I haven't eaten supper at my apartment one time in the last five days? It amazes me."

They all laughed and then had a nice walk in the park. Afterward they went to a nice little cafe that Maria knew about for supper, where they enjoyed a good meal and she told them all about her new boss and office, and how God was working things out for good. "And if you can believe it, Julie, I have actually remembered to pray concerning wisdom and guidance for your decision about teaching. Right now, I feel sure he has something outstanding planned for you to do in your future."

After everyone had completed their shopping, Ted loaded the chairs and other things in the trunk. They drove to Maria's apartment building where they helped Maria get her purchases up to her apartment. She quickly went and got the cash to pay back her loan and thanked them for a lovely evening.

They thanked her for the same, said good-bye, and went home to unload and put their purchases away. What a week this had been! They were looking forward to the small group meeting tomorrow and decided they would get to bed early. They could do a quick cleanup and prepare the room and refreshments in the morning.

*****

On Friday evening, Jason Beckett did look up some of the verses that Maria had listed in her note, but he was so distraught that he could not concentrate. He decided he would try it again another day. Nothing about this situation made any sense to him. He thought he had everything so well planned out, and was looking forward to courting and winning Maria. But everything went wrong. There didn't seem to be any possible way he could fix it like he usually did, and have things go his way. This was a dead end, a brick wall, totally insurmountable in his opinion.

*****

Everywhere There's a Sunrise, Let's Tell The Good News!

That evening after supper and dishes, Mindy told her dad, "I really wish you would meet and marry a wonderful Christian woman so you could be happy again, and so I could have a mother. You're a wonderful dad, and I'm very grateful for you. I just wish you could feel happy again. I really like helping Anita with the daycare and being able to spend time there. She is a great friend and I would like that to continue, but it would be nice to have a wife for you and a mother for me here in our house."

He responded, "Thank you for telling me how you feel, Mindy. I can't promise you anything right away, except that I'll pray about it and be open to what Jesus wills for us."

"Thank you, Dad. You're the best!"

He answered, "And you're the best too!" She hugged him and went to do her homework.

After she left, he put his head down on his arms at the table and cried. Even after four years without his special wife he could not imagine himself with any other woman. But he knew that was unfair to Mindy. She was getting to the age when a girl really needed a mother.

Finally he was able to pray. "Father in heaven, please forgive me for waiting for so long to pray about this situation. Change me in whatever way you need to, in order that if you desire for me to marry again and thus provide a mother for Mindy, I would be able to accept and even enjoy it. May your perfect will be done in our lives. I pray in Jesus precious name, Amen."

*****

Chapter 6

Isaiah 55: 10,11, *For as the rain comes down, and the snow from heaven, and does not return there, but waters the earth and makes it develop and bud, that it may give seed to the one who sows, and bread to the one who eats, so shall my word be that goes forth from my mouth. It shall not return to me void, but it shall accomplish that which I please, and it shall prosper in what I desire.*

Saturday

Don and Anita were the first to arrive at the Blakes apartment on Saturday morning. They brought in the hymnals and Bibles and then helped move chairs and set up the new ones in a circle in the living room while they listened to a summary of what Maria had told Ted and Julie last night about her new boss. They were all quick to praise the Lord for his goodness. While Julie and Anita set out the refreshments in the kitchen, Ted and Don sat down in the living room to pray for the small group time and then visit. Just in time, Julie was ready to answer the door, and Anita went to sit beside her husband. All the people arrived by ones and twos and they were ready to start on time. Ted had saved Julie a place and had her little notebook and a pen ready for her to use for the new people's names and to take notes on the teaching time.

Pastor Don started with, "Welcome everyone! I'm glad to see that everybody was able to come today. I would like to introduce our hosts, Ted and Julie Blake to all the new members. They just moved to Pine City a couple weeks ago. Now would you new members tell them your names, where and what hours you work and how long you've lived in Pine City? Julie is going to take notes."

"Hi, I'm Larry Kelsey. I work at Triple A Plumbing and Heating from 8 to 5 M-F."

"I'm Jane Kelsey, and I'm a midwife and do Lamaze training, so my hours vary. Presently I'm on vacation. We've lived in Pine City for 27 years."

"Hi, I'm Clara Morgan. I attend the university for nurses training in the morning and work from 1 to 9 PM, M-F at American Furniture Warehouse. I've lived in Pine City most of my life."

"I'm Roy Foster, and I work from 6 AM to 2 PM M-F, at Home Depot, then take care of our identical twin girls and our home the rest of the day. We've lived in Pine City for 7 years."

"Hi, I'm Sherry Foster. I take care of our girls and home while Roy is at work and then I go to work at Wal-Mart from 2:30 to 10:30 PM, M-F. Right now Hope and Joy are at the pastor's home with Timmy and Mary, with Mindy taking care of all four of them. They should have fun playing together."

"Hello, I'm Antonio [Tony] Valdez. I work at Fiesta Espanola Restaurante from 12-9 PM, M-F. I've lived in Pine City for about nine years."

Don added, "Tony was just recently promoted to Assistant Manager there, so that's our first praise report. He is too humble to tell us so I helped him out." The rest of the group clapped and thanked the Lord. "Are there any other praise reports? I need to emphasize that everything we talk about in this group goes no further, and we don't share praises or oral prayers that involve some person by name, who does not attend this group."

Matt jumped right in with, "Yes, Fiona is back home, and I get to court her again!" That was followed with shouts of praise, and lots of smiles, while Fiona smiled and blushed.

Roy said, "We were able get our work hours changed so one of us can always be with our twins, and Anita worked it out so Mindy will baby sit for them during small group time." More clapping and thanks to the Lord. Julie was glad that she now knew not to share about Maria. That kind of sharing could turn into gossip.

Nobody else had a praise, so Don brought up the idea of training Jeff and Karen Spencer to take over the guidance of this small group in about a month. "Let's pray about it and then hear any discussion you members might have. Father in Heaven, we ask for your wisdom, direction and assistance as we consider this plan. We'll wait here in silence for a couple minutes so you can speak to us."

After that, Larry started the discussion with, "As I remember in other groups, the facilitator is usually not the pastor, because he has so many other obligations. When he does start a group, he turns the guidance over to a couple who is willing to do it and has been trained."

Matt added, "I agree with what Larry just said and I know that Jeff and Karen are mature Christians who could do a good job of leading a small group."

Sherry mentioned, "Roy and I were in a group with the Spencers two years ago and they always had good things to add to the meetings."

Ted shyly added, "I think that since Pastor Don suggested the idea, we should agree to it."

The other people were nodding at various points during the discussion and Don decided it was time to bring it to a vote. Everyone agreed that it would be a good plan to have Jeff and Karen train and become this group's new facilitators.

"Thank you all for helping in this decision, and thank you Lord that we can have unity about it. Now let's sing hymns that go well with Easter time. So they sang, "Thine is the Glory," 1Corinthians 15:54b, 55; and "He Rose Triumphantly," 1 Thessalonians 4:14. Then they sang "One Day," Romans 5:6, which is about Jesus birth, life, ministry, death, resurrection, and that he will come again.

After that, Pastor Don explained that in place of the teaching time this week, all the small groups were having communion to honor and remember Jesus and what he did for us. He asked them to open their Bibles to Luke 22:7-14,19,20. They followed along as he read. *Then the day of unleavened bread came, when the Passover must be killed. He sent Peter and John saying, "Go and prepare for us the Passover, so that we may eat it." And they asked, "Where do you want us to prepare it?" He answered, "When you enter into the city, a man carrying a pitcher of water will meet you. Follow him into the house that he enters. Say to the man of the house, 'The master says to you, 'Where is the guest chamber, where I shall eat the Passover with my disciples?' He will show you a large upper room, which is furnished. Make it ready there." And they went, and found it as he had said, and they prepared the Passover. When it was time, Jesus sat down, and the twelve disciples were with him. ... Jesus took bread, and gave thanks and broke it, and gave it to them saying, "This is my body which is given for you; do this in remembrance of me." Likewise also the cup after supper, saying, "This cup is the new testament in my blood, which is shed for you."*

Then Don and Anita passed out the little pieces of unleavened bread and read verse 19 again before everyone ate the bread, remembering Jesus. They passed out little cups of grape juice and Don read verse 20 again. Then they all drank it and bowed their heads, remembering all that Jesus had so willingly done for them. It was a very precious and meaningful time for them all. After that, they sang the hymn, "One Day" again and it meant even more to them this time.

Many of them felt solemn and kept thanking Jesus silently. Don summed it up for them all when he started the conversational prayer time with, "Jesus, we are so grateful for your great love and all you did for us by willingly taking our place and making our salvation possible, and for this season on our calendars which focuses on that time in your earthly life."

Anita added, "We're also very thankful that you didn't stay dead, but were resurrected the third day and appeared to so many of your followers who wrote about it in the Gospels and Acts so that we could read and believe, be saved, and have eternal life with you."

"Yes, and thank you for this new small group where we can, in unity, take communion in such a meaningful way," Tony said. Then Ted mentioned his own gratefulness for being able to be in this city, church and group.

Fiona continued the subject by saying, "Please help us as we go out into our little worlds to take your love to those who don't know you yet. May our lives show them your love and make them hungry to know you as their own personal Savior." Julie wrote that request and the next in her notebook.

Tomo thought this might be a proper place to pray for his children, so he asked God to send loving Christians into their lives who would witness to them and that the Holy Spirit would open their hearts to accept Jesus. Ami added that if that would include bringing them back to Pine City to live, it would make her very happy because she missed them so much.

Jane said, "Larry and I agree with Tomo and Ami in that prayer, knowing that you are able and willing to answer it affirmatively as you did with our children by bringing them to the realization that they needed Jesus as their own Savior."

Roy added, "Please help those of us who have young children to train them in all the knowledge that they need to make their own decisions to accept Jesus as soon as they are able to recognize their need." Sherry, Anita, and Don all nodded to that.

Karen changed the subject by saying; "I feel that Jesus is urging me to give a word of knowledge to Julie. May I do that, Julie?" She nodded and said of course, so Karen continued, "Okay, Jesus says that you are a very good teacher, and that a new teacher is needed soon in the Grace 'n' Faith Christian School."

Julie responded, "Wow! I'm blown away by this word of knowledge. Thank you, Jesus, and thank you, Karen, for telling me. I had been waiting for an appropriate time to pray out loud here for guidance about whether to go job-hunting in Pine City for a teaching position sometime soon, but it seems like now I won't have to. Where can I find out more about the school and its need?"

Don spoke up, "I can tell you about it after the group meeting is over. This may be an incredible answer to prayer. I thank you also, Jesus, that by your Holy Spirit and Karen's willingness to let you use her voice, many prayers could be answered and a need taken care of. Amen. This has been an incredible meeting today! It is amazing to watch how God works through people in His church! If nobody else has a prayer or comment, shall we break now for refreshments?" Everyone nodded and stood up.

Ted and Julie welcomed them all into their kitchen where there was stand-up room for everyone and they enjoyed the cookies and their choice of coffee, tea, cocoa or ice water. People paired or grouped off and visited while they ate. Julie managed to talk to Karen and thanked her again for speaking up. Then Julie found Ted alone for a moment and suggested that they take Don and

Anita and their children to MacDonald's for lunch and then the children could play on the equipment while the pastor explained about the school.

After all the others had thanked them and left, Don and Anita agreed to that idea and said they would meet at MacDonald's in about 20 minutes so they could get the children buckled into their own car seats after checking with Mindy to see how the time went with the twins added to her daycare group. She told them that all had gone well.

Then, they all arrived at the same time at MacDonald's and Julie helped Anita with Timmy and Mary. The children wanted to play before lunch for a while and that gave Don a chance to get started, "First, I would like to ask about your experience with teaching. I assume you were in a public school?"

"Yes, I taught third grade one year and fourth grade the next year. Then the city cut back on funding, and I wasn't rehired the third year, so I went to work as a receptionist in a dental office," Julie answered.

Don was excited and said to himself that this could not be more perfect. But he started by explaining to her about the school and how it operated. "The church has a K-3 Christian School which is accredited and therefore needs licensed teachers. The school building is separate from the church building with a covered walkway connecting them. On Saturdays and Sundays the schoolrooms are used for children's Sunday school classes with the lunchroom held in reserve for small groups, which have no home available for a meeting.

"The school day for the teachers goes from 7:45 to 5:15, which is longer than a public school day, but that way it includes day care for parents who work 8 - 5 jobs. For teachers, the salary is lower than the public school, and there is no retirement fund. They must contribute to Social Security instead. But there are no evening or weekend hours needed because there are no busy work or drill papers to be checked.

"There are very few parent-teacher conferences needed, because most mothers and/or fathers volunteer often in the classroom and can watch their child's progress for themselves. Parents are motivated to volunteer because it takes dollars off the tuition. It's like they're being paid to come help in the classroom. Only working parents will need conferences twice a year. There are report cards, but they're simple and they and other 'paper' work can be done on the computer during recesses and other

Everywhere There's a Sunrise, Let's Tell The Good News!

times because the teachers have no recess or lunchtime duties. Lessons are already planned, and teachers just follow the directions. Hopefully you can be included in Ted's health insurance plan where he works. Are you still interested, or have I scared you away, Julie?"

"I'm <u>very</u> interested and have a lot of questions, but it looks like the children are on their way back over here and are probably hungry," answered Julie.

"Right. Here is a booklet that explains more about the school. Maybe you could read it while we go order and while we're all eating," Don said.

She nodded and took the booklet, but called Ted back, "Would you please give them your order and mine and some cash to pay for theirs and ours also, then come and read this with me? I need <u>you</u> to know everything that I do before we can make any decisions."

"Sure, honey. I'll be right back," he answered. When he returned, they started reading, and learned the following:

****

The motive for having a Christian school is taken from Psalm 78:1-8 which says in summary, *Give ear, O my people to my law, incline your ears to the words of my mouth. ... We have heard and our fathers have made known to us things that we will not hide from our children, showing to the generation to come the praises of the LORD and his strength, and his wonderful works that he has done. He commanded our fathers that they should make them known to their children, so that the generation to come might know them, and declare them to their children: that they might set their hope in God, and not forget the works of God, ... and not be stubborn and rebellious, but have hearts that are right and steadfast with God.* And from Deuteronomy 6:4-7a, *Hear, O Israel: The LORD our God is one LORD: you shall love the LORD your God with all your heart and soul and might. And these words, which I command you today, shall be in your heart. You shall teach them diligently to your children.*

All schools in Pine City are year-round, because many studies have been done which indicate that there is much learning lost over the summer vacation months, and it's hard for the children to get back into their studies after that much time off. Instead, there is one week for spring vacation to coincide with the week before Easter, a week off during the Fourth of July holiday, and another for the week that includes Labor Day, two days off for Thanksgiving, and two weeks for Christmas/New Years. The new school year starts when the children return from those two weeks. This plan gives a lot of vacation time, but not all at once.

There are no more than 25 students per room. Each room has one licensed teacher and a parent volunteer to help all day. When signing the contract, the teacher must agree to <u>not</u> become pregnant during the school year because the students need the stability of one teacher for the whole school year. Each school year, the teacher will sign a new contract still agreeing to the above. The parent volunteer will probably not be the same each day, but will be on a rotating schedule. This assures that the parents will be able to notice the progress his or her child is making.

The school curriculum includes all subjects covered by the public schools plus Bible and Christian Living training. It emphasizes Creation by the Triune God, and that evolution is just a theory. The children are taught how to deal with the teaching of evolution before they go into the public schools in fourth grade. They will know what it is and to basically ignore it, because it does not help to argue with the theory that makes it possible for humanity to not have to be answerable to its creator.

All the skills needed to pass each year's proficiency tests are taught, drilled and learned so that most children do well on those tests. If a child is not ready for the next level, he or she might need more extra help at the next level to become proficient in some of the skills. It is not called failing. As much as is possible we do individualized teaching and learning for those children, but most children move forward in small groups.

Fourth and fifth graders will come back on Wednesday afternoons after their early dismissal time to assist in K-2, or to help third graders with research reports and later in the year to answer third graders' questions about being in the public school next year. They also enjoy coming back to see their teachers and be encouraged themselves.

(A summary of the **curriculum for each grade level** is in the addendum at the end of this novel.)

****

Everywhere There's a Sunrise, Let's Tell The Good News!

By the time they had finished eating, they were also finished reading the booklet. "What do you think, Julie?" Ted asked.

"I really like it, especially the part about a child not failing or having to repeat a grade. That has always bothered me and I'm sure it's even harder on the child. It's especially important to let the eyes develop before forcing them to learn to read. The Bible and Christian Living Curriculum sounds wonderful also. In fact the whole idea is ideal!" she quipped. "What do you think?"

"I think you're fun, and I love you!" he laughed. "I also agree with all you said. Pregnancy is not an issue for us. So you can easily agree to that. Shall we go talk to Don some more?" She nodded, so they threw away their trash and went to join the others. It worked out well that the children were also finished and ready to go back and play for a while.

She didn't wait to be asked, but stated, "I'm very impressed, and most of my questions were answered. In fact, I can't think of any right now, except what's the next step?"

Pastor Don answered, "On Monday at the pastor's small group meeting, we were told the news about one of the third grade teachers needing to resign as soon as possible. I won't go into the reason, but they need a replacement very soon. I will need to talk with the person in charge and set up a time when she can interview you. After that, you might want to visit the school. The timing might be a little difficult with your work hours, but it will work out. I assume you'll need to give your present employer some kind of notice, but that's getting ahead of ourselves. Let me see what I can find out and I'll get back to you as soon as I can."

Julie next asked, "May I tell Maria about this since she's been praying with me about it all?"

"I would like to say that it would be fine, but I think it would be better to wait until we know more about what will happen. Do you agree?"

She nodded and replied, "Yes, that would be much better. Is there any chance I could tour the school during my lunch hour on Tuesday or Wednesday, which is from 12 to 1 o'clock? That would give them a day to settle in after a week of vacation. I remember how that goes."

"That sounds like a good plan, so I'll ask about that also. Thank you both for the good lunch and our time of talking about this possibility. I think it's time to get our children home for their afternoon rest time. We'll see you in church tomorrow. It's Resurrection Sunday! He is risen!" stated Don.

"He is risen indeed!" both Ted and Julie said in unison. Then they all got ready and left.

*****

Matt ate lunch after the Saturday morning group, and even had time to clean up his apartment before changing into work clothes to go spade in the garden. He arrived at the O'Connor's house at 2 PM and Fiona was waiting on the porch, also dressed for garden work. After greeting one another, they went out into the back yard where Glenda and Patrick were already digging.

"Wow! With all four of us spading, this should get done quickly!" said Patrick. "Greetings, Matt, and thank you for coming to help us. It's a beautiful afternoon for working outside."

"My pleasure. I'm glad I can assist, especially on such a nice afternoon. Now, where's my shovel?" Glenda handed hers to him and she and Fiona went to get two more from the shed.

They all worked well together with lots of talking and laughter to speed the job along. By the end of three hours they were all hot and tired, but the garden was all spaded. They went up on the shady porch and the two ladies brought out refreshments for all of them. That helped to revive them, and Matt said he would bring the blue prints from the pick-up so they could look at them. He answered any questions they had about the house, and they continued visiting for a while until Matt looked at his watch and announced that he needed to get home. With thanks and good-byes and waves, he was soon on his way, glad for a good, profitable time together.

*****

As Jeff and Karen Spencer drove home from the small group meeting, they were quiet. Both were thinking about how marvelous their God was, plus the unanimous acceptance of their training to be facilitators for the small group, and word of knowledge Jesus had Karen give. They were also praying for help in their training, for Julie's decision about teaching, for people raising children, and for adult children who need salvation.

During lunch they talked about the meeting and how meaningful it was to have communion together at this special time of the year. Then, after cleanup, they decided to go do all the shopping for the week. It would also let them get some exercise after sitting for so long.

*****

Larry and Jane Kelsey went home after the small group meeting and did some house and yard work for a while, before eating lunch. Jane mentioned, "I thought the time of communion was especially significant today, and the words of the songs were, too."

Larry agreed and added; "Karen's word of knowledge was so timely during the conversational prayer time. She could not have known that Julie was going to pray for direction about job-hunting for a teaching position in the public schools, or that the pastor thought it might be an answer to prayer. He didn't go into detail, but it sure was interesting. Father, thank you for all that happened at the small group meeting and that we were privileged to attend and be a part of it. Please work out all the details for Julie and for the church school."

Jane continued, "Yes, and please help the families who are raising children, to teach them to love and believe in Jesus so they can be witnesses for the Kingdom. Please send people to witness to those adult children who don't know Jesus. In your name we pray, Amen."

"I was just thinking," said Larry, "would you like to ask the Suehiros over for supper tomorrow evening, if they're not busy someplace else because of Easter?"

She answered, "It's a great idea! I would like to get to know them better, and maybe we'll find out some more information so we can pray in a more intelligent way for their adult children. I think their phone number is in the church directory, so we can call them after doing dishes."

They did that, and the Suehiros were happy to say yes.

*****

Maria spent her Saturday doing housework, laundry, some baking, and Bible study, plus writing in her journal. She wrote about the things she had learned during the week, including a new insight that even if Jason had been a believer, he was in a different league than she was. She doubted that there could be much unity between two people with such different ideas about spending money. She was glad she didn't have to think about dating a person like that. But she spent some time praying for his salvation and healing. Then she prayed for Julie again about what she had shared on their first exercise walk last Monday, that she would have God's guidance and peace about whether to try to find a job teaching in public school, or just have an 8 to 5 job.

*****

Ted and Julie stopped at a park on the way home from lunch with the pastor and his family. As they walked along the pathway, they discussed the amazing small group meeting and the church school some more. Julie started by saying, "Communion with the small group was so much more meaningful than the ones we've had in the churches we've attended. The words of the songs, and since it's Resurrection Sunday tomorrow had something to do with it, and just being in a small group helped also."

He agreed and said, "I like the conversational prayer time. I didn't know what to expect, but it's just like everybody was talking to God like he was a part of the group, and they added to what was just prayed or changed the subject as needed."

She smiled and agreed, "Talk about a change of subject! I still can't get over the fact that Karen could _not_ have known what was in my mind without God telling her. That proves to me that it _was_ a word of knowledge, and that God cares about me personally, and of course about the church school. I'm excited to see what will happen."

"So am I! Have you had any other thoughts about the whole idea?" he asked her.

"Yes, and I need to know how _you_ feel about it. It would be less money than I could earn by teaching in a public school, with longer hours at the school. But there would be less impact on home life, since I would not have to bring work home in the evenings or on weekends. That _was_ a concern I had if I went back to teaching at a public school," she answered.

"The money you could earn isn't a problem and you're already included on the insurance plan where I work. Also, you would be earning more at the church school each day than you do at the dental office, since your workday is half an hour longer, and the wages are a little higher. You'll actually be paid for nine and one half hours of working, instead of eight, since you would work through lunch and most of your break times. We were doing fine on the other amount and we can continue to tithe on the amount of money you'll earn at the school, and what I make where I work. You'll have five weeks off when school is on vacation, but you'll get two of those weeks as paid vacation time that you would not get at the dental office. So that is a step up from the dental office. Having said all that, we've always agreed that this life isn't all about making money. The best thing is that this would be a tremendous ministry opportunity for you," he explained.

"That's for sure! Just think of being in a Christian school that wants me to teach the children all those things that were written in that booklet. In public school I had to be so careful about anything I said for fear of having a lawsuit or getting fired. Wow! It sounds better all the time!" she exclaimed.

Ted continued, "Yes it does! If it does work out for you to go to work there, I'm all for it, because I know how much you like teaching and what a good teacher you are. You're already used to year-round school, so that's no problem."

"Right. Thank you for your vote of confidence and the compliments!" Julie responded. "I like the idea of having two adults in the classroom at all times. It might be a little stressful with parents there all the time, and having them rotate. But since the year is already a third finished, and the parents know what has been happening, it might help me to get acclimated better. This has been a very helpful conversation. I really appreciate your input. Let's go home now. I have some housework to get done."

*****

Chapter 7

Luke 19:10, *For the Son of man came to seek and save that which was lost.*
Luke 24:34, *The Lord is risen indeed ...*

Resurrection Sunday, the second Sunday in April

On Sunday morning, many of the members of the small group were busy catching up on some of their housework, and fixing lunch and maybe starting something for supper in a crock-pot. Then they got ready to go to church for a Resurrection Sunday celebration. Ted and Julie were in the entryway and greeted members of the small group as they arrived. When Maria entered, they all agreed to meet as usual for their exercise walk on Monday after work, and then the three of them went inside and sat together.

Fiona sat with her parents in their usual area and she took a little time to look around. The sanctuary was about three-fourths full today, not like last Sunday. Then she realized that since it was Easter Sunday more people would be attending, since it's a time when many people go to church, even if they don't attend any other Sunday of the year. She also remembered that other years the people in small groups would receive little invitations at their small group meetings two weeks before Easter, to pass out to friends, acquaintances and even just people they saw in stores. This happened for all twelve churches and was a great outreach idea. It looked like it had really worked!

Matt came in and sat with Fiona and her parents and she welcomed him with a smile. It was nice to see him any time, but especially dressed nicely for church. Her heart gave a little flutter of happiness to think that he cared for her!

She looked at the list up front and saw that they would be singing more songs this morning than the other weeks, and they were all such good ones. She took out a Hymnal and looked up "Easter Song" based on Mark 16: 6,7, the angel at the tomb of Jesus said, *You are looking for Jesus of Nazareth, who was crucified. He is risen. He is not here: look at the place where he was. But go and tell his disciples and Peter that he will see you as he said in Galilee.* They also sang "Christ the Lord is Risen Today," 1 Corinthians 15:55; "Christ Arose," Acts 2:24; and "God Incarnate," Matthew 1:21 and 1 Corinthians 15:20, which tells the gospel story.

After an inspiring time of singing, Pastor Don began by welcoming all the visitors. Then the message started with 1 Peter 1:3,4. *Praise be to the God and Father of our Lord Jesus Christ, who according to his abundant mercy has made us be born again unto a living hope by the resurrection of Jesus Christ from the dead, and to an inheritance that is incorruptible, not defiled, and that does not fade away, which is reserved in heaven for us.*

"What a wonderful hope that is for people who believe in Jesus. But maybe you're here today and you don't have that hope, because you haven't heard about it before, or you don't understand it, or you think it could not be for you.

"Think about the story told in the last song we finished a few minutes ago. I'll explain it: Jesus came as God incarnate, which means as God in a human person. He came to bring salvation to us because of our sins for which the penalty is death. So that means he came to give us life. He died on the cross to pay our debt, because we could not pay it ourselves, since we are sinful. Now we can be forgiven and free. The message of Easter or Resurrection Sunday is that Jesus didn't stay dead. God raised him to eternal life to prove that he accepted Jesus sacrifice as payment for the sins of all men if they will believe in Jesus. So now we can have peace and hope instead of fear and dread. That is <u>indeed</u> something to celebrate!

"Turn with me to Acts 10:36-43 and follow along as I read it. *God sent his Word to the children of Israel, proclaiming peace by Jesus Christ who is Lord of all. That Word was published all through Judea, beginning in Galilee after the baptism which John preached: that God anointed Jesus of Nazareth with the Holy Spirit and with power, and that he went around doing good and healing all who were oppressed by the devil, because God was with him. We, (his disciples) are witnesses of all the things he did in the land of the Jews, and in Jerusalem. They killed him by hanging him on a cross, but God raised him up from the dead the third day and he appeared openly, not to all the people, but to us, the witnesses he chose beforehand, who ate and drank with him after he rose from the dead. And he commanded us to preach to the people, and to testify that <u>he</u> was ordained by God to be the judge of the living and the dead. All the prophets give witness of him that through <u>his</u> name, **whoever** believes in him, shall receive the forgiveness of sins.*

"Did you see and hear that word, 'whoever'? That means **you** who don't have that hope, because you haven't heard about it before, or you don't understand it, or you think it could not be for you. **YOU** can, if you'll just believe. Then you can say with other believers that Jesus was wounded, and died for me on the cross and now my sins are gone, and I am free. And you can say that Jesus has risen up from the grave and is forever alive and prays for me, until the day he comes back from heaven to take me and all other believers to live forever with him in Heaven.

"Let's all bow our heads and close our eyes while we thank our Savior for all he did for us and while I lead anyone who wants that hope in a prayer that they can repeat after me silently. I'll say it slowly so you can think about it and keep up. God, I realize that I am a sinner. ... ... I confess these sins to you. ... ... Name silently, the ones you think of. ... ... Please forgive me. ... ... Thank you that you already paid the price for my sins by dying on the cross, ... and that God raised you from the dead. ... ... I believe in you and ask you to be my Savior. ... ... Amen. ... ... Now I'm going to add another song that's not on our list up here. Please find "Hallelujah, What a Savior!" Now let's stand and sing it because it's such a good summary of what Resurrection Sunday means."

After they sang it, he said, "If any of you prayed that prayer with me silently a few minutes ago, please tell somebody here about it. And if you'll come and tell me, I have a booklet that I would like to give you that explains more in detail what it all means and what steps you will want to take next. Now let's all go in the joy of the Lord, because Jesus is risen!"

And the congregation answered. "He is risen indeed!" It had been a thrilling service. The people all began moving around and went especially to greet the visitors in the congregation and to find people that they wanted to greet or talk to. Maria said good-bye to Ted and Julie and then went over and met Ruth's sister, Esther, and they talked for a little while. Jeff and Karen found Ted and Julie and asked them if they would like to come to their house for supper that evening. They thanked them and said, "Yes".

Many people told others about their prayer and were congratulated and welcomed into the family of God. Then they went to talk to the pastor and receive the little booklet he had offered. He was ecstatic and told them how glad he was for them. The booklet had a little card inside that said, "Please fill me out and bring me back to church and give me to the pastor next week if you would like a visit from the pastor or would like to join a group especially for new believers." It had a place for name, address, and phone number. New believer groups would be started to teach these people how to live the Christian life, and most of them would continue as regular small groups.

Pastor Don managed to catch Jeff and Karen before they left, and gave them a booklet to read about being small group facilitators. They thanked him and told him they would read it. Then he asked them to come over to his house on Tuesday evening so they could discuss what the booklet said and ask any questions they might have.

*****

After church, Matt decided to drop in and visit Walt and Betty. They were home and were delighted to see him. When they were all seated, he started by saying, "I came to see how you are both feeling. Did you get an appointment with the doctor, Walt?"

Everywhere There's a Sunrise, Let's Tell The Good News!

"Yes, I'll be going tomorrow afternoon at 3 PM," he answered. "I feel pretty good after resting a lot this weekend. Maybe it's nothing to worry about, but I know Betty and you will be pleased that I'm finally going to go. I think you both worry too much, but I thank you for caring."

"You're welcome. How are you, Betty?" Matt asked.

"I'm relieved that he's going to see the doctor, so I feel good," she replied. "How are you, Matt?"

"I'm relieved too, and I feel fine, thank you. Yesterday, I was able to help Fiona and her parents spade their garden, so now it's ready to mark the rows and plant as soon as the danger of frost is past. It was a good time of getting better acquainted with Patrick and Glenda. I had never known them well enough to go by first names, but that's what they said they want now. It was Fiona's idea that we do some things with them as a family. She is an amazing person. Betty, how's your next project coming?" asked Matt to get the attention back on her.

"Not so good. I keep procrastinating because mending isn't something I enjoy doing. But since you asked me about it, I think I'll get a good start on it tomorrow. I know I'll feel better about doing it after if see the pile starting to shrink, one item at a time," she laughed. "Walt, tell him what you did this weekend while you were resting."

"Okay," he responded. "I sat in my recliner and looked up all the Bible references that book has had in it so far. It was fascinating. I read them aloud to Betty whenever she would sit down and rest. She is always busy around the house and of course that's why she's such a good homemaker. We aren't ready to talk about the book to you yet, but we're getting closer."

"Oh, I didn't come over here to rush you, or even question you about it. Take as long as you need. But I'm glad to hear that you're reading the book and looking up the Bible references. Well, I think I had better mosey on home and get caught up on some of my own housework. I'll see you tomorrow at the work site, Walt," said Matt as he let himself out of their house and then drove to his apartment.

*****

As soon as the Kelseys arrived home after church, Jane checked on the food cooking in the crock-pot and found that it was coming along nicely. It sure smelled good. They worked together to straighten up the house and set the table and get ready for the

Suehiros to arrive at about 5 PM. Jane made a salad and put in it the refrigerator until it was time to put it on the table.

Larry and Jane greeted Tomo and Ami when they arrived and ushered them into the living room, where they sat for a little while and got better acquainted. Jane said, "We didn't get to hear your introduction because we weren't at the first group meeting. Would you tell us now?"

"Of course," answered Ami. We've owned and operated Ami's Japanese Restaurant for the last 20 years. My name means friend, so we named it Ami's. We've lived in Pine City for 25 years and raised our children here. Their names are Aneko, which means older sister, and Yoshi meaning quiet or shy. Both of them have grown up and moved away from Pine City. They're both still single. Tomo has a twin brother who is a few minutes younger than he is because he was born after him. His name is Afta which means just that."

"It's really interesting that his name sounds so much like the English word, 'after'. I always wished I had a twin. What was that like, Tomo?" asked Larry.

"Well," he answered. "It was great growing up with a brother and playmate my age. We were very close and always did things together, except that we couldn't be in the same classroom at school. That bothered both of us, but I guess it was for the best, because it forced us to make other friends also, besides each other. What's more, we were identical twins and the teachers would have had a terrible time telling us apart. My parents had no problem with that, and we could not get away with switching places with them around."

Larry said, "Thank you for telling us about having a twin brother. It is much like I thought it might be. I would like to meet him. Does he live around here?"

"No," answered Tomo. "Just after we graduated from high school, Afta got married and moved pretty far away to be near his wife's family. We don't get to see much of each other anymore. We talk on the phone regularly but it's not the same somehow. Ami and I just came to the Lord a little over three years ago, and it's been so good for us. The only problem is that nobody else in our close or extended family knows Jesus and none of them wants to talk about him, including our two children who had already moved away from Pine City before we got saved."

"Oh, that's so sad! Would it be okay with you two if we all pray about your family now?" asked Larry. They nodded and Larry started, "Father in heaven I'm so glad that Tomo and Ami know you, but you just heard what he said about his family. We know that you want them to be saved even more than we all do because you are patient, and don't anyone to perish but all to come to repentance, as it says in 2 Peter 3:9b."

Jane added, "Thank you for that, Father. Please send people into the lives of all the people in Tomo and Ami's close and extended family who will be able to talk to them about you. Give them the words to say that will show how much God loves them and wants them to be in his family. Holy Spirit we are glad that you can draw people to Jesus and ask that you do that for this whole family."

Ami was in tears, but she also prayed, "Yes, thank you for that, and help me remember that they're all in your hands, and you know how to reach them."

Then Tomo said, "Please help us to rest in you and have peace as we continue to pray for them and wait for the miracles of their salvation. We pray and agree together in Jesus precious name, Amen. Thank you Larry and Jane for praying with us. We feel better knowing there are others agreeing with us in prayer. I'm really glad a new small group has started up that meets at a time when we can attend."

"Me too. I was feeling rather isolated. The church times are very good, but it's hard to get to know people with just 15 minutes to visit after services. Thank you for asking us over to supper. This is a nice way to get acquainted. Jane, how do you like being a midwife?" Ami asked.

"It is very rewarding, most of the time, and it's hard work, but also very sporadic. I never know when I'm going to be called away from whatever I'm doing to go help deliver a baby. I have just returned from a city in a warm southern state where I delivered my own daughter's first baby, a healthy boy. My daughter's name is Lucy. They named their boy Jonathan. I spent two months with her just so I could enjoy them and help out for a while. So right now I don't have any clients. I'll have to admit that it's nice to have a vacation. Shall we continue our conversations while we eat? I, for one am getting hungry," Jane said as she got up and led the way into the dining room.

"You have a beautiful home. It feels so comfortable and welcoming," Ami commented as she followed Jane.

"Thank you," replied Jane. "I'm glad you like it. If you two will sit on that side of the table we'll sit facing you and then we can see each other better while we're talking. Larry and I will be right back with the food for our supper."

They came back quickly with the crock-pot, salad, bread, butter and dressing. Larry prayed, "Thank you Lord, for this time we can share with Tomo and Ami, and thank you for this food. Please bless it to our bodies and use us in your service. I ask in Jesus name, Amen. Now if you'll hand me your plate, Ami, I'll dish some of this up for you since the crock pot is rather hard to pass around." Soon everybody was served and the rest of the things were passed around so they could start eating.

Jane started the conversation going again by asking, "What did you like about the small group meeting on Saturday?" They had a lively discussion about that with everyone sharing one or more things. Then they talked about various other topics while they ate supper and dessert. When they were finished, all hands made short work of the cleanup in order that they could all go back into the living room for more visiting before the Suehiros went home.

*****

Ted and Julie's time at Jeff and Karen's for supper was just as nice, with conversation centering on the word of knowledge given by Karen and what Ted and Julie had learned about the school by talking to Pastor Don and reading the booklet about the school. Julie started by admitting that she had not even known that the church <u>had</u> a school. She told them she was very excited about the possibility of teaching there, but had no idea whether it would happen since Don had to contact the school and find out what the next steps would be. The four of them spent a long time praying together for God's will, and for wisdom and patience while they waited to find out. Julie promised to call and tell them when she knew anything for sure.

*****

Monday

Pastor Don awoke on Monday morning realizing that he had not asked for a volunteer to host the next small group meeting. So they decided to call and invite all the members to come to their house for the meeting on this coming Saturday morning. Anita volunteered to make all the phone calls while the children were playing quiet games where she could keep an eye on them. Don gave her the list of phone numbers before he left for his job at the Local Grocery.

*****

During the morning, Maria was able to finish up several of the tax returns. Just before lunch, she took them up to Ruth so she could send them over by courier to William. As she handed them to Ruth she said, "I left a plastic grocery bag of my belongings in the bottom drawer of the desk in his office building. Would you ask William to send them over here to me with the courier when he returns?"

"Certainly. Are you ready to go to lunch? Esther said she would like to join us today in the park. It looks like a beautiful day out there, but it's hard to tell how cool it might be. I notice it also looks a bit windy. We'll meet you in the lunchroom with our coats. Then we can take our lunches and see if it's warm enough to eat outside," responded Ruth.

"That sounds like a good plan. If it's not warm enough we could go for our walk first and then come back here and eat in the lunch room," said Maria. Ruth agreed and they went to get their coats and meet in the lunchroom.

"Hi, Esther, I'm glad you're going with us today. We barely had a chance to talk yesterday," Maria said.

"For sure, but at least we got started, and we can continue today. Let's take our lunches out of the refrigerator and get started," said Esther.

Out on the sidewalk, Ruth exclaimed, "Burr! That wind is really chilly today. How about a really short, fast walk to get our blood moving and legs stretched before we return here to eat?" They all agreed and put up their hoods, tied them and set out with Ruth leading the way. They managed to walk all the way around the block one time and hurried back inside where it was warmer and they would have a chance to talk as they ate their lunches in the lunchroom.

"That was kind of fun anyway," Esther said as they sat down, "and now I'm really hungry. Maybe it would be best to walk before eating every time. I've heard that's better for digestion anyway. Father, thank you for the food we're about to eat. Please bless it to our bodies, and our bodies to your service." They all said, "Amen," and began to eat.

"I like that idea. It gets us up and moving after sitting all morning at our desks," said Maria.

"We might have to reinvent the wheel when we go out with other co-workers, though," Esther commented, "because they didn't just have the experience we did. Many of them like to go to cafes or fast food restaurants, and they usually drive."

Ruth added, "Right you are, and if we want to make friends with them and have opportunities to share our faith, we'll have to plan on doing as they do, like that saying, 'When in Rome, do as the Romans do.' What do you think, Maria?"

She answered, "I think you're absolutely correct. And that means I need to be willing to go out to eat which is something I seldom do. I will need to rework my budget and figure out a way to make it work. It's very important to me that I get started here on the right foot, if I'm going to be able to share my faith with my new co-workers. At Jason's office none of the workers ever did anything together. This is all new for me, but it will be good for me. How do we get started?"

"Ah, that's the BIG question!" replied Ruth. "It's even harder for me, because the others don't feel comfortable being friends with the boss. For some reason that's forbidden for them, and I don't know what the reason is. Let's pray like we do in small groups. Father, thank you for sending Maria to this office so she can work with us. Maybe this will be an opportunity for us to make friends with the other workers. Show us how to get started."

Maria continued, "Yes, Lord, I'm very grateful to still have a job, and to have the chance to work with a Christian boss who has the desire to witness and share the Good News with her employees. Please help to break the barrier of them not wanting or daring to be friends with the boss, and help me to know how to be friendly but not pushy."

Esther added, "Father we're asking you for wisdom and for the Holy Spirit to fill us with boldness and just the right words to say at the right time. Maybe I should keep on as I have, just slowly asking one at a time if they would like to go to lunch together and we talk about what they want to until a friendship develops. Please help the few seeds I've planted to take root and grow."

Maria said, "Father, it sounds like Esther has a good plan for herself. Please help Ruth and me to figure out a plan we can try. We're all in agreement here and ask these things in Jesus name." In a few moments she said, "Here is an idea I just had. Since I'm the new employee here, could Ruth introduce me to one person a day at 4:50 PM? She could invite us both to join her for lunch the next day so we can get acquainted. Then Ruth can ask whether the person would like to bring a lunch and go for a walk before eating, or if they would like to go out to eat."

"I like that plan," replied Ruth. We can try it this afternoon and see how it goes. What do you think, Esther?"

"I think it makes good sense," she responded. "We could plan to bring our lunches on Friday and the three of us meet to discuss how our plans are working and pray some more."

"Another good idea," Ruth agreed. "Thank you Father, and thank you both. This has been an enjoyable and productive lunch hour. Now we had better all go back to our offices and get back to work."

Maria worked extra hard and finished two more tax returns, leaving only three for tomorrow and she would be done. She took the two finished ones up to Ruth at 4:45 so she could send them to William before he left his office. Then Ruth took her to meet one of her co-workers and they were able to set up a get-together for lunch the next day at a nearby cafe. So far so good.

When they returned to Ruth's office she handed Maria the grocery bag with her things in it. Maria thanked her, and said, "I'll see you tomorrow." Then she put on her coat and drove home, noticing that it was starting to rain. Her phone was ringing when she entered her apartment. Julie had called to cancel their exercise walk, hoping that the weather would be better on Wednesday. Maria was thankful that she had at least walked 4 blocks at noon. She would have even more to tell Julie when she next saw her.

*****

During Don's lunch break, he called the church's school to talk to the principal and set up an interview for Julie Blake. She informed him that she would have to do a background check on Julie and get back to him. She did it so rapidly that she was able to call back in 15 minutes. She said the interview time would be 5:15 on Tuesday. He also asked her to set up a tour of the school for Julie, if the interview went well. Then he called Julie who was also on her lunch hour and told her the time for her interview with the principal, Miss Beth Davis, would be on Tuesday, at 5:15 PM.

After Don's lunch break, he worked for about an hour and since being alert was part of his job description, he was always looking and listening for anything unusual going on. As he was stocking shelves, he heard a rasping noise near a back wall of the store, so he quickly put down the cans on the shelf and quietly headed that way. From behind a shelf, he was able to see a young girl with colored chalk writing on the wall. She had a banana sticking out of the side pocket of her dirty, torn jeans. She finished writing, and then hurriedly went around a corner and disappeared.

Silently, he headed that way and by looking through an opening in another isle he could see the toe of a tennis shoe just barely showing on the other side of a large trashcan. Pretty soon a hand threw a banana peel into the can and then there was a sound of cellophane rattling and being torn. He quickly called store security, described her to them, and told them to catch her if she managed to get away from him. He could smell the banana and then peanut butter and even hear chewing as he quickly walked to where she was sitting on the other side of the trashcan, with the last of the peanut butter packet and crackers in her hands.

Don took a firm but gentle hold on her arms and lifted her up. He hushed her when she started to scream, and said to her, "Okay, Missy, I've been watching you."

She interrupted, "I'm not Missy, I'm Candy Smith. Oops!" She had looked scared and then rebellious.

He continued, "You didn't pay for the things you've been eating here in secret, and you have the evidence inside you, and in your hands, and in this trash can. I also saw you writing graffiti on that other wall!" She was crying now. "Let's go sit in this lunch room and talk." He led her to a chair and let her cry for a while, then handed her some tissues. "Would you like to tell me why you did this?"

"The kids who were letting me live with them told me I had to do this or else starve. At first they had taken care of me and let me eat their food, then they took me with them to watch and learn how to shoplift, and get out of a store without getting caught. When I got good enough at that, they stopped giving me food and said I'd have to pass one more test if I wanted to continue to stay with them. I would have to graffiti a wall in a store and eat the food I stole there without getting caught. I really didn't want to do it, but I was hungry and scared. They told me that if I got caught, I could not come back to them. They said they would have to move someplace else so I couldn't rat on them and lead the police to them. They also said they would have a lookout watching, so they would know if I got caught. I <u>did</u> get caught, and now I don't have any place else to go," she finished. She was crying again.

Don let her cry for a time before he quieted her, got her attention and stated, "Now you have two choices, Candy. You can face the charges and pay for what you did, or you can try to escape by running away from here <u>and</u> from everything else for the rest of your life until you're caught anyway. If you run now and try to escape, the security officers who are inside watching for you might catch you. Then you would get a bigger penalty. Even if you did escape, your gang won't take you back because you failed their test."

"No, they'll beat me and send me away just like my parents did when I couldn't make money for them, … oops!" Candy said and then put her face in her hands.

Don said, "It isn't an 'oops' to tell the truth. I'm glad that you told me your name and about your parents. Since you know that it will do no good to try to escape, let's look at your other option of facing the charges and paying for what you did. One way you could do this is to spend a set amount of time in Juvenile Hall, which is like a prison. The other way is to clean up the mess you made with the graffiti and then work the rest of my workday with me to earn enough money to pay for the things you stole. I think you have now learned that everything you do has consequences, so what do you think is your best choice, since you've made this <u>big</u> mistake?"

Candy answered, "I can't go 'home' or go back to the gang and I don't want to do either of those anyway. I don't want to go to prison either. Would you really let me clean up the mess I made with the chalk, and work here to pay for what I stole?"

"Yes I will, but you'll have to agree to two conditions," he replied.

She asked, "What are they?"

"Number 1, you will never do graffiti or steal anything again, and that includes shop lifting! Number 2, you will go to live in a Safe/Care House where you will be cared for and loved, and where you will do your share of the chores, and you will go back to school and attend church with them," he answered.

"Really? Be loved and cared for? Just for doing chores and going to school and church? Wow! It sounds like paradise! What's the catch?" she asked.

"There <u>is</u> no catch. The people I would take you to, <u>want</u> to help kids like you, because Jesus loved and helped them," he answered.

"I'll do it! I promise, I will never steal or do graffiti again, and I'll go there to live, do chores and go back to school and go to church with them. Thank you, Mister. Where's the cleaning stuff? And when the wall is clean I'll work with you the rest of today to pay for the food I stole," she said very seriously.

"You're welcome. Candy Smith, you just made a very good choice, and I'm glad. Now let's go get the cleaning supplies and get you started," Don responded feeling very relieved. He watched from a distance while she cleaned the wall and he also called the security officers and reported what she had decided.

Then he called the couple who would be taking Candy into their home to live. He made arrangements to settle her in with them. After that, he called Social Services and reported what her parents had done, and where he was placing Candy. Don also called the police and alerted them to the fact that a gang was moving to a new place after a failed initiation attempt. They and Social Services were used to getting calls from Don Ross and appreciated the way he was able to get many children off the streets and out of gangs. He was glad to be able to serve the Lord and the city this way, and that the Local Grocery encouraged him to do it. But it was very stressful, so he prayed for strength and peace to carry on and do it well.

When he saw that Candy was almost finished he went over to praise her good job. They put the supplies away and they both went and stocked shelves until 5 PM. Then they went and found a package of crackers, a peanut butter packet, and a banana, which they took to a clerk up front to pay for them. She paid for them with the money Don gave her for working with him the rest of the afternoon. Then they went and put the items back in their places.

While she was getting buckled up in the seat, Don called his wife to tell her he would be late getting home today. Then he drove to the home where she would start her 'new' life. He could see that she was nervous. He told her not to worry about things like clothes and belongings because this would be like starting over with a clean slate. "Keep making good choices and doing the right things and life will be much better for you." When they got there, he went inside and introduced them, got her settled and was finally able to go home. What a day!

Don and most of the other pastors and many church members were stockers in various stores around the city. They all had agreements with their employers to be alert to look for shoplifters and try to catch them in the act. Then they would try to talk them into working to pay for what they had stolen and agree to stop stealing. If necessary, they would be placed in a Safe/Care Home, depending on their situation. The goal was to shrink the gangs in the city and especially to catch new members and get them on a better road, hopefully leading them to accept Jesus as their Savior and become useful members of society. New members were usually easier to catch because they had not become as skilled as the others. It was an important ministry, and he was thankful that this one had turned out so well. He was also glad they would get to go to the pastor's small group meeting after supper.

*****

Chapter 8

Romans 8:28 again, *We know that all things work together for good to them who love God, and are called according to his purpose.*
James 1:17, *Every good and perfect gift is from above, and comes down from the Father of Lights, who has no variableness or shadow of turning.*

Tuesday

When Jason arrived at work that morning, he walked past the office where Maria had worked for about two years and really missed seeing her there. "I wish I had not said anything or transferred her to the other office. Maybe I would have still had a chance with her. Well, it's too late now. I already ruined it somehow and can't undo it now. It's just so wretched!" he exclaimed, slamming his door for emphasis. Then he realized he was at work and all the other employees would be arriving soon so he had better get control of his actions.

*****

Matt rose early on Tuesday, glad that he had done his laundry already on Monday. He would have extra time to work on his house today if it had not rained too hard last night and wasn't too cold. April could be an unpredictable month. He was also wondering what Walt had found out at his visit to the doctor yesterday afternoon. Maybe they would have a chance to talk when he got to the job site. He looked at the weather forecast on the web and was pleased with what he saw, so he ate a good breakfast and got dressed to go over to his house and do as much as he could in a couple hours. It went well there and he hurried home to fix a big lunch, eat it, rest a while, and then go to the work site.

Walt came right over to him, <u>not</u> looking very happy. "The doctor did a lot of tests and then told me I had better plan on cutting back on my work, because my heart is <u>not</u> up to this hard work."

"Oh, I'm sorry to hear that!" exclaimed Matt. "Did the doctor have any suggestions about how you could do that?

"Yeah," he answered, "but it don't like them. He said I could get another foreman, and just supervise a couple hours a day or I could retire. He also said I need to change my diet big time, and develop an easy exercise routine that's not as demanding as working all day. I told him I don't work all day, but he said seven hours <u>is</u> all day even if I do rest in the afternoons. I'm not old enough to retire! I have a lot of plans and things I want to accomplish before I retire. I don't like this!"

"I can understand that. It's not easy to be told that you have to change your whole lifestyle and give up on things you've planned to do. But what's the alternative? What can happen if you don't follow his instructions?" asked Matt.

"I know, I know, that's what Betty asked me too. Are you two in cahoots? That's three against one! I'm out voted before I even get started!" Walt complained.

"Whoa!" Matt cautioned gently. "Please don't get upset with us. We only want what's best for you and we want you to be around for a good many years yet, so I hope you will consider all the options and choose what will help you the most. Would it help if I come over to your house for a while after work and we can talk about it? I could stop on the way, and get something to eat for my supper while I'm there."

"Thank you, Matt. I'm sorry I blew up at you. Yes, please come over tonight. I'll rest this afternoon and we'll reconsider all the options. It will help to have you come and discuss them with Betty and me. Now here is what's planned for this afternoon here on the job site."

While he worked that afternoon, Matt prayed off and on for Walt and that he would have wisdom talking with him tonight.

*****

Everywhere There's a Sunrise, Let's Tell The Good News!

Julie worked all day Tuesday at the dental office with a feeling of anticipation and some uneasiness about her upcoming interview with the principal of the church school. A couple minutes before 5, she went to the restroom to freshen up before driving to the school.

On the way to the school, she thought about the news she had received the day before at work. The woman she had replaced had given birth early to a healthy baby daughter on Wednesday last week and felt so good that she wanted to get back to work next Monday. Her mother had talked her into letting her do daycare for her baby, and she could to pump enough milk for the baby in the morning before going to work. Then Grandma would bring the baby over for the lunch hour to be with mommy and to have some more. She could pump some more milk to last the afternoon.

Therefore, Julie would be out of a job at the end of <u>this</u> week. Julie had prayed with Ted last night and they had left the whole situation in God's capable hands. She had felt at peace then, but right now she had butterflies in her stomach. By now she had arrived at the school, so she prayed again asking for God's will to be done and that he would take away her nervousness.

She was composed by the time she reached the principal's office and introduced herself. "Hello, Miss Davis? My name is Julie Blake and I'm here for an interview."

"Welcome. I'm glad to meet you, Julie. Come in and sit down. Please call me Beth unless there are children around. Then of course adults are titled," Beth began.

"It's a pleasure to meet you Beth. Until Saturday, I didn't even realize there was a school connected with the Grace 'n' Faith Church, but I was thrilled to find out. I have read the booklet Pastor Don gave me about the school and my husband and I are in full agreement with all that it says. It sounds like a lot of wise planning has gone into the set up and operation of this school," responded Julie.

"Yes, there was, and it's working very well. Pastor Don called me at noon today and told me a lot of things about you, and about Karen's word of knowledge on Saturday morning at your small group meeting. I was amazed! I have a few questions to ask you," said Beth. She continued by asking questions about several different topics, which Julie answered with no problems. Beth finished by asking, "How much notice do you have to give at your present job before you would be able to come to work here?"

"Friday this week, is my last day at my present job. I just found that out yesterday." Then Julie told her what she had learned on Monday. "So I could be ready to come to work here this coming Monday if you decide to hire me for this position."

"That would be perfect. The teacher who needs to leave for personal family reasons is in a hurry, but can stay through Friday this week. Next week, we might have to get a substitute. If you have time today, I can take you on a tour of the school right now," responded Beth.

"Yes, I have time right now and I would like to see the school," Julie replied.

Beth showed her through the school, which was set up with two wings off the main office and lunchroom area. Kindergarten and first grades were in the first wing with a hallway between them, and second and third grades were in the second wing with a hallway between them. There were four classrooms for each grade level. It was a much bigger school than Julie had imagined. All of the children were gone by now, and only a few teachers remained to straighten up their rooms.

Before going into the last wing, Beth asked Julie, "Do you think you would like to work here?"

"Yes! I'm very impressed with all I have seen and what I have read about this school," Julie answered.

Beth stated, "Good. Then you're hired! I will now introduce you to the teacher who is leaving and maybe we can set up a couple of noontime visits when you can talk with her and get some insight into what she's been doing. I asked her to stay late today just in case."

"That's a very good idea. I'm sure it will help me a lot. Thank you for hiring me!" Julie said as they arrived at the classroom.

"You're welcome." Upon entering, Beth said, "Miss Green, this is Mrs. Blake. I have just hired her to take over your position when you leave. She has to work at her present job through Friday, but is able to start work here on Monday. Could you set up a couple of noontime visits when you can talk with her and give her some insight into what you've been doing in your classroom?"

"Mrs. Blake, it's a pleasure and a relief to meet you!" exclaimed Miss Green. "Yes, I can meet with you here every day the rest of the week, and if you can bring your lunch we'll have more time to talk."

Julie replied, "Miss Green, I'm glad to meet you and really appreciate your generous offer. I'll be glad to come the rest of the week on my lunch hour so you can help bring me up to speed to step into your position since you have to leave."

"We'll let you go now, Miss Green. Thank you for staying over today to talk with us. I'll see you tomorrow. Now, Mrs. Blake I have some things to send home with you, which you can study at home. They should answer a lot of your questions, and I'll be glad to answer the rest as you go," continued Beth as they walked back down the hallway to her office.

"First, I need to let you read and sign the contract for the rest of this school year." Julie did that, and then Beth said, "I collected all of these memos and the notebook that has all the information new teachers need to know, this morning so they would be ready to give to you. These are yours to keep. So you can underline things, write comments, highlight, or do anything else you need to do. If you can read as much of this as possible before your meeting at noon tomorrow, I think it will help you understand much of what Miss Green will be telling you."

"I'll do my best," responded Julie. "Thank you very much, Beth. I'll see you tomorrow. Do I need to check in at the office when I arrive a little after noon?" Beth nodded, and waved goodbye. Julie almost skipped as she went outside to get into her car. "You did it, Lord! You brought me a job when I didn't even know I would need one. I'll be a teacher again, and it even helps the other teacher. Please help her with whatever her family problem is."

Julie drove home carefully and Ted was waiting at the door to greet her. He could tell by her big smile that she had good news, so he took her things and set them down before he gave her a big hug and kiss. Then while they were eating the supper Ted had fixed for them since he figured she would be late, she told him all about the interview, tour and meeting the other teacher. After supper she showed him what she needed to read before noon tomorrow.

Without her having to ask, he volunteered to do the cleanup after calling the pastor and also Karen, to let them know how it had all turned out. That way she could have that time to read. As it turned out, when he called the pastor, Jeff and Karen were there also, so the pastor put it on speaker phone, so they could all hear the news. They were all thrilled, of course!

Julie smiled and hugged Ted and expressed her thanks to him and then got right to work reading. Some of it was a review of what the booklet had said, but the rest was a detailed explanation of everything she would need to know about the school building, the school day, her job description, and what the parent volunteers were expected to do. There were short job descriptions of the principal, secretary, nurse, custodian and lunchroom supervisor. All that information would have taken several hours in a teachers meeting in the public school. This had only taken about an hour and a half to read and she could remember it better. Plus she would be able to go back and read it again as needed. What a good and efficient way to get necessary information across. As she read, she highlighted the especially important parts and wrote a couple question marks by hard to understand parts.

She got up to stretch and walk around and find Ted so she could thank him again and tell him how much she appreciated his help and understanding. She still had a lot to read, but she needed a break and wanted some quality time with Ted. The next few days would be very intense for her, she was sure, but it would all be worth it. When she found Ted, she shared all that with him, and said, "I'm overwhelmed at the way God has orchestrated this whole situation. I will not be even <u>one</u> day without a job, and teaching is definitely my job of choice." They took time to thank and praise God for his amazing leading, and to ask for strength and wisdom as they started this new part of the adventure they had begun by moving to Pine City. Then she went back and read until bedtime.

*****

By lunchtime on Tuesday, Maria was finished with two more tax returns, so she told Ruth she had only one more to do and would then be able to do whatever else Ruth would like her to do. Ruth and Maria agreed to give thanks silently before eating, so they would not alienate the other person. They met with the other co-worker and walked to the cafe. They were all glad for the exercise before eating. Ruth was able to dispel the feeling of apprehension the co-worker had about being friends with the boss, and they all had a nice time of getting acquainted and visiting while they ate lunch.

Ruth told the co-worker the plan of introducing Maria to the other co-workers one at a time and going to lunch if they wanted to. They were at a nice cafe, and it was a good change from the sack lunches that Maria was used to bringing to work. She had reconciled spending the extra money to buy lunch by considering it a part of her ministry.

Everywhere There's a Sunrise, Let's Tell The Good News!

They returned to the office and got back to work. In two hours, Maria was finished with the last tax return, and she took all three up to Ruth's office with a feeling of accomplishment. They were all finished before the deadline and Ruth could send them over to William's office. Ruth thanked her and gave her some other work to do. Maria was pleased that it wasn't more tax returns. She was rather tired of them.

At 4:50, Ruth came to Maria's office to take her for another introduction and invitation. They were successful again, and this time they would take a sack lunch to the park if the weather was nice enough or else eat in the lunchroom. Both of them were very satisfied with the way the day had gone, and they went home in great spirits.

*****

Don got home from work in time to talk to Mindy before her dad came to pick her up. He asked, "Mindy, is there a chance that there's a girl named Candy in your class at school?"

"Yes," she answered. She wasn't there for about two weeks, but today she was back."

"Candy has had a pretty hard life and some extra problems lately, and I think she needs a good Christian friend at school. Don't tell her I told you anything about her. Just be nice to her, try to be her friend, and pray for her," he said.

"Okay. I'll do my best. She's been kind of a loner in the past and I've never tried to even talk to her, but I'll see what I can do," promised Mindy.

"Thank you, Mindy. I know God will bless your efforts," Don replied as he left the room.

*****

After work, Matt left the job site and stopped at a fast food drive-up to pick up a supper to take with him. Betty greeted him at the door and apologized for them not having offered to fix him supper. He said, "Please don't worry about it. It's not a difficulty for me. I just would like to be able to come here and help Walt feel better about what he will have to do. Can we all meet in the kitchen while I eat this so we can talk?"

"Of course. I'll go tell Walt you are here and we'll meet you in the kitchen," she answered.

"Hi, Matt. I feel bad about having you come over here after work and you had to bring your own supper to boot. I wasn't thinking well at all today because I was so upset," Walt apologized.

Like I told Betty, don't worry about it; it's no trouble for me. You're too important to me to not be here for you. Are you feeling any better about the doctor's orders?" asked Matt.

"Yes, Betty and I have talked about it off and on this afternoon, and I'm not quite so upset. But I'm glad you came. Maybe you'll have some ideas or suggestions that we've not thought about," said Walt.

"Maybe. But first I would like to hear what you two have thought about," said Matt.

He responded, "Betty and I agreed that it would be better for me if I didn't work so hard, since I tire so much more easily than I used to, and I do need a better diet and a well rounded exercise program. The doctor gave me the names of a dietitian and exercise coach. I'll call them tomorrow. But I don't think that I want to retire yet if I can help it. I like construction, and don't want to give it up, but I don't see how I can keep myself from working if I go to the job site. What are you thinking?"

"Okay, here are some thoughts I had while I was working," Matt responded. "First of all, I would like you to take care of yourself so you'll be here many years to be here as a husband to Betty, a dad to me, and a grandpa to the children I plan to have with Fiona. ... No, I haven't asked her to marry me yet. I need to give her some more time. But I want you to keep that in mind as a goal."

"What a good goal, and it is very important to me. It will give me the incentive to do the hard things that the doctor talked about," agreed Walt.

"Secondly you need time to finish that book and get all your questions answered so that you can make the right decision about Jesus when you are ready. With those two goals in mind, here are a couple ideas on <u>how</u> you might cut back at work. You could consider yourself the <u>supervisor or superintendent</u>, not a co-worker when you go to the job site in the mornings. I know the morning shift is one hour shorter than working an 8-hour day, but that is still too long for you. I know what a hard worker you are and so do all the men. You don't need to prove anything to anyone. Just buy yourself one of those directors chairs and sit in it while you explain to them what the doctor said you have to do in order to protect your heart," Matt recommended.

Walt actually laughed and said, "Can't you just see me, Betty, sitting on my **throne** and telling all those men what to do?"

"Yes, I can! And I think it would be a good idea. You know what needs to be done and can keep watch <u>even</u> <u>better</u> from a director's chair to make sure all of them are doing what they're suppose to be doing," she stated emphatically, totally surprising Walt.

He nodded and agreed, "You're right, like you usually are, my dear wife. It will just take a lot of getting used to after all these years of being physically involved in everything that goes on."

Matt commended them saying, "Now that's good thinking, both of you. How about trying that, and the new diet/exercise program out for a while and see if it keeps you from getting so tired. If it does <u>not</u> help enough, you could let me be the foreman of the first shift, and hire Jeff Spencer to be foreman of the second shift. I've been watching him, and am convinced that he would do a good job of it. You could still be supervisor, but only for an hour or so in the morning and an hour or so in the afternoon and therefore you would <u>not</u> be retired yet, either way. You just need to find the way that works best for you."

Walt conceded, "All right. I'll try it the way you both say. Tomorrow I'll set up appointments with the dietitian and exercise coach, and tonight Betty and I will go to Wal-Mart and buy me a throne! I'll take it to work tomorrow and put up with their laughs and teasing. They will just have to get used to it."

"Good for you, Walt. That's the right attitude. You can make it work. I'll see you tomorrow <u>on your throne</u> and you can tell me how it went and then what the plan is for the afternoon," responded Matt before leaving. He prayed for Walt all the way home, and again as soon as he woke in the morning.

*****

Wednesday

Wednesday morning, before leaving to work on the house, Matt called Fiona. "Good morning, Fiona! This is Matt. ... ... I was wondering if you would like to take a ride with me after breakfast tomorrow, up to that beautiful viewpoint that overlooks the valley and the mountains. ... ... Great. If it's nice enough outside we can walk along the pathway. If not we can sit and visit in the car.

What time is good for you? ... ... Okay, I'll see you at 9 AM tomorrow. ... ... Bye and God bless you." He was elated to be able to look forward to a couple hours with her and time to talk without the family or a group around.

*****

It was no trouble for Julie to pack a sack lunch on Wednesday morning to take to the school because that's what she did every day anyway. When she arrived early at work, she went in to talk to the person who had hired her for the job, and had told her of the other woman's desire to return to work on Monday. "I have good news!" she stated as she sat down. "I've already been hired for another job which begins on Monday, so you don't need to feel bad about the other woman wanting to come back to work so soon."

"That's <u>excellent</u> news," he replied. "Would you like to tell me about it?"

So Julie took that as an opportunity to give God the credit that belongs to him alone, and shared an abbreviated account of what had happened. She also mentioned that she would be taking her lunch hour the rest of the week to meet with the teacher who was leaving, so she could get information that would help in the transition.

"<u>Amazing</u>! What church did you say it was?" She told him and invited him to come, giving the time for the service and the address of the church, before hurrying to her desk just as the first appointment arrived.

The morning flew by even faster than usual. Julie hurried to the restroom, grabbed her lunch and coat and drove to the school. She checked in at the office, told the principal she had read all the material last night, and then went to the schoolroom. "Hello, Miss Green. I got here as quickly as I could, and I brought a notebook so I can take notes if that's okay with you."

"Good idea. Please call me Pam when there are no children around." she answered.

"Okay, and you please call me Julie when the children are not present," agreed Julie.

Then Pam thanked God for the food they were about to eat and asked for him to help her remember everything she wanted to tell Julie. She talked between bites, and Julie wrote while she was chewing. It turned out to be a good way to hear and write down a lot of information. When they finished eating, Pam showed Julie how the lesson plans worked.

"What a unique idea for lesson plans!" Julie exclaimed. "I really like it. They'll be easy to follow and keep track of where I leave off each day. I just hope I can keep up with where I'm supposed to be, and not get behind. How do you do that?"

"It isn't really very hard," she responded. "You will soon see where there are places you can speed up or combine some things to get up to where you're supposed to be. Don't let it worry you. You'll do fine."

"Thank you so much for all the time and information. I'll see you again tomorrow," Julie said, smiling as they waved good-bye and Julie hurried to her car and back to work. On her afternoon break, Julie called the principal and asked if it would be possible for her to stay after the children came in from their lunch on Friday, so she could meet them. It might help them with the transition. Beth Davis liked the idea and said she would ask Miss Green what she thought. She would call Julie this evening with an answer.

*****

Walt was smiling when Matt walked up to his 'throne' and bowed on Wednesday. "It went very well today. Nobody laughed or teased me. They were very understanding. I was busy all day watching and answering questions when they came to me. And I'm definitely not as tired as I usually am by this time of the day," he stated.

"I'm so glad to hear that. It sounds like you're adapting very well to being the supervisor. Now what's the plan for the afternoon?" asked Matt. When they finished talking and Walt went home, Matt was relieved and prayed that Walt would continue with his good resolve every day.

*****

That afternoon Mindy confided in Anita, "You know that I go with Dad to his small group. Last night I happened to look at Miss Nelson, the nurse at the church school, after Dad said something. She was smiling with admiration about what he had said. Then Dad looked at her and smiled, too. It hit me that they might make a perfect match."

"Why do you think that?" asked Anita.

Mindy answered, "Miss Nelson and I became good friends after my mother died when I was in third grade. She helped me a lot to get through the grieving process. Since she had taught health in all my grades at the school, she was a person I could trust and talk to about any problems I was having. I still like her a lot even though I've been out of that school for almost three years already."

"I'm glad she was there for you and was able to help you through that hard time in your life," responded Anita. "She does sound like a very possible good fit."

"I think they're pretty close to the same age. Could we pray about it?" she asked.

"Of course." Anita prayed first, "Heavenly Father, you heard all that Mindy just shared with me. Please help Mindy's dad to be open to getting better acquainted with Miss Nelson, and let you lead them to do your will."

Mindy added, "Yes, please help us to know if she would be a good wife for my dad and a good mother for me, and if we would be a good family for her."

"Yes, we agree and pray in Jesus name, Amen," finished Anita, thinking about how mature Mindy sounded.

*****

Ted and Julie picked Maria up at her apartment and they drove to a different park to take their walk. Julie asked Maria to be the first to tell about how her week had gone so far. Maria was enthusiastic about the new office and about their lunchtime plan, which had worked very well for two days already. "I've always wanted a ministry of some kind and it's extra good to be able to have it right where I work. The other office was very unfriendly and people never did anything together. It was a pretty lonely place to work. So this has turned into another blessing. I'm so thankful. And no, I haven't heard anything from or about Jason, and this is a blessing also. I don't want to think about that situation, except that I pray for his salvation and healing every day. Now, please tell me about your news. I can tell you have some just bursting to get out."

"Oh, Maria, you're so right!" Julie was exuberant as she told her all the details of the Saturday small group meeting, their lunch with the pastor's family at MacDonald's afterward, waiting to hear more about it, finding out on Monday about the other woman wanting her job back this coming Monday, her interview on Tuesday, being hired and reading like crazy last night, listening to the teacher at noon and taking notes, with plans to do the same on Thursday and Friday. "I'll be a <u>teacher</u> again on Monday, and not out of work even one day! Isn't God amazing? I'm overwhelmed that he could make it all work out like this!" They had finished the walk and were back at the car. Ted joined them and Julie took both of their hands and they all lifted them in a cheer of praise to their awesome God.

Then Julie's cell phone rang. It was Beth saying the answer was yes, and telling her what time the children would be back in the classroom, and that if she could take a little longer lunch hour, she could take time to tell the children about herself and answer any questions they might have. Julie said that sounded great and she would try to work it out with her present boss, and also that she had a couple questions about the things she had read. She found out she could ask them when she arrived tomorrow. She had the speaker on so Maria and Ted could both hear it. Everyone said, "Wow!" when the call was over.

They left Maria at her apartment and hurried home to fix, eat, and clean up after supper. Then Julie skimmed the parts that she had questions about and figured out the answers. She went over her notes from Mrs. Green and wrote down a few questions to ask her. It seemed like a race to get as much information as she could before Friday was over. Then she realized that Miss Green wasn't the only one who could help her. There were three other third grade teachers and also Beth Davis who would all probably be glad to assist her. So she relaxed and went to spend some time with Ted and ask him how his day had gone.

*****

Amelia arrived at The Garden Shop right on time Wednesday, greeted her mom, and hurried over to where Fiona was working and started helping her with the plants. "I'm getting better at timing how to fix and eat supper before I need to leave to get here on time," Amelia said, smiling and feeling proud of herself. "Now, I won't get so hungry before I get home tonight. I was even able to study while the food cooked and while I ate it. I really want to be able to keep my grades up so I can continue to work here."

"Fantastic!" exclaimed Fiona. "You figured out very quickly how to make supper time into a time to study and still get here on time without being hungry. I don't think you'll have any trouble keeping your grades up. Just keep using all your time wisely like that and you'll do great. The next two questions are ones I ask myself off and on during the week. Are you getting enough sleep at night? Do you feel tired the next day after working here?"

"No," she answered, "I don't feel tired the day after I work here, because I go to bed early on Wednesday night. On Friday night I stay up a little longer because I can sleep in on Saturday morning. So yes, I think I'm getting enough sleep at night. But you're right. I should monitor that off and on and make sure to get enough sleep every night. I didn't realize how much learning is involved in getting a job. But it's good learning and will help me to grow up."

"Good thinking, and every job brings new learning. Even going back to work here after two years of being away, I had new things to learn; especially because of the change in the hours I work. But like you said, it's good learning and helps us grow up. I know I still have a lot to learn," added Fiona. "What subjects do you like at school?"

"This might surprise you, but I like all of them. It's fun and interesting to learn new things. I especially like science courses like biology. I can even see some overlap in what I've learned here, as far as what plants need in order to grow. I'll be taking chemistry next year, and I look forward to it. Math is a little hard for me at times, but I finally am getting so I understand algebra and geometry better. Next year I'll need to choose whether I want to take trigonometry and calculus or take business math instead. What did you take?" asked Amelia.

"Since I knew by the time I was a senior that I wanted to work with plants, I chose business math, because I might eventually need to know how to keep a business running if I ever would want to open a flower store of my own someday. I didn't think trig. or calc. would help me out that much. Have you thought very much about what you want to do after high school?"

"Well, ... no, I haven't, but now that you mentioned it, I guess it would be a good idea to think about that, so that I can plan whether to do college prep or just get into the work-a-day world. Did you go to college, Fiona?" asked Amelia.

"No, I went directly to full time work here at The Garden Shop, and came back to it after taking care of my great aunt. College would have been interrupted for me, and besides it would not have done me any good for this job or for taking care of my great aunt. That was like an education itself," answered Fiona.

"Would you tell me about it, or does it make you feel too sad to think about her? I'm sorry about her passing away," said Amelia.

"Thank you, Amelia. I <u>was</u> sad, and still am at times, but knowing she's in heaven and not in pain any longer helps a lot. I'd be glad to tell you about my time there," responded Fiona, and as they continued working, she told her the same things she had told Matt when he had asked her.

"Wow! I can see what you meant when you said it was like an education itself. You had to learn so many new things in a short time so you could know how to care for her, besides a whole new life style of being unable to go any place. I'm glad she was such an appreciative and loving person. That probably made everything easier for you. Thank you for telling me about it all," said Amelia.

"You're welcome. Yes, it did make it easier, and I'm grateful for the whole experience. It helped me to grow up while I was there. Oh, my, look at the time! We've nurtured a lot of plants and had a nice time to visit, and now it's already time to close up and go home," Fiona exclaimed, and suddenly smiled thinking about the date she would have with Matt tomorrow. She would go to bed early so she would be alert.

*****

Thursday

Thursday morning, Matt woke early and went for an early morning run since he would not be working on the house today. When he returned, he took a shower, shaved, and dressed for his date with Fiona. He ate breakfast and arrived right on time. Fiona was ready as usual. He appreciated that and told her so.

She replied, "I'm grateful you always arrive on time also." That got the date off to a very good start as he escorted her to his pick-up, opened the door, and made sure she was ready before he closed it again. Then they drove up to the viewpoint that overlooked the valley and the mountains.

"Do you think it's warm enough outside for us to walk along the path for a while," asked Matt.

She answered, "Yes, I dressed extra warmly this morning because I like to take in the view as we walk. It's a much better view that way, than from the windshield."

"I agree, just let me come around and open the door for you, and we'll be off," he replied and then he jumped out, ran around the pick-up and opened her door. Then they set off up the path. The view was extraordinary as usual, and they both enjoyed it, stopping every once in a while just to gaze at it. As they walked, Matt told her, "Walt had a doctor appointment on Monday and was told that he would have to slow way down at work or else retire. He was very upset about it when I arrived at work on Tuesday, so I went over to their house after work last night. He had settled down by then, and the three of us worked out some ways he could try. He was in pretty good spirits yesterday when I got to work. Would you please remember him in your prayers?"

"Of course," she agreed. "I'm glad you were willing to take your time to go and help him out. He doesn't have much family around here, does he?"

"No, they weren't able to have any children, and both of their siblings live very far away. They've kind of adopted me, not legally of course but they've really helped to take some of the place of my parents after their fatal accident four years ago. Since they aren't believers, I can't really bond with them, but I know that I can keep praying for them that they'll make the right decision. They've both said that they would like to meet you sometime. What do you think? Would you be comfortable meeting them?" he asked.

"Certainly! I feel as though I know them a little already from the things you've told me about them. They sound like very nice people," she responded.

"They are. Maybe we could take them out to eat on a Saturday afternoon sometime soon," he suggested.

"That sounds good, but not this Saturday. My parents and I would like to have you come over for lunch after the small group meeting and then we can either play croquet outside or some board game inside if it's not nice enough outside," she responded.

"I would like that very much. Speaking of outside, the wind has picked up and it's getting cool. Let's go back to the pick-up." They walked quickly and got inside where it was warmer. Then he asked, "How's your job going at The Garden Store?"

Fiona told him all about it including the new name for the business and that the manager's daughter, Amelia, was working there with her two days a week from 5-8 PM. "She is a fast learner and is doing very well. We had some nice discussions while we worked last night. How's your job at the site?" she asked.

"We're probably about three quarters finished. Somehow the last fourth always seems to go slower, and the people are anxious to get moved in, but they'll just have to wait. How are your parents and your brother?" he asked.

"They're all fine. Riley has grown up a lot over the past two years. He even called especially to talk to me. It was a nice surprise!" Fiona replied.

"Indeed!" Matt agreed, "I feel like I missed out on a lot by being an only child. I always wanted a brother or a sister, but they couldn't have any more children after they had me. They were good parents though, and I learned a lot from them, so I'm very blessed."

"Good parents <u>are</u> a big blessing. I've learned so much from mine, also. Not everybody has good parents. I feel like I've really been sheltered from the bad stuff that goes on in this world and I'm so thankful," she finished. "Oh, look at the time. We both need to get home and have lunch before we go to work. Thank you for bringing me up here to see this gorgeous view and have such a pleasant conversation."

"My pleasure. Any time spent with you is a delight for me. Thank <u>you</u>, Fiona!" he replied.

*****

At noon Julie took her lunch with her and hurried over to the school. She stopped in the principal's office after checking in. There were students within hearing so she said, "Hello, Miss Davis. When I start working here will I still need to check in at the office?"

"No, Mrs. Blake, this is only because you're coming in at noon and haven't started working here yet. We like to know when people enter the building during the day," she answered.

"I like that idea. I figured out the answers to the questions I had while I reviewed the materials last night, but I have another one. My boss said that I would be able to spend the <u>whole</u> day here tomorrow. He told me that the woman who wants to start working on Monday is so grateful to me for being understanding, that she volunteered to come in a day early and still let me be paid for that day. I could hardly believe it! Will it be okay with you and Miss Green for me to come all day tomorrow?" Julie asked.

"Yes, that would be just perfect! The students will have a chance to get to know you better and feel more comfortable with you being there on Monday morning," she answered.

"Thank you. I know I will be helped by watching Miss Green in action with the students and see how she teaches some of the lessons. God is so good! Would it be possible for me to meet the other three third grade teachers tomorrow morning, before I go to Miss Green's room? That way I would not feel so awkward when I come in on Monday morning," Julie said.

"Excellent idea," Miss Davis answered. "I was just going to ask you if you would like to meet them. I'll have them come to the office at the beginning of the day, so they'll be here when you arrive tomorrow."

"Thank you, Miss Davis. Now I'll hurry to see Miss Green," said Julie as she left the office. She hurried down the hallways to her room, the first one on that wing where she greeted, and was welcomed by Pam. First, Julie told her about the good news of being able to be here all day tomorrow, and then gave thanks for their lunch and took notes while more things were explained to her. Each classroom had one computer, mostly for the teacher to use, and there was a computer lab where each class could go on their scheduled days and times. The classroom computer had all the student pictures, profiles and records and it also took the place of a grade book. It would be useful in preparing report cards. Thankfully, that had already been done for the first quarter of the year and those were included for each student.

Julie asked, "Would it be all right if I bring a thumb drive tomorrow and copy this information to take home and study over the weekend?"

"Yes," Pam responded. "In fact that's what all the teachers do over the two week vacation at Christmas and New Year's, to 'get acquainted' with the new class that comes to them right after the new year. It is always a big help. I have a thumb drive that belongs to the school, and I'll download the information right now. That way, you can study the pictures and names tonight so you'll know who is who tomorrow. This would have been my third year here, and it's so hard for me to leave!"

"I can understand that, and I'm so sorry. May I ask you what I can tell the children about why you have to leave? Pastor Don didn't tell me anything about it and neither did Miss Davis," explained Julie.

"Of course. I'll tell you just what I've told my class. My mother had a stroke last week and it's caused paralysis on her left side. She'll be coming home from the hospital on Monday and I need to be there to help care for her. While I'm there, I'll get training on how to care for her and also how to help her do physical and occupational therapy which might assist her to regain some use of the left side of her body and/or how to adapt to what she still can use," she replied.

"I'm so sorry about your mother, <u>and</u> that you have to leave this school. Thank you for explaining it to me. I'll remember to pray for you both. I see that it's time for me to leave. Tomorrow, I get to stay all day so that I can meet the children and they can meet me. Thank you again for all the information about the classroom, the subjects, and other things about teaching here. This will be a great help for me," Julie responded.

"You're very welcome, Julie! Getting to know you has relieved much of the worry about leaving the children. I can tell you'll be a very good, caring teacher for them. I'll see you tomorrow," she replied as she hurried to let the children come into the classroom.

*****

Julie worked the rest of Thursday afternoon at the dental office and didn't feel very sorry to be leaving that job even though she had enjoyed it. She was looking forward to being a teacher again. At the end of the day, she asked her boss to thank the woman for her and told him, "I've enjoyed working here even though it's been for such a short time. I put my belongings in this little bag to take home, so they won't be cluttering up her desk. I hope to see you and your wife at church this Sunday!"

"We're planning on it. I've never seen so many things work together for the good of so many people in my life!" he exclaimed.

"I haven't either. It says somewhere in the Bible that all good and perfect gifts come from God. He surely has been giving a lot in these situations. Good-bye, see you Sunday," she said.

When Julie arrived home, she and Ted talked about how their day had gone and thanked God for the way he had been helping in this transition for Julie. Then she asked, "How would it be if I call Maria and cancel our exercise walk for tomorrow? As a matter of fact, the timing won't work out as well for any day during the workweek, since I get off later and will sometimes be staying a little longer to finish something or get ready for the next day. Maybe we could plan to have an exercise walk after the small group time on Saturdays or after the church service on Sundays. It would feel good after sitting for so long. Once a week will be enough walking exercise for me since I'll probably get plenty of exercise while I'm teaching. Which day would work better for you?"

"Either one will be fine for me. Let Maria decide which one will be better for her," he answered, and then stated, "I'm married to the most amazing woman in the world! I'm glad you can figure things like this out, because I never even thought about how your new job would impact the exercise walks. I'm sure that Maria and you would like to continue at least once a week so you two can have some time to converse."

Julie called Maria, who decided that Sundays would be the best day. Maria told her that she was getting to walk almost every day just before eating lunch, so she didn't need the other three afternoons, either. It was one more thing that God worked out for the good of them both, along with all the other miracles that had been happening in the last week.

*****

When Pastor Don got home from work, Mindy told him that she had been able to eat lunch with Candy, and she had seemed to enjoy it. He thanked her and asked her to keep up the good work. After supper, he went over to the Safe/Care Home where he had taken Candy on Monday, so that he could check with them on how she was doing, and talk with her so she would know that he cared about her. She told him that she liked it here and thanked him again for bringing her to this home. Then she excused herself and went to finish her homework.

The couple that had taken her in gave him a good report. She had gone to school with no grumbling and was thankful for the clothes and food. She did all her chores well and without complaining. The other girl that was staying with them took her under her wing so to speak, and that had helped her with the transition. So far, it's very good. Don thanked them for their good work and went home to share the good news with Anita and play with his own sweet children for a while.

Julie called them to give them an update on her time at school the last two days at lunchtime, and excitedly told them about how it had worked out for her to be able to spend the <u>whole</u> day there tomorrow.

*****

Everywhere There's a Sunrise, Let's Tell The Good News!

Chapter 9

Proverbs 20:11, *Train up a child in the way he should go, and when he is old, he will not depart from it.*
Matthew 19:14, *Let the children come to me and don't forbid them, for of such is the kingdom of heaven.*

Friday

Julie packed their lunches and left a few minutes early to go to the school, because she wanted to be there on time to meet the other teachers. When she arrived, she greeted the secretary, telling her she would be there all day today and then every day beginning Monday. Then she went directly to the principal's office where she met the other three third grade teachers who welcomed her to the school. They all told her they would be glad to help her or answer questions.

Julie said, "It's a pleasure to meet you. Thank you all so much for making me feel welcome and for your generous offers of help. I'm sure I'll need your help off and on. I feel blessed that I've had these days to talk with Miss Green and receive her help, also. I'll see you on Monday."

Then she hurried to the classroom. First, she was shown where all the books, teaching materials, and supplies, were kept, and that she could get more supplies, when needed, from the secretary. Then Julie asked, "After I meet the children, could you demonstrate to me with your class how you use the hands-on materials that help them understand adding, subtracting, multiplying, and dividing fractions? I would love to see how that works in action."

"Of course. This will work out just perfectly since we've been doing that this week and they have all the materials in their desks right now. We have Math in about an hour this morning. They'll enjoy performing for you," Pam answered. "The parent volunteer for the day just arrived. I'll introduce you two, and then explain to him what he will be doing today." She gave him a written plan for the day and asked if he had any questions. Then she showed him where to locate the materials he would need.

After that she told Julie which child was his. When all the children were seated, Miss Green said, "Children, this lady is Mrs. Blake. I told you about her yesterday afternoon. She'll be taking my place this coming Monday, as the teacher in this classroom. I'm sure you'll help her as she gets used to a new school since I know what good children you all are. She's taught in another school for two years, and I know that she is a good teacher. Now she would like to talk to you for a few minutes."

Julie said, "Good morning, children. I'm very glad to meet you. I just moved here to Pine City at the end of March, but I already like it a lot. I'm delighted to see that each of you has on a name tag. I'll be able to learn your names more easily this way. Perhaps after today, you could keep them in your desks and wear them again on Monday. Starting Monday, we'll begin working together to keep learning the things you've been working on so far this year. I've taught third graders before, and know many of the things you learn in third grade, so that should help us both. I'll be here all day today so that I'll be able to watch the way you are doing things in this classroom. Then we can continue doing those things for the rest of the school year. Now it's time for you to begin your school day."

They all stood and pledged allegiance to the American and Christian flags. This morning, they sang, "God Bless America." After that they said the Lord's Prayer together. Then they sang a song about questions to ask as they read the Bible. The questions were about the meaning of the verse, how it might help them, and what God wants them to do. Then it had a prayer asking the Holy Spirit to help them understand what they were reading.

When they sat down, they took out their Bibles and notebooks, which had the title, "My Bible Study Journal," printed on the front. They all started reading and writing without needing to be told. Each child had a laminated book mark with the questions to ask about what they were reading, a reminder to look in the dictionary if they needed to look up the meaning of a word and write it down, and to write down a sentence or more about what they learned from the verses they studied.

Miss Green explained, "Today, I'll be giving details to Mrs. Blake off and on about how we do various things. Now both she and I will walk around and notice what you're reading or writing. If what you're writing is very personal, you remember that you may cover it up when we get to your desk, and we'll just look at what you've been reading. This is also a time that you may ask us questions or share comments about what you've been reading. In about 15 minutes we'll break into our small groups since this is Friday, so you need to be ready to share at least one thing with your group that you've learned this week."

Both teachers circulated in the room taking about a minute at each desk. Some of the children were brave enough to ask Mrs. Blake a question or share a comment. She responded appropriately and went to the next child. She was pleased and surprised at their level of capability; even their spelling was mostly correct. Some of the things they had written in their notebooks had real depth of thought.

"It's time now to get into your small groups. Remember to <u>not</u> put your Bibles on the floor if that's where you choose to sit. We like to show respect for God's Word," Mrs. Green reminded them.

The teachers again walked around listening for a short time, to each group of four students. When the beautiful, big, round clock at the front of the room chimed the half hour, the students all rose and walked back to their desks where they carefully returned their Bibles and notebooks to their desks. Then they sat facing the front of the room with expectancy. Miss Green read a story to them from Keys for Kids devotional book and then they discussed various things about the story and the Bible verses that were in it. After the story, she said, "Let's stand up and sing that song about loving Jesus all day long." The children stood up and sang that song as they walked in place. Then they sat back down.

After that, Mrs. Green told them, "Today, I'm going to give you a short oral quiz on what we've learned so far about what to do when you are taught about evolution next year in fourth grade in the public schools. Who can tell me what is the best thing to do when you don't agree with what's being taught?"

She called on a boy who answered, "I'll listen politely and not disagree out loud. I'll just ignore what they're saying and remember that the Triune God is the creator of whatever they're discussing."

"Very good. Why do we <u>not</u> disagree out loud?" she asked.

A girl answered, "It is because it never helps to argue with the theory that makes it possible for humanity to not have to be answerable to a creator. But what does that mean?" asked the girl.

"I'm very glad you asked that question. Can any of the rest of you explain what that means?" asked Mrs. Green.

Another girl raised her hand and said, "I think it means that many people who live in our country don't want to have to answer to anybody for their actions, so they would rather believe the universe just happened by evolution. If they believed that the Triune God created it, they would also have to believe and do all the Bible says to do, like confessing their sins, believing in Jesus and living the way he says to live."

"Exactly!" her teacher commended her. "Now, here is one final question. What do you do if somebody <u>asks</u> you what you believe about evolution vs. creation? Please turn to your partner and take turns answering that question to each other. Be sure to be polite but enthusiastic about what you say." She and Julie walked around the room listening to the pairs as they shared. Then she asked, "Who would like to pretend that the teacher asked that question and wants you to get up in front of the whole class and say what you just told your partner?"

A boy raised his hand and then walked up to the front of the room and said, "I'm grateful that you asked me to share what I believe, because it's so important to me. I believe that the one and only all-wise God created the universe He created it like it says in Genesis chapter 1 in the Bible. The reason I believe this is because I have studied many animals and plants and even some of my own human body parts. I realize the only way any of these could exist and continue living is that an engineer who knew how to make them whole and complete from the very first designed them. If all the intricacies of a butterfly or a rose or a person had to depend on the chance of evolution, then each species would have died off before they even got started. In closing, I'll quote from Romans chapter 1:19,20, in the Creator's book, the Bible: *That which can be known of God has been shown to men. The invisible things of God, like his eternal power, are clearly seen from the creation of the world, being understood by the things that are made.* If you would like, I could bring some essays that I've read about some plants, animals, and human body parts that illustrate what I have just said."

"Thank you. That was very well done with a respectful manner and sincerely. Your older brother was in my class last year, and I can tell he's been doing a good job of teaching you what to say. Please tell him I'm proud of you both. Now maybe you can start teaching the rest of the class." He smiled and nodded.

She continued, "What we have to remember is that many people won't agree with what we say, and they might make fun, tease, mistreat or in some way make us miserable. This is called 'persecution,' and the Bible says we will probably have to endure that for the sake of Jesus. We can do like the disciples did in Acts 5:41, *And they departed from the presence of the court, rejoicing that they were considered worthy to suffer shame for Jesus name.*

Remember, it's actually a privilege to be persecuted for believing in Jesus and the Bible. But, it's not good to suffer shame for doing wrong or bad things. Let's stand up and sing that song that says that God made the world with all the right things in it."

Next, she showed Julie how to quickly pull up answersingenesis.org on the computer, and have it displayed on a big monitor at the front of the room. The children learned some interesting facts about the gecko lizard and how its feet were designed to be able to walk right up walls and on ceilings. There were pictures to go along with the teaching. When it was finished, she asked the children to give her any facts they could remember from watching. She listed all of them on the board and then gave the children time to copy them into their special spiral notebook, which they had titled, "Proofs of Creation." These facts could be used later to write essays with the help of fourth and fifth graders who came on Wednesday afternoons to assist them. After copying those facts into their notebooks they stood up and sang a pretty song that was a prayer asking God, who made creation so beautiful, to please help mankind to keep it that way.

During this part of the day, the parent volunteer was making flashcards or other learning materials for use in the classroom later in the day. During math and other subjects, the volunteer would call one student at a time to come and drill on whatever extra practice she or he needed.

The clock chimed. What time is it, class?" asked Miss Green. They all answered that it was nine o'clock and time for Math. "Correct! First we'll show Mrs. Blake how we exercise for a little while after sitting still." They all stood up, and did each of the following things 7 times each: jumped up and down and then raised their arms and hands above their heads, and then lifted up one foot and leg at a time out in front of them, and finished by jumping up and down some more. Then they sat down again, ready for Math.

Mrs. Blake said, "I like that exercise. I've asked Miss Green if I could watch while you show me how you add, subtract, multiply, and divide fractions using the materials you have in your desks." As Julie watched the children, she was astonished about how much the materials helped to make clear what each process meant and how it worked. Then she saw how well it transferred to paper and pencil practice.

"Since you'll be using these materials some more next week, please put them carefully back into the Baggies and into a safe place in your desks," instructed Miss Green. "Next, we'll show

Mrs. Blake another way we exercise after sitting and working for a while." The students all stood by their desks and went through a routine of rolling their shoulders ten times, marching in place while crossing their hands to touch the opposite knee ten times, doing ten jumping jacks, and then taking ten deep breaths, holding them and letting them out slowly before sitting down again, ready to go on with the next part of Math time.

    They were working on memorizing the multiplication tables. Today, they practiced the fives. Yes, it was old fashioned, but very necessary and good for the brain. While they did that, Miss Green wrote some simple multiplication problems on the board. Then the children copied them in their Math notebooks and figured out the answers. If they needed help in figuring out the answer, they got out a different baggie that had many cardboard strips, which they used to make sets of for example, 5 times 4. They would group five sets of four and then count them up. Or they could add four five times on their papers and get the answer that way. Volunteers went up to the board and wrote the answers on the problems she had put on the board, and if any answer was wrong, hands went up, and one student was chosen to come up and politely show why it was wrong and then fix it.

    Next they practiced counting, by doing another exercise break during which they counted each step, starting today from 451 and stopping on 530, as they walked counterclockwise around the room. Then they did adding and subtracting of three-digit numbers with carrying and borrowing. They took out the materials they had in their desks for counting and to use in adding and subtracting three-digit numbers. Amazingly enough, each desk was clean and orderly, so there was no time lost in finding whatever was needed by the student. They were pretty adept at setting up the packs of hundreds, tens and ones and then adding or subtracting whatever their teacher wrote on the board.

    Julie was sitting up front where she could clearly see all the students, so when she didn't have to concentrate on the how-to of teaching, she was able to start memorizing names with faces. It did help that she had worked on it the night before with their pictures and names on the computer. She realized this day was giving her a jump-start for Monday, and she was very grateful. At 9:45 the volunteer and the children went outside for recess, after using the restrooms in the classroom if they needed to. During recess the teachers got drinks, used the restroom, and prepared for the next part of the day.

Everywhere There's a Sunrise, Let's Tell The Good News!

*****

Friday morning, Matt worked on his house for three hours before going home to rest and eat lunch. Then he went to the job site. Again, Walt was doing well from his director's chair, and had a good attitude. Matt and the second crew made a lot of good progress on the house before time to go back home. He was looking forward to the small group tomorrow morning and then lunch and fun with Fiona and her parents. The past week had flown by like a jet airplane.

*****

Maria packed her sack lunch and left for work wondering how the week had gone so fast. She was enjoying her time in the new office, and was looking forward to lunch today with Ruth and Esther. At noon, they met in the lunchroom got their lunches and headed out the door. The day was lovely, so they enjoyed the quick walk to the park and around it for about 20 minutes before sitting down on a bench to give thanks and then eat and talk.

Ruth asked, "Esther, how has your week gone?" (Maria was thinking, "<u>Where </u>had it gone?")

Esther answered, "Really well. The last three days I've gone to lunch with 3 different women and had nice visits with each of them. Building friendships takes a lot of time and I think I might need to spend more than just one day a week with them. I felt like I was spread kind of thin."

"That's probably very true for you and what you're doing. After I've met all the employees here I think that would be a good idea for me also," inserted Maria. "What do you think, Ruth?"

"I agree," she said. "Lord, we remember that, 'Rome wasn't built in a day.' We need to just keep at it one day at a time and with one person for as long as it takes to build a relationship and then continue to keep it going. Father, thank you for the progress we've made this week. Help us keep at it and not get discouraged because it seems to take so long to make a friend."

Esther added, "Yes, help us remember that since they are not believers, we don't have the same important connection with them as we do with each other, so it will take longer."

Then Maria prayed, "Thank you so much for these two precious friends who share my faith. Unity is such an important factor in any relationship. Keep us strong and vigilant so we don't form tight bonds with these co-workers until they come to believe in you also." They all said, "Amen."

Ruth looked at Maria and asked, "Would you be willing to pray with Esther and me about Jason?"

She answered, "Certainly! I pray for his salvation and healing daily, but I know it would be more effective with the three of us agreeing in prayer." So they spent some time asking God to open Jason's mind and heart to the scriptures Maria had written down for him to look up, since he had told his dad he would do it, and that he would see his need for a Savior, rather than relying on being a good person to get to heaven.

Ruth looked at her watch and said, "We'll have to walk quickly to make it back to work on time." As they walked, she continued, "Jason told Dad that he had tried to look up some of the verses the other day, but he was still too upset about his plan failing. We're all hoping that this upset will drive him to God for help and he will realize that he can't always have things his way."

Esther said, "I would like to have lunch with the two of you again on Mondays and Fridays to start the weeks with prayer and planning and end them with debriefing and prayer. Besides, if we try to plan something with a co-worker on Friday for Monday, it will most likely be forgotten over the weekend."

Maria and Beth both agreed just as they got back to the office where they worked.

*****

Off and on during the morning, when she wasn't too busy with the children, Anita wondered how the day was going for Julie. Each time she wondered, she sent up quick prayers that God would help both of the teachers and also the children to work well together during this transition. She also thanked and praised him for the way he had worked everything out so far.

Before the morning rest time for the children, Anita helped them sing and do the actions to the song, "Climb, Climb Up Sunshine Mountain," and then read a story out of a nice Bible Story Book. It had beautiful pictures to go along with the story. She showed the pictures to the children as she read to them. Then they sang together a song that went along with the story. Afterward each child unrolled his rest time mat out on the floor and laid down on it. The younger ones needed some help getting their mats unrolled and positioned where they wanted them. They were required to have sufficient space between them that they could not talk. This was nap time for most of them and most of them did go to sleep.

While they were napping or just resting, Anita was able to get a little quiet housework done or mending, knitting, or even have her own Bible study time.

When rest time was over, the children were eager to play some active games. When it was warm enough outside they would get to go out and play in the big back yard. But when it was too cold, Anita would organize some active inside game, after reminding them about ways to act that would help them get along with each other. If a problem came up during the game, she would stop the game and they would talk about what happened and how to fix it. The children learned to say they were sorry if they were in the wrong, and how to forgive if they were the one who was wronged. In this way, the daycare took the place of preschool, but was even better, because the group of children was smaller and they also got to hear Bible stories and sing Christian songs for children.

Anita wasn't the only mother who did daycare in her home. Many mothers in all twelve churches took care of their own children and up to seven more belonging to working mothers in the churches. The church supplied a notebook to each daycare mother. It had daily lessons including which Bible story to read, what songs to sing to go along with it, organized games to play and ways to teach children how to get along with each other. Then if the children went into the Grace 'n' Faith Church School when they were old enough, they had already learned many stories, songs and skills which would make them feel comfortable going to the school where they would continue doing more of the same.

*****

At the school, it was ten o'clock. The students returned to the classroom, hanging their coats on their hooks, and sitting down at their desks. The next subject was Reading, so each student took out the book he or she was currently reading in, opened to the right page which had a pretty hand-made bookmark of their own construction, and started reading. Miss Green called a group of seven children to the round table. They brought their books with them and got a drink before sitting down. Then the parent volunteer called another group of eight children who got drinks on their way to a table in the back of the room where they drilled with flash cards for sight words.

The rest of the children took turns getting drinks and then stayed at their desks reading. For half the time, Julie watched the group at the round table as each one read aloud with expression and then the teacher asked them some questions about the story. Miss Green had told her that she could take a low rolling stool around to each desk and listen to the children read out loud to her. As she did that, she took notes on how each was doing before going to the next child. Later in the day, she would enter those notes into the computer like in a grade book.

At the end of about 15 minutes, a different group of children was called to the round table, while others went to work on different flash cards in the back. Julie kept listening to the other children read orally for a while and then watched the drill on the flash cards before going back over to the round table. After another 15 minutes the remaining children went to the round table while the first seven who had been at the round table went to drill on another set of flash cards. Julie was able to listen to most of the ones left at their desks and notice what books and levels the groups were in and what each group was working on.

For the next 15 minutes, each child read silently from a different book in his/her desk while Miss Green used the rolling stool to go around to as many as she had time, to ask comprehension questions about what they had been reading and to see if there were any questions that needed to be answered. The clock chimed eleven o'clock and they all quietly put their books away and stood up beside their desks. Their teacher said, "Let's sing "We're Marching to Zion" as we march around the room."

"What time does the clock say now?" They answered that it was ten minutes after eleven. "Time for _____?" she asked. And they all said that it was time for Penmanship! They had special lined paper with the letter already written on it, so they could copy it later. The teacher carefully explained how to make the new cursive letter of the day. They had reviewed all the printed letters the first months of the year and were excited now to learn how to write in cursive. So they listened carefully and watched as the letter was made three times by the teacher. She had them stand up and trace the letter on the board in the air. Then she said that they could try one on their own. They were to compare theirs with the one on the paper. If they had trouble with it they would raise a hand and she would go and help them. They practiced that letter for one whole line and then took out a folder from their desk that had other letter pages in it. They could choose another letter page to practice another letter they had learned before. "Remember, we're not in a hurry. The purpose of this practice is to see how nicely we can make each letter. We don't want to get sloppy like many doctors who write prescriptions we can't even read!" she stated. They all laughed.

Fifteen minutes later it was time for Spelling. "Let's show Mrs. Blake how we do a spelling bee. Take your places. We'll use words from the last three weeks," she said. The students quickly made a line around the room, with the beginning of the line being close to the teacher's desk. Miss Green would say a word and give its meaning. The child would say the word, and then spell it. If correct, she or he would stay in place. If not, Miss Green would spell the word correctly and the child would go to the end of the line. After each child had spelled one word, the ones who had gone to the end of the line were given another chance to correctly spell the word they had missed. They even had to remember what it was.

"Okay, now, go back to your seats and get ready for the spelling test on this week's words. You'll <u>print</u> them, because using cursive right now, takes too much concentration and you might spell the words wrong because of it. Take your time and print nicely." Each child had a "pad" of spelling test papers in a special place in his/her desk so all that needed to be done was to take out the pad, tear off the top page, put their name on it and number to 15. She said each word, its definition, and repeated the word, then waited till they had time to print it, before going to the next one.

At the end of the test, she said, "Now, trade with your partner and use your green pencil to write any corrections or a star if they are all correct." The students took a green pencil and their spelling books out of their desks, opened to the correct page, and checked each other's work. After looking at their own test, they passed the papers up to the front desk and she collected them across the front of the room. The results would be entered into the computer later and the papers would be returned to the students.

While the students took and checked the spelling test, Julie sat at the teacher's desk studying the lesson plans. They were in a big three-ring notebook, and she noticed that the teacher took pages out leaving the notebook open to the correct page. She then carried the pages with her as she taught, in case she needed to look at them during the lesson. She had the spelling test page now with the words and definitions on it.

"Since our next subject is English Grammar and Creative Writing, and we need an exercise break, show Mrs. Blake how we sing about being thankful for things we have by standing up and jumping straight up each time we say the word 'have,' to emphasize that word. We do that to help us remember that we don't use the word 'got' there because it's not good English grammar." When they finished, she asked, "Why else do we sing this song so often?" A girl answered that it's to remind them that they have so much for which to be thankful.

It was so delightful and cute to watch and listen and sing with them that Julie almost burst out laughing. She could tell this way of teaching was going to be fun, and good exercise, too.

There was no book for English Grammar. Each day the lesson plan book had sentences that the teacher would say the wrong way and the students would raise their hand and when called on he or she would politely correct the sentence. Then the teacher would say, "Thank you" and the student would say, "You're welcome." Sometimes she would hand the page from the lesson plan book to a student and have them read the incorrect sentence so she could politely correct it and then be thanked by the student. It looked like a good way to teach respect and proper manners also.

The rest of the morning was spent doing creative writing in another of their special notebooks. The teacher had them read aloud from the chart on one of the bulletin boards to remind them to write neatly, spell correctly and use proper grammar. Miss Green stood at the chalkboard to print any words they needed help spelling, and to answer any questions about grammar. The students started writing where they had left off yesterday. They weren't allowed to write in cursive yet. They had to wait until they knew all the letters and how to connect them properly.

Since it was close to lunchtime as they wrote in their creative writing notebooks, the teacher called rows to use the restroom and wash hands so they would be ready when it was their turn to go to lunch. Everybody, including the teachers and parent volunteers brought sack lunches that needed no refrigeration. In order to keep costs lower, there was no kitchen, so there were no cooks in this school.

Miss Green had the children line up with their coats and lunches, in an orderly manner with a small "no touch" space between them and then walked with them to the lunchroom. There was an adult lunchroom monitor in the lunch room who kept order, answered questions, and made sure the lunch of each one was finished before dismissing that one to go outside and play. The parent volunteer ate lunch with them in the lunchroom and then went outside to supervise the playtime and organize some physical education type games when most of the children got there.

*****

Fiona and her mother were having a lovely Friday morning, even if it <u>was</u> doing spring-cleaning. It was just so nice to be together again. Both of them were aware that the time they had been apart had actually drawn them closer together. They were more thankful for each other and were getting to know each other better than they had before. "I'm really glad I decided to take a few months off from working, so we could spend more time with each other," said Glenda. "While you were home before, I never took the time to <u>just be with</u> you. I would like for us to be friends, not just mother and daughter. Mother and daughter are important, but if we can be friends also, it will make our relationship more full and special. I desire that we talk to each other about whatever topic either of us chooses, like friends do. What do you think, Fiona?"

She answered, "I think it sounds fantastic! Most of my school chums have either moved away or gotten married and we don't associate much any longer, so I need a friend, and I can think of nobody I would rather be friends with than my own mother. So, on what topic would you like to start?"

"I'm wondering whether you're happy with your choice to not go to college, but to work at The Garden Shop instead," her mother said.

Fiona responded, "I'm very glad I made both of those choices. With the timing of going to help Great Aunt Cara, I would not have been able to graduate anyway. Besides, many college graduates are not able to find work in their field of expertise anyway. I'm grateful that I don't have college loans hanging over my head. Plus, I really do enjoy working at The Garden Shop enough that I could do that for the rest of my life, unless God has something else he wants me to do."

"I'm relieved to hear that, and you're totally right in everything you said. Let's get these drapes hung out in the fresh, spring air after we shake the dust out of them. I refuse to take them to the dry cleaners and pay their expensive price only to have them come home smelling like the chemicals they use. Then we'd have to hang them out there anyway just to get the smell out," Glenda stated.

"That's for sure!" Fiona exclaimed. Later she asked, "What do you use to wash the windows and the casings around them?"

"Whatever window cleaner and other cleaners are under the kitchen sink, I guess. Only I don't like the smell of them either. Do you have any ideas?" Glenda queried.

"If you have some distilled white vinegar, it can be used to wash both the windows and around them. I know it does have an odor while you're using it, but as soon it as has evaporated the smell goes away and just leaves everything sparkling and clean smelling. Great Aunt Cara taught me that you could use it to clean just about anything. Sometimes you use it undiluted to disinfect something, but for general cleaning and washing windows, three parts water to one part vinegar works well," explained Fiona.

"Sounds good to me, and it's more environmentally friendly also. She was a smart woman," responded Glenda.

They worked on the windows and casings while they covered other topics, and then Fiona playfully asked if there was another topic her mother would like to talk about, successfully hiding the smile from her lips but not from her eyes or voice.

"Well, I would like to know how it's going with you and Matt," her mother replied a little bit shyly.

Fiona replied, "It's going very well. He seems to understand that I desire to move slowly, so he's not acting impatient or being pushy at all. As you suggested, I invited him over for lunch on Saturday after the small group meeting. I would like us to play croquette outside if it's nice out, or a board game inside so that I can see what kind of a winner or loser he is, and how he treats us as a family for an afternoon together."

"That sounds like a really good idea. He worked well in the garden last week. Playing a game will show other things about his character," replied Glenda.

"My thoughts exactly. He is very polite to all of us, especially me. He is gentlemanly and opens and holds doors for me, helps me on with my coats, walks beside me to assist when needed, slows down so I can keep up, asks me for my opinion, or if I'm warm enough. He listens carefully when I talk, and never puts me down. He's so special that sometimes I wonder if he's real. I don't want any unpleasant surprises after marriage if I can help it. I want to know him very well before I say 'yes,' if possible," she finished.

"He does sound almost perfect. Of course there's no way to know everything about another person. Even after living as a married couple for years, there are still things I don't know about your father. Yes, he _is_ a wonderful person, and I love him dearly, but there are times when I don't understand why he says or does whatever, in a given situation," Glenda clarified.

"In other words, maybe there will be things I can't find out before we are married, but hopefully they won't be things I cannot accept and deal with. I know Matt isn't perfect, but I sure do like him a lot. Now, I would like some motherly advice. What are some things I need to be _sure_ about before I say 'yes' if he does ask me to marry him?" she inquired.

Her mother answered, "Notice how he treats other people and how he talks about them when they're not present. If he's critical of others, then he might become critical of you also. Besides, it would be very hard to live with a critical person. Of course you already know he's a believer, so you're safe there. If he ever becomes pushy about things you're not ready for, or even suggests that you go to bed together before marriage, I would hope you would drop him like a hot potato. He would not deserve such a pure woman as you've kept yourself."

"If he ever makes fun of anything you say or do, pull back, and observe carefully to see if that's a pattern or just a one-time occurrence. It would be very difficult to live with someone who would make fun of you, ignore you, not listen, or not try to understand, or use what you've said against you later. Also try to find out what he watches on TV or the Internet, and what movies he prefers. That tells a lot about a person."

"Thank you, Mother! I'll be on the lookout for those kinds of things any time we are together. I can see how some of those things would devastate me, so I'll be very observant," affirmed Fiona.

"Good. Also, unity is so important in a marriage. You're both believers, but what place does God have in his life? Be sure you discuss and _agree_ on what church and small group to attend, how much money you want to give to the Lord's work and where you want it to be given. Does he like to spend a lot of money on himself? That might indicate a selfish element of his personality. Even if he wants to lavish gifts on you, that might not be the way God desires the money to be spent," she continued.

"I can see that we need to spend a lot of time talking and be open and honest with what we say. I'm glad I wasn't asked to promise anything before I left two years ago," Fiona said with a sigh.

"I don't mean for you to start questioning everything about Matt. We think he's a wonderful person so far, but I do want for you to be very careful, and I'm glad you asked me for this advice. I only wish that I could be sure that I've covered everything I needed to talk about. Father in heaven, only you know what else Fiona needs to look out for. Please show Fiona, as she continues to get to know Matt, what her answer should be if he asks. Put up a big red or green light to direct her way. Keep my Fiona safe and happy," prayed Glenda.

"Yes," continued Fiona. "You know I only want to do your will, Father, so make your guidance very clear and easy for me to follow. Keep my emotions under your control and help me to progress at the best speed possible. Make me very observant to any red flags in this relationship. What exactly do you have for me to accomplish in your Kingdom. My first and foremost wish is: I desire to be used by God," she sang the chorus as she finished her prayer. "Is there a book or a place where all the advice you've given me is written down? I don't want to forget any of it."

Her mother answered, "Yes, I have just the one, plus another one about love languages that would be helpful for you to read as you continue on this quest. The first book, I bought for you just after you left for Aunt Cara's home, and have been waiting for an appropriate time to give it to you. The other one, your father and I got at a weekend marriage retreat. They're both very good books. I'll get them for you as soon as we get these windows finished and the drapes back up." Soon they were done, and Glenda gave the books to Fiona who had time to look at each of them while she ate her lunch before going to work.

*****

During the Friday noon lunch break while Pam and Julie ate in the classroom, Julie learned that the grade level teachers do their own music and art projects, usually connected with something they're learning in the classroom. These lessons were in the lesson plan book. There is no physical education teacher, because of recess times and all the active learning times in the room. The parent volunteers who supervise the recess times organize games once every day after lunch that were very much like PE anyway. It makes for a better use of time.

She also learned that the nurse, Miss Lora Nelson, comes into the classroom three times a week, on Mondays, Wednesdays, and Fridays, for half an hour to teach age appropriate health, hygiene, nutrition, systems of the body, safe use of medicines, the dangers of drugs, alcohol, and smoking, plus exercise routines they could do on snowy/rainy inside days and that they could teach all of these things to their parents. The teacher stays in the room in case the nurse is called away for an emergency, but the secretary usually could handle small things. The teacher uses the time to enter progress into the computer.

The principal, Miss Beth Davis, comes into each class two times a week, on Tuesdays and Thursdays, for half an hour to teach History and Geography, while the grade level teacher stays in the room to continue entering progress into the computer. In this way, the students get some variety in teachers every day, and the grade level teacher gains half an hour each day to enter data into the computer at school, rather than having to take work home at night. It also enables the principal and nurse to learn the names of all the children in the school, in order to be considered resources, friends, counselors, and for the children to become acquainted with them. Julie thought the plan was excellent.

Pam also showed her how to enter grades and comments into the computer's grade book. They were able to enter all the spelling tests and Julie got started on the comments she had written about their oral reading. She would finish them later.

Lunchtime with its recess lasted 45 minutes. When the children entered the classroom they hung up their coats and lunch bags, got drinks, used the restroom if needed, and then sat down on a nice carpet to have a class meeting during which they could ask questions, report and <u>solve</u> (not just complain or gripe about) problems they may have had at lunch or recess, or discuss and fix anything the teacher had noticed that needed attention, or make announcements. That took about fifteen minutes, and when the big clock chimed one o'clock, they got up and went to their desks for Science.

They were in the process of learning about the scientific method. Today they would investigate and gather data about ice melting. During the class meeting, the parent volunteer had put one ice cube in a clear plastic glass for each student on the two long counters in the room, which were just the right height for the students to stand there and work. They took with them their science notebook and a pencil and observed what was happening to the ice. While they waited, they wrote on the paper the title: Ice Melting. Nothing seemed to be happening so they wrote: It is cold and slow to melt. The teacher suggested that they hold the bottom of the glass on the palm of their hand. Their hands got cold, so they wrote that down. "Let's try blowing on it," one of them said. So they did that and a little water appeared in the glass, so they wrote that down.

Miss Green said, "Since it is so slow to melt, let's go have story time now, and then look at it again afterwards. Mrs. Blake, would you like to read the story to the class today?"

"I would love to!" she answered. "I would like for us to go over and sit on that nice carpet where you had your class meeting." She led the way over there and as soon as they were settled, she showed the book cover and read the title. "Look at the clock now, and we'll time how long this book lasts, so that we'll have an amount of time to write on your data sheets about the ice." As she read the book to them, she held it so they could see the pictures and read it with good expression to make the story interesting. When she had finished, she asked what they liked about the story, and received some interesting answers. "This story was a realistic story, not make believe. We can tell that, because the things that happened in the story could happen in real life. "How long has it been now?" she asked. A boy answered, "20 minutes." She stated, "That should be long enough for something to have happened to the ice. Stand up carefully and walk over there to look. Then you can write down what you observe."

They went to look and there was more water in the bottom of the glasses. There were plastic rulers there and they measured the water after writing down that they had waited 20 minutes. They wrote the measurement down also. Miss Green told them to leave their notebooks and pencils there and return to their desks for the next subject, which was Social Studies. They would check the ice again after they worked with the maps of the United States that the parent volunteer had placed on each desk.

"Can you point to a place on this map where there would be a lot of ice?" asked Miss Green. The children pointed to areas that had mountains and to the northern and central states. "So you can realize why it's important to understand that ice is slow to melt and that blowing warm air on it helps. There are other ways to speed it up. We'll try one after we finish with these maps.

Everywhere There's a Sunrise, Let's Tell The Good News!

Now, everyone touch North on the map. Good, now West. Yes, where is South? And now find East. Find the compass rose on this map. Most maps have North at the top of the map, but there are some that don't, so it's always important to look at the compass rose before you answer any questions about directions. We didn't do that this time, because along with a compass rose, this map also has the directions written on the edges of the map. Watch out! During the next few weeks, I have a feeling that Mrs. Blake will have you look at other maps which have North in a different place on the map. If you don't look at the compass rose, or the edges of the map, you'll get the wrong answer!

"Raise your right hand and then point to the right side of the map. What direction is on the right side of this map?" They all answered that it was east. She continued with left being west, top was North, and bottom was south. "Does this occur on every map?" she asked. A couple students looked confused but most of them were shaking their heads, "NO!" "You're right to think, 'NO'. What does it depend upon? Point to the one place on this map that answers that question." They all pointed to the compass rose and nobody looked confused now. She continued by having them point to the state where they lived and the city. Then she asked other questions like what state is east of us, or what direction would you travel to get to X state or city.

Then she looked at the clock and said that it had been another 20 minutes, so they could go look at the ice cubes again. They went and wrote down the time, the water measurement, and that the ice cube looked smaller now.

"Earlier I said that there were other ways to speed up the process of melting ice. Does anybody know of one?" she asked. A girl said that salt could be used to help melt ice. "Right. So let's try that, and we'll also try sugar. You'll notice that our parent volunteer has written some words on the glasses. One of them says plain, another one says salt, and the third one says sugar. Now, you will be in groups of three. One of you will take the salt and measure one forth of a teaspoon. Mix it with the water in the glass that says 'salt'. Another of you measure one fourth of a teaspoon of sugar and mix it with the water in the glass that says 'sugar.' The other person does not have to do anything because the glass labeled 'plain' is called the control. We need it to compare with the other two glasses. I'll have two different groups put twice as much salt and sugar into their ice cube glasses. Carefully pick up a thermometer and put it into your glass. We won't read the thermometer yet because it will take awhile to respond to the temperature of the water. Write down everything you just did in your notebooks."

Just as they were picking up their pencils to write, one girl knocked over her glass with the sugar added to it. "Oh no!" she exclaimed, and almost started to cry, but the two children beside her comforted her and helped with the cleanup. Miss Green explained reality discipline to the children emphasizing that it wasn't punishment, but to help us all learn. This time the reality discipline would be that the girl would not be given another glass since so much time had passed in the experiment that it would not do any good. That group would just have to look at their neighbor's glass with sugar added to it, and compare that way instead. She commended them for doing such a good job of cleaning up the mess and reassuring the girl who had the accident. She reminded them that nobody is perfect, and accidents happen. She led them in singing, "Everyone Makes Mistakes."

"If it had been done on purpose, a different type of discipline or even punishment would have been needed," she told them.

Then she asked them if they understood, and they all said, "Yes, Miss Green."

When they finished writing, she had them go back to their seats. "That all took about ten minutes. We'll leave the ice there again for about 10 minutes more and then look again, because 10 plus 10 equals ___?" They all said, "20." As they went to their seats, she said, "I'll set the timer this time, and we'll have silent reading time, but it will be 5 minutes less than usual since the ice cube accident, cleanup, and discussion took about five minutes. Read in whatever book you've chosen. If you've finished the last book you were reading during silent reading time you may take it back to the shelf where you got it and choose another book. While you're reading, Mrs. Blake and I will walk around and stop now and then to ask a question for you to answer. Or if you have a question about what you're reading, raise your hand and one of us will come and answer it." She quickly explained to Mrs. Blake that this was one example of how to keep up with the lesson plans. Just readjust the timing as needed.

When the timer went off, they returned to look at the ice cubes again. The ice cube was very small now and there was now much more water in the glass that had salt in it. The glass that had sugar in it and the one that was plain had more water than before, but less than the glass that had salt in it. The ice cubes were smaller than before but not as small as the one that had salt in it.

"Write down what each thermometer says for its corresponding glass. Now hold each glass steady with one hand and use your pointer finger of the other hand to feel the temperature of the plain water, the sugar water, and the salt water," Miss Green instructed. They all noticed that the salt water felt colder than the others. "Go over to the two last groups and write down the temperatures that go with each of their glasses. Notice that the ice cube in the salt glass is very tiny and there's more water in that glass. If you want to, you may feel the water in their glasses also. The salt lowers the temperature at which water melts/freezes, and that's why it melted the ice faster and felt colder. When even more salt is put with the ice cube, it melts even faster and the water gets even colder," she explained.

They wrote down their observations in their notebooks, and had a discussion about what they had observed and learned, while they took turns carrying the glasses over to the classroom sink, to dump and stack them. The parent volunteer washed all the glasses, removing the words also, since they were put on the glasses with washable markers. He left them to dry in a drainer, and then went and cleaned up the counters. Julie realized how much help the parent volunteers were going to be and was again very grateful.

At 2:15, the school nurse, Miss Nelson came into the classroom, and she and Julie were introduced. Before she started her lesson, she taught them another exercise routine of pretending to lift weights while standing in place. She reminded them to do the exercises slowly, and just start out with four apiece. They could work up to ten, adding one time each week. She added a balancing exercise also, standing on one foot then the other. They could keep a hand or finger on their desk if they needed to. After that she reviewed what they had learned about good nutrition.

The other two teachers had gone over to the classroom computer so Julie could learn some more about record keeping and then finish entering comments about the oral reading she had heard. Pam told her that she would need to keep track of the ones she had not heard yet and start with them the next school day. Today she had been able to listen to a lot of them because she wasn't teaching groups at the round table. With only one teacher in the room, it usually took a week to be able to hear each one, unless she had them read aloud at the round table. It was a good practice to alternate those ways of listening, because some students were nervous reading in front of others in the group. They needed that practice also, but a better picture of progress could be gained by listening both ways.

There was an emergency about 25 minutes later that the nurse had to go take care of, so Miss Green went and finished the nurse's lesson. At 2:45, the children again went out to recess. Julie was shown where the Health and also the History and Geography lessons were located. Pam suggested that each day, Julie should open to those lessons and quickly skim them, so she could take over if there was an emergency like there was today. She also showed Julie where the daily plans were for the parent volunteers. Then she showed Julie where the intercom was located.

*****

This Friday, Walt returned home from the job site and ate the delicious lunch Betty had ready for him. "This new diet is very tasty, the way you fix it, Dear," he complimented.

"Thank you, Honey. It is probably better for both of us than the things I had been fixing. It was easier the old way, but I think I had gotten into a rut. Learning new recipes and different kinds of foods to eat is good for my brain. I don't want it to get sluggish," she added.

After cleanup, they went into the living room and continued reading the book Matt had loaned to them. They were about half way through it now, and they were learning a lot.

*****

At break time Friday afternoon for Karen at Subway, she went into the break room with one of her co-workers to rest and eat a mid-afternoon snack. They began talking and Karen asked her how things were going. She told Karen, "It's about the same as the last time we discussed it. I get so discouraged, because before and when we were first married he professed that he was a Christian and things went very well for a while. If I had known he was going to change, I would have never married him, but since I couldn't have known that, I'm stuck. Now it's not only Christianity that we can't agree on, it's lots of things. It seems like I can't say anything but what he disagrees with it. If only I could remember to keep my mouth closed, there wouldn't be so many arguments."

Karen suggested, "Let's pray some more right now." She nodded. "Heavenly Father, thank you that you know all about this situation and have heard what she just said about how it's going. We don't understand why it keeps on going like this, but you do, and even if it doesn't look like that to us, you are still in control. We know that you can change people, but that you don't force them to against their will. We ask again that you will bring her husband to a true relationship with Jesus as his Lord, and until that happens, give her the grace she needs to respond to him as you would. Help her keep quiet when needed, and to say the words you give her at the appropriate time. Fill her with your peace and joy so that she can live above these circumstances and be a living testimony to her husband and any other unbelievers who are watching. We pray these things in Jesus precious name, Amen."

With a new smile on her face, the co-worker added her prayer of acceptance, thanked Karen, and they both went back to work.

*****

Friday's recess was over at 3 PM, and the students came inside and immediately started working to finish an art project that had been started earlier in the week. It was a surprise for Miss Green and she knew she was not to see it until it was finished. Miss Davis had gotten them started on it Tuesday, and said they could work on it during their art time until Friday when they needed to be finished with it so they could give it to Miss Green. (The parent volunteer was available to help with anything a student might need.)

Miss Green sat at her desk and called one student at a time to her desk to be tested on their memorization of the multiplication tables up to fives. Mrs. Blake joined in this endeavor after watching the how-to for a few minutes. They were able to get through the whole class before the art time was up one-half hour later.

All but a few students were finished with their art projects, and they took them up to Miss Green at her desk, where she looked carefully at each one, exclaiming how pretty and nicely made they were. Each student had made a special card to thank and say good-bye to his or her teacher. Everybody, including Julie was in tears by the time it was over. What special memories for Miss Green to take with her!

Julie could see that Miss Green needed some time to get control of her emotions, so she took the next page from the lesson plan book and started the lesson in Music. This gave the rest of the students time to finish and deliver their cards to their teacher, also.

"Children, those are beautiful cards and I know Miss Green will treasure them. Go back to your desks now and we'll begin Music by singing some songs out of the hymnals you keep in your desks. Who has a favorite to begin our singing time"? Mrs. Blake asked. A boy chose "Jesus Loves Even Me." They sang all the verses. Using the lesson plan, she asked, "What was last Sunday?" They all answered that it was Resurrection Sunday. "Let's sing some of the songs that were included in the service last Sunday." So they sang, "Easter Song," "Christ Arose," and "Christ the Lord is Risen Today."

"Now find 'God Incarnate, Jesus Came,' and read the words to this song silently and see if there are any words or parts of the song you don't understand. When you're ready, you can raise your hand and I'll call on you to ask your question." She answered the first question and for the next ones asked for volunteers who thought they could answer, but she helped as needed. To finish up the lesson, they stood and sang several action songs that were listed in the lesson plan to start the blood circulating again and get rid of the wiggles.

When they had finished the music lesson, Miss Green was ready to teach again, and started by saying, "Thank you all very much for the beautiful and special cards you each made for me. I'll keep them and treasure them with fond memories of our time together the first part of this year. What you made for me is a good example of our Bible lesson for this afternoon." She read a Bible verse aloud and then another story from the children's devotional book called Keys For Kids. They spent some time discussing and commenting on the story. "Can anybody tell me the reference of one of our memory verses that reminds us to be thankful?"

A boy answered, "1 Thessalonians 5:18." Then all of them recited it in unison: *In everything give thanks, for this is the will of God in Christ Jesus concerning you,* 1 Thessalonians 5:18.

After that, she played a selection on an SD card from Storybook Room with Uncle Bob. This time he was interviewing the cornea of the human eye. It is an unusual way to tell a story, pretending that the cornea is speaking and answering all the

Everywhere There's a Sunrise, Let's Tell The Good News!

questions Uncle Bob asks and giving additional information that proves that only a caring, wise creator could have made something so complex. The students took notes again in their "Proofs of Creation" notebooks. That interview was followed by Tim, who was "talking" to "Faith" in the Bible and learning what faith meant and why it was important. There followed a discussion about both stories, with the students asking questions about anything they didn't understand.

Then it was time for sharing and prayer time on the nice carpet in the corner. Miss Green started the time by using a puppet to encourage them to share, and then asking some questions. They liked talking to the puppet. After a while, she put the puppet away and reminded them what conversational prayer was, and that everything they shared and prayed about during this time was confidential, which means private and not to be shared with anyone but their parents.

Each child had the chance to add a sentence or two to the prayer time, but it was not required. Several of them asked God to bless and help Miss Green as she went back to her hometown to take care of her mother. Others thanked God for the time she had been their teacher. Still others thanked God for providing another teacher for them so quickly. Some of them asked God to bless and help Mrs. Blake as she took the place of their other teacher. A few of them asked for him to help this class to work together with Mrs. Blake as she gets used to this new school and class of students. Mrs. Blake had been invited to join in this time on the rug, so she thanked God for the opportunity to teach such a nice group of third graders, and for all she had been able to learn by spending the day with them. Miss Green closed the prayer time by thanking God for the months she had been able to be with this class and that he had provided such a good teacher to take her place. There were tears in many eyes again before they finished.

The next 20 minutes before school was out for the day, were spent saying memory verses to their partners while the partner looked at the verse on a file card the other one handed him. They would say the reference, then the verse, and then the reference again. They took turns like this until each person had said four or five verses. Julie walked around listening to them reciting, with good expression and word perfectly, verses about God creating the earth and the whole universe. Some of the verses were: Genesis 1:1; Psalms 33:6&9; Proverbs 3:19,20; Isaiah 41:20; 45:12; Romans 1:20; Colossians 1:16,17. Additional verses could be used to show people the way of salvation, such as: Romans 3:23; 6:23; 10:9,10; John 3:16; and Ephesians 2:8,9.

At the end of this time, Miss Green handed out their spelling tests so they could take them home to put with the other tests they had taken this year. She reminded them to review the words often because these were words that they would be using all their lives, and there would be review tests off and on the rest of the year. Some of them would be announced, but others would be like pop quizzes. Mrs. Blake would know when and which kind to have, because they were already in the lesson plans.

At ten minutes to five, she had them gather up anything they needed to take home, and stand in line at the door. She reminded them to keep everything in their hands while they ran or walked around the playground as they waited for their parents to come pick them up. This was not a normal playtime, because they needed to be on the lookout for when their parent arrived. At five o'clock, she said good-bye one last time and gave a hug to any who wanted one. Julie watched as they walked or ran around the playground following the directions about their belongings carefully. (Their parents arrived in a spread out fashion and pretty soon only a few children would be left waiting.)

Julie gave Pam a few minutes to dry her eyes, before going over to ask if there was anything she could help with before she left. She offered to help carry things to the car and mentioned that she had her own puppet to use for sharing time, so if the other one belonged to Pam, it would be no problem if she took it with her, so she did. They had only a few boxes to load and then Julie said, "Thank you again, for sharing your last class day with me. I learned so many helpful things that will make my first few days here go much smoother. I'm sure it will be easier on the children also."

"That's so true, and I'm immensely grateful to God for arranging it so that you could spend this day with us. I can leave at peace, knowing this class is going to be in good hands. Thank you, Julie, for stepping in and taking over the music lesson. I needed that time to get control of my emotions. Also, thank you for offering to pray for me as I take care of my mother. I know it will help me a lot. I'll be praying for you as you teach here, also and for the children that they will adjust quickly to their new teacher. Would you like to keep in touch by e-mail?"

"Yes, Pam!" answered Julie. "I feel like I have known you for more than just four days, and I would like to be able to tell you how the children and I are doing. I'd also like to know how things are going for you. Here's my e-mail address." She wrote it on a piece of paper and gave it to Pam.

"Good. I would like that, Julie," responded Pam.

"Did you attend a small group while you lived here?" Julie asked.

"Yes," she answered. "That, and the church are other very hard things for me to leave. My small group is all coming over tomorrow morning to help me finish packing up all the things in my apartment and load it in a rental trailer so I can leave early Sunday morning to drive to my parent's home. My parents are not believers and don't attend church. I'm not sure I'll have time or opportunity to attend while I'm there caring for my mother. I worry about feeling cut off and not having a support group."

"Oh!" Julie said excitedly, "you won't <u>have</u> to feel cut off, because the church has a web site where you can listen to each Sunday service of church #1 on your computer. I have a friend who did that when she had to be out of town some weekends. She said that church #1 always has a salvation message on the web site as an evangelistic outreach, so people searching or just surfing can hear the Good News. It's not quite as good as being there in person, but you can hear the music and even could look up the songs in your hymnal and follow along. If you need to keep the house quiet, you could use earphones."

"Wow, I never thought of that. It would be a big help to at least have the church services!" Pam agreed.

Julie continued, "And for a small group, maybe mine could have you as an absentee member. I could record the teaching time and attach it to an e-mail, or more than one, if it's too big to fit. If you would like us to, we could pray for you and your parents during conversational prayer time."

"Another excellent idea, and one I would have never thought of. But since we're going to keep in touch by e-mail, and be praying for each other, all I have to do is give you permission to include me and my parents in your small group prayer times and it will be almost as good as being there. Feel free to share with them my reason for having to leave my teaching position at the school. Thank you so very much, Julie, for caring enough to think up ways to help me. I already feel a little better about the whole thing. Now, I must get ready to leave or I'll be crying again." She said good-bye and gave Julie a hug, which she returned gladly.

Julie went to tell Miss Davis that the day had gone very well and that she would see her on Monday. She met her in the hallway on <u>her</u> way to say farewell to Miss Green, so she told her there in the hall, and then went home.

    Ted was at the door to meet her, and he took her in his arms and said, "You've been crying. What happened, Honey?"

    She told him about the tearful prayer time and the last good-bye. "I could see how much they all loved each other and how hard this was for all of them. I couldn't help but join in the tears. But it was a very good and profitable day. I can tell you all about it after supper. How are you, my dear husband?" she asked.

    "I'm relieved to know that nothing bad happened to you, my precious Jewel. I can understand how a sensitive, caring person like you would feel those emotions along with them. I'm fine, and my day went well. Supper's ready. I'm glad you told me you might be late this afternoon. I'll bet you helped her load her things and stayed to talk for a little while," he responded as they went into the kitchen to eat, and she nodded.

    After supper and cleanup, Julie made sure to call Pastor Don and Anita, and Jeff and Karen, so she could tell them what had happened this week as she had promised to do. Then she told Ted all about her day and how thankful she was that she was able to spend the <u>whole</u> day in the classroom. She finished by saying, "If a picture is worth a thousand words, then being able to watch and participate, ask questions and receive on the spot instructions, and get a little bit acquainted with the children was worth a whole college course. This way of teaching is very different from my other years, but it's <u>so</u> much better! I feel much better prepared to go in there on Monday and take over where Miss Green left off. I even get to take my koala puppet, Kippy, to school and use him there like I did in my other two classes. That will be such fun again. And I <u>know</u> I'm going to love those children!" she exclaimed.

*****

Chapter 10

John 1:18, *No man has seen God at any time, the only begotten Son, who is with the Father, has made him known.*

Saturday

Everywhere There's a Sunrise, Let's Tell The Good News!

Saturday morning dawned bright and fair, and all the small group members woke after a good night sleep looking forward to the meeting of the small group at the pastor's house. They all got as many things done as they could before they went over there. It was such a nice morning, that many of them decided to leave early enough to walk the few blocks from their homes.

Mindy Jones had come 15 minutes early so she could get things ready for her four charges in the kitchen and outside. They would plan to spend as much time outside as possible as soon as it warmed up a little more. She would have quiet activities for them to do in the kitchen while they needed to be inside. Providentially, the house was arranged so that the children could get into the bathroom without going through the living room where all the people would be.

Today, the twins, Hope and Joy, arrived only five minutes early, so Mindy had ten minutes to get ready with only Timmy and Mary, who "helped" her. All four of them were so cute that Mindy really enjoyed this time of having them together. The first thing she had them do was color a picture they could give to their parents at the end of the meeting. She made sure that they did a nice job on it so they could feel proud when they presented their picture. By then it was warm enough to go outside and play tag for a while and then swing on the swing set, or go down the slide.

She had hidden several items in the yard before Timmy and Mary saw her. After they had played for a while on their own, she gave them some clues and sent them on a treasure hunt. Surprisingly, Mary was the first one to find one of the items. She ran to Mindy to show her, while the others kept looking for the rest of the items. Hope and Joy were next. Each of them had found one apiece at the same time even though they were in separate places in the yard. Then Timmy ran up with the last one, which had been hidden in a rather obscure place, so he felt good about it even though he was the last child to find one. "Now, Timmy, run and hide yours in a different place while these three hide their eyes so they can't see where you go." She had each of the three others do the same thing with their item while the others hid their eyes.

Mindy said, "Okay, listen carefully. This time you have to find a <u>different</u> item than you found the last time. In other words, you may not bring me the one you just hid. Do you understand?" They all nodded their heads, and they were off again. Timmy quickly found the one that Mary had hidden. Then Joy found the one Timmy had hidden. Mary found the one Hope had hidden, and Hope found the one hidden by Joy.

"Come and sit here on the porch and each one of you make up an imaginary story about the item you just found. When you're ready you can stand up and tell us your story." The first story was so hilarious that Mindy was worried that the people inside the house might hear all the laughter and it would bother them, so she moved them over to the part of the back yard that was the farthest away from the living room before the next child told his or her story. Each story seemed to get funnier than the one before it.

*****

While all that fun was going on for the children, Pastor Don and Anita welcomed all the members of the small group to their home, started the meeting with prayer and then asked if anybody had a praise report. Julie didn't want to go first but the rest all kept quiet and looked at her. So she smiled and enthusiastically told the group a summary about all the miraculous things God had done in the past week concerning her new job as a third grade teacher in the church school. She even added that her former boss and his wife were planning to come to church this Sunday because she had told him about how God had worked so many things out for the good of so many people. She told Don that she didn't know if they were believers or not, but just in case, he might want to include a salvation message for them to hear. There was much clapping and cheering and loud praises to God for all he had done.

Then Ami Suehiro said, "We received phone calls from both of our children this week. Each one told us separately that he or she missed Pine City and was seriously considering coming back to look for jobs here." That announcement was greeted with more clapping, cheering and loud praises to God, especially by Larry and Jane Kelsey and the Suehiros, since they had prayed about it again last Sunday before supper.

Jeff Spencer said, "Karen and I have been learning a lot about how to be facilitators of a small group by reading a booklet about it and then getting all our questions answered by Don and Anita. We praise God that they're such good teachers." There was more clapping, cheering and loud praises to God.

"Are there any other praises?" If not, I have an announcement. I've decided after reading that booklet again, that it would be a good idea to decide where our next meeting will be held, right after we finish praise time so we don't forget, like I did last week. Are there any volunteers? Singles could pair off, if that would be easier for them. The lunchroom is available in the school for singles who don't have a big enough apartment for a meeting."

Karen spoke up, "Jeff and I would like to be the next hosts. You can write down our address and phone number."

They did that and then Don said, "Next week I'll have a list of all the names, addresses and phone numbers of the members of this group so that we don't have to write one down every week. I should have thought of that before too, but I forgot, since things have been so busy the last few weeks. That was in the booklet also, but I had not read it for quite a while. So, now you see that your pastor is human too."

They all laughed. But Matt encouraged, "Don't be hard on yourself. This <u>has</u> been an unusually busy time for you, and we can all understand how that goes!"

"Thank you, Matt. I needed that reminder and encouragement," Don responded.

Then it was time to sing. They sang some more songs to celebrate Jesus resurrection since Easter had just been last Sunday. The songs included: "Hallelujah, Jesus is Alive," Acts 1:3; "Jesus Lives and So Shall I," John 14:19; "Celebrate Jesus," Luke 24:5,6; and "Our God Reigns," Isaiah 52:7.

After the singing, Julie got ready to record the teaching time. She had already asked Don if she could do that and e-mail it to Pam Green and he had agreed. Don said, "Our teaching this week is continuing on the topic we started two weeks ago about the Holy Spirit and his work in the church, and also about the church being the body of Christ. Today I would like to focus on who Jesus is, was, and will be, what he's done for us, and how we became members of the body of Christ. I've written some Scripture references on pieces of paper and I'll give a different one to each person starting here and going around the circle. If you don't wish to read aloud, just tell me, "No," and I'll pass you by. Please look up your reference now and practice it silently a couple times so you can listen to the others as they read rather than practicing yours as they read. Use your piece of paper as a bookmark so you can quickly find the scripture again that you're going to read.

"These Scripture references are all interrelated as cross references about some of the verses in Colossians 1:12-23a. Follow along as Anita reads those out loud now. *"We give thanks to the Father, who has made us able to be partakers of the inheritance of the saints in light. He has delivered us from the power of darkness, and has translated us into the kingdom of his dear Son, in whom we have redemption through his blood, even the forgiveness of sins. He is the image of the invisible God, the firstborn of every creature. For he created all things that are in heaven and in earth, visible and invisible, whether they are thrones, dominions principalities, or powers. All things were created by him and for him, and he is before all things, and by him all things consist. He is the head of the body, the church. He is the beginning, the firstborn from the dead, that he might have the preeminence in all things. For it pleased the Father that in him should all fullness dwell. Having made peace through the blood of his cross, to reconcile all things unto himself. ... And he reconciled you who used to be alienated and were enemies in your mind by wicked works. He reconciled you by his body, through death, to present you holy and blameless and not able to be reproved in his sight, if you continue in the faith, grounded and settled. Don't be moved away from the hope of the gospel, which you have heard and which was preached to every creature, which is under heaven."*

Don said, "Thank you, Anita. Keep your Bibles open to the Colossians passage. Now, I'll say <u>just</u> the cross reference and the verse or verses in Colossians that go with it. Put your finger on the verse or verses it goes with in Colossians while you listen to the cross-reference. Whoever has that cross-reference, please read it while we listen and then look to see how it adds understanding to the verse in Colossians. You might have to look for only a part of the reference that goes with a part of the verse or verses in Colossians, but I found this to be a very helpful exercise as I was studying this week. If we can use God's Word to help us understand other places in his Word, it's more meaningful, and often more correct than just hearing or reading some person's interpretation of God's Word. That's why so many Scripture passages are include in the teaching times here and at church.

"John 1:1-3 goes with verses 16 and 17. *In the beginning was the Word, and the Word was with God, and the Word was God. The same was in the beginning with God. All things were made by him, and without him was not anything made that was made.*

"John 14:6-11 goes with verse 15 and 19. *Jesus said, 'I am the way, the truth, and the life. No man comes to the Father, but by me. If you knew me, you would also know my Father, and from now on you know him and have seen him. 'Philip said to him, 'Lord, show us the Father and it will be enough for us.' Jesus said to him, 'Have I been such a long time with you, and still you have not known me, Phillip? He that has seen me has seen the Father. How can you say 'Show us the Father?' Don't you believe that I am in the Father, and the Father is in me? The words I speak to you I do not speak of myself, but the Father who dwells in me does the works. Believe that I am in the Father, and the Father is in me, or else believe me for the sake of the works.'*

"2 Corinthians 4:3,4,6 goes with verses 21 and 12 and 13. *If our gospel is hidden, it is hidden to those who are lost. The god of this world has blinded their minds so that the light of the glorious gospel of Christ who is the image of God should shine unto them. For God, who commanded the light to shine out of darkness, has shined in our hearts, to give the light of the knowledge of the glory of God in the face of Jesus Christ.*

"Hebrews 1:1-3 goes with verse 16,17 and 21,22. *God, who at various times and manners spoke in the past to the fathers by the prophets, has in these last days spoken to us by his Son, whom he has appointed heir of all things, by whom also he made the world. Jesus being the brightness of God's glory and the express image of his person, and upholding all things by the word of his power, when he had by himself purged our sins, sat down on the right hand of the Majesty on high.*

"Acts 26: 22,23 goes with verses 12 and 18. *Having therefore obtained the help of God, I (Paul) continue to this day, witnessing both to small and great, saying no other thing than that which the prophets and Moses said should happen: that Christ would suffer and that he would be the first who would rise from the dead, and show light to the people of Israel and to the Gentiles.*

"Ephesians 1:19b-23 goes with verses 16- 18. *(God's) mighty power was used when he raised Christ from the dead, and set him at his own right hand in the heavenly places, far above all principality and power and might and dominion, and every name that is named, not only in this world, but also in that which is to come. And he has put all things under his feet and has made him head over all things for the church, which is his body, the fullness of him who fills all in all.*

"Romans 5:8-11 goes with verses 20-22. *But God commended his love toward us, in that, while were still sinners, Christ died for us. Much more then, being now justified by his blood, we shall be saved from wrath through him. For if, when we were enemies, we were reconciled to God by the death of his Son, how much more, being reconciled, shall we be saved by his life?*

And not only so, but we also have joy in God through our Lord Jesus Christ, by whom we have now received the atonement.

"Ephesians 5:25b-27 also goes with verses 20-22. *Christ loved the church and gave himself for it, so that he could sanctify and cleanse it with the washing of water by the word, in order to present it to himself a glorious church, not having spot, or wrinkle or any such thing, but that it should be holy and without blemish.*

"Colossians 2:6,7 goes with verse 23. *As you have therefore received Christ Jesus the Lord, so walk in him, rooted and built up in him and established in the faith, as you have been taught, abounding in it with thanksgiving.*"

The readings were followed by a very good discussion of the way many of the verses were enlightening and added much understanding to the Colossians passage. It was excellent to have the opportunity to go back and forth between them, looking for similarities or how they went together or added more information or insight to both passages. They all agreed that they had a much better understanding now of who Jesus is, was, and will be, what he's done for us, and how we became members of the body of Christ.

Don suggested, "You can do this kind of study on your own at home if you have a Bible that has center references or references in footnotes. You might want to find answers to questions that come up while you're reading, by looking up cross-references before reading the study notes that are included in many study Bibles. Those notes can be very helpful, also. Just don't rely on them all the time. Now it's time for Conversational prayer."

Julie interrupted, "Before we start, may I ask a question?" He nodded and she went ahead, "The teacher I'm replacing at the church school, desires that she and I keep in contact by e-mail and I told her I would be praying for her in this situation. Then I asked her if I could share it with my small group, and she gave me permission to include her and her parents in our conversational prayer times. She told me to feel free to share her reason for having to leave. So, could we have her as an absentee member of our small group?" He nodded again, and she continued, "Then as time goes on, if she has other requests, she can e-mail them to me and we can include those also. I can keep encouraging her with the e-mails I send in reply. We can kind of take the place of the small group she had to leave."

Don agreed, "Yes, Pam Green can be an absentee member of our small group since she's given you permission, so why don't you start off our conversational prayer time with her as our first topic today?"

"May I also record the prayers we say for her?" He agreed again, so she turned on her recorder and then prayed, giving a short summary of Pam's need to return to her parent's home to care for her mother who just had a stroke, and the other things they had talked about. "Please give her traveling mercies as she drives to their home tomorrow pulling a rented one-way trailer with her belongings."

Karen added, "Heavenly Father, since you've worked out so many things for the good of so many people in this whole situation, please continue by using her mother's stroke to bring Pam's parents into your family, and if it's your will, heal her mother and then use her to be your witness and bring many more into the Kingdom. Please turn this bad news into good news for your glory."

Clara continued, "Let Pam feel your presence, and know that she's not cut off from her church or small group. Thank you that she can listen to the church service via the web, and that Julie cares enough to be her go-between, so that she can still belong to a small group."

Then Ted prayed, "Father in heaven, thank you so much for all the amazing ways you've worked in this whole situation just during this last week and since you are the source of all good and perfect gifts, I ask that you will continue giving them to help Pam as she adjusts to living with, and helping her parents. Give her peace about her class at school with the knowledge that Julie is a very good teacher and will take good care of them."

Fiona added, "Heavenly Father, I thank you for all the help you gave to me as I cared for my great aunt, and now I ask that you will give that same kind of help to Pam Green. She'll need even more help since her parents are not believers."

Matt continued, ""Yes, please help her remember that she can do all things through Jesus who gives her the strength. Help her to learn quickly how to care for this stroke victim. Keep her cheerful and may her parents see you living through her with your love and grace."

Jeff added, "Thank you LORD for this caring small group and the way we've bonded in such a short time. Thank you for the unity we have, and that we can agree to even pray for someone we barely know, but who needs your help. As Karen and I learn how to be facilitators of this small group, direct us and give us your wisdom to be all that you want us to be and to do your will in everything."

Tony continued, "LORD, thank you that your answer to Jeff's prayer is already 'YES' since anything we ask according to your will we receive. I'm glad they're willing to take on this responsibility. Please bless them."

Sherry prayed, "Thank you heavenly Father that I can see into the back yard right now, and see that the four children are having such a good time with Mindy, and none of them even know that I can see them. It's a blessing and answer to my prayer that these Saturday mornings will be profitable and fun for the children, also."

Roy continued, "I agree with that prayer and thank you also. I can see that they're learning how to share and get along, and that's something we as parents haven't been able to provide as an opportunity."

Tomo added, "LORD, thank you for caring, Christian parents for small children. Continue to give them the guidance they need as they raise their children to know and love and serve you."

Ami prayed, "Father in heaven, thank you that we know that you will continue to work in the lives of our grown children also. May your will be done."

Larry and Jane both said at once: "Yes, LORD, we agree with all these prayers."

Don and Anita got up and motioned for Jeff and Karen to follow them to Julie's chair. He told her, "We would like to lay our hands on you as in Acts 6:6, and consecrate you to your new teaching position." She agreed, started the recording again so Pam could hear it, and bowed her head.

They asked God to: "Bless her with wisdom, grace, and the knowledge needed to handle every situation every day, and thanked him for her willingness to step in and take over for a needy fellow Christian and church school classroom partway through the school year. Give her peace and the ability to take over this position in such a way that she and the children all feel comfortable with the transition. Thank you that Julie was able to spend the whole day with the class on Friday, so she learned a lot about the different way of teaching, and that the class is already starting to feel comfortable with her. Take away any remaining awkwardness that any of them might feel, and assist them to all work together right from the start and throughout the rest of the school year." And everybody said, "AMEN."

Anita inquired, "I can see that we're running a little late. Would it be satisfactory with everybody if we invite Mindy and all the children to come inside and eat refreshments with us?" They all agreed, and she went to call them inside. The children were thrilled to get to come eat with all the grown-ups, and Mindy was pleased, also. The adults enjoyed visiting and watching the children as they interacted with each other and their parents. The twins were a little shy with the people they didn't know, but Timmy and Mary came right over and visited with Ted and Julie since they had seen them several times recently. Mindy went over to stand by Fiona so they could visit for a while. She had known her before she left and was glad to see her again. Fiona was pleased that she remembered her and they had a nice talk.

After the meeting, the ones who had walked also enjoyed the walk home and many of them commented on how awesome God was and how good the teaching time was with such a good suggestion of a way they could do a better job of studying at home. They were thankful for the pastor's practical ways they could improve their study times. The prayer time was awe-inspiring also. They even had a new member even though she would be an absentee one. They were amazed at the love they could feel for someone they barely knew. They would continue to pray for her and her family, and of course they would remember to pray for Julie as she started teaching on Monday.

*****

Roy and Sherry exclaimed over the nice job Joy and Hope had done on their pictures, and as soon as they got home, Sherry put them up on the refrigerator. Then she asked, "What did you enjoy about the morning at the Ross house? Hope, you answer first this time."

Hope responded, "I liked when Mindy hid things in the yard for us to find. After that she had each of us hide the thing we found so the others could look for it. We had to find a different thing than the one we hid."

Then Joy added, "It was really fun making up funny stories about the second thing we found. We made so much noise laughing about them that she made us move to the far side of the yard, so we would not bother you guys. At first I didn't like coming inside to eat with all the grownups. It was scary. But then everyone was nice to us, so it was okay then."

"Timmy's story was the funniest. He's a very nice boy and always shares things with us," added Hope.

"Mary is so cute. She tries to be big enough to play with us and when she can't do something, all three of us try to help her. Mindy says that it's important for us to learn how to get along with each other," said Joy.

"Yeah," agreed Hope. "Since three of us will be in kindergarten this coming year, I'm glad we get to practice with Mary and Timmy on Saturdays."

Roy concurred, "Yes, we all thank you, heavenly Father, for that blessing, and that Joy and Hope are enjoying their time at the Ross house. Now, how about a nap for you two while your mom and I fix lunch?"

They both yawned and said that was a good idea, as they hurried to their room.

Sherry gave Roy a big hug and kiss. Then she said, "You were right. God did work it all out, and it's so much better than I could have ever planned it to be. Our girls are getting some of the benefit of Anita's daycare teaching from Mindy, Timmy, and Mary. What a blessing!"

*****

Matt and Fiona had walked separately to the meeting, but of course they walked to Fiona's house together, and as they walked, they talked. Fiona said, "I feel an extra connection to Pam Green since her situation is somewhat like mine was. But hers will be so much harder, since her parents are not believers. I remember meeting her at church, but didn't have much chance to get to know her. This would have been her third year at the school and I was gone for two of them. Oh well, I don't need to know her well to pray for her. We have all the information we need to know about her to continue to pray for her, and Julie will keep us informed about new things she learns in e-mails. Isn't our world amazing?"

Matt agreed and suggested that they pray together about Pam and Julie both whenever they got to spend time together. Fiona agreed, and it was the beginning of a very nice afternoon.

When then they arrived at the O'Connor home, Glenda hugged Fiona like she had been gone a week, and then enthusiastically greeted Matt because she was also genuinely happy to see him again.

A little later Matt complimented Glenda, "This is a very delicious lunch. I'm always so glad when someone invites me to eat a meal with them, because my cooking is definitely not good. You're a fantastic cook, Glenda, and so is Fiona."

"Thank you for the compliments, Matt. This lunch <u>was</u> a joint effort and we're glad you like it," Glenda replied.

When the meal ended, Glenda tried to get them to just leave the dishes until later so they could have more time outside playing, but Matt disagreed, "If we <u>all</u> help, it won't take us long and they're so much easier to clean up before they get dried on. Please let us all work on it together so we can enjoy the play time without dirty dishes hanging over our heads." He talked her into it and in very short order everything was washed and put away.

Fiona asked him, "Do you like to play croquet, Matt?"

"Yes!" he responded. "It used to be one of my favorite lawn games and your lawn is just right for it." Then he suggested to her parents, "How about if Fiona and I go out and get it set up while you two relax inside?"

Patrick answered, "That sounds like a good idea. Thank you, Matt."

Matt carried the equipment, following Fiona out into the back yard. They set up the stakes and wickets and laid out the mallets and balls where the players could choose their color. He asked Fiona what her favorite color was so he would be sure to <u>not</u> choose that one. Then they went inside to tell Patrick and Glenda that everything was ready. When they got outside, Matt told them, "Your yard is beautiful, so well cared for and inviting. I hope when I get my yard landscaped it will look as nice at yours does."

Patrick thanked him and they all chose the color they wanted and started the first game. Matt noticed that Fiona <u>did</u> get to have her favorite color. The games were fast and exciting, with each player having the fun of knocking another ball away from its place on the lawn. After four games Matt had lost three times and won once, and remained contented either way. Fiona had won twice and lost twice and laughed each time. The group picked up all the equipment and while Patrick put it away, Matt and Fiona carried refreshments out to the porch where they continued visiting while they got refreshed. Glenda asked Matt what he thought about the sermon last week, and he had nothing but positive comments about it and about the small group meeting that morning. Fiona agreed, adding her share of accolades. Patrick and Glenda both agreed about the Sunday service and they all praised God for the people who had made their decision to ask Jesus to be their Savior.

After Matt had gone home, Glenda asked Fiona if Matt had passed all the tests for the day. She nodded and answered, "Yes, he passed with flying colors, and this morning when Don was berating himself, Matt told him not to be hard on himself. I still think he's wonderful."

*****

When Matt got home from the O'Connor's house, he was very pleased with the way the afternoon had gone. It had been fun and uplifting. They were nice people and he enjoyed spending time with them. Suddenly he thought about another family which he had not remembered since Fiona had returned. So he called the Clay household and asked to speak to Ben. "Hi, Ben, this is Matt. How are you? ... ... I want to apologize for not calling you lately. My mind has been occupied with Fiona being back home. ... ... Thank you, Ben, for your forgiveness and understanding. Now that she and I have been able to talk and do some planning, I know that I will either have Saturday afternoons, or Sunday mornings to work on my house, and I would like to hire you to help me one partial day a week. ... ... But a workman is worthy of his wages. ... ... Okay. If you're sure. It <u>would</u> be a good way for you to learn about building. That way we can talk and I can answer any of your questions while we're working. ... ... Yes, I do have tomorrow morning free, but the forecast is for rain tomorrow. ... ... Could you come over to my apartment at 9 AM and we can get caught up on whatever questions you may have desired to ask the past couple weeks? ... ... Great, I'll see you here tomorrow morning about 9 and if you want to bring a lunch we can talk longer and go to church together after that. ... ... Good-bye."

*****

The third Sunday in April

The Sunday after Easter, Jason woke to the sound of rain on the roof, so he rolled over and tried to go back to sleep. He didn't like rain. In fact lately, he didn't like much of anything. Nothing seemed to be going the way he wanted it to go. He tossed and turned for a while, finally gave up, got out of bed, and went to take a long hot shower to cover up the noise of the rain. That worked for a time, but the water started cooling off, so he had to stop. Then he turned on some classical music and all it did was remind him of how Maria had seemed to enjoy the music at the restaurant that Thursday when all his plans had gone down the drain.

He finally fixed and ate breakfast. Then he had to clean up the mess he had made because everything he tried to do while he fixed breakfast went wrong. Breakfast had not even tasted good. He could feel his emotions spiraling downward and finally remembered he had forgotten to take his medicine. He took it, and it made him sleepy so he went back to bed for a couple hours. When he woke up, he decided to skip church because he was already late.

Later in the morning, he opened up the Bible Maria had given him and read the note again. The last few times he had read it, he had gotten angry all over again, not at her but at her father. Today, he didn't feel as angry, so he decided to look up the verses and try to read them. They still didn't make sense to him, so he decided to try it another day.

*****

The Sunday after Easter it was raining, but the congregation was thankful for the moisture since it had not rained much lately. Pastor Don noticed that Mindy whispered something to her dad, and then they maneuvered so that Mindy could sit next to Candy who smiled and said, "Hi." Don was pleased and knew that Mindy was really trying.

Ted and Julie stood in the entry to watch for her former boss and his wife so they could welcome them to church and ask if they would like to sit with them. Maria had already agreed to go and sit with Ruth and Esther, so their visitors would not feel awkward. Julie was thrilled when they entered. She hurried over to greet them, meet his wife, and then introduce Ted. They were glad to be able to sit with someone they sort of knew. Julie sat beside his wife and whispered a few helpful instructions to her about the songs being in the hymnals with the titles and page numbers on the display board at the front of the sanctuary. "You're welcome to stand or sit during the singing time." She finished. After that she had time to find the first song and read through the verses before the singing began.

Today they sang more songs about the resurrection of Jesus: "Hallelujah, What a Savior," Isaiah 53:3; "Jesus is Alive," Matthew

28:6; and "Wounded for Me" 1 Corinthians 15:3,4. Since their guests remained seated for the singing time, Ted and Julie did also, so their guests would not feel embarrassed.

Pastor Don began his teaching time by saying, "Did you ever wonder why the resurrection of Jesus Christ is so important? Look up Romans 1:2-4, and follow along with me." *The gospel of God was promised by God's prophets in the holy scriptures, concerning his Son, Jesus Christ our Lord, who was of the seed of David according to the flesh, and declared to be the Son of God with power, according to the spirit of holiness, <u>by the resurrection from the dead</u>.* "That one makes the answer pretty clear. Now find Acts 2: 24, and read it aloud with me: *God Raised Jesus up, having loosed him from the pains of death, because it was not possible that he could be held by it.*

"King David prophesied that the promised Messiah would *not see corruption,* that is in Acts 2:27, and in verses 30-32 it says, *Therefore, being a prophet, and knowing that God had sworn with an oath to him, that one of his offspring would sit on his throne. David, seeing this before, spoke of the resurrection of Christ, that his soul was not left in hell, neither did his flesh see corruption. God has raised up this Jesus, and we (his disciples) are all witnesses.* So, the resurrection proved that Jesus was the Son of God, and also proved that he was the Messiah who had been prophesied so many times in the Old Testament.

"Today I would like to read to you about three people who were told by <u>eye witnesses</u> about Jesus being raised from the dead, but they would not believe it at first. Please turn in the Bible to Luke 24:13-48, and follow along with me. *On the afternoon of the day Jesus had risen from the grave, two of his followers were walking to a village called Emmaus. ... As they walked, they talked together of all the things which had happened, and while they were talking, Jesus himself came near to them and went with them. But their eyes were kept from being able to recognize him. He asked them, 'What are you talking about as you walk and are sad?' One of them whose name was Cleopas answered, 'Are you only a stranger in Jerusalem, and have you not known the things which happened there the last few days?' Jesus asked, 'What things?' They answered, 'Concerning Jesus of Nazareth who was a prophet mighty in deed and word before God and all the people; and how the chief priests and our rulers delivered him to be condemned to death, and have crucified him. But we had hoped that he was going to redeem Israel. Beside all this, today is the third day since these things were done. Besides that, some women of our group astonished us by going to the grave early this morning and could not find his body. They came and said that they had seen angels who said that he was alive.' ... Jesus said to them, 'O fools, and slow of heart to believe all that the prophets have spoken. Didn't Christ have to suffer these things, and enter into his glory?' And beginning at Moses and all the prophets, he explained to them in all the scriptures the things concerning himself.*

"As they drew close to the village, he acted as though he would go further, but they constrained him, saying, 'Stay with us, for it is almost evening.' So he went in to stay with them. As they were ready to eat, he took bread and blessed it, and broke it and gave it to them. Then their eyes were opened, and they knew him, but he vanished out of their sight. They said to each other, 'Didn't our hearts burn within us, while he talked with us on the way and opened the scriptures?' They got up that same hour and returned to Jerusalem where they found the disciples gathered together, and others who were with them saying, 'The Lord is risen indeed, and has appeared to Simon.' The two told what things were done on their way and how he was made known to them in breaking the bread.

"As they were telling this, Jesus himself stood in the midst of them and said, 'Peace be unto you.' But they were terrified and frightened and supposed that they had seen a spirit. He asked them, 'Why are you troubled? Why do thoughts arise in your hearts? Look at my hands and my feet. See it is I myself. Handle me, and see, for a spirit does not have flesh and bones as you can see that I have.'

"When he had spoken this, he showed them his hands and feet. And while they still believed not for joy, and wondered, he said, 'do you have any meat here?' They gave him a piece of a broiled fish, and of honeycomb. He took it and ate it before them. Then he said to them, 'These are the words which I spoke to you while I was still with you, that all the things must be fulfilled, which were written in the law of Moses and in the prophets and in the psalms, concerning me.'

"Then he opened their understanding of the scriptures, saying, 'It was written that Christ must suffer and to rise from the dead the third day, and that repentance and remission of sins should be preached in his name among all nations, beginning at Jerusalem. You are witnesses of these things.'

"Now turn to John 20: 24-31. *But Thomas, one of the twelve, ... was not with them when Jesus came. The other disciples therefore said to him, 'We have seen the Lord.' But he said to them, 'unless I see the print of the nails in his hands and put my finger in to the print of the nails and thrust my hand into his side, I will not believe.' And after eight days again, the disciples were within, and Thomas was with them. Then Jesus came, the doors being shut, and stood in the midst of them and said, 'Peace be unto you.' Then he said to Thomas, 'Reach here your finger and behold my hands, and reach here your hand and thrust it into my side. Do not be faithless, but believe.' And Thomas answered, 'My Lord and My God.' Jesus said to him, 'Thomas, because you have seen me, you have believed. Blessed are those who have not seen, and yet have believed.'*

"Perhaps you've heard the Easter story often, and have wondered if it could really be true, just like the three people I just finished reading about in the Bible. If that's the case for you, Jesus will probably not come and show himself to you like he did to those three, but you can be blessed like Jesus said, because even without seeing him in the flesh, you can still believe that he is risen, and that he is the promised Messiah and Savior. You can also agree with all the words in the hymn we sang earlier that Jesus was wounded and dying and risen for you, and is now living in Heaven and is praying for you to believe in him so that he can come for you also, when he returns for all other believers.

"If you would like to believe in Jesus as your own personal Savior you can do that right now. Let's all bow our heads and close our eyes while we thank our Savior for all he did for us and while I lead anyone who wants to believe in Jesus, in a prayer that they can repeat after me silently. I'll say it slowly so you can think about it and keep up. God, I realize that I am a sinner. ... ... I confess these sins to you. ... ... Name silently, the ones you think of. ... ... Please forgive me. ... ... Thank you that you already paid the price for my sins by dying on the cross, ... and that God raised you from the dead. ... ... I believe in you and ask you to be my Savior. ... ... Amen. If any of you prayed that prayer with me silently, please tell somebody here about it right after the service is over. And if you'll also come and tell me, I have a booklet I would like to give you that explains more in detail what it all means, and what steps you'll want to take next.

"Now I have a special song that tells the story about the two followers walking toward Emmaus. It is based on Luke 24:13-48 which I read to you earlier. If you are believers in Jesus and all he did for us, feel free to praise and thank him in a way that you would like to, after the song is over." Pastor Don played the song, which ends with such a joyful celebration that all the believers in the congregation did join in by either raising their arms to heaven or kneeling to worship or praise Jesus out loud for being their redeemer and filling them with such joy. After a while it quieted down and he reminded those who had prayed the prayer with him to tell someone about it and to come see him. He also reminded the ones from last week to come and give him the card that was included in the booklet. Then he dismissed them by saying, "Now let us all go in the joy of the Lord, because Jesus is risen!"

And the congregation answered. "He is risen indeed!" It had been a thrilling service again, like the one last week had been. As the people got up and started moving around, Julie's former boss and wife told Ted and Julie that they had prayed that prayer. Julie hugged them both and Ted shook their hands and then welcomed them into the family of God, telling them that everyone who believes in Jesus is a child of God. Then they took them to the pastor and introduced them to him, staying with them while they told of their decision. They filled the card out on the spot and gave it back to the pastor, stating that they could hardly wait to get to know more about the great God who made so many things work out for the good of so many people last week.

Many others came up to the pastor and told him they had prayed the prayer also, including a few who had been attending the church for months, but had not been convinced until today, that they needed Jesus to be their Savior. Pastor Don was overjoyed and welcomed each of them into God's family. He gave each person or couple a booklet with a card to take home. Then, others came to give him the cards they had filled out from last week. He told them he would call them very soon about a meeting time and place for their first small group meeting.

*****

Maria waited at the back of the sanctuary for Ted and Julie. They had big smiles and hugs for her too. There was no need to tell her about the couple who had visited and sat with them. She had seen them go up to talk to the pastor, and was thrilled for them, also. When they looked outside, they could see that it was still raining, so they decided to drive to the inside mall and walk back and forth in there for half an hour. This time Ted just walked along with them because they had asked him to listen to all they had to share with each other about the days since Wednesday.

Maria shared, "I'm really enjoying working for a Christian boss and becoming friends with Ruth and Esther. Our plan to make friends with our co-workers is working well so far. It is going to be slow, but eventually we'll have a chance to witness to them. Just think; if it had not been for the situation with Jason, none of these other things would have happened. Maybe it was all a part of God's plan and not a big mistake we all made, after all. Ruth, Esther and I all prayed together at lunch on Friday for Jason's salvation and healing. We're all hoping he will be driven to God by his upset over not being able to control this situation."

"That sounds like a good thing to hope for," responded Ted. "It <u>is</u> amazing how God can work things out for the good of many people in such a short time."

"For sure!" exclaimed Julie. "When I told my former boss about the word of knowledge and then how God had worked out so many things for good, he decided to come to church so that he could get to know a God like that, and now he and his wife are believers. He's another Christian boss in the workplace. I have a feeling he will do a good job of witnessing to his co-workers too. I just realized that I now have a Christian boss also. We need to pray that Ted's boss will become a believer too." Then she gave Maria a summary of how Thursday and Friday had gone for her. "I'm overwhelmed by the greatness and goodness of our God. Did you know Pam Green, Maria?"

"Yes," she answered. "She was in my small group on Tuesdays. She told us that she had to resign her teaching job and go take care of her mother who had just had a stroke. We all went and helped her pack up her things on Saturday so she could leave this morning. Oh, wow! <u>She</u> must be the one you're replacing. It never dawned on me that she taught in the church school. I thought she was in the public school system."

"It sure is amazing, the way it all worked out," commented Julie. "But she's going to need our prayers for all she's going through. She and I will correspond by e-mail. May I tell her you'll be praying for her also?"

"Of course. I wish I had thought to tell her that before she left," lamented Maria.

"Don't kick yourself about it, Maria," cautioned Ted. "God will take care of it all. Just look at what he's already done! Now, our walking time is up, so I need to get Julie home so she can study

Everywhere There's a Sunrise, Let's Tell The Good News!

names to go with the faces on the pictures she has, and some other things she needs to do in order to be ready for her first day of teaching those precious third graders tomorrow."

They walked back to their cars and said good-bye. "I'll call you sometime this week to let you know how it's going, Maria. God bless you," said Julie.

"And I'll continue to pray for you this week too, Julie. God bless you both," replied Maria.

*****

While the twins were having an after-church-nap, Sherry said to Roy, "Since we were at the Ross house for the small group meeting on Saturday, and I saw how well the children all got along, an idea has been growing that I would like to try if you agree to it. It would be wonderful if they could spend a couple mornings a week with the whole group in the daycare. I would like to call Anita tomorrow and ask her if she has any work I could do for her on Tuesday and Thursday mornings like from 8 AM until noon. During that time the girls could be a part of her daycare, and the work I would do for her would pay their way. I would take them home for lunch and the rest of the day with me and then you. It would give Hope and Joy a chance to learn some of the songs and hear some of the Bible stories that are a part of the church daycare program, and that will be continued in Kindergarten. Plus they'll learn how to get along with a larger group of children."

"It sounds like you've really thought this idea through and your reasons are very good. I like the idea, but I wonder if you really have that much time of your own to give to the project. Will you have time to do your own work at home, and might you be too tired to work well at your evening employment after working all morning?" he asked.

"Those are both very good questions which I have asked myself over and over. I think that I can rearrange my routine for those two days and work extra hard at home on Mondays, Wednesdays, and Fridays, so that I can keep up with my own housework. I always rest while the twins are napping in the afternoon, so I should be fresh enough to do my work at Wal-Mart in the evenings. My energy level is very good, for which I'm thankful. We could try it for a week or two and see how it works. We'll never know unless we try it," she finished.

"Okay," Roy gave in, "as long as you're willing to stop doing it if you begin to feel too tired. I'll be willing to pitch in and help more on Tuesdays and Thursdays in the afternoons when I get home from work, as long as you give me something I think I can do. I would like to see the twins have that extra opportunity also. Father in heaven we ask that you will guide us with this idea and for your will to be done."

"Thank you, Roy, for agreeing, and for praying for us," said Sherry. "Do you think you could run the vacuum on Tuesdays, and clean the bathrooms on Thursdays. Those take the most energy and time, but I don't wish to overwork you either. So you must tell me if you're getting too tired also."

"Yes, I could do both of those things. This whole project is a joint, team effort for us as parents of twins. I know we both want the best for them, but we must also do what's best for us as a married couple. This idea is only for the rest of this year anyway, since they'll start school in January, so maybe it won't be too hard for us to do," Roy mentioned. "Let's try it and see how it goes for a couple of weeks if Anita agrees to it, that is. If not we've had a good discussion in any case."

*****

The Clays were having a nice quiet Sunday evening meal with just the four of them and time for conversation about various topics. Ernest started by saying, "I'm surprised and pleased about all the new believers, especially this Sunday! I'll bet there will be a baptismal service sometime soon."

"For sure. That was a very good teaching time, and I'm so glad that some of the people who have been attending the church services for a few months have now joined us as fellow believers," Connie agreed.

"The song Pastor Don played at the end is one of my favorites and so is that story in the Bible. It must have been so exciting for the disciples to be able to see that Jesus had indeed risen from the dead!" Amelia exclaimed.

Ben agreed with her and added, "I saw a girl from my class at school go talk to the pastor with her family. I'm so glad for them. It is extra special, because I gave her one of those invitations a couple weeks ago. They didn't come last week, but they did this week, and now they're part of God's family!"

"Wow! That _is_ thrilling," responded Connie. "I think Easter is my favorite holiday and it's such a good time to explain to people about why Jesus came to earth and lived a perfect life so he could be a perfect sacrifice and provide salvation to all who will believe in him." They all agreed with her, and then she asked, "Amelia, how is your new job going? We haven't had much time to talk lately."

She answered, "I really like it. It is especially enjoyable to work with Fiona, but I'm also fond of working with all the different plants. They're very pretty and it's nice to know that I'm helping to nurture them and keep them looking nice so people will want to buy them and have them in their own homes to enjoy. Also it was fun to do your grocery shopping on Thursday, since you had such a good list made out. I was able to buy a couple things I have needed. How are things going for you Ben? With my new job, I don't see as much of you as before."

He responded, "School is fine, particularly since I decided <u>not</u> to do 'college prep.' and therefore I don't have those hard math courses. They would not help me in building anyway. Matt called me last evening and apologized for not having as much time as he did before Fiona came back to Pine City. Then he asked me to come over to his apartment this morning so that we could get caught up on any questions I had. He would like me to work with him on his house either Saturday afternoon or Sunday morning each weekend, depending on which time he's not on a date with Fiona. He offered to pay me, but I told him the experience and having him answer my questions and teach me what he knows will be plenty of pay. It might even help me decide which branch I want to major in, or if I would want to become a contractor."

"Super!" Amelia exclaimed. "I'm glad for you. Matt seems like a very nice man, and I think he and Fiona make a nice couple. I haven't had the nerve to ask her how their time together is going. It's really none of my business anyway."

"I like your good thinking, Amelia," her dad praised her. "She'll probably volunteer some information on her own after she knows more about the relationship herself, and when she gets to know you better. They're both extremely nice people and I'm glad you both get to spend some time with them separately."

"Thank you all for sharing in our Sunday evening meal conversation time. During the week we don't have much time to be together for meals with all the funny hours at The Garden Shop, so this has been a lovely evening. Who would like to help me with the cleanup?" Connie asked.

They all volunteered and since it went so fast, they had time for a fun Bible board game together before bedtime.

Linda L. Linn

*****

Before going to bed Sunday night, Julie checked her e-mail, and found one from Pam. She excitedly opened it and read: "Hi, Julie, I arrived safely at home after eight hours of driving mixed with a few stops for various reasons. I'm tired, but I thank God for a safe trip. My dad was pleased and relieved to see me. He said he didn't know what he would have done if I had not been able to come home to help. He thanked me for coming, and told me to thank you for helping make it possible. Of course I could not say that it was God who made it <u>all</u> possible. Maybe some day I'll be able to tell him that and a lot of other things that I learned while attending church and small groups in Pine City. I already miss it, but when I get settled in, I intend to look up the church's web site and listen to the service. I'm so glad you gave me that idea! I think I'll go to bed now. I'll be praying for you and the third graders. I'll pray that God will bless and help you all. Good night from Pam."

Julie answered it right away: "Hi, Pam, I hope you're sleeping right now, but I wanted to answer your e-mail as soon as I could, and send you the attachments of our small group teaching time, plus the prayers that were said for you and the consecration prayers that were said for me. I think we're both in God's <u>good</u> hands and that he will continue to help us both. I'm glad to hear that you had a safe trip and that your dad appreciates you coming. If you want, you can tell him that I said that he's welcome and that I was glad to be used by God to make 'it' possible. Maybe you could tell him my part of the story and how God worked out so many things for the good of many people." Then she told him about her boss agreeing to bring his wife to church and their decision to receive Jesus as their Savior today. "I'm so pleased, thankful and amazed at all God has done in these situations. We'll all keep praying for you and your family and I'm anticipating more miracles. Oh, Maria Gomez, who is in the same small group as you were, told me to tell you that she'll be praying for you also. Thank you for praying for our third graders and me. So long for now. I'll look forward to your next e-mail. God bless you, from Julie"

*****

Chapter 11

Everywhere There's a Sunrise, Let's Tell The Good News!

Read the words of the hymn, "Take My Life and Let It Be"

Monday

    Julie woke early Monday morning and got up, since she was too excited to go back to sleep. It wasn't because she was nervous, because she felt confident and at peace. She was just eager to get started. After packing her lunch and Ted's, she put a book about koalas and her koala puppet into a small backpack to keep them clean as they were carried to school along with her lunch and a suggestion/comment box that she had used in her other classes. Her purse was always carried separately. Then she made a nutritious breakfast for them to enjoy.

    Ted came into the kitchen when breakfast was ready and gave thanks for the food and for his wonderful wife, and asked God to bless her with wisdom and the grace to handle this first day of her new teaching position.

    Julie passed around the food and stated, "Ted, you're definitely my treasure. I'm so blessed to have such a caring, godly husband, who prays for just the things I need. Thank you, and I know that you'll pray for me off and on today also. Remember that my work hours are now fifteen minutes earlier and later than they were before so we'll have to adjust to that. But I don't think it will be very hard."

    "No, we'll do just fine. God is faithful and will give us the help we need," Ted agreed. "This is a delicious breakfast. Thank you for making it. I'll do the cleanup. Go ahead and finish getting ready for your day, so you can leave a little early."

    "Thank you so much, Ted, for your good idea," she agreed. "I need to ask Beth a question on the way to <u>my classroom</u>. Wow! It sounds <u>so</u> good to be able to say that again."

    "I'm very glad for you and I'm really proud of you," he said as he hugged her before she left for the school. Then he cheerfully did the cleanup and took his lunch with him as he walked to his own employment.

*****

    Mid-morning, on Monday, Sherry Foster called Anita Ross while her girls were having their morning nap so that they would not hear her and be disappointed if the plan didn't work. She was in hopes that the daycare children were resting right now also.

She told Anita that she had discussed an idea with Roy on Sunday, and had gotten his approval to try it for a couple weeks and then continue if she didn't get too tired. Then she went on to explain her idea, like she had to Roy. Anita liked it and said she did have some housework and projects that would fit into the plan perfectly, since she knew what a good seamstress Sherry was. She would need to ask Don when he got home. If he agreed to it, she would call Roy, since Sherry would be at work by then and he could tell her when she got home. If they got a green light, Sherry could start tomorrow. Anita took a few minutes to explain what she would like Sherry to do when she arrived, since she would not have time to do it in the morning with a houseful of children. She also reminded Sherry to bring mats for the girls' nap time.

*****

 Matt was pleased with this sunny, warm Monday morning because he would have a chance to work on his house some more today. Things were progressing a little faster than they did before Fiona returned, and he was sure that it was because he had so much more incentive, now that she was back home. As he worked he tried to figure out whether it would be best to try to plan to always work on the house on Saturday afternoons, or Sunday mornings, and which day would be best to plan for time with Fiona. His mind just went round and round about it, so he decided to pray and ask God to help him know what would be <u>God's will</u>, and of course that would be the best.
 He returned to his apartment after about two and a half hours of productive work, and checked the weather forecast on his computer. Tomorrow looked like another nice warm, sunny morning so he decided it might be a good day to take Fiona to a park to practice throwing Frisbees. He called her and they set the time for 9:30 the next morning. It was nice to have that to look forward to as he ate lunch and got ready to go to the job site.

*****

 After saying "Hi" to the secretary, Julie stopped at the principal's office and greeted her. Then she asked, "Is it okay if I bring some of the teaching materials I have at home, so I can use them here? Today I brought my puppet since I told Miss Green she could take hers with her."

Everywhere There's a Sunrise, Let's Tell The Good News!

"Certainly," answered Beth. "Just be aware that you might not have time to incorporate very many of your own materials into the already very busy lesson plans. But it _is_ nice to have something extra to fall back on if you finish a project early. I'm glad you have your own puppet so she could take hers when she left. She was much more at peace when she left. I think it helped her that you could spend the day here on Friday."

"I'm glad to hear that. I know it helped _me_ immensely!" Julie said.

Beth asked, "You know where the intercom is located in your room, don't you?" Julie nodded. "If you need me, just call and I'll be there. That goes for the rest of the year also. It is good to have a plan for emergencies."

"Thank you, Beth. It _is_ good to know that," Julie responded. "I'll go now and get ready for the children."

Julie felt like skipping down the hallway to _her_ classroom, because she was so enthusiastic. She put the book and Kippy in his new 'home' near the nice carpet, and her other things in the closet. She would just bring a few things a day from home in her backpack so that she could put them away more quickly and easily than a whole box at a time. Next, she looked at the lesson plans for this date and got things ready for the first hours, and then took out the plans for the parent volunteer also and read through them so she could answer any questions there might be.

Just as she was finishing that, the volunteer arrived and they introduced themselves. The parent told Julie how thankful he was that she was here as the permanent teacher and not just a substitute. He informed her which child was his, and then looked over his plans for the day. Since he didn't have any questions, he went and got right to work. Therefore Julie had a chance to do a few more things to be ready for the first part of the morning until recess. She would get to prepare for the next part of the day during recess.

As the children came inside, many of them said, "Good morning, Mrs. Blake," and she greeted them by name. After the opening pledges, song and prayer, when they were seated, she asked them if they knew the difference between Miss and Mrs. and Mr. They nodded, and she left it at that. She could tell that they missed Miss Green, but that they were also glad to see her now familiar face. She thanked them for putting on their name tags, and the way they were going to help her by being patient as she got used to the new school. The morning went very well and very rapidly.

After lunch, at the class meeting, there weren't very many problems to discuss and solve so Julie showed them a small box with a slit in the lid and a lock on the clasp, and explained, "This is a suggestion / comment box with the words, 'Dear Mrs. Blake,' on the front. If you have a comment you want only me to hear or you have a suggestion of something you would like to do or learn about, please write me a note about it. Put your name on it, so that I can talk to you about it the next day, after I pray about it at home. I'll put the box back here on the counter beside the classroom sink, so you can put your notes into it on the way back to your desk after getting a drink. Now, what time is it, class?"

They answered, "It's one o'clock and time for Science." They went quietly to their seats and were ready to watch a video about ice, which went very well with the experiment they had done on Friday. When it was over they discussed it and volunteered things they would like to add to their science notebooks about ice, while their new teacher printed them on the chalkboard. They copied the facts neatly into their notebooks.

After some exercises, they met at the carpet for story time. She read the book listed in the lesson plans, and they discussed it. Then with a little extra time left over, she read the book she had brought about koalas. The title was "I'm Not a Bear." The book has many facts and photographs about koalas that she wanted them to understand before she introduced her puppet at sharing time.

The rest of the afternoon went as well and as fast as the morning had, and already it was sharing time. When the children were all seated on the carpet, Mrs. Blake explained that Miss Green had taken her puppet with her since it belonged to her. "Today I brought a puppet that belongs to me, and he really is eager to see you." Then she introduced her puppet. "This is a koala puppet, and his name is Kippy because one of the meanings of 'kip' is to nap or sleep, and koalas sleep a lot. So does Kippy. Say his name, and notice that your face smiles as you say it. Now, say "Hi, Kippy.'"

They did, and he responded, "Hi, children, I'm *so* glad to see you. I really like listening and talking to children. Does anybody have a question to ask me or something you would like to share?" They listened and watched the puppet moving and didn't seem to notice or care that Mrs. Blake was the one moving and talking for him. She made her voice sound like a small animal might sound. It was fun to pretend that he was doing it by himself.

Everywhere There's a Sunrise, Let's Tell The Good News!

The children and Kippy spent several minutes with questions, answers, and things to share, and not one of them goofed and asked, "Are you a bear?" One said he was better than a bear, even though he was a boy and didn't have a pouch like the mama koalas did. Some even shared a few of the facts they had learned about koalas from the book Mrs. Blake had read to them at story time. Julie was impressed as she put Kippy back in his 'home' and was glad that the children had enjoyed their time with the new puppet.

Then it was prayer time. Several of the children were thankful that they had gotten to meet Mrs. Blake on Friday, because it wasn't as scary today as it would have been. Others were grateful that they didn't have to have a substitute until a permanent teacher was found. A couple even thanked God for the cute new puppet. Many of them remembered to pray for Miss Green as she took care of her mother. One of them thanked God for the new things they were learning every day. Another was thankful for nicer weather making it more fun to play outside. Mrs. Blake added, "Thank you, heavenly Father for this excellent class of third graders and the way they've helped me today. Please continue to help us work together and learn all the things we need to learn this year." Everyone said, "Amen."

The day concluded with practicing scripture memory verses with their partners, as their new teacher, Mrs. Blake happily walked around and listened to them. During that time she was also able to go over and thank the parent volunteer for his good help that day. When they were lined up, ready to go home, she reminded them about keeping everything in their hands as they walked or ran around the playground while they waited for their parents. Just before they left, she said, "Bye, see you tomorrow!" Many answered the same way. It was a much happier closing to the day than Friday had been, and she was relieved that they had accepted her so easily. Beth came in briefly to ask her how her first day had gone, and she was glad to tell her that it had been very good.

After putting a few things away and straightening others, Julie was able to leave just after 5:15, hurry home, help Ted finish fixing supper, and enthusiastically tell him all about her first day back as a teacher. She was tired, but it was a good tired, and she didn't even have a bunch of papers to check!

Instead after clean up, she checked her e-mail and found one from Pam: "Hi, Julie. Mother came home from the hospital today, and it's so hard to see her now unable to do most things for herself. She is very frustrated and depressed. I don't blame her a bit. What a shock to be fine one minute and the next your whole lifestyle had been altered. I can tell your prayers are helping me to deal with the situation. Please keep them up. While she sleeps I've been studying about how to care for her. How did your school day go today? I think I need a diversion, so tell me a lot. Thanks, from Pam."

Julie answered immediately: "I'm so sorry that you and your parents have to be going through this hard trial. I can't even begin to imagine how hard it must be for all of you. Yes, I'll continue to pray for all of you. Okay, here is how my first day of teaching went." Then she gave a subject-by-subject description of the day, including cute things the children said and their prayers for Miss Green. She ended with: "All of them are precious. I love them already! Get a good sleep tonight and remember that Jesus is always with you and will help you. Bye for now, from Julie."

*****

Right after Monday's supper cleanup, Anita told Don about Sherry Foster's idea and was very glad when he agreed to it. She called Roy so that he could relay the message to Sherry. Then she and Don spent some time playing with Timmy and Mary before they told them that Joy and Hope would be coming to spend time with them and the other children on Tuesday and Thursday mornings this week. As they expected, the children were overjoyed, because they liked the twins. Then the family all got ready to go to the pastors' small group meeting.

*****

Tuesday

At breakfast on Tuesday morning, Don and Anita discussed their small group meeting of the night before. Don remarked, "I'm glad our main pastor is the one keeping track of, and planning for things like baptisms and new believer groups. I'll need to study the instructions again for new believers and get ready for the meetings." I've been so involved in the other things that have been occurring these last few weeks that I might forget to make these additional things happen.

Everywhere There's a Sunrise, Let's Tell The Good News!

"I can understand that!" Anita replied. "These have been the busiest weeks we've had in a long time. It was nice of Matt to caution you about being hard on yourself. God understands."

"You're right. Thank you, Honey," said Don. "So I need to choose a couple to be co-facilitators with us for three weeks and then to continue on their own. We will want to have the first meeting this week for those who returned their cards on the last three Sundays, and add the others who will return their cards this coming Sunday, so we can teach them about water baptism before the special evening service that churches 1, 2, 3, and 4 combine to have on Tuesday the week after next. The other churches will combine to use Wednesday and Thursday evenings that week. We can announce the special service at church next Sunday for those who would like to attend, especially if they know any of the people who will be baptized. Any small groups who meet on Tuesdays are welcome to come to the service in lieu of their group meeting."

"Right," she agreed, "and it's our turn to make sure the men's and women's showers and dressing rooms beside the baptismal are cleaned and in order for that night, and that the baptismal behind the stage is filled and the water is warm. It is so exciting, and I'm really pleased that God is adding to his church those who are being saved!"

"Amen to that. His plan and the way he carries it out is always the best. All we have to do is follow his leading and do the things he says to do. Did I tell you that Candy came and told me that she prayed the prayer with me this Sunday, and she is so thankful that I caught her stealing in the store and put her in that wonderful Safe/Care home. She's a believer now! One more branch rescued, and it is now grafted into Jesus, the true vine," Don exclaimed.

"Praise the Lord! That *is* wonderful. Mindy told me yesterday, and we had a nice praise time together," she said.

"And already the word of knowledge that Karen gave to Julie has brought in two new believers, besides being an answer to many prayers. Thank you heavenly Father," Don added. "I had better go get ready, or I'll be late for work. Please think about some ideas of couples who could be co-facilitators for the group and we can call them this evening."

"Okay. Here is your lunch. I love you. Have a good day," she responded with a hug and a kiss.

Just then her first daycare children arrived and she was off and running on her own busy day. At 8 AM Sherry and the twins arrived. Anita introduced them and their mother to the other children. Some of them asked, "How can we tell them apart?" The twins answered in unison that they would help them learn which one was which. Then Sherry went and got busy with the first sewing project of making a new dress for Mary. This was going to be fun for her also! Sewing without interruptions was unheard of after the twins had been born, not that she cared. The twins were precious.

*****

Tuesday, morning at 9:30 Matt arrived at Fiona's house and she was ready to go. The weather was just right for their plan to practice with Frisbees. They talked about various things as they went to the park, and remembered to pray together for Pam Green and Julie Blake before they got out of the pick-up.

Matt commented as they walked in the park, "It is such a beautiful day today." Then he started to sing, "Did you ever see the lawn so green, or the sky this blue? I think I got some of the words wrong there, and that's all I can remember of the song, but I just felt like singing this gorgeous spring morning."

She responded, "Oh, I couldn't agree more, and you're such fun to be with. I almost started to sing the song with you, but I couldn't remember the words either."

"Maybe we'll go see that movie again sometime. It was a funny one," he added as they walked along throwing their Frisbees up in the air and then catching them as they came down.

"That would be fun. Do you have any hints for me on how to throw this thing so it goes where I want it to go?" Fiona asked.

"No, I think we're like the blind leading the blind as far as these things go. Maybe I should have bought a book about how to do it, or at least looked it up on the web," he answered laughing.

"Oh well, let's find a big tree we can aim at and see what happens," she replied. So they located a nice big tree with a tall chain link fence behind it to help keep the Frisbees in the park. "If we start out pretty close to it, we might have half a chance to hit it. But let's not hit it too hard. I wouldn't want to damage the poor thing!"

"You're so fun and such a good sport," complimented Matt. "We can have fun with these things, even if we don't know how to throw them. The object of <u>this</u> game is to get close to the tree, and not go over the fence!"

Everywhere There's a Sunrise, Let's Tell The Good News!

They were almost in hysterics after about fifteen minutes of throwing the Frisbee but not getting anywhere near the tree. A couple of times the Frisbees almost went over the fence. They were having fun, but decided that it might help if they would drive over to the library and look up on the web just <u>how</u> to throw them.

They did that and when they got back to the park with their new knowledge, they were much more successful, and it wasn't even as tiring as before.

"I brought some apple juice in a cooler with some glasses. Would you like some while we sit on a bench and rest for a few minutes?" asked Matt.

"That sounds delicious!" Fiona exclaimed. "Thank you for being so thoughtful."

"You're welcome," he responded as he poured the juice for them.

As they were finishing the juice, Fiona suggested, "Let's go over to the Frisbee golf course and watch the players for a while. Maybe we can learn some more from observing, and my arm can rest. I don't want to tire it out so much that I can't do my work this afternoon and evening."

"Great idea. Neither of us should overdo throwing. We need to work up to it slowly," he agreed.

So they drove over to the course and were glad to see a foursome going around the course. They did learn a lot, mainly that the people didn't have Frisbees. One of the people explained, "You can use Frisbees on the course to practice, but if you want to compete, you'll need to have these special disks. That's the reason it's called 'disk golf.'"

After thanking the person for the information, Matt and Fiona decided to stick with just the Frisbees and to wait until Saturday afternoon or Sunday morning to practice again so their arms would have a chance to recuperate. He took her home and they thanked each other for a fun morning.

*****

This Tuesday, all the other people in the Saturday small group and Maria were having their normal days either already at work or getting ready to go if they had afternoon shifts. It was such a beautiful day that many of them were wishing they could be outside and enjoy it instead of working inside. Spring fever was affecting them. But everyone was thankful for their jobs, and decided to do everything as for the Lord, and to not complain.

Linda L. Linn

*****

    For some reason, Matt arrived at the work site fifteen minutes earlier than usual, and he was amazed to find that the first shift construction crew was already gone, and so was his boss. What had happened????? He looked around to see if a note had been left, but he couldn't find one.
    The next thought that entered his head was "Go check at the hospital." So, he locked up the house, and ran back out to his truck. Then he drove safely and quickly to the hospital, parked, and ran into the emergency entrance. "Has Walter Evans been admitted here today?" he asked the receptionist.
    "Yes, the ambulance brought him in just ten minutes ago. I assume you're Matt. His wife is in the waiting room and asked me to send you to her if you came in," she answered.
    "Thank you very much. I'll make a quick phone call and then go to her," he responded. Then he called Jeff Spencer, asked him to call everyone on the second shift and tell them to stay home because Walt is in the hospital. Then he asked Jeff to please hurry over to the hospital as soon as possible.
    When Betty saw Matt come into the waiting room, she rushed over to him, crying and babbling something about Walt waiting too long. Matt gave her his handkerchief and then took her into his arms and let her cry. When she had calmed down enough, he led her back to her seat and sat down beside her. "Can you tell me what happened?" he asked her.
    She was still crying, but she managed to say, "One of his co-workers called me from the job site and told me that Walt might have had a heart attack. They had called for the ambulance and wanted me to meet them here at the hospital. I haven't heard anything from the doctor yet. It seems like I've been here for hours, but I know it's not that long. Thank you for coming here."
    "You're very welcome. I arrived at the work site fifteen minutes earlier than I usually do, and nobody was there. I think the Lord told me to come to the hospital," he explained.
    Her tears started coming faster now, and she gasped, "What if he dies, or is already dead? He waited too long to decide to ask Jesus to be his Savior and he won't make it to heaven! We had talked about it again just last night and he wanted to wait until he could get you to pray the prayer with him, so he could get it right. Now it might be too late! I think I'm more upset about that than

anything else. Before I went to sleep last night, I prayed the prayer in the book and I know that Jesus is my Savior. I just wish he had joined me."

She was sobbing now, so Matt put an arm around her shoulder and pulled her close to him as he began to pray, "Father in heaven, thank you that Betty now believes in Jesus and he is her Savior. Please help her right now to feel your presence as you comfort her and fill her with your peace. Now we put Walt into your hands, knowing that you want his salvation even more than we do. May your will be done in this situation. We ask these things in Jesus name, Amen."

Betty was much more calm now and thanked Matt again. So Matt went over to talk to the two men who had followed the ambulance over from the job site. They told him about what had happened and when. "About 11:00 we had a kind of an emergency and he came over to help get everything back where it belonged and hold up the board that needed to be nailed back in place. Then he just naturally kept on working with us and none of us remembered that he was supposed to be sitting in his director's chair, and I guess he didn't either. Everything seemed to be going fine until around 12:00, when Walt grabbed at his chest and fell to the floor moaning. Somebody called 911 and the ambulance was quick to arrive. Everybody else went home a little early and we followed over here. Oh, no! We didn't think to get the key off Walt and lock up the house!"

"Don't worry. I locked it up just before I drove over here. Thank you for telling me about what happened." Matt replied, and went back to sit next to Betty.

Just then, the doctor came in and called for Betty. She took Matt's hand and took him with her. The doctor said, "Please come with me, Betty."

She answered, "I need to have Matt come also, since he's like a son to us."

The doctor agreed to that and they went into a small conference room, where he told them, "Walt has had a massive heart attack and is not expected to live. You may both come into his intensive care room, but he's not conscious right now, and he might not regain consciousness. I cannot give you much hope, but it will help if you can keep from loud crying and hysterics."

"Yes Sir," she replied. "We <u>will</u> control ourselves, because we do want to see him."

The doctor said, "Okay, then, follow me."

At least the doctor had prepared them to not expect him to be conscious when they saw him, but it was awful to see him unconscious with all the tubes, wires, and equipment around him. "I'll leave you with him for a few minutes, then we will need to continue working with him without you in here." With that statement the doctor went out and shut the door.

"Come with me to his bedside, Betty," said Matt. "We're going to pray together that God will heal Walt, and I need you to put your hands on Walt with me and agree with what I pray, because the Bible says that if two or more people agree about what is being prayed for, they will receive it." She did that willingly, and nodded and said, "yes" off and on. "Father in heaven, we ask in Jesus name that you will totally heal Walt's heart and give him the chance to accept Jesus as his Savior. **Walt, in Jesus name be healed!**" Matt said that last sentence more loudly than the rest, and Walt immediately opened his eyes and looked at them.

"Where am I, and what is all this stuff on me, and what are both of you doing here?" he asked.

Matt explained it all to him, including how upset and worried Betty had been about him not praying the prayer with her last night. Then Matt asked him, "How do you feel?"

"I feel perfectly fine, and I would like to pray with you right now to accept Jesus as my Savior."

The doctor came back in at that moment, and Betty went over to him with her finger to her lips to silence him. She whispered to him, "Please let Walt and Matt finish praying before you say or do anything else." For a wonder, he agreed.

Matt prayed, "Thank you heavenly Father for healing Walt and that he now wants to accept Jesus as his Savior." Then he said to Walt, "Just repeat after me: Jesus, I know that I am a sinner. ... ... I confess my sins to you, ... I ask you to forgive me. ... ... I know that believing in you, Jesus, is the only way to get to heaven. ... ... I do believe, and I accept you as my Savior. ... ... Thank you, Jesus, Amen."

Walt repeated each part with tears in his eyes until the last part when a huge smile lit up his face, and he exclaimed, "Yes, thank you Jesus for a second chance. Now I'll live the rest of my life for you! Betty, where did you go?" She hurried over to him and he said, "I'm sorry I didn't pray with you last night. It would have kept you from all the worry and upset you went through today."

"Hush now, I forgive you, and I'm just so relieved and happy that we're both believers now," she calmed him. "Doctor, thank you for letting them finish."

"You're welcome. I'm also a believer and I welcome both of you into God's family. God had done three great miracles here," he said. "Walt, we will need to keep you here at the hospital for observation over night and to perform the tests that will prove to the other doctors and nurses that God has healed you. Will you cooperate with us?"

Surprising Betty and Matt, Walt said, "Yes Sir! I'll be glad that we can give the glory to God for healing me and saving my soul!" The other three thanked and praised God for these miracles.

Betty and Matt returned to the waiting room, and found Jeff there talking to the other two men from the morning shift. All three of them came over and were surprised to see Betty and Matt standing there smiling and laughing with relief and joy. First Matt told them that the doctor had said that Walt had had a massive heart attack, and that he was not conscious and they didn't expect him to live. "He left us alone with Walt for a few minutes, so Betty and I prayed for God to heal Walt's heart and give him another chance to accept Jesus as his Savior. Praise God he did."

Jeff joined in the praise session after he heard about God healing Walt's heart and his decision to ask Jesus to be his Savior. Then he turned to the other two men and asked them if they would like to accept Jesus as their Savior also, and add two more miracles to the other three. They all sat down facing each other. Jeff and Matt explained the gospel to the two men. Then Matt and Betty and Jeff took turns answering their questions. It wasn't long before they both prayed the same prayer that Walt had. What a time of praise and thanksgiving and rejoicing they all had then!

The doctor walked through the room right at that time and they called him over to relay the good news, so he joined in the praise. Then Betty asked him, "May I go tell Walt about these two before I go home? And what time can I come take my husband back home in the morning?"

He answered, "Come at 9:30 with clean clothes for him and he will be showered and ready to put them on. It would be best if he didn't go to work tomorrow, because he might not get very good sleep here tonight. And yes, you may go and tell Walt about these two more miracles, and that you'll see him tomorrow morning."

She said, "Thank you Doctor, for being here today and for all you've done for Walt, and for us." The others all agreed, adding their thanks.

"You're all very welcome. I'm always very pleased to be able to witness God's miracles like I have today. God can take bad news like what I told you, and turn it into very good news," he replied as he waved at them and left the room.

Betty went in by herself to tell Walt and to say that she would call the first shift people and tell them not to go to work tomorrow morning, but to come on Thursday. It was nice to have a few more minutes with him before leaving to go home and get his clothes ready for tomorrow and then to rest. It had been a demanding time, but she was very thankful.

*****

Matt and Jeff stayed to talk a little longer with the other two men, and to invite them to come to church on Sunday at 2 PM, and to bring their wives. Then Jeff gave the church address and waved good-bye as they left. Matt asked Jeff, "Do you think we should call the second shift people and have them come in for the rest of the afternoon. Betty said she would call the first shift and have them come on Thursday, but we could probably go ahead and work today and tomorrow anyway. I'd like to go work off the stress of the last couple hours."

"Sure, we have to call them anyway to tell them how Walt is doing. I'll call half of them and you can call the other half and we can tell them we'll meet them there in half an hour," he laughed at his many uses of "half."

Matt joined in the laughter, helping to relieve the stress the last couple hours had heaped on them. He was so grateful and relieved that they could be laughing instead of grieving over the loss of a friend and a soul. Four more souls had been added to the kingdom of God and he had a feeling that Walt would be an enthusiastic soul winner now. Wow!

*****

After supper cleanup Tuesday, Anita told Don that it had worked out very well to have Sherry come with the twins for the morning and showed him the progress she had made on the new dress for Mary. He was pleased. Then she gave him a list of couples that might be possible co-facilitators for the new believers group, and he got started making phone calls. The third couple was delighted that he had called them. They did some planning on the phone. Then Don decided to call all the ones who had returned their cards so far, to see if they could come this Thursday at 7:00 PM to the Pastor's home for the first group meeting.

Anita helped him make those phone calls and almost all of them could make it. The others promised to come the next Thursday so they would be ready to be baptized the following Tuesday.

In the midst of the phone calls, Matt called and got their consent to stop by when he got off work at 9 PM. When he arrived, he was all smiles and said, "I have the most amazing praise story to tell you, but first I need to get three of those new believer booklets and cards, so I don't forget." Then he told them about his afternoon and the salvation of Betty last night on her own, and then Walt's massive heart attack and how God had healed and then saved him. When two of Walt's co-workers who had followed the ambulance to the hospital heard about the miracles for Walt they also were saved. "I assume there will be a baptismal service soon and would like to give them all a chance to get into a new believers group so they'll be ready. That's why I need these booklets and cards. I've told you before about Walt and Betty and how reticent they've been, but now they're both believers!"

They had a good time of praising and thanking the Lord. Then Don told him about the first meeting of the new believers being at 7 PM Thursday, here at their house.

"I'll tell Walt and Betty about the meeting when I go see him at his home tomorrow morning. I'll have him call you if they're going to come. The main emergency room doctor, who was there today, is also a believer. They're going to keep Walt overnight for observation and tests to prove to the other doctors and nurses that God has really healed him. Walt can give these other books and cards to the two men at work on Thursday and then they can call you if they want to come. I hope you'll have room for four to six other people. I don't know if the two men's wives are believers or not, but if not yet, they might be soon," Matt finished, thanked them, bid them good-bye, and then went home.

"That was a good point, Matt made about hoping we have room for the extra people. We probably will have for the first meeting, but not for the next. It would be good to meet at the church for the next one anyway, so we can show them the dressing rooms and showers connected with the baptismal and what it all looks like. For the following meetings, we'll probably need to find another couple that can continue with a group in their own home. So I'll get busy and call some more from your list until we find that other couple. Thank God for such a wonderful problem!" he exclaimed. After four more calls, he found another couple that would be honored to come and to help facilitate the other group.

*****

Wednesday

On Wednesday morning, Betty arrived at the hospital at 9:15 to take her husband back home. She came early, because she didn't know whether he was still in the room he had been in yesterday or if they had moved him to another room. She checked at the information desk and they told her which room he was in. By the time she got there, it was 9:25. A nurse took the clothes from her so he could get dressed. So she waited in the hallway.

"You can come in now," the nurse told her. She went in and saw him, and he looked so good to her, standing up, smiling, and healthy. She would have run right to him for a hug and kiss, but the room seemed like it was full of doctors and nurses, including the doctor from yesterday, and Walt's own doctor who had told him to slow down. Actually there were only four doctors and five nurses, but the room seemed full. She looked at Walt and then at the doctor from yesterday with questions written all over her face.

Walt came over to her and said, "Everyone, I would like you to meet my dear wife, Betty." They all smiled and said things like, "Pleased to meet you," "It's a pleasure," "How do you do," and "Hi." She smiled and waited.

Then Walt explained to her, "I asked them all to be here when you arrived so they could tell you what they told me."

Then in unison, they all said, "After seeing the shape he was in when he arrived yesterday, we didn't think he stood a chance to survive, but God had the last word. It is very obvious to us that God has healed Walt and he's perfectly healthy. We ran all the tests, and his heart is like that of a healthy 20-year-old. We have seen God do things like this before and we're always amazed. To God be the glory!"

"Definitely!" Betty exclaimed. "Thank you all for telling me. I'm also amazed, and very thankful."

One doctor and a nurse added that they had been skeptical when they heard of this happening before, but now that they had seen this miracle personally, they had decided God was for real, and Walt had helped them pray the same prayer he had prayed. Betty smiled and thanked God for those miracles, also.

After that, all the nurses and doctors left, except for Walt's own doctor. He was the skeptical one who now believed in Jesus. He said to Walt, "You may continue to work in construction and don't need to slow down or just be a supervisor. Start back slowly though, because your muscles are not used to working like you used to. As with any exercise, start with a little bit and build up so you don't over-stress your muscles. Explain that to your co-workers, and maybe they can help you remember. Just be careful to not have an accident, because you still have a human body that could get hurt. None of us want to see you back in here! I would also recommend that you continue on that good diet and do the exercises to keep your body in shape."

"Yes Sir! I agree with all of that, and I'll do my best to be careful. Thank you for coming here this morning to tell Betty and me that." The doctor smiled, and shook Walt and Betty's hands before he also took his leave.

Finally, Betty could hug and kiss her own dear husband and relax in knowing that he was alive and well. It had been very good for her to hear that fact from all of them, so that it left no doubt. She could live without worry now. Walt picked up his bag of belongings and he and Betty walked down the hall and out of the hospital to their car. He would follow the doctor's orders and go home and rest, since they <u>had</u> kept him awake most of the night doing all their tests.

Matt was there when they arrived, and he went inside with them where he heard from both of them what the doctors had told them. He was overjoyed right along with them and did his share of praising and thanking God for the miracles. He gave them the booklets with the cards and explained what they were for, showing them Pastor Don's phone number so they could call him if they wanted to go to the meeting on Thursday at 7 PM at the pastor's house. Before leaving he said, "I won't stay, so that you can go get the rest you didn't get last night. Don does not get home until after 5 PM anyway, so will you a chance to sleep for a while, and read the booklet later."

Matt drove home, went for a run, and then called Fiona to tell her all about what had happened since he saw her on Tuesday morning, which seemed like days ago, not just yesterday! She was thrilled with all the good news and joined in with her own thanks and praise to God. Later, Matt ate lunch and went to work at the job site, where he and the crew accomplished a lot.

*****

Late in the afternoon, Walt and Betty read through the little booklet and filled out the card that went with it. Then they called Pastor Don Ross to tell him they would plan to be at the meeting at 7 PM on Thursday evening. Afterwards, they went through the booklet again noticing how much of it agreed with what Matt had told them all along, and how closely it followed parts of the book he had loaned to them.

"How could we have waited so long?" Betty asked. "It all makes so much sense now."

"I think I was being stubborn for a while, and then I erroneously thought I needed Matt to help me pray properly. I can see now, that was a lie from the devil, because he didn't want me to be saved. I'm so grateful that God had the last word and gave me another chance," said Walt.

"Me too!" exclaimed Betty. "I was so upset when I thought you might have died already and had been lost. If Matt had not been there to pray and settle me down, I might have been hysterical. He is such a good friend and always seems to know the right thing to do and say."

"You're right," he agreed. "Tomorrow morning I'll take these other two booklets and cards to those two co-workers who were at the hospital. Did you happen to get their names?"

"No, I didn't, and I'm sorry, but I think they'll be among the first to greet and welcome you back tomorrow. They were quick to understand and believe after they heard about your miracles," she answered.

*****

Jane Kelsey was busy doing housework and thinking as she worked on Wednesday afternoon. For the last couple weeks, she had thought about advertising the beginning of a new Lamaze class. She could put an advertisement in the newspaper for a week. But she never got around to writing it. If she <u>did</u> advertise and enough people were interested, it would mean that she would gain new clients and get her business started up again. But for some reason she could not get motivated about doing that. She decided she had better pray about it some more and discuss it with Larry.

So, after supper and cleanup, she told him her thoughts, ending with, "I think I'm enjoying just being a homemaker and I'm not sure I want to give it up yet."

Larry responded, "Dear, you don't <u>ever</u> have to give it up. We have enough money with just my wages, so that you don't ever have to start up your business again. You can if you really desire to, but you don't <u>have</u> to. Maybe God has something else planned for you to be doing along with homemaking, or maybe he would just have you rest and be ready to do whatever else he directs. I don't know, but <u>God</u> does, and he will tell us in his own good time. So, relax."

Jane replied, "Thank you, Honey. That is all very good advice and I will take it. Now, how was your day?"

"I had a good day. The work is steady and since I'm working for somebody else, I don't have the worry of how to keep the job going from week to week and month to month. I would not like being a self-employed person. This is much easier for me to do, and I enjoy plumbing and heating. The people are so appreciative after something is fixed. Consequently, it's a rewarding kind of job to have," he told her.

*****

Wednesday had been another very good day at school for Julie. She was getting used to the routine and knew all the children's names by yesterday, so they didn't need to wear name tags any longer. They were a very good class and she enjoyed teaching them. She really liked the methods this school used. The children seemed to learn and remember things much better and they enjoyed it too.

When she got home she had many fun things to tell Ted while they worked together to fix supper. She began with, "Some of the students have written comments or suggestions already for the little box I showed them. Yesterday, one of them said he wants to learn how to fly a real airplane and be a pilot when he grows up. When I talked to him today about it, he did seem serious about it and he realizes that it will be a long time before he can start learning how to fly, but he plans to study hard all the way through school so he will be ready for the training when the time comes."

"He sounds like a serious boy who knows already what he wants to be when he grows up. Maybe God has plans for him to fly for some missionary group who needs pilots," responded Ted.

"Maybe so. He will probably be a good pilot, since he's so serious and determined," Julie agreed. "Today, a girl suggested that we have two more story times during the day, and the boy who told Kippy he was better than a bear wants to have two times a day to share things with Kippy. I like both of those suggestions, but we would need a longer day to implement them, because the days are already planned to be very full of learning activities. I hate to disappoint those two children. I'll pray about it and maybe God will give me an idea of how to do at least part of them."

"That's a good plan. I'm so glad we can always ask God for wisdom, and he promises to give it to us," Ted said.

Then they sat down to eat, and after they gave thanks Julie asked, "How was your day today, Honey."

"It was a really nice day. After Maria told us about Esther's plan to eat with one person at a time and try to make friends with the hope of being able to witness to them eventually, I decided to try it myself. Besides, it will be nice to have some other friends in our new city. This week I've managed to eat lunch with the same man each day and we're getting acquainted. I know it will be slow going, but it will be worth it," he answered.

"For sure, and that makes me think. Even though the other teachers in the school are all Christians already, maybe I should make more of an effort to get to know some of them, especially the ones in the third grade classrooms. Now that I'm adjusting to the way of teaching, I might have time to eat with one at noon some days. They _have_ been gracious to answer my questions and that has been a big help to me. It would be nice to have a friend or two more here," commented Julie.

"That sounds wise. Remember the quote about 'no man is an island.' God is our real help, but often he works through others for our benefit and maybe theirs also," Ted agreed.

"Right. After we get things cleaned up, I'll call and talk to Maria, like I told her I would. Then I'll check to see if Pam has answered my last e-mail. I still can't get over how nice it is to _not_ have papers to check!" she exclaimed.

She had a good talk with Maria and answered another nice e-mail from Pam. Then she took some time to pray and ask God for wisdom about the two suggestions the students had made. She listened for a time, but remembered that often his answers came

Everywhere There's a Sunrise, Let's Tell The Good News!

as she was doing routine housework, so she got busy with a project that needed to be done.

The answers did come to her. They could listen to a story while they practiced making cursive letters. It could be a long book without pictures, and each day's reading could take about as long as the time they were practicing. That would only be one more story time a day, but this time, the girl would have to compromise and be thankful for one instead of two extra story times. And if someone needed help with a letter, they could interrupt the story. For the other suggestion, they could share, and Kippy could listen and talk during the class meeting time as well as the sharing time. She would check with Beth before school tomorrow and see if those ideas would be acceptable. The last thing she wanted, was to do something wrong. She realized that she desired to be able to teach in this school for many years to come.

*****

Chapter 12

Acts 2:47b, And the Lord added to the church daily those who were saved.

Thursday

Walt was feeling very well physically on Thursday morning, plus he was rested after sleeping much of the day and all night Wednesday. He took the two booklets and cards with him to the job site. Betty was correct, the two men who were at the hospital with him were the first ones to come and welcome him back. He applauded their decisions to ask Jesus to be their Savior and gave each of them the little booklet and card. Then he asked, "How about your wives?"

One of them answered, "My wife and I spent the afternoon with him and his wife. We told our wives the whole story, about what had happened at work and the ambulance taking you to the hospital. When your wife and Matt came out of your intensive care room, they told us that the doctor had said it was a massive heart attack and you were not expected to live, but they were smiling and laughing. That made no sense to us, until they explained about the miracle God did for your heart, and that he gave you a second chance to accept Jesus as your Savior, which you did.

Then we told our wives about Betty, Matt, and Jeff answering all our questions and helping us to pray and ask Jesus to save us too. We included all our questions and their answers, and by the time we were finished, both our wives also prayed, and now all four of us are saved. According to Matt, that adds two more miracles to that day."

"Thank You, Jesus!" Walt exclaimed. "There's a meeting tonight at 7 PM at the house of the pastor of the church that Matt attends. It's especially for new believers like us six. Betty and I are going and I hope you and your wives will come also. Go back home for long enough to read the books with your wives and decide if you want to attend. If so, just call the pastor's wife and tell her you'll be there. Then you can come back to work."

"Okay. We'll see you in a little while," they said as they left.

While the men had been talking to Walt, the other co-workers had gathered around and were listening to them and Walt. After those two men left, the others wanted to hear the story from Walt in person. They really had not expected to ever see him again, but here he was looking very healthy and extremely happy. Walt sat down in his director's chair and began. Some of the men sat on the floor while others remained standing as they listened. Walt told them what he had been told by Betty and Matt about what the doctor had said about his massive heart attack and that he was not expected to live, but how Matt and Betty had prayed for God to heal his heart and give him another chance to accept Jesus as his Savior.

Walt continued, "The healing was immediate, and right after that, Matt helped me to pray a prayer to ask forgiveness of my sins and to say I believed that Jesus was the only way to get to heaven, and to ask Jesus to be my Savior. Betty had prayed that prayer the night before, and I'm sorry for the worry I caused her by waiting. If God had not healed me, I would have died without believing, and I would have been lost for all eternity, instead of being on my way to heaven like I'm now.

"I hope I can help you all to understand how important this decision is for you as much as it was for me. Betty and I listened to Matt explain the gospel many times, but we always had questions and were hesitant to take the big step. He loaned us a book which we had finished reading and agreed with, but even after Betty prayed on her own Monday night, I still wanted to wait and have Matt pray with me. I was mistakenly afraid I couldn't do it right. I almost missed my chance forever by believing that lie from the devil. But God was merciful and gracious. He totally healed me and gave me a second chance. I will be forever grateful.

"The doctors kept me in the hospital overnight to do tests and prove that my heart really was healed. They kept me up almost all night, but they all agreed that I now have the heart of a twenty-year-old. One doctor and one nurse were so amazed and convinced that God had done this miracle that they both decided to believe and ask Jesus to save them too. So, what do you think, men? You saw how I looked on Tuesday, and how I look now, and you've heard all that God has done for me. What's keeping you from believing and accepting Jesus for yourselves?" Walt asked.

*****

Matt awoke at 6 AM that Thursday, and could not get back to sleep so he got up planning to eat breakfast and get ready to go do some extra work on his house when he had a very distinct direction: "Call Jeff and tell him to dress, eat breakfast and meet you at the work site at 7:10 AM." Matt instantly obeyed by informing Jeff, and then dressing and eating so he could meet him. When they arrived, they entered quietly and got to listen to Walt telling the story of his miracles to his co-workers.

Just after they got there, the Mayor and his wife also arrived to take a tour of the house and see how it was coming along because they were eager to get moved in. When they saw everybody sitting or standing around listening, they didn't look very pleased. But Matt and Jeff motioned for them to stay quiet and come listen. So they listened beginning at the point of Walt's heart attack through the part about the doctor and nurse also believing and being saved, and Walt's question for the men.

*****

The men began asking questions and Walt was able to answer a lot of them, but then the questions got beyond what he had learned or could remember from reading the book Matt had loaned him. Just then he saw Matt and Jeff in the background and motioned for them to come and help him answer questions, which they gladly did. The Mayor and his wife came closer and joined the group also. Walt welcomed them, assuring them that they would not be charged for the time this was taking, but that this subject was very important and he desired that all the men be given a chance to decide for themselves what they would do about Jesus.

    The questions and answers continued for another fifteen minutes and then there was quiet consideration about what they had heard. One by one all seven co-workers decided the only logical and appropriate thing for them to do about Jesus was to believe in him and ask him to be their Savior also. Even the Mayor and his wife came to the same decision. And as a result, there were nine more miracles added to the other eight. What a time of thanksgiving, and praise they all had together and when the other two returned from their homes, they joined right in!

    Matt told them he would go over to his pastor's home and bring back booklets that these people could take home and read. When he returned he handed them out, and he also told them about the New Believers groups that would be forming. The one tonight was already full, since the first two workers and their wives had just joined, but they would have another one either on Tuesday or Wednesday next week to accommodate the new people, plus a second meeting, also next week, for all of the people together which would meet at the church on Thursday at 7 PM. Matt said, "This will give you other seven men a chance to talk to your wives this afternoon. If any of you need help in answering the questions your wives might have, call Walt this afternoon, or bring them over here to the work site and Jeff and I will take unpaid time off to answer their questions."

    Then Matt invited all of them to church on Sunday where they could give the cards to Pastor Don. He gave the address and the time, and then said to the Mayor and his wife, "If you would like to right now, Walt can give you a tour of your house while Jeff and I get these nine workers up to date on what the second shift workers did the last two days, while they had some unpaid time off because of Walt's emergency and miracle. Then they can get back to work."

    After that, Jeff went back home and shared with his wife all that had just happened and she also thanked and praised the Lord for all he had done. Matt went over to the hospital to see if he could find the doctor and the nurse who had become believers because of the miracle God had performed for Walt. He was glad to find the doctor who had been there on Tuesday, and asked him about the other two. The doctor went to bring them out to the waiting room, where Matt gave each one a booklet with a card from the extras he had picked up that morning. He invited them and anyone else who didn't already have a church home to come to church on Sunday and told them the place and the time. He also told them about the small groups that were being started for new believers, and that the first meeting would be next week.

Then he went and worked off the excitement at his house site. While he was doing that, he had another idea, which he put into effect when he went to the job site after lunch. "Walt, how did the rest of your morning go?" he asked.

"It was great. I followed the doctor's orders about getting my muscles used to working again little by little, and the men all helped me remember to do it. They're a good bunch of men, and now, we all have this wonderful new belief that we share, so it's drawn us closer."

"I'm glad to hear that. I agree. It is extra special to be able to be in unity, especially with your co-workers. Do you have enough energy to stay here and talk to the second shift people like you did to the first shift this morning? They all have heard about what happened from Jeff and me, but I think it would have more impact if they could hear it from you. Who knows, maybe some or all of them might also come to Jesus for salvation."

"Yes!" he exclaimed. "I'm glad you thought of that. I'm so thankful to God for what he did for me that I want to do everything I can to help others realize their need for him, also. So I'll tell you what's planned for the second shift and then stay to talk to the men when they arrive."

The men were a little surprised to see Walt, but agreed to sit and listen to his account of what God had done for him. Many of them had the same questions as the others had, and got the same answers from Walt, Matt, and Jeff. Seven of the eight men accepted Jesus as their Savior right then. They were filled with thankfulness, peace and joy. One of them was not "ready" yet, but said he would think about it.

Matt had picked up some more booklets and cards before he came to work, and gave the seven men each a booklet and card, explained about them and invited all of the men to church and to the new believer groups that were forming. "I hope you'll tell your wives and ask them to join you in your decision. Call Walt or Jeff or me and we can either come to your house, or talk on the phone, if your wives have questions that you can't answer. You can give the cards to Pastor Don after church on Sunday." Then he told them the church address and the time of the service.

Linda L. Linn

*****

    As Maria drove to work that Thursday morning, she was thinking about the great telephone conversation she had with Julie the evening before. Julie seemed so much happier than when she was working at the dental office and also than when she was teaching in the public school in the other city. This sounded like a much better place and way to teach than the other was, so she was very happy for her friend. And she was grateful that they could still converse on the phone and on their walks on Sundays. They were both very busy now with their own lives and that was a good thing.

    Maria was also looking forward to going to lunch with yet another co-worker and Ruth. Each time they had lunch with a new person, Maria learned so much about people in general besides the new person, more about Ruth and sometimes, even more about herself. It was like taking an interesting college course in human personalities. Since today looked like it would be sunny and warm, she was glad they had planned to walk to and around the park before eating. Walking together was a good way to become acquainted before eating. Then, the conversations flowed easily during lunch.

    As she walked into the office building, Maria prayed that God would bless this lunchtime also. Then she got to work, thinking that her life was so much more full and more meaningful than it had been before, so she thanked God for that blessing also, since he had brought many good things from that difficult situation. That brought Jason to mind, so she prayed for him, too, that God would soften his heart, and draw him to salvation and healing.

*****

    Before Karen left for her job at Subway on Thursday, Jeff called Tomo Suehiro, "Hello, Tomo. This is Jeff Spencer. I'm in the Saturday morning small group with you. ... ... I was wondering if we would be too late for you to fix and serve us the evening meal if we got to your restaurant at about 8:15 PM. ... ... Good, then I'll plan a day when my wife and I can come. Do we need reservations? ... ... Okay, and is there any day that would be better for you, like when you have fewer customers at that time of the evening? ... ... So, any day except Friday. ... ... Thank you, we'll see you sometime soon.

Everywhere There's a Sunrise, Let's Tell The Good News!

"What do you think, Dearest? Would you like to go this evening or wait until a day next week?" he asked.

"I would love to go this evening. Thank you so much for remembering to call him about the timing. I had kind of forgotten about our discussion about going there. I'll look forward to dining with my caring husband at the friendly Japanese restaurant after our jobs today," she responded.

Jeff hurried home after being excused from work an hour early, changed clothes and took his attractively dressed wife out to dinner. Both of them agreed that it turned out to be the most delicious meal they had had in a long time. Besides, they had been long overdue for a date together. They had to admit that it <u>was</u> rather hurried, but they did get out of there a couple minutes before nine. Tomo and Ami had been very pleased to see them and waited on them in person, so they felt extra special.

On the way home, Karen asked, "Would you like to have them over to lunch or supper on a Sunday sometime?"

"That would be nice. I <u>would</u> like to get to know them better. We can ask them to come whenever it would be best for you," he replied. Then he shared with her the good news about the seven men who had accepted Jesus at the job site this afternoon. Of course she was as thrilled as he was.

*****

When Sherry arrived on Thursday morning at the Ross home, Anita was embarrassed to ask her to postpone working on Mary's dress so she could clean the bathrooms and dust the living and dining rooms in preparation for the small group meeting that evening in their home. Sherry said, "I'm glad to do <u>whatever</u> will help you the most, Anita. Please don't worry about it. I'm just so grateful that I can do this for the twins, and that you're willing to add two more children to your workload while I'm here. Just tell me where the supplies are and I'll get right to work."

"Thank you, Sherry, for putting me at ease," replied Anita, and then she showed her the supplies.

When Sherry was finished with those jobs, she only had about 20 minutes left, so she gave the kitchen a quick cleaning also, before collecting her girls and taking them home to lunch.

While they ate lunch, they told her about the Bible story and the songs they had sung that went with it. Then they explained how to play a new game they had learned. They thanked their mother for taking them to be with that group. She gave them both big hugs and said they were welcome. After cleaning up the dishes and the kitchen they all went to take their afternoon rest. The girls would sleep until about 3PM, but she got up at 2PM to greet Roy when he got home and to get ready to go to work. It was nice that he could also get a little rest before they woke up. They didn't have much time together as a couple, during the week, but both felt it was worth it so that Joy and Hope could go to the Christian school next year, and through third grade. It would give them such good Christian preparation for the rest of their public schooling and lives. When children are well trained when they're very young, they usually stick with it the rest of their lives. And this school trained them very well!

*****

Just as soon as Don got home from work Thursday, he started preparing supper while Anita finished her time with the daycare children. When they had all gone home, he greeted Anita and his children with hugs and kisses, and then they all sat down to eat and he listened to Timmy and Mary tell some things that had happened that day. Timmy said. "The first day Joy and Hope were here, Mary and I were the only ones who could tell them apart. Today everybody could, because Hope told them that she has two freckles on her right cheek and Joy has none." Everyone laughed.

Mary said, "Me and Timmy like having the twins here for extra days."

Don corrected her gently, "Say Timmy and I." She smiled and repeated it. "I'm glad you both like it. How was your day, my dear wife?"

"It was wonderful because Mrs. Foster willingly cleaned the bathrooms and kitchen and dusted the living and dining rooms so they would be ready for the meeting tonight, while Timmy, Mary and I got to enjoy having the twins join our daycare for the morning. I'm glad you did the vacuuming last night. How did your day go, Dear," she asked.

"It was good to have a normal day working at the Local Grocery. I didn't even have any phone calls to make. It's nice to have a job that allows me to do that when I need to though," he answered.

After supper and a cookie from the refreshments for dessert, they all helped with the cleanup. After the extra chairs were set up in the living room for the New Believers group meeting, Timmy and

Mary helped put out the Bibles and hymnals. Don spent some quality time with Mary and Timmy while Anita got the refreshments ready and put out onto the dining room table. Then they both helped the children get ready for bed and gave them permission to play quietly in their rooms until their 8:00 bedtime. Just as they finished that, the doorbell rang, and they went to meet their first guests.

As soon as everyone had arrived and had been seated, Pastor Don welcomed them and introduced the co-facilitators, saying that they would be taking over the guidance of the group in a few weeks. He had the group members introduce themselves to the group by telling their names and when they had accepted Jesus as their Savior. Before the singing time, he recommended, "It would be good for each family to buy a used or new Bible and a used or new hymnal to use at home, because the Bible verses and the words in the songs we sing at church and in these groups are so meaningful that it's helpful to review them from time to time." Then they sang: "Wonderful Grace of Jesus," 2 Corinthians 8:9; "I Will Sing of the Mercies of the LORD," Psalm 98:1; and "His Name Is Wonderful," 4:12. Don interrupted the singing to say, "I would like to dedicate our last song to Walt Evans who was saved on Tuesday afternoon just after being healed from a massive heart attack and, and who now has 'A Perfect Heart:' Ezekiel 36:26, both physically and spiritually."

Walt added, "There was one doctor and one nurse who asked Jesus to be their Savior because they saw the miracle that God did for my heart. They might come to the next meeting." The group members all made a variety of exclamations of awe and then sang the song thinking of its extra significance.

After they finished singing "A perfect Heart." Pastor Don said, "All of you new believers have perfect spiritual hearts in God's sight now because Jesus made them clean and he rules in them. Then they sang the song again, and it meant even more to them when they considered their own hearts.

Pastor Don started the teaching time by saying, "I want you all to know that I'm overwhelmed with joy that you're all now a part of God's family, because as it says in John 1:12 *To as many as received Jesus, God gave power to become his children even to those who believed on Jesus name.* I'm also very glad that you all agreed to come to this first meeting of the new believers group. We'll begin by having you ask questions about things your read in the booklet."

They spent about 15 minutes with their questions and his answers, and then he went on to define some terms that they would be hearing in the church services, group meetings and when they read the Bible. Those terms included: believer, Christian, follower, disciple, and he used a Bible dictionary to define them. Then Pastor Don suggested, "If any of you like to take notes, it would be fine with me if you bring a notebook and pen with you next week.

"Now, I'd like all of you to find 2 Corinthians in your Bibles. Right now it might be difficult and slow for you to find places in the Bible, but with practice it will get easier and faster. You can use the table of contents in the front of the Bible. There are Bibles, which have thumb indexes or tabs along the right edge of the Bible with the names of the books on them. That can be very helpful, or you can memorize the names of the books and learn to locate the books that way. Whichever way you choose will be fine. Just do not get discouraged and give up.

"This is a very important book for you now that you are believers. It is a book that you'll need to read every day so that you can learn how God wants you to live this new life. You'll notice that the books are divided into chapters and verses. Find chapter five and go to verse 17. Please read it with me. *Therefore if any man is in Christ, he is a new creature. Old things have passed away, behold, all things have become new.* Think about what that means for you. Before you accepted Jesus as your Savior, what was your old life like? Since you accepted him, how have you changed already? This book, the Bible, will tell you what your new life will be like here on this earth, and it will also tell you some things about what your eternal life will be like when you go to heaven. Are you beginning to understand how important this book is?" he asked. All heads nodded emphatically.

"Let's think about feelings," he continued. "How many of you have felt happy and excited since you asked Jesus to save you?" Many hands were raised. "How many of you have had joy and peace since you accepted Jesus as your personal Savior?" Most hands went up. "Feeling happy or excited are nice feelings. But feelings come and go, as you've learned in this life. We cannot live our lives by feelings. But you have joy and peace now, and they're not just feelings. They are part of the fruit of the Holy Spirit. He produces them in you. If you go just one book to the right in your Bibles you'll find Galatians. Then go to chapter five and verse 22 and 23. Listen as I read them, the *fruit of the Spirit is love, joy, peace, long suffering or patience, gentleness, goodness, faith, meekness, temperance or self-control; against such things there is no law.* Read those verses over again to yourselves and think about them. This valuable fruit of the Holy Spirit will start to become more and more a part of your lives as you surrender your will to him.

"The Christian life is not trouble-free with nice feelings, although we <u>will</u> also enjoy good feelings when we have them. There will be trials, and some things will seem to go wrong. This is why Jesus told people to count the cost when they wanted to follow him. But he says he will always be with us and will help us. Many times we won't feel happy and elated, but we live by faith. Faith is what you used when you believed in Jesus and asked him to forgive you and be your Savior. Faith is what you will continue to use the rest of your life. You'll believe by faith that *God will work all things together for good for those who love him and are called according to his purpose,* as is says in Romans 8:28.

"Since the Holy Spirit is living inside of us now and is producing his fruit, we can believe by faith that we can still experience his peace and joy even when things don't go the way we want them to. We can love and be patient with difficult people in our lives by faith that the Holy Spirit is producing that fruit in our lives. We can be self-controlled and gentle instead of angry, by faith with the Holy Spirit's help.

"It won't all happen at once. Change takes time and sometimes our own will gets in the way, but we can confess when we fail and he promises to forgive. Find 1 John near the back of the Bible and look at chapter 1 verse 9. Read it aloud with me. *If we confess our sins, God is faithful and just to forgive us our sins and to cleanse us from all unrighteousness.* Yes, we'll still sin from time to time. Maybe you've heard the saying, 'Christians are not perfect; they're just forgiven.' I don't know who said that but it's true. Don't be too hard on yourselves, and don't expect yourself or others to be perfect. The only one who is perfect is the triune God: the Father, Son, and Holy Spirit. You'll learn more about the Trinity and many other things as we go along.

"I don't want to overwhelm you at this meeting. Our next meeting will be at the church next Thursday, at 7 PM and we'll have some new members joining with us there. At our next meeting, you'll be learning more about water baptism. That topic is also introduced in your booklets, but we'll add to it. Do you have any questions about what we've covered today?" Don asked. There were several, and he answered them and then said, "We have some refreshments ready for us in the dining room. Please come and enjoy a time of getting better acquainted with each other as we eat and drink."

After everyone was finished, they expressed their thanks and went to their homes. Don and Anita felt like the meeting had gone very well and realized that they would need another one just like it on Tuesday or Wednesday to get the other new members caught up to where these were. Anita said, "We've never had this happen before. But like you said, it's a good problem. The other couple can probably be with us for the next meeting since they could not get to this one."

"You're right. I think we can wait until tomorrow to call them about it and decide which day will work best. I know you checked on the children a couple times during the meeting, but let's go see if they were able to stay asleep with all the people in the house." They were both asleep and looked so peaceful.

Don and Anita put away what was left of the refreshments and were able to quietly put most of the chairs back where they belonged. There would not be time in the morning to do very much of that kind of thing before the daycare children arrived. This was a very busy life they felt that God had called them to live. He was giving them the energy and ability to do it.

*****

Friday

Matt was able to work for a couple hours on his house Friday morning. When he got back home, he called Fiona to see which day would be better for their time together this weekend, and what she would like to do. After she talked with her mother about her plans, she called him back, putting her phone speaker on so she could continue the mending project she was working on. She asked, "Would it work to go home right after church and change clothes so we and my parents can all go to the park? They both want to try throwing Frisbees, now that I told them how much fun we had. Mom and I will bring a picnic supper that we can eat after we get tired of the Frisbees."

Matt answered, "That sounds enjoyable and delicious. I hope the weather will cooperate." Then he told about what had happened at the work site yesterday morning and afternoon.

Everywhere There's a Sunrise, Let's Tell The Good News!

"Wow!" Fiona exclaimed. "Thank you, heavenly Father, for bringing so many more people into your Kingdom. The miracle Jesus did for Walt has helped a lot of people to realize who you are and that they need you too. We praise you for the way you draw people to yourself."

Matt added, "Yes, Father, you are awesome and amazing. We ask that you will help the other man to get past what ever is holding him back, and bring him into your Kingdom soon. Amen."

Fiona agreed, and told Matt she would see him at the small group tomorrow. Then they said good-bye.

Matt always felt elated after talking with Fiona. It was so wonderful to be able to share things and pray together about them, even just on the phone. Besides, he could now look forward to some time with her and her parents on Sunday. They were nice people and he was glad for the chance to know them better. Suddenly he realized that he would have Saturday afternoon <u>and</u> Sunday morning both to work on his house. He would call Ben when he got home from work and ask if either or both of those times would be good for him to come and work with him if the weather was good enough.

Fiona was also feeling extra good after that phone conversation. She was most pleased with his news about all the people who had just become believers in Jesus. She smiled when she thought about the rejoicing that went on in heaven each time a sinner repented. The fact that Matt was involved in this evangelism also delighted her, because it showed that he was letting God use and direct him. Each time she had anything to do with Matt, he showed her some new facet of his life and character. So far they had all been good. She felt herself liking him more and more.

Her mother was glad to hear about all the good news Matt had told her, and agreed that she liked him more all the time also. The next thing her mother said blew her away. "We got a letter yesterday from your great aunt Cara's lawyer. It took this many weeks to finalize the distribution of her assets after the house and furnishings were sold. After you had been with her almost a year, she was so grateful to you that she had her will changed. Her only child had no interest in helping her in her time of need and he seldom even called her. But you became like the daughter she never got to have. So she left three-fourths of her assets to you and only one-fourth to him. He contested it, but her change in the will stands. Enclosed is a check for you, Fiona."

Fiona looked at the amount and gasped. "Wow! Oh, Mother, I never expected or even wanted anything for what I did for her. I was blessed by just being able to be with her and learn so many things from such a godly woman."

"Your father and I know that, and discussed that last evening after we opened the mail, she said. "We were just as astonished as you are. We had no idea! We need to get this put in the bank in an account for you, right away."

"Yes, indeed we do. It's not good to let a check like that lay around the house. Let's go do it right now, and we can pray on the way there and back for God to show me how to use it in the best way for his glory," Fiona responded.

Glenda mentioned, "The lawyer said to leave a specific amount in a separate account to pay the inheritance tax, consequently, we need to open two accounts, so the tax money does not get spent before April 15, next year."

"I'm glad he told us about that. It's something I would never have thought of doing," replied Fiona.

"We wouldn't have either. Neither of us has ever inherited anything," her mother said as they went and got in the car. They were both prayerful as they went to the bank. Two savings accounts were quickly opened and Fiona left there with two receipts to show it had been done. They continued to pray on the way home.

When they were back in their house Fiona said, "I would like to give all of the inheritance except the tax, to the work of the Lord. There's nothing I need, and I don't wish to squander it away buying frivolous things that would spoil me and ruin my desire to live a simple life. I desire that any <u>extra</u> money be given to the Lord. Do you have any ideas, Mother?" she asked.

"I think we should make an appointment with the main pastor of the 12 churches and ask him about areas of need and ministry. Then we three can all pray about it and see where God leads," she answered.

Fiona responded, "That sounds like a good idea." Then she ate lunch and went to work with a smile on her face.

*****

Jeff and Karen spent Friday morning cleaning the house and finding their extra folding chairs so there would be enough places for everyone to sit during the small group meeting the next morning. Then Karen left Jeff to finish setting up the chairs and went to bake a couple dozen each, of two kinds of cookies for refreshments. Jeff and she could enjoy some of them for their lunch today. She liked Julie's idea, and had bought individual packets of hot and cold beverages so the people could choose their favorite, and just add hot or cold water to their cup or glass. It was a good plan to keep the refreshments simple, since lunch wasn't far away after the group meeting. Next time they met here, they might have fruit, or vegetables with a dip. She wrote that down so she wouldn't forget.

Pastor Don had called them before he went to work this morning and told them about all the new believers groups that were forming. It was going to be so busy the next couple weeks that he felt he needed to bow out of facilitating the Saturday group a week early. He also told them he felt that they were ready to take over, so this Saturday would be the last time he and Anita would be facilitators. The first part of the conversational prayer time would be used to dedicate and consecrate Jeff and Karen as the new leaders. This was exciting and a little bit scary when they thought of the responsibility, but they prayed together that God would help in every situation and detail.

*****

Ted and Julie had a nice supper Friday evening, telling each other how their days had gone. Ted told Julie, "A co-worker and I fixed a car today that had been damaged by a small tree falling on its trunk. It was pretty badly crinkled but we were able to straighten it out, fill in a few low spots and repaint it so it looks almost as good as new. I think that's why I like this kind of job. Being able to fix something so it's still usable and looks nice makes this a valuable occupation. However, I <u>would</u> like to find a ministry of some kind that I can do maybe at the church."

"I agree completely. I'm very proud of you and the work you do at your job. Heavenly Father, please provide a ministry for Ted to do for you." He added his prayer to hers and smiled. Then Julie told him the outcome of her ideas for story time and an extra sharing time with Kippy. Beth had approved of both ideas and had thanked her for asking first. The two children were thrilled that their new teacher would agree to their suggestions, and the rest of the class was happy to have an added story time and more time with Kippy. It was nice to have things settling down to a routine again after the eventful week before.

Since the weather was so nice, they planned to take a picnic lunch with them tomorrow and go to a park in the city where they had not yet been after the small group meeting. They could walk around and admire the flowers and blossoming trees before they ate.

After supper cleanup, Julie went to look at her e-mail and found a couple prayer requests from Pam. She copied them down so she could take them to the small group tomorrow morning. Then she prayed about the requests before she answered the e-mail. She told Pam how the rest of the week had gone at school and ended with, "The children are all doing good work and have adapted well to the change of teachers. I almost had to laugh out loud when one of them said. 'You work us just as hard as Miss Green always did.' I guess he was hoping I would be easier on them. They all said, to tell Miss Green 'Hello, and we miss you,' when I write to you. I'll be taking your prayer requests to the small group tomorrow morning and we'll pray about them. I'll record the teaching time again. I'm glad you enjoyed listening to the last one, and I'm also glad you can listen to the weekly service times. Keep on with the good work you're doing there and remember that God is pleased with your service. Bye for now. Julie."

*****

Chapter 13

Mark 6:7a, *Jesus called the twelve to him and sent them out two by two...*

Saturday

On Saturday morning, Matt was the first one to arrive for the small group meeting at the Spencer home. He wanted time to thank Jeff for all he had done to help out this week with Walt and the new believers. He also thanked Karen for being willing to have Jeff be gone for that extra time. Then he went in and sat down in the living room anticipating his view of Fiona when she arrived. She had a way of lighting up the room when she entered.

Don and Anita came next, and Matt got up to help them put the Bibles and Hymnals on each of the chairs. He was glad they had a rolling suitcase in which to carry all of them to and from all the meetings.

Soon everybody else had gotten there and they were seated and ready for the meeting. Don opened with prayer and asked if anybody had a praise to share. He asked everyone to hold his or her applause and praise until the end, after every person had shared. Sherry started with praise that she could work for Anita in exchange for some preschool type training for Joy and Hope two mornings a week. Anita added her praise that Sherry had been such a big help already. Larry was thankful that his wife, Jane, could be home and not plan to start up her Lamaze business any time soon. Julie praised the Lord for the salvation of her former boss and his wife, for a very good week of teaching and that the children had adjusted well to the change of teachers. Tony praised God that his new position as assistant manager was going well. Clara thanked God that he had helped her do a good job on a test that week. Tomo said that Ami and he praised God for the beauty of springtime. Fiona thanked God for the times she got to be outside and enjoy spring.

Don said, "I asked Matt to wait until the end of the praise reports because his will take longer." So Matt thanked and praised God for all the miracles that had happened that week for his boss and many other people. He gave a summary of the happenings of the week and finished by saying that God is awesome, powerful, loving, and works in ways only he could perform. Fiona noticed how humble Matt was as he was telling his praise, and that he gave all the glory to God. When Matt was finished, Don told the group members that they could clap and praise God now, for all the praises they had heard, which they did enthusiastically.

Anita announced, "Now it's time to get a volunteer for the meeting next Saturday. Here is a list for everyone. It has names, addresses and phone numbers of all the group members." She passed out the papers to everyone.

Jane Kelsey stated that the group could meet at their house next week, so that was settled.

The singing time was longer this time and included the following: "Living for Jesus," 2 Corinthians 5:14,15; "Faith Is the Victory," 1 John 5:4,5; "Under His Wings," Psalms 91:4; "People Need the Lord," John 4:35, and Matthew 9:13b; "I Will Serve Thee," Colossians 3:24; and "Go Ye Into All the World," Matthew 28: 19,20.

Julie turned on her recorder when Don started the teaching time by saying, "Our main reason for being on this earth is to do what Jesus said to do in Mark 16:15,16a. Find it, and read it aloud with me. *Go into all the world, and preach the gospel to every person. Those who believe and are baptized shall be saved...* Jeff's and Matt's involvement in the miracles surrounding his boss' heart attack, healing, salvation and the salvation of the many others, is a good segue or transition into the topic of the ministry the small groups are all doing.

"We've been building the foundation for this new group and now it's time for <u>this</u> group to get started doing what Jesus told seventy of his followers to do in Luke 10:1,2 which I'll summarize. Jesus said for them to pray that the Lord of the harvest would send workers out into his harvest, and for them to go two by two. In verse 9, he told them to heal the sick and to say that the Kingdom of God is near. In Matthew 10:8, he added to raise the dead, cleanse lepers, and cast out demons, and to do it free of charge. He said other things for them to do which don't relate to us. We probably won't encounter lepers either. These disciples were to go before Jesus into cities where he would come and this would get them ready to hear him.

"The miracle of healing that happened this last week was a catalyst for the salvation of many people. There's no way to know how many, or if any will be saved when we pray and then go out listening and doing what Jesus, by means of the Holy Spirit tells us to do. Did you notice how many times Matt was told to do something last week. It is important to do what we are told to do immediately. Timing is of the essence. If Matt had waited too long, the opportunity would have been gone. Matt and others of you've been doing these kinds of things for a long time, and you know when the Spirit is speaking to you.

"For others of you, this is new, and probably sounds intimidating. With practice, you'll learn. Furthermore, you won't be alone. You'll go with someone who knows how, so you can learn by watching, like the disciples watched Jesus as it says in Acts 10: 38,39a, *God anointed Jesus of Nazareth with the Holy Spirit and with power and he went around doing good, and healing all who were oppressed by the devil, for God was with him. We disciples are witnesses of all the things he did....*

"The reason to go two by two was also made clear in Matt's praise story by Matt having the wife of his boss, even though she was a new believer, agree with him in prayer. Or when Matt was told to have Jeff come to the work site. They both needed to be there to answer questions and it added credence to what they were saying. You won't always need two people to witness to others, like what happened when Julie told her boss about all the things God had worked together for good for so many people. She invited him to church and he and his wife came. Both of them accepted Jesus last Sunday. Also, Matt had been witnessing on his own, to the boss and his wife for a couple years, preparing for this time.

"Let's look at the scriptures that go with the songs we sang today. Turn to 2 Corinthians 5:14,15 and read aloud with me. *The love of Christ compels us, because we judge that if one died for all, then all were dead. He died for all so that those who live should not continue to live for themselves, but for him who died for them and rose again.* Believers desire to live for Jesus because we love him and appreciate what he did for us, and because lost people need him. John 4:35b says: *Look at the fields. They are ready to harvest.* Matthew 9:13b says: *I came to call sinners to repentance.* Colossians 3:24b reminds us that *it is the Lord we serve.*

"Next, I must remind you that whenever you serve the Lord and do things to bring others to him for salvation, the devil will oppose you in numerous ways, but our victory is guaranteed. Read 1 John 5:4,5 with me. *Whoever is born of God overcomes the world, and faith is the victory that overcomes the world. Who overcomes the world? He who believes that Jesus is the Son of God.* The devil is ruling the world right now, so we overcome him by our faith. If we are persecuted or even martyred, we know that for us *to live is Christ, and to die is gain,* as it says in Philippians 1:21.

"Now find Ephesians 6:10-18 and follow along as I read. *Be strong in the Lord, and in the power of his might. Put on the whole armor of God so that you may be able to stand against the wiles of the devil. For we wrestle not against flesh and blood, but against principalities, powers, the rulers of darkness is this world, and against spiritual wickedness in high places. Therefore, take the whole armor of God, so that you may be able to withstand in the evil day. ... Stand therefore, having the belt of truth, the breastplate of righteousness, and your feet covered with the preparation of the gospel of peace. Above all, take the shield of faith, with which you can quench all the fiery darts of the evil one. Take the helmet of salvation and the sword of the Spirit, which is the word of God. Pray always with all prayer and supplication in the Spirit, with perseverance and supplication for all the saints.*

"We need this armor on all day, every day, no matter what we're doing, but especially when we go out to do battle for the souls of people. Anita and I have drawn a picture of a Roman soldier in his armor with each piece labeled. Here it is. We put it in one of those protective clear plastic holders to keep clean and dry and hang it in our bathroom by the mirror. We go through the list each morning as preparation for the day. Your homework for today is to make a list of the armor we just read about and consciously put it on every day.

"In closing, listen to 1 John 4:4. *We are of God ... and have overcome ... because greater is he that is in (us) than he that is in the world.* And in John 16:33b, Jesus said, *be of good cheer, I have overcome the world.* At the end of Matthew 28:19,20 it says that Jesus would be *with them always, even to the end of the world.* He is the one who works through us to accomplish his will."

Anita gave booklets to Tomo and Ted to be read later, while Don continued, "So the next step is to choose partners and at least one morning or evening each week that you can go out into the world and as you go, ask Jesus by his Spirit in you to guide and tell you what to do. Ted and Julie will need to partner with Larry and Jane, because their work hours coincide, and Ted and Julie need to be with people who know how to do this. Tomo and Ami will need to choose a couple that also has experience so they can teach them. It would be good for them to partner with Jeff and Karen. Roy and Sherry are both busy all day during the week, so they'll probably have to use the weekend and take the twins with them. The rest of you can choose partners who will work with you.

"Now for an announcement. Anita and I won't be available to be partners, because this is our last week as facilitators of this group. Since God has brought so many new believers into our church the past few weeks, I'm going to be very busy getting new believers groups going, and there will be a baptismal service the week after next. Since the seven men and their wives from Matt's second shift all accepted Jesus on Thursday, there will be a need to have another Saturday small group for the 14 of them. They all called Anita on Friday morning, saying they would like to be in a new believers group. And there might be 16 in that group when the other man and his wife believe. I'll be guiding that group with another couple, starting this afternoon and next Saturday so they will all be caught up to where the others will be and be ready for the baptismal service. Like Anita and I have been telling each other, this is a very good 'problem' to have. We just had to figure out a way to have enough time to get everything done!

"Conversational prayer time is next and I would like to start it by having everybody come with me to lay hands on Jeff and Karen, so we can consecrate them to their position as facilitators of this wonderful small group." Everyone gathered around them and were able to lay at least one hand on one of them, while Don prayed, followed by Anita and others.

Prayer time continued with Matt asking God to encourage the new believers to come to church regularly, get into the small groups being formed, learn how to live the Christian life and become soul-winners. Jeff, Don, and Tony all agreed with that and Jeff added his request that the one man who had not been "ready" yet, and his wife would soon become believers also. Julie turned on her recorder and prayed for Pam's requests, and Fiona, Clara, Roy and Sherry all agreed and added their prayers for Pam. Tomo and Ami prayed again for their unsaved grown children, followed by Larry and Jane agreeing with them, and adding to their prayers. Then Larry prayed about the church music group's need for a bass singer to replace one who had just moved to another city. Ted followed that by thanking the Lord, and saying he would talk to Larry about it.

Then Jane changed the subject by saying, "I feel that Jesus would have me share a word of knowledge with you, Clara. Would that be okay with you?" Clara nodded, so Jane continued, "It is time for you to stop working and to speed up your nursing education and evangelistic training. The harvest is ripe and the workers are few."

Clara looked overwhelmed, but she said, "Thank you Jane, and thank you Jesus. I would really like to be able to do that, but I don't have the money to pay for even a slow education and for daily living, without working."

Jeff and Karen smiled at her and he explained, "We are on a special committee for Church #4 and there's money available to help you with living expenses, while you add classes to accelerate your education. There's an evangelism training class starting soon and it will be paid for also, from money donated by believers who have extra money and like to have it used to train and get people out there to work in the harvest fields. We'll talk with you more about it after refreshments." All Clara could do was smile and nod her head. In her mind, it was another amazing miracle!

Following Jeff and Karen into the kitchen, the group members all enjoyed the homemade cookies and a beverage of their choice. Many of the women asked Karen if they could have her recipes for the cookies because they were delicious. She answered that she would bring copies to the next small group meeting. There was much pleasant fellowship as they got to know each other even better. The remaining people picked partners for going out two by two. Some of the couples would be going out four by four until the ones new to it learned adequately how to continue on their own.

Then Fiona asked Julie, "Would you ask Pam if it would be okay for me to have her e-mail address so that I can write and encourage her and maybe give her some of the ideas I learned while I helped my aunt."

Julie replied, "That would be great. I think she's feeling rather cut off and another friend might be very welcome. You would be just the one to be able to help her with taking care of her mother. I've never had any experience."

Ted found Larry and stated, "I'm a bass singer and I love to sing. I would be interested in finding out more about that need, and the possibility of being able to help."

Larry was elated, and said, "I'll tell you all about it when we meet together on Tuesday at 7 PM to talk about our four by four ministry time. This has been another incredible meeting! I'm so glad we get to be in this group."

*****

Jeff and Karen asked Clara, "Would you be able to stay at our house for lunch today and to hear more about the money which is available to help you expedite your education?"

Clara was still astonished, but gladly answered, "Yes! Please! I can hardly wait to find out how this is going to work. At the rate I've been going, it would take at least four more years to become a practical nurse. I think they need nurses in the small city where my parents went back to live. I could use any of my extra time to evangelize there. My parents don't have any money to help me, so I've been doing this on my own."

"God knows that, and I'm sure he's pleased with your efforts and progress. Now he wants to step in and help you. He is so marvelous! He used Jane to tell you what to do and now he will use the funds available from the church to get you going faster. Besides, he knows how tired you must be, trying to keep up with a full-time job and schooling also," said Karen.

Jeff suggested, "Let's sit down and we can tell you all about it. People who have extra money donate it, and it's kept in a foreign and home missions fund, to be distributed to qualifying people.

You qualify, because God said so today, by his word of knowledge through Jane. We'll need you to present your current budget and a projected budget that will include the extra nursing classes that you will start soon, plus the cost of the evangelism classes. Just add your current living expenses to that. Add whatever other money you need, to buy some of the necessities you've been going without lately. We know you won't be extravagant like some people would. We have to keep people accountable so you'll need to keep receipts and records of everything you spend. Karen and I know how honest and trustworthy you are, so we're not worried about you, but the rules of this fund have to be followed, especially since some people might tend to spend more than they need."

Karen continued, "We'll tell you the cost of the evangelism classes and their hours so you can plan your other classes around them. We know that your studio apartment is as inexpensive as they come in this city, so you don't have to look for something cheaper. And you've told us that you like it there, so you won't have moving added to everything else."

Clara sat there and listened and smiled and had all she could do to keep from clapping and shouting. Then she thanked them, and praised the Lord for more than meeting her needs. She helped get the lunch on the table and they all enjoyed eating while she asked questions and they answered them.

Jeff stated, "The timing of this word of knowledge is incredible. But we're coming to expect this kind of thing from God, who does all things well. How much notice do you need to give your present employer?"

Clara replied, "Only one week. There isn't as much business in the evenings as there used to be, and I have a feeling they were going to cut my hours pretty soon, so this will probably help them out also."

"Perfect, so this coming Friday will be your last day and you can start the evangelism class the following Monday evening, if you give them notice this Monday."

She asked as a final question, "What are the evangelism classes like, and how many people will be in them?"

Jeff answered, "The first four months of classes are already over and you'll be skipping them because you already know everything in them. They are for the foreign students who come here with very little knowledge of the Bible. The class just starting on Monday, will be about several different ways to share your faith one on one, and ways to get acquainted with the area that will be your harvest field. The class size will be up to its limit of thirty students. You and nine others will be new members who didn't need the first four months of training. Since you will also be doing ministry by going out in little groups with people in your class, you won't have time to partner with somebody in the Saturday small group."

"Nevertheless, you certainly can continue coming to this group," Karen explained.

Clara responded, "All right, I'll call Fiona and tell her I won't have time to be her partner in their four by four group. I guess they'll just have a three by three group."

Karen replied, "That should work out fine for them. They'll be happy for you."

They all enjoyed another cookie or two apiece and then everyone helped put things away and clean up. Karen went to get two of this church's well known booklets that explain everything about a certain topic. "This one gives all the details about the way the fund works and how to keep records, and the other one makes everything clear in relation to the evangelism classes, Clara. They're yours to keep and use as references. After you read them, get in touch with one of us if you have any questions."

Clara responded, "I'm sure I will have some, but for now, I'm about saturated. Thank you for the scrumptious lunch and more cookies, and for patiently telling me all about this magnificent plan!"

Jeff replied, "It was our pleasure. We enjoy being on this committee because we get to talk with people like you who are dedicated to serving Jesus in his harvest fields." They said their good-byes and Clara went home to read and rejoice. She still could hardly believe how blessed she was.

*****

Jason woke early to a warm, spring Saturday morning, and went out for a nice long walk, feeling better than he had in many days. The new green grass and leaves on the trees that were starting to bloom along with the tulips and daffodils added to his enjoyment. Without thinking, he ended up at his parent's house and decided to stop in for a visit. They were delighted to see him and had him join them for breakfast, which was just about ready. It all tasted delicious to him for a change. They had good conversation while they ate.

Jason said, "I had such a nice walk over here. The weather is perfect this morning and I think spring has become my favorite season. Of course I'll probably say that for summer and autumn when it's their turns."

His mother, Anna, laughed and said, "I notice that you left winter out. Not that I blame you. I don't enjoy being cold, although the snow is pretty coming down and makes a 'fairy land' of the trees and bushes."

"Yes, you and I were the smart ones to stay inside while the girls and Dad went out to 'play in the snow.' I guess that the winter is needed to help me appreciate the springtime more," Jason agreed.

"Both of you are correct. Winter can be beautiful in its own way, but even I don't like being out in the cold as much as I used to. I guess I'm getting old," William said.

Next Jason asked, "Do you both have some time right now to answer some questions?" Both of them nodded, so he continued, "I've tried several times to read the verses Maria wrote in the Bible she gave me, but I can't seem to make any sense out of them. At least I'm not feeling as angry at her father anymore. I'm just confused. What does it mean when it says that good works don't save us? Isn't there a verse that says we are to do good works? That's the way I've tried to live my life, believing that since I'm a good person, I'll go to heaven. The verses she wrote down don't agree with that. So either she's wrong, or else I am, and I've never liked being wrong."

His mother sat there praying with all her might, silently, while his dad answered, "I agree with you. None of us likes to be wrong. But sometimes it's for our best good when we find out and admit we're wrong. Remember the time when I used to think seat belts were stupid and a waste of time? It could have been very dangerous for me to continue thinking that way because I was putting my whole family and myself at risk if we had an accident. I could have been dead wrong for me or for all of us. I was very grateful for the class I had to take in safe driving where I learned how wrong I was in time to keep all of us safer. In the same way, if you find out that the verses she wrote down are right and you are wrong, you're still alive and have time to admit that you're wrong. You can change to the correct way of thinking in time to choose the only way to be sure that you will go to heaven."

"Okay, I'll be open to being shown that I'm wrong. Are there other verses that can prove it to me?" Jason asked.

His dad answered, "Yes. Do you have a list of the verses Maria gave you? If so we won't spend time reading them again right now."

"Yes, I wrote them down so I would not have to turn back to the front of the Bible each time I was ready for another verse. I have it here in my shirt pocket," answered Jason and he handed it to his dad.

"Thank you for bringing us our Bibles, Honey. I'll start with Titus 3:4-7, *After the kindness and love of God our Savior toward man appeared, he saved us, not by works of righteousness which we have done, but according to his mercy. He saved us by the washing of regeneration and renewing of the Holy Spirit, whom he shed on us abundantly through Jesus Christ our Savior, that being justified by his grace, we are made heirs according to the hope of eternal life.* Here is a paper and pen. Please write the reference, Titus 3:4-7, so we can keep track of these as we go." So Jason wrote it and the others on the paper as they were stated.

His dad and mom went back and forth adding verses to the ones Maria had listed.

Anna read Galatians 2:16,21b. *We (Jews) know that man is not justified by the works of the law, but by faith in Jesus Christ. We have believed in Jesus Christ that we might be justified by faith in Christ, and not by the works of the law. For by the works of the law shall no flesh be justified. ... If righteousness came by the law, then Christ died in vain.*

William read the next one, Romans 3:20,24-28. *Therefore by the deeds of the law there shall no flesh be justified in God's sight, for by the law is the knowledge of sin. We are justified freely by God's grace through the redemption that is in Christ Jesus, whom God set forth to be a propitiation through faith in his blood, to declare his righteousness for the remission of sins that are past, through the forbearance of God, ... that he might be just and the justifier of the ones who believe in Jesus. Where is boasting then? It is excluded, not by the law or by works but by faith. Therefore, we conclude that man is justified by faith without the deeds or works of the law.*

Jason listened carefully and stated, "I guess that works of the law are the same as good works because if a person keeps everything in the law, he's doing good works."

Anna agreed, "True, but no person has ever been able to keep the whole law all his life, except for Jesus. James 2:10 says, *For whoever shall keep the whole law, and yet offend in one point, he is guilty of it all."*

William agreed and read 2 Timothy 1:9, *God saved us and called us with a holy calling, not according to our works, but according to his own purpose and grace, which was given to us in Christ Jesus before the world began, but is now made manifest by the appearing of our Savior Jesus Christ who has abolished death, and has brought life and immortality to light through the Gospel.*

"I get it! According to these verses, nobody can be good enough to get to heaven by being a good person. I was wrong. I've been wrong all my life. How futile! It's been a wasted effort. What is the Gospel that the last verse you read spoke about?" Jason asked.

His dad read 1 Corinthians 15:1-4. *(Paul) declared the Gospel which (the Corinthians) received and by which they were saved ... ... For I delivered to you first of all ... ... that Christ died for our sins according to the scriptures, and that he was buried, and that he rose again the third day according to the scriptures, and that he was seen ...* by many witnesses. "Because God knew nobody but Jesus could keep the whole law, he sent Jesus to pay the penalty for every person's guilt, whether it would be many terrible sins or just breaking one of the laws. The Gospel means the Good News. None of us has the ability to get to heaven on our own efforts, but because of the Gospel, we don't have to even try. We just need to believe and accept Jesus as our own personal Savior."

Jason thought about that and the other verses for a while and then excitedly said, "The other verses that Maria talked about and all the ones you read have the Gospel in them! Dad, may I use your Bible to re-read the verses Maria wrote down? I want to see if they make sense now." His dad smiled and handed him the Bible and the list of verses. He looked up each one and read them out loud. As he went, he reiterated almost everything she had said with each verse, and he became more convinced that every verse and everything she had said was true and he was the one who was wrong. "Now I can see what she meant, but at that time my pride and anger got in the way. I got angry when she intimated that I would not go to heaven. She was right and I was wrong. But I don't have to <u>stay</u> wrong! I can believe the Gospel and know for sure that I'll go to heaven when I die. Will you two help me pray the prayer so I can do it right?"

"Of course, Jason. We'll be glad to!" they both said. In a short time they were finished and Jason had the peace and joy of a believer. Anna turned on a hymn called "Verily, Verily" which has many of the words from John 3:16-18, and John 5:24 as she handed the hymnal to him so he could follow along as his parents sang. By the third verse Jason was singing with them. He realized that he had done what the hymn said.

Then William said, "I would like to encourage you about the good works you've done. They are not futile because they've helped you gain some good habits that can continue in your new life as a believer on his way to heaven. Listen again to Ephesians 2: 8, 9, but this time I'll add verse 10 also. *For by grace you are saved, through faith, not of yourselves. It is the gift of God, not by works so that no man can boast. For we are his workmanship, created in Christ Jesus to do good works, which God has intended before that we should do.* When you hear all three verses together, what do you understand?" his dad asked.

"That God has good works for us to do, but they're not what gets us to heaven! Wow! It's so clear to me now."

Anna added, "There's another verse that agrees with that one. It's Titus 3:8 *This is a faithful saying, and I want you to affirm these things constantly, that those who have believed in God will be careful to maintain good works. These things are good and profitable to men."*

"Thank you so much, Mom and Dad, for your patience and for helping me see that I was wrong. It's scary to think that I could have gone on and on like that and have been eternally dead wrong. Thank you, Jesus, for my good parents and for Maria and especially for all the verses in the Bible that set me straight."

His parents continued by thanking and praising God, "for bringing our dear son into his family!"

Suddenly, Jason asked, "Do you think Ruth and Esther would come over here so that I can apologize to them?"

Anna answered, "I think they would be thrilled. I'll call them right now." When she finished, she told him that they were on their way. They were there within 15 minutes, and came in with looks of anticipation on their faces.

Jason immediately stood and walked over to them. Taking their hands in his he said with tears running down his face, "Ruth, Esther, my dear sisters, I'm so very sorry for the way I treated you. It was uncalled for and totally rude. Will you please forgive me?"

They both said at the same time, "Of course, Jason. We forgive you. Thank you for your apology." He thanked them for their forgiveness, and then the three of them joined in a three-way hug, while he told them what had happened to him this morning.

After that, the whole family had a great time of rejoicing, and thanking and praising the Lord.

William then said, "Jason, I think there's something else Jesus would like to do for you. He wants to heal you of your bi-polar disorder. Would it be all right with you if each of us puts a hand on your shoulder or back, and I put mine on your head while we pray that he will do that?"

"Yes," he answered. "I would love to be free of that disorder!"

So they gathered around him and put their loving hands on him and prayed in agreement. Then William finished with, "Jason, Jesus Christ heals you completely of your bi-polar disorder. It is gone in Jesus name."

In a few moments Jason said sincerely, "Thank you all for praying, and thank you Jesus, for healing me!" The rest of the family joined in with their thanks and praise.

William continued, "I talked to your doctor a couple weeks ago, and asked him what we should do if Jesus heals you. He told me to tell you to continue your medication until the day before the appointment you make so he can spend a day with you to do tests and observe you without medication. He said that this new medication you've been on only takes a day to get out of your system. I guess that's why it was so obvious to you when you forgot to take it. Going to the doctor for the tests will prove to the medical community that you are healed, and don't need to take any more medication. And we'll also have a chance to give God the glory for your healing."

Jason agreed with that, and the family continued to visit for a while. Anna gave Jason one of those booklets and cards that the pastor gives to new believers and explained about it, and then invited him to join them in church tomorrow where he could give the card to the pastor. "I'll be there," he said. "And now I'll walk back to my apartment and get some work done and be sure my suit is ready for tomorrow."

"Sounds like a good plan. Feel free to wear what ever you would be most comfortable wearing. Some men come dressed casually, and others wear suits. The service your mom and I attend starts at noon. We'll see you tomorrow at church. Would you like to come here for lunch after church?" his dad asked.

"Yes, I would like that very much," he answered. After Jason had left, the rest of the family spent some more time praising and thanking God for the miracles he had performed that morning, and talking over how wonderful it was.

Linda L. Linn
*****

    Ted and Julie were glad that the weather was still pleasant, and that they had planned and prepared a picnic lunch to take with them after the small group meeting. When they got to a park that was new to them, they strolled around to admire the flowers and blossoming trees before they ate. While they walked they reviewed what had happened in the small group.
    Ted said, "I'm so amazed by the things that keep happening in our small group, and not just in the group, but also in the church and now in the hospital and the workplace. This is the type of thing we were looking for before we moved here. Now we're hearing about it from eye witnesses and even seeing it for ourselves in your case with the teaching position at the church school."
    Julie agreed, "That's for sure! I feel almost overwhelmed after hearing Matt's story and the teaching time today. I'm amazed and thankful and praise God. But, are <u>we</u> really supposed to go out there and do things like that?"
    "I think we're both feeling intimidated by this new assignment. I'm very relieved that we won't be expected to go out there and try it on our own. Larry and Jane will be with us and we can watch and learn. They'll probably explain a lot to us along the way. And remember we have another of those well-known booklets about this topic to read and it will help us understand things better. This time it's called, 'I Can Do All Things.' The Lord will know when we're ready to try it on our own," Ted responded.
    "That <u>is</u> a relief!" said Julie. "There I go again worrying about the what, when, where and how. I know the why. Don did a great job teaching about that today. I just need to remember that Jesus lives in me by his Holy Spirit, and that he is the one with the power, know-how, timing and guidance. This won't be something that I have to try to <u>make</u> happen. It will all be up to HIM. All I have to do is be wherever he says to be, and do whatever he says to do."
    "I think you hit the nail right on the head," said Ted. "Everything is up to him and he gets all the glory for it. There's nothing we can do on our own. Even our daily lives depend on HIM, so we don't need to worry or wonder. This will be good for us, because it will stretch us and strengthen our faith."
    Julie continued, "Yes, you're right. It's all part of growing and learning to trust Jesus. I'm also very happy for Clara, because

Everywhere There's a Sunrise, Let's Tell The Good News!

God is stepping in to help her. I don't know her very well, but it's seemed that she's looked a little more tired every week than when we first met her. Now she won't have to work full time to pay for classes and daily living both, along with trying to study. God is so good, and his timing is always perfect, even if it does not look like it to us at the time while we're waiting and not knowing what to do. He proved that to me by the way he put me into this wonderful teaching job, and worked out all the details in such astonishing ways. I'm happier teaching in this school with these methods than I ever was when I taught in the public school."

Ted added, "God is the giver of perfect gifts. I'm extremely glad for you, my Jewel. I like seeing you happy with your career. This has been a good move for us. Just think about how far we've come already."

"You're right again, my treasure. I'm very grateful," Julie responded, and then she turned around and doubled over laughing. Ted looked at her like she had lost her marbles.

When she could stop laughing, she quipped, "Just look how far we've come ... away from our car and our lunch! All of a sudden I'm very hungry. Those cookies we ate at the group seem very far away now!" At this point, they were both laughing so hard there were tears streaming down their faces.

Ted exclaimed, "You're so much fun to be with, Honey. Race you back to the car! First one there gets to unlock the doors." With that they took off running and of course Ted won. He had such long legs.

They enjoyed their picnic lunch even more because they were extra hungry and it all tasted better out of doors. When they finished, they put the leftovers back in the container and headed home to read the "I Can Do" booklet. The title is taken from Philippians 4:13 which says, *I can do all things though Christ who strengthens me.*

Here are some of the things they found out: Julie read, "It is church policy to go out in groups of two or more, for accountability and always with at least one male in the group for the safety of the women."

Ted commented, "I'm really glad to hear that, because I don't like the idea of two women being on their own, except for in stores and shopping malls."

Then she read, "Usually married couples go out together two by two, but any time another couple needs training, they should go with a couple who has experience, and it is always four by four, for obvious reasons. It is not a good idea for unmarried couples to go alone. They need to have at least one more male or female, preferably another couple to keep them accountable.

"There are many and varied scenarios like praying while walking around in a park or neighborhood, or down a street in the business part of the city, all the while being alert for any opportunities to begin a conversation with one or more people, or possibly offer to help them in some obvious need. It is usually best to try to develop rapport with the people before offering to help. But always follow the Holy Spirit's leading and do what he says to do." She put the book down and said, "It doesn't sound too hard so far."

Ted agreed and then took his turn reading. "If you see somebody in a wheel chair, there <u>could</u> be an opportunity to pray for their healing, but as stated before, you need to develop rapport with them before offering to pray. You could easily offend someone otherwise. Handicapped people usually like to think they're doing the best they can and want to feel confident of being as independent as possible. Many of them don't want sympathy, or even offers to be helped. It is best to treat them as much like normal people as you can." He looked up at Julie and stated, "These are really positive and useful things to know. I would never have realized them on my own."

"I wouldn't either. I'm very thankful for the booklets the church has on so many subjects. It is especially valuable to have all the information in print so we can review it as needed. I could never remember all these things if someone were giving a lecture or teaching on it. Let's read silently together and comment or ask questions as needed. It goes faster that way, and I think I remember it better."

Ted nodded and later, he remarked, "Here is an exciting point: 'When there has been an obvious healing, be sure that Jesus receives all the glory for it and try to lead the conversation to the Gospel message and encourage them to let Jesus heal their souls and spirits as well. If there have been other people watching and listening, include them in the conversation. This is where and when the evangelism opportunity is the greatest.' That's exactly what happened with Matt's boss after God healed his heart. He was more than ready to accept Jesus salvation, and so were his co-workers!"

"You're so right. That's exciting, and I remember Don saying that Matt's praise report was a good transition into the subject of the ministry the small groups all do. It's beginning to make sense.

It will be so thrilling to be involved in somebody being healed and then saved too, as a result!" exclaimed Julie.

"Exactly," agreed Ted. "But it might take time to build a relationship with the people who need it, kind of like what Maria, Ruth and Esther are doing at their workplace. So we'll need to be patient and not pushy. It could turn people away from Jesus instead. I think I need a break for a while. How would you like to take some time for housework and I'll do some car care? We can read some more later." Julie agreed and they went and got a lot accomplished.

*****

Don and Anita went right home after the small group meeting, to give Mindy a few hours off before she would need to come back for the new believers small group meeting, which would be here at their house, from 2:30 to 4:30. They listened to the children tell about their morning of fun with the twins and Mindy, and then it was their nap time.

"Let's lie down and rest for 30 minutes before we fix lunch," Anita suggested. "It's going to be a busy afternoon and evening since the children might be finished with their afternoon naps by the time the group is over."

"I like the sound of that. That new Saturday morning small group has been extraordinary every week, and we need some time to regroup before lunch and the next meeting," Don agreed.

After a nice rest and a good lunch, they still had time to play a game with Timmy and Mary before they set up the chairs and put out the Bibles and hymnals. They would follow the same basic plan that they had on Thursday evening, so Don was ready for it. He helped Anita to set up the refreshments in the kitchen. Mindy got there at 2:20, and since it was such a nice spring day, she took the children outside to play in the yard until about 4 PM when it would be time for their naps. She would read them a quiet story just before that. Don and Anita were very thankful that Mindy was willing to spend her Saturday doing daycare and that they had the money to pay her. Today Anita would not have to get up periodically to go check on them like she did on Thursday evening.

The group members all arrived close to on time, and the meeting went very well. They had a few different questions about things in the booklets, but other than that, it was very much like Thursday's meeting. The co-facilitators answered some of the questions and had enough input that the group could be used to them when they took over on their own in a couple weeks.

Just before refreshments, Don said, "We'll meet again next Saturday, but it will be at 9:30 AM, and it will be at the co-facilitator's home." He gave the address and continued, "We'll talk about water baptism, cover some other topics and answer any other questions you might have. Come now and join us for a few refreshments and a time of visiting."

When all the people had left, Anita took Mindy to her home. Don and Anita put all the leftover refreshments, the Bibles and hymnals, and the extra chairs away, as they talked quietly about how the meeting had gone and what else needed to be done. "I still need to find co-facilitators for the other new believers group that will meet on Tuesday or Wednesday next week. I guess I could make some phone calls right now. His first call produced a couple that would be glad to help guide a group for new believers. They decided on Wednesday as the best day for the group, since the baptismal would be on Tuesday of the following week and they would miss out on a meeting that week if they chose that day.

After that phone call was over, Anita speculated, "I know the churches don't share numbers, but still I wonder how many new believers resulted from the special 'Christ in the Passover' meetings done by Jews for Jesus. They were at three of the Saturday church services the weekend of Palm Sunday. I'm so glad they were able to come this year! The Jewish population in Pine City has grown in the last few years. I have always had a special caring in my heart for the Jewish people."

"I know you have, and I think it's a very good thing. I know we won't hear how many, but they'll be included in the baptismal services the week after next. It's a good thing that the churches don't share numbers, because our work is for Jesus, not for us to feel proud. It is not competition, as you know, but like it says in Philippians 2:3a, *Let nothing be done with strife or for vainglory...* Our purpose is to show unity, like Jesus prayed just before he died for the world: John 17:21, *I pray that they all may be one, as you Father, are in me and I am in you, that they also may be one in us, so that the world may believe that you have sent me.* I'm glad the Lord is the one who adds people to his church. It takes all the pressure off us. But I'm very grateful that you didn't give up trying to get Jews for Jesus to come do their 'Christ in the Passover' meetings," Don stated.

"Me too. Their web site, jewsforjesus.org, was very helpful. The meeting we went to see that Saturday was very well done and helped me to understand how the Passover is such a good picture of what Jesus came to earth to do for people," Anita replied.

"I agree," said Don. "Maybe you could look to see if they have any other programs they could do here."

"Great idea!" she exclaimed. "I'll go look, hopefully before the children get up."

Don said, "Okay, I need to call the main pastor and tell him how many new believers we might be baptizing so that he can make any changes before we announce on which day the service will be. I'm not completely sure until after tomorrow, but I know how many booklets I handed out and how many people usually bring their cards back, so I can estimate. I'll call him right now and tell him my estimate so he can make any changes he needs to make."

The main pastor was pleasantly surprised at Don's estimated number, and he told Don that he could still announce Tuesday of the week after next for the special baptismal service for church #4 which would be with churches #2 and #3. Church #1 would move over to Wednesday, since the numbers for Wednesday were lower.

"So far, so good," said Don after hanging up the phone, which had been on speaker so Anita could hear also. "We can go ahead as planned for Wednesday and Thursday and Saturday next week. We'll need to see if Mindy can do daycare for us on Thursday evening while we're at the church, and for Saturday again."

Just at that point the children woke up from their naps and came sleepily out of their rooms to cuddle on one or the other of their parents' laps. It was a special time of the weekend since they didn't get to do that on weekdays. Don and Anita enjoyed it, also. It was good to be able to give additional positive attention to each child. Anita would look at that web site later.

*****

Matt and Ben spent Saturday afternoon and early evening working on Matt's house. The weather was just right, and they accomplished a lot, along with plenty of questions getting answered and explanations about the way things were done.

"Have I over worked and overloaded you with information today, or would you like to come back tomorrow morning if the weather permits, and work some more?" Matt asked Ben.

"Yes, I would like to come back tomorrow morning, and I'll bring my lunch and clothes to change into for church. I've learned a lot today, and I like it. It wasn't too much for me. I think all of this will give me a good background for my schooling next year. It was great to help frame in that wall and then help set it up. This house is starting to take shape now. It would go so much faster if we could just work on it every day," Ben answered.

"I agree, and I would like that myself, but I have my regular job, and you have school, so we'll just have to be content with the few hours we do find to work on it. Let's go to my apartment now and fix us a bachelor supper."

"That sounds like fun. I'm hungry," agreed Ben.

*****

On Friday, Patrick had called the pastor of church #1 and set up an appointment for Glenda, Fiona, and himself to come ask some questions on Saturday at 3 PM so that all three of them could be there. The pastor told them about several areas of ministry that were often in need of funds to do their work and then mentioned, "There is one other idea that we've been considering, since our churches are growing very quickly in the last few weeks. Many of our 12 churches will be getting very close to the maximum of 275 pretty soon and that's wonderful, but we need a creative way to care for all the people and keep growing and reaching out to the unsaved people in our city. The best idea we've had, is to build a second church like this one and a school to accompany it and hire 12 more pastors and 16 more teachers. Then we can have volunteers go as members of the new churches, keep operating like we have been and keep growing. This idea is <u>not</u> common knowledge, but it's something you could pray about," he finished. They thanked him and went home to do just that.

*****

Chapter 14

John 13:35, *By this shall all men know that you are my disciples, if you have love one to another.*

Everywhere There's a Sunrise, Let's Tell The Good News!

The fourth Sunday in April

    Sunday morning was another beautiful spring day with puffy white clouds in a deep blue sky. The mountains in the distance looked so majestic with snow still on them. They had gotten a lot of snow the past winter and it would probably take its time melting. That would be a good thing since it would be more useful by melting little by little, and it would fill up the reservoirs again.
    Matt and Ben were able to work some more on the house again, and it was nice to see the progress. They enjoyed working together, and it was helping both of them. Ben was so appreciative, and Matt liked explaining things to Ben the way Walt had done for him. It made him feel like he was doing something positive and not just being so focused on doing something for himself.
    Of course he would have to admit that he <u>was</u> building this house for himself and hopefully for Fiona, if he ever felt free to ask her to be his wife. <u>They</u> were moving <u>very</u> slowly. He reminded himself to just be patient and enjoy the process. Plus, he could look forward to sitting with her in church this afternoon and then spending the rest of the day with her and her family. It would be fun to practice throwing Frisbees again, and then eat what he knew would be a delicious picnic supper.
    Jason went for another long walk in the morning, and this time the grass seemed greener, the sky bluer, and the flowers and birds more colorful than ever before. After a while, he returned home, ate breakfast and then took a shower. He spent a little extra time getting dressed for church. He even looked forward to going. He had finished reading the booklet and had filled out the card, so it would be ready to give to the pastor. He decided that it would be good for him to join a small group of new believers with a leader who could answer questions and get them started on this new life. For the first time in a very long time, he could be hopeful of better times ahead. It was time for some positive changes in his life. He didn't know what they would be, but he felt peaceful considering them. Thoughts of change usually were accompanied by fears and doubts, but not now. It was good and freeing to be rid of fear and doubts, and he wondered if it was because Jesus had healed him. He felt like a new person! He thanked Jesus and then determined to enjoy the freedom and peace.
    Roy and Sherry took Joy and Hope to a nice park in town after breakfast and explained to them, "You may play on the equipment

while we walk around the edge of the play area. We'll keep an eye on you and if you need us because of an accident you can call for us." Then they started walking and praying and looking for anyone they might be directed to in order to talk with them, or help them with something, or whatever else the Holy Spirit might say to do. There were several parents there with their children, and they tried starting a conversation with small talk, but didn't get very far. Some days were like that, and it was okay. They knew they just had to be available and let the Spirit guide them. After about an hour, they went to play with the girls for a time before taking them back home to get cleaned up, eat lunch and then go to church.

Walt and Betty were nervous about going to church for their first time ever. Matt had called them last night and said he would wait for them at the entrance and they could sit with him and Fiona and her parents. He wanted them to meet Fiona anyway after the service. They were grateful that he was so thoughtful and had anticipated their anxiety about going to church. He had also told them they didn't need to dress up, or for Walt to wear a suit. They could come in casual clothes if they would rather. Either way was fine with this church. In fact he had told Walt that he had called all his and Walt's co-workers to tell them there was no dress code for the church.

*****

Matt and Ben were standing together in the entryway of the church before the Sunday 2 PM service. Ben saw his family come in, so he went to be with them, and Matt waved at them. Not long after that, Walt and Betty came in and smiled to see that Matt was exactly where he said he would be. He went right over to welcome them and lead them to seats in the same row as Fiona and her family. He had called her the night before and asked if she would save three seats for him and the Evans couple. He greeted Fiona and her parents. Then Walt and Betty and he sat down. He showed them where the Bible and hymnals were located and the big display board up front that had the names of the songs they would sing. They looked comfortable about that and Matt assumed they had learned how to use these important books at the new believer group on Thursday. Those groups were so helpful to people who had had no background in church. He had many reasons to be grateful for this church and the good things it did.

Everywhere There's a Sunrise, Let's Tell The Good News!

Pastor Don came in and smiled at all the people in the congregation. He welcomed all the new believers especially, and then they started singing. The songs this week were: "Then Jesus Came," from many verses in the Gospels; "I Heard the Voice of Jesus Say", Matthew 11:29,30; "Praise Him! Praise Him!" John 10:2; "Jesus Paid It All," 1 Corinthians 6:20; and "Jesus, Name Above All Names," Philippians 2:8-11.

The teaching time started with the scriptures that go with the songs. Don said, "Our first song today was how Jesus came with his compassion, mercy and healing power to heal, restore sight, forgive or do whatever a person might need. There are many verses in the Gospels, Matthew, Mark, Luke, and John that tell of those times, but we'll only look up one today. Please find Mark 1:30,31 and listen as I read. *The mother of Peter's wife was sick with a fever and they told Jesus about her. Jesus came and took her by the hand and lifted her up. Immediately the fever left her and she served them.*

"The words of our second song are a summary or a testimony of what each one of us as believers did when we decided to believe in Jesus and ask him to be our own personal Savior. They're certainly an encouragement every time we sing or read them. Take your Bibles and find Matthew 11:28-30. Follow along as I read. Jesus says, *Come to me all you who labor and are heavy laden, and I will give you rest. Take my yoke upon you, and learn about me, for I am meek and lowly in heart, and you shall find rest for your souls. My yoke is easy and my burden is light.* These verses go very well with that song. He gives us rest, and as we learn about him, we'll find that being yoked with him makes our burdens light.

"The third song was a great way to praise Jesus for all he is and has done. It is another good summary and can be used as a testimony to tell others what Jesus did for us. In John 10:2, it tells about Jesus being the shepherd of the sheep. Real shepherds take very good care of their sheep. Many places in the Bible compare us people to sheep. I'm glad we have a real and very good shepherd.

"1Corinthians 6:20 says: *You are bought with a price. Therefore glorify God in your body and in your spirit, which belong to God.* Jesus paid that price, and now because he loved us that much, we want to live the rest of our lives for him. This is basically what the fourth song said.

"Here is a summary of Philippians 2:8-11 for the last song. Jesus humbly died on the cross, and therefore God exalted him and gave him a name, which is above every name, and one day everyone will bow to him, and confess that he is Lord.

"I went through the verses that go with today's songs to remind and/or to teach you that they usually only go with part of the song. I'm sure that there are other verses that could be chosen to go with the songs. That might make a good Bible study for you to do sometime.

"I would like to welcome all the new believers again, and tell you how happy we are to have you here as a part of this congregation and of the family of God. Now, for the main part of today's teaching. We really are a family. The following Bible verses will remind us old timers and teach you new believers how God desires his family to act. Please find 1 John near the end of the New Testament. Look at chapter 3, verse 1. *Behold what manner of love the Father has bestowed on us that we should be called sons of God ...* Next go in the same book to 4:7-11, and 19. *Beloved, let us love one another, for love is of God, and everyone that loves is born of God and knows God. He who does not love does not know God, for God is love. This is how the love of God was shown to us: God sent his only begotten Son into the world that we might live through him. This is love, not that we loved God, but that he loved us, and sent his Son to be the payment for our sins. Beloved, if God so loved us, then we also ought to love one another,* and verse 19: *We love him (God) because he first loved us.* Turn back a page to chapter 3, verse 23 which says, *this is (God's) command: Believe on the name of his Son, Jesus Christ, and love one another ...*

"Here are some more verses. You don't need to look them up, but you might wish to write down the references, and then just listen. Galatians 5:13b tells us to serve one another by love. 1 Thessalonians 4:9b says, *we are taught by God to love one another.* 1 Peter 1: 22b says to *love one another with a pure heart fervently.* We desire to show the world how much we love one another so that they'll want to have what we have.

"Besides love, there are some other things we need to be doing for one another. Colossians 3:13,14 says: *bear with or be patient with one another, forgive one another like Christ forgave you, and above all, love.* Ephesians 4:32 says almost the same thing. *Be kind to one another, tenderhearted, forgiving one another, even as God for Christ's sake has forgiven you.* And 5:2 says, *Walk in love, as Christ also has loved us, and has given himself for us as an offering and sacrifice to God.* Romans 12:10

says, *be kindly affectionate to each other with brotherly love, in honor preferring one another.* Verse 16a says, *be of the same mind (or in harmony) with one another.* Romans 15:7 says, *Receive one another, as Christ also received us to the glory of God.* Hebrews 3:13a says, *Encourage one another daily.*

"Now, we're not going to sing this yet, but please open your hymnals to "They'll Know We Are Christians by Our Love," John 13:35. Let's read the words out loud and think about what they say. ... Now, read it again, but this time read the chorus using the word believers in place of the word Christians.

"I've used the word love a lot today. Here are some synonyms for love as a noun: affection, devotion, respect, allegiance, and loyalty; and as a verb: to cherish, to value, to be loyal. This time read through the whole song, silently, replacing the word love with some of its noun synonyms. It helps me a lot to do this with hymns because I have to focus more on what the words say and mean. Now let's sing the whole song as it is written."

When they finished singing, Pastor Don said, I have a very important announcement for our new believers. The week after this one, on Tuesday at 7 PM, there will be a special baptismal service here in this sanctuary for all our new believers and anyone else who hasn't been baptized in water. Other people who attend this church service time are invited to come also, especially if you know one or more of the people who are going to be baptized. Come and hear the results of the Good News. Any small groups that meet on Tuesdays may come and this can replace your usual small group meeting.

"This week the new believers groups will contain teaching about what water baptism means, why it is important, and how it is done. For those of you who are new believers but haven't returned your cards to me, please see me right after this service and when you give them to me, I'll give you a paper with the time and place of two meetings that you'll need to attend this week, so that you can be ready to be baptized.

"Now let's go show the world that we are Christians by our love!" finished their pastor.

Many people went up to the pastor, returned their cards and received a paper with the days, times and places for the new believers group meetings. Then Don was able to catch Matt and Walt before they left so he could urge them to let the men on the second shift go home at 5:30 so they could eat, shower, and dress in time to be at the church at 7 PM on the day of the baptismal service.

Walt agreed, "That's a great idea! Since Matt is in charge of that shift, it will be up to him to remember to send them all home at 5:30 PM on Tuesday next week. This is all very exciting to me. Thank you, Pastor Don."

The regulars greeted each other and made sure to welcome and talk with the other new believers. Ted sought out the first and second shift men and their wives, while Julie went to talk with her former boss and his wife. They wanted them to feel at home here like they had the first times they had come to this church.
Because of the pastor's teaching, they could understand why they liked this church so much. The people really did show their love for each other.

*****

After the service, Maria, Julie and Ted went for a longer walk in the park, with Ted following and praying. Julie had so much to tell Maria about, but she insisted Maria go first. Maria stated, "It's all very much like it was last week, which is wonderful, but nothing new has happened, so please go ahead and tell me all your news.

So, as they walked, Julie told Maria about the Saturday group and all the miracles that had taken place during the week, being careful not to mention any names. Then she shared about a very good week at school, and told Maria the two prayer requests that Pam had sent in her last e-mail. Then they enjoyed the green grass, new leaves on the trees and the flowers that were blooming along the pathway.

While the ladies were talking, Ted had met up with Tony, so he had someone to walk and visit with, also. He explained to Tony about wanting to walk with the ladies so he could be sure they stayed safe.

Tony mentioned that was the same idea for having two by two or four by four groups for projects, to keep the ladies safe and to be accountable to each other. Ted agreed that he remembered reading that in the booklet.

Then Ted asked Tony if he had met Maria. Since he had not, Ted introduced Maria and Tony to each other when they arrived back at the cars. "Maria, this is Tony Valdez, and he's in our small group on Saturday mornings. Tony, please meet Maria Gomez, who attends Church #4, and is our good friend."

Everywhere There's a Sunrise, Let's Tell The Good News!

"Mucho gusto," they both said at the same time, laughed, and then went on conversing in Spanish for a few minutes with Julie listening and understanding all they were saying.

But Ted finally interrupted and said, "No fair! I don't know enough Spanish to keep up with you, and you talk so fast anyway, that I don't have a clue about what has been said."

They apologized and Tony translated for Ted, "We were just saying that we had seen each other at church, but had never had the chance to meet and talk before. Then we both said where we work, what our hours are, and how long we've lived in Pine City. Just like we do at the first meeting of all the small groups."

Ted responded, "Thank you, Tony. Maybe all three of you who speak Spanish so well can teach me so I can join into the conversations. I can see now that it would be a useful language to know."

"Your wife speaks Spanish also?" asked Tony.

"Yes, Julie studied Spanish in high school and then minored in it during college. While she and Maria were roommates in college, she became very fluent by conversing with her. I never had those opportunities," Ted lamented. They told him they would be glad to teach him and then he had an idea, "Since we are all still dressed nicely for church, we could all go to a nice restaurant for supper. Is anybody interested? And if so, who has a suggestion about where to go? I haven't lived in Pine City long enough to have any ideas."

Julie and Maria both said that they would like to go out for supper but didn't care where.

Tony suggested, "If you like Spanish cuisine, Fiesta Espanola Restaurante, where I work has very tasty food. I would enjoy eating there instead of working for a change."

"Great proposal!" said Ted. "Is it close enough to this park that we can walk, or should we take the cars?"

"It's just across the street from here, at the end of the block there. I live close enough to the church and my job and shopping that I don't even own a vehicle. I just walk or ride my bike or take the bus. It saves an amazing amount of money for me to do it that way," Tony explained shyly.

Maria responded, "I really like that idea. I would do it myself if I could, but my job is too far away from where I live, and I realize that it would not be a safe thing for a woman to do anyway." She had seen Ted stiffen and frown so she wisely added that last phrase. She was pleased to see him relax again. "Shall we go?" They all nodded and started to walk to the corner.

Before long they were seated in a very nice establishment and were looking around and enjoying the ambiance. Tony told them a little about the history of the restaurant and how long he had been working there. Then Ted congratulated him for his recent promotion to assistant manager. Tony thanked him humbly, and then a waiter came to pour their water and give them menus. Everyone studied the menu and chose an entree by the time the waiter returned to take their orders.

Then Julie instructed, "This will be your first Spanish lesson, Ted." Holding up her glass of water she stated, "Este es un vaso de agua. That means, This is a glass of water. Repeat that sentence." He picked up his glass of water and repeated the sentence in Spanish, even though he did feel a little embarrassed. Then his three instructors took turns holding up an item from the table and saying a sentence to go with it, which he repeated. When they had finished all the items on the table, they said the word in Spanish and he was to pick up the item they said.

Since he had a good memory, he did very well, but soon grew tired of being in the limelight, so he proposed that they just converse in English for a while. He asked, "What did you like about the service this morning?"

Maria answered, "I was pleasantly surprised by all the new believers there today. I know some of them accepted Jesus in the last two or three church services, but I'm glad Julie was able to tell me about the miracle that happened last week that resulted in so many people coming to Christ."

Tony said, "The man in our small group who told the story was so humble about it and gave all the glory to God, which of course is where it should go, but I was glad he didn't act proud about it."

Julie added, "Me too. I liked the teaching today about how we are to love, be patient, forgive, and be in harmony with one another. I can't remember all the things he said, but it makes sense to show the world that we are Christians by our love for fellow believers. Ted and I really like the way the people in this church show their love. They made us feel so welcomed and cared for when we first got here," said Julie.

Ted agreed with her and at that point their food arrived. It was all delicious, and they enjoyed more dialogue about various topics as they ate. As they finished eating, Tony suggested that Ted review the words he had learned at the beginning of their meal. He surprised them all by picking up each item, saying what it was, and getting all of them right.

Everywhere There's a Sunrise, Let's Tell The Good News!

*****

At a different park on the other side of town, Matt, Fiona, and her parents were enjoying the nice weather while they practiced throwing Frisbees as they walked around the whole park. They even remembered to look at the flowers as they went and managed not to hit any of them with the Frisbees.

Matt mentioned near the end of the practice session, "I think all of us have gotten better than when we first started today. It is definitely harder than it looks, but I think that with a couple more practice sessions we'll be ready to take on the course and do a pretty good job. What do you think, Glenda?"

"It is pretty fun. Although, I think I might have a sore arm tomorrow," she answered.

"Oh, I am sorry. We should have stopped sooner. I have some special gel in the pickup. It always helps me when I overdo things. I'll just run and get it. Be right back." He hurried back and told the ladies to go over to the restroom and slather a light layer on what ever felt sore. Then he asked, "How are you doing, Patrick?"

"I'm fine, thank you, Matt, and thank you for caring and having something to help the ladies," he answered. Fiona's and my jobs at The Garden Shop, keep us in better shape than the housework does for Glenda, but she's eager to try things anyway. She is a wonderful woman. God has really blessed me!"

"I'll say!" agreed Matt. "Your daughter is also a wonderful woman and I hope some day to be able to ask her to be my wife. She just isn't ready for that question yet, so I'll try to be patient."

Just then the women returned and Glenda said, "My arm already feels better. Thank you very much, Matt."

"You're very welcome. I'm glad that it helped. You can keep that tube and use it again several times this evening and again tomorrow. I have another tube at home. How's your arm, Fiona?"

"It's fine. I've been practicing off and on and I think it helped," she replied.

"I'm glad to hear that. No wonder you're hitting the targets better than I am. Good for you. Keep up the good work. I'll try to get in some additional practice this week, so I can improve also."

Patrick said, "Let's go eat. I'm getting hungry enough to eat the picnic basket," he joked. They all laughed as they went to get it out of the car and set things up. "This fresh air and exercise does make me extra hungry." Everybody agreed with him.

Everything tasted as delicious as Matt had imagined it would. He had enjoyed the afternoon immensely and was sorry when it ended.

*****

Monday

Matt woke on Monday to another spring rain and even some snowflakes earlier in the morning, but they melted as soon as they hit. He was thankful for the nice weather on the weekend and all the work he and Ben had gotten done on his house. The rain made it easier for him to take his dirty laundry over to the laundromat and get that chore over and done with. He'd have to admit that it was nice to have clean clothes. It was even nicer to be able to look back on the fine time he had yesterday afternoon with Fiona and her parents. It was good to be able to get to know them better by doing fun things or working together on a project. Matt's mind stayed on her, while he finished his laundry and went back home.

*****

While Ted and Julie ate breakfast Julie remarked, "It was a fun afternoon and evening with Maria yesterday. I have a funny feeling that you were playing matchmaker though, which is very unusual for you."

"Would I do a thing like that?" he teased. "Well, maybe so. Tony is a very nice young man, and he's a committed Christian. I just thought I would introduce them and then take everyone to supper so they would have a chance to get acquainted. God can take it from there."

Julie smiled and replied, "I thought it was a very good idea. Maria is too shy to reach out and initiate anything on her own. They seemed comfortable with each other and conversed easily. It will be interesting to see what happens. She needed a positive experience after that fiasco with Jason. I should pray for him more often."

"Me too. Well, we better hurry and get ready to go to work," said Ted.

"Right. Oh, look, it's raining, with a few snowflakes mixed in. Would you like to get ready early and have me drop you off at your job?" asked Julie.

"No, I won't melt, but thanks for offering. I'll clean up the breakfast things and then go. Thank you for making such good lunches for us to take to work."

"You're very welcome, and thank you for all your help with the housework," she added, and gave him a quick hug and kiss before hurrying away to finish getting ready for school. She decided not to take any teaching materials with her today so they would not get wet.

*****

Maria had gone to bed wondering if Ted had set up that meeting on purpose, but he didn't seem the type to be a matchmaker. She woke up Monday still wondering. They did all have an enjoyable evening at the restaurant and it had been a good way to get acquainted with a stranger. Tony seemed like a nice, polite person, and he was easy to talk with. And at least she knew that he was a believer. There was nothing said about any future times together, and he had not asked for her phone number, so she would not waste time speculating. Instead, she spent time praying and put the whole thing in God's very capable hands. Then she ate breakfast and went to work.

She was surprised to see Ruth and Esther both in her office when she arrived and wondered if something might be wrong. Then she wondered why her thoughts were always about what might be wrong. Maybe they had good news about something instead, so she hurried in to find out.

Ruth and Esther both started talking at once and Maria couldn't understand what they said. So she held up her hand and asked for just one of them to talk at a time. Esther zipped her lips and nudged her sister to talk. Ruth excitedly declared, "Jason became a believer on Saturday morning. Mom called for us to come over to their house because he wanted to say he was sorry to us for the way he had treated us. On top of all that, we all prayed for him, and Jesus healed him! He will go to his doctor for confirmation this week."

Esther continued, "We just couldn't wait until lunch time to tell you and thank you for praying with us about him. And we also thank you for your testimony to him at the restaurant, and for writing those verses in the Bible you gave to him. God used it all to get his attention and then he had questions for Mom and Dad on Saturday. He wanted them to tell him of other verses that would prove people are not saved by being good people. He went to church #1 with our parents and us on Sunday with a card to return, and he will be baptized next week on Wednesday."

"Wow!" exclaimed Maria. "I'm astounded by the goodness of God, and how quickly he's answered our prayers. Of course, I know you all have been praying for him for years, so it does not seem as fast to you. I'm so happy for all of you and for Jason too. Thank you for telling me right away this morning. Maybe we can talk about it some more at lunchtime. I suppose we should all get to work now."

They did all talk about it at lunchtime as they ate in the lunchroom at the office building since it was still raining outside. She was surprised again, when Ruth suddenly stated, "Maria, you could let Jason court you now, since he's a believer. He didn't say anything. And neither did any of us. The idea just hit me this minute! What do you think?"

"Oh, my! Give me a few minutes to think," she answered and they ate for a while in silence. Then she hesitatingly said, "I'll be completely honest. When Jason arrived at my little apartment building in a newer BMW, and took me to the most expensive restaurant in the city, I could tell right then that he is in a completely different league than I could ever be comfortable with. I do make good wages at this job, but I've chosen to live very simply so that I can give more to the work of God's Kingdom. Could we pray about this new scenario together and wait to see what God would want me to do?"

Ruth answered, "Certainly! Forgive me. That was a thoughtless thing for me to say to you. Prayer is the very best thing we can do. Jason will need time to become grounded in his new beliefs without thinking about wanting to court you. Furthermore, you would need time to hear how he changes. Father, we ask that you will keep Jason's mind on you and not let him even think about Maria unless and/or until you want him to. Plus we ask that you will put Maria's mind completely at peace and erase what I said to her, since it was way to early to even consider."

Maria continued, "I do forgive you, Ruth, and I will be at peace about it. Heavenly Father, thank you so much for Jason's salvation and healing. Now please help him become a committed follower of Jesus and to change and do whatever it is your will for him to do. Keep my mind fixed upon you instead of on a possible 'boyfriend.' Guide my every thought and decision since I don't even know for sure what your will is for me about singleness or marriage."

Esther finished for them, "Father, I ask for that last request especially for me also. It is hard to go back and forth between desiring a godly man who would love me, and wondering if I could do more for your kingdom as a single woman. Thank you that Ruth has peace about remaining single. Please guide Maria and me. Thank you. Amen."

*****

This Monday was the first rainy day for Julie as a teacher in the church school. She got to find out about one of the weekday uses of the church sanctuary. Recess and lunch play times and even before and after school were spent in there instead of out on the playground if the rain continued all day. Julie walked over there during the first recess, just to see how they handled it. The covered walkway kept her dry. The chairs were stacked up out of the way, and there was plenty of room. It <u>was</u> pretty noisy, but they were playing active games and having fun. She only stayed a few minutes and then hurried back to get things ready for the next couple hours of class time. She was relieved to know that they had a chance to get rid of some of their pent up energy, and would be ready to listen, learn and study. They were a good class.

*****

Tony awoke early on Monday morning realizing he had not slept very well. Maybe it was because of a meal that was bigger than he usually ate for supper. Or, maybe it was because he could not get his mind off the beautiful woman he had met that evening. She had immediately begun talking to him in Spanish and it was such a pleasant change to be able to converse in his own main language.

Of course, Ted had put a stop to that, because he could not understand them, but he seemed to want to learn Spanish himself. Maybe he could figure out a way to help him learn. Ted had looked a little embarrassed at times with his audience of 3 people trying to teach him. Tony liked Ted, from what he could learn at the small group, and if he could come up with a way to teach him alone, it might be a way to gain another Christian friend. Their hours were different, so it would have to be on the weekend.

He wondered if the three of them went walking together often on Sunday afternoons. Well, he had Ted's phone on that list that Anita had handed out at the small group meeting, so he could call him some evening as soon as he got home from work, or at his supper break time, which would be better, than calling so late in the evening. So he would copy the number and take it to work with him today.

Of course, that might not get him back in touch with Maria, and he had not had a chance to get her phone number. On the other hand, he wasn't even sure he wanted to. He better get busy and pray about that topic again, because he still wasn't sure whether God wanted him to stay single, or if maybe he had a good Christian wife for him. Here he was, 26 years old, and still he didn't know.

*****

After her morning classes and eating an early lunch, Clara took her supper in a paper bag and went to work for her last Monday at the American Furniture Warehouse. She arrived ten minutes early and stopped in to see her boss who motioned for her to come in and sit down.

"I came early today, because I want to thank you again for being so understanding and changing my hours when the new quarter started at the university, so that I could work here and still be able to attend classes in the morning," she said.

"You're welcome. How's it going?" her boss asked.

She answered, "I've been doing pretty well, although it makes for a long and busy day. I have what I hope will be as good news for you as it is for me. Two days ago, at a meeting of my church's small group, I was told, as a message from the Lord, 'it is time for me to stop working and to speed up my nursing education and evangelistic training. The harvest is ripe and the workers are few.' I was overwhelmed when I heard that, and thought it would be impossible, but they told me that there's a special fund set up by the church to help people like me to be able to hurry up their education so we can get out there and help win people to the Lord, since it might not be very long before Jesus comes back.

"Anyway, the money will pay for my living expenses and the extra classes I take, plus obtain the training the church gives to people who want to go out as missionaries. I'm planning to work as a nurse and tell the Gospel to needy people in my parents' hometown. So, since you need one week notice before I stop working here, I stopped in today to tell you that this coming Friday will be my last day to work here. I'm hoping that this won't put an extra burden on you or any of the people in this store."

Her boss exclaimed, "Wow! <u>That</u> is an exceptionally amazing story. You have told me other things that have happened in connection with your church's small groups, but this one top's those. Yes, this is very good news for me, because the evening hours have slowed down so much that I really don't have need of as many employees as I did when I hired you. I didn't want to lay you off or cut your hours because you're a very good worker, and I know how much you needed the job. Now neither of us has to worry about it, because your Lord has taken care of it, for both of us. You've asked me to come to your church before and I never did, but now I'm convinced that I need to learn more about a God who cares enough to work out important things for people like you."

"Thank you, Sir," Clara answered. "God is wonderful and he's blessed me a lot. I'm really glad you'll be coming to church. My pastor, Don Ross, will be glad to answer any questions you have. Church starts at 2 PM and I think I already gave you the address. Now I had better go get to work."

*****

It was after supper and cleanup was finished Monday evening, when the phone rang at the Blake residence. Maria had called to tell Julie all about Jason's salvation and healing, and then about what Ruth had said and all the rest of their conversation and prayer time. Maria told Julie that sometimes she felt she was in a maze and that she didn't know which way to go. Add to that, the meeting with Tony and wondering if Matt was playing matchmaker, and put <u>it</u> on top of the fact that she still didn't know what God's will was for her about singleness or marriage, and she felt totally lost.

Julie prayed with her about all of it, and promised to continue to pray. She encouraged Maria to rest in the Lord, and when it was his time, he would take her hand and lead her out of the maze. Julie did admit to her that Ted said that he was just giving her an opportunity to become acquainted in a safe setting, and see where God took it from there. He wasn't trying to push her into a relationship. Julie also said that <u>she</u> wanted Maria to have a positive experience with a good Christian man. In addition she told Maria what Ted had said about her needing to be more careful about walking outside alone.

A short time after she hung up the phone, it rang again. This time it was Tony wishing to speak to Ted. He explained to Ted his idea about teaching him Spanish without so many people being teachers at once. His idea was to meet at the same park on Sundays after church and they could walk behind the two ladies while he and Ted worked on Spanish. Ted told him he thought it was a great idea and they could start this coming Sunday if the weather would cooperate and not rain on them.

When Ted told Julie what Tony had suggested, she commented, "That was very nice of him. He seems like a caring person, and that will be a much better way for you to learn Spanish."

"I'll have to admit that I was a little embarrassed at the restaurant yesterday with three teachers at once," he said.

She continued, "I could see that and I understand. I just remembered that I still have all my Spanish text books from my high school and college courses. If you really <u>would</u> like to learn Spanish, I'll get the first one out for you and it will give you a head start for our next walk. Then you can go through the other books as you're ready for them."

"Yes, I really do want to learn Spanish and your idea is an excellent one. Thank you," he said.

She went and got the first book for him and said, "I'd be glad to help you with pronunciation or whatever else you might need. I'm glad you decided to learn Spanish. This will be another thing we can enjoy doing together."

*****

After their small group meeting with the pastors, Don and Anita stopped at Jeff and Karen's house to give them an SD card with the music, and a paper with the song titles and teaching for the Saturday small group. Starting next week, all that would be sent by e-mail on Tuesday morning. They didn't stay because they needed to get the little ones home and put to bed, but said to call if they had any questions. Jeff and Karen read over the paper and it seemed very straight forward, so they didn't need to call. They agreed that it should not be very hard to be facilitators, especially

Everywhere There's a Sunrise, Let's Tell The Good News!

with a group as nice as this one, and the plans for the meeting already made by the main pastor. This church had some very good ideas and clear-cut ways to implement them.

*****

Chapter 15

Matthew 8:3,4, *Jesus touched him saying, "Be clean."*
And immediately his leprosy was cleansed.
Jesus said to him, "Go show yourself to the priest
and offer the gift that Moses commanded, for a testimony to them."

Tuesday

    It was still raining off and on Tuesday morning, but that wasn't too unusual for this time of the year. Jason woke to another day of rain and was thrilled to recognize that it didn't depress him like it used to. He had called his doctor on Monday morning, and had gotten an appointment for today, so he had not taken his medication yesterday as the doctor had directed him to do. Before his healing, he would have been feeling very low this morning with the continued rain, especially without his medication, so he already knew that the doctor would be able to agree that he had been totally healed. What a miracle it was, really two miracles! One was for his soul, and the other for his mind. He was filled with thanksgiving as he went to shower and get ready to spend the day at the doctor's office after he opened up the office building and made the coffee for his workers.

    When he arrived at the doctor's reception area, he was asked to fill out a bunch of papers. That usually upset him, but today he was fine with doing it. He answered all the questions truthfully and thoughtfully, and returned the pile to the receptionist. It wasn't long before he was in the doctor's office explaining what had happened to him on Saturday. He also mentioned his observations about the rain and about filling out the papers without his usual upset. The doctor listened politely and typed that information into the computer. Then he read through the papers Jason had filled out. His expression looked very pleased when he finished. After that he asked Jason a series of questions, and listened carefully to the answers, typing comments into the computer as he went.

Next, the doctor told him that the technician would do a sequence of tests on him in another room, and then give him a chance to rest for a time while the results were analyzed. Jason decided that the tests were interesting, but wondered what they would prove. Maybe the doctor would tell him. If not, he might ask. He was thinking these things as he relaxed on a comfortable bed in another room. He got so relaxed that he fell asleep. They let him sleep there for about an hour, since that was a positive part of the examination. He woke feeling rested and peaceful.

Jason had not even noticed what time it was, so he was surprised when the doctor suggested that they go have lunch together. They had a nice visit over a delicious lunch at a cafe close to the office. When they returned the doctor explained the results of the morning tests and said he was pleased with them. After that, the technician did some more tests for about two hours. They would have been tiring if he had not had such a nice nap and lunch. It was turning out to be a much better day than he had anticipated.

After another short rest in a comfortable chair, he was called back into the doctor's office, where the doctor with pleasure told him that all the papers he filled out, questions he answered, and tests that were done proved to him that Jason was completely healed of his bipolar disorder. He handed Jason a paper that explained the techniques that had been used to ascertain the healing.

"I'm so delighted for you. I'm glad to tell you that you no longer need to come here to see me, and you do not need to take any more medication. Just dispose of any you have left at home at one of the drop off places for old medications in town. Now, the technician and I have a few more questions for you," stated the doctor, as he called him on the intercom. The technician came in and sat down when the doctor opened the door for him. The doctor brought his chair around and joined them in a conversation grouping, and then he inquired, "Your dad called me a couple weeks ago to ask what you should do if you got healed. I told him, and you did what he said. What's going on?"

Jason replied, "Dad told me he had called you. He told me he knew that if I would let Jesus save me, then Jesus would also heal me."

The doctor asked, "How do you know that it was Jesus who healed you? Could it have been just a natural change that sometimes, but seldom, happens in cases like this?"

Jason answered, "The reason I <u>know</u> that it was Jesus who healed me, is that my family all laid their hands on me and prayed for Jesus to heal me, after I had accepted Jesus as my Savior. Dad laid his hands on my head while he prayed, and I could feel a strange sensation of power going through me. When they finished praying, I felt completely different than I had ever felt before. We all thanked and praised God and gave him all the glory for the two miracles he had performed for me. I'm a new person spiritually, <u>and</u> mentally. I have the desire to serve Jesus because he loved me so much, and I'm filled with gratitude and love for him. Now, I have a question for both of you. You've known and treated my condition for many years, and now it's been proven to you that I'm completely healed. Is there anything keeping you from believing in Jesus as your <u>own</u> personal Savior?"

They both answered that they didn't understand how to do it.

Jason said, "I would be happy to explain it to you. If you have a Bible in the office, I have a whole list of verses here with me that helped me to believe." The doctor went to his bookshelf and got a Bible to hand to Jason, who started with the verses his parents had used and then all the ones that Maria had written in his Bible. He explained things like she had between verses. Then he answered the questions they had, and let them think about it for a few minutes. He could see when the light dawned and they understood what the verses had said, so he asked if they would like to pray and accept Jesus. Both of them did, and then the three of them had a nice time of rejoicing and thanking God.

Afterward, Jason told them the things he could remember from reading the little booklet for people who had just accepted Jesus. It explained that now they were a part of God's family, with the full assurance that since they believe in God's son, they have eternal life, starting now and lasting through eternity. Nothing and nobody could take them out of Jesus' hands. Their lives on this earth would be different now and there are many things they would need to learn. The best place to learn these things would be in something called a "new believers small group." There was a new one just starting that would be meeting tomorrow evening at 7 PM at the pastor's house. He offered to go get booklets and cards for them from his mother. They agreed and he said he would hurry.

He went and told his mom a quick summary of his day, and said he'd be back. She gave him the booklets with a hug and invited him to supper so he could tell his dad. She would invite his sisters also, so they could all hear about it at the same time. He readily concurred with those ideas, and then hastened back to the doctor's office.

    He told them, "It would be best if you would call the pastor and ask if there's room for you. Maybe after you tell your wives about the miracle of my healing, and then tell them about your own miracle of salvation, they'll desire the same salvation for themselves, and will want to attend the meeting with you. I truly hope so, and that you and they will come to church on Sunday at noon. You know where the church is. Now, I need to go over to my office building to check on how the people did today and then lock it up after they all leave. Then I've been invited to my parents' house for supper and to celebrate all the good news of today, including that both of you are believers now, along with me."

    The doctor and technician both thanked Jason for explaining how to have Jesus as their Savior, for answering their questions, for going to get booklets for them, and for the invitation to the group and to church. They were both obviously very thrilled about how the day had gone. Jason told them it had been his pleasure and a privilege.

*****

    Ted and Julie drove over to Larry and Jane's house after supper on Tuesday, so they could learn more about the two by two and four by four small group evangelism ministry. They were welcomed inside and sat in their comfortable living room where they visited for a little while before Larry said, "We'll answer any questions you have about the ministry groups first, and then I'll tell you, Ted, about the music need, while the women talk about whatever they want to."

    "How many times a week do you usually go?" Julie asked.

    Jane answered, "We usually only go as a ministry once a week, but when we go shopping or on a pleasure walk we pray and try to be alert to any opportunity or leading the Lord gives us. We used to shop separately, but now we try to go together so we have the benefit of two or more being in agreement and Jesus being in the midst of us as we try to minister to people in any situation. The shopping takes longer that way, but it's worth it."

    Ted commented, "I can see how that would be a very good idea. We'll try it. Julie and I read through the booklet and it does a good job of explaining the ministry, and how to go about it. When would you like to go with us?"

Everywhere There's a Sunrise, Let's Tell The Good News!

Larry replied, "If Tuesdays work for you, we would like to go next Tuesday."

Ted and Julie looked at each other and nodded, and then he said, "Tuesdays would be good days for us also. We'll be able to read the booklet again. Then we can watch and learn more about the process as it happens."

"Great! Now, Ted, if you'll come with me into my office, I'll tell you about the church music group. The ladies can stay here and visit." So Ted excitedly followed Larry to his office, where Larry continued, "The lead pastor chooses the songs to be sung for the church services, and also the ones for the small groups and they can add up to seven or more. The instrumentalists and singers receive the list of songs and piano music playing four-part harmony, by e-mail on Mondays and start practicing the songs on their own.

On Thursdays, they come with their instruments, and the singers come to a special room in the church that is set up for recording music. It is sound proofed, so that no outside noise can penetrate. Each song is played all the way through one time while the singers listen to the instruments. We all practice it until the director says it's good enough to record. Then we sing it again and it's recorded. The director usually has different instruments play for each song to give variety, and often has the singers arranged in different ways. We do that for all the songs for the church services and for the small group meetings, and it usually takes a little over two hours."

"It sounds like an efficient way to provide music for all twelve church services and many small group meetings. Is there a way I can be of help?" asked Ted.

"I've been listening to the singing time at the Saturday small group meetings, and I could tell there was one man with a good bass voice. I just could not figure out who it was, until you told me on Saturday that you sing bass. I called the director today and told him I found a replacement for that man, and he was thrilled. So you are our new member."

"Wow! That was fast and easy. I thought I would have to audition with a lot of others and perhaps be chosen. But you said that it's already decided. Thank you for your part in this. I've been wondering how the music was prepared for the church. I do like to sing, and the songs chosen are always good ones!" Ted said enthusiastically.

Larry responded, "You're welcome, and I know you'll do a good job, because I've watched you singing and you're very sincere and don't miss words. Here is a list of the songs we'll be singing and an SD Card with a piano playing them in four-part harmony so that you can practice the words and your part tonight and tomorrow. From now on, they will be e-mailed to you on Mondays, if you'll give me your e-mail address."

"It sounds like a good plan," Ted responded and wrote out his e-mail address for Larry.

"I'll show you how it works now and we can practice a song or two together," said Larry. As they did that, Ted could understand how easy it would be to practice.

Then Larry added, "We meet at 7 PM by the way, and I thought maybe we could carpool, plus give our wives a chance to visit, taking turns. One week I would come pick you up, bring Jane and drop her off at your home. The next week you come here and pick me up and drop Julie off. We can ask the ladies separately in the privacy of their homes so that they can think about it and agree or disagree with that part of the idea."

Meanwhile, the ladies were enjoying a good visit in the living room. They had covered a couple topics and then Julie asked, "Is there anything being done through the church to evangelize the children in the public schools? I'm so impressed with the church school curriculum. By the time they reach the end of first grade, most of the children have received Jesus as their own personal Savior. But, I know for a fact, that children who don't attend church with their parents, or go to Sunday school have no exposure to the gospel. I also know that on Wednesdays, the public schools are let out early so that the teachers can have meetings or training of some sort. That results in a lot of children either being home alone, or worse, being out roaming around."

"That is a huge problem, I agree," responded Jane. "Yes, there are many people in Pine City who have Bible Story Groups for the elementary age children and Bible Study Groups for middle and high school levels. The groups meet in homes usually on Wednesday afternoons. So a lot of children have an opportunity to attend one of those. I've heard that there's always a need for more women to have such a group in their homes. But I have never felt that I had time to do one. Now that I've decided to not start up my Lamaze business again anytime soon, I would have time for one or possibly two. I could have one of each on Wednesdays, covering both age levels."

Everywhere There's a Sunrise, Let's Tell The Good News!

"What a great idea! Does the church have materials for people to use, or do you have to come up with things on your own?" asked Julie.

Jane answered, "I'll find out and let you know." Just then the men came into the living room and they all visited for a while before it was time for Ted and Julie to go back home. When they got there, Ted told Julie all of what Larry had shared about the music, and showed her the list of songs and the SD card. She could tell he was very pleased, and she told him that she was delighted for him..

*****

Wednesday

Ruth and Esther were waiting in Maria's office again on Wednesday morning, and they told her all about Jason's doctor appointment and all the good news they had heard at supper last night. Maria was pleasantly surprised to hear that he had used his parent's verses plus the ones she had written in his Bible, and even some of the things she had said to explain to them the plan of salvation. It was especially wonderful that both the men had also been saved. The three ladies had a short time of praise and thanksgiving before they went to work.

At lunchtime she and Ruth were meeting with the next to the last of the co-workers that she needed to be introduced to. That would leave just one more for tomorrow, and then she and Ruth would be on their own, doing like Esther was doing. They had to keep reminding themselves that this kind of evangelism takes time, and to be patient. At least it had stopped raining and was warm enough outside so that they could walk to and from the cafe for lunch. Maria was glad she would be getting a little exercise again.

*****

Matt and Fiona had arranged to go to the Frisbee Golf Course this morning and see how well they could do after their time on Sunday at the park and further practice the next few days. They had read over the rules again on the web, so they were fresh in their minds. But before they got started, they remembered to pray for Pam and Julie. After that Fiona went first and fell short of the goal. Then Matt overshot and went past it. Making up their own scoring method, the score was 0 to 0. The next one must have been easier, because they both hit it, making the score be 1 to 1. They decided to do only nine instead of all 18, so they would not tire out their arms. By the time they finished #9, the score was tied 4 to 4.

Matt said, "It looks like we need more practice, but I think we're getting the hang of it a little better."

"I agree, and I think if the weather is good we could do this again next Sunday after church and even try more than 9, because we'll have more time and if we practice every other day, it will keep our arms in shape," said Fiona.

"That sounds good to me, Fiona. Wow! Look at the time! We had better get going or we won't have time to eat lunch before we go to work," Matt replied.

"Time flies when you're having fun, and we have been!" exclaimed Fiona.

When she got home, her father had just gotten home for an unusual lunchtime at home. They all had wanted some more time to pray together about the ideas the pastor had given them on Saturday afternoon. So they prayed some more and then ate lunch.

While they were eating Fiona said, "The idea that appeals the most to me is the last one he talked about. Our city is so large that it could easily need 3 or 4 churches that operate like ours does now. The money is earning good interest now and will grow until it's needed for that project. Then it could give them a good start for a building fund. I'm pretty sure many people will desire to donate money for such a project."

"I agree with your good thinking, Fiona," replied Patrick. "I wonder what Matt would think about you giving all that money away. It would be a good thing to find out. If he seems very upset or disagreeable about it, you might have a problem in your relationship. Let's pray about it. You can look for an opportunity to discuss simply the idea of giving all the money away, <u>not where to</u>, right now, since that project isn't common knowledge yet."

"You're so right. It will be another test for him to pass. So far he's done very well," she responded.

*****

That evening Don and Anita did a repeat of all the actions and preparations for the new believers small group meeting as they had done last Thursday evening, and also on Saturday afternoon, including reminding them about the meeting at the church tomorrow evening. They all said they would be there. Everything went just as well as the other times, so they were grateful. On Tuesday, Anita had asked Mindy if she could come on Thursday evening and then as usual on Saturday morning, and she had agreed. She liked taking care of Timmy and Mary and the extra spending money was nice too. They had changed the new Saturday group to the morning time, and told the people at the end of the meeting about the time change and the location being at the home of the co-facilitators. They were glad they taken care of that item, so they didn't have to call everybody in that group. If they could remember to do all the little details so that everything would run smoothly, they would be very grateful.

*****

After work, Ted and Julie discussed their time at the Kelsey home. Julie said, "They're both very nice people. I'm glad we get to partner with them for the four by four projects. It isn't as intimidating to me now as it was at first."

"That's good. I think it will help a lot to be able to watch how they do things. I learn best when I can see something demonstrated," he replied.

She agreed, "I do also. But I do want us to read the booklet again before next Tuesday."

He nodded in agreement, and then commented, "It sure didn't take very long for God to answer our prayer about a ministry for me! As usual I'm amazed by the way God works. I'm glad that I get a turn at being the one to take somebody's place and help the church. I couldn't be more pleased about my new ministry being in music preparation. I've wondered how they do it ever since our first Sunday here. They do such a good job, and it always sounds wonderful. It helps me to worship and praise God. Now I get to be a part of helping to prepare it. Thank you very much, Father in heaven!"

"Yes, Lord, I thank and praise you, also," Julie added.   "I'm so happy for you, my treasure. Now I'll be able to hear your voice double during the singing times. I will especially enjoy having it right next to me while we sing instead of having you up in the choir and me sitting alone down in the congregation!" she said as she grinned, and he laughed. "Well, you do have a wonderful, full, low, mellow bass voice and I love you and it both. I think it will be a high-quality addition to the other voices."

"Thank you, Honey. I value your compliments. And I thank God for the voice he's given me and now for this opportunity to use it for his glory and to help the church. "Oh, I forgot to mention this after we got home last night. Larry had the idea that we could carpool to the church on Thursdays, and if you would like to, when it's my turn to pick him up, you could come along and spend that time with Jane, and vice versa. What do you think?"

Julie answered, "I think it sounds perfect. We were enjoying some good visiting when you guys finished sooner than we thought you would last night. If we do this idea, it would give us over two hours together each week. I would probably benefit from having her as an older friend. Maybe we could do some needlework while we visit. I know I have a lot of mending that needs to be done. Shall I call and see what she thinks about it?"

Ted replied, "No, I think it would be best if I call Larry and ask him what her opinion was. He had said that we would ask separately at home so each lady could feel free to agree or disagree with the idea."

"That was thoughtful of him. It is easier to think without the pressure of the other person watching and wondering what your answer might be. Maybe we should say that I would like to try the idea and see how it works. Then if we run out of steam, we would have a way out."

"Okay, I'll call him right now." When he finished the call, he laughed and said, "Jane said the same thing you did. Maybe you have found a kindred spirit. He will bring Jane over here tomorrow and pick me up at 6:45 PM."

"When are you going to practice your part for the songs?" asked Julie.

"I did last night in the shower, and again this morning after you left for school," he answered.

"Good and if you would like, we could also sing together sometimes," she suggested.

He responded, "I like that idea. How about every Wednesday after supper cleanup? That will give me a chance to practice alone first for a couple days each week."

*****

Everywhere There's a Sunrise, Let's Tell The Good News!

It was getting easier and easier for Amelia to come home from school, do her homework, fix her supper, and study for a test if necessary while she ate, and then go get ready to go to work at The Garden Shop. When she got to work that Wednesday, she told Fiona that as they worked, and added, "I really like working here with the plants, especially when I see someone buy one of the ones I've helped to nurture."

"I know just what you mean," answered Fiona. "For me it's like I have a little part in adding beauty and enjoyment to their homes and lives."

"That was well put. I never understood why Mom and Dad seem to like this place and work so much, but now it makes sense. That is what they're doing, and it's like when you do something nice for others, it becomes a blessing for you also. Besides, working with plants is working with a part of God's creation and that's a wholesome thing to do. I enjoy looking at all the flowers on my way inside and walking through the shop. They're all so beautiful and there's such a variety that I never get tired of them. They remind me of the one who created them and I give him praise."

"Wow! Amelia, I agree with all you said and I feel very much that way also. You expressed it all so well. I hope I can remember all you said and write it down when I get home so I can remember it," exclaimed Fiona.

They worked in silence for a little while and then talked about various topics until the subject of dating came up. Amelia commented, "I think I'm looking forward to dating next year when I'm a senior. I'm glad my parents are old fashioned enough to say that juniors are too young. It bothered me at first, but I can see that it is best. I hear all kinds of stories at school, and I'm not positive that even seniors are old enough for the responsibility. All the kids want is a good time. They don't want to be responsible for their actions."

"You're so right!" responded Fiona. "My parents would only let me go to church group activities or at the very most double dates and not until I was a senior. It is a lot easier to stay responsible that way. The whole idea of dating for most young people is to go out with many different people, have fun and see how far you can go without getting in trouble. Lots of feelings get hurt when one person gets tired of the other and dumps him or her. Add to that an unwanted pregnancy and all the fun is over."

"Yeah, that's the scariest part of the whole idea. I've heard stories of girls who said 'No.' and then got dumped, or the boy pushed and pushed until they agreed. I don't want any of that in my life. Your parent's idea of just church activities and double dates would probably help. And my small group has been teaching the importance of only dating people you are sure are believers. That should help also."

"Yes, and here is another idea. When I was taking care of my aunt, I heard some radio or TV programs by believers that suggest people should not date at all, until they're sure that God wants them to be married, and then only after they've gotten to know the person by watching how he interacts in large and small group activities. A lot can be learned by watching how people treat others, listening to how they talk, and even what they laugh about, and especially what they criticize," Fiona mentioned.

"Now that all makes good sense to me," responded Amelia. "How can we know if God wants us to be married or to stay single? I was reading in 1 Corinthians chapter 7 about marriage and singleness, and it's not very clear, but the part that hit me the most was in verse 28, where it says something like if you marry you will have many troubles. That does not sound like very much fun to me."

"I agree. I've been reading two books that have helped me a lot in answering the question about God's will for us. One of them explains what that verse means. Plus it tells us what to look for in a mate if God does desire for us to marry," Fiona replied.

"Good. Would you write down their titles? I'll buy them the next time I go to the Bible Book store. I feel like I'm going to need all the help I can get. Growing up is a serious matter for me, and I want to do it right."

"I'm glad you feel that way, because too many young people just muddle their way through and end up making a mess of their lives," Fiona said, and then wrote the titles and gave them to Amelia. "Maybe we could discuss what we're reading in the books while we work here and it will help us both,"

"Thanks, I think that's a very good suggestion. I'll shop at the Bible Book store before I grocery shop for Mom tomorrow on the way home from school. I might even get a chance to start reading one of the books if I don't have very much homework tomorrow. Then we could talk about what I've read on Friday. I'm feeling better already. Thank you, Fiona for listening to me and for your thoughts and suggestions," finished Amelia with a shy smile.

"That's what friends are for, and I'm glad that we can be friends. This will help me, too. When I was in high school, our church and the group for young people were very small, and none of us knew very much. I'm especially glad for my parent's rules for me that helped me to stay pure. I actually didn't do even double dating then," said Fiona.

"Thank you for telling me that. Oh, look at the clock! It's already almost 8 PM. We need to get ready to close up and go home," stated Amelia. The time goes so fast when we work and visit. I can hardly wait until Friday so we can talk some more."

*****

Chapter 16

Acts 8:36b, The man believed and said: *"See here is water. What hinders me from being baptized?"*

Thursday

Sherry and the twins went over to the Ross home on Thursday morning where she was able to finish the dress for Mary, since the meeting was at the church this evening, and she didn't have to clean.

Meanwhile, the twins played and learned some more. Another child was playing with a toy that looked intriguing to Hope, so she went and took it away from the child, without asking, and started to play with it herself. The other child started crying. Anita came and led them both away from the group so they could settle the problem.

"Hope, who had the toy first?" Anita asked.

"He did, but I never played with one like this before and I wanted to try it," answered Hope.

By this time the boy had stopped crying and said, "She didn't ask for it. She just grabbed it. She pulled it away from me and it hurt my hand."

"Oh, I'm sorry it hurt you. Is it bleeding? Do you need to put something cold on it for a while?" He just shook his head. "I didn't know I was supposed to ask. Here you can have it back." Hope gave the toy back to the boy. He thanked her, and after Anita prompted him, he told Hope he forgave her. Then he took the toy back to where he had been playing. "I have a lot to learn," Hope said to Anita.

"Yes, we all do, Hope, but you did the right thing by saying you were sorry, and trying to help him with the hurt. Besides, now you know that you need to ask. What should you do if the child refuses to give it to you?" asked Anita.

"I think I should go play with something else and wait until he's done with it," she answered.

"Good idea, or you could just watch him play with it and maybe learn how it works before you try it later," Anita suggested. "Are you ready to go back to the play area?"

"Yes, Mrs. Ross. Thank you for helping me to learn without being mad at me," answered Hope.

As she walked past the boy with the toy, he called to her, "Hope, do you want to play with me?" She gladly sat down and they had a nice time playing with the toy together.

In the meantime, Timmy and Joy had been putting a puzzle together. If Joy got frustrated when a puzzle piece didn't fit, he would say, "Just be patient and it will fit someplace else later." Or, "Look for a piece that has the same colors that are next to the hole you want to fill."

"Oh, those are good ideas, and they really work. Look, here's the right piece!" exclaimed Joy.

During their lunch at home, the girls told Sherry what they had learned today.

*****

Thursday evening Mindy arrived a few minutes early and that put Anita and Don at ease about the children, so that they could get ready to go over to the church and set everything up for the meeting. The other two co-facilitators met them there and they all made short work of the preparations. They had brought refreshments just like they had promised, and put them in the lunchroom for after the meeting. They put on name tags, and had time to talk and pray before the members of the groups arrived.

Anita asked, "I wonder if Walt's other co-workers would like to stay together as a group or to have part of them join Walt's group exchanging places with some in that group."

Don replied, "I'll ask Walt privately and then we can talk about it to the whole group if he wants the blending of the groups. I think I'll wait until refreshment time so their minds can be focused on the teaching time."

At that point, the people started arriving, put on name tags, and took seats in the big circle that had been set up.

Everywhere There's a Sunrise, Let's Tell The Good News!

    Pastor Don welcomed them all and explained that the name tags would take the place of introducing everybody, since there was a lot to cover tonight. After a prayer to get started, they sang: "If Any Man," Matthew 16:24; "Take the Name of Jesus With You," Colossians 3:17; and "More About Jesus," 2 Peter 3:18. Then he reminded them again about the importance of buying a Bible and hymnal, and that if they were interested in used ones to see him after the meeting.

    The teaching time began with a time for the people in the group to ask any <u>other</u> questions they had about the reading in the little booklet or about the church service.

    There weren't very many questions, so the pastor said, "Let's talk about what water baptism is." He told them about John the Baptist and how his baptism differed from believers' baptisms. "John was getting people ready to meet Jesus by having them repent of their sins and be baptized publicly to show they had repented. When believers are baptized, it is in obedience to Jesus who said in Matthew 28:19 for his disciples to baptize *in the name of the Father, and of the Son and of the Holy Spirit.* Colossians 2:12 says that we are *buried with Jesus in baptism, and are also risen with him through faith in God who raised Jesus from the dead.* And 3:1 states: *Since you are risen with Christ, seek those things, which are above, where Christ sits on the right hand of God.*

    "Now, please look up Romans 6:3-6, and follow along as I read. *When we were baptized into Jesus Christ, we were baptized into his death. Therefore we are buried with him by baptism into death, that just as Christ was raised up from the dead by the Father, even so we also should walk in newness of life. For if we are like him in his death, we shall also be raised like his resurrection. Knowing that our old man is crucified with him ... so we no longer serve sin.* Skip to verse 11. *Likewise consider yourselves to be dead to sin, but alive to God through Jesus Christ our Lord.* That does not mean that we'll never sin again though, because that won't happen until we get to heaven. But when we do sin we do as 1 John 1:9 says, *If we confess our sins, God is faithful and just to forgive us our sins, and to cleanse us from all unrighteousness.*

    "Here is the reason why water baptism is so important. Water baptism is a representation of being buried with Jesus when we go all the way down under the water, and of being raised with him when we come up out of the water. It is also a public testimony to the people we know, that we have decided to believe in, follow, and obey Jesus for the rest of our lives. Besides that, it is something we can look back on. When we remember what it means, it can help us to live our lives for Jesus.

"Since most of you haven't seen a baptism in process, I'll show you a video clip of two people, a man and then a woman, being baptized here in our church. By seeing it, you will be able to understand how it's done." He showed the clip and then asked, "Did you notice that the people put their hand up to gently squeeze their noses shut? This will help to keep the water out of your nose. Be sure to keep your mouth closed as well." Then he explained, "If any of you wear hearing aids, or anything else that should not get wet, be sure to take them off in the dressing room. We'll show you the dressing rooms later. Also, if for any reason your doctor has told you to not go swimming or be immersed in water, tell us after this meeting and we'll arrange to do your baptism an alternate way.

"It is <u>very</u> important that you take a shower before coming to the church. Wear <u>clean</u> dark colored clothing that cannot be seen through when it's wet, but it should be light-weight, so it won't weigh you down when it gets wet, as you noticed in the video. We need to keep the water clean because all twelve of the churches that share this building will be using the same water all week. Two of the churches will be joining us on Tuesday. The other churches will have their special services on Wednesday and Thursday.

After you are baptized, you can take another quick shower before you dress in dry clothing. Be sure to bring your own towels and dry clothing for this purpose, and especially to dry your hair. Ladies, don't worry about trying to curl your hair before or after, and please don't use hair spray or makeup before you're baptized. Be sure to bring everything you need with you, and arrive here at the church a few minutes before 7 PM so you won't miss any of the songs we'll sing. Be prepared to tell all the people watching that you believe in Jesus as your own personal Savior. Please keep your testimony short, because we have a lot of people to baptize that night. Did I forget any thing? Are there any questions?"

It was totally quiet after he asked that. "Have I inundated you with so much information is such a little amount of time? Maybe the church needs to have a little booklet that will explain all of this so you have time to take it in and think up your questions. I think I will suggest that to them for the next groups. Let's tour the dressing rooms, showers, and baptismal area now, and you can think of any questions you have while we do that. Ladies, please follow Anita, and you men can follow me to the other side."

On both the ladies and men's sides, there were four small private dressing rooms and four showers with enclosed dressing areas to dry off and get dressed after showering. There were also two small restrooms and a large waiting area with chairs while waiting for a turn in the dressing rooms, and a turn to get baptized. There were outlets for the women to use their own hair dryers after being baptized and showering, so they would not get chilled, especially on winter nights. Anita made sure to point those out since Don had not mentioned them. The women felt free then to ask other questions and Anita answered all of them. There were stairs leading up to the baptismal reservoir, which would be filled with warm water, and steps leading down into it with hand rails so they would be safe. When finished, they would turn around and go back up the stairs where a helper would assist them down the stairs and to a shower. The nice, warm water of the shower would make them feel warm again.

Questions were all answered by seeing the facilities and asking without the other sex listening. Don would remember that for the next group and maybe even have a hand out ready for the Saturday group. Everyone went to the school lunchroom where the refreshments were enjoyed and the people got a chance to visit while others had time to tell Don and Anita of special needs. They took notes so they would not forget anything.

Then Don asked Walt about Anita's idea, and he called his group of co-workers together so he could ask them. They discussed the idea for a while and then motioned for Don to come and answer some questions, finishing with, "What do you think would be best for us?"

He answered, "Either way would be okay, but I can see at least two benefits of having five couples of your co-workers in each group. You would have an opportunity to meet people you don't know yet, and they would have the chance to hear about the miracle that helped to bring salvation to so many people."

Walt responded, "That sounds very good. How will the other people like the idea?"

"Good question. Let's go ask them," replied Don. After he explained the idea and the benefits for everyone, they all agreed and quickly split into the groups that would continue together after tonight. Then he reminded them about how important it would be for them to continue attending the new believers small groups. "There's so much to be learned, and it's very helpful to be able to listen to each other and ask questions. We'll have one more meeting for each group with co-facilitators and then Anita and I might need to start other small groups if you all go out and witness and bring more new believers to the church! You'll continue in these groups until January, when all the couples in all the groups will be put into new groups containing people you probably won't know yet. It is a very good way to meet and make new friends in the church.

"Now I'll announce the next group meeting places and times. For lack of better names for your groups, #1 will meet at the home of your co-facilitators on Thursday, at 7 PM. They'll hand you a piece of paper with their address and phone number on it. Likewise for #2, but you will meet on Wednesday at 7 PM. Remember that these meetings are in the same week as the baptismal service. We like to keep up the momentum of what we're learning and not miss a week in between. Be sure to attend church this coming Sunday and every Sunday that you possibly can, because there's so much to be learned in order to live the Christian life. Now we can get back to eating and visiting. And if anybody would like to, you can buy used Bibles and hymnals right now, or if you have any other questions, come and ask us."

A few people came with more questions they had just thought of, and many came to buy Bibles and hymnals. Most of the couples that did, bought a Bible for each person, and a hymnal to share. Everyone had a nice time and enjoyed the refreshments. There was an aura of excitement and anticipation about the upcoming special baptismal service. Not one of them heard, or had any idea that music was being practiced and recorded right then in the same building.

*****

Larry dropped Jane off to spend Thursday evening with Julie, and he and Ted went over to the church for Ted's first meeting with the music preparation group. Ted was surprised at the large room. Not only was it soundproofed; it was actually a very nice recording studio with professional quality equipment. Next, he noticed a large colorful banner placed where it could be easily seen upon entering the room. It had the words of Psalm 33:1-5 from the New International Version of the Bible in large calligraphy letters with colorful pictures of musical instruments and musical notes scattered around it. As the instrumentalists arrived with their instruments, and all the singers along with them, Ted could understand why they needed such a large room. When every member had arrived, they read the verses on the banner in unison. Then after an opening prayer, Ted was introduced as the new bass singer, and they got started practicing.

    Talk about beautiful! Even the practice sounded good. And what a wonderful way to spend an evening! They were singing meaningful *psalms and hymns and spiritual songs, with grace in (their) hearts to the Lord,* Colossians 3:16b. By the time they had successfully recorded all the songs for the coming week, they were tired, but Ted was elated. He could not imagine a better ministry for himself. He was very glad that they would be meeting every week like this.

    Meanwhile at his home, Julie and Jane were having a nice visit. Jane had found out that the church did have materials available for people to use in their homes for the students' after school groups. She had gone to the church office yesterday and they loaned her some of the materials and gave her one of their well known booklets, this time about everything you would need to know to get started and continue having either or both of the age groups in your home. She brought them with her to show Julie who was very impressed. The materials were good quality, and obviously people used them carefully so they stayed in good condition. It was like a library where they could return what they had used and check out another set. There was no charge for using them unless somehow they got ruined. Then you would pay to have them replaced. They even had a logical order in which to use the materials from the first meeting, and for several years down the road. The materials were age appropriate, so a person who did both age groups would need two sets for the Wednesday groups.

    "This is amazing! Everything this church does is first class, good quality, well thought out and practical!" Julie exclaimed. "Did they tell you how many groups are in progress at this time in Pine City?"

    "Yes, but I forgot what they said. All I remember is that there's a big need for many more. I'll be talking to my friends and acquaintances that don't have jobs outside of the home and see if I can convince some of them to start one or two. It really is a great opportunity to minister to the children of our city. And usually the younger they are, the more likely they are to accept Jesus as their Savior, and serve him the rest of their lives, if they have ongoing follow-up by continuing to attend the groups and learn more about how to live for him. I'm very excited about this as a ministry opportunity for myself and for some of the people I know."

"Do you think you'll have for us time to meet together every Thursday, or will you need that time to study and prepare and call people?" asked Julie.

"Don't forget that I'm home all day, so I'll have plenty of time for all of that. I like being able to talk and visit with you on Thursdays, and I would like to continue it. Maybe we could use at least part of our time to knit or mend or do other handiwork. Then we could accomplish something while we visit," suggested Jane.

Julie responded, "It's a great idea. In fact, I mentioned something like that to Ted when he told me about Larry's idea. This is going to be a great addition to my week. Since I don't have school work to bring home and finish during the evenings I'll look forward to spending time with you and getting caught up on some mending."

When Ted arrived home, Julie could tell he was tired, but very delighted. He told her all about it after Larry and Jane had gone home. She hugged him and told him how glad she was for him. Then she told him how much she had enjoyed her evening with Jane. After that they went to bed early, since tomorrow was another workday.

*****

Friday

Now it was Friday morning and Maria went to work looking forward to eating lunch with Ruth and Esther. She worked rapidly all morning and accomplished a lot. Ruth was good at giving her varied accounts to work on and since the income tax deadline was over for the year she would not have to do those again for many months.

It was another rainy day, so they walked up and down the stairs a few times before going into the lunchroom to eat lunch. Their co-workers seldom ate in the lunchroom especially on Fridays, so they were able to have it all to themselves.

Maria asked them, "Since I have now met all my co-workers in this office building, we had said that we would start doing what you've been doing, Esther, with one person at a time. But do you think we should be walking to lunch just in pairs?" They had no opinion. So she explained, "I read the "I Can Do" booklet over again about needing at least 3 people if it's just women doing ministry, for safety reasons, and I remember that a friend of mine was upset whenever I mentioned walking someplace alone. He won't even let his wife and me walk as a pair without him being along as a 'bodyguard.' So I felt that I should discuss the issue with both of you during lunch."

They readily agreed with her and decided to change their plans to include at least two other workers each time they walked to the park or to a cafe for lunch.

That issue settled, Maria asked, "Are you two busy on Sunday afternoons after church?" "If not, maybe you would like to join Julie and me as we walk in a park after church. She is my former college roommate and I would like you to meet her and her husband."

Esther answered, "We're not busy this coming Sunday afternoon, and it would be a good way to get some exercise if it's a nice day."

Ruth agreed, "I think we could plan on that for this week at least."

"Great! I'll ask Julie and Ted if that will work for them, also. We went to a very nice park near the church last week, and if you would like we could all ride to church in my car. That way we would only have to find parking for two cars at the park instead of three," suggested Maria.

"That sounds good also," answered Ruth. "Let's hope that it will be a nice day. Now I suppose we better all get back to our offices and get to work."

After supper that evening, Maria called Julie and got an okay about having Beth and Esther join their walking time on Sunday after church.

*****

When Clara arrived for her last day of work, her boss called her into his office and asked her to sit down. Then he said, "I've watched you during the years you've worked here and I want to thank you for a job well done. You always find a way to keep busy even on the slowest of evenings. You have a very good work ethic, and I think you will do very well as you finish up your nurses training and learn to be a missionary for your parents' home town. In this envelope is your full paycheck for this week, and as an added bonus, I'm giving you this day off. Go home and rest, or do whatever else you need to do to get ready for your accelerated education and training." Then he handed her the envelope.

"Oh! Wow!" she exclaimed. "Thank you very much, Sir! I <u>do</u> need some rest, and I'll get it right after I finish up my current budget and projected budget, now that I know how many classes I'll be able to add to my afternoons, and what the cost will be. I'm so excited."

"And I think you should be," he agreed. "I'm very happy for you. I'll see you in church on Sunday and introduce you to my lovely wife."

"I'll look forward to meeting her and seeing you there. I'll wait for you at the entrance, and you can both sit with me. Thank you again for everything, and especially for this day off with pay. I've never had anyone do something that nice for me before," she said as she was leaving.

When she arrived home she called Anita to have her tell Pastor Don that she expected her unbelieving boss and his wife to be in church with her on Sunday, so he could have a salvation message ready. Then when Karen got home from Subway, she called and told her how nice her boss had been to her, and that she now had her budgets ready, and had even taken a nap that afternoon. She would bring the budgets to the small group the next day.

*****

During supper, Julie asked, "Ted how was your week at work?"

"It went well, but I don't remember very much about it since our time on Tuesday and Thursday was so different and interesting. I'm still blown away about how they prepare the music for church, and how easy it was for me to be able to join them. That had to be God working it all out, even before we prayed about it!" he said with great feeling. "How was your week at school? We haven't had much time to share our thoughts this week."

Julie agreed, and then said, "My week at school was delightful! The students are so well behaved and are motivated learners. I'm sure it's because they come from Christian homes, and have received good training at home."

After cleaning up the supper dishes, Julie went to check her e-mail, and finally there was one from Pam. "Hi, Julie, I'm sorry I haven't been able to write to you all week. It's been a very busy week with lots of doctor and therapist appointments for my mother, and more things for me to learn about helping her to do the therapy. Maybe things will settle down a little bit now. At least I might get to rest up over the weekend, since there are no doctor appointments on weekends. Please pray that I can remember everything I'm supposed to do for the therapy. They talked so fast, and I tried to take notes, but I should have taken a recorder with me. I'm glad to hear from you that your teaching is going so well and that the children are doing well also. It gives me joy to pray for all of you. Sincerely, Pam."

Julie answered right back. "Hi, Pam, I admit, I was getting a little worried about you and I prayed all the harder for you since you had not sent an e-mail. I can understand why you didn't have time. Here is an idea about the therapy. Maybe you could look on the web for the same kind of therapy. On YouTube, there are videos explaining many different topics also. If all else fails, maybe you could call the therapist and have her fill in the gaps. We'll pray for you at the small group meeting tomorrow. Be sure to listen to the church service on the web, this weekend and do get lots of rest. I'm sure you will need to keep your energy up and stay well. Sincerely, Julie."

*****

Saturday

It was Saturday morning, and time for the new believer small group. Don and Anita left Mindy in charge of Timmy and Mary and the twins, and went to the home of their co-facilitators with Bibles and hymnals for the meeting. They were relieved that they didn't have to take care of the refreshments. Everybody made short work of setting up the chairs in a circle and putting out the Bibles and hymnals, so they had time to talk and pray before the meeting.

All the members arrived on time and the meeting was almost a copy of the one on Thursday evening except that they weren't at the church, and Don had made a hand out with all the information that he had given verbally. He gave them time to read it and ask questions. Then he gave them a floor plan of the baptismal, dressing rooms, etc. since they couldn't meet in the church, because of the other churches' services there today. They split into men's and women's groups so all the questions could be answered by seeing floor plans of the facilities and asking questions in separate men/women groups. The meeting went very well because of the extra planning.

Linda L. Linn

*****

Meanwhile, the other Saturday morning group was meeting at Larry and Jane's house. Jeff had remembered to get enough Bibles and hymnals from Don and they had bought a rolling suitcase to carry them in from house to house. Jeff and Karen helped get the chairs set up with the books on them, and had time to pray before anybody arrived. Then the stereo boom box they had bought was set up and ready to play the music for the songs.

When the members had all arrived on time as usual, Jeff led in an opening prayer and asked if anybody had a praise to share. "Let's continue to wait until the end of <u>all</u> the praises before we clap and praise out loud because it saves valuable time."

He looked directly at Clara to encourage her to be first. Clara gave a summary of what she had learned from Jeff and Karen, and then shared what her boss had said and the bonus he had given her, plus that he and his wife would be in church tomorrow. Ted praised God for the opportunity to be a part of the music preparation group for the churches and small groups. Larry praised the Lord for providing for the need of the church music group. Jane thanked the Lord for the Wednesday Bible groups she was getting ready to start in her home for the children and young people of the public schools. Ami thanked God that Aneko had called and would be arriving this afternoon to spend the week job hunting. Matt praised the Lord that his boss and so many other people would be baptized this coming Tuesday evening. Sherry was thankful for the things Hope and Joy were learning from two mornings a week in the daycare, and the work she was able to do to pay for it. When nobody added more Jeff led the clapping and all joined in with applause and oral praises to their wonderful God.

Announcements included, "The baptismal service is at 7 PM this coming Tuesday. I know most of you won't be able to get off work to attend, but I hope those of you who can, will, because it's a very special occasion for the new believers and a chance for us to show them our support and love. Next topic: who would like to host our next small group meeting?" asked Jeff.

Tony volunteered, "I called Clara this morning and asked if she could bring cookies, and I'll take care of getting the lunchroom ready in the school, plus bring the beverages."

"Thank you Clara and Tony. We'll look forward to that for next Saturday. We'll need to park on the other side of the school so we'll be out of the way of the Saturday church service people. Now let's read the verses that go with each song before we sing."

The songs were "Open My Eyes," Psalm 119:18, *Lord, open my eyes that I may behold wondrous things out of your law.* "Praise the Savior," Ephesians 2:13-19, *In Christ Jesus we who were far off are made near by the blood of Christ. For he is our peace, who made both one and broke down the middle wall of partition, having abolished in his flesh the hostility, ... to make in himself one new man of the two, thus making peace. He reconciled both to God in one body by the cross, ... and came and preached peace to us who were afar off, and to those who were near, for through him we both have access to the Father by one Spirit. Therefore we are now no longer strangers and foreigners, but fellow citizens with the saints, and of the household of God.* And "His Name Is Life," John 14:6, *Jesus said, "I am the way, the truth, and the life. No man comes to the Father, except by me.*

"Now please turn to Mark 4:20 which is the end of the parable of the sower. It says, *The seed that was sown on good ground is like those who hear the word and receive it and bring forth fruit, some thirty fold, some sixty, and some one hundred.* Then in verse 23 Jesus said, *If any man has ears to hear, let him hear.* How do those verses go with the song "Open My Eyes?" Jeff asked.

Fiona answered, "When we read or listen to God's Word we should ask him to help us see whatever he wants us to learn and to make us fruitful in his work."

"Thank you, Fiona. Look next at Luke 11:28, which says that *we are blessed if we hear and keep the word of God.* Look up Psalm 9:10 and read it aloud with me. *They that know your name will put their trust in you, for you, LORD, have not forsaken those who seek you.* In the Bible someone's name often revealed his character. This is very true of God the Father and God the Son. Look at the verses in the song "His Name Is Life," and somebody say some of the names of Jesus in there."

Tomo read, "Savior, Prince of Peace, Shepherd, Lamb of God."

Jeff wrote those names on a big chart and asked the people to give him other names they could think of for Jesus. They had a long list by the time they finished. "Think of the name, Savior. The verses we read for the song, 'Praise the Savior,' go into great detail about what Jesus, our Savior, did for us. Everybody take one of the names you gave me to put on the chart and look up a verse or two that go with it that tells about that name. I'm glad these Bibles have good concordances in the back to make this easier."

The rest of the teaching time was spent with this activity, and it turned out to be a blessing to all. Then Jeff said, "Now you have another idea to add to your Bible Study times. Add to this list or use names for God the Father the next time you do it. In fact, this will be your homework for our next meeting. Come prepared to share at least one name and a scripture reference to go with it."

Julie commented, "I'm very glad I was taking notes today. I'll tape this into my notebook when I get home." At that point everybody else got out their paper and pens and copied down all the names on the chart, and the verse references that Jeff had printed beside them.

When they had finished, Karen began conversational prayer time with, "Jesus, it's so good to be here with you and one another. Thank you for all the names we found in the Bible that help us to know you better. We praise you for everything that you are."

"Yes, my Savior, I especially thank you for all you did for us as listed in the Ephesians verses we read today, and in so many other places in the Bible," added Larry.

Clara said, "Jesus, my provider, thank you for taking care of all my needs through the people that you've given extra money to, and they've given it to help people like me. Holy Spirit, please draw my boss and his wife to salvation."

"Yes, and use all of us to tell others about your free gift of salvation as we go about our daily lives and when we go out two by two, three by three, and four by four," Fiona prayed.

Matt followed with, "Thank you that Jeff and I will be able to attend the baptismal service this Tuesday, since my boss and most of our co-workers will be there. Not enough left at the site to work!" he chuckled, and so did the rest.

"Holy Spirit, please draw that last co-worker to Jesus. Do whatever it takes to make him ready," added Jeff.

Roy continued, "Thank you, Jesus that I can come and bring the twins to the baptismal service. This will be a good thing for them to learn about."

And Sherry agreed, "Yes, and then they can tell me all about it the next day! That will be fun, since I can't come."

Ted added, "Lord, I'm grateful that Julie and I don't work evenings, so we'll get to come see all the baptisms."

Karen said, "I just realized if I go straight from work, I'll only miss about an hour of the service. Thank you, Lord for helping me see that."

Julie turned on her recorder and prayed, "Jesus, I ask that you will help Pam remember everything she needs to in order to help her mother do the exercises the therapist told her to do. Also, give her the rest she needs and keep her in good health. Remind her that she can do all things through you, because you give her the strength."

Fiona added, "I agree with that, Jesus, and ask that you will fill her with the knowledge, peace, and patience she needs as she cares for her mother."

Tony prayed, "'Please help Pam to remember all she learned while she attended this church and small groups."

Clara added, "Yes, and may that give her joy even when situations seem hard."

Ami prayed, "Please have Pam's mother show appreciation for what Pam is doing, and to cooperate when she's doing the therapy. Holy Spirit, please draw her parents into the family of God."

Jane continued, "Please help Aneko to find a job that's just right for her so she'll want to stay in Pine City, and please bring her and Yoshi to a knowledge of you as their own Savior."

Tomo concurred, "Yes, and please give Ami and I all the right words to say at the right time. Help us to not be pushy, but patient and let you do your work in their lives." When Ami said Amen to that, and the rest did also.

Then Jane invited everybody to come into their dining room for refreshments. There were vegetables all cut and ready for several different kinds of dips. It was all very refreshing and the time to visit was also.

Ted and Julie talked to Larry and Jane about skipping their four by four activity this week so all four of them could go to the baptismal service. They agreed. Matt, Fiona, and Tony discussed when they could go out and do three by three ministry, and decided on Friday mornings at 9:30. This week they would meet at the park near the church. Then Ted conversed with Tony and said that he was looking forward to walking with him and learning Spanish. Tony looked pleased. Fiona and many others told Clara how happy they were for her and that they were glad she was going to continue to be in this small group. Clara gave her budgets to Karen in an envelope. The ones who could not get off work to attend the baptismal service asked others if they could call them and be told "all about it" like the twins would do for Sherry. Karen handed out recipes for the cookies to the ones who had asked her for them. It had been a very nice small group meeting. Jeff and Karen were delighted that it had gone so well.

*****

Matt went directly over to see Walt and Betty after the small group meeting. They welcomed him inside, and he said, "I sure do miss being able to work with you every day, Walt. At least we have a few minutes between shifts, so I should not complain. How have things been going for you this week, Betty?"

"I've had a very good week, thank you. The new believers small group meeting was extra interesting this week, since we got to go to the church and see the facilities for the baptismal service on Tuesday. That helped to put my mind at ease. It was especially helpful that they played a short video of a man and then a woman being baptized," said Betty.

Walt continued, "That's for sure. They say a picture is worth a thousand words, well, I think a video must be worth about ten thousand!"

"I'm glad the video helped you both. Do you both have your testimonies ready for Tuesday evening?" asked Matt.

"Yes. Don said to keep them short, but I made mine long enough to give the glory to God for all he did for me. I'm hoping there will be some unsaved people there who will believe in Jesus as a result," replied Walt.

"Good idea, Walt. I'll ask Don if it would be a good plan to make an announcement for people to bring some of their unsaved friends with them and for him to be ready with a gospel message. I know the time will be rather tight because of all the people who are being baptized, but it would be worth running a little bit late."

Betty agreed, "I think you're right. People these days are in too big a hurry."

"You're right, Betty. But I'm going to hurry home and eat lunch because I need to meet Ben who is going to help me work on my house for the rest of the afternoon. I'll see you both in church on Sunday. Fiona and I will save seats for you in about the same area as we were in last Sunday," said Matt as he rose to leave. They nodded and laughed.

Matt called Don as he was fixing his lunch, and told him about Walt's idea. Don said it sounded great, and that he would call right away and see if the lead pastor agreed. He did, and called all the rest of the pastors so they could announce it in church the rest of the weekend.

*****

    The Suehiros had asked Jeff and Karen to come to their house for lunch after the small group meeting so they could ask questions about the four by four ministry and decide on a day that would work for all of them to go together. So the Spencers loaded all the books and the boom box into their car and went to have lunch with Tomo and Ami.
    "If you like to eat outside, we have a covered patio, and it's warm today," suggested Ami.
    "We would enjoy that. How can we help?" asked Karen.
    "We're having all cold foods that we fixed yesterday morning and put them in the refrigerator so they would be ready for today. You can both help us carry the things out to the patio," Tomo explained.
    It didn't take long to get things in place for their meal. Tomo asked Jeff to give thanks, and then they visited while they ate all the delicious food. "That was an especially delicious lunch!" exclaimed Karen. Ami thanked her for the compliment.
    After putting the left over food away, and cleaning up the dishes, they all settled in the living room where all the questions could be answered. Ami started with, "How often do you go out and do ministry?"
    "We try to go out once a week, but stay alert when we're out together doing other things or errands. The idea is to be listening and looking for opportunities wherever we are, even if we're alone inside a store doing some shopping. You might think of it as lifestyle ministry. That's kind of what Jesus did when he was here on earth," explained Karen.
    "I get it," said Tomo. "That makes good sense. It isn't just a once in a while project, but something you're ready for all the time." Then he asked, "What do we need to bring with us?"
    "We like to have a small Bible along with us in case they ask any questions we might need to look up. It is a good idea to be ready to explain the Gospel and know how to lead a person to Christ for salvation. You might want to practice that on each other. Plus, we always carry some of those little booklets and cards like Don gives out to new believers at church in case someone <u>does</u> decide to believe," answered Jeff.

Then Ami asked, "Will we pray before we meet together or wait until when we're together?"

"Both would probably be best. We can use all the help we can get," Karen replied.

"What day would be the best one for both of you to go?" questioned Tomo.

After some discussion, they decided that Sundays after church would be a good time for all of them to go out and do ministry together. They could leave right from the church and not have to worry about cooking a meal for a couple hours. That would not work this coming Sunday, because Aneko was going to be here, arriving later this afternoon. They would get started the next Sunday.

*****

After nap time and lunch, Roy and Sherry took Joy and Hope to a different park than last week, where they prayed for direction and for God to use them. This time they were at least able to converse with the parents of a little boy who was in a wheelchair. It seemed best to them to just keep the conversation general this time.

"Do you come to this park often?" Sherry asked at one point.

The mother answered, "Yes, it's the best one in town that's equipped with a place for wheelchairs. So we try to come here whenever the weather permits it."

Roy commented, "It looks like our girls are having fun playing ball with him. He's a good catcher, and throws the ball gently so they have a better chance of catching it. How old is he?"

The father responded, "He's seven years old. We have worked on catching and throwing a lot, and he enjoys playing with balls. How old are your girls?"

"They'll be five near the end May, and it looks like they could use some practice," Sherry answered.

At that point, the mother noticed that her son was getting tired, so they decided to take him home. The twins, who had told him their names and learned his, thanked him for playing with them and said "Good-bye." Roy and Sherry planned to get here a little earlier next week hoping for a longer time to talk with his parents.

*****

Everywhere There's a Sunrise, Let's Tell The Good News!
The first Sunday in May

    The weather had been perfect for working on the house yesterday afternoon, and this Sunday morning was just as nice, so adding them together, Matt and Ben were able to get almost a whole day of work done on Matt's house. So they made good progress that both of them were happy to see. They stopped in time to eat lunch and get cleaned up for church.

    Julie sent an e-mail to Pam with the teaching and prayer time for Pam's requests. Then she asked her if she could give Fiona, one of the members in the small group, her e-mail address, because she had some ideas to write to her. Pam answered right back and told Julie that would be fine. So Julie called Fiona and gave her Pam's e-mail address. Fiona got busy right away and wrote down as many things as she could think of that had helped her while she was caring for her great aunt. She ended with an encouraging scripture verse, and told Pam she would be glad to answer any questions, or just be another correspondent. Pam wrote right back and thanked her for the good ideas, and agreed that it would be very nice to have an additional person to communicate with.

    Jason was walking again on this gorgeous morning, going over in his mind all that had happened since his salvation and healing, and trying to decide what to include in his baptismal testimony. Soon he had it figured out. His feet had carried him over to his parent's house again and he decided to visit with them and try out his 'speech' on them. They were pleased, as usual to see him, but even more so now that he was a believer. Their relationship had grown much closer now.

    Jason started, "I would like you both to listen to my baptismal testimony and help me improve it if needed. Here it is. I'm so thankful that God sent a special woman to tell me the real way to be sure that I would go to heaven when I die, even writing down the verses for me in a Bible she gave me. Those verses and the verses my parents told me helped me to see how wrong I had been all my life, thinking that all I needed to do was be a good person. So I repented, confessed my sins, and believed in Jesus. He saved me and also graciously healed me of my long-standing bi-polar disorder. I'm a new person now that I'm a believer, and I <u>know</u> I'm on my way to heaven!" They both clapped and said it was a perfect testimony. "I hope there will be some unbelievers there to hear it," Jason added.

Tomo and Ami were having a lovely morning visiting with their daughter, Aneko. It was just so good to see her again and hear all about her adventures in the city where she had been living.
Finally Tomo got his courage up and said, "We've been attending a very good church for the last three years. The service starts at 2:00, and we'd love to have you go with us."

Aneko surprised them by saying, "I would like that. I tried a few churches near where I live but I didn't like any of them. The people seemed phony to me."

Then Ami asked, "Which one of your favorite things would you like to have for lunch?"

She answered, "You pick it, Mom, and I will come and help you cook it."

*****

It was Clara who was waiting in the entryway of the church this Sunday. She wanted to greet her former boss and his wife, so they could sit with her. When she saw them come in, she happily hurried over and was introduced to his wife. Then she had them follow her to her usual place in the fourth row of the middle section. She made sure she was sitting beside his wife so she could explain how to find the songs in the hymnal by looking at the display board at the front of the sanctuary. It was just easier for her to talk to a woman.

The singing time started with "All That Thrills My Soul Is Jesus," Colossians 3:11 and 1John 3:1. Then they sang "Praise the Name of Jesus," Psalm 18:2; "Fairest Lord Jesus," Isaiah 33:17; and "Jesus is Lord of All," Acts 2:36.

Pastor Don started his teaching time by reading, Acts 2:36 which says, "*Therefore let all the house of Israel know assuredly, that God has made this same Jesus whom you have crucified, both Lord and Christ.* That means that he is Lord of everything including our past, present, and future. Colossians 3:11b says, *Christ is all ...* that little part of this verse really says everything that needs to be said, so I could just dismiss us now." Everybody laughed. "But I won't, because I like to talk about this topic.
"People who believe in Jesus as their own personal Savior could use the hymn, "We Come, O Christ, to You," as their own personal testimony. We didn't sing it this morning, but I would like us to focus on the words in it. Please find it and read all the verses silently.

Everywhere There's a Sunrise, Let's Tell The Good News!

"These verses make a sermon all by themselves. They tell the story of who Jesus is and what he's done for men. Believers can count on him for guidance and provision. In turn, we can live our lives for him so that others can see him in us. It isn't always easy, and sometimes it seems to take so much time to obtain his guidance, but he is the one with all the wisdom and his timing is always best, as I'm sure many in this congregation can agree.

"Please open your hymnals now to the song, 'Jesus Is All the World to Me,' which we did sing this morning. Read the words silently and think about them. For believers, this song is a testimony of how he gives us a new life, joy, and strength. He is our friend during trials and gives us blessings and meets our needs. Our love for him causes us to want to live our lives for him and follow wherever he leads. The best verse is the last one that speaks of a believer's eternal life and eternal joy with Jesus. If you're not a believer you don't have this hope, but you can have it.

"1 John 3:1a says, *Behold what manner of love the Father has given us that we should be called sons of God.* Believers are called children of God because of what it says in the Gospel of John 1:12, *As many as received (Jesus) were given power to become the sons of God, because they believe on his name.* Acts 10:43 says, *all the prophets witnessed about him that through Jesus name anyone who believes in him shall receive the forgiveness of sins.* This is the Gospel, or the Good News. No matter what your sins, you will be forgiven when you believe in Jesus name. His name means everything that he is, like the verse in Colossians 3:11b says, *Christ is all,* and he has done everything God required, by dying on the cross to be a perfect blood sacrifice that would pay for all of our sins.

"But, it's not automatic. There is a part that people need to do in order to become a child of God. They need to believe and ask for forgiveness and for Jesus to be their Savior." At this point Pastor Don continued as he had many of the other Sundays, to lead any who wanted to do that, in a prayer they could say silently. "If you prayed that prayer with me, please tell someone about it right after this service, so they can rejoice with you, and then come tell me so that I can give you a little booklet to read that explains more about what it means to be a believer.

"Remember the special baptismal service at 7 PM Tuesday this week, and if any of you have friends who don't know Jesus, see if they would like to come also. I know that some of the testimonies might speak to their hearts, and I'll be ready with a salvation message," the pastor finished, and then said, "Let's sing

'Jesus Is All the World to Me' again, and then you may be dismissed."

After the song, Clara rejoiced with her former boss and his wife who told her that they had prayed the prayer with the pastor, and she went with them to introduce them to Pastor Don, so they could talk to him. Then she quickly went to tell Jeff and Karen. After that, she told Jane about it.

Tomo and Ami were overflowing with joy when Aneko told them she had prayed the prayer. They were waiting to introduce her to the pastor as soon as the others had left. Clara had gone back to be with her guests and they were filling out the card to return to the pastor. She asked them if they would like to be baptized in water on Tuesday evening, if the pastor could get them ready in time. They said they would, so she went with them to ask. Tomo was asking the same thing for Aneko so they joined in by listening.

Pastor Don said, "This is unusual, since the time is so short, but I think we can manage it. In fact, I have all my notes here from the first two new believers meetings. Would all of you please come with me to the church office? I'll get copies made so that you can read the notes after you read the booklets this afternoon. Then if you three can come to my home at 7:30 this evening, I can answer all your questions and get you ready to be baptized in water this coming Tuesday evening at 7 PM." They told him they could, and thanked him profusely, before leaving, and then went to their homes and started reading.

*****

Matt and Fiona had dressed for an active afternoon, so they headed to the Frisbee Golf Course as planned. Before getting out of the truck, they prayed for Julie and Pam for a while. They made it three fourths of the way around the course before deciding that it was enough for the afternoon. So they sat on a bench for a while discussing some different topics.

This was her opportunity, so she grabbed it and prayed that God would do his will, and that she would accept it. "Matt, I haven't had a chance to tell you about the surprise I got last week." She gave him a summary of the unexpected inheritance she had received from her great aunt. She included the amount and the expected taxes.

"Wow!" he inserted at that point.

She continued, "After praying a lot about it I told my parents that I would like to give it all, except the taxes, to the work of the LORD." She watched his face carefully to see what his reaction would be.

He smiled at her and said, "That much money would go a long way to help almost any ministry. I commend you, Fiona. You walk your talk. Too many people would just spend it on whatever they wanted to buy for themselves."

She almost sighed with relief and was so thankful that he had passed another test with flying colors. They talked some more about this and that.

Toward the end, Matt asked, "Would it work for you to go with me and take Walt and Betty out to supper next Sunday evening? I haven't asked them yet."

She replied, "Yes, that would be very nice. We didn't have much time to talk today or last Sunday, but it was nice to have them sitting with us. Where shall we take them? I wonder what kind of food they like."

"They like all kinds of food, but the doctor told him to stay on a good diet to keep him healthier, so how about that new restaurant that has many of those choices?" he inquired.

"Good idea. I'll look forward to it. Maybe I can learn some things about a healthier diet, also," she responded. Then they made plans to have a tennis match on Wednesday morning, as he drove her back to her home.

When Fiona went in the house she was smiling, and immediately went to tell her parents the good news about Matt's response to her wanting to give away all of her inheritance. They were also thrilled, and they all praised and thanked God together.

*****

After church, Maria, Ruth, and Esther were waiting in the entry for Ted and Julie, where they were all introduced. Later, Ted told Maria that Tony would be there at the park also, to walk with him and teach him Spanish. At least <u>she</u> knew that in advance. This might be a little awkward. They drove their cars over to the park so they wouldn't take up spaces in the church parking lot. When they arrived Tony was there waiting, and <u>he</u> was the one surprised at all the <u>females</u> who were there.

Maria introduced Tony and Ruth and Esther to each other. They talked for a few minutes and then since the plan was to walk and get exercise, they all started out. Ted and Tony stayed back about ten steps from the ladies, and got started on Spanish.

Julie explained to the other ladies about Tony offering to teach Spanish to Ted. That made sense to them, and they all started conversing in Spanish. Maria was blown away because she had not known Ruth and Esther could speak Spanish. It just had never come up in their conversations. She found out that Spanish was one of their main languages even though their last name didn't attest to that fact. Their mother, Anna, was originally from Spain, and she had gone there to visit relatives. She had met William there when he had come on a trip to visit his mother's relatives living in Spain. When they both had returned to the states they dated and fell in love. So after courtship and marriage, it was natural for them to teach their children both languages. They were all having such fun, and Julie joined right in along with them. Again, she was so happy that she had become fluent in that beautiful language.

They walked for about 45 minutes before returning to some benches, set up in a circular grouping, near where their cars were parked. Everyone sat down and all but Ted began talking in Spanish. Julie quickly translated for him so he wasn't left out. It was like a mini small group, and when they were finished with basic information, they knew a lot about each other, and were able to continue talking about various topics, including some of the things they had liked about the church service. After about half an hour, they all decided that they should go home and fix their own suppers. Julie invited Ruth and Esther to join them again any time they would like to get some exercise after church. And Tony told them and Maria that he would look forward to seeing them again.

*****

When Pastor Don and Anita got home with their children, they all changed into comfortable clothes and Timmy and Mary went out to play in the back yard while their parents watched from comfortable chairs on the back porch where they could talk. Don told her about the new decisions for Christ and the people's desire to be baptized on Tuesday.

"Amazing and wonderful!" she exclaimed. "I'm so thankful for the many new believers Jesus has added to his church in the last few weeks. I thank and praise you, Jesus, that we can have a part in building your Kingdom."

Don added, "I join Anita in her praise and thanks, Lord. You are marvelous!"

Then Anita confirmed, "You said they would meet at 7:30 at the pastor's house?" After Don nodded, she said, "Good planning, Honey. That way the children can have their nap, we can rest, and then we can fix supper, eat it, and clean up, and still have a little time to spend with the children before the people get here. Timmy and Mary can play in their rooms until I go to their rooms at about 8:00 to put them to bed."

"Yes, and I think I have a couple copies of the floor plan of the baptismal area, so we can go over that separately, you with the ladies, and I with the man. We won't need to set up any additional chairs tonight," he added.

By 7:30 they were ready when their guests arrived, and they welcomed them inside. It only took about 15 minutes to answer their questions, and then they went over the floor plan as they had intended. Then Pastor Don told them about the small groups for new believers. Clara's former boss and his wife would be in the group meeting on Wednesday nights, and Aneko would go to the one for late shift people, meeting on Saturday mornings. After a little while of visiting, they were out the door by shortly after 8 PM. So both parents were able to put the children to bed.

*****

Aneko told her parents all about the short meeting when she got home and they shared some of their memories of their own baptisms three years ago.

"I'm so excited about being baptized and starting my new life as a believer," stated Aneko. I've known for a long time that there was something missing from my life. This has filled that void. I'll be attending the small group for new believers that meets on Saturday mornings. Now I can understand what you both meant when you tried to tell me about your salvation."

Tomo responded, "Your mother and I are also excited and very grateful to God for answering our prayers for you, our dear Aneko." They shared a three-way hug, and prayed that God would bring Yoshi and the rest of their extended family into his family very soon.

*****

Monday

Tony carried his dirty clothes to the Laundromat inside his apartment building, always thankful that it was so handy. This was one advantage to having an afternoon and evening job. Most of the other people in this building had regular daytime jobs and that left the mornings open for him to do his laundry without having to wait his turn.

As he put his clothes in the washers, he thought back on yesterday afternoon. All those women being there at the same time had astonished him. They were all beautiful, intelligent, articulate, kind, and interesting. Of course, Julie was already married, and that was good. The other three were single and he was overwhelmed with the possibilities. He wondered if Ruth and Esther would ever come walking again, but felt sure that Maria would be there next Sunday. "What is going on, Lord? Are you trying to tell me something? Which one would you have me choose to get better acquainted with, if any?" No answers were forthcoming right away, so he chose to leave it in God's expert hands.

Then he thought about Ted, and the good progress he had made already in learning Spanish. It would be a great help that he was going to study in Julie's old textbooks. Since Julie translated for Ted while Tony and the other ladies were conversing in Spanish, Ted didn't have to feel left out. It had been an enjoyable afternoon.

*****

Ruth and Esther were waiting in Maria's office again with big questioning grins on their faces. She guessed what it probably was, and she was right. "Did you know that Tony would be there in the park yesterday?" asked Esther.

"I had <u>no</u> idea!" she exclaimed. "I was only thankful that Ted warned me before we got there. I thought it might be a bit awkward but since you both speak Spanish, it turned out to be rather fun. I thought I might be embarrassed, but he accepted my explanation, and you two fit right in."

Esther said, "He seems to be a very nice person. I could tell by the things he said that he's a committed Christian. May I ask you a question, Maria?"

"Sure," she answered, knowing by the look on Esther's face what it was going to be, but she would let her ask.

Ruth interrupted, "That question needs to wait until lunch. We must go get to work, before our co-workers think we're wasting time." They agreed and quickly got to work.

Lunchtime could not come fast enough for Esther, and somehow she didn't want to admit the reason, even to herself. So she made herself concentrate on her work instead.

They met in the lunchroom, took their lunches out of the refrigerator and since it was a beautiful day, they walked to, and around the park where they were finally able to talk. "Are you interested in him?" Esther asked Maria.

Maria had never been one to tease or make someone wait and wonder, so she honestly answered, "I was a little bit last Sunday, until I got to work and you both told me about Jason's salvation and healing. Then I was totally confused. To go for so many years with no prospects, and try to accept <u>singleness</u> as God's will for my life, and then have <u>two</u> possibilities to consider, has me in a quandary. I don't know what to think. I told Julie the other day that I feel like I'm in a maze, and I'm totally lost in there. But she told me that when it was God's timing, he would take me by the hand and lead me out of it. So I'm trying to wait patiently and trust him to do just that."

"And he will for sure!" Ruth responded.

"So, what does that look like for me?" asked Esther. "I admit that I'm interested in Tony."

"Let's all pray about it just before we eat," answered Maria. They did that adding thanks for their food, and when they were almost finished eating, she suggested, "Since Tony has decided to teach Spanish to Ted on Sunday afternoons during our walks, I think you should join us, Esther. You also, Ruth, if you want to walk, although I know you're not interested in Tony. We can let Tony decide which person he's interested in, or give him some information that might help him decide. I feel like I need to give Jason a chance to become what God wants him to be and then court me if he still wants to. So, Tony is all yours, Esther."

"No wonder, Jason thinks you're so special, Maria," Ruth told her, and Esther nodded. "And he doesn't even know you as well as we do."

"For sure!" added Esther. "You're so kind and understanding. If I were in your place, I think I would want to keep <u>both</u> options open, but you're willing to step back, not even knowing how things might turn out for you. I for one would feel very blessed to get to have you as a sister-in-law!"

"I feel just the same way," agreed Ruth.

"Thank you, both for the complements. I <u>know</u> I'm blessed to have you as sisters in the Lord, and if it's the Lord's will, I know you would be great sisters-in-law. But, I have no idea what kind of husband Jason would be. Now I suppose we better hurry so we can be back to work on time," said Maria.

*****

Aneko set out job hunting in the morning, and then went to the restaurant in the afternoon about 3:00 to help her parents until closing time. When they got home that evening she told them, "I didn't find anything today that I could enjoy working at, until I got to the restaurant and started helping both of you. Is there any chance you need another employee?"

Tomo replied, "Yes, indeed! In fact we've been talking about that for several weeks now. It's been getting busier than we can keep up with, and we don't like to keep people waiting."

Ami added, "We can think of nobody else we would rather hire than our own daughter! Consider yourself hired."

"Thank you both so much! I've missed you and our family life. Could I live here with you for awhile?"

"Of course!" Ami exclaimed. We've missed you also, and we'll be thrilled to have you home again!"

"I'll expect to pay for my room and board," Aneko added, but her parents looked aghast.

"No way!" declared Tomo. "This is your home for as long as you want to live here! Welcome home!"

"My feelings exactly!" added Ami. "This house has seemed so big and empty since you both moved away. It will be so good to have you here again."

"What wonderful parents I have! Thank you, thank you, thank you!" Aneko said. "I'm so glad I came to visit and job hunt. And I'm overjoyed that I went to church with you and finally have peace with my Father in Heaven!"

*****

Clara spent the whole day in nursing classes at the university. The timing had been perfect for her to fill her days with classes for the new quarter that was just starting. Plus, she didn't even have to worry about paying for all those classes, plus her rent and food, and other needs besides. God had abundantly provided for her.

Everywhere There's a Sunrise, Let's Tell The Good News!

She would be attending the evangelism classes in the evenings. It was still a very full schedule for her, but she had been able to work it out so she got home in time to rest before supper and cleanup, and then go to the evening class. She was one very grateful student!

*****

Tuesday

It was a normal busy day for everybody at their jobs, and the rest of daily living. Many were looking forward to the evening when they could attend the special baptismal service either to watch or to be baptized. Those being baptized had learned how important it was, because of all the good teaching they had received.

Pastor Don showered as soon as he got home and dressed in lightweight dark colored clothes so he would be ready to baptize the new believers in church #4. The family hurried through supper so they could get over to the church in time to prepare the dressing rooms and fill the baptismal tank with warm water. Timmy and Mary were being cared for by a volunteer who would also look after the other pastors' children. Everything was ready when the first people started arriving for the special service.

Most of the people were early and it was going to be a large crowd, including people from two other churches, plus all the new believers from all three churches. Matt was in his place beside Walt and Betty, wishing Fiona could have joined him, but knowing she had to be at work. All of their co-workers and their wives were in the rows behind them, and were joined by Jeff and Karen. Walt's doctor and his wife, and the Mayor and his wife were also sitting beside Walt, ready to be baptized.

Tomo and Ami had closed the restaurant at 6 PM after the three of them ate their own supper there. Aneko had had time to shower and dress and was sitting with her parents.

Candy was sitting beside Mindy and her father, Vern, with her foster parents on her other side. The rest of Vern's small group was also in attendance, sitting beside and in front of them. Mindy saw Miss Nelson look over at her dad a couple times, but he didn't seem to notice. Mindy prayed in her mind that God would wake him up.

Julie and Ted sat beside her former boss and his wife. The whole evangelism class had come to watch the baptisms, so Clara was able to sit with her former boss and his wife. Larry and Jane sat on the other side Clara. Roy was there with the twins, wishing that Sherry could have joined them but the twins would tell her all about it. Ernest, Connie and Ben were sitting next to the family he had invited to church. Maria and her entire small group were seated together. Several people had given notes to Don alerting him to the presence of unbelievers. All three pastors had announced to their congregations to bring unbelievers to the baptismal service.

Don and one of the other two pastors took turns leading the singing. They sang only two songs, but the words in both of them were sermons in themselves: "We Bless the Name of Christ the Lord," Matthew 3:15; and "Come Holy Spirit, Dove Divine," Romans 6:4-14.

The new believers from church #4 were dismissed first to go get ready in the dressing rooms. During that time, the third pastor read the scripture verses that went with the two songs. When he finished Pastor Don and the first new believer were ready in the baptismal tank. It was set up with good microphones that would pick up what he and the people would say.

Walt was first, and his testimony was: "I thank God for giving me a second chance, and saving me after healing me of a massive heart attack. He made my physical and spiritual hearts both perfect. I choose to serve him the rest of my life. I only wish I had not waited so long! If any of you people in the audience haven't asked Jesus to be your Savior, I hope that you'll do it soon!" Then, Pastor Don baptized him in the name of the Father, and of the Son, and of The Holy Spirit.

Betty was next and said, "I'm grateful for a friend who would not give up on us, but kept talking to us about the Good News and praying for us until we believed in Jesus. He knew that we needed the Lord."

When it was Candy's turn, she said loud and clear, "I thank God for Pastor Don who caught me red-handed doing graffiti and stealing, but who was kind enough to let me work with him to pay my debt and then he put me into a wonderful home. I came to this church where I learned about the Savior, Jesus, who forgave me for all my sins and made me into a new person. If you don't know Jesus, I hope that you will soon." Pastor Don unashamedly wiped away tears of joy, before baptizing her.

Julie's former boss stated, "I'm so glad that I got to see that God could work out so many details for the good of many people that I knew. I came to church to learn more about him, and so far, I've learned that I've only scratched the surface. His love and the salvation he gave me are more than precious. I'll have the rest of my life to continue learning about this great Almighty God." His wife said almost the same thing.

Clara's former boss and his wife gave testimonies that were very similar to those.

Aneko said, "I thank God for sending Jesus to be my Savior and for the peace he's given me and for filling up the void inside me that nothing else could fill. The hymn titled, 'Satisfied,' has the rest of my testimony if you want to read it sometime."

One of Walt's co-workers testified, "After seeing my boss have a massive heart attack, and then Jesus healing and saving him, the only sensible thing I could do was to believe in Jesus to save me also. I'm so glad my wife and I did."

Another of them said, "Thank you Jesus for saving me and my wife. We will love and serve you forever."

Another said, "I thank Jesus for the unity we feel on the job since all of us believe in Jesus."

One of the wives said, "Our marriage was good before, but now with Jesus as the head of our home, we have the best marriage ever."

Another wife said, "I'm so thankful that Walt sent my husband home to tell me about Jesus, and that he saved me too. Now we pray that our grown children will come to know his salvation also."

Many of the co-workers and their wives testimonies were similar to those in some ways.

Walt's Doctor said, "I thank Jesus for showing me his power and grace in healing and saving Walt. My wife and I could not help but believe in him as our Savior also." The Mayor and his wife said something very similar.

Other testimonies focused on how believing in the resurrection of Jesus had opened their hearts to believe in Jesus as their own personal Savior.

Still others were thankful for the person who was willing to give them an invitation to church at Easter time, and because of that they heard about how Jesus had died for them and was raised to life by God, so they could be saved.

Others were being baptized because of the witness of friends or family, and still others as a result of a miracle that God performed for them when a pair of believers was out doing ministry.

Church #3 was dismissed to go get ready, as Pastor Don continued to baptize the rest of the people who had just received Jesus in the last few weeks in church #4. When he was finished the next pastor came to take his place and Don went to shower and get dressed so he would be ready to give a short salvation message after all the rest of the people were baptized.

The continuing testimonies were individualized and told of the way God had been working in the other two churches the past few weeks also. It was wonderful to realize that God could do all these miracles not just in these three churches, but in all 12 here, and in countless others around the world. God was adding to his church like it says in Acts 2:47!

As soon as the last person was baptized, Pastor Don went up on stage and gave a short message about the Gospel and how to become a believer in Jesus. Then he led the people in a prayer much like those on the last few Sundays. When those who prayed it with him went up to tell him, spontaneous applause and praise to God erupted all over the sanctuary. He and the newest believers joined right in, then he gave each family or individual a booklet and a card to return to the pastor of the church they were with. It looked like there would be several new believers small groups starting very soon, and another special baptismal service not too far off.

*****

Chapter 17

Colossians 1: 9b-11a, *Paul prayed that: you might be filled with the knowledge of God's will in all wisdom and spiritual understanding; that you might walk worthy of the Lord, being pleasing ... and fruitful in every good work, and increasing in the knowledge of God, strengthened with ... his glorious power ...*

Wednesday

It was time for a tennis match between Matt and Fiona and the weather was just perfect for it. It was nice to have mornings off, because even in the summer the earlier mornings would be cool enough for outside activities. This time they had waited until ten o'clock so it had a chance to warm up. Before getting out of the truck, they again prayed for Julie and Pam. From Julie's praises at the small group meetings, they could tell she was doing fine, so they spent more time praying for Pam's requests and salvation for her parents.

When they got out of the truck, Fiona said, "I'm out of practice, but this is going to be fun anyway."

Matt agreed, "Me too. We always have fun together, and I'm so grateful to have you back in Pine City. We probably should keep this match short so we don't get too tired and sore from using muscles that are not used to it yet."

"Good idea," she responded. "I appreciate the way you're so thoughtful."

"You're welcome. Are you ready? Here comes my first serve," he replied.

"Thanks for the warning! It went past me before I even registered what you had said," she laughed. "Okay, serve it again, and this time I'll be ready."

A little later he said, "Hey, you're doing great now. I should have let you get ready before. I guess that was a little bit of the scamp coming out in me. We both used to do that when we played ping pong," said Matt.

"Right. That was fun, too. We can add ping pong to our list of activities if you still like it," she suggested.

"I do!" he exclaimed thinking of another time he would like to say those two words. "Okay, here comes another of my serves. Are you ready?"

"Yes, go for it," she replied. And they finished the match in quiet concentration. Matt won it by two points. It looked like they were still pretty closely matched in tennis. "I'm ready for a rest. How about you? I brought some fruit juice for us today."

"Yummy. I forgot all about something to refresh us. I'm glad you remembered," he responded. You still play a very good game, Fiona."

"Thank you, and so do you, Matt," she replied. "I'm very glad to be back in Pine City, and that I get to spend time with you again." By way of answer, he reached over, picked up her hand and kissed the back of it. She felt a tingle go all the way through her as she smiled at him and blushed.

He gave her hand a little squeeze and put it down. Then he changed the subject so he could stay in control of himself. "I asked Walt and Betty if they would like to go out to supper on Sunday after we all go look at the flowers in the botanical garden, weather permitting. If not, we'll go to their home and visit until time to go to the restaurant. Will that work out for you?"

"Yes, I'll be looking forward to it," she replied. "It was so good to hear about both of them being baptized last night and have you tell me their testimonies on the way over here to the tennis court."

"I had a hard time not getting up and cheering for them both. It was a long time in coming, but they finally made it, and I'm so thrilled. Now all four of us can build a deep relationship with each other based on our belief in Jesus the Messiah. It's been hard for me to hold back. Now I don't have to," he explained.

They played another game after finishing their juice. This time it was a tie. Then it was time to take her back home so she could eat lunch before going to work. He needed to do the same. They both wished the time didn't have to end.

*****

Don got home from work on Wednesday, and finished getting the supper ready that Anita had started. They enjoyed their meal together and everyone helped with the cleanup. Mindy's dad had picked her up to go home and eat, but he would bring her back by 6:30 to take care of Timmy and Mary. The children visited with their parents while they got ready to go to the third new believers small group.

When Mindy got there Timmy and Mary ran up and hugged her like she had been gone for days. Then she said to Don and Anita, "I'm amazed by the change in Candy. She really is a new creation in Christ. We're becoming good friends, and I'm so happy for her. I would never have had the nerve to say what she did in front of all those people, but it was a very good testimony."

Pastor Don replied, "I know! I could not keep from crying tears of joy about her. God is so good. I'm glad she and you can be friends."

"Thank you for coming to be with Timmy and Mary, today and tomorrow, and this coming Saturday. We're very blessed to have you be here. They enjoy you so much," stated Anita.

"You're welcome," replied Mindy. "I enjoy <u>them</u> very much too."

"We should be home by about 9:30. I'm glad you brought your homework so you can do it after they go to bed," said Don. Then they all said, "See you later."

When Don and Anita arrived at the co-facilitator's house, they were pleasantly surprised to see the chairs already set up with Bibles and hymnals on them. They had brought some along just in case, but this couple was all set. They had time to pray and visit for a while before the group members came.

This third meeting started with a prayer, and then many praise reports about how God had made the baptismal service so meaningful. It would be a precious memory for them to cherish.

Next, Don explained how small groups usually worked and asked, "Would any of you like to be hosts for the meeting next week?" Walt and Betty were quick to volunteer, and he thanked them. "Now it's time for singing."

They sang "I Am Resolved," John 6:68. The rest of the songs and the teaching were very much like the first small group meeting Ted and Julie attended. Don taught them about the Holy Spirit and the way he worked in the lives of believers and in the church. After that, Anita handed out the small booklets that told more about the Holy Spirit. Their homework was to read the booklets before the next meeting so that any questions they might have could be answered then. At that meeting they would follow the schedule of an ongoing small group. He also reminded them that this was the last meeting with Don and Anita as co-facilitators, and took time to pray for all of them as they went on together. Then they had a pleasant time of refreshments and fellowship.

*****

Thursday

On Thursday, Maria went to work as usual with plans to go to lunch with the same two coworkers as on Tuesday and Wednesday. On Tuesday, they had driven to a small restaurant some distance away, and had a nice lunch while getting to know each other better. Wednesday they had brought lunches and walked to and around in the park before eating. The weather had been so nice. It was lovely to be outside. They shared small talk, and every one seemed to be at ease. Today, at noon, they walked to a nearby cafe and had a pleasant time visiting. So far, so good, but it seemed to move so slowly. As she got back to her office, she asked God to give her patience and guide her words.

*****

The pastor's family had an evening almost like the one last night, and the meeting for the other new believer's small group was basically a copy of the night before. Don and Anita were thankful that everything went so smoothly. They were glad to get home and thank Mindy. Then Anita took her to her home. Then they went in to look at their two children as they slept peacefully, and asked God to continue blessing them. After that, they hurried off for their own rest.

*****

Jason attended his third new believers small group, which was very much like the ones Don had co-facilitated that night and the night before. Jason was taught about the Holy Spirit and his role in the church and in believers. He and the rest in his group learned that since they were filled with the Holy Spirit, they would never feel alone again. The pastor of church #1 also prayed for the co-facilitators and the group, since this would be his last time with them.

Jason was learning so much every day and especially at church and small group meetings. Now he had another little booklet to read and learned more about the Holy Spirit. He had begun a daily time of reading in the Bible and praying, especially asking for guidance and help to live this new life.

*****

When Ted and Julie got home from her visit with Jane, and his time at music preparation, he had a surprise for her. "Look what I have! Hold out your hands." He filled them with SD cards to use in their stereo players around the apartment. There were dates going back to when the church had started preparing music this way.

"Oh Ted! These are wonderful!" exclaimed Julie. "Now we can have beautiful music wherever we are in the apartment." I'm so glad these are available."

"Me too. When I asked the technician after the meeting, about whether there were any recordings that people could purchase, he told me about all of these, and that they only cost as much as the SD cards cost the church. I bought all the ones they have made so far. Plus, they're not copyrighted so we can make copies or send the songs over e-mail to people who might want some. I immediately thought about Pam."

"Right! I'll ask her if she would like some, and if so, I can send one at a time when I e-mail her," she said. That's very thoughtful of you, my treasure! Not only can we enjoy them, but she can also. I'm glad this church is so generous. Just think of all the booklets they've given to us since we got here, too."

"I agree. Thank you, heavenly Father for all the blessings we've enjoyed since we moved to Pine City!" he exclaimed.

Julie added her own thanks and then said, "I'll go check my e-mail and see if Pam has any requests for the small group Saturday, and ask her if she would like to have any of this music." She found one request and a praise to share.

*****

Friday

Matt, Fiona, and Tony met at the park near the church to pray and plan and then walked around to see if they would get any directions from the Holy Spirit today. After they had walked and prayed for a while, they could see that the park didn't get much use on Friday mornings. There were hardly any people besides them in the park today.

Tony suggested, "Maybe we would see more people if we went to stores where people are shopping. Since I don't have a car, because I don't desire one, how would it be if we would meet at the grocery store on that corner over there next Friday at 9:30 AM. We could take a shopping cart and put a few things in it so we look like we're shopping. In fact I could shop for some of what I usually buy there, so it will be truthful."

Fiona replied, "That sounds good to me. What do you think Matt?"

Matt answered, "I like it. Then after we're finished, I can do my grocery shopping there, also." When that was settled, they went their separate ways.

*****

Ernest and Connie went to work at the same time today, both of them wondering where the week had gone. Time seemed to be moving faster and faster for them. With their busy lives, it was no surprise really, and both of them would tell you that they were thankful to be busy instead of being bored like some people they had heard about.

The morning and afternoon went very well. Connie was able to answer questions for many customers, so she was certainly enjoying her day. She also got to talk with Fiona, and that was also a highlight of her day. "How are things going with Amelia?" she asked her.

"It's wonderful," Fiona answered. "She's opened up and shared about many topics. She seems very comfortable talking with me and is still enjoying her work. Did she tell you about the books she bought?"

"Yes, and I'm so pleased that you suggested those two books. They're a couple of the best on that topic. I feel so much better about her than I did before, and wanted to thank you again for being a friend to her," Connie said.

Fiona responded, "It's my pleasure to be able to see you more peaceful, and to feel like I'm doing something useful along with taking care of the plants. She and I <u>have</u> become good friends. We've had some very good discussions about the books, since I'm reading them also. It's helpful to have someone who is interested in the same topic. We can bounce ideas off each other."

"I'm very glad. Thanks for telling me about it. I better go get back to work. It's almost time for me to go home soon, and Amelia will be arriving soon. Have a good evening!" said Connie.

"You do the same! See you Sunday at church and then on Monday," replied Fiona.

*****

Julie could hardly believe it was already Friday. She was having such fun teaching in this school, and was very thankful that God had arranged for her to be able to teach here instead of in a public school or work in another dental office.

Today, she had made plans to eat lunch with the teacher in the classroom just down the hall from her. Julie gave thanks for their food, and they had a nice time getting better acquainted and just visiting while they ate. The time flew by and Julie said, "Maybe we can do this again sometime soon." The other teacher nodded as Julie waved and went out the door and back to her own classroom.

The students came inside in their usual orderly fashion, and she met them on the nice carpet where she and her koala puppet, Kippy, were ready to listen and talk about whatever problems or good times they had experienced so far that day. The class meeting time had become a more positive sharing time because problems were very few and it felt pleasant to talk about happy things instead.

One girl raised her hand, and Kippy called on her. "I just wanted to tell you how nice the weather is outside, Kippy, since you never get to come outside with us for recess."

Kippy responded, "Thank you. I'm glad it's so nice out there. Spring is a beautiful season."

Mrs. Blake agreed, "Yes, in fact, it's my favorite season! I always like seeing the new green grass and leaves and all the beautiful flowers and blossoming trees."

Then Kippy asked, "Who has a different favorite season to tell us about?"

A boy raised his hand and Kippy called on him. "I like winter the very best, because I like to go out in the snow and make snowmen and snowballs for a snowball fight, or go sledding at the park with the big hill!"

"Wow!" exclaimed Kippy. "That does sound like fun, but I'm afraid I would get too cold."

The boy said, "No you wouldn't. You have a very nice fur coat to keep you warm."

"Oh, yes, I suppose I do, but I needed some excuse so that I could stay inside and take a nice nap," replied Kippy.

Mrs. Blake laughed, "I guess that means you want to go back to your napping place now." Kippy nodded and the class laughed too, while their teacher put him in his place, and they all went to their seats.

The rest of the afternoon passed quickly, and of course Kippy 'woke up' for the end of the day sharing time. All the children had quickly come to be fond of him, and it was fun to have two times a day to 'talk' with him.

*****

When he arrived at the work site, on Friday, Walt was looking very pleased when he told Matt, "It looks like we might be able to finish up this house by the end of next week! If you can come over to our house on Saturday next week for lunch, I'll be able to tell you about my plans for the next project."

Matt responded, "Thank you, I would enjoy that. There is no better cook in this city than Betty! I hope the restaurant Fiona and I take you to this Sunday for supper will be good enough."

"I'm sure it will be. Don't worry so much, Matt. We'll enjoy being with you and getting to know Fiona. It's been nice to sit near you and her at church," said Walt.

As he was working during that evening, Matt was thinking about Fiona, and wishing he could be with her more often. When he recalled kissing the back of her soft, small hand, it filled him with longings to have her be his wife, but then he realized he better just go slowly and be patient, waiting for God's best timing. He could look forward to seeing her at the small group tomorrow and then time with her and Walt and Betty on Sunday.

*****

Saturday

Mindy came a few minutes early on Saturday morning and said, "Candy and I have been sitting across from two other girls during lunch this week. Yesterday, she told them her testimony, and they really listened. I got to give them my testimony also, and they said they would think about what we had said and we would talk some more next week. Her boldness is helping me to be bolder. Please pray with me that these girls will come to Jesus too."

"Of course we will!" exclaimed Don. "That's fantastic. Father in heaven we agree with Mindy in asking you to draw these girls to Jesus. Have them think and remember what was said over the weekend. Continue to give Candy and Mindy holy boldness to share and answer questions so they can lead their new friends to Jesus."

Anita added, "Thank you Lord, for helping Mindy and Candy to share their faith with those two girls. Please bring them into your kingdom soon."

Mindy continued, "And thank you, Lord, for saving Candy and making her into a new person. May others see that and want the same thing for themselves. Help us remember to make friends before we share, so the kids won't be offended by what we say."

At that point, Timmy and Mary entered the room and ran to greet Mindy with a hug and excited hellos. It would be extra fun, because today Joy and Hope would be with them also.

They all said good-bye when Don and Anita left to drive to the co-facilitator's home where the third new believers small group was meeting. This was the group that was for those who worked the evening shift. Aneko would be a new member of this group, so she would be introduced, and everybody would be wearing name tags so she could start learning their names. Anita had made name tags for all of them and placed them in plastic holders with strings attached so they could put them over their heads and wear them around their necks. The members would bring them back to the next several meetings in order to help Aneko get to know them.

When Don and Anita got to the meeting place, they helped their co-facilitators finish putting out the Bibles and hymnals, placing a name tag on top of each pile. As the members arrived they were told to find their name tag, and put it on before they sat down, since they would have a new member today.

After the introduction of Aneko as their new member, the rest of the meeting was very much like the other two meetings earlier in the week. During the refreshment time many people, especially the wives, welcomed Aneko to the group, telling her how glad they were that she had joined them. She thanked them and mentioned that she would have to miss the next meeting so she could move her things to Pine City. She was given a list with the facilitator's names and all the members, plus addresses and phone numbers so she could call and find out where the meeting would be when she returned.

*****

The other late shift small group was meeting in the church school's lunchroom. Tony had arranged chairs in a circle so they would not have to sit on benches at the tables. He had put beverages of several kinds on one of the tables. Clara had brought several kinds of cookies and Tony and she had gone out early on the bus to a field outside of town to gather some wild flowers to make a couple bouquets. The room looked welcoming and cheery.

Jeff and Karen arrived in time to put Bibles and Hymnals on the chairs and still have time to pray with Tony and Clara for the upcoming meeting. Before long, all the members were there and the meeting was underway.

There were many praises and thankfulness for the baptismal service on Tuesday evening from those who had been able to attend, and even from those who had heard about things second hand. Tomo thanked God that Aneko had asked Jesus to be her Savior and had found the job she wanted to have right in Ami's Japanese Restaurant, and would be living at home again. Fiona thanked the Lord that Pam had been able to put into practice some of the ideas that she had given to her when she sent an e-mail to her, and that they had been very helpful. Sherry thanked the Lord that she and Roy had been able to talk to the parents of a seven-year-old boy who was in a wheel chair. Ted thanked God for the beautiful music that was available on SD cards from the church just for the price of the card it was on. Then they all joined in applause and oral praise to the Lord.

"Who would like to be our hosts for the next meeting?" asked Karen.

Roy spoke up, "We would like to invite you to our home for next week." Karen thanked him.

Jeff put an SD card into the portable stereo player and said, "Let's sing." The songs this week were: "How Majestic Is Your Name," Psalm 8:1; "Great Is Thy Faithfulness," Lamentations 3:22,23; "El Shaddai," Genesis 17:1; and "Praise to the Lord, the Almighty," Daniel 4:37. Julie was able to hear her husband's mellow bass voice beside her and in the prepared music both. She smiled at him often.

"How many of you did your homework?" Jeff asked. He was amazed when everybody raised his or her hand.

Someone said, "And if we hadn't done it, we could find several right here in the songs we just sang! They are great. Like right here in the verse that goes with this last one, God is called the 'King of heaven,' Daniel 4:37."

"Good job! Who would like to be next? Just call yours out and tell me which column to write it in, plus the scripture reference you found." The chart he was writing on looked something like this:

Names of God the Father

The LORD and the Lord: many places
King of heaven: Daniel 4:37
El Shaddai: Genesis 17:1
The God Who Sees: Genesis 16:13
The LORD Will Provide: Genesis 22:14
The LORD My Banner: Exodus 17:15
The LORD My Shepherd: Genesis 49:24
The LORD Who Heals: Exodus 15:26
The LORD of Hosts: 1 Samuel 1:11
The LORD is Peace: Judges 6:24
The LORD our Righteousness: Jeremiah 23:6
God Almighty: Genesis 17:1
God Most High: Genesis 14:22

Everywhere There's a Sunrise, Let's Tell The Good News!

Names of God the Son

Jesus: Matthew 1:21
Lamb of God: John 1:29
Savior: 1 Timothy 1:1
Prince of Peace: Isaiah 9:6
Good Shepherd: John 10:14
Light of the World: John 9:5
King of kings: 1 Timothy 6:15
Bread of Life: John 6:35
The Word: John 1:1 and 14
Wonderful Counselor: Isaiah 9:6
Emmanuel: Matthew 1:23
Son of Man: Luke 6:5
Lord of lords: 1 Timothy 6:15

    People kept busy copying down names and verses for their own charts as others called out more of them. When everyone had added at least one name, Jeff commented, "This was a wonderful time together. I learned a lot from it, and Karen and I even get to take this chart home and hang it up in our house. I can imagine somebody getting some nice poster board and colored markers and writing these in calligraphy. Or someone else typing them into a word processor with all the scripture references quoted. Maybe some of you ladies who are good with needlework might make these into a beautiful wall hanging. I'm sure there are many other ideas out there. This won't be homework, but if any of you do make something, please bring it to one of our meetings to show us."
    Then Jeff started conversational prayer time with, "Father in heaven and Jesus, thank you for your names, which are so meaningful to us. Thank you for all we've learned today."
    "King of heaven, I'm so thankful that you are in control of everything that you made," continued Karen.
    Tomo added, "Jesus, my Savior, thank you that you are now Aneko's Savior. Please make that true for Yoshi and the rest of my extended family very soon."
    Clara prayed, "My Provider, please continue to provide me with the intelligence to learn all I need to become skilled at being a good nurse and soul winner."

Roy continued, "Dear LORD Who Heals, please heal the boy in the wheelchair when you show us it's time to pray for him."

"Light of the World, shine through us as we go out by twos, threes, and fours, this week to do whatever you guide us to do in your name, so many others will want to have you as their Savior before you return," Larry prayed.

Jane added, "Jesus, we look forward to the time when you return to this earth as King of kings and Lord of lords!"

"Emmanuel, Jesus, thank you for sending your Holy Spirit to be with us always, since you rose from the dead and returned to heaven," continued Ted.

Julie turned on her recorder and prayed, "Please have Pam's mother and father be willing to listen to the church service on the web along with her, especially since the service is recorded by church #1, which always has a gospel message and invitation to pray included during the teaching time."

"Please draw them both to Jesus very soon and give them unity as a family," continued Matt.

Ami added, "Please, LORD Who Heals, completely heal Pam's mother and use it as an impetus to help her and the father and any extended family, plus their friends believe in Jesus as their Savior."

Fiona continued, "Wonderful Counselor, I'm thankful that you used me to give Pam some ideas that were helpful to her. Please teach her and remind her of things to do that will be a blessing."

Sherry added, "Jesus, our Savior, and heavenly Father, God Most High, thank you for how meaningful it is to pray to you using some of your many names in the Bible."

Tony concluded with. "Bread of Life, thank you, that you are our true food, and now please bless these refreshments to the nourishment of our bodies and our time of fellowship to our spirits. We pray in Jesus name, Amen."

With that, everyone stood and moved over to the tables that held the refreshments. Paper plates and cups would make for easy clean up when they finished. They enjoyed both the fellowship time and the refreshments, and nobody even noticed that they were in a school lunchroom instead of in a house.

*****

Roy and Sherry went to the Ross residence and picked up the twins who had just finished an early morning nap time and claimed to be starving. They had napped earlier than usual because all four children had acted extra tired after playing hard outside for an hour. Mindy was good at noticing the signs and talking them into early naps.

As soon as they got home and ate lunch they were raring to go again. That was just what their parents wanted, so that they could get to that park that was wheelchair accessible earlier than last week. Maybe the people would be there again and this time they could build up more rapport for their two by two ministry. The girls even had brought one of their favorite balls in hopes that they could play with the nice boy again.

When they arrived, the family was just getting out of their vehicle. Hope and Joy got to watch as the van elevator lowered the boy in his wheelchair to the sidewalk. They were fascinated, and would have run right over to talk to him and see it closer, but their parents kept them next to them instead. They explained that they wanted to have time to talk to the boy's parents, so it would be best to wait until the boy was in his place on the play area. "Come and we'll push you in the swings for a little while," suggested Roy. They were all for that, and put their ball down in a safe place, so they could run to the swings. Their parents hurried over so that they could push the swings as soon as they were seated.

When Sherry noticed that the family was all settled, they helped Joy and Hope slow the swings down and get off safely. They ran to get their ball and hurried over to ask the boy if he wanted to play with them. Of course he did, and they were soon having fun together.

Roy and Sherry walked over to his parents and noticed that one set of his grandparents were also there. They introduced themselves and learned all four of their names. Roy had brought some lawn chairs so they could sit almost facing the people and be able to converse better, but still be able to keep an eye on the children. It worked well, and they got better acquainted with each other. After a while of small talk they felt free to ask some questions and learned that the boy, Cory, had been born with his lower legs paralyzed, but the doctors didn't know why, and had said there was no way to help him.

At this point, Roy sensed that it was time to pray, so he asked, "Would you be willing to have us lay our hands on his legs and ask Jesus, the Great Physician, to heal your son's legs?"

The parents and grandparents looked shocked for a while and then looked hopeful. The boy's father answered, "Yes. Please do."

All six of them got up and walked over to where the children were playing. At a signal from Sherry, Joy and Hope held their ball still, and sat down to watch and listen. By this time there were a couple other families who had gathered nearby to see what was going on.

The father introduced Roy and Sherry to their son, Cory, and explained what they wanted to do. He looked very excited and agreed. Roy and Sherry hunkered down to be on his level and they both put their hands on his legs. Roy started by praying, "Jesus, since you're the creator of everything and the Great Physician, you know all about how legs are supposed to work and how to fix these two legs that are not working correctly. We ask in Jesus name that you will heal Cory's legs so that he can walk and run and play, and live a normal life." Then he spoke directly to the legs, "Legs, be totally complete, whole and strong in the name of Jesus!"

Both Roy and Sherry felt the power of God going through their arms and hands and into the legs they were touching. They knew Cory could feel it because he looked surprised and then said, "I can feel something in my lower legs! They want to move!" Sherry and Roy quickly got out of his way as he extended them out in front of him. "I want to get up and walk!" Both of his parents came to him and held out their hands to help if needed, but he stood right up and started walking! Then he ran! "I can walk and I can run!" he shouted as he came back to thank Roy and Sherry. "Thank you, thank you so much!"

But they said in unison, "Thank Jesus instead, he's the one who healed you. All we did was let him work through us when we prayed for you."

"How can I thank him? I can't see him," Cory asked.

Sherry explained, "We can't see him either, but you felt his power go into your legs while we prayed, and now you can pray to him and thank him. To pray just means to talk to him. He's here listening even though we cannot see him and he probably won't answer in a voice we can hear."

Cory prayed, ""Thank you, thank you so much, Jesus, for making my legs work!" Then he smiled. "He heard me. I know he did, because he's the one who healed me!"

Everywhere There's a Sunrise, Let's Tell The Good News!

Roy agreed, "Yes, Cory, Jesus loves you so much that he wants you to be able to walk and run. But even more than that, he wants you and all the people who were watching the miracle that just happened, to know that he loves you all so much that he came to earth, lived a perfect life so he could die on the cross in your place in order to forgive all your sins. Sins are the bad things all people do. Sins are what separate people from a holy God, and keep people from going to heaven. God raised Jesus from the grave to show that Jesus perfect sacrifice was accepted." Cory's parents asked a few questions and Larry answered them and explained the Gospel some more.

Then, Sherry continued, "If you and your family and the rest of you people would like to have your sins forgiven and to know that you will spend eternity in heaven with Jesus and God the Father, all you have to do is confess your sins, ask for forgiveness and believe in what Jesus did. How many of you would like to do that?"

They all nodded their heads, so Roy led them in a prayer very much like Pastor Don used in the church service so many times. He had them repeat after him out loud.

Cory said, "He heard all of us. I know he did, because he's here listening."

"Yes, he is and he will always be with you and your family, and the rest of these people, listening any time you pray to him," agreed Sherry.

"Now, I really would like to walk and run and play for a while. May I play with your girls?" he asked.

"Of course!" she replied. "The rest of us will go back to our seats so we can watch." His dad pushed the wheelchair over by the benches, only then realizing that they would not need it any longer. They wouldn't need the new one they were planning to buy since Cory had just about outgrown this one. They did watch in amazement as Cory walked and ran and played like a normal, healthy seven-year-old. When all three children got tired out they came and sat on the grass near their parents, and other people who were asking questions about all that had just happened. Roy and Sherry happily answered them, and then gave each couple a little booklet that would explain even more to them. Then they invited all of them to come to church the next day at 2 PM.

"If you would like to get into a small group especially for new believers, fill out the card and bring it with you. You can give it to the pastor after the service is over," suggested Roy. "Sherry and I will be standing in the entry way of the church to greet you and we can all go in and sit in the same area inside. After the service, we'll introduce you to Pastor Don."

"We can't begin to tell you how glad we are that you both came to this park and talked to us and then prayed for Cory. Now he's healed, and we all believe in Jesus! Thank you, thank you, thank you, Jesus!" exclaimed his mother. Everybody there joined in with his or her thanks and praise.

Joy and Hope were overjoyed that their new friend could walk and run and play now. Their parents were grateful that God had worked through them to do this miracle and bring many into his kingdom.

*****

The second Sunday in May

Matt was so thankful for the continued fair weather. He and Ben had been able to work Saturday afternoon and Sunday morning on the house and it was shaping up faster than he had thought possible. Ben was excited to see the progress they were making and continued to thank Matt for the privilege of working with him on his house. The outside walls were all framed. They had been raised up and were all connected together. It was beginning to look more like a house! Soon he would need to order rafters.

Matt wondered if and when it would be appropriate to show Fiona the progress that was being made. He was trying very hard to be patient and not even appear to rush her in any way, but it seemed like it got more difficult daily. So he prayed for extra help, and realized that all this was working together to build his character and growth in the Lord.

*****

Roy and Sherry got to the church early for the Sunday 2 PM service and he gave Pastor Don a note saying that they expected several new believers to attend the service today. They would have cards to give to him after the service. Then they hurried to wait in the entryway where they greeted Cory and his parents and grandparents, and the two other families who had been in the park on Saturday, who had also accepted Jesus. All of them went in and sat in the same area. Roy and Sherry showed them where the Bibles and hymnals were so they could use them during the service.

Songs included: "All People That on Earth Do Dwell," Psalm 100; "I Am Trusting Thee, Lord Jesus," Proverbs 3:5; and "He Who Began a Good Work," Philippians 1:6.

Pastor Don began, "Our teaching time today should be encouraging and uplifting to all of us, especially to the newest of our new believers who haven't had a chance to be in a small group yet. We're so glad to welcome you into the family of God and to our church.

"Please open your Bibles to Psalm 100 and notice that the first song we sang is totally based on this Psalm. Follow along with me as I read it and make comments on it. *Make a joyful noise unto the LORD, all you lands. Serve the LORD with gladness. Come before his presence with singing.* That is what we've just finished doing. Since we're believers, we have joy, and gladly want to serve the Lord. Singing is one way to serve him. Verse 3 says, *Know that the LORD is God. It is he who made us and not we ourselves.* That means he's our creator. It seems ludicrous to think that we could have made ourselves! Every part and intricate system of our bodies could only have been made by a creator who has all the wisdom and knowledge of how to make it all work and keep it working. Verse 3 goes on to say, *We are his people and the sheep of his pasture.* Being sheep does not seem very appealing to us, but we need God's care as much or more than sheep need the care of a shepherd. Verse 4 says, *Enter into his gates with thanksgiving, and into his courts with praise. Be thankful to him and bless* or praise *his name.* Gates and courts here refer to the Old Testament temple, but we can enter our church or any place we happen to be, praising the LORD and being thankful to him. Verse 5 gives the reason: *For the LORD is good. His mercy is everlasting, and his truth endures to all generations.*

"The second song we sang was about trusting Jesus our Lord, and <u>only</u> him for his great free salvation, for guidance that he alone should give, and power to live and speak his words during all of our lives here on earth. It's a very good song for all of us to remember. It would make an excellent morning prayer on days when there's something we need extra help doing.

"Now I'm going to read some verses from the Psalms and Proverbs that speak of trusting the LORD. You might like to just write down the chapter and verse so you can look them up later. Psalm 13:5 says, *I have trusted in your mercy. My heart shall rejoice in your salvation.* Psalm 62:8 says, *Trust in God at all times, you people. Pour out your heart to him. God is a refuge for us.* Psalm 84:12 says, *O LORD of hosts, blessed is the man who trusts in you.* Proverbs 3:5,6 says, *Trust in the LORD with all your heart, and do not lean to your own understanding. In all your ways acknowledge him and he shall direct your paths.* And Proverbs 16:20b says, *Whoever trusts in the LORD is happy.* All of those verses give us good reasons to trust in the LORD.

"Our third song is based on Philippians 1:6, which says, *We are confident of this: he who began a good work in you will perform* or complete *it until the day of Jesus Christ.* Find Colossians 1:9-12, which tells us some things about this good work. *For this cause we ... do not stop praying for you, desiring that you be filled with the knowledge of his will in all wisdom and spiritual understanding, that you might walk worthy of the Lord, being pleasing and fruitful in every good work, and increasing in the knowledge of God, strengthened with all might, according to his glorious power, unto all patience and long suffering with joyfulness, giving thanks to the Father who has made us able to be partakers of the inheritance of the saints in light.* That's a long list. We need to remember that it is God who helps us do these things.

"In the same chapter, verses 13-20 tell us more about who Jesus is. *The Father has delivered us from the power of darkness and has brought us into the kingdom of his dear Son, in whom we have redemption through his blood, the forgiveness of sins. His Son, Jesus, is the image of the invisible God, the firstborn of every creature. For by him were all things created, that are in heaven and that are in earth, visible and invisible, whether they be thrones, dominions, principalities, or powers. All things were created by him and for him, and he is before all things and by him all things consist,* or hold together. *He is the head of the body, the church. He is the beginning, the first born from the dead, so that in all things he would have the preeminence. For it pleased the Father that in Jesus all his fullness would dwell, and having made peace through the blood of his cross, by him to reconcile all things unto himself, whether they be things in earth or things in heaven.*

"This Jesus is the one we trust in for our salvation and for guidance and power to live the lives he wants for us! He is the mighty creator, our redeemer who paid for our salvation with his blood by dying for us on the cross. God raised him from the dead, and we celebrate this at Easter time. He is in heaven interceding or praying for us. He is the head of the church and the one we trust. Let's sing that second song about trusting Jesus again in closing. I know there some very new believers here who have cards they would like to give me, so when we finish that song, please come up here to the front to give them to me."

At the end of the service, Roy and Sherry went with the new people to introduce them to Pastor Don. Cory's father told him everything that had happened Saturday afternoon, with the rest of the people nodding and adding a tidbit or two here and there. Pastor Don was thrilled, and welcomed them into the family of God and to the church. Cory raised his hand like he would in school and when Don called on him, he said, "The Jesus you were reading about in the Bible and told us about is the same Jesus who healed my legs so I can walk and run and play and live a normal life. I know he's the same one, because the man who prayed for me said he created everything and knew how to make my legs work. After Jesus healed me, my family and I each asked him to be our Savior too. I'm so thankful for Jesus!"

Pastor Don smiled and agreed, "You're completely right about all of what you said. Would you do me a favor and tell all the people who are still here what you just told me? I know it would help them to be thankful to Jesus also."

Cory nodded, so Don grabbed the microphone and got the attention of the people so they could listen to Cory's testimony. He handed it to Cory and with amazing self-assurance he repeated what he had just told the pastor. The people broke into spontaneous applause and thanks to Jesus, with Cory and all the rest of the people up front joining in. All the couples that had come with Cory gave Don their cards, and he told them he would be calling them soon about when and where the new believers small group would be meeting.

When they were finished talking to the pastor the people who had accepted Jesus at the baptismal service came to give him their cards and he happily told them the same things.

*****

Tony was waiting at the park when Ted, Julie, Maria, Esther and Beth arrived, and again he felt surprised by all the beautiful women together in one place. The ladies took off on their walk, with Ted and Tony following about ten steps behind continuing their Spanish lesson.

Ruth asked, "What do you think we should say to Tony, Esther?"

"I have no idea. I felt tongue tied, just seeing him again. He's very handsome," answered Esther.

"I thought he looked a little awestruck when he was looking at all of us ladies," stated Maria.

"Maybe he was feeling outnumbered and really wanted to bolt," added Julie.

"You three are no help at all, but at least I feel like laughing now," Esther said. "I can't very well just tell him I'm interested in him, and want to get to know him better. He needs to spend time with just me if he's going to learn enough about me to decide if he would like to see me again. How do we let him know that Ruth and Maria are not interested?"

Finally, Julie understood what Esther was getting at, even though she had not been in on that conversation when those three were at work. She suggested, "Here is an idea," and she went on to tell them.

"Okay," said Esther, dragging the word out. "I'll feel embarrassed, but here I go." She dropped out of formation and the other three kept walking. She walked toward Ted and Tony. When she reached them, she walked beside Ted and said loudly enough for Tony to hear also, "Ted, Julie sent me back here to have you catch up with her and explain something to Ruth and Maria as they all keep walking. Then, Ruth can tell me about it later and you, Tony, will still have someone to walk with."

"I'll be glad to," replied Ted, and he took off running to reach the other ladies.

"How's the Spanish lesson going for Ted?" asked Esther, hoping she would be able to think clearly enough to keep the conversation going on interesting topics.

Tony replied, "It's going very well. Ted has a very good memory and is learning vocabulary quickly."

"I can't imagine trying to learn a new language now. When we were growing up, it was easy to learn both Spanish and English, because we were around them both all the time. It just came naturally,"

"That must have been a great help to you. I grew up knowing only Spanish and I didn't learn English as my second language until I attended public school. I still have an accent and I'm not as fluent in English. On the other hand, you are very fluent in both languages," Tony complimented her.

"Thank you, Tony. If you would like to, we can continue our conversation in Spanish," Esther suggested.

Everywhere There's a Sunrise, Let's Tell The Good News!

"Thank you, I would like that. I don't have many chances to communicate in my native language," he answered. The rest of their time walking together was spent conversing about many interesting topics in Spanish. By the time they returned to the starting point of the walk where the others were waiting, they were wishing the walk wasn't over, but Tony <u>had</u> gotten Esther's phone number.

*****

Jeff and Karen went with Tomo and Ami to a residential area near the middle of Pine City, for their first four by four ministry time. The ladies walked together about half a block ahead of the men and as they walked, they prayed for the families living in each house, and kept their eyes open for anyone who might want to visit or might need help with a project in the yard. It was a pleasant afternoon to be outside, but it appeared that most of them were either not home, or were inside watching sports on TV.

Well, at least they had a chance to pray for many people and had a good walk in the process. They would have to keep track of the sports schedule, if they were going to see any people outside.

*****

Matt and Fiona went to pick Walt and Betty up in Matt's crew cab pick-up, which he had been keeping clean and vacuumed out since Fiona had returned to Pine City. They spent over an hour visiting as they walked and viewed the flowers in the city's botanical garden. The flowers were beautiful, and the labels helped when names could not be remembered. Later, they went to eat supper at the Healthy Eating Restaurant. It was a good thing Matt had gotten reservations for them since there were many people waiting to be seated. It appeared that there were many who were curious about this new restaurant.

"Anderson, party of four," the seating hostess called out, and they followed her to a comfortable booth. They were given menus to look at while a waitress got water for them.

Betty mentioned, "I might get some new ideas for our <u>own</u> meals. Some of these entrees sound delicious."

"Your own cooking is so good, that I'm concerned that this place might not measure up, but at least this is one night that you don't have to cook," Matt replied.

"Thank you, Matt. I'm glad that you like what I cook, and that Walt does also," she responded. "Let's each try something different so I can get a look at four different entrees."

"Good idea, Dear! Then we can each give you an evaluation of the one we tried," agreed Walt.

Fiona had hers picked out by this time, and the others were ready when the waitress came with their water. They gave their choices, and then Fiona asked, "Betty, what are some things you like about being a homemaker?"

"I like being the wife of a loving, caring husband, and living in the comfortable, practical, well built home my dear husband built for us. He custom built many things just the way I asked him to, especially the kitchen cupboards, counters, and sink, with plenty of counter space for cooking and baking. It makes it so much easier to prepare meals. I also like being able to sew in a separate room just for sewing, where I don't have to put everything away at the end of every day. I can just close the door and get back to it when I have time. Plus, I like our yard, which is just the right size for a small vegetable garden and flowers scattered around the edges of the yard. I enjoy being outside in the cool morning hours to care for the plants or harvest whatever is ripe," Betty explained.

"It sounds delightful," Fiona responded. "As you already know, I work with plants all week at The Garden Shop. My family has had a vegetable garden every year for as long as I can remember. I get great pleasure from observing and nurturing plants. Your kitchen and sewing room sound ideal. I would like to see them sometime."

"How about tonight after supper?" asked Betty.

"That would be great. Will that work out for you, Matt?" inquired Fiona.

He nodded emphatically, just as their entrees arrived, and he gave thanks for the food. They all exclaimed over how delicious the food looked and tasted. "This is almost as good as yours, Betty," he complimented.

"Thank you, Matt. But eating here with all of you is even better, because I didn't have to cook this, and because of the pleasant conversation we're having," she responded.

Walt continued, "I'm enjoying my entree a lot because I get to see my dear wife relaxing for a change. She is a very busy and exceptional homemaker!"

Fiona smiled at them both, enjoying the way they showed each other <u>how much</u> they were loved and appreciated. She thought about that, and prayed that if she and Matt ever married they would have the same enduring love all through their life together. A feeling of excitement floated through her, and she had to look down at her partly eaten meal to hide her feelings or else the others would read it all over her face.

Without her knowing it, Matt had been watching her as the emotions played across her face and he wondered what she was thinking about. Well, time would tell. It wasn't his place to ask her, and this wasn't the time even if it were. He might just have to wait until she was ready to tell him. But he had a feeling that he could reveal his heart to her in the near future, and it would not be as scary for her.

Both young people realized at the same time that it had grown very silent, and Matt decided to get the conversation rolling again. So he asked, "What did you like about the church service today, Walt?"

Walt answered, "The singing! The songs are so meaningful and all of them went very well with the teaching time. Besides, I like listening to you and Fiona sing. You make a pretty duet."

Fiona <u>did</u> blush at that statement, but responded, "Thank you, Walt. I enjoy singing beside Matt. His tenor and my alto do blend nicely together, I'll have to agree." Walt looked at Betty and she nodded, sharing some unspoken communication. Matt smiled thinking that he knew just what they were communicating.

The way Fiona looked quickly back down at her plate, he knew she must have seen all three of them, so he tried to rescue her by saying, "I think this has been one of the most beautiful springs we've ever had in Pine City. What do you think, Betty?"

"Oh, I agree!" she responded. "And it was made even more beautiful when Walt and I let the great Creator, Jesus, bring the springtime into our hearts. Matt, I'm so grateful that you didn't give up on us, but continued to talk to us and answer our questions and pray and wait patiently for us to come to Jesus."

"Jesus does this for each of us, and I'm glad he helped me to be like him," Matt replied, humbly.

Fiona added, "I was so thrilled when I heard about your miracle of healing and believing in Jesus. What did you both like about the baptismal service?"

Walt answered, "Again, the songs were very meaningful and beautiful, and I got to testify to the whole crowd how Jesus had healed and saved me."

Betty continued, "I was overjoyed when I saw all those people go up at the end of the service to tell Pastor Don they had prayed that prayer and asked Jesus to be their Savior. What a joy to know those people will be in heaven too!"

"Yes, I was glad when I heard that he included the gospel and that prayer when all the baptisms were finished," responded Fiona.

They finished the rest of the meal and a light dessert in companionable dialog, and Christian fellowship. After that, they all went over to the Evans' home so Fiona could admire their house and yard.

Afterward, on the way to Fiona's house, Matt asked, "What do you think of Walt and Betty?"

"They're just as nice as you said they were and our visit was very interesting," she answered.

"I could tell that they like you too," said Matt. "They were very relaxed, open, and shared easily."

"I like the way they showed each other how much they love and appreciate each other," she mentioned.

Matt responded, "I do too. They do that often, and I think it's part of what makes their marriage so special. I want to remember to do that myself."

"Same here! Oh, are we at my house already? That was quick," she said.

"It sure was! When would your dad like to have help working on the back porch?" he inquired.

"Come on in and you can ask him, if they're home, that is," she responded. They were home and it was decided that he could come for a couple hours before supper to work on Saturday, and then eat supper with them. And before that, they would have another practice session on the Frisbee course on Wednesday morning, weather permitting. If it turned rainy and cold again, they would go to another museum.

*****

Chapter 18

Acts 4: 10,12 (summary) *Be it known to you all, ... that by the name of Jesus ... this man stands here whole.*
Neither is there salvation in any other, for there is no other name ... whereby we must be saved.

Everywhere There's a Sunrise, Let's Tell The Good News!

Proverbs 18:22 *Whoever finds a wife finds a good thing, and obtains favor of the LORD.*

Monday

When they arrived at the school on Monday morning, Cory's parents asked to see the principal, and then explained to her what had happened. They asked if they could go into his classroom with him on his first morning at school after his healing miracle. The principal agreed and said that she would come also. They were all a little nervous about how the teacher and children would respond.

As expected, all of them were completely shocked when they saw Cory <u>walk</u> in with his parents, and none of them could think of a thing to say. Cory had asked his parents if he could be the one to explain, so he raised his hand and the teacher gathered enough of her wits to call on him. "I would like to tell all of you what happened to me on Saturday afternoon at the park where I usually go to play." He told them every detail, including that it was Jesus who healed him, because the people prayed for him in Jesus name. Then he told them why Jesus had healed him. He included all the facts Larry and Sherry had told them about the Good News of Jesus, including his dying for them so they could be forgiven and know they would go to heaven. He finished by saying, "I know prayer is not allowed in public school, but if any of you listening would like to ask Jesus to forgive you and be <u>your</u> Savior, I would be glad to meet you by the big shade tree on the playground at recess and help you to pray."

The principal and teacher both thanked Cory for sharing what had happened, and said his offer to meet at the big shade tree was a good idea. They also told him and his parents how glad they were for Cory that he could walk and run and play now. The children all joined in with their claps and cheers. That seemed to break the ice. Cory walked over to the place where his handicap desk was and raised his hand again. When his teacher called on him, he asked, "May I have a regular desk now?"

She answered, "Of course! There's an empty one right in the middle of the second row. You may choose someone to help you move your belongings and school books to that desk right now." That only took a couple minutes and Cory was glad to be able to stand for the flag pledge and to sing the "Star Spangled Banner." Then, during the regular morning class time, he was able to stand or sit as necessary, and walk to the reading table, etc, just like the rest of the students.

At recess time, Cory <u>ran</u> over to the big shade tree, and many from his class ran with him. They were still amazed. Even his teacher came, but she walked of course. The principal had asked her to keep an eye on him at recess. Knowing the shortness of recess time, Cory got right to the point, explaining what each person needed to do, and then he led them to pray out loud by repeating what he would say. He did it just like Larry had done in the park that day. His memory was very good, and since the teacher was there, nobody heckled him. His teacher prayed right along with the rest.

At the end, Cory said, "Now all of you that prayed that prayer with me are members of God's family and are on your way to heaven. I have a lot to learn about what that all means, so I'll be going to church and a small group that will explain it all. Tomorrow I can bring some little booklets and cards like the pastor of the church gave my family. Then you can read the little books and talk to your parents. Tell them about what happened to me and ask them if they would like to have this wonderful Jesus be their Savior too. The booklet has a prayer like we prayed in it so they can pray it too. Then you can all decide if you want to come to church and a small group also."

At that point the bell rang and they all ran to line up, except for a few girls who walked back with the teacher.

*****

Early Monday morning found Maria in Esther's office. "I expect a full report on your time with Tony while we have lunch today!" she exclaimed. "I suppose you already told Ruth."

Smiling, Esther replied, "Yes to both statements. And Ruth even told me everything Ted explained to you and her. It was interesting. See you at lunch!"

Maria nodded, waved, and hurried back to her own office, well satisfied, and looking forward to hearing what Esther would have to say. Maria was glad that she was an accountant because she enjoyed the work and the time passed quickly while she was busy. Soon she, Ruth and Esther were walking to and around in the park.

Esther started by saying, "At first I thought Julie was crazy, but it worked so well that now I think she's a genius!"

The other two started laughing so hard that it took several minutes before Esther could continue, "Hush you two! Or else we'll run out of time before I get to tell you. Okay, now that's better. Tony and I started conversing in English but soon changed to Spanish because he's much more fluent in his native language. We discussed many topics and I learned a lot about his family, childhood, growing up years and how he became a believer. Of course I told him the same things about myself. Somewhere in there I mentioned that Ruth has decided to stay single, and since he didn't ask about you, Maria, I said nothing. I decided he does not need to know about that. When he asked me if he could call and spend some more time with me, I gave him one of my cards, with my cell phone number and work number. I don't think he will call me at work though. He is much too polite to do that."

Maria exclaimed, "Sounds like you and he made some very good progress in what was left of the walking time! I'm very glad for you, Esther. Will you keep us informed as the time goes on?

"Thank you, Maria. Yes, I will, if he ever actually does call me. Sometimes these things just fizzle out you know," lamented Esther.

Ruth said, "Let's pray for the Lord's will to be done. Remember, we don't really want anything else!"

"You're right big sister. Thank you for reminding me," she said humbly.

Maria jumped in with, "Ted's explanation about how the music is prepared for the church services and small groups was very interesting. I never knew about it before, and I intend to buy several of those SD cards so I can have those meaningful songs in my apartment. Some of the music on the radio is just not worth listening to these days."

"Oh, I agree!" Ruth chimed in. "Esther and I are going over there during our lunch break tomorrow instead of out to lunch with coworkers. Would you like to join us?"

"Yes!" Maria answered. "Two of us can eat while the other person drives and another can drive back while the first driver eats. I can hardly wait to enjoy some of that music at home!"

*****

Just before supper there was a phone call at the Ross home from Cory's mother explaining what had happened at the recesses at his school. "Where can I get some more of those little booklets and cards so that Cory can give them to those who would like them? He didn't think to count how many, but his class alone has 30 students plus his teacher. At lunch and last recess there were some children from the class he was in last year."

Anita had answered the phone and said, "Wonderful, now if you can get over to our house within the next hour and a half, we'll have the booklets and cards ready to send with you. I'll make sure there are about 50, and you can keep any extras to use later on, as you need them." Then she gave the address of their home.

Right after supper, Pastor Don and Anita were again planning for the other new believers groups. They looked at each of the cards they had received Sunday and made piles for two new groups, trying to get an assortment of ages in each group. They would be sure to keep Cory together with his parents and grandparents.

While they were working on this, Cory and his parents rang the doorbell. Don and Anita invited them inside, and listened to their excitement, joining in with their own. Don suggested, "If these people desire to be in a small group, have the parents call us by Wednesday, and we'll try to get groups organized by Friday. It would probably be best to hand these booklets out during the last recess of the day tomorrow on the playground."

"I'll be sure to do that, Pastor Don. Thank you," replied Cory. He acted so polite and grown up for a seven-year-old.

After they had left, Don made phone calls to find co-facilitators for each of the other groups. One group would meet on Wednesday evening and the other on Thursday evening. They planned to meet this week, since it was important to get these people started learning about the Christian life right away. The first meetings would be at their home again. So they called all the people who had returned their cards and invited them to their home this Wednesday or Thursday.

When that was completed, they hurried to get ready and go to their own pastors' small group meeting, where they would praise God for all the new believers. During announcement and question time Don could ask when the next special baptismal service would be held so they could make plans for it. Praise time contained many praises and thanks for the new believers who were baptized, and their testimonies, plus for all the new believers who resulted from people inviting unbelievers to the service where they heard the testimonies and the gospel.

There were so many of them that Don didn't have to ask <u>when!</u> It was part of the announcements! The next special baptismal service would be in three weeks, giving time for two meetings each for the new small groups to be ready. Thanks were also given for the new believer who had had the idea of inviting unbelievers to come. Don joined right in with his own silent thanks for Walt's idea and his desire to have others come to Jesus for salvation.

*****

Tuesday

When Sherry arrived at the Ross home with the twins, she was again asked to clean bathrooms and to dust the living room and dining room, and clean the kitchen. Anita explained, "I'm hoping it will stay clean enough for the Wednesday meeting. Then on Thursday, you'll only have to do a little touch up work for the meeting on Thursday."

Sherry responded, "I'll be glad to. In fact it's rather fun to clean your house for a change. Besides, Roy is taking care of our bathrooms at home for me so I can work here. So in that way he is also serving here. This is working well for both of us, and neither of us is getting too tired. We're both very thankful."

"I'm grateful for your help here also. Roy's a good husband. I'm glad you have that blessing. I hear Mary calling me so I'll go see what she wants."

"Mommy, <u>may</u> we play outside?" she asked emphasizing that word "may."

"I'm glad you remembered to use the word 'may' when you asked. Yes you <u>may</u>, and so <u>may</u> all the others." Anita answered.

The others cheered, and Joy exclaimed, "Oh, goody! I like your back yard. It's even more fun than ours."

"Let's go out and see if it's warm enough out there that we don't need our coats," suggested Anita. It was, so Anita organized a group game that they played for a while and then everyone could have fun in other ways of their choice.

Those who were four years old grouped off by themselves this time and those who were three, played nicely together also. Pretty soon the younger ones wanted to be pushed in the swings, so the older ones did it and were even careful. When it was time, she took them inside for a little snack and a Bible story and singing, before their naps.

Anita was thankful for this occupation that allowed her to be with her own children and also care for others whose parents both needed to work outside the home. She was also grateful that she could have all three, and four-year-old children in her group. Then, when both children were in the church school she could volunteer there several days a week and that would keep the tuition down to something they could afford. The money she was earning during these years at home was being put into savings and would help to pay the rest of the tuition. She was also glad that the pastors' families weren't given preferential treatment and big salaries, but instead were like the others in their congregation. It helped keep them closer to their "sheep." They could understand their lifestyles and trials better and be able to relate to them in a more helpful way. "Just like Jesus did when he came to earth the first time," she thought.

That evening when Don got home from work, Mindy told him, "The girls Candy and I have been witnessing to, accepted Jesus as their Savior. We gave them booklets and cards, and if their parents agree they want to join one of the groups for new believers. They might call tonight. I already told Anita."

"That's fantastic news! Praise the Lord!" exclaimed Don. "You girls are doing good work for the Lord. Keep up your excellent efforts!"

"We plan to. Please keep praying for us," she requested.

"Certainly, and you pray for all the rest of us believers as we tell the Good News to others too," he answered.

*****

Mindy was very observant as she accompanied her dad to their small group that Tuesday evening. She also prayed silently that God would get Miss Nelson and her dad together soon if it would be his will.

During refreshment time at their small group, Miss Nelson came over to talk to Mindy and Vern. "How are both of you doing?" she asked.

"We're fine," Vern answered.

Mindy replied, "I was just thinking about you the other day. I'm very thankful for all the help you gave me when I was in third grade, Miss Nelson."

"You're welcome," she responded. "It was my pleasure, and I'm glad to know that it helped you."

Vern added, "Yes, it really did help her, so I thank you also. How have you been?"

She answered, "I'm fine too. The weather has been so enjoyable this spring. Mindy, I would like to have you call me by my first name, Lora, from now on, since we're not at school, and besides we have been in the same small group since January."

Mindy replied, "Okay, thank you. I would like that also, Lora. Do you like to walk in the park or go on hikes? The weather has gotten warm enough to do those kinds of things again."

Lora responded, "Yes I really enjoy doing things outside when the weather is nice. What do you think, Vern?"

He hesitated a moment feeling awkward, but knowing that Mindy would enjoy doing those things, he answered, "I think we could plan to do some of those things as a threesome." He was thinking he would need to accompany them to be sure they stayed safe.

Mindy was delighted. Maybe this would start to wake him up.

*****

On Tuesday evening the Blakes and Kelseys met at the shopping mall for their first four by four ministry time. Both couples had prayed before they went into the mall. The Blakes followed them at a short distance and observed what they said and did. The Kelseys appeared to be conversing together, but were really praying quietly out loud for the people they saw as they were walking. After a while, they approached a young man who was sitting alone and looked depressed. The Blakes walked around to the side, where the man could not see them, but close enough that they could see and hear what happened. Larry began with small talk, and Jane listened and prayed silently.

Pretty soon they sat down on the bench with the young man and listened as he poured out his story. He had just lost his job, and his wife had gone home to her parents, taking their two small children with her. "I feel like such a failure, as a man, and as a husband and father. Can't seem to keep a job long enough to provide for my family. For a while it seemed like drinking and drugs helped me feel better, but now I'm hooked, and don't have the money to buy any more."

Larry commented, "That last statement is probably the best thing that has happened to you."

The man looked astounded and almost angry when he asked, "Why? How could that be a good thing?"

Larry stated, "Because <u>now</u> you'll have to look for some other place to help you feel better."

"Where?" he asked cynically. "It looks to me like I've lost everything and have no place to go but further down!"

Jane asked, "Do you really desire to get off the drugs and alcohol, and become the man your family needs?"

He looked at her as if she had asked something really stupid. Then he replied, "Of course I do. I certainly don't want to go on like this."

"Good!" she responded. "I asked that question because we've talked to some people in a situation similar to yours who just wanted pity and a handout, but weren't willing to do the work to make positive change happen."

"So, what do you suggest?" he asked looking to Larry for the answer.

Larry replied, "There's only one person who can really help you, and he wants to help you, but you have to do your part."

The man looked interested and asked, "Who is it and what is my part?"

"It is the Lord Jesus Christ, who came to this world almost 2000 years ago to seek and to save people just like you, and worse." Then Larry told him a summary of the Gospel and added, "He is the only one who can get you out of the mess you are in, and make you into the man, husband, and father your family needs. Your part is to believe in him, confess all your sins to him, and ask him to forgive you, and then ask him to be your Savior and make you into the man he wants you to be. Are you willing to do that?" asked Larry.

"Yes, I'll do whatever it takes. Do you really think it will work?" he asked.

Larry said, "Yes! But it won't be easy. You've come down a long way and it's always harder to go uphill than down, but Jesus will help you if you'll believe in him and ask him to. Would you like me to help you pray?"

"Yes, please," he answered. So Larry led him in a prayer much like Don used at church, but made sure the man prayed out loud and listed all of his sins before asking for forgiveness. When he was finished, he looked up with a smile and said, "I've never felt such wonderful peace. Thank you, Jesus! Now, what do I need to do next?"

Larry explained, "Since you don't have a job, or a place to live right now, our church has a special fund that will pay for your room and board and rehabilitation in a program that will help you stay off the drugs and alcohol and teach you the skills you need to have in order to get and keep a good job. But you have to be willing to follow their rules, and do whatever chores they need to have you do to help keep the place cleaned up and functional. How does this sound to you?"

"Unbelievable! Why would any church want to do that for a failure like me?" he questioned.

Jane answered, "They want to do it for Jesus, because of all the ways he's helped them, and because they love him and want to serve him by helping people like you. Are you willing to go there, follow their rules, do chores, and work hard to do whatever Jesus asks you to do?"

Silence. The four by four group waited and prayed that he would agree.

"Yes! Since Jesus loved me and saved me like you two told me, then I'll work as hard as I can, knowing that Jesus will make me into the man he wants me to be," the man said.

"We're very glad," Larry responded and then asked, "Do you have any belongings to pack and/or any person to tell where you're going?"

"No, she took all our stuff to her parents when we were put out of the apartment, and she does not want to ever see me again, because this has happened too many times. I can't say that I blame her," he finished.

"Okay then, if you'll come with us, we'll take you to the place I told you about," said Larry.

He got up meekly and followed Larry with Jane behind them. She turned and waved to Ted and Julie with a smile of victory. Another branch grafted into the good olive tree as it says in Romans 11:24!

*****

Wednesday

While the children played inside on rainy days, Anita was usually able to sit on the sofa and do a little mending, but not today. As soon as she sat down, the phone rang. She was glad she had taken it with her. "Hello, Ross residence. ... ... How wonderful! How many people will that be, and what are their ages? ... ... Please tell me the names again. ... ... What is the best phone number for us to call you back? ... ... Good, thank you. I got that all written down and we'll call you as soon as we can with the time and place for the group to meet. Good-bye until then."

Anita lost count of how many times that happened during her busy day, but she got all the information written down on a stack of cards so they could plan for another group or two. She wondered how they should conduct these groups with parents and young children. They probably needed to be kept together, like they had decided for Cory and his parents and the other two families who had one child each, and had been at the park that day. Something like this had never happened before. What an interesting situation. She would ask Don what he thought about it when he got home from work.

Between phone calls, she sang with the children, read them a Bible story, played group games with them, had them take their naps, fed them lunch, and all the other things this job entailed. She was understandably tired by the time all but her two had gone home. Don had taken over answering the phone as soon as he got home, and they took turns while they were eating the supper Don had fixed.

"How do you think we should handle the groups with parents and young children?" she asked Don.

"They're too young to have separate groups, so we'll need to keep them together," he answered.

Anita replied, "I thought the same thing. We will probably continue getting phone calls during the small group meeting tonight. I'll keep the phone with me and turn it on 'vibrate' so it does not interrupt the meeting. I'll just get up and go into your office to answer it and write down all the information."

"Good idea, Honey. Thank you for your help with all of this, especially while you're caring for little ones during the day. I don't know how you do it!" he exclaimed.

"God is my helper and I'm going to have Sherry bake lots of cookies when she comes tomorrow, for the meetings Thursday, Friday, and probably Saturday, since most of these cards equal three or more people each," Anita explained.

Don and Anita followed the same routine as they had a few weeks ago for this Wednesday evening's newest, new believers group. Everything went very well, and at the end, he had a booklet ready to give them about the what, why, when, where, and how of water baptism, so that it would not be so much overwhelming information to give them all at once in the meeting with the other group at the church. It even included the floor plan of the baptismal area, dressing rooms, etc. Two weeks ago, he had talked to the Grace 'n' Faith church's main leader and suggested that a booklet would be helpful for the new believers. Low and behold, at the end of Monday's small group meeting for pastors, the leader had handed out as many copies as each pastor would need for their new small groups. They would need to get some more now, for what they had started calling the "school groups."

Don and Anita had scheduled this meeting and tomorrow's meeting for 8 to 9:30 PM, so that their children could already be in bed, and not have an hour on their own. It worked very well, since there wasn't as much to cover in this first meeting. For the combined meeting at the church on Wednesday next week, Mindy had agreed to come and play with Timmy and Mary for an hour before putting them to bed, and then do her homework, so the 7 - 9 PM time would be just fine, since that meeting might take longer.

When they looked at the list for the Thursday meeting, they noticed that there would be room for two more families with children in that group. It was the same group that Cory was in, so it would work very well. Therefore they called two of the school children's families at random and invited them to the small group at their home the next evening at 8 PM.

*****

It was raining, so Matt and Fiona went to the museum this Wednesday, instead of to the Frisbee course. Each was actually relieved, because of wanting some quiet uninterrupted time together, but in a nice atmosphere like this art museum would provide. So they prayed for Pam's requests and thanked God for Julie's praises, before they went inside. For a time, they looked at, and discussed some of the art work, and then they sat down on a comfortable bench facing a large painting of a quiet stream running through a meadow at the edge of a forest just as the sun was rising and painting the clouds with every shade of salmon and pink the artist could add. In fact, it looked very realistic.

Fiona sighed and relaxed. Then she smiled at Matt and said, "I really like this painting. It almost feels like we're right there enjoying the real thing."

Matt replied, "I agree. It helps me to relax. We've been so busy lately. It is nice to be here and just take pleasure in being together." They sat in silence for a few minutes doing just that. Then he continued, "I want you to know that God has first place in my life, and he is the head of my life. I desire to do his will in all things."

"I'm glad to hear that, because I feel the same way," responded Fiona.

Matt continued, "I've been praying about you and me, and I feel that it's God's will that we are together. Fiona, I enjoy being with you _so much_, and my feelings have grown much deeper for you since I've been courting you again. When we're apart now, I miss your smile and the fun, intelligent things you do and say. I count the hours until I can see you again. I would like to tell you my feelings about you right now, and hope it's not too soon." At this point, Matt got down on one knee in front of her and declared, "I love you, Fiona, and I desire very much to spend the rest of my life with you, showing you how much I love you. Will you marry me, dear Fiona?"

"O, yes, Matt. I would be honored and overjoyed to marry you!" she exclaimed.

He got to his feet and helped her get up so he could give her a gentle but adoring hug. Kissing would have to wait until later, as they had agreed some time ago. They sat back down and Matt pulled a little blue velvet covered box out of his pocket. "Do I need to wait to give this to you until after I ask your father for your hand?"

"I'm afraid so, because he is still very old fashioned, but I would _love_ to look at it." So he opened the box and showed her the beautiful, delicate diamond ring. "Oh Matthew, it's splendid. I've never seen one that is so delicate and yet so impressive. Thank you so much!" Fiona said with much emotion.

"And I thank you, my dear Fiona, for consenting to be my wife. You have made me one _very_ happy and blessed man. Now I can continue building OUR house with the joy of knowing that we'll be in it together for the rest of our lives. I desire to custom build it just for you, Dear, making it a home that you can be as happy in as Betty is in the house Walt built for her. So, sometime soon I would like to show you the progress that has been made lately, and get your thoughts about how you want things to be. I'm glad you got to see Walt and Betty's house. Maybe that will give you some ideas, and we can go look at show homes and books and magazines, and make this into your dream home," he responded.

"Thank you, dear Matt," replied Fiona knowing she needed to be very careful of his feelings on this issue. "I know how important this house is to you, and I very much appreciate that you desire to make it be everything I would want it to be. I hope you'll find out that I'm very easy to please, and I'll enjoy whatever is practical and works. But first and foremost, I desire for you to know that wherever we would live, it is YOU I love, and not what you can do for me or give me, although I do understand those are ways to show love. I don't like the idea of a lot of money being spent on me. I'm glad that we agreed a couple weeks ago that we would live simply and give our tithe plus another ten percent to help win souls to Jesus. It will be fun to plan things together as you build, though. I've been wishing recently, that I could see how it's progressing."

"Is it any wonder that I love you so much, Fiona? You said all that so well, that I can have no doubts about your precious love for me, and not for things. I desire to give you that same kind of love, my dear. When can I ask your father for your hand?"

"Could you come to breakfast tomorrow morning at 6:30 AM, since he has to be to work at 8 AM? If you ask him right when you get there, we can all enjoy talking about it all through breakfast," she suggested.

"Then you're not worried that he will say 'no'?" he asked seriously.

"No way. No worries, Mate, as the Aussies would say. My parents both like you a lot. They'll both be thrilled to have you as their son-in-love!" Fiona exclaimed. "I'm so excited that I feel like I could fly! You are my dream come true. Since I returned to Pine City I've been able to get to know you so much better, and I've been very favorably impressed by each new thing I've learned about you." She happened to glance at her watch just then, and gasped. "We had better hurry or we'll both have to go to work without lunch." That brought them both back down to earth and they did HURRY. Both of them got to eat before going to work, but they wondered how much work they would really get done!

*****

Maria had kept a list of the names of the co-workers she and Ruth had gone to lunch with as she was being introduced. She had even written down some of their interests as soon as she had returned to her office each day. So on Tuesday before going home, she made arrangements with two on the list who had similar interests figuring that might help get conversation started. She had checked the weather forecast that morning so she suggested they go to a cafe in her car, since it might rain the next day.

When it was lunchtime on Wednesday, she and those two ran in the rain out to her car and she drove them to a cafe, which was a favorite for Maria. She got them started conversing about one of their interests, and after a little while managed to introduce the topic of dying, which is something most people dread. After they had each made it clear that they definitely did dread it, Maria stated, "This may surprise you both, but one thing I can look forward to is dying."

One of them exclaimed, "You've got to be kidding! I've never heard anything so weird."

The other one asked, "How could you possibly look forward to dying? Even survival instincts go against that."

Maria laughed and said, "I don't have a death wish, but because of the way I believe, I know that when I die, it won't be the end for me. In fact it will be the beginning of a glorious new life for eternity in heaven. And heaven is better by far than anything can be here on earth. I got this idea from one of the authors in the Bible."

Both of them were still looking skeptical at this point, but Maria decided to continue anyway. So she explained, "His name was Paul, and he was in prison in Rome. He wrote to some people in a city called Philippi. He very much wanted to get out of prison and go back and visit them and help them learn more about Jesus, but he also knew there was a real possibility that he might be executed instead. He wrote to them that he was in a dilemma of desires, because for him to die would be gain, since he would be with Jesus, but he also desired to get out of prison and be able to return to their city and teach them more about how to live for Jesus. If you would like to read about it, it's in the first chapter of Philippians in the New Testament. In fact, since we're running out of time today, we can continue this discussion tomorrow during our lunch in the park after you read about it tonight."

"Okay, I'm game. I'll have to admit you have sparked my interest," one of them said, and the other one nodded.

*****

Thursday

Matt rose early, showered, shaved and dressed carefully so he would be ready to ask Fiona's father, Patrick, for his daughter's hand in marriage. He had butterflies in his stomach, even though she had told him not to worry. He was glad that breakfast would come after he asked. Maybe by then he would be able to settle down, and even eat something. He was so excited. It all actually seemed rather sudden after all the waiting and wondering if she would ever be ready for him to ask.

He pulled up in front of their house at 6:25, and spent a few minutes in prayer before going up to the door. Patrick answered the door smiling, which immediately put Matt at ease. "Come right this way. Glenda is waiting for us in the living room, since Fiona told us you have a question to ask," he invited.

"Good morning, Glenda and Patrick. Yes, I do have a very important question to ask. May I have Fiona's hand in marriage? I love her dearly and promise to take good care of her," Matt stated.

Patrick answered right away, "Yes, Glenda and I have already discussed that possibility and are in agreement that you will make a very good husband for our precious daughter." Then he called loudly, "Fiona, would you please come into the living room?" She looked lovely, as usual, and gave them all a smile and greetings. "Fiona, Matt came this morning and asked for your hand in marriage. Are you willing to marry this man?" he asked her.

"Yes, I'll be very pleased to marry Matt," she answered, smiling and blushing a little.

"Good. Your mother and I gave him our permission and now we'll leave you two alone in this room so that he can propose and give you his pledge to complete this engagement. Then, Matt, we would like you to stay and have breakfast with us," said Patrick as he ushered Glenda from the room.

"Oh, Fiona, I'm so happy," Matt said hugging her after they left. "Is there a proper Irish way to propose? And I'm not sure what my pledge is suppose to be. Please tell me so that I can do it correctly."

"The way you proposed yesterday was perfect. And the ring is your pledge, so let's repeat what you did yesterday, only this time you do get to give me the ring," she explained.

"Oh, that will be easy. Thank you for telling me!" he said. He asked her to sit on the couch and knelt in front of her where he repeated his proposal and then took out the ring and placed it on her slender finger. They both admired it. Then he tenderly kissed the back of her hand, remembering that they had agreed to save all other kissing for the wedding and after.

Subsequently, he helped her to her feet and they went to join her parents in the dining room for a delicious breakfast. The formality fell away and they did "talk about it all through breakfast," just like Fiona had said. Her parents expressed their delight about the beautiful engagement ring.

After breakfast and helping with the clean up, Matt asked, "Would you like to go see the progress that has been made on our house?" It felt so good to be able to call it our house! He felt like he could fly and carry her there!

"Yes! I would love to go and see it. I'll be ready in about 5 minutes," she said as she hurried to the restroom and to grab a light jacket.

When they got there she exclaimed, "Oh, Matt, you've done so much more than when I saw it last time. It's going to be just perfect. I love it already."

That was just what he had been hoping to hear from her. He wanted only to please and take care of her. He took her hand and helped her up the temporary steps. "We'll walk through the 'rooms' and if you notice anything you want changed be sure and tell me, because now is the best time to make any modifications. I'll go get the blueprints and we can make any notes right on them as we go through the house."

As they walked and talked about it, Fiona did notice a couple things that she would like better if they were changed, so she mentioned them and he wrote them down. He said, "This is going to be even more fun with you to give me ideas. Your input is invaluable! I love you so much!"

"I love you too! It feels so good to be able to express our feelings to each other," she stated.

"That's for sure. I've wanted to for a long time. This is wonderful!" he agreed.

Fiona was beaming when she arrived at work and immediately pulled Connie into the lunchroom so she could share her good news with her without all the customers listening in to what she said. Of course Connie was delighted and gave Fiona a great big hug. Then they went out to nurture some plants and Fiona was able to tell her the whole story as they worked. The same thing happened when Amelia arrived on Friday. Fiona told her that she still would like to discuss the books as they had been doing, even though she felt that Matt had passed all the tests with flying colors.

When Matt got to his work site, after lunch, he told Walt his good news. Walt was thrilled, and almost blurted out his plans for the new project right then, but stopped short, and instead he reminded Matt to come to lunch on Saturday. Then he explained what needed to be done that afternoon. It did indeed look like they would be finished with this house tomorrow evening. So much was happening all at once, that Matt felt a little overwhelmed. But he prayed and put it all in God's capable hands and asked for his help to do his part well. Then he got to work to help get this house finished by tomorrow evening. At break time he shared the good news of his engagement to Fiona with Jeff and told him to be sure and tell Karen also.

*****

Maria met those two co-workers in the lunchroom where they took their lunches out of the refrigerator and then walked over to the park. As they were walking around the park, which had been freshly washed by the rain yesterday, Maria asked, "Did you have a chance to read that first chapter in Philippians?"

They both nodded, and one replied, "There's a lot more in that chapter than just the little part you told us about."

"I agree," said Maria. "I couldn't remember the exact verse numbers to tell you yesterday, so I just had you read the whole chapter. What did you think about it?"

"Well, you did a good job of telling about his dilemma. But I cannot imagine a person feeling like he did," she stated.

"Would you like to hear what I think about that?" asked Maria.

"Yes," the other one said, "because I can't imagine feeling that way either."

"Okay. I'll try to keep it short," and she gave them a summary of Paul's life before and after he met Jesus on the road to Damascus, what he learned from Jesus, his missionary journeys, and of his knowing a man who experienced the glory of the third heaven. "Since Paul had been so terrible and was so totally changed for the better by Jesus, he loved Jesus and wanted to serve him until the time he would die and go to be with Jesus in heaven.

"He said that for him to live was Christ living through him, and to die would be gain. Jesus became his whole life while he lived, and he knew that when he died, his spirit would go to be with Jesus. When Jesus returns to earth to gather and change the bodies of all the people who are living and believe in him, all those who have died, and believed in him will be raised from the dead and their spirits will be reunited with glorified bodies and will spend eternity in heaven with Jesus. Paul tells about that in 1 Thessalonians chapter 4 if you would like to read about it."

"Wow! You're better than some of those TV and radio preachers I've heard sometimes. I know we're out of time again today, but, could we continue this some more tomorrow?" asked the first one and the other one agreed.

"Of course! Let's bring our lunches again, since it's been so nice out here today," answered Maria.

*****

Right after supper clean-up time, Don and Anita sat down with the pile of the cards from the phone calls. A few more calls had come today. After putting the two they had called last night in a place by themselves, they divided the rest of the cards in half and then counted the people represented by each pile. Amazingly enough they came out with an equal number of people. Both groups would be larger than normal small groups, but they would probably work out all right. So now they had a Friday "school group" and a Saturday one also. Before the meeting that evening Don and Anita both used their cell phones and made all the phone calls necessary to get co-facilitators, and invite all those people to their house for their first new believers small group meetings. The Saturday group would meet at the morning time, and Mindy had agreed to care for all four children again, for the next three Saturdays.

The Thursday evening meeting went very well. Cory was thrilled that two of his best friends were in his small group with him. It <u>was</u> rather unusual having children in a small group setting. And there would be even more in the Friday and Saturday groups. Don practiced on this group trying to use more easily understood words. He also told the children they could raise their hands and ask questions if they didn't understand something.

*****

The same evening, Larry told Ted and Jane told Julie how the rest of their evening had gone on Tuesday. The man they had led to the Lord had been crying tears of joy as he told the people at the special house all that had happened to him that evening. He was very grateful to be able to receive help and promised to follow all their rules and do whatever chores they needed him to do. Ted and Julie were glad to hear about the happy ending.

Everywhere There's a Sunrise, Let's Tell The Good News!

*****

Very late that evening, when Sherry got home from work, Roy was still up so after their usual greeting and hugs and kisses, she told him, "Just before I came home yesterday, Anita told me that she had lost count of how many phone calls she had gotten from the families of children in Cory's class in the public school he attends. There were even some from those in his class last year. They're all brand new believers because of the testimony Cory gave in his classroom and the invitation to meet by the big shade tree and pray for Jesus to be their Savior. The children from last year's class had all gathered around him at lunch recess and heard the same testimony. Many of them received Jesus during the last recess."

"Wow! Exclaimed Roy. "I never could have imagined that happening. How did they know to call Anita?"

Sherry answered, "Apparently he told the children about the booklets and cards, also. On Monday night he and his parents stopped at the pastor's house and picked up 50 of them! Although, they might not have used all of them."

"Remember how self-confident he was at church on Sunday, speaking to the whole congregation?" he asked.

"Yes, it was amazing. Anyway, today, Anita had me bake dozens of cookies for meetings on Thursday, Friday, and Saturday, and that's not counting the meeting they had on Wednesday. We need to pray that they'll have the stamina and energy and wisdom for all these groups. Some of them will have children in them," she explained.

"Wow again! Let's pray for them right now, and then off and on whenever we think about it." So they did, and then Roy continued, "I wonder if we can share this news with our small group Saturday and have them join the prayers since they'll have still have two more weeks with four meetings a week before the co-facilitators can take over."

"I don't know about telling our group about that part. Who can we ask?" inquired Sherry.

"You could call Anita tomorrow morning," he answered.

"Good idea. I'll do just that and let you know what she says," she replied.

*****

Linda L. Linn
Friday

    Early Friday morning found Maria in Ruth's office to quickly explain what had happened on Wednesday and Thursday at lunch time and ask that she and Esther pray for her when they had lunch together in the lunchroom, as she continued to explain some more to these two co-workers at lunch today in the park. Ruth told Maria that they would be glad to pray for her.
    As Maria and the co-workers walked around the park before eating, one of the two said, "I read that chapter, and it's clear that the people he wrote that to, didn't have to be grief stricken like other people are when someone dies. I think I understand <u>that</u> to mean that those people didn't need to fear and dread dying, because they knew heaven came next and that they would all be reunited."
    "Exactly!" exclaimed Maria. "The only reason to dread death is if a person does not know for sure they will go to heaven when they die. The alternative is <u>dreadful</u> indeed! How about you two, do you know where you'll go when you die?"
    The other one answered with the question, "Can we know for sure?"
    "I'm glad you asked that." Then she proceeded to tell them the Good News, much like she had told Jason. When she had finished she asked, "Would you like the peace of knowing for sure that you <u>will</u> go to heaven when you die?" After they both nodded, she helped them pray out loud a prayer much like Don used in church. She had picked up some booklets and cards when she was at the church buying music on Tuesday, so she gave each of them a booklet and a card, and invited them to come to church at 2 PM on Sunday. They agreed and she said, "I'm so happy and so glad to have two new sisters in Christ! You see, both of you now are in the family of God, so that makes us sisters. I'll be waiting in the entryway of the church on Sunday, and we can all sit together. Then I'll take you up to introduce you to Pastor Don, and you can give him your cards if you would like to join a small group and learn how to live this new life."
    They both thanked her and they all walked joyfully back to the office.
    At the end of the workday, Maria grabbed Esther and they ran up to Ruth's office where she told them both the good news. "I'm so excited and thankful! This is the first time I've ever gotten to lead anyone to Jesus for salvation. What a privilege! They were

both so filled with joy and peace. It was wonderful to see," she finished.

"Tell us all about it!" they both exclaimed.

So Maria explained what they had talked about each of the three days after picking two co-workers who had similar interests to get the conversation rolling. I have a list of their interests if you would like to use it."

"That sounds like a very good plan," commented Esther. It seems like small talk can just go on and on, and even after three days with the same two people there have been no openings to share the gospel."

"I thought the same thing after last week, so I tried something different," agreed Maria. "It seemed to work well this week. Those two were really easy to talk to and even read the scriptures I suggested when they went home, before going to lunch the next day. It might not work out that way every time, but God, we ask you to keep giving us ideas that will work."

Ruth added, "Yes, Lord, now that we've broken the ice with all of them, please help them be open to hearing the gospel. And if they've already hardened their hearts for some reason, send your Spirit to soften them."

"We praise and thank you for these two co-workers who have joined your family. Help them to grow in you and be ready to witness along with us to the rest of our co-workers," prayed Esther.

*****

Tony, Matt and Fiona met at the grocery store on the corner as they had planned, for their three by three ministry time. They got a cart and Tony put a few of the things he usually bought into the cart as they walked along together and prayed for guidance and for the people they were passing in the isles. They walked and shopped and prayed all the way through the store, but nobody seemed to need any help or look despondent or anything else that they could help with today. Matt had been putting the things he usually bought in a separate place in the cart, so when they had made one round, they went to check out, each paying separately for their purchases.

Outside, they talked over what had happened. "Stores in the shopping mall don't open until 10 AM on weekdays, so we would have to change our meeting time from 9:30 to 10 AM. We could try that next time if it's close enough for you, Tony," Matt suggested.

"The inside mall would give us more opportunities and we would not even have to shop. I could ride the bus over there, so we might try that next Friday at 10 AM. Would that work for both of you?" asked Tony.

They both nodded and agreed to try that next week. They all said, "See you tomorrow at small group!"

*****

That evening, Jason was thinking about all the things he had learned at the new believers small groups and even by listening to the testimonies at the baptismal service. The church services also added to his knowledge, plus now he was able to understand the Bible when he read it at home every day. The words to the hymns and songs that were sung at church and small group meetings were also significant to him. He had bought a hymnal so he could read them over at home. He read some of the other hymns in it also, and learned several more things from them.

He wondered how he could have been so blind all those years, and was sorry he had wasted so much of his life. So he confessed that and prayed about it. He remembered hearing about how God could restore the years the locust had eaten so he went to his concordance to look up the verse. He found it in Joel 2:25a. *And I (God) will restore to you the years that the locust have eaten.* He accepted God's forgiveness for those wasted years, and chose to believe that they would be restored and for his life to be useful to God now, like it was meant to be. Then he read the words to the hymn, that begins: "Take my life and let it be ...," and he decided that every verse in it would be the goal of his new life as a believer in Jesus. That would be a complete changeover for him, but he also knew that with God's help he could do it.

*****

Friday's most recent new believers group was rather crowded in the pastor's house. Most of the children had to sit on the floor, but there were no complaints and even <u>they</u> were very good listeners. They had even more questions about the little booklets than their parents did, but Don and Anita answered all questions very patiently. It was interesting to watch them try to find the songs in the hymnals, but by the last one most had gotten the hang of it with a little help from their parents. The Bibles were much harder, and they finally stood beside their parents to follow along in one of their Bibles.

Don encouraged the children; "Finding verses in the Bible will get easier with practice, so don't give up. The Bible is like your mother's cookbook or your dad's 'How To ... book.' It has all the directions you'll need in order to live this brand new life as part of God's big family."

The rest of the meeting was much like the first one of the other new believers a few weeks ago, and it went very well. The people and especially the children enjoyed the cookies Sherry had baked for the occasion. The children all knew each other from school so they talked together freely, but the parents used the time to get acquainted with each other.

By the time it was all over and everyone had left, Don and Anita were very tired, but also very pleased.

*****

Chapter 19

2 Peter 3:18, *Grow in grace, and in the knowledge of our Lord and Savior Jesus Christ. To him be glory both now and forever. Amen.*

Colossians 3:15, *Let the peace of God rule in your hearts, ... and be thankful.*

Saturday

Morning seemed to come very soon at the Ross house on Saturday, but they woke rested and energetic, quickly straightening up the chairs and books on them for the next meeting. Timmy and Mary were interested in seeing many more chairs than usual in the living room and Mary said, "Looks full!"

"You're right. It *is* very crowded and will be even more so when everyone gets here. Joy and Hope are coming today to play outside with you two and Mindy," Anita told her.

"Oh, goody! Fun with them!" exclaimed Mary, and Timmy agreed with her.

The children were all outside when their first guests arrived. The meeting was very similar to the one the night before. By the time the people had all left, the four children and Mindy were eager to come inside and have a cookie and milk.

"These cookies are yummy!" exclaimed Timmy.

"Yes they are," agreed Hope. "Mommy baked them on Thursday while she was here."

Joy added, "She baked some more just like them at our house yesterday morning. We got to eat one for lunch dessert yesterday."

Timmy continued, "We each ate one after supper last night. It's fun to do almost the same thing as you did."

Joy said, "I'm glad we get to be friends with you and Mary."

Just then, Roy and Sherry came to pick them up and they both remembered to say thank you to Mindy, and to Don and Anita. Then the Ross family all decided it was time for a nap before lunch.

*****

Before breakfast, Julie checked her e-mail again to see if Pam had sent anything, but there was still nothing there. So Julie wrote her a short note saying they would pray for her at the small group meeting that morning. Julie was a little worried about her since this was the first week with no correspondence at all. She prayed for her while she fixed breakfast, and commented on it to Ted when they were eating, "I'm concerned about Pam, because she hasn't written all week. She did that last week until Friday, but finally sent one."

Ted replied, "Maybe she's still extra busy, like she was last week and the week before. We can pray for her at the small group even without specific requests."

"Yes, I told her we would pray for her in a short note I sent just before breakfast," agreed Julie. Now, tell me how your week was. Time goes so fast since we're so busy."

My week at work was very good, as it usually is. Coming home to spend time with you is the best part of it," he answered. "How did your week go at school?"

Julie replied, "You always say such sweet things to show me how loved I am. Thank you, my treasure. My week at school went very well and very fast. Yesterday I ate lunch with the teacher next door to me and we had a pleasant visit." Then she told them about the fun time the children had with her koala puppet, Kippy.

"I'm so happy for you that you're enjoying your teaching position, my Jewel, " he responded.

Julie quipped, "And just think, I get paid for doing it, too!" He laughed as they finished breakfast. Then they cleaned up the kitchen before they left for the small group meeting.

*****

Sherry had taken Joy and Hope over to the Ross home so that they could play with Timmy and Mary while Mindy took care of them. Then she had hurried back to finish helping to get the house ready and refreshments set up for the Saturday small group meeting at their house. Roy had cleaned, dusted and arranged the chairs last night while Sherry was at work. Sherry had baked cookies on Friday morning. Of course she didn't bake as many as she had needed to bake Thursday at Anita's house. She couldn't imagine having small group meetings four days in a row.

"Oh, I forgot to tell you, Roy. Anita said it would be very helpful to know that our group would be praying for them. We don't need to go into all the details, just a quick summary. Will you do that, Honey? You're better at summaries than I am," said Sherry.

"Sure, Dear. I'll be glad to. I'll do part of it as a praise and the rest during conversational prayer time," he said.

"Thank you," she said as the doorbell rang. Jeff and Karen had arrived to put the Bibles and hymnals on the chairs and have a time of prayer before the other members got there.

Everybody arrived pretty close to on time. It was a good way to show respect for each other's time. No time had to be wasted waiting for latecomers. Jeff opened with prayer and encouraged the members to share praises and thanksgiving. Again, he reminded them to hold group applause and praise until the end of the sharing time.

Matt and Fiona stood up and said together, "We praise and thank you LORD, we're engaged!"

Spontaneous applause and cheers and congratulations followed that announcement and praise.

Jeff laughed and said, "I guess there will be times when we just can't wait until the end, and that's fine."

Ted settled things down by singing the Doxology, and they all joined in.

Julie said, "I praise and thank God for another delightful week teaching at the church school."

Ami continued with, "Praise God that Aneko will be moved back home by this coming Wednesday, and will only miss the one small group meeting of today. She'll be working with us at the restaurant."

Larry shared what their four by four group had done on Tuesday evening, thankful that Ted and Julie had been there to pray for them as they shared the gospel with the needy alcoholic, drug addicted, husband and father. His life was turned around for the better, all because of Jesus saving him!

Clara said, "I thank and praise you, LORD, for the renewed energy to take on extra classes and learn faster."

Roy had waited until he was sure that the others were finished, and he said, "Sherry and I took Joy and Hope with us to the same park two weeks in a row for our two by two ministry time." Then he gave a summary of what had happened there. "You got to hear the boy who was healed when he talked at the end of the service Sunday." Roy gave a summary of what had happened at the boy's school, when he gave his testimony in the classroom, and then had the children meet him by the shade tree at recess. That resulted in two more new believer's groups, which include children and their parents. "Sherry and I praise and thank you Jesus for using us in this miracle and harvest, and we give you all the praise and glory."

He and Sherry led the applause and oral praise to God, and they ended by singing together, "Our God Is an Awesome God."

Karen asked, "Are there any announcements?" Silence. "Okay, then who would like to volunteer to host the next small group meeting?"

Matt looked at Fiona and she nodded. He said, "Fiona and I would be pleased to have you join us at the church school lunchroom next Saturday." Karen smiled her thanks to them.

"Did anybody make a handiwork of some kind for the chart we constructed last week?" Jeff asked.

Jane pulled a 16 X 24-inch poster from beside her chair and held it up for all to see. It was done in perfect calligraphy and in all colors of the rainbow. Lots of "oo's and aah's" expressed appreciation for the artwork.

Karen said, "I understand that some other types may take a lot longer to complete, so when you have something ready to show us, do it as an announcement."

Today the songs were: Psalm 22: verses: 1,7,8,14,15, and 18, set to music; "When I survey the Wondrous Cross," John 19:37; "Praise the Lamb of Glory," John 1:29.

"Today our teaching is about the Last Supper, and we will partake of communion together. You probably guessed that from the songs we sang," Jeff told them. "Let's read John 1:29 together, *John the Baptist saw Jesus coming to him and said, "Behold the Lamb of God, who takes away the sin of the world."* Now we'll sing 'Praise the Lamb of Glory' again and really focus on the words as we remember everything he's done for us.

The rest of communion was very much like the time they had on the Saturday before Easter last month and just as meaningful, if not more so, since they had all gotten to know each other better. This group had become very unified during their short time together.

Karen started the conversational prayer time. "What a privilege it is to meet and take communion together, Lord."

Jeff continued, "Please enable us to remember and thank you for all you've done every day, not just during our times of communion in our small group."

Tony agreed, "I agree with that very good idea. Make gratefulness a part of our daily lives, please."

Jane continued on a different subject. "Please give the children I contacted the desire to come to the Wednesday afternoon Bible Story or Study groups this week, and to continue coming. Please draw them to yourself, Jesus."

Julie agreed, "Yes, LORD, there are so many children in this city who have never heard about Jesus. Please speak to other people to get more groups started." Then she turned on her recorder and prayed, "Father, you know what Pam needs even though she didn't send me an e-mail this week. Please meet her needs, give her peace and strength as she continues to take care of her mother."

Ted continued, "I agree, and it is our privilege to be able to pray for Pam, even though she's in another state. You are omnipresent, and therefore you can work in both places at once. Pleas bless Pam with whatever she needs."

Clara added, "Yes, and we continue to ask you for a miracle of healing for her mother, and salvation for her parents."

Fiona continued, "Also please help Pam to stay focused on you, and be encouraged that you are in control of every situation that she needs to deal with. Fill her with your wisdom, and guide her words."

Jeff spoke directly to her saying, "Pam, this is Jeff, the facilitator of this small group, and I feel that Jesus desires to have you put your hands on your mother's head and speak to her brain to be totally healed in Jesus name. If you like, my wife, Karen and I could be on the phone agreeing with you like that Bible verse says." Then he gave his phone number. "We'll be home all afternoon if you choose to call. I'm sure Julie will e-mail these prayers to you, as soon as she gets home this morning. Yes, she's nodding emphatically."

Next, Tomo prayed for safe travel when Aneko drove home on Wednesday, and Larry added his agreement.

Roy prayed for Don and Anita, giving a summary of the four small groups for the newest believers, and Sherry added her agreement before asking the whole group to keep them in prayer the next few weeks. "We pray that they'll have the stamina, energy and wisdom for all these groups. Some of them will have children in them."

Matt finished by praying, "Father in heaven, thank you for Don and Anita and their pastoring skills. Please strengthen and encourage them as they feed your sheep. We also rejoice in all the brand new believers. Help all of us to reach out to them with love, welcome them into your family, and to help them in any way that you show us."

And everybody said, "Amen!" and "Wow!" It had been another amazing meeting.

Then they all met in the kitchen for fellowship and refreshments.

*****

Jeff and Karen went directly home and prayed for Pam and for wisdom for themselves if she called. Then they spent the rest of the morning and the early afternoon near the phone, wondering if Pam would call them.

He said, "It always seems like with things such as this we have to stick our necks out, and then wonder if we've said or done the right thing."

"Oh well, better to do that, than do nothing at all." she stated. "Let's be patient."

After about another hour, the phone rang and they both jumped, and then laughed at themselves for being startled. It was Pam. Jeff turned the speaker on so they could both hear. Pam requested, "Jeff, would you please explain to Mother and Father what you meant for me to do? I have the phone's speaker on so they can hear also."

"Of course," he answered. "Mr. and Mrs. Green, my name is Jeff Spencer, and my wife is Karen. We facilitate the small group in Pine City of which your daughter, Pam, is an absentee member. We've been praying for her and you, Mrs. Green, since we heard about your stroke. Today, I felt that Jesus was telling me to have Pam put her hands on your head and speak to your brain to be healed in Jesus name. You see, Jesus did things like that when he was living on earth almost 2000 years ago, and the people were healed. He promised that people who have faith in him would do things like he did. He also promised that where two or three people agree about what they ask for, his Father in heaven would do it for them. So we are here on the phone to agree with Pam as she asks for your complete healing."

"Okay, Pam, you can do that," consented Mrs. Green.

"Thank you, Mother. I will very gently place my hands on your head. I know how it's been hurting you lately. Now, I'll pray. Jesus, you are the Creator and Great Physician and we are in agreement as we ask that you will completely heal my mother from all the causes and effects of that stroke. Brain, in Jesus name, be healed!" She could feel Jesus power going through her hands to her mother's head and she heard Jeff and Karen agreeing over the phone.

Her mother looked startled and she reached up her hands to cover Pam's hands on her head. "My head and whole body feel warm, and all the pain in my head is gone!" she exclaimed. She took Pam's hands in hers and held them in front of her, squeezing them both with the same strength. Then she smiled a big smile using all the muscles in her face. After that she proceeded to do all the physical therapy movements perfectly with both sides of her body. "I'm no longer paralyzed! I can move all my body parts and do everything normally! Thank you, Jesus, for healing me!" Next she got up and walked around for a while. "Now would you please tell us again how to be saved?"

Pam shared the Gospel like she had before, including verses from the Bible. Her mother and father asked questions which Pam, Karen and Jeff took turns answering. When her parents understood what they needed to do, Pam led them in a prayer much like her pastor used, and both parents gladly repeated after her. Then all five of them gave thanks and praise to Jesus.

Afterward, Jeff asked, "May I make a few suggestions?"

Her father answered, "Please do."

So Jeff continued, "I would like to send you some of the little booklets our church gives out to new believers. They're on several different topics, and will answer many of your questions as you're learning how to live your new lives in the family of God. Also, it is important that you find a church in your city that teaches the Bible and has small groups like the ones explained in one of the booklets."

Pam's father and mother both agreed, "Yes, please send the books, and we'll find a church and small group."

Jeff said, "Very good, I'll get the booklets in the mail Monday morning. Pam, I think it would be valuable for you to stay there for a week or two and help them as they look for a good church and small group to attend. Also, please stay in touch with us on the phone and with Julie by e-mail so we, as a small group can give you the support you might need."

"Thank you for all those good suggestions. I'll do my best," answered Pam. "Thank you both for being here on the phone with us today."

Jeff and Karen both said, "It was our pleasure!" Karen added, "We're so glad that Jesus healed you, Mrs. Green, and that you and Mr. Green are now believers in Jesus!"

After that, they all said good-bye and ended the phone conversation. But you can be sure there was much dialog in both families about all that had happened.

When she got a chance later that afternoon, Pam sent an e-mail to Julie telling her of the miracles of healing and salvation that had taken place that afternoon for her parents and how Jeff and Karen had helped over the phone. Of course Julie was overjoyed to hear about it. Pam also apologized for not writing all week. She explained that she had been so discouraged that she couldn't bring herself to even write about it all. She was worried that all she had been doing was complaining and making prayer requests. She thanked Julie for sending the e-mail with the small group prayers for her, even though she had not sent any requests, and for Jeff's instructions. Now she was overflowing with praise and thanksgiving.

After sending a reply to Pam, filled with praise and thanksgiving to God for his gracious miracles, Julie called Fiona to let her know also, since she had been sending e-mails and had told her how she and Matt had been praying for them every time they went on a date together. She encouraged her to share this news with him, and thanked them for all their prayers. It appeared that they would not need to continue the prayers any longer.

*****

Matt took Fiona home after the small group, telling her, "Walt invited me over for lunch to discuss his next building project. What time should I get to your house to work on the porch this afternoon?"

She answered, "It doesn't have to be exact. Sometime between 3:30 and 4:00, should give both of you time to complete that little repair job before supper. Wow! You get to eat out twice today!"

"Yes, and it's a very real blessing since my cooking leaves much to be desired. I'll look forward to seeing you and your parents later this afternoon then," he said

"And I'll look forward to seeing you! I enjoyed the group's applause and congratulations today. It's going to be fun to be engaged," she added.

"I'm sure you're right! Everything I do with you is a pleasure, Honey," Matt said enjoying being able to use a name of endearment for her, and to see her smile and blush as he helped her down from his truck at her house. "I'll see you this afternoon," he said giving her hand a gentle squeeze.

He drove right over to Walt and Betty's house and they greeted him warmly. Their whole relationship had taken on a deeper level of love and caring since they had both come to Christ. They were feeling more and more like family now, and Matt really enjoyed that. Betty ushered him right into the dining room since lunch was ready.

Walt gave thanks for the food, and then the hot dishes were passed around. It all smelled so good, it made Matt's mouth water. "Betty your cooking just gets better and better. This is all delicious!" exclaimed Matt.

"Spoken like a true bachelor," laughed Betty. A home cooked meal would be much better than anything a normal bachelor would fix. But thank you Matt for the compliments."

"You're welcome. How are your sewing projects coming along?" he asked next.

"I'm glad to be able to say that all the mending is caught up! Talk about a good feeling! I'm out from under that load," she answered.

"And, I have all my old favorite work shirts back again. I didn't even out-grow them, because it really didn't take her that long to get them finished," said Walt. Then he asked, "How's the work coming on your house, Matt?"

"Actually, pretty well. Ben has been helping me on the weekends and it's starting to look more like a house. The weather has been nice enough that I can get a couple hours of work done on some of the weekdays also. I have had more incentive since Fiona returned home," explained Matt.

"I've been pleasantly surprised the few times I have driven past it during the last couple weeks. This morning, I showed the Mayor and his wife their newly finished house and told them they could move in any time now. They were both very pleased and told me to thank all the workers for a job well done."

Matt inserted, "We do have very good workers on both shifts."

Betty asked, "Shall we have our dessert and some coffee in the living room?"

"Sounds good, and then I can tell Matt about our next project." When they were seated and Matt had put down his coffee on the side table, Walt began, "Betty and I had planned this project several months ago, so it would follow the completion of the Mayor's house. After you told me your good news about becoming engaged to Fiona, we were even more certain of the timing. Our next project is to have both crews work on your house so that it can be finished and ready for you and Fiona to move into right after your wedding. It's our wedding present to you both!"

It was a good thing Matt had set his coffee down, because he would have dropped it in his surprise. For once he was speechless and just sat there with his mouth hanging open.

Betty jumped right in before Matt could say anything. "Fiona is such a sweet girl. We couldn't be happier for you, Matt. When she saw my kitchen, her eyes lit up with admiration. We would like the house you are building to contain as many custom built things as she and you would desire. We know you've been trying to keep costs down to a minimum, but we really desire to make your home as nice as ours is."

Walt continued, "We've saved money all our lives to do something special for the children we could never have, and when we met and got to know you, we just adopted you in our hearts. You and the men will still be paid your regular wages as we work on this project, because we saved more than enough to cover that and the materials.

"Wow, you guys! I'm totally overwhelmed with your love and generosity. What can I say? ... I know! The only appropriate thing I <u>can</u> say is THANK YOU BOTH VERY MUCH!!!" exclaimed Matt.

Walt replied, "You're very welcome. I'm glad you will accept this gift, because we've been looking forward to doing this for a very long time."

"As I was growing up, my parents wanted me to call them Daddy and Mama. I still miss them and probably always will, but it's been much less, since I have known both of you. Would it be fitting and proper and acceptable to you both if Fiona and I call you Dad and Mom, since that's what you've become to me?" asked Matt.

They both had tears of joy in their eyes as they met together in the middle of the room for a big three-way hug.

"That's exactly what we both would like and enjoy and wish for," answered Walt. "We'll be very happy to have you two as a son and daughter. And when you have children, they can call us Grandpa and Grandma. You can explain to them why the last names are different, and be sure to tell them about their blood grandparents also."

Betty said, "Now, we know that you carry a set of the blueprints for your house around in your pick-up. Walt wants to study them and have you explain some things so he will be ready for Monday morning."

Matt jumped up and ran out to get them and bring them in. "Please let me help you clear the table and clean up the dishes while Walt looks them over. By the time we're finished, he will be ready with his questions."

Walt smiled and said, "Great idea. We appreciate your thoughtfulness and willingness to help."

They spent the next couple hours doing questions and answers. They discussed many aspects of the plan and Walt gained in his mind what he needed to know to get going on Monday. "Talk to Fiona and get her input on everything that she desires, so we can put it into the plan now, when it's easier to accomplish, rather than having to change things later."

"Okay, I'll tell her about your gift and get her thinking about it this evening after we have supper with her parents. She'll probably be just as surprised as I was," said Matt. "I see that it's almost 3:30. I need to run home, change into some work clothes and help her father with some repairs on the back porch, before supper. Otherwise I would love to be able to stay here longer. Thank you for the delicious meal and the fabulous surprise gift!

See you in church tomorrow. I love to be able to say that, and know that we'll all spend eternity together!"

*****

Tony had waited all week to call Esther, because their work hours didn't mesh, and because he was so nervous he could not make himself do it. When he got home from the small group meeting, he made another excuse. It was too close to lunch, next: how much time should I wait after lunch, and what if I interrupt something important? On and on he went with excuses and questions until he almost talked himself out of it altogether. But then he took the phone in hand, and decided to go ahead and call. It was either now or never! Was he ever surprised that she answered and even sounded glad that he had called! They talked about this and that for a little while and then he asked her if she would like to go out to eat supper this Sunday evening, explaining that he had agreed to teach Spanish to Ted during the walk in the park on Sunday afternoons after church, so it needed to be after that, so could he meet her at her apartment at 5PM tomorrow? He hadn't even stopped to take a breath so he could be sure to get all of it said. It ended up being a pretty long, run-on sentence. She graciously agreed, and Tony had a DATE!

*****

Matt changed, grabbed another set of blueprints, and made it to Fiona's house by 3:50. He was thankful that she had given him some margin on the time today. He wanted to maintain his good record of being on time. He and Patrick got right to work on the porch repair and it was finished in less than two hours. Meanwhile Fiona and Glenda finished supper preparations and they enjoyed a tasty meal together, with pleasant conversation. Matt was eager to have some time alone with Fiona, but he hid it very well, even helping with the cleanup after the meal.

Then he asked, "Fiona do you feel up to a walk to the park this evening?"

"Yes, that would be delightful. The weather is just perfect for a walk," she answered. On the way she shared what Julie had told her on the phone earlier this afternoon. He was elated and they praised God on the way to the park.

Everywhere There's a Sunrise, Let's Tell The Good News!

When they reached the park, Matt led her to a bench and asked her to sit with him for a few minutes. "Later we'll continue walking, but I have some big news to share with you." He sat down on the other end of the bench and turned to face her. She also faced him. He wanted to see her response to this news about the house.

"After lunch with Walt and Betty, they told me about a wedding present they desire to give to us. The house we were working on was completely finished on Friday, and today he told me about his next project."

Matt told her every detail they had told him, and her look of surprise was just what he had expected. She was speechless. But her hand covered her mouth so he couldn't see it hanging open.

"Before you think or say anything, I need to explain to you how important it is for them to be able to give us this gift. They were never able to have children, but they've been saving money all during their marriage in order to do something special for those children. When they met and got to know me, they adopted me in their hearts, and they've already done the same for you. I asked if we could call them Dad and Mom, and they agreed with tears of joy in their eyes. This is a dream come true for them. At first I didn't know what to say, but I realized that the only appropriate thing to say was THANK YOU BOTH VERY MUCH!!! It is hard for me to receive such a gift, but I will do it graciously and let them have the joy of giving," he explained.

Fiona responded with her characteristic grace, "I understand what you mean, and you know from what I said the other day that I didn't want a lot of money spent on me. But this is different. They wish to bless us with their love and generosity. Therefore, I will enjoy this gift. How can I do that in the best way?"

"Thank you for understanding. You'll need to think of everything you would put into a custom-built home to make it be exactly what you would like it to be. We can work together on this, and it needs to be done soon before very much more work is done on the house. Betty said that you admired her kitchen. Decide if you would like one just like it or if you would make some changes. When could we get together and see what we need to modify?" asked Matt.

"Whenever we can work it out for both of us. This is the beginning of our life together. It is important that we do this. Where would be a good place for us to meet?" she asked.

"Well," he pondered, "Tomorrow is Sunday, I could take you to the house in the morning after breakfast, say 8:30, with a set of the blueprints, and we can discuss in more detail any changes that need to be made before the crews start working tomorrow. Then I can let Walt know by Sunday evening. If we dress for church, I could take you to lunch again before church at our favorite restaurant as a celebration of our engagement and this gift."

"That sounds really good! Do you have an extra set of house plans that I could study this evening?" she asked.

"Yes I do, right in the pickup. Your idea is great! When do you think we should tell your parents?" he asked.

"Let's walk back there and tell them right now. They'll be excited and thrilled for us," she answered.

And they were! Matt had grabbed the blueprints on the way in, and everyone wanted to look at them again. He left them with Fiona who spent the evening studying them and making a list of everything she could think of that would make a good house even better. It was hard for her to ignore the expense that some of her ideas would cost. When she stopped for the night, she placed her hands on the pages she had written and asked God to guide her about what to keep and what to cross out. Spending money on herself went against everything she had been taught, but she reminded herself that this was a special gift, and she needed to accept it graciously.

In the meantime, Matt had spent the evening doing the same thing, making some changes that would make this house extra special for him too. He was hoping that Fiona would really be able to add the things that would make this her 'dream' house, just like he had wanted to do for her, but he knew she would never have been comfortable with accepting that from him, especially after all the discussions they had had on living simply, so they could give more money to God's work. He totally agreed with her, and was glad they could agree on that subject. But this way, he could see her enjoy all the custom built extras because of Walt and Betty's gift. It seemed almost like God was blessing them this way because, ----. Why? Because he is the giver of every good and perfect gift. Wow! So, then Matt spent some time in thanksgiving.

After that he called Ben to tell him the good news about becoming engaged to Fiona and that Walt was going to have both crews working during the following weeks on his house as a wedding present. "You and I won't work there tomorrow, but we'll probably get to some other weekends and you'll get to see fast progress then!" Matt finished. Ben was ecstatic over Matt's good news, even though he had heard about the engagement from his mother and sister when they had come home from work on Friday.

*****

The third Sunday in May

Fiona was ready when Matt arrived right on time after breakfast. She brought the blueprints and her neatly written list of ideas with her. For some reason, God didn't have her cross anything out.

When they got to the house the sun was shinning right on the mountains. What a welcome! They went directly to the dining room and checked to see if the sliding glass door would be in the right place for them to be able to eat while enjoying the view. He had a couple of chairs, which he placed side by side with elbowroom for both of them. They sat down to see if the door was correct. It was just right!

Fiona prayed, "Thank you Great Creator for all of your creation and especially for these magnificent mountains that we'll be able to see while we live in this wonderful house!"

Next they checked the window in the kitchen, and it was also perfect. The same thing happened in the living room, master bedroom, and the office they would share. As she checked those off her list, she said, "You already have made all these things just right. I can tell you were building with me in mind! Thank you so much!" she exclaimed.

"My pleasure, my dear," he replied.

They went back into the kitchen and she told Matt, "I really did like the way Betty's kitchen was set up, and I would like for this one to be the same, <u>except,</u> since I'm left handed, I would like most of her plan to be flipped over."

"Betty will be so happy that you like hers that much and so will Walt," Matt said.

"Another change I would make is to have a side by side refrigerator-freezer, instead of one with the freezer on the bottom. That kind dumps all the cold air right out on the floor every time it's opened, because of all the holes in the basket that gets pulled out," she explained.

"Good thinking, Dear, I can tell that I'm marrying a very intelligent woman," he responded.

"Thank you, Honey! Could we put the nursery right near the master bedroom, instead of the sewing room, so we'll be close when the baby cries? We could put a door from our bathroom into the nursery. Plus, I would like a door from the sewing room into the nursery in order to be able to hear and be near the baby while I'm sewing."

"Of course! That makes perfect sense," he said as he was making changes on the blue print.

"Also," she read from her list, "if possible, I would like to have the sewing room made large enough to hold not only my sewing machine cabinet, but also have room for a Bible study desk and a cutting table. Betty's sewing room was very nice otherwise, and I would like to have all those cupboards and drawers. Some of them will need to have locks on them to keep little fingers out of things that could hurt them. We could even put a playpen in there so that I can sew and still keep an eye on the little one. As they get older they can play on the floor or at the cutting table. We can call it an activity room and make it seem to belong to everyone. I know that will take quite a bit of extra space, but the utility room, and children's bedrooms could each be a little smaller and not hurt them. Later when we don't need a nursery any longer, we could swap the functions of the nursery and activity room, and let the other one be a bedroom, since they're side by side, but only if you make the shelves and cupboards movable and both rooms the same size."

"I can tell that you really thought all of this over in detail last night, and I agree with every change you've suggested. I also really like to hear you talking about our children and planning for them. I'm so glad we have a chance to change all these things now before inside walls and plumbing, etc. have been put in place. The timing of this gift is just perfect since we have time today to make the big changes. Walt will be pleased to see all the thought you have put into this," responded Matt.

Thank you, dear Matt," she said. "It does me a world of good to know you like the changes. I liked the house plan just the way you had made it, but when I got to thinking about how to make it an easier place to live and keep house, all these ideas came to mind. I even asked God to help me know what to scratch out if I put too many things down, but he didn't have me scratch anything out."

"I'm glad he didn't, because in order to make this gift work the way Walt and Betty want it to, we should put in everything we really desire into the house right now as it is being built. There may be some things we can't think of right now and we'll have to change later or go without, but that's okay," he explained.

"Again, I thank you. The last thing I thought of that I would like, is to have the children's bedrooms on the other side of the entryway and main bathroom with the utility room right across from the kitchen so I can work in both places at once, so to speak, without having to run from one end of the house to the other. That's an exaggeration, I know, but you get the picture. Besides, when the children get older and have their loud music playing, it will be nice to have it further from our living areas."

"Wonderful ideas! These changes will make our home a place to enjoy and live in easily. You said that was the last thing, so I assume it's my turn." She nodded, so he continued, "I'd like to put a high window in the master bathroom, so we can have some fresh air ventilation along with the fan, and a view from that side of the house if we wish to stand there. I think we should not have a sky light in the walk in closet since that might make the clothes fade," he said.

"Those are both great ideas! In fact, I think I'd rather not have sky lights anywhere in the house, since the sunlight can cause problems in some of the places it might shine during the day." she exclaimed. "My future husband is a very smart man."

"Thank you, Honey. I agree about not having sky lights anywhere in the house. Also, I would prefer easy care, long lasting flooring, and no carpets in any room," he added.

"Another very good point!" she exclaimed.

"I've seen some vinyl flooring that has a cushioned back which is comfortable for walking and standing. It comes in very nice patterns. We would never have to worry about spills, or snow being tracked into the house," he said.

"I like that idea very much. Carpets are much harder to clean and never do get really clean," she commented.

"Those are my feelings, exactly! I've been thinking about the way the kitchen on this plan is so far from the bathrooms and utility room plumbing. If we swap places with the kitchen and living room we could get all the plumbing much closer together. And since the winters here can get very cold, I would like to keep all the plumbing away from outside walls to cut down on any chance that they might freeze. That would also get the plumbing closer together. But then you would not have the sink under the kitchen window, just a counter. Here is what it would look like. What do you think?" he asked.

"Brilliant! Besides all your reasons, it will also save money in the long run, because the hot water won't have so far to go to reach the sink and dishwasher," she replied.

"Exactly! This plan has the kitchen, dining, living room, and family/exercise room in an open concept with no walls, but I can't help but wonder what the exercise equipment will look like sitting there in the middle of that open space. What if we made some free standing book shelves that go high enough to shield the equipment from view?" he asked.

"That's a fabulous idea!" exclaimed Fiona. "It could be our library. I've been wondering where we could put all the books we already have plus others we will surely buy along the way."

"Right. It would make a nice library. Next, think about the garage. I had not planned to have an entrance into the house right from the garage, but if we don't, it will be quite a long way from the door out of the garage to either the front door or the sliding door into the dining room. That would not be very pleasant in the snow or the summer heat."

"I definitely agree. Where would you put the door?" she asked. He showed her on the plan and she nodded her agreement.

"Since the garage is going to be over-sized, I had planned to build a workshop area in it later, but I've decided to let that be part of Walt's gift to us. That way I can keep all the messy jobs out in the garage and it will keep the house cleaner," he explained.

"Oh, I'm so glad you decided to build your workshop now and not wait. Usually, with that kind of waiting, the thing gets put off so often, that it never gets done. Since you're a builder, you <u>need</u> a workshop!" she stated.

He <u>almost</u> impulsively threw his arms around her to give her a big hug, but stopped in time. He'd have to be very careful until after the wedding. "I appreciate you so much!" he said with great emotion. "I think we should go to the restaurant now. If you think of anything else, let me know so I can inform Walt this evening."

"Okay. Oh, I know another thing, right now. Could we use LED lights all through the house, plus get all energy efficient appliances?" she inquired.

"Yes, I had planned on that, but I'll write it down now so we don't forget to do it. All this thinking has made me hungry. I'm ready whenever you are."

*****

Everywhere There's a Sunrise, Let's Tell The Good News!

By now, everybody was used to seeing Matt and Fiona sitting together in church with her parents, Patrick and Glenda, and usually with Walt and Betty on the other side of Matt. They were no longer speculating since it was common knowledge by now that Matt and Fiona were engaged, and everyone was happy about that.

Maria was waiting in the church entrance on Sunday for the 2 PM service, after asking Julie to save three seats beside her at the end of the row for herself and two guests. She had called Pastor Don alerting him that she would introduce him to two new believers after the service. When they arrived, she welcomed them and led them to the seats Julie had saved. She introduced them to Julie and Ted, and then showed them the Bibles and Hymnals and display board up front, sitting between them so she could help both of them more easily. They had time to look up the first song, and were ready just in time.

The songs today were: "All Creatures of Our God and King," Psalm 148: all 14 verses; "At the Name of Jesus," Philippians 2:5-11; and "Majesty," Hebrews 2:9.

Pastor Don began the teaching time by saying, "Open your hymnals again to the first song we sang, and scan it for some of the things that I'll read about in Psalm 148 that goes with it. *Praise the LORD, Praise the LORD from the heavens. Praise him on the heights. Praise him all his angels; praise him all his hosts. Praise him sun and moon; praise him all you stars of light. Praise him, you heavens of heavens, and you waters that are above the heavens; let them praise the name of the LORD, for he commanded and they were created. He has also established them forever and ever. He made a decree that shall not pass. Praise the LORD from the earth, you sea creatures and all deeps, fire, and hail, snow and vapors, stormy wind, fulfilling his word; mountains and all hills, fruitful trees and all cedars; beasts, and all cattle, creeping things, and flying birds; kings of the earth and all people; princes and all judges of the earth; both young men and maidens, old men and children: let them praise the name of the LORD, for his name alone is excellent. His glory is above the earth and heaven. He also exalts the horn of his people, ... the children of Israel. Praise the LORD.*

"I love it when so much scripture goes with a song that we have just sung. It's fun to compare them. Notice that the author of the words of the song was St. Francis of Assisi, many years ago. William Draper translated them.

Linda L. Linn

"Next please find Philippians 2 and follow along as I read verses 5-11. *Let this mind be in you, which was also in Christ Jesus, who being in the form of God, ... equal with God, made himself of no reputation and took the form of a servant, and was made in the likeness of men. Being found in the fashion of a man, he humbled himself and became obedient unto death, even death on the cross. Therefore, God has highly exalted him, and given him a name that is above every name, that at the name of Jesus, every knee will bow, things in heaven and in earth and under the earth, and that every tongue will confess that Jesus Christ is Lord, to the glory of God the Father.* Our second song was based on these verses, and both are very good places to find things for which to praise the LORD. He is <u>so</u> worthy of all praise!

"Now, please find our last song, "Majesty," again and let's read the words out loud together as an invitation to praise Jesus. Turn over just a couple pages to "King of Kings," and let's read that out loud as praise to Jesus. Here is some homework for you. This week use your Bible and hymnal to find places where you can read praises out loud to Jesus. If you need to, you can personalize the words to be your own praise to him. Many scripture verses and songs are an invitation, or are like commands to praise the Lord or Jesus, but by changing the wording a little you can make them into personal praise verses or songs. For example, find 1 Chronicles 16:25. It says, *For great is the LORD, and greatly to be praised. He also is to be feared above all gods.* You can make that be a prayer of praise to the LORD like this: *LORD, you are great, and greatly to be praised. You are to be feared above all gods.* That does not change the meaning, it just personalizes it for you to use in praising him.

"Now, you try it. You can use the concordance in the back of the Bible and look up words like: praise or worship or thanks, or the Lord, or Jesus, or an attribute of his that you would like to use. I'll give you a few minutes to find something. When you're ready with something you would like to share with the rest of us. Just stand up, and I'll bring this microphone over to you so everyone else can hear your praise. Tell us the scripture reference so we can all write it down."

Many people found verses to personalize and share. It was a lovely time of praise to the one and only ONE who deserves all praise, worship and thanksgiving.

"Now let's sing 'At the Name of Jesus,' again before we close the service."

Then he closed with prayer, and Maria introduced her two co-workers to him. They gave him their cards, and he took them into the office where he gave them the notes for the first meeting that had already happened last week plus a little booklet about water baptism so they would be ready for that meeting. Then he invited them to join the second meeting that would be on Wednesday at 7 PM, they wrote down the address and thanked him. Maria said, "I'm so glad you came today. Good-bye and I'll see you at work tomorrow."

Then Esther came up to tell Maria, "Ruth and I won't be walking with you and your friends today because I have a supper date with Tony. He *will* be there in the park to teach some more Spanish to Ted. And yes, I'll tell you all about it on Monday. See, you didn't even have to ask. I know you pretty well already!" They all laughed.

*****

Since it was a warm day, Mindy asked, "Dad, could we go ask Lora if she would have time and would like to go for a walk with us in the park right now?"

Inwardly he groaned, because he'd rather not go, but he agreed.

They went to where she was standing in the sanctuary and Mindy asked her the question. She answered, "That sounds like fun. I have walking shoes on today so where shall we meet, since we need to get our vehicles out of the church parking lot?"

Vern suggested, "How about the park by the river?"

"I like that one and I've heard that lots of flowers are blooming right now!" Lora exclaimed.

Mindy said, "Neat, I like the springtime. We'll see you there."

They followed her and parked behind her car. They got out of their cars and the path was wide enough for them to walk three abreast. Vern ended up in the middle, so he had to pay attention and add to the conversations. He ended up really enjoying the time they had together. Lora was an intelligent woman who was fun to be with and Mindy was enjoying herself also.

When they returned to the vehicles, Vern commented, "That was a lot of fun. Lora, would you be able to go with us for a short hike next Saturday after lunch if the weather permits? If it's too cold, we could go to a museum."

She answered, "Yes, either one of those ideas would be enjoyable."

"Good. If you'll give me your phone number, I'll call you Saturday morning about 10 AM so we can make final plans depending on the weather." Lora wrote her phone number on a piece of paper and handed it to Vern. He said, "Thank you."

Mindy added, "Have a good week at school. I'm looking forward to Saturday."

Then they all said, "Good-bye."

*****

Roy and Sherry and the twins went right over to the same park as last week to see if Cory would be there so they could follow up and visit, since they had no home address for the family. They had been glad to see them all in church again this Sunday, but didn't get a chance to talk to them. Yes, they were there, and Cory was out there playing extra hard as if to make up for all the time he had not been able to play. Joy and Hope ran to play with him and Roy and Sherry went to visit with his parents who were enjoying being able to watch their son living the normal life of a seven-year-old.

Roy greeted them and said, "We just wanted to check with you and see how things are going for you."

Cory's father answered, "Thank you, we were hoping to see you again. We're still overwhelmed with all that has happened: that God would be so good and powerful, that you would be willing to let him work through you to perform a miracle that we had never even imagined could be possible, that Jesus would save us and my parents too, that Cory could testify to so many of the children at school and they believed along with their families, that we are now in a very good church and a small group learning how to live this new life, and even that you cared enough to come back here and check on us. We thank and praise God for all the good results of his Good News."

Cory's mother continued, "We would like to keep on becoming acquainted and be friends with you, if you would like to, and I know Cory would enjoy being able to play with Hope and Joy."

Sherry responded, "I know that the twins and Roy and I would like that also. We're all part of God's family of believers, and it will be wonderful to be friends. Could we exchange addresses and phone numbers so we can keep in touch, and get together off and on to visit?" She nodded and they both wrote down the information on pieces of paper that they exchanged. Then they all sat back to watch the children play while they visited.

*****

When Jeff, Karen, Tomo and Ami met for their four by four ministry time, Sunday, right after church, Tomo mentioned, "Aneko arrived Wednesday evening, has gotten settled in, and she was happy that she got to go to her small group on Saturday, and come to church today."

Karen said, "I'm glad she had a safe trip, and it's wonderful to have her as a part of the family of God. She looks like such a sweet girl."

Ami smiled with pleasure as she agreed, "We sure think so! What are we planning to do today?"

Jeff answered, "Let's start with prayer and then we'll drive to a little park in the center of the city." So they all prayed together for the direction of the Holy Spirit and for him to work through them. Then they followed the Spencers to the park. There were a lot of people walking around in the park, enjoying the lovely weather. One in particular caught their attention. He was a young man walking with his parents, but trying to learn how to navigate with a white cane, so he was obviously blind, but had not been so for very long. The four by four group sat down on a bench to observe and to pray for clear leading.

Jeff said, "Tomo and Ami, since these people look like they're Japanese, from what I can see from back here, I think it would be best for you two go walk and talk with them. Just get acquainted with them and try to build up some rapport with them. Karen and I will walk behind you all and continue to pray. After you've built up rapport, if you feel that Jesus wants to use you as his hands to heal the young man, just do whatever Jesus tells you to do, and we'll be praying in agreement with you. If you need us to come help with something, just motion to us and we'll come."

"Okay," they said, and went to approach the three-some so they could introduce themselves. As they got closer to the people, and were able to see them from the front, Tomo got very excited and almost yelled, "Afta, is that really you? Or am I seeing things?" Then he ran and embraced his twin brother for a long time. "I've missed you so much, Afta. It's so good to see you and your wife, Hana. And this must be your son, Denji. How do you all happen to be in Pine City? Could we find a place where we can sit and you can tell me all about yourselves?"

The group went to sit on some benches where they learned the story. Afta said, "Tomo, it's very good to see you again, also. It's been too long. Our son, Denji, is a good boy, but he was out riding around with some friends when a drunk driver hit the car they were in. Denji was the only one injured in the accident, and was in a coma for several weeks in a special hospital in the big city just west of here. When he came to, he could not see anymore. It's been an awful shock for all of us, and I didn't call you because we were uncertain of the outcome. Denji's other injuries have healed now and he's gone through much therapy and is learning how to deal with his blindness. We came to this park from our hotel so he could practice with the cane and get more comfortable with it before we called you and made arrangements to come and visit with you before we go back home."

Tomo thanked Afta for sharing all that information, and then knowing how opposed he had been to everything Tomo had said about Jesus, Tomo went directly to his nephew. "Denji," said Tomo, "Ami and I are very sorry to hear about your terrible accident and injuries and blindness. We came to this park today to see if there would be anyone here who had a need we could pray about to Jesus, the Creator and Great Physician. He made your eyes in the first place, and he can make them work again. Would you be willing to have Ami and I place our hands on your head and ask Jesus to do that for you?"

"Yes, I would," Denji answered.

Ami stood up and walked over to him and they placed their hands on his head. "Jesus, we come to you in agreement and ask that you would restore Denji's sight. Denji, receive your sight in Jesus name." They kept their hands in place for a few more moments as they felt Jesus' power going through them to Denji. Then they told him he could open his eyes and look around.

He did that and shouted, "I can see again, even better than before! I don't even need glasses anymore! Wow! Thank you Uncle Tomo and Aunt Ami for praying for me."

"You're very welcome, and we're both glad Jesus would work through us, but Jesus is the one who healed you and you can thank _him_," explained Tomo. Meanwhile, Afta and Hana were watching with astonishment.

"I felt a strange sensation going through my head as your hands were on it. What was that?" Denji asked.

"That was the healing power of Jesus going through our hands and into your head as Jesus healed your eyes," Tomo answered.

"And now Jesus desires to do something even better for you and Afta and Hana."

"What could be better?" he asked incredulously.

"He desires to save you all from your sins, make you part of his family, and give you eternal life!"

"Could you explain that to me. I've never heard about things like that before," said Denji. At that statement, his parents looked ashamed, because they had decided not to tell their son about the things Tomo had shared with them.

"Of course, I'll be glad to explain all of that to you!" said Tomo. He and Ami sat down again and Tomo proceeded to tell his nephew everything he needed to know about the Gospel. He finished, "You see, Jesus loved you so much that he died in your place so your sins could be forgiven if you'll believe in him and accept him as your Savior." Looking at Afta, and Hana, and Denji, Tomo said, "If each of you three will do that, you can be sure that you're a part of God's family, and will have eternal life. Would you like to do that?"

All three said "Yes."

So Tomo led them in a prayer with them repeating after him. Afterward he said, "Now would be a very good time for you to thank Jesus for your healing and salvation, Denji."

"Jesus, thank you very much for giving me back my sight and for saving me and my parents!" exclaimed Denji. His parents joined in with their thanks and so did Ami and Tomo.

At that point, Tomo motioned for Jeff and Karen to come join them, so he could introduce all of them. They talked for a while, before Jeff and Karen left. And then Tomo and Ami invited Afta and his family to get their things from the hotel and stay the rest of their time in Pine City with them in their home. "Aneko is home and will be thrilled to see all of you. Do you know how to get to our house?" They nodded, and Ami continued, "We'll just go ahead home and get two rooms ready for your visit. Please stay as long as you can!"

*****

Tony was at Esther's apartment promptly at 5 PM for their supper date. He had been kicking himself every moment as he walked over there for even imagining that he could date such a fine woman with her own car and a very good job. He didn't even have a car to take her to supper in, let alone any place else! Who in the world would consider making his date walk to supper?

Nobody but himself! How could he have been so stupid? Well, it was too late now. He would just have to make the best of it. At least there was a nice restaurant within close walking distance. Besides, <u>this</u> <u>is</u> who he was, and if she didn't like it, so be it. He punched in the number for her room and she said she would be right down.

"Hi, Esther. You look lovely this evening," Tony greeted her and was glad to see that she had on walking shoes.

"Thank you, Tony," she replied. "You look very nice yourself."

After that very stilted exchange he offered her his arm and said, "Thank you. May I escort you to dinner, Esther?"

"I would be honored." And then in an effort to rescue them both, she said, "Las flores son bonitas." From there on, they spent the rest of their time conversing in Spanish and it was much better. They both were able to relax and take pleasure in their time together.

*****

Matt and Fiona went back over to the house after church. They prayed for God to show them anything else that needed to be changed and then combed through the blueprints to see if there was anything they had missed. They wanted everything to be added or changed before the building continued on Monday. It was so exciting! They could hardly believe all this was really happening, along with so many other blessings since Fiona had returned to Pine City! They spoke about each blessing together as a praise and thanksgiving offering to the LORD who had made all of them possible.

After that, they both went to see Walt and Betty and tell them about all the changes they had made in the floor plans, and even added a few more at Walt or Betty's suggestions.

Walt instructed, "Now, both of you go to your respective homes and get some rest. And Matt, I don't want to see you at the job site until 1:30, so you can get your own chores finished and rest some more. That way you'll be fresh to work the entire second shift. I don't want you getting sick over all this excitement!"

"Yes, Sir!" answered Matt as he saluted. They all waved and then Matt took Fiona to her house. They decided to wait until Wednesday morning to meet at the library to look at books with ideas they might like to include in their home.

Everywhere There's a Sunrise, Let's Tell The Good News!

*****

Chapter 20

Psalm 31:3b, ... *For your name's sake lead me and guide me.*

Monday

Maria knew better than to go to Esther's office first thing in the morning. Instead, she got busy working and looked forward to lunchtime when she could hear all about Esther's date with Tony.

She had enjoyed her walk with Julie very much the afternoon before, and was glad it was back to just the two of them. They had spent the time getting caught up on how their lives were going. She knew that Ted and Tony had also enjoyed their time together by the laughter she had heard from time to time.

Lunchtime finally came, and since it was nice outside they walked to and around in the park where Esther told her about supper with Tony. "It started out with both of us being very nervous, but when we started speaking in Spanish we both relaxed. We walked to that nice restaurant which is pretty close to where I live. The food was delicious, and we discussed a lot of topics while we ate. After that, he walked me home and I thanked him for a delicious meal and nice evening. He thanked me for being willing to walk to supper. I could tell he was embarrassed, so I tried to put him at ease about that issue. I don't know if he will call again."

Ruth prayed, "Father, we ask that your good and perfect will be done for both Esther and Tony."

Then Maria and Esther discussed husband and wife qualities they had read about in some good books their mothers had given them. They must have read the same books that Fiona had, because most of the qualities were the same as what she had been looking for in a man and trying to develop in herself.

Then Ruth told them some of her ideas about singleness. Most of them came right out of 1 Corinthians 7:7,8, and 25-35, and 38. "I'm just glad for myself that I don't have to think about it any longer. I know how frustrating it can get to not know what you're supposed to do. By the way, Maria, Jason is growing in his faith by leaps and bounds. Dad, Mom, and we are so proud of him. He seems very focused on learning everything he can about how to live a life worthy of his Savior. Please keep praying for him."

"I'll be glad to do that. Prayer is the very best thing any of us can do for somebody else," responded Maria.

At the end of the day, Maria stopped by the offices of her co-workers who were new believers, to ask them if they would like to go to lunch together again tomorrow. They both said they would. She decided that it would be a good idea to do that off and on so they could build up a closer friendship and they could ask her questions if they wanted to.

*****

The morning at the Suehiro home just continued the celebration that they had started as soon as their guests had arrived from the hotel yesterday afternoon. They had enjoyed much conversation catching up on the years they had been apart, and took pleasure in a delicious meal that they all worked together to fix for supper. Aneko had been thrilled to see her relatives, and was glad to learn that they planned to stay for several days.

Tomo and Ami had been able to answer many of the questions that came up from reading the little booklet they had given them for new believers. Afta said, "It looks like the first thing we need to do when we go back to our home, is to look for a church and small group we can belong to, so that we can keep learning. It would be nice if they would have one for Denji's age group also."

"That <u>would</u> be nice, but the group we are in has many different ages in it," explained Ami.

Aneko added, "The group I was able to join is for new believers and has couples of several different ages. I'm the only single in the group. But it coincides with my work hours at the restaurant. They all accepted me graciously, even though I joined the group two weeks after it had started."

Tomo continued, "The most important thing is to find a church and group that believes the same things that are talked about in the Bible, and in the little booklet, which is based on the Bible."

Hana commented, "There are a lot of different churches to choose from. How will we be able to find a good one?"

Aneko answered, "While we are at the restaurant working today you could use my laptop computer to look up churches in your city. Most churches have a web site, and if you click on 'About Us' and then on 'What we believe,' you'll be able to compare that with the list in the booklet. It should give you a good head start for when you go back home. They usually have a place that tells about their small groups also."

"Or," said Tomo, drawing out the word, "You all could just move to Pine City and attend church with us. They would put you in a group for new believers and you would be all set."

Afta laughed, "I knew you would find a way to try and talk us into moving here. In a way we would like to, but our jobs are there and Hana's parents are there also."

Tomo replied, "You're right. But I just <u>had</u> to try anyway. Let's all pray about it. Maybe her parents will accept Jesus also when they hear about the miracles of Denji's sight being restored and all three of you being saved. That would be a wonderful result of you going home, and I'm sure you have many other friends and other relatives who might also be willing to learn about Jesus. It <u>is</u> a great ministry opportunity for all of you. I think I was just being selfish."

Afta responded, "We can talk more often on the phone after we go back home. Now that we believe like you do, we have more in common and we can stay close."

"Let's do your very good idea," replied Tomo.

*****

Tony walked to work thinking back on his time with Esther yesterday. She had quickly put them at ease by changing over to Spanish, and it had not seemed to bother her to have to walk to the restaurant and back afterward. But that didn't mean they were meant for each other, or that he was even supposed to get married. He was no closer to an answer about that than he was before. All this thinking was keeping him from his usual Bible study and close fellowship with Jesus. This could <u>not</u> be a good thing.

As he arrived at the restaurant where he worked, he left all those thoughts outside and focused on his job, in order to continue to be the good worker and assistant manager they had hired him to be. He knew Jesus would want him to do his best. "Do everything as for Jesus," he repeated to himself.

*****

After school Lora talked to Beth about the walk she had enjoyed on Sunday with Vern and Mindy. Lora finished, "Mindy is still such a sweet girl, and her dad, Vern, actually relaxed and enjoyed the walk with us. He even suggested a hike or going to a museum for the coming Saturday afternoon depending on the weather. He said he would call to finalize plans on Saturday morning."

Beth responded, "Wow! I'm surprised. I hope that means that he's healing from his sorrow. I remember Mindy from her years here at the school. I'm glad you were able to have such an enjoyable walk. How do you think Mindy is doing?"

"I think she's doing very well. She thanked me again at the small group meeting for my help to her in third grade. Vern agreed that it really had helped her and also thanked me," replied Lora.

"Well, keep me posted on how things go. It sounds very interesting," stated Beth.

*****

During the Monday evening pastors' small group, the lead pastor again discussed the idea of building a second church and school like the one they already had, saying that Pine City was a large enough city that it would need not just one more but many like this to reach all the people in the city with the Gospel. The members all voted to pursue the idea without delay since the churches were all growing quickly right now. It was the most creative solution they could think of, and they felt like God had given them that idea. They could use the same blueprints for the sanctuary and school, but they needed to find property that would be appropriate. Also, they would need to accelerate the growth of the building fund.

In the meantime, they would place some of the newest groups of new believers into the churches with smaller numbers immediately so all pastors would have only two new believers groups meeting during the week. Don and Anita almost sighed audibly with relief! That would be a big help, and besides, then the sanctuary would not be getting full as quickly. When they had started sharing this building with 12 churches, very few of them thought they would ever reach the point of having their church's sanctuary filled. But, a number of them would be getting close, if they didn't move some of their new people out into the other churches. In the last few weeks, God's miracles had resulted in many people being saved, and most of them were becoming faithful attendees of the church services and small groups.

Everywhere There's a Sunrise, Let's Tell The Good News!

All the pastors had been told to bring their lists of people in the newest small groups and to decide which ones would be the best to put into other churches. After working on that for a while, they were given the names, phone numbers and addresses of the new meeting places so they could call the people in those groups, explain the reasons, and tell them where to meet instead of what they had said last week. All the pastors would be praying that the people would accept and like this change. It really would be for the best of all concerned in the long run.

*****

Tuesday

When Sherry arrived that morning, Anita sent the twins in to play with the others, and then she took time to tell Sherry about the decision of the pastors' small group. "They immediately put some of the most recent groups of new believers into churches with smaller numbers. As a result all the pastors would have no more than two new believers groups meeting during the week. Don and I were so relieved! Thank you for having the small group pray for us."

"I'm glad you told me about their good decision. It's a relief to me also to know that you won't have to facilitate four groups for the next two weeks," replied Sherry.

Then Anita requested, "Please call Jeff so he can tell the other members their prayers have been answered and we'll be able to keep up now. I'm very grateful for your willingness to clean the house again last week, so it would be ready for the Wednesday and Thursday meetings."

Sherry responded, "You're very welcome. I'm glad I was able to help you."

"Here's a pattern and material to make a new shirt for Timmy," Anita said.

Since the children were playing well in the next room, they also made plans for a birthday party for all the May birthdays in the daycare group. It would include Timmy, Mary, Hope and Joy. If they had the party on Thursday this week, it would fall on a day between those birthdays, and also not on either of the other two. It was very unusual for a daycare to have that many birthdays in one month.

During the day, Anita called many of the people in the two "school" groups for new believers and explained to them the reasons that they would be going to church in the same building, but at a different time. There would be different facilitators and they would meet at their house for the next small group meeting with the same group of people. Most of them were very understanding and agreed readily. A few weren't too happy, but Anita explained that the church met in the same building, just at a different time and with a different pastor, but it would be very much like the service they had attended Sunday. After her explanation, they were more amenable.

When Don got home from work, he fixed supper for them so they could eat as soon as the daycare children had gone home. After cleanup, he made some more phone calls to those who weren't home when Anita called them. They both took a break to go outside and play with their own children for a while. They felt a great relief that they would not have two more weeks with four new believers small groups. Instead they would only have two groups. Before the children's bedtime, they had managed to reach every family in those two big school small groups, and everyone had agreed.

*****

Clara was really enjoying her classes now that she didn't have to work full time in the evenings just to try and make ends meet. She liked going to the evening evangelism classes also, and was learning a lot. She had been able to add time to her personal Bible study time and enjoyed reading more hymns.

She was very thankful and used some of her extra time to praise and thank the Lord who had provided for her so abundantly, and helped her to not be so tired. Next she called Jane, "Thank you again for telling me that word of knowledge from Jesus. I'm able to take twice as many classes and that will cut the time to finish my nurse's training in half."

Jane replied, "You're most welcome. I'm always amazed and pleased when I can be used to help someone. I know that you're going to be a very good nurse and God will use you to minister to and bring many people into his Kingdom in the future. God bless you, Clara."

Following that conversation, Clara called Jeff and Karen and told them many of the same things.

*****

Everywhere There's a Sunrise, Let's Tell The Good News!

After supper, Ted, Julie, Larry, and Jane met again for their four by four ministry time at the shopping mall after supper. This time it would be up to Ted and Julie to look for and follow Jesus leading about people to serve. They all walked and prayed like last time and soon Ted noticed an older woman who was having a hard time carrying her shopping bags. She had just set them down on a bench and sat down beside them. He and Julie approached her, and talked for a time about the weather and beauty of spring. When he sensed that she had relaxed, he asked, "Could we help you carry your purchases to wherever you are going?"

"Oh, yes, please. I bought too much today and my arms are just not as strong as they used to be," she explained.

"Well, we would be happy to lend a hand," Julie responded. "Just let us pick up the bags, and you can lead the way with us walking on either side of you."

They walked and talked as they left the mall and went out in the parking lot to her car, where they loaded all the packages into the trunk, and then made sure she was settled inside ready to drive home. She put the window down and asked them, "Why would you take your time and energy to help an old woman?"

Ted hunkered down beside the window and answered, "Because we came here today especially looking for someone we could help for the sake of Jesus, the Messiah. He came to this earth almost 2000 years ago to serve the people he had created, and he's asked us to do the same thing, so people will know about his love for them. He loves you and wanted you to see some of that love in us."

"Well, I certainly did see love in what you did, and if this person, Jesus, loves me, old and useless as I am, then I would like to know him better," she said.

Julie suggested, "Look, there's a nice bench in the shade. Would you like to lock up your car again and sit there with us so we can tell you more about Jesus?" She nodded, got out and locked the car, and joined them on the bench.

"Are you Jewish?" she asked. "You mentioned the Messiah. I'm Jewish."

Julie prayed for more help and was glad they had gone to one of the Saturday Christ in the Passover services the week before Easter. She answered, "No we aren't Jewish, but we do believe in the Jewish Messiah."

Ted continued, "I would like to quote to you something that I memorized that was said by a Jewish man over 1900 years ago.

His name was Paul. It will explain to you who Jesus is and why we believe that he is the Jewish Messiah. *Paul stood up and motioned with his hand and said, "Men of Israel, and you who fear God, listen. The God of the people of Israel chose our fathers, and he made them great when they lived as strangers in Egypt. With his mighty arm he brought them out of Egypt. He put up with their behavior for forty years in the wilderness. When he had destroyed seven nations in the land of Canaan, he divided the land to them by lot. Then he gave them judges until Samuel the prophet. After that the people desired a king, and God gave them Saul,... of the tribe of Benjamin who ruled forty years. When God had removed Saul, he raised up David to be their king, saying, I have found David son of Jesse, a man after my own heart. He will fulfill all my will. From this man's descendants, God, according to his promise has raised unto Israel a Savior, Jesus. ... ... Men and brothers, children of Abraham and whoever else among you fears God: it is to you that this word of salvation has been sent. For those who lived in Jerusalem and their rulers, did not recognize Jesus or even the prophets, which are read every Sabbath day. But they fulfilled all that the prophets had said by condemning Jesus. And though they found no cause of death in Jesus, they desired that Pilate would have him executed. When they had fulfilled all that was written about him, they took him down from the tree and laid him in a tomb. But God raised him from the dead. And those who had come with him from Galilee to Jerusalem saw him many days. They are now Jesus' witnesses to the people. We declare to you the good news that the promise which was made to our fathers, has been fulfilled by God to us their children, because he raised Jesus up from the grave, as it is written in the second Psalm, "You are my Son, this day have I begotten you." The fact that God raised Jesus from the dead never to decay fulfills this: "I will give you the sure mercies of David." It is also stated in another Psalm, "You shall not let your Holy One see decay." For after David had served his own generation by doing the will of God, he fell asleep and was buried with his fathers, and his body decayed, but the one, Jesus, whom God raised from the dead did not see decay. Therefore I want you to know, that through this man, Jesus, the forgiveness of sins is preached to you. By him, everyone who believes, is justified from all the things, which you could not be justified from by the Law of Moses."* (Acts 13:16-39)

Everywhere There's a Sunrise, Let's Tell The Good News!

"Well, young man, that was very well spoken and most of it is Jewish history. I've heard about Jesus, and have been told that Jewish people cannot believe in him and still be Jewish. I've believed what they said all my life, but if the rest of what you said is true, then maybe I could. What prophecies were fulfilled?"

Julie answered, "Jesus was born in Bethlehem in the land of Judah as was prophesied in Micah 5:2, and was taken to Egypt to escape being murdered by king Herod, and then was called back to Israel after Herod's death as in Hosea 11:1. Jesus genealogy is found in Matthew chapter 1, and it clearly shows that he was the son of David, and all the way back to Abraham. While Jesus was on earth, he fulfilled the prophecy of Isaiah 61:1-2, by preaching the good news, and in chapter 35:5,6 where it says he would open the eyes of the blind and ears of the deaf, and heal the lame.

"And now I would like to read to you out of Isaiah chapter 53, which contains many of the things the people did to Jesus. *He was despised and rejected of men, a man of sorrows, and acquainted with grief. We hid our faces from him. He was despised and we did not esteem him. Surely he has born our grief and carried our sorrows, yet we saw him stricken, smitten of God and afflicted. But he was wounded for our transgressions; he was bruised for our iniquities; the punishment that brought us peace was upon him, and with his stripes we are healed. All we like sheep have gone astray; we have turned every one to his own way, and the LORD has laid on him the iniquity of us all. He was oppressed, and he was afflicted, yet he opened not his mouth. He was brought as a lamb to the slaughter, and as a sheep before her sheerer is dumb, so he opened not his mouth. He was taken from prison and from judgment, and who shall declare his generation? He was cut off out of the land of the living. For the transgression of my people he was stricken. He made his grave with the wicked and with the rich in his death. He had done no violence, neither was there any deceit in his mouth. Yet it pleased the LORD to bruise him. ... ... He shall bear their iniquities.* These are only a few of the prophecies that were made about Jesus, but if you listen to the way they crucified him you'll hear many of them fulfilled." Then Julie read to her from Matthew 27: various verses, and compared them to some of the verses in Psalm 22.

The lady did listen carefully and agreed, "Yes, I see what you mean. All the rabbis have told us to not listen to people who talk about Jesus, but you two young people know our history and our Scriptures and have proven to me from those, that this Jesus you tell me about really <u>was</u> the Messiah. I'm so sad that they did all those horrid things to him."

Ted concurred with her, "We are sad about that also, but remember that God allowed all of that to happen in order to fulfill all those prophecies and to make it possible for all people who will believe to be forgiven for all their sins, without having to offer animal sacrifices any longer. Also remember what I quoted earlier said that God raised Jesus from the dead. He lives, and was seen by those who had been his followers. Later he ascended to heaven where he lives at the right hand of God praying for people. He loved you and all people so much that he was willing to go through all those horrid things in order to make a way to forgive sins and justify people. All you have to do is believe in Jesus and what he did, and you will be justified. Jesus will be your Messiah and Savior and Friend. Would you like to do that?"

She looked uncertain and frightened, so Ted said, "Just think about it, and listen while I sing a song" Then he sang, "I Will Serve You." The song tells of Jesus dying on Calvary for heartaches and broken people, how he gives life to people who believe, and that Jesus' love is the reason we want serve him.

His soothing voice and the words of the song erased the fear and uncertainty from her face, and she answered, "Yes, I do very much desire to have Jesus be my Messiah and Savior and Friend." Then she surprised them by praying, "Jesus, I'm sorry for what my people did to you, but I thank you for being willing to go through all of that horror to make a way for people to be justified from all they could not be justified from by the law of Moses. I'm glad you didn't stay dead. I believe in you, Jesus, Messiah, and what you did, and I ask you for that justification. Please be my Messiah and Savior and Friend."

Julie put her arms around the lady and hugged her saying, "We are so glad that Jesus is now your Messiah also. You see, you <u>can</u> believe in Jesus and still be Jewish. In fact, you are even more Jewish now than before, because you believe in the real Jewish Messiah, Jesus. There are a lot of Jewish and other people who also believe like you do now!" The lady hugged her right back.

"At first I was afraid to believe in Jesus, because my family does not, and they'll be very upset with me. But if Jesus could go through all he did, because he loved me, then how could I do less than that? I will do just what your song said, and maybe some of them will eventually believe also," the lady said.

Ted agreed, "Yes, that's a good plan. We will pray for it to happen. We know of Jewish people who believe in Jesus and who attend a church and a small group for new believers. It might help you to meet them and learn more about Jesus." Handing a small book to her, he continued, "This little booklet will explain a lot of things to you, and if you would like to go to that church and small group, you could fill out this card and I'll deliver it to the pastor of that church who will call you to tell you where and when they meet."

"Oh, that would be wonderful. Thank you both so much for loving me. I'll fill this out right now." Then she gave the card to Ted and got up to go get in her car. "Thank you again," she said.

Julie responded, "It was our pleasure! May God go with you."

When she had driven away, Larry and Jane came over and they all had a praise session right there in the parking lot. God was adding to his church, and all of heaven was rejoicing too.

*****

Wednesday

After breakfast, Pam called Jeff and Karen turning on the speaker, so she and her parents could both hear. "Hi, Jeff and Karen. This is Pam. I called to let you know how things are going so far with the search for a church and small group for my parents."

"Hi, Pam," answered Jeff. "We're glad you called. Tell us all about it."

Pam, responded, "We spent a good part of the afternoon on Saturday after the miracles, thanking and praising Jesus, and then, we prayed for God to help us find just the right church and small group. We looked up a bunch of churches in this city on the web. We found a couple with beliefs much like Grace 'n' Faith, and one even told about having small groups. So we went to that one on Sunday, and we liked it. After the service we went to the information desk and asked about the small groups. They had many, including one for new believers, which had just started last week. We went to it last night and my parents were welcomed graciously."

Karen said, "Great news, it sounds like you won't have to look any further."

Jeff asked, "Do any of you have questions that we might be able to answer?"

Pam's father said, "Yes, the booklets arrived already in the morning mail. How did you do that so fast?"

"I had a set of them here at home and Karen packaged them up on Sunday morning and took them to the post office early Monday morning, asking for the fastest delivery. They did get there quickly!"

"Well, we'll start reading them, and call you if Pam can't answer our questions. She has a storehouse of knowledge in her brain from the years she spent going to church and small groups in Pine City. We're very proud of her and so thankful that she was willing to give up her job to come here and take care of me!" exclaimed her mother.

Her father added, "Could we pray together on the phone that God will give her a good job soon, so she can get on with her life?"

"Yes, that's an excellent idea. We'll continue in conversational prayer style, like we do in our small groups," said Jeff. "Father in heaven, you heard all we've said and we ask that your will be done about getting a job for Pam, in your best timing and in the best place for her."

Karen continued, "I agree with that prayer and ask that you will guide Pam as she begins to think about searching for a new job, and as she continues to answer her parents questions, and do whatever else you desire for her to do."

Pam added, "We've talked about having my parents friends over for an evening of visiting and testifying about what great things God has done for us as a family. Please guide in that decision."

Her mother continued, "Yes, please show us who to invite and then give us the right words to say."

Her father added, "We thank you again for the miracles in our lives, and ask that you will use what we say to convince others that they need Jesus, also."

Jeff closed with, "Thank you, Jesus, that these people desire to have others come to you for salvation and to give you the glory for all you've done. Please work it all out in accordance with your will. In Jesus precious name we all pray in agreement, Amen."

They all added their Amen's and said good-bye for now.

In the afternoon, Pam sent an e-mail to tell Julie about the phone call. Julie answered the e-mail right away after supper, thanking her for writing, and rejoicing in the way God was leading her and her parents. She closed with, "I'll be praying that God will give you the very best job. I know that he is very pleased with the way you continue to help your parents," Julie closed and clicked on "send."

*****

    That morning after they prayed together for additional guidance, Fiona and Matt went into the Public Library to look at books with ideas for "building your dream home." The librarian helped them locate the books and congratulated them on their engagement. They thanked her and got right to work looking at separate books, and writing down ideas and page numbers they could share with each other. They were both very organized with separate notebooks where they wrote down the name of each book, so they could find it again if need be. At the end of 45 minutes they whispered the ideas they had liked and put stars in the notebooks by the ones they were really fond of. Then they left everything where it was and told the librarian they would be back in about 20 minutes after taking a walk so they could talk for a while.
    Fiona asked, "How does it feel to be working on your own house with your co-workers?"
    "Almost too good to be true! I sometimes feel as if I'm dreaming all of this and I don't want to wake up and find out it's just a dream," he answered.
    "I could reach over and pinch you," she teased.
    He laughed uproariously and then said, "No, don't. I don't ever want to wake up. I'll just go on dreaming and enjoy every minute of it. Actually, I know in my head that all this is true, and <u>you</u> are the very best part of it all. It will just take a while to really penetrate the rest of me. As for the work at our house, I'm more than pleased with the way everyone works together. Since all but one of them are Christians now, everything seems to go so much better. We're in unity, and they're all so happy for us, it makes it seem like <u>more</u> than just another job building a house for someone. This is much more personal for all of us."
    "I'm glad. Being unified, and not envious makes all the difference," Fiona agreed. Shall we go back and look at another book apiece? It was nice of the librarian to find them for us."
    "Yes, let's go. Some of these ideas will have to wait until we're further along with the building, but it will be good to keep them in mind."
    So they returned to the books and kept writing down ideas that they would discuss as they walked back to Fiona's home. They

thanked the librarian and decided to check out two books apiece so they could continue looking and writing down ideas. As they walked home, they realized that today they had not found anything that would require structural changes in the house.

*****

Jane had practiced off and on all week in preparation for her first Bible Study and Bible Story groups. The middle school and high school students would come first since they started daily school an hour earlier than the elementary ones. Each meeting would last for 50 minutes, with the last 10 minutes spent for refreshments.

Ten students arrived about five minutes late and a couple more a few minutes later. Jane said, "Welcome to our first meeting. "My name is Mrs. Kelsey and I'm so glad you were able to come." As she spoke, she had been handing out name tags and markers so each could make his or her own name tag. "These will help me to be able to learn your names more quickly, and you can leave them here and use them the next few weeks, also. What are some of the things you would like to learn about the Bible?" she asked.

Nobody answered, so she resumed, "Well, here are some of the things you'll be learning: what the Bible is, who wrote it, why it's important, and how it can help us. Later we'll play some fun games to help us learn the names and order of books in the Bible and how to find them quickly. For this first meeting I'll show you a video that will give you a lot of information about the Bible. Then we can discuss what it said."

They watched the video attentively and then had a good discussion about it. By then it was time for refreshments and after that, they left their name tags with her, thanked her and she said she would see them next week. Jane was pleased with how it went.

In a few minutes the elementary students arrived. It was a larger group of about 15, and noisier. She had them make their own name tags also, and then started off with a flannel graph Bible story, which introduced some of the facts that were in the video the older children had watched. She asked them questions as she went along and could tell that they were paying attention by their answers. Next she taught them a song with actions about the Bible. They enjoyed singing it a couple times and then had their

Everywhere There's a Sunrise, Let's Tell The Good News!

refreshments. They thanked her, gave her their name tags and said they would be back next week. They looked like they had enjoyed the time, and she had also.

"Thank you, Lord, for your help. Please give them all the desire to continue coming so they can learn about you, and make the decision to believe in Jesus," Jane prayed.

*****

Don and Anita and their co-facilitators got ready for the second meeting of the new believers small group. They had decided to have this week's meeting at their house so Anita could put the children to bed at their regular time after they played for half an hour in their rooms. They decided to flip-flop the teachings and do the one on water baptism next week so it would be closer to the special baptismal service the Tuesday after next. He introduced Maria's co-workers as new members, and everyone wore name tags to help them learn names.

"Just like at school," commented Cory to his friends. All the people near them smiled.

Pastor Don prayed and then they sang the same songs and had the same teaching as the other small groups had in the meeting after their water baptism.

The next evening, the Thursday new believer's small group meeting at the Ross home went about the same as the night before except that there were no children or new members in it.

*****

Thursday

All the daycare children were excited about the big May birthday celebration since five of the children in the group were born in May. Three of them would be five years old, and the other two would be four years old. There would be no gifts exchanged, but they would play extra games that would be additional fun. Later they would have birthday cake and ice cream. The five birthday children wore birthday crowns that they could take home with them.

They all sang to each other that wonderful birthday song about feeling Jesus near every day of the year. It is so much more meaningful than the other birthday song.

Linda L. Linn

This celebration didn't take place on any of the daycare children's actual birthday. Each of them would have or already had a family celebration with their own families on the real birth date.

*****

For several mornings, Julie had been teaching about fossils in general, including the fossils of dinosaurs. It was a fascinating subject, and everything <u>she</u> had been taught in public education settings (like fossils were millions of years old), was completely different from what she was learning from this school's lesson plans and resources like creation.com. And <u>this</u> made so much more sense. Besides, it helped to provide evidence that the earth was created in six days just like the Bible said. It taught that fossils were formed as a product of the global flood during the lifetime of Noah, about 6,000 years ago.

She read the book called, "I Really, Really, Really, Like Fossils" to her class. Most fossils are found in sedimentary rocks and are formed when dead plants or animals are covered by sediments that settle out of the water. The sediments become rock by the pressure on them. The song by Buddy Davis, called "Billions of Dead Things," contains much of this information in a fun and interesting way. The children were quickly memorizing it.

Their task today was to write what they had learned about fossils in their own words so that they could share it with anyone who would listen as an introduction to telling the Good News. If people would listen to this much, without becoming argumentative, they might be interested in listening to a presentation of the Gospel. The children decided that a good way to start might be to sing that song to the people. So they practiced singing it a lot.

A student asked, "Mrs. Blake, what are some places or situations where we might use this song and the speech we're going to write?"

"That's a good question," she answered. "Let's brainstorm some ideas and I'll write them on the board." They came up with the following ideas: in the public schools, like in science or other classes, or on the playground, or in the lunchroom or hallway (but don't sing), walking to and from public school with friends, visiting museums (but don't sing), visiting national parks or memorials or other places that have fossils, especially if a ranger or guide has given a speech about them. "It would be best to wait until he or she has finished the presentation and then ask a question about fossils at the end, since it's not polite to interrupt somebody's presentation."

They all copied these ideas into their notebooks called, "Proofs of Creation." They would title the talk they would give, "Fossils." On the other side of the chalkboard, were all the facts they had learned about fossils the past few days. Mrs. Blake said, "Let's put numbers by each fact to show the order in which it happened." So they did that, and it was a good review. "Now, copy all these facts in numerical order in your notebooks," she instructed. When they had finished copying the facts, she had them get up and do some exercises.

"Next, use each fact, but put it in your own words to write a report or talk you can give in one of the situations we listed earlier. Be sure to include how you will tell them the Good News. Write it in a way that will show you are humble but enthusiastic. Write it first on a piece of tablet paper. This is called a rough draft. Get as much done as you can in the next 20 minutes. I'll help with spelling if you need it. Tomorrow and next week we'll finish them and proofread and edit them.

"A fourth or fifth grade partner will be here on Wednesday next week to help with the final editing. When your talks are finished and fixed, you'll copy them into your notebooks. Then just like you are memorizing the song, you'll memorize your talk so that you'll be ready when an opportunity comes to share it. After you've memorized it, you'll get to practice it here in the classroom with each other," she told them.

*****

While Ted and Larry were at the church preparing music, Jane told Julie about the meetings with the children on Wednesday afternoon, and they prayed together that the children would continue to come and that they would be drawn to Jesus for salvation.

"It's amazing to think that none of those children know as much about the Bible as the children in the Grace 'n' Faith school know by the time they get to second grade. I'm so glad you're willing and able to help them learn," commented Julie.

"It _is_ good, and I enjoyed it after I got over being nervous. I think I've talked two other women into joining the ranks. I called them yesterday again and told them how it went. We went together over to the church to get materials for their first meetings and my next ones," responded Jane.

"Wonderful!" exclaimed Julie. "Keep up the good work. I've caught up with all my mending, and I would like to make a copy of your beautiful calligraphy poster of God's and Jesus' names so that I can transfer it to a piece of material and embroider it."

Jane commented, "That project might take years to complete, but it would be beautiful. How would it be if you bring the material you wish to use here and I'll write all the words on it instead of you trying to copy them? I've tried doing things like that before, and it's hard to keep the original and the one over it lined up correctly."

"You'd do that for me?" asked Julie incredulously.

"Of course. I like doing calligraphy," she answered.

"Thank you. That would be great. I'm sure the finished project would look much better that way. I'll drop it off tomorrow on my way home from school," Julie said.

*****

Friday

Fiona and her parents prayed together Friday right after breakfast, "Heavenly Father please keep my parents safe as they drive to Riley's college graduation and as they bring him back home."

Patrick continued, "Yes, and please keep our Fiona safe as she's here alone, coming home from work and then helping to host the small group tomorrow at the school lunchroom."

Glenda added, "Thank you that Patrick can work his regular hours and then we can still drive all the way there in the daylight. Thank you that Riley has made it to this milestone."

"Thank you also that we'll be able to drive all the way home in the daylight Saturday and be here for church on Sunday," said Patrick.

Fiona continued, "Please help Riley as he begins to look for a job next week. It would be very nice if he could find just the right job here in Pine City. May your will be done about that." Then they all said, "Amen."

Afterward Fiona commented, "I'm glad I called Riley yesterday and he agreed he would like to get acquainted with Matt during a supper at our house some Sunday evening."

Everywhere There's a Sunrise, Let's Tell The Good News!
*****

Tony took an early bus so he would be sure to be on time at the shopping mall. He was fifteen minutes ahead of their planned 10 AM time, so he sat down on a bench outside to wait. He used the time to pray about their ministry time, ask God's blessing on Matt and Fiona as their relationship progressed, and then he asked what he should do about Esther. He had not been at peace ever since he had asked her out and had felt like such a brainless person for even thinking he could date anyone without having a car, plus all the usual spending money that went along with dating. None of that agreed with the lifestyle he had selected for himself, choosing simplicity as the best way he could serve his Lord. He could not ask anyone, especially Esther to step down to his level of living. She was from a very wealthy family! Maria had some of the same values as he did, but she also had a car and a good job. Her hours didn't mesh any better than his and Esther's did. How could he have ever thought it would be a good idea to get to know either one of them?

His thinking was growing stronger and stronger, that he should just remain single and be available to do whatever God wanted him to do, without trying to develop a relationship with any female. Here I am, Lord, please use me in the work of your Kingdom, and keep me focused on you instead of wanting a girlfriend. Make me content again with the simple lifestyle I chose in order to be ready to do your bidding.

He was so involved in his thinking and prayers that he didn't see Matt and Fiona until they were almost next to him. But he greeted them without showing his surprise, inviting them to sit and pray together before they went into the mall. After that they went inside and started strolling and praying for the people they saw, asking Jesus to guide them by his Spirit in them as to what they should do. They saw many interesting people since it was pretty busy for a Friday morning.

After a while they sat down on a bench inside to watch. There was a man in the corner with a temporary booth set up. It was very difficult to see what he was doing. Pretty soon Tony said, "I feel that Jesus wants me to go over there, introduce myself and get acquainted."

Matt responded, "Go ahead, we'll stay here and pray for you. Motion for us to come, if you want us to join you there."

So Tony walked over to the booth and said, "Hi, my name is Tony Valdez, and I just came over to meet you and see what you're doing."

The man smiled and introduced himself in very broken English. Then he continued speaking in fluent Spanish, explaining to Tony what he was doing. He said that Jesus had told him to go set up his booth in the shopping mall this morning, because he was going to send a Spanish speaking man who also knew English to help him continue in this ministry that he had been trying to do on his own for about a month.

When he finished, Tony told him he had some friends who would also like to meet him, so he motioned to Matt and Fiona to come on over. Tony introduced the three people and gave a quick summary of what the man was doing. "He usually sets his booth up in a park or in an outside walking mall, and then he tells Bible stories and the Good News to any children who will listen. He uses flannel graph stories and big story books. He wants to also have someone with him who can tell the stories in English, because many times there are children who speak only English. He works the same hours I do, but in a different restaurant, and goes to church #3, he said we could have this be our two by two ministry, except that we would do it more often than once a week. He hasn't found anyone in his small group who could help him."

"That sounds like a great opportunity for you, Tony. What do you think about it?" asked Matt.

"If it would be acceptable to you and Fiona to go two by two now that you are engaged, I think Jesus would like me to join this man in his ministry," Tony answered.

Fiona commented, "It sounds like Jesus arranged this meeting for the two of you so you could work together for him, and I think it's great."

The man motioned for Tony to listen to him in Spanish, and then Tony translated, "He said that he heard the word engaged and had seen that we came here today as a three by three group. He said that it would not be appropriate for you to go two by two until after you are married, and until that time, you should do whatever you need to do to prepare for your wedding. But if you are 'dating' in public places until then, you could still be ready to minister whenever Jesus tells you to do something for him."

Matt nodded and prayed, "Thank you, Jesus, for your leading, and for guiding all of us in this situation. We will all do as you have instructed, and we pray for your blessing on these two men as they minister to the children for you."

Tony translated that to the man who smiled and shook their hands. Tony stayed there, and Matt took Fiona home.

Tony was thrilled to have more than just a once a week two by two ministry. He had extra time in the mornings because of the way he chose to live. He told the man he could work with him two or three times a week. On Saturday afternoons, they could focus more on elementary school age children. They talked about the possibilities and made plans to go to a popular park tomorrow, Saturday afternoon. He could even ride his bicycle to the park and lock it to the back of the booth while they were telling stories. Tony went home with a couple of stories that he could practice so he would be ready by tomorrow afternoon.

*****

This Friday, Julie asked the other teacher to bring her lunch into her classroom. They talked about this and that, and then the teacher told Julie, "My husband's job is being transferred out of state and we need to move in two weeks. I'm just sick about it. That makes two teachers, and both third grade ones, who could not honor their contracts this year, and it's not even their fault. It's so unfair to the children too."

Julie responded, "Oh. That is so sad. Let's pray that God will work it all out for the best of all concerned."

She replied, "Yes, let's do that." So they spent the rest of their lunchtime praying about this need.

When the lunchtime was over, both teachers went and welcomed their students back from lunch and continued with a lively afternoon of learning. Kippy was ready to listen and respond to the things the children shared. One of the girls said, "It's getting warmer and warmer outside, Kippy. You would probably be too hot if you came out there with all your pretty fur."

"Thank you for the compliment, and I agree with you. I much prefer to be right here in this comfortable classroom where I get to listen and talk with such nice students," he replied.

Another girl asked, "Do you ever get tired of sleeping so much?"

Kippy answered, "No, you see, <u>that</u> is the way God made koalas, and when God makes an animal or a person in a certain way he also helps them be content with the way they were made, that is, if they don't complain about it."

They all laughed and someone thanked him for the reminder to not complain. Then they all stood up and sang the song "Why Complain?"

The rest of the afternoon went in its usual fast-paced way, and soon it was time for them to go home. After dismissing her students and straightening up the room, Julie gathered her things and stopped by the principal's office.

"Beth, what do you know about the teacher next door to me?" asked Julie.

She answered, "Her husband's job is being transferred out of state and they need to move in two weeks."

Julie said, "She told me about it as we ate lunch together today. Have you heard from Pam Green lately?"

"Not for more than a week," Beth answered. "The last e-mail she sent sounded like she was very discouraged."

Julie agreed, "I know she has been. But then on Saturday, … " and Julie told her all that had happened Saturday and Wednesday. "Is there any chance that Pam could come back here and take over the position of the other teacher who has to leave?"

"Wow!" exclaimed Beth. "Thank you Lord! That would be perfect. The timing is just right also. Isn't God amazing? When it seems like everything is going wrong, he comes in with the best solutions. Yes, I'll call her right now and turn the speaker on so you can hear what she says."

So she dialed the number and Pam answered, "Hello, this is the Green residence."

"Hello, Pam, this is Beth Davis at Grace 'n' Faith School. I just learned from Julie Blake about the miracles God has performed for your parents, and wanted to tell you how thrilled I am for all of you," said Beth.

"Thank you very much. We all praise God for everything he has done," replied Pam.

"Now, I have some news for you, and an offer which I hope will work into your plans." Then she told her about the other teacher and how it makes an opening for Pam to return and teach in third grade at this school, but it would be with a different class than she had before.

Almost in shock, Pam managed to answer, "Oh, Beth, I can't begin to tell you how happy that will make me! Jeff and Karen and my parents and I all prayed in agreement that God's will be done about getting a job for me, in his best timing and in the best place for me, and I know Julie added hers later. And right now, he already has answered. I'm overwhelmed, and so grateful. Yes, Yes, Yes! What time do you need me to be there?"

Beth laughed, "I love your enthusiasm, and couldn't be more pleased than to have you teaching here again. If you would like to spend the day in the classroom like Julie did with you, on the other teacher's last day here, then you would need to be here, say Wednesday of the second week from now, with your belongings to get settled into an apartment and then spend Friday in the classroom. You would start teaching the following Monday, right next door to Julie, who is here listening, and she's just about jumping up and down with joy for you."

Pam almost shouted, "Oh, Julie, I can hardly wait to see you and everybody else there! I'll finish helping my parents here like Jeff suggested and then be on my way back to Pine City. I've really missed you all. My parents are here listening to this whole conversation also, and they look just as elated as I feel. They are being so encouraging. God is so good! He knew all along what would happen, and I've learned so much."

"I'm so delighted for you, Pam, and for the school, and for me, too!" exclaimed Julie. Next she asked, "Do you want to call Jeff and Karen, or would you rather have me share this as a praise in our small group tomorrow morning."

She replied, "Let's do both. I'll call them first thing tomorrow morning because I want to thank them personally for all their prayers and support and you can share it with rest of the group also. I wonder if I could join your group when I get there. I'll ask Jeff and Karen. It's been great being an absentee member and I know it would be even better to be present. And thank you, Julie, for all your wonderful caring and e-mails and prayers."

"You're most welcome! I look forward to seeing you soon, and now I suppose we should let Beth go home," Julie suggested.

"I'm glad I got to listen to the two of you," responded Beth. "It sounds like you two have developed a precious friendship through all that has happened in the last few weeks. I'll look forward to seeing you soon, also, Pam. God bless you."

Then they all said good-bye and Julie couldn't help but give Beth a hug, which was gladly returned.

*****

Linda L. Linn
Chapter 21

Psalms 73: 24, *You shall guide me with your counsel, and afterward, receive me into glory.*

Saturday

"I'm so excited about Pam coming back to Pine City in a couple of weeks, and I get to tell her praise in the small group this morning!" Julie said to Ted. "I know, I already told you all about it all when I got home last night, but it's all working out in such an unbelievable way, that I just can't stop thinking about it."

"I agree, Honey. And I think God used you to help bring parts of it to fruition. You never would have known about the other teacher leaving if you hadn't reached out to make friends with her. And you would not have known about Pam needing extra prayer and instructions from Jesus through Jeff, if you hadn't been trying to keep in touch with her by e-mail. Then you had the courage to go talk to the principal about the possibility of Pam filling that vacancy, and she was glad you did. I'm so thankful to have you for my wife, and that I get to see God working things out for you and then for others that you come in contact with in your day to day life. Of course, God is the **amazing** ONE, but I'm delighted that you're available for him to work through," finished Ted.

"I never thought about it like that. Like I'll paraphrase Romans 8:28, God worked all these things together for good because we love God and have been called according to his purpose. Plus he included several miracles in the mix. And he is the only one who deserves the praise for all that has happened. I'm glad he could use me for some of it though," said Julie.

"We get to praise him with Larry and Jane about the Jewish lady who accepted Jesus as her Messiah at the mall on Tuesday, when we go to the small group also. It's a great privilege to have the God of the universe working through us," added Ted. He started singing the chorus of "Channels Only," and Julie joined right in.

When they got to the small group meeting in the school lunchroom that morning, they were surprised to have three visitors, and it was no problem figuring out who they were, since Tomo and his brother were identical twins. Tomo introduced them and then, as the first praise, Tomo, Ami, Afta and Hana let Denji tell what had happened to him. He gave all the praise to Jesus for bringing him through the accident, healing the other injuries and restoring his sight, plus saving him and his parents, and re-establishing the relationship with his uncle and aunt and cousin, Aneko.

Everyone listened in amazement to the other praises about the results of the Gospel that had happened through other people that week, like Pam's mother being healed, and both parents becoming believers. Added to those was the phenomenal wedding present given to Matt and Fiona, Jane's groups off to a good start, Tony's new ministry, and then Ted and Julie were able to share their praises humbly, also, and give all the glory to God. At the second small group meeting, Julie had started writing down all the praises in her notebook. It was good to be able to look back and see all the things God had done just in this small group and know that he was active in all the others in town also. They had a long, loud praise session when the last person had shared.

"I have an announcement," Jeff said. Julie praised the Lord about Pam Green moving back to Pine City to teach in a different third grade class in the church school in a week and a half. Pam asked if she could join our group when she gets here, and I said, 'Of course!'" That caused some more clapping and praise. "Are there any other announcements?"

Nobody else had one, so Karen asked, "Who would like to host our small group for next Saturday?"

Julie looked at Ted and he nodded so they volunteered.

They sang "Channels Only," 2 Corinthians 4:7 and John 4:10; "Great is the Lord," Psalm 145:3; "All Glory to Jesus," Philippians 2:9,10; and "Only One Life," Matthew 10:39b.

"Our teaching today is about the greatness of our God as it says in Psalm 145:3: *Great is the LORD, and greatly to be praised, his greatness is unsearchable.* Then in Philippians 2:9,10, it says, *God highly exalted Jesus and gave him a name which is above every name, that at the name of Jesus, every knee should bow, of things in heaven, and things in earth, and things under the earth, and that every tongue should confess that Jesus Christ is Lord, to the glory of God the Father.* I'm glad we serve such a great God. Think for a minute about the gods that other people serve. There is no comparison!"

Jeff had everyone look up 2 Corinthians 4:7 and follow along as he read: *We have this treasure in earthen vessels that the excellency of the power may be of God and not of us.* "As all of you were sharing your praises today, I know that God was very pleased that you gave all the glory and praise to him because he had worked through you. We all know that we are nothing without him working through us. We're channels through which his living water can flow to others. I can see that all of you understand that idea very well.

"Matthew 10:39b tells us that losing our lives for Jesus sake actually results in us finding it. Think back over your lives and see if you can find an example of this in your life. Now let's read the words of our last song, 'Only One Life,' again. In your notebooks write down the parts of your body, and other parts of your life, that are mentioned. Then notice how the author gives those things to Jesus to be used to bring others the gospel, and live only for Jesus. It might sound like a big loss of our own life, but really, as you do this for him, you'll see how he enriches your life by the things you do in his name to serve others and bring the lost into the Kingdom of God.

"If you think back through our praises for today, I think you'll see how the lives of our members have demonstrated how this concept works." Everyone nodded and then Jeff started the conversational prayer time with, "Jesus, I ask you to continue to help us as we live our lives for you, and then give you all the glory for everything you accomplish through us."

Larry continued, "Remind us that the time is short, the harvest is ripe, and we ask that you will send us and many other laborers out into the fields to work for you."

Jane added, "Make that especially true for the harvest of the young people and children in Pine City."

Tomo prayed, "Thank you that Yoshi is coming this afternoon to visit for the weekend. Please help all of us in our house to let you work and love him through us."

Ami added, "Yes, please draw him to you. May our lives be a light and be channels you work through to bring him to belief in you, Jesus."

"Please use me and my parents to help convince Yoshi of his need for you," prayed Denji.

"Yes, Father, you know that everyone here agrees with these prayers for Yoshi," added Matt.

Julie turned on her recorder and prayed, "We thank you so much, Father, that you've worked out this situation for Pam and her parents for good, even though it all was so hard in the process."

Fiona agreed, "Yes, and thank you for all the things she learned, and that she gets to come back to Pine City to teach again in the church school."

Ted added "I agree with that, and we're glad that Pam will no longer be an absentee member after next week."

Karen continued, "Please help her as she assists her parents with the gathering of their friends so they can witness to them about what Jesus did for them."

"Use these miracles to be the catalyst that will bring many of them into your Kingdom," agreed Sherry. "And thank you for working out a way for each pastor to have no more than two new believers small group meetings a week."

Roy prayed, "Thank you, Jesus for bringing Tony and this other man together so they can minister to some of the children in Pine City. Have the children listen and understand. Draw them to yourself."

Tony added, "I agree, and please help me to improve my English so they will listen. Use me today at the park."

Clara continued, "Please help Tony to realize that his English isn't that bad, and that reading these stories will help his English improve the way he wants it to be."

Matt agreed, "I like listening to Tony. His use of English has already improved just in the short time this group has been meeting. Please give him peace about that."

Then Fiona prayed, "Please bless my brother as he's graduating from college today and my parents as they're attending the graduation. Keep all of them safe as they drive home to Pine City from his college. Now please bless these refreshments to our bodies and our bodies to your service, in Jesus name, -- "

They all said, "AMEN." Then everyone gathered around the tables and enjoyed the fresh fruits Fiona and Matt had brought. The fruits of many varieties were so juicy and refreshing that they made separate drinks unnecessary. The tables were beautifully decorated with flowers from the O'Connor's house and yard.

Everybody enjoyed the fruit and time of fellowship. It had been another very good small group meeting.

Fiona and Matt of course, stayed to clean up the lunchroom and put it back the way they had found it. Then he helped her take all the leftovers and flowers back to her house. She had used some of the smaller potted plants so as not to cut any flowers for just the two hours in the lunchroom.

Jeff and Karen told Tomo and Ami they would be praying for them as Yoshi's visit would take the place of going out together today for their four by four ministry time, and that Jeff and Karen would go out on their own.

*****

Roy and Sherry went to pick up the twins at the Ross home and were surprised when Anita answered the door, instead of Mindy! "Oh no!" exclaimed Sherry. "It never entered my mind that you would be home, since you only had two small groups this week and none on Saturday. How could I have been so thoughtless? Please forgive me. We'll try to figure out another babysitter for Saturday mornings."

Don had come up behind Anita and now they were both laughing so hard that they couldn't speak. Sherry got very quiet and just stood there looking puzzled.

Anita finally got control of her laughter and explained, "There's nothing to forgive. We just got home ourselves. Mindy enjoys caring for the four of these children so much that she still wanted to keep coming on Saturdays. So Don and I decided that it would be a good time for us to go on a 'date,' and since we haven't had one of those in years, we really enjoyed it. Maybe on some of the Saturdays, we'll go out for our own two by two ministry time, since it would be easier that way than with the children. Anyway, you don't need to apologize or find another babysitter."

Don said, "We apologize instead, that we didn't tell you in advance and that you were distressed when you got here."

"I forgive you, and I'm very relieved," replied Sherry. "Your idea sounds like a great one. I'm so pleased that Hope and Joy get to have such fun on Saturday mornings with Timmy, Mary and Mindy. I can hear them outside right now and I feel so blessed."

Roy continued, "We miss you at our small group! It is going very well and I hope you get to talk to Jeff and Karen so they can tell you all the great news that we get to hear every Saturday."

The children came inside with Mindy right then and Sherry asked her, "Have they napped yet?"

"Not today. We were having a jolly time and never even thought about it," explained Mindy.

"Fine, I just wanted to know what to plan for when we go home," Sherry clarified. "Thank you for taking such good care of the children and helping them to enjoy themselves so much."

"You're welcome. It really *is* my pleasure. I can't think of a more fun way to spend my Saturday mornings, and I really mean that!" stated Mindy.

Roy said, "Then we're very glad that it benefits all of us so well. Here's the money for our part for today."

"See? I even get paid for having such fun!" she exclaimed.

The twins came up to her right then and said in unison, "Thank you Mindy, for all the fun."

"You're welcome." Then she said to Roy and Sherry in her grown-up way, "And *that* is even better pay than money!"

"We agree! And now we'll go home for lunch and naps before we go to the grocery store to shop and do our two by two ministry for this week," said Sherry.

*****

Saturday morning Vern called Lora and they decided that the weather was nice enough for a hike that afternoon. He asked for her address and they picked her up after lunch.

"Hi, Vern and Mindy," greeted Lora. "I'm so glad the weather is cooperating. A short hike will be just perfect for this afternoon."

"I think so too," replied Mindy. "Where will we go today, Dad?"

"There's a nice little lake in the foothills not too far from here and even if it's cooler because of the elevation gain, we should all be warm enough since we have jackets with us," he answered.

They talked as Vern drove toward the lake. "I can see that we all agree about being prepared when we go hiking," Lora said.

Mindy agreed, "Dad told me he learned about that in boy scouts, and told me about how important it is to always be prepared and stay safe especially when we're hiking. It's more fun that way too."

"That was very well said, Mindy," Vern praised her. "I used to help lead a boy scout troop besides being in one as a boy. They do teach a lot of valuable lessons."

Other topics were discussed along the way, and then they parked near the lake.

"Oh, this is a delightful place. Spring has even reached this altitude," Lora mentioned as they started along the path around the lake. "The grass has turned green and a few wild flowers are already blooming."

"Yes, and look!" Vern exclaimed. "The goslings have just hatched are following their mother to the water."

"Oh yes, I see them! I'm glad I brought a camera," said Mindy as she took pictures of the geese, the lake and of her dad and Lora. It turned out to be one of the happiest afternoons she could remember in a long time.

*****

When all the Suehiros got home that morning from their small group meetings, Yoshi was already there. He had left earlier than he had planned, and his drive had gone faster than usual, so he had come in, gotten settled in his room which had twin beds, and had rested for a while, wondering what it might be like to share his room with his cousin. He was a bit nervous about a reunion with his uncle, aunt and cousin again because it had been so many years since he had seen them. Then too, he was a quiet, shy person, just like his name meant in Japanese.

Just before they arrived he was almost wishing he had not come. But seeing his parents helped him to relax again. They came in and welcomed him home just like they always did. Afta and Hana were nicer than he had remembered the last time he had seen them, and Denji had grown up a lot. And then his older sister, Aneko, got home from her small group meeting and he knew everything would be all right. They had always been very close, and she could sense how he was feeling.

Aneko asked him, "How was your drive today?"

"It went very well, and the scenery was even prettier than I remembered. There's still a lot of snow on the mountains and they show up very well from the highway when I drive this direction," he answered.

"I know! Those mountains are part of the reason I decided to move back to Pine City. I had really missed them," she said.

Tomo suggested, "Shall we all go into the living room and get comfortable as we continue our visiting?"

Aneko answered, "Yes, let's! Come on Yoshi, I'll race you to our favorite chair!"

"No fair!" exclaimed Yoshi, seeing her run right to it while he had to look for the chair. "It's been moved since last time I was here!"

"You're right, Yoshi. That wasn't fair of me, so please come here and sit down. I'll sit in the one right next to you," said Aneko, surprising Yoshi by not gloating over winning like she used to do.

"Thank you, Aneko. That's very nice of you," he said.

She responded, "You're welcome."

Then Yoshi requested, "Denji, Mom told me on the phone a little about your accident and the other things that happened, but I would like to hear the whole story from you if you don't mind."

"Certainly. I'll be glad to tell you all about it," replied Denji, and while the others prayed, he proceeded to describe everything he had experienced, including how he had felt in the hospital, especially when he had found out that he was blind. "For many days I was convinced that I didn't want to live since I could not see any longer. I had a lot of therapy and it helped me work through that terrible time, so I became determined to do the best I could. They started teaching me Braille, and it was like going back to elementary school to learn all over how to read and write.

"Also I was starting to learn how to walk places with a white cane so I could be somewhat independent. That's what your dad and mom saw me practicing in a park here in town so I could get proficient with it before we called and came to visit. AND that's where JESUS came and restored my sight by using your dad and mom's hands on my head while they prayed and commanded me in Jesus name to receive my sight. When they told me I could open my eyes, I could SEE even better than before the accident. I no longer even need to wear glasses!"

Yoshi stated, "I would have a very hard time believing that you were telling the truth if it weren't for my parents and your parents both sitting here nodding in agreement. I have read in the Bible about Jesus healing blind people while he lived here on Earth almost 2000 years ago, and I guess that is a fact of history. But I had no idea things like that could happen during the present time!"

"But the best part is still to come," inserted Denji. "Uncle Tomo told me that Jesus wanted to do something even better than just restoring my sight, and I asked him, 'What could be better?' He said, 'He desires to save you all from your sins, make you part of his family, and give you eternal life!' I had never heard of anything like that before." At that point, he related everything Tomo had told him about the Gospel. "Then he had us repeat a prayer after him, and Jesus saved all three of us and made us a part of his family and we now have eternal life! I agree with him that that really is better. Now I have salvation plus my sight, and I couldn't be happier! Is there any reason you cannot join us in this wonderful salvation, Yoshi?"

Silence hung heavy for a few moments while Yoshi was thinking, and all his relatives were still praying silently. Then Yoshi answered, "No, there's no reason. I've been stupid for waiting this long, after all that Dad and Mom have told me. I should have done this years ago." He got up from his chair and went to kneel in front of his parents and asked, "Would you please help me pray that prayer you told me about before, so that Jesus can be my Savior also?"

Tomo and Ami both answered, "Of course!" Then they did just that, and now everyone in the room was a part of the big family of God, besides being part of an earthly family who all believed in Jesus. What wonderful rejoicing followed!

Yoshi stated, "Now, I can see what you meant when you tried to tell me how wonderful this is. I've never felt such peace and joy before in my life! Denji, thank you very much for telling me all about what happened to you."

He replied, "You're very welcome and I'm very glad that you now believe in Jesus too!"

Everybody agreed, and thanked and praised God some more, and then Ami told Yoshi about all of heaven rejoicing when someone becomes a new believer.

"Wow! That's amazing. I know I have a lot to learn now, so where's the best place for me to start?" inquired Yoshi.

Aneko stood up and said, "I'll let you borrow the little booklet the pastor gave me right after I believed. Then you can get one of your own right after church tomorrow, when you meet the pastor of our church." Then she ran to her room, came right back with it, and handed it to Yoshi. "Dad and Mom can answer your questions, if you have any."

*****

The fourth Sunday in May

Matt had called Ben and made arrangements to show him the progress of one week with both crews working. It definitely was moving fast now, and Ben was suitably impressed. Then they spent the morning working together to see what they could add to that progress. They accomplished a lot by lunchtime and on this occasion Ben took Matt home with him to eat lunch with his family, because he had invited him the night before.

Matt enjoyed his time with the Clay family. Of course they all congratulated him on his engagement to Fiona. "Have you set a date yet?" asked Ernest.

"No." answered Matt. "I think we'll need a better idea of when the house will be finished before we set a date, since completing it is a wedding gift from my boss. He wants it to be completed so we can move in right after we're married."

"Wow, that's a BIG wedding present!" exclaimed Amelia.

Matt replied, "I know. I could hardly believe it, when he told me." Then he explained Walt's reasons.

Connie said, "Wonderful, we're so pleased for you. They must have been saving for many years and had better jobs than we've had."

"Right. We could never give a gift like that to even one, let alone two children!" exclaimed Ernest.

Then to get out of the spotlight, Matt asked, "What did you like about the church service last week?"

Ben answered, "I liked the verses people looked up and turned into personalized praises to the LORD."

Connie added, "I liked the songs we sang, because they were all about praise to the LORD."

Amelia commented, "The songs are always beautiful. The music that goes with them is so good that I would like to be able to buy some just like them to listen to at other times."

Matt responded, "I know that you can buy that music. A man in our small group told us about it just a little while ago. Just stop at the church office sometime during the week and tell them you would like to buy some. The music comes on those little SD cards that you can insert into a boom box like they use at small groups. The music only costs as much as it does for the church to buy the SD cards."

"Great, I'll stop by there on Monday right after school," replied Amelia.

After that they discussed various topics until it was time to help with the clean up and get ready to go to church.

*****

Jason went walking again on Sunday morning after calling his parents to see if he could have the pleasure of breakfast with them and ask a few questions about things he had been reading in the Bible. He enjoyed walking in this part of the city at this time of the day.

While they were eating he asked, "Which father do you think Maria meant when she wrote that note in the Bible she gave me? I've been reading in 2 Corinthians. Verse 6:14 says: *Do not be unequally yoked together with unbelievers, for what fellowship has righteousness with unrighteousness? And what communion has light with darkness?* Do you think she could have meant her heavenly Father? And if so, do you think he might let me court her now that I'm a believer? I know my faith is new, but it is very genuine. If she meant her earthly father, do you think he might reconsider? Or do you think I should not pursue that relationship at all? I've never stopped loving her, but I thought it had to be completely over until I read that verse. Now I'm not sure."

William answered, "Well, you certainly do have some very important questions. And for once I don't know any of the answers for certain. When she talked to me, I assumed she meant her heavenly Father, but it's never good to assume."

"That's for sure!" Jason exclaimed. "I've been learning that by this situation. So maybe I should not assume that it has to be totally over. Maybe I should find a way to ask her."

Anna suggested, "Let's pray and see what Jesus might say to us about what to do."

Jason nodded and began, "Jesus, you know that now I only desire to do your will in every part of my life. You know that I messed up big time when I talked to Maria at the office, and then on that date. But I know you can work all things together for good, and that is what I ask you to do now, in accordance with your will."

William continued, "We thank you so much for the good that you've already done by using those verses to get Jason to question his opinion, and then receive you as his own Savior."

Anna added, "And we're very thankful that you healed Jason and that he's growing to be the Christian man you want him to be. Now we ask for your guidance and your answers to his questions about Maria. We will be listening as we quietly finish eating breakfast."

After they finished eating, William suggested, "Maybe we could have her come to our house for a meal here if she consents to answer your questions, then you can ask her with us here as a buffer for that first meeting. Your sisters have told her about your salvation and healing, and she had readily agreed to pray with them about that before it happened. She rejoiced with them when they told her about your miracles."

"It sounds like that there's a possibility that she might agree to your suggestion. Would you be willing to ask her, Dad?" inquired Jason, humbly.

"Yes, I'd be glad to do that for you, Jason," answered William. "I'll call her this evening."

"Mom, what do you think about the idea, and if you agree with it, what can I do to help prepare the meal, and get the house ready for our guest?" asked Jason.

"I like the idea," she answered. "I would like to meet Maria. Let's make it for this coming Saturday at noon, and you can come first thing in the morning to help with the dusting and bring some flowers for a centerpiece. Then you can help me with the cooking like you used to do so often. What would you like us to serve?"

"I think something simple and not too spicy. I noticed that she chose an entree that would be easy to digest, probably because she was nervous, when we were at the restaurant. It had chicken in it so we would be safe cooking something with chicken," he explained.

"Good thinking. We could have baked chicken with mashed potatoes, garden peas, and a tossed salad with choice of dressings," she recommended.

"It sounds delicious," said William. "It makes my mouth water just hearing the menu!"

"I agree. Mom, you're such a good cook. I'll be delighted to be able to help you. You're the best parents a person could ever hope to have! Thank you both," said Jason with great emotion. Then he helped with the dishes and walked home to get ready for the service at church #1, feeling more hopeful than he had for weeks about Maria.

*****

As the weather continued to warm up, the people were thankful for the air conditioning in the sanctuary. The room wasn't as full as last week since the two new believer small groups that had so many school children in them had been placed into two different church times. Cory noticed and wondered about it, thinking maybe he could ask Pastor Don about it at the next small group meeting.

The church service songs were: "There Is a Redeemer," 1 Corinthians 1:30; "What a Gathering," verses 2 and 4; 1 Corinthians 15:52-54; "Christ Returneth" verses 1, 2, and 4, 1Thessalonians 4:16; "Jesus Is Coming Again," verses 1 and 2, John 14:3; and "We Shall Behold Him," 1 John 3:2.

Pastor Don started the teaching by saying, "Today is nearly forty days after Resurrection Sunday. Some people used to call the fortieth day, 'Ascension Day,' to honor the day when Jesus went back to heaven after his resurrection, subsequent to showing himself to his followers for forty days. You'll see that <u>The Second Coming of Jesus</u> would be a good title for our teaching today as we read Acts 1:9-11. *When he had spoken these things, while they were watching, Jesus was taken up, and a cloud received him out of their sight. While they looked persistently toward heaven, as he went up, behold, two men in white clothes stood by them. One said, 'You men of Galilee, why do you stand gazing up into heaven? This same Jesus, who is taken up from you into heaven, shall also come in like manner as you have seen him go into heaven.'* Right after Jesus had gone, the disciples were reminded that he would come back again, just like he had promised when he was with them, as in John 14:3, *If I go and prepare a place for you, I will come again, and receive you to myself, that where I am, there you may be also.*

"In addition, to that verse, is what Jesus told the disciples and many other people in Matthew 24. Verse 27 says, *As the lightning comes out of the east, and shines to the west, so shall the coming of the Son of man be.* Verse 30b says, *They shall see the Son of man coming in the clouds of heaven with power and great glory.* Verse 36 says, *But of that day and hour no man knows, not even the angels of heaven, but my Father only.* Then verse 44 says, *Therefore be ready, for in such an hour as you think not, the Son of man will come.*

"The following one is a little scary in parts, but it's one we need to remember. 2 Peter 3:9-14 states, *The Lord is not slow concerning his promise, ... but is patient, not willing that any should parish, but that all should come to repentance. But the day of the Lord will come as a thief in the night, in which the heavens shall pass away with a great noise, and the elements shall melt with fervent heat. The earth also and the works in it shall be burned up. Seeing then that all these things shall be destroyed, what manner of people should you be in all holy living and godliness, looking for and hastening the coming of the day of God. ... Nevertheless we, according to his promise look for new heavens and a new earth, in which righteousness dwell. Therefore, beloved, seeing that you look for such things, be diligent that you may be found by him in peace, without spot, and blameless.*

"But we don't have to try and do this on our own. 1Peter 1:5,7b,13 states that, *[believers] are kept by the power of God through faith unto salvation ready to be revealed in the last time. ...*

so that they may be found to the praise and honor and glory of Jesus Christ at his appearing. ... Therefore, ... be sober and hope to the end for the grace that is to be brought to you at the revelation of Jesus Christ.

"Other verses give us ideas of the way we're suppose to be living in view of Jesus return. 1 Timothy 6:11-14 says in summary, *You ... follow after righteousness, godliness, faith, love, patience, meekness, and fight the good fight of faith, lay hold of eternal life, ... keep these things without spot, indisputable, until the appearing of our Lord Jesus Christ.*

"And Titus 2:11-14 says, *For the grace of God that brings salvation has appeared to all men, teaching us that, denying ungodliness and worldly lusts, we should live soberly, righteously, and godly in this present world, looking for that blessed hope, and the glorious appearing of the great God and our Savior Jesus Christ, who gave himself for us, that he might redeem us from all iniquity, and purify for himself a people who are his own, eager to do good works.*

"Paul prayed for the Thessalonians, in 3:12,13, *The Lord make you to increase and abound in love one toward another, and to all men, ... may he establish your hearts blameless, in holiness before God, our Father at the coming of our Lord Jesus Christ with all his saints.* Then in chapter 5:1,2, and 23,24 he says, *But of the times and the seasons, brothers you have no need that I write to you. For you know perfectly that the day of the Lord comes as a thief in the night. ...* The verses between 2 and 23 tell how we should live while we're waiting for Jesus return. Then verses 23,24 say, *... May the God of peace sanctify you completely, and I pray that your whole spirit and soul and body may be preserved blameless unto the coming of our Lord Jesus Christ. Faithful is he who calls you, who will also do it.* In 1 Corinthians 1:7-9 and in Philippians 1:9-11, you'll find something very similar, which you can look up at home.

"Patience is encouraged in James 5:7,8 which says, *Be patient therefore, brothers, until the coming of the Lord. See how the gardener waits for the precious fruit of the earth, and has patience for it, until he receives the early and later rain. You also be patient, and establish your hearts, for the coming of the Lord draws near.*

"The next three scriptures we will look up are among my favorites. 1 John 3:2,3 states, *Beloved, now we are the sons of God, and it does not yet appear what we shall be, but we know that when he shall appear, we shall be like him, for we shall see him as he is. Every man who has this hope in him purifies himself the way Jesus is pure.*

"We're familiar with these verses in 1 Thessalonians 4:13-18, and they are a great comfort and hope when a loved one dies. They say, *I would not have you to be ignorant, brothers, concerning those who are asleep, so that you do not sorrow as others do that have no hope. For if we believe that Jesus died and rose again, even so those also who sleep or die in Jesus will God bring with him. For this we say to you by the word of the Lord, we who are alive and remain at the coming of the Lord shall not go before those who are asleep. For the Lord himself shall descend from heaven with a shout, with the voice of the archangel, and with the trump of God. And the dead in Christ shall rise first. Then we who are alive and remain shall be caught up together with them in the clouds to meet the Lord in the air, and so shall we ever be with the Lord. Therefore comfort one another with these words.* Be sure to read 1 Corinthians 15:51-58 at home because they explain more about this.

"And the last scripture is in Philippians 3:20, 21a and 4:4-9 and it's very hopeful. *Our citizenship is in heaven. We look for our Savior the Lord Jesus Christ from there. He shall change our bodies so that they may be fashioned like his glorious body. ... Rejoice in the Lord always, again I say rejoice. Let your moderation be known to all men. The Lord is at hand. Be worried about nothing, but in everything by prayer and supplication with thanksgiving let your requests be made known to God. And the peace of God, which passes all understanding, shall keep your hearts and minds through Christ Jesus. Finally, brothers, whatever is true, ... honest, ... just, ... pure, ... of good report, ... virtuous, or praiseworthy, think on these things. ... Do the things you have learned, and the God of peace shall be with you.*

"I didn't include any of the verses in Revelation, because I feel that it's best for each of us to make time to read the whole book and be blessed, as it says in verse three of chapter 1. So your homework for this week is to ask the Holy Spirit to help you understand it as you read the whole book.

"Now let's sing 'We Shall Behold Him' again, and then you are dismissed."

All of the Suehiros went up to the pastor, and Tomo introduced the rest of his family to Pastor Don, who was thrilled to meet them and hear all the good news. He gave Yoshi his own copy of the new believer booklet since all the others already had theirs. Tomo explained, "Afta, Hana, and Denji need to return to their home this week. They'll be finding a church with beliefs like this one and small groups. They will also be baptized in water there, but Yoshi would like to be baptized in the next special service this church has."

"That will be fine. Aneko do you still have all the notes I gave you about water baptism?" he asked.

"Yes. I'll go over all that with him when he returns, since he has to go back to work tomorrow. But he will be back for the special baptismal service," she answered.

"Great! The service will be the week after this, on Tuesday evening at 7 PM. I'll need to announce that next week during church," he said. Then the Suehiros thanked him and left.

After that several parents with young children took their cards up to the pastor, who rejoiced with them and took them into the office to get them notes about the first small group meeting. Then he invited them to come to the next meeting and gave them the address and time of the meeting.

*****

Maria, Julie, Ted, and Tony met for their afternoon walk in the park after church. The weather had been getting warmer every week so Julie suggested to Maria, as they walked, "Maybe we should consider changing our walking time to before breakfast on Sundays. But I don't know how that will affect Tony."

Maria answered, "We could ask him at the end of our walking time."

"I like that plan. How did your week go?" asked Julie.

"Well, it wasn't as exciting as last week when I got to lead two co-workers to Jesus for salvation, but the three of us did go to lunch a couple times this week and we got to know each other better and I was able to answer some of their questions, also. And of course Esther told us about her supper date with Tony last Sunday evening, but there wasn't much to say except that he was embarrassed about not having a car," said Maria.

"Well, she knew about that ahead of time, so it wasn't a shock to her. I'm sure she handled it very well. I'll be interested to see what happens," responded Julie. Then she told Maria about all that had happened for Pam and her parents and that she would be coming back to Pine City to take the place of another teacher who has to leave. "Please keep all of this confidential. She'll be joining our small group since she's been an absentee member during this time," Julie finished.

"Wow!" exclaimed Maria. "You surely do have an exciting life since you moved to Pine City, Julie!"

"I know! Isn't God amazing to do all these miracles?" asked Julie. "I feel very blessed to be able to witness them. On top of those things, on Tuesday, Jesus used Ted and me to lead an older Jewish lady to Jesus to be her Messiah and Savior! She was such a sweet lady and is now going to one of the other churches and a small group for Jewish new believers."

"Praise the Lord! Yes, _he_ is totally awesome. I'm glad we can go to this church and small groups which encourage us to let Jesus work through us to do his work here on earth until he comes back," responded Maria.

"That thought goes just right with the teaching time for today. I long for his return, but I also want to see as many people as possible brought into his family before he comes," said Julie.

Meanwhile, Tony had been explaining to Ted about his new ministry, "Yesterday afternoon, as you know we went to a park and set up his booth. Several Spanish children and their parents came over and listened to a story using the flannel graph. It was about Jesus telling the disciples to let the children come to him, plus many of the things he did while he was on earth. Then he explained the Gospel and gave an invitation to ask Jesus to be their Savior.

"While he took the ones who wanted to do that to a park bench where they could pray, I took over the story telling with some English speaking children and their parents. They were good listeners, even when I fumbled with some of the figures. I told the same story in English and several of those children and their parents went with me to help them pray to ask Jesus to be their Savior. We gave them little booklets from church to read with their parents, and bring to church on Sunday. I saw the families go up to Pastor Don and give him their cards. It's such a wonderful feeling to be used by Jesus to tell others about him and have them respond positively."

Ted replied, "I'm so glad for you. God answered 'Yes' to our prayers for you!"

"He certainly did, and I thank and praise him for that. Now I have a question for you. Even though I've been enjoying these walks and teaching you Spanish, would you mind if we stop doing it so that I can go to parks with that man on Sunday afternoons also, and that way we can reach even more children?"

"That would be fine with me, Tony," Ted answered. "I've enjoyed these times also, but I would rather have you go and be used by Jesus to win more people to Jesus. Julie can help me to continue learning Spanish. Go, and God bless you, Tony!"

"Thank you, Ted. I knew you would understand. May I still consider you a friend, and maybe we can get together sometimes?" asked Tony.

"That sounds good to me. Call me whenever it would work best for you," answered Ted.

By that time, they had all arrived back at the starting point, and Ted told the ladies about Tony's plans. They smiled and wished him God's blessings and help, all the while feeling relieved that their question had been answered.

*****

When Tony got home, he called Esther and thanked her for her gracious acceptance of his not having a car and that he had enjoyed their time together. She thanked him again for the delicious meal and pleasant evening. Then he explained to her that after praying about it a lot, he felt that God wanted him to remain single so he could continue his simple lifestyle and be available to serve Jesus however he might lead. Then he told her about his new ministry that just started on Friday, and what had happened on Saturday afternoon. She praised the Lord with him and said she would pray for his ministry to flourish. They said good-bye and Tony prayed that she would not be hurt. He felt at peace that he had done the right thing, however.

*****

At about 7PM Maria's phone rang. It was William who asked her how she was doing and then after listening to her, and answering the same question from her, he said, "Jason has some questions he would like to ask you. Since you told me what happened that night, I suggested that my wife, Anna, and I and Jason could invite you to our house for lunch this coming Saturday. Then he could ask you his questions, and you would have Anna and I as a buffer. It might not seem so intimidating to you this way if you're willing to see him again and answer his questions. He really is a new creature in Christ now, and is growing rapidly as I'm sure Ruth and Esther have told you."

"Yes, they have, and I praise and thank Jesus for the miracles in Jason's life," responded Maria. "I would like to call my pastor and ask him for his opinion before I reply to your invitation, which is most kind."

"Good idea, I'll be here all evening, so call back at your convenience," he replied.

So Maria called Don, and asked him to have Anita listen also. She explained what William had said and asked them for their advice. They all prayed first.

Don answered, "I remember that all of us were pretty hard on ourselves that evening, but since God worked it all out for the good of all concerned, especially your friendship with his sisters and Jason's salvation and healing, and since I know that his parents are very good Christians, then I think that it would be very safe for you to accept William's invitation. It would be a good way for you to see Jason again, but only if you're very sure you really _desire_ to see him again. You don't _have_ to you know."

"Yes I do know that, and I'm very nervous about the whole idea, but I had told his sisters that I feel like I need to give Jason a chance to become what God wants him to be, and then court me if he still wants to. They've told me that he's growing in the Lord by leaps and bounds. I think I would always wonder or regret it, if I didn't give him a chance to at least ask his questions," explained Maria.

Anita said, "It sounds to me like you've really thought the possibilities through. Just be very careful of your own heart. Be sure you get all _your_ questions answered before you would agree to let him court you if he does want to."

"Thank you, Anita, for an excellent idea. I'll have this whole week to think of questions and make a list of them so I won't forget anything. There's no need to even be courted if we would not be compatible. I don't wish to hurt his feelings in any way, but this is a life long decision and needs careful consideration," she stated.

Don responded, "That's for sure! You could run this idea past Ted and Julie since they were in on the ground floor and I'm sure you've kept them updated. They might have some additional input that would be valuable."

"Thank you, Pastor Don and Anita. I'm so blessed to have you in my life. I'll call them right away. Bye for now," Maria said, and immediately called Julie who answered and got Ted to listen while she gave them the whole story, and then asked them to pray.

After they had all prayed, Julie responded, "Pastor Don is right when he says you don't have to see Jason again. Only do this if you really desire to see him again. I'm going to be completely honest with you and tell you that I think you and Jason make the most unlikely couple I can think of, because you're poles apart in the area of finances and who knows what else. I don't want to see you get hurt again. The last time was very scary," she trailed off.

"Thank you, Julie. I agree with your assessment of Jason and me as a couple, and have often thought of the same things, but he's now a new creation in Jesus and maybe he's completely different. He just wants to ask me some questions and if he says he still wants to court me I'll have a whole list of questions to ask him before I answer, " she stated, sounding more sure of herself than she was.

Ted inserted, "You did mention that his parents will be there, so this won't need to be scary. I know that Pastor Don said they're very good Christians, so you'll be safe. We just don't want you to open yourself up to getting your heart wounded in any way shape or form."

"Thank you, Ted. If either of you have a word from the Lord that says I should not date Jason or that I should remain single, please tell me now! If only I knew for sure, then I would tell William that fact and this whole thing would be over. But so far, I haven't had an answer to that question even though I ask it almost every day," Maria replied.

"I'm sorry, Maria," said Julie. "I'm so worried about you getting hurt that I forget that you're still waiting for guidance in this area. Maybe the guidance will come by you going to see Jason again and answer his questions. It sounds like something you feel you need to do in order to not have any regrets or speculation on you part."

Maria replied, "That's exactly what I told Pastor and Anita. You don't have to be sorry, Julie. I thank you for your concern, and I did call you for your advice, which is invaluable. Would you and Ted write down some questions that I should ask Jason if he still wants to court me? Call me sometime this week so I can write them down."

"Okay, we'll do that, and we'll keep praying for you. We love you. Bye for now," said Julie.

After Maria said good-bye, she called William and accepted his invitation to lunch on Saturday.

Linda L. Linn

*****

Monday

    The Suehiros were up early Monday, so that Afta, Hana and Denji could catch an early flight back to their home. It had been a very nice visit, and though it was sad to see them leave, they all cheered each other up by promising to call often, and travel to visit every chance they could get.
    It was a very quiet house though, since Yoshi had left the afternoon before so he could go back to work. But his plans were to give his boss a week's notice and be back the next weekend to go over all those notes with Aneko so he would be ready for the Tuesday baptismal service. He would also start looking for a job in Pine City.

*****

    Mrs. Blake (Julie) got a lot of pleasure from teaching her third graders about creation and God the creator. She continued to use materials from creation.com, answersingenesis.org, and audios with Uncle Bob interviewing various creatures or body parts on Nature Corner, plus lots of songs and some books like "It Couldn't Just Happen."
    This morning she asked, "What are some of the songs you've enjoyed that go with God's creation? I'll write them down in this notebook and some days when we have extra time we can sing one from the list."
    "That's a good idea. One of my favorites is 'Fearfully and Wonderfully Made.' I like to sing," said a girl.
    "I really like the one about God's big wonderful world. He made everything just right," another girl answered.
    A boy said, "I like 'All Wild Things of God's Creation.' It says that he put them here with care."
    "There's a song by Buddy Davis that talks about Jesus being King and the creator, and another one that says he made the earth and heavens in six days. I like those," added another boy.
    A girl said, "I like the one that talks about us believing by faith that God created us. And there's another one that says we're made in God's image. I like it also."

"My favorite is the one that has a prayer asking God to help us keep creation beautiful," added another girl.

Mrs. Blake said, "Thank you for all those good ideas. I enjoy singing with this class. You sing well and with enthusiasm."

*****

Maria met with Ruth and Esther for lunch, and since it was raining today, they ate in the lunchroom. Esther seemed a little quiet, but Maria refrained from asking her about it. Maybe she would share on her own. Instead she commented, "I really enjoyed the teaching at church yesterday about the second coming of Jesus. It was good to be reminded about everything all those verses said. Sometimes I get so wrapped up in things that happen in everyday life, I forget that Jesus really could return very soon."

Ruth agreed and added, "It really is a blessed hope we have. I pity people without our hope. What a hopeless way to live, no pun intended. But when I think about it, it would work both ways." They all chuckled.

Esther continued, "Yes, our blessed hope is reason enough to rejoice and continue working for Jesus even when some things don't go the way we desired. Tony called me last night." She told them word for word what they had said during the conversation. "He was very gentle about it and I know he didn't want to hurt me. He didn't hurt me. It was my own dreaming that caused me to be sad. It felt like the death of another dream. I had built castles in the air and they all came tumbling down. Of course it's better to know about it right away, rather than getting to like him even more. I do understand why, and I'm proud of him for being up front, and for choosing to obey and do what God wants him to do."

Maria got up and went to sit by Esther so she could put her arm around her for a hug, then she prayed, "Father in heaven, thank you for Esther. She and Ruth have become such wonderful friends to me. Please give Esther your peace and comfort in this situation. Show her how this can work for her good as well as his. Maybe you have someone even better for her, or maybe you'll give her the same peace that Ruth has about remaining single. Please guide Esther and also guide me as we wait upon you for your answers."

Ruth added, "Thank you that Tony got such clear guidance from you and that he was honest and careful in sharing that with Esther. Please comfort her. Help her to learn whatever lessons you have for her in this situation, and to grow even closer to you because of it."

Esther agreed, "Thank you Father for Ruth and Maria. Their prayers have helped me to put things into a better perspective. I know you are in control. Forgive me for wanting my own dreams, and help me to only desire your will for my life. Give me patience and discernment as I wait for you to reveal your will to me."

They finished eating in a comfortable silence and contemplation and then went back to work. Maria didn't mention the phone call and invitation she had received from William last night. This way she could keep her mind on her work all week and not have to answer their questions or have them speculating about the situation.

*****

Don and Anita enjoyed the pastors' small group meeting where they heard praise reports from other pastors about the way the people who had been moved into their churches had settled in and were content. They were reminded to announce the special baptismal service day and time to their congregations on Sunday.

A committee reported on what they had found so far as they had been looking for a suitable piece of property to buy where they could build an additional church building and school. There just wasn't much open property in the center of this city. Somebody suggested that they might be able to remodel a couple of buildings if there would be enough parking available. The committee agreed to look for that possibility the rest of this week. Another person recommended looking for some very old rundown buildings that could be torn down and replaced with beautiful new buildings. They agreed to look for that option also and thanked the people for their ideas.

*****

Everywhere There's a Sunrise, Let's Tell The Good News!

Chapter 22

Proverbs 3:5,6, *Trust in the LORD with all your heart, and do not lean on your own understanding. In all your ways acknowledge him, and he shall direct your paths.*

Tuesday

Maria was reading her Bible while she ate breakfast and found herself reading 1 Corinthians chapter 7 again for the umpteenth time since Jason had declared himself to her in his office. As she finished it and breakfast about the same time she prayed again that Jesus would make his best will very plain to her. "I need a big red stop sign in the middle of his forehead, or over the word marriage, or some other clear word from you, Jesus, like maybe a green GO light over the word single."

Then she laughed at herself and got ready to go to work, thinking as she drove, about all the questions she had already written down to ask Jason, plus the ones Ted and Julie had told her last night when they called. They were all good ones, and the wrong answer to even one of them would be that stop sign. She was thankful for such good friends.

*****

After resting on Sunday and Monday, Riley would begin to look for a job today. Riley asked his family to pray for him after they finished breakfast. He said, "It sure would be very nice if I could find just the right job here in Pine City. I like it here so much more than before I went away to college. Father in heaven, please guide me in my job search and help me to find the best job where I can serve you and use what I learned in college"

Patrick added, "Thank you, Father, for the way you helped Riley recover from his skiing injuries. I agree in asking you to direct him to the job that will be best for him and will also serve you."

"We ask that you would give him that job here in Pine City so we can enjoy being together as a family again," continued Fiona.

Glenda agreed, "Yes, please heavenly Father, I agree with all those requests and ask that you'll do your perfect will. We pray in Jesus name, Amen."

"Thank you all. I'll be on my way now," Riley said. Part of his resting time on Monday had been used to do a web search for job possibilities. He took out the list he had made and went to the first one on the list.

When he came home that evening, he had appointments for several interviews during the week.

*****

Julie had been praying off and on, for the other teacher who had to move, and decided to have lunch with her again today if she was willing, so she could share a couple ideas with her. After they gave thanks for their lunches, she decided to see if the other teacher would start the conversation. She did, "Beth came to my classroom yesterday morning and told me all about the miracles that happened for Pam's parents, and that she agreed to come back to Pine City and take over my position. I'm so relieved, and happy that my class will have a good teacher who already knows how to teach the way this school requires."

Julie agreed, "Things really have worked out well for her and for your class. I just pray that they'll work out as well for you."

She replied, "Oh, I think they will. My husband gets a promotion <u>and</u> a raise because of this move, and the living expenses in that city are lower than they are here. We were planning to start a family after this school year is over anyway. Now we can get a head start. I can get a job there doing something besides teaching, and we can continue saving money so that I won't have to work after the baby is born. I'm not feeling as bad about it all as I was on Friday. In fact, I'm getting excited about it."

"I'm glad to hear that. May God bless everything you do!" Julie exclaimed, and decided there was no need for her to share her ideas.

*****

Larry, Jane, Ted and Julie met in their own neighborhood to walk and pray during their four by four ministry time. It was a lovely evening and many people were outside, either working in their yards or sitting in the shade. Ted and Julie led the way this time and they saw something interesting in one of the yards, so they stopped in an inconspicuous place to watch. They realized the young woman was speaking to her father in sign language, and he answered back with sign language, so she must be deaf and not able to speak.

They felt led to walk over and introduce themselves and just get to know more about them, trying to build up rapport, and see what Jesus would have them do, and when.

They were able to find out the names of the people and meet the mother also. Small talk was the order of the day, with the father or mother signing to their daughter what was being said. Ted and Julie didn't stay very long. Larry and Jane had stopped in the shade half a block away to pray for them. The two couples kept walking and praying for another half hour and then went back to Ted and Julie's apartment for refreshments and to talk and pray about the evening.

Larry stated, "I think you two are ready to go on with your own <u>two by two</u> ministry. That family you met today is a very real possibility for a miracle and salvation. Keep praying for them and follow up with another visit or two while you wait to see how Jesus will lead you. We'll be praying, also. Let us know how it goes."

"Okay. Thank you both for all your help and encouragement," said Ted.

"Yes," added Julie. "We're very grateful for all you've done to get us started on this ministry."

Jane responded, "It's been our pleasure, and I'm glad we can still get together on Thursday evenings."

"Me too," replied Julie. "See you Thursday!"

*****

Wednesday

Matt and Fiona met at her house right after breakfast so they could go over the other books they had checked out and ideas they had written down. They sat at the kitchen table while Glenda was busy sewing in another room. "Most of the ideas in this book have to do with decorating inside after the house is finished. Mom and I looked at some of the ideas and decided that we could work on some of them before the wedding. For the curtains and drapes, all I need is the dimensions of the windows and sliding doors."

"I'll write those down for you right now, since I brought the plans inside with me," offered Matt.

"Oh, thank you. That was quick. Would you like to accompany me to shop for the material?" she asked.

"Well," he hedged. "I know nothing about fabric, style, design, etc. I think I would just get in the way and hold you back. Why don't you just show me the pictures of the ones you like and then get whatever material you like to make them? Are you sure you want to do all that sewing? We could get ready made ones if you would rather."

"Dearest Matt, I don't think I've ever seen you so flustered or ill at ease about anything. But I think I understand how you feel. This isn't something you've ever dealt with before. I think I would feel the same way if you asked me what grade of wood I would like to have for the cupboards or something else. Yes, I really do desire to do the sewing and Mother would like to help. This way I can choose material that's easy care and does not need to be dry-cleaned. The ready made ones are never the right size anyway and would need to be remodeled. Here are some pictures of the styles I like. What do you think about them?"

"I really like the ones on this page. Even the colors are nice, like the out of doors in the springtime. Do you like these colors?" he asked her.

"Yes, very much, and that was one reason I decided to make ours, so we could have colors we would like, since the ones we could order don't come in these colors," she answered. Then she took a picture of that page.

"Wonderful. I knew I would like whatever you would choose," he said, greatly relieved.

"Thank you. Now which pillows would you like to have on the couch and chairs? I can buy enough material so they'll match the drapes in the living room," she explained.

He looked at all the pictures and decided, "I like these simple ones. They look like they could be removed, washed and replaced easily."

"I agree," she said taking a picture so she could buy a pattern for that type of pillow cover.

Then he said, "Here is a complete change of subject. What about a wedding dress for you?"

"Oh, I'm so excited and pleased." Fiona replied after a big smile, "Mother had me try on her wedding dress, and it fits me perfectly. It's gorgeous and she's going to give it to me to pass on to our daughter hoping it will fit."

"Wow!" he exclaimed. "That is a huge blessing and one that makes your mother happy also."

Then they got back to work with the other books, this time taking pictures of the things they would like to include in their house. It was a quick easy way to remember and not have to go back to the books later.

Fiona suggested when they finished, "Let's walk over to the library to take these books back and take some pictures of the things we had decided on in the other books so we can have them all together."

"Yes, let's do that," he agreed. When they finished he walked her back home, where they made plans to go on a fun hike Friday. She had time to eat lunch and go to work. He went back to his apartment and did the same.

*****

Don and Anita combined the two new believer small groups, and they all met at the church in preparation for the special baptismal service next Tuesday. Mindy was glad to come and take care of Timmy and Mary, put them to bed at 8 PM and then do her homework for the next day. The meeting went even better than the one last month, since the people had read the new little booklet, which had floor plans right in them. They were divided into men/women groups to ask questions. The people were looking forward to this next step in their new lives.

Before refreshments, they prayed for the facilitators who would be taking over on their own after the baptismal service next week. The facilitators wrote down the address of the home where they would meet.

At the end, Cory came up to Pastor Don and asked, "Where did all the other people and children go who were in church the week before?"

Don hid his surprise about the question well, and answered, explaining about the 11 other churches that use the same building, and why the leaders had decided to put one group each in two of the other churches which didn't have as many people."

"Oh, that makes good sense. I get to see those kids at school anyway. I just wondered," he explained.

"It is always good to ask questions when you wonder. I'm glad you asked," said Don.

*****

Linda L. Linn

Thursday

About 10 AM on Thursday, Pam called Jeff and Karen and said, "I just wanted to share our good news with you and thank you for praying for us. Last evening we had about a dozen of my parents close friends over for an evening of visiting. They had all come to see Mother after her stroke and knew what bad shape she was in. Father and Mother explained how Jesus had healed her completely and they were all astonished. Then Mother told them that even more importantly, Jesus had saved them. She and Father made the Gospel very clear to them and every single one of them accepted Jesus also!"

"Fabulous!" exclaimed Jeff and Karen.

"We called the church and they're going to start a new believers small group for all of them to be in, starting next week on Wednesday evening. It's so wonderful that they'll have friends with them as they learn and grow together. Now I don't need to worry about them when I leave, because the church and small group will help to guide them in their new lives in Christ," finished Pam.

"We thank and praise Jesus with you and your parents," said Jeff.

"Would you like us to help you look for an apartment near the school? We could get some ideas to show you when you arrive on Wednesday, and then help you move in, when you decide on one," suggested Karen.

"That would be so nice of you! All I really need is an unfurnished studio apartment or a small one bedroom one. I prefer to be on the ground floor, because they're cooler in the summer, and I don't like stairs or elevators. I'm hoping to find one that has pretty low rent also," Pam added.

What time do you think you'll arrive?" asked Jeff.

"It takes almost 8 hours to drive the distance pulling a rented trailer," she trailed off.

"I get off at 8 PM so if you could come to our house, about that time, I can take you to see the apartments we've found. Then when Jeff gets off work at 9 PM he can join us. When you decide on one you like, we can move enough of your things into the apartment and get your bed made so you can sleep there. Then we'll come in the morning to help unload the rest of the trailer and you can take it to the dealer," Karen recommended.

"Wow! You have it all planned out and it sounds great. Thank you both so much. I'll plan to see you on Wednesday at about 8 PM. That will give me time to rent the trailer and get it packed here that morning," agreed Pam.

"Bye, Pam. Greet your parents for us," said Jeff.

*****

Jane told Julie, "I was pleased that most of the children came back to the Bible study and story groups after school. This week the study and story contained the Good News message and an invitation. One of the older children and two of the younger ones responded to the invitation and stayed to pray after refreshments."

"Praise the Lord!" exclaimed Julie.

"I sent little booklets and cards with those children and encouraged them share them with their parents and call me if they had any questions. I had printed my phone number in the back of the booklets. I also invited them to come to church on Sunday, giving the time and address. Needless to say, I'm delighted!" stated Jane.

"Me too, and I know there was rejoicing in heaven also," agreed Julie.

*****

Friday

Matt and Fiona drove to a trail head in the mountains for their hike on Friday and got there about 9 AM. Only a few other cars were parked there, so they were glad that it would not be crowded on the trail.

"This is lovely. I've never been here before. Look, the sign says the trail goes to a waterfall and it's only one mile. We should have plenty of time to hike there, enjoy it, and get back before we need to go home for our lunches and go to work," said Fiona enthusiastically.

"Yes, it's lovely, and so are you! I enjoy your excitement and ability to see the beauty in nature and have fun. I found this trail last summer, and thought of you as I hiked alone. Today will be so, so, _so_ much better with you here to join me! Here's your canteen, and we probably will want our jackets, at least for a while," Matt responded.

"Thanks. I brought my camera today so we can have memories of all the beauty and our time here together," she said as they started up the trail.

The trail followed a rushing stream, and every now and then a small bridge took them to the other side or back again. The wildflowers were just getting a good start, since spring comes later at higher elevations. Fiona stopped occasionally to take pictures of the flowers, the stream and of Matt. Then he asked for the camera and took a few pictures of her, also. They walked and talked until they reached the waterfall.

"Wow! It's spectacular!" The water came shooting over the cliff and made a free fall to the pool below with a mighty roar. It was too noisy to be able to talk, and they were getting wet from the spray as it hit some rocks in the pool.

Matt tapped her shoulder and motioned for her to follow him back a ways where there was a bench away from the spray. She took several pictures from that vantage point, and a nice woman took their picture as they stood in front of the waterfall.

Then they walked to another viewpoint a little further away and Fiona took some more pictures. It was quieter here, so they could talk about the splendor of God's creation. "Last summer most of the snow had melted by the time I got here, so the waterfall wasn't so big and loud, but it was special anyway," added Matt after they had discussed the surroundings.

"Oh, could we plan to come back here later this summer? I'd enjoy seeing it that way too," she requested.

"Sure, I would like that. This hike has been a nice break from all the planning about the house. We should plan to get away into nature at least once a month so we can be renewed and refreshed," suggested Matt.

"I couldn't agree more. I'll look forward to that every month for the rest of our lives!" she exclaimed.

He laughed and stated, "Me too!"

That afternoon and evening, Connie first, and then Amelia got to hear about the hike, the fun of being engaged, the house Matt was building now with the help of Walt and both crews, plus some of the changes they had made, and some of their plans for decorating. And of course they were told about her mother's gorgeous wedding dress. Fiona felt like she was just bubbling over with joy and excitement. It was a good feeling!

*****

Everywhere There's a Sunrise, Let's Tell The Good News!

Finally at the end of Friday's lunchtime with Ruth and Esther, Maria shared what William had told her last Sunday evening, and that she would be going to lunch at their house for lunch tomorrow to answer some questions that Jason had. They all prayed together about it and Esther asked, "Would you please be ready to tell us about it at lunch on Monday?"

Maria replied, "I'd rather call you after I get home on Saturday, so I don't have to wait 'til Monday."

"Good idea! We'll both be home all afternoon and I'll turn on the speaker so we can both hear what you say," responded Ruth.

*****

At suppertime, Don and Anita listened as Timmy told them, "I liked the story today about Daniel in the lion's den. I especially liked that song called, "Here Kitty, Kitty." The lions didn't hurt him at all. I'm glad God kept the lions from hurting Daniel."

Don agreed, "Yes, that was a big miracle, and it caused the king to believe in God."

"Mary, tell about what Mindy did to all us kids in the backyard today," directed Timmy.

She said, "Mindy turned the sprinklers on and we all got wet. It cooled us off. It was fun."

Anita explained to Don, "Mindy had asked me if she could do that, and since it was so warm out, I said she could, but only for a few seconds. They didn't get very wet and dried off quickly in the warm sun, before you even got home."

"Mindy is a good girl. We're blessed to have her spending time with us," responded Don.

*****

After supper cleanup, Julie called Maria, with Ted listening. Julie asked, "How are you doing? Remember that we'll be praying for you this evening and tomorrow. In fact we've been praying for you all week."

Maria said, "Thank you. I know it's helping and will continue to help. At least this time I'm going prepared with a list of questions written down that I can refer to if I need to. I'm sure glad that William and his wife will be there. I cannot imagine facing Jason alone, even though he's a believer now."

Ted encouraged, "Be strong and courageous, like God told Joshua, because God is with you. Try to not let your feelings show on your face, and be sure to get answers to your most important questions. If he fails on one of those, you won't need to go on with the rest. You'll have your answer, which is: <u>don't let him court you</u>. If he passes all of them with flying colors, you'll also have your answer, which is: <u>proceed with caution</u>."

"Thank you both, so very much. It's wonderful to have good Christian friends who back me up with prayer and encouraging words and advice. I know I would much rather remain single all my life than marry a man who might make my life miserable. I pray that God's will shall be done," responded Maria.

*****

Saturday

Ted and Julie had the chairs all set in place for the Saturday small group meeting. Cut vegetables and dips in the refrigerator were ready to be set out on the table beside the plates and napkins when it was time for refreshments. Most of the members walked to their apartment since it was such a cool, delightful morning. They might be wishing for their air-conditioned cars when they had to walk home, however.

Jeff and Karen arrived a few minutes early to get the books placed on the chairs and have time to pray with Ted and Julie before the meeting. They enjoyed those few minutes with the host couple every Saturday, and were glad it was the plan to have different hosts for each meeting.

Praises started with Tomo and Ami saying in unison, "We praise and thank the Lord that our son Yoshi asked Jesus to be his Savior last Saturday afternoon!"

Jane continued, "I thank and praise the Lord that he used me to bring three children into his kingdom."

Tony said, "Thank you Jesus for helping me with English and saving several children and their parents."

Karen added, "We praise and thank you Jesus for helping Pam and her parents with their evening of witnessing to their friends and neighbors. About a dozen came, and all of them asked Jesus to save them!"

Roy said, "We praise Jesus and we were all very happy when we returned to that same park, and got to talk with Cory and his parents. They're all doing well and would like to be friends and to continue to see us off and on."

Fiona bubbled over as she shared, "I praise God for his marvelous creation and thank him for the ability to hike and enjoy it. The mountains, flowers and stream were so beautiful and that waterfall was in itself a crescendo of praise."

Jeff led the applause and oral praise. "Are there any announcements? No, ... then who would like to be the hosts for our next meeting?" The Suehiros said they would be glad to have everyone at their home again.

Next, Jeff said, "We'll use Fiona's praise as an introduction to our first song today: 'Joyful, Joyful, We adore Thee,' Psalm 139:14." After that they sang "Blessed Be the Name," Hebrews 1:4; and "My Tribute," Psalm 115:1.

"If you look at the second verse of our first song, you'll notice many of the things Fiona mentioned in her praise, so it was a good introduction. All of those things go very well with Psalm 139:14b where David said, *I will praise you...marvelous are your works.*

"Turn to Hebrews 1:1-4 and follow along. *God who at various times and in diverse ways spoke in the past by the prophets, has in these last days spoken to us by his Son, whom he has appointed heir of all things, and by whom he made the worlds. His son is the brightness of God's glory, and the express image of his person. He upholds all things by the word of his power. When he had by himself purged our sins, he sat down on the right hand of the Majesty on high, being made so much better than the angels, as he has by inheritance obtained a more excellent name than they.*

"Now read the words to our second song, and notice how well it goes with those scripture verses. All our praise goes to God the Father and to his Son, Jesus. <u>They</u> are worthy of all praise.

"Think about the words in the song, 'My Tribute,' as I read the first part of Psalm 115, verse 1. *Not to us, O LORD, not to us, but to your name give glory.* I'm so glad we can do that in this group. I really enjoy our praise reports and the songs we sing. It's all such a relief from the way the world does life, grabbing for all the glory they can get for themselves. What an empty way to live. But we have the privilege of telling them the right way to live. It is the life that Jesus came to give abundantly. We thank and praise you Jesus!

"Let's sing 'Joyful, Joyful, We adore Thee,' again. I love the music for this one. It is the melody from Beethoven's Ninth Symphony, and is called 'Hymn to Joy.'"

The conversational prayer time started off with some people choosing praises from the songs they had sung.

Julie kept her recorder turned on and prayed, "Father, please bless the next days that Pam and her parents have together. Help her as she gets ready to return to Pine City to teach in Grace 'n' Faith School."

Then Karen prayed, "I agree with that and ask that you give her traveling mercies on Wednesday."

Jeff added, "Please help Karen and me to find the best place for her to live by the time she arrives."

Fiona continued, "Thank you that next Saturday she'll be here in person and the rest of us will get to meet her. Help us to give her the support she needs. And I thank you for the safe trip my family had last weekend, and that my brother has found a job here in Pine City that is just right for what he learned in college and it will be a way to serve you."

Larry changed the subject again with, "We thank and praise you again for the salvation of so many people in the Suehiro family, and ask that you continue that work as Afta and his family share the gospel in their home city."

Ami added, "Tomo and I agree with that, and ask that you'll help Yoshi find just the right job when he comes home to look this week."

Ted closed with, "We thank you Lord, for the privilege of meeting together like this every week, and now we ask that you would bless our time of fellowship and refreshments."

Julie said, "Please join us in the kitchen, where the refreshments are still in the refrigerator staying cool. It will only take a few minutes to set them out on the table."

Everyone followed, talking on the way, and then enjoyed the vegetables and dips, again not needing something extra to drink, because they were all so juicy.

Julie cornered Karen and asked if she could be of help getting Pam settled. Karen told her what they had planned, and gave her Pam's cell phone number so she could call and ask her if she needed additional help Thursday after school. Then Fiona joined them and gave Karen the phone number of a family in the church that has a small one-bedroom apartment in a walkout basement that they would like to rent to a quiet Christian single woman who already has a permanent job.

"That might be perfect! I'll call them as soon as we get home, and we'll go look at it," Karen said.

Everywhere There's a Sunrise, Let's Tell The Good News!

*****

Jason got up early, showered, ate breakfast, packed a clean set of casual clothes and set out walking to his parents house, stopping on the way to buy a small but pretty bouquet for a centerpiece. He almost felt like skipping, and laughed out loud. He could not remember the last time he had skipped. When he arrived, he was handed a duster by his mother who took the bouquet and exclaimed, "This is exquisite! It is just the right size and has some of my favorite flowers. Thank you, Jason."

He was pleased with her assessment, and replied, "You're very welcome. I wanted it to be special for you because you're such a special mother. Now I'll get busy and dust. Which rooms do you want me to dust?"

"Just the living room and the dining room, and then clean the main bathroom, since I ran out of time yesterday while I was making your favorite dessert, since you're such a special son." They both laughed at the way she copied how he had said almost the same thing to her. Then he got to work. In about an hour he was finished, and ready to help in the kitchen.

"Here I am, ready to help you cook. It's been a long time, so you'll probably have to coach me," he said.

"Okay. The chicken is in the refrigerator. It needs to be washed and cut into pieces like you used to do. It will all come back to you as you do it, so don't worry," she instructed.

She was right. He remembered how to do that task, and all the others she gave him afterwards. They had a very nice time working together to cook this special lunch.

Jason said, "This has been fun, Mom! I hope we can do this more often."

She responded, "I agree. Just tell me when you have time and we'll plan it!"

"Would you mind if I go take another shower? The one I had early this morning is of no use right now, and I would like to feel fresh when I see Maria." He said her name with adoration, and his mother understood.

"Sure, go right ahead, and use the upstairs bathroom so this one will stay fresh and clean if she desires to use it," his mother answered.

He showered quickly, dressed in his fresh clothes and was back downstairs to finish setting the table and make the salad before Maria arrived.

William answered the door with Anna beside him so introductions could be made. That accomplished, Jason came and welcomed her and thanked her for coming. She felt completely tongue tied as she had before, but, Anna rescued her by taking her by the hand and leading her into the dining room, and seated her across from where Jason would be sitting at a small table with room for one on each side.

"Anna, you have a lovely home and this centerpiece is charming," Maria was finally able to speak.

"Thank you, Maria," replied Anna. "Jason and I will bring out the dishes and then we can pray and eat."

William prayed, "Father in heaven, we thank you for the delicious food that Anna and Jason prepared this morning, and ask that you would bless it to the nourishment of our bodies, and our bodies to your service. We pray this in Jesus precious name, Amen".

Then they passed around the baked chicken, mashed potatoes, garden peas, and a tossed salad with choice of dressings. It was all delicious. Maria schooled her features and made herself enjoy every bite, making appropriate statements about how good it all tasted. Every now and then she fingered the list of questions in her pocket, and sent up another prayer for guidance and peace.

When all of the main meal had been eaten, Anna said, "I'll be right back with Jason's favorite dessert." He actually blushed and looked embarrassed, but he smiled at her as she returned with chocolate chip cookies. "He has never outgrown his childhood favorite, and I'm glad, because I always know just what to bake," she explained. Everybody laughed and it helped to break the ice and they enjoyed the dessert.

"Now," William instructed, "we'll adjourn to the living room, where we have comfortable chairs in a circle so we can all see each other. We'll leave the clean up for later since the leftovers are already put away, so we can get right to the questions Jason would like to ask." He led the way and the others followed and got seated.

Jason started, "Before I ask any questions, I want to tell you how sorry I'm for getting angry and fuming about what you said in the restaurant. It is no wonder you left me there."

"Thank you for the apology. I forgive you," Maria replied.

"Plus, I wish for you to know how much I appreciate you sharing the Gospel with me and helping to wake me up to that terrible error in my thinking," he added.

"You're welcome. I'm glad I was able to be of help," Maria responded.

"Also, since Jesus has saved and healed me completely, I won't get angry again. In addition to that, I'm sorry that I came on so strongly about my feelings for you in the office that day, because I should have waited. But I need to tell you that I still feel the same." Then he continued, "Thank you so much, Maria, for being willing to come here today and answer my questions. My first question is: Which father did you mean when you wrote that note in the Bible you gave to me?"

Maria answered, "I meant my Heavenly Father, but I know my earthly one would have felt the same way."

Next he asked, "Do you think he might let me court you now that I'm a believer? I know my faith is new, but it's very genuine."

Maria replied, "I'm so glad that you're now a believer, Jason, and that Jesus has healed you also. In view of that, I know my Heavenly Father would say you could court me. But since you have already made your feelings very clear to me, I find that I need to be very careful. I don't wish to hurt your feelings in any way, but this is a life long decision and I need to give it careful consideration. Therefore, I will need to ask you some questions before I can give an answer about being courted."

"Please feel free to ask me whatever you want," he responded.

"Okay, here is the first one. What is your view on finances?"

Jason looked puzzled and then a light bulb went on. "I see that I also need to apologize to you about that first date. I was trying to impress you, so I rented a newer BMW, and took you to the most expensive restaurant in the city. At that point in my life, all that mattered to me was showing you how much wealth I had, so you would know that I could take care of you. But what I did there was a lie and would not have shown you anything. I'm sorry I did that."

"Thank you for the apology. I forgive you and I need to apologize to you also, because when you complimented me for not complaining about going out of town to work on that confidential job, I didn't say anything then, but the night before, I had complained about it to my cat." They all got a good laugh about that. "I'm sorry I wasn't honest then."

Jason said, "Thank you for being honest about it now, and I do forgive you."

"I ask this <u>next</u> question of myself also. "Do you think Jesus would like for you to be married, or might he want you to remain single?" asked Maria.

"I definitely want to be married, if it can be to you!" Jason said emphatically.

Maria kept her face unreadable and continued, "What is your view about marriage?"

"One man and one woman joined for life," he answered.

"And what do you believe about having sex before being married?" was her next question.

"It's not a good idea," he replied.

Then she asked, "What do you think God wants you to do with your life?"

Jason stated, "You ask hard questions. I guess I don't know."

Next, Maria asked again, "What is your view on finances? I don't think that question was answered."

He responded, "I work hard and honestly for the money I make, and I tithe 10%. I desire to use the rest to make it possible for you to live like a queen, never having to work another day of your life. I wish to love and cherish you and spend whatever it might take in order to prove my love to you."

With great effort to keep her face calm, she asked, "Did you have any other questions you wanted to ask me?"

"No," Jason replied, wishing he could ask her right then if she would marry him!

So Maria, surmising that he was thinking that very thing, decided she would have to be very honest even if he did get hurt feelings. She plunged in, her face showing just how stressed she was. "Jason, I thank you for answering my questions and I'm honored that you desire to love and cherish me, but it would be unfair of me to let you court me, because I know I could <u>never</u> live the life you described to me just a minute ago. I'm very sorry. I didn't want to hurt your feelings."

"Please explain what you mean," he requested.

"I think that you are in a completely different league than I could ever be comfortable with. I don't like having money be spent on me," she explained. She realized she would have to tell him why, so she added, "I desire to live simply in order to give all my extra money to win others to Jesus. I would <u>not</u> desire to quit working, because I've just recently found a way to witness to my co-workers. Thank you for your part in fixing such a delicious meal. Again, I'm sorry."

All he could say was, "Oh."

Maria then turned to her hostess and asked, "May I please help you with the clean up?" She nodded and the two ladies went to the kitchen, where they made short work of the dishes.

Then Anna took Maria's hands in hers and said, "Thank you for being honest with Jason. I know it was hard for you to do, but it's so much better than leading him on like some women might."

"It <u>was</u> very hard, because I hated to have to hurt his feelings. Thank you very much for the delicious lunch and for you and William being here as a buffer. I don't know if I could have said all that needed to be said, if I had been alone with him," Maria responded.

"You're very welcome and I hope you and I can be friends. Please visit again sometime. I'll have Ruth and Esther ask you to come with them at a time when Jason won't be here. Don't worry about him. He will get over it. He still has a lot to learn, and it's good you realize that you are not the one to teach him," said Anna.

Maria nodded, left by the kitchen door, got in her car and drove home, totally relieved that the ordeal was over!

In the living room, Jason was crying, grieving over the loss of his dream. He asked his dad, "What went wrong? I thought all women yearned to be treated like a queen and be lavished with gifts. Not Maria! She asked me very hard questions and then turned my last answer against me, effectively shutting the door forever. I know she didn't do it on purpose to hurt me. Her face had looked very pale and distressed." Finally he prayed, "Father in heaven, please heal my broken heart and help me learn whatever you want me to learn from this situation. In Jesus precious name, Amen."

His dad responded, "Jason, I'm so proud of you. You worked through all of those thoughts without becoming angry but in a logical manner. And best of all was your prayer at the end. God will answer it in his time and you'll be all the better for having gone through this class in his school of experiences."

*****

Karen called about the apartment as soon as they got home from the small group meeting. The people said they could come right over and look at it, so they did. It was small, and unfurnished, but very clean. Pam had furniture, and with it all in place it would be very comfortable and private. The ceiling and walls had been soundproofed so she would not even hear the footsteps or whatever was going on above, in the rest of the basement, or in the garage next to it. The rent was a little less than for a normal one bedroom apartment in a complex, <u>and</u> it included the utilities. There was a parking place just around on the side, and a nice view of a small park from the sliding glass door and other windows.

Karen called Pam immediately and told her all about it. "I love it already," Pam said. "You don't have to look any further. It sounds perfect, more like a little house than an apartment. What about laundry?"

"Laundry is included, but you'll have to share the facilities with the owners and they'll help you plan when you can use them. They're also in the basement," said Jeff.

"The kitchen is so cute and has a place for a table with a view of the park. It is facing south, so the snow won't take very long to melt in the winter," explained Karen.

"Can you put down a deposit or whatever they need, and then I'll pay you back and pay the rest of the rent when I get there?" Pam asked.

"That will be fine. I like picturing you in this cute little home. We'll see you on Wednesday. Bye for now," said Karen and she ended the call after Pam thanked them again and said her good bye.

Jeff and Karen made all the arrangements with the owners after telling them all they needed to know about their new renter. In the car, they called Fiona to thank her for the information and how they and Pam had liked it so much. Then they thanked and praised the Lord before going to lunch at a nice quiet little cafe.

*****

Once at home in her comfortable little studio apartment with her calico cat, Maria looked around and smiled. She liked it here and she liked her lifestyle, because it allowed her to do whatever her Master, Jesus would tell her to do. Now she would be able to continue with the ministry of sharing her faith with her co-workers.

She knelt beside her sofa and thanked God for the big red stop sign about being courted by Jason, and she thanked him for her friends and pastor who had prayed for her and given her good advice. Then she prayed, "Jesus, my Lord and Master, I commit myself to your service as a single woman for the rest of my life if that is your will. I desire to be available to do whatever you ask me to do and not waste time even thinking of finding some man to marry. Take my life and help me be consecrated to you. May everything I say and do bring you glory and further your kingdom, in Jesus name, Amen." She got up from there filled with a great peace.

After that she called Pastor Don and Anita, then Ted and Julie, and last Ruth and Esther, telling them everything that had happened, and how relieved she was that it was all over, but that she was glad she had gone to lunch and talked with Jason. Now she would not have to wonder or regret. She even told all of them about her commitment to remain single if God willed, so she could give her full attention to serving Jesus.

She agreed with Julie that Jason and she would have been a very unlikely couple, and thanked them again for the questions they had suggested. The one about finances was the clincher.

She said to Ruth and Esther, "I hope you won't be angry with me and I hope we can still be friends --- "

They both interrupted her and said, "Of course we'll still be friends, and we're sisters in the Lord besides!"

"Thank you both so much! That means a lot to me," replied Maria, very relieved.

Then she went and took a second shower in the same day to get rid of the nervous perspiration. The nap she had after that was soothing and restorative. She woke feeling rested and full of peace and joy. She put on a CD with the song, "I'd Rather Have Jesus," and sang along with it with great feeling and agreement.

*****

That Saturday afternoon, Vern, Mindy and Lora visited the zoo. The weather was just perfect.

Mindy commented, "It's a good idea to come to the zoo when it's not so hot. It smells a lot better than in the middle of the summer."

Vern laughed, "I remember. Last year we waited too long and it wasn't nearly as pleasant."

Lora joined in the laughter. "Which animals do you enjoy watching the most, Mindy?"

"The zebras, because they look so much like donkeys and horses except for their stripes," she answered.

"Let's go there first then, so we'll be sure to see them. After that we can just go from group to group of animals until we run out of time," suggested Lora.

"That's a very good idea," Vern replied. "It's almost like eating dessert first!"

Everybody cracked up and it was a good way to start their visit to the zoo.

*****

The first Sunday in June

After breakfast, Ted and Julie decided to go walking in their neighborhood again while it was cool. As they walked, they prayed that those people would be out in their yard again and they would have a chance to build up more rapport and see what Jesus might tell them to do. Julie had told Ted she would like to learn some sign language so she could communicate directly with the young lady. So they had gone on the web and she had learned to say, "Hello," and ask, "How are you?"

So she was glad when she saw them out in the yard. She practiced it again on Ted and then they went in and greeted the parents. Then Julie explained, "I learned a little sign language and would like to try it but I won't know what your daughter answers, so will you translate?"

Her mother answered, "Certainly. Go ahead and try it."

Julie got her attention and signed, "Hello. How are you?"

She smiled and answered in sign language. Her parents translated and explained to her that Julie only knew that much, but would like to learn some more. They spent the next half an hour there being taught and practicing some other phrases and words. It was fun, and they all enjoyed it. As they left, Julie said, "I'll try to learn some more before we see you again." Then they prayed for those people all the way back home where they looked up some more words and phrases to learn and practiced the ones they had learned in the yard.

*****

Matt and Ben were busy again working on his house. When they had arrived on Saturday afternoon, Ben had exclaimed, "I'm overwhelmed with the progress that has already been made on this house since the two crews have been working here full time! I wanted to see it move faster, and it sure is. I just wish I could be here every day. I know I can't, because school is more important. Someday, if it's the Lord's will, I'll be doing this for a living."

"What a worthy goal, and I, for one, believe you'll reach it. You're a very good worker. If I were a boss, I would hire you," stated Matt.

Ben smiled and said, "Thank you for the compliment."

"You earned it. Now let's see how much we can add to what they've already done," replied Matt.

*****

Maria was waiting for Ted and Julie in the entryway of the church. Maria told them her plan to have them meet and walk together in the mall where it would be cool. Meanwhile they would enjoy the service.

The songs today were: "Revive Us Again," Psalm 85:6; "Share His Love," Romans 8:32; "Pass It On," 1 John 4:11; "Til He Comes," Romans 10:9; "Bring Them In," John 10:16.

"I know most of us are already doing what these songs say to do, and what the teaching instructs, and I'm so glad. Keep up the good work! Please write down all the references that go with the songs we sang today. Read them at home. Next think of any other verses that go with this topic. Write those down too. You can use them as encouragement to keep going if you need to build up your confidence.

"Last week's teaching was about The Second Coming of Jesus. This week is a follow up to that teaching, and is meant to encourage us to harvest while there's still time. I especially like John 10:16 which goes with the last song we sang. It says, *I (Jesus) have other sheep, which are not of this fold. I must bring them also and they shall hear my voice, and there shall be one fold, and one shepherd.* We have the privilege and responsibility to be Jesus' witnesses as he said in Acts 1:8, and to help him bring those other sheep into the fold. Thank you for helping to bring them in.

"Now, we'll use the rest of our teaching time today to have as many people as we have time for, read one of their favorite scripture verses about this topic or any other one, into this microphone so we can all enjoy hearing them together. Take the next three minutes to look one up and practice it, then keep your finger in the place so you can make a line here behind the podium and take turns reading into the microphone while the podium holds your Bible. When you finish reading go ahead back to your seat.

While you're not in line you might like to write down the references. If someone takes your favorite verse, go ahead and read it again. Repetition is a good teacher."

Silence, except for turning pages and then murmurs of people practicing for three minutes and the first 'brave' people went up on the stage to form a line behind the podium. It was very special to listen to God's word being read by fellow members of the church, knowing it was one of their favorite verses. Julie chose to stay at her seat and write down <u>all</u> the references, so as to not miss any, but most of the congregation had time to go read a verse.

When the time was up, Pastor Don said, "I have an announcement. There will be a special baptismal service this Tuesday at 7 PM. If you know any of these new believers, please come and support them as they follow Jesus in water baptism. And, like we did last time, invite some unbelievers. The lead pastor will be giving a gospel message and invitation at the end."

Then he had them sing "Pass It On" again and prayed a dismissal prayer before they left. Many people went up to tell him how much they had gotten out of listening to the people read their favorite verses.

*****

Jeff and Karen had invited the Suehiros including Aneko to go for a walk in the park after church, to discuss the two by two ministries. Jeff said, "I think that it would be good for you to have a three by three ministry, and I don't think you'll need our assistance any longer. You handled that last one just fine on your own."

Tomo responded, "I think your idea good. Yoshi can join us too, and he and Aneko can read our "I Can Do" booklet. If they have any questions that we can't answer, may we call you?"

"Of course! And we can still get together to visit or do other things together," answered Karen. In fact, when Yoshi gets moved back to Pine City we would like to have all four of you come to supper some Sunday evening."

"We would enjoy that," replied Ami.

*****

Maria met Ted and Julie at the mall, where they walked and talked for about 45 minutes. It was relaxing to just share small talk after the stress of the last week, and to know that they didn't have to rehash any of it again.

"I thought it was very nice of Pastor Don to compliment the congregation on doing a good job of evangelizing and to encourage us to keep up the good work," Ted commented.

Julie agreed, "Yes, and I liked the idea of having people read their favorite verses out loud. I enjoyed that so much that I stayed at my seat and wrote down all the references so I can go over them again sometime."

"We're very blessed to have such a caring pastor and his wife. They've helped me many times," added Maria.

Later, Julie mentioned, "I like walking in here where it's cool. This will probably work out well for our weekly exercise and sharing time until it cools off again in the fall."

"I agree. I think I'd rather keep Sunday mornings the way they are now," replied Maria.

"Besides, we can all keep our eyes open for a ministry opportunity here in the mall on Sunday afternoons, since Julie and I are on our own now. If you would like to, we could add you and make it three by three," suggested Ted.

"That's a great idea," agreed Maria, and Julie nodded emphatically. "When Pam left, my group lost its third member. This is why I'm so happy to have a ministry at work."

"Maybe Pam will want to join us," suggested Julie. "We can ask her after she gets settled."

*****

Matt was a little nervous before he arrived at Fiona's house for supper that Sunday evening. Since he had never met Riley, he prayed for peace and the right words to say all evening and then went up the walk. Fiona and Riley were waiting on the porch and right away, Matt noticed that Riley was smiling and eager to meet him.

"Welcome!" he said. "I'm so glad Fiona chose you to be my brother-in-love. I've always wanted a brother, and from what Fiona has told me, you'll make a perfect one."

"Thank you, Riley. The feeling is mutual, and I'm glad you're home from college so we can get acquainted before the wedding. I was glad to hear that you found a job you like so quickly here in Pine City," said Matt relieved that everything was going to be all right.

Fiona invited, "Come on inside you two. You can visit in the living room while Mother and I finish getting supper ready."

They all had an enjoyable time during supper and the evening following it.

*****

Chapter 23

Isaiah 58:11a, *The LORD shall guide you continually.*

Monday

Matt drove past his house on the way to the Laundromat, still amazed that Walt and Betty would want to do something so nice for Fiona and him. The first shift was already busily at work. He waved and continued on his way. When he was finished washing and drying all his clothes, he decided to drive to his apartment a different way so they wouldn't think he was checking up on them. Walt insisted that he <u>not</u> come and work extra time during the week in the mornings. He was trying to figure out other things to do instead, so he prayed for guidance.

He called Fiona, when he got home and turned on the speaker so he could finish folding his clothes while he talked. "Hi, Fiona. How's my fiancée this beautiful morning?" he asked.

"She is very well. How's my fiancé?" she playfully asked right back.

"He is feeling super, but is trying to figure out a puzzle. I would like to spend as much time with you at least like we've been doing, and still give you time with your mother. Walt doesn't want me to work extra time on the house during the week, so I won't get too tired. But it's okay with him if I work part days on the weekend. Ben Clay likes to help me on the weekends when it works out. So here is the puzzler. Would it work out for you to have our time together on two mornings a week, like Tuesdays and Thursdays, and have Ben work with me on Saturday afternoons and Sunday mornings?" inquired Matt.

"Certainly," she answered. "I like that idea, because we'll also be together at small group and church. What did you have in mind for activities on Tuesdays and Thursdays?"

"I was thinking that one of those days we could do something fun, and the other one we could work on planning for the wedding and for the interior of the house or the landscaping," he replied.

"Great ideas. We can play it by ear depending on the weather, and what fun things we might wish to do. But if we need to work both days we could do that instead of something fun," she suggested. "And, if we desire to do something with my parents, Sunday evenings would be open for that."

"I'm so glad I called you. I love to hear your voice, and you helped solve the puzzle for me on top of that. Thank you my dear Fiona. What would you like to do tomorrow morning?" he asked.

"I would like to go to a landscaping place and get some ideas for our yard," she answered right away.

"Good plan. They might have some books we can look at, or photographs of things they've done for other people. Let's go right after breakfast. May I pick you up at 8:30?" he inquired.

"I'll look forward to it!" she responded enthusiastically. "See you in the morning!"

He told her good-bye and they hung up, both very pleased with the plans they had made. His laundry was all folded so he went to put it away, and do the rest of his housework.

*****

At lunchtime, Ruth, Esther, and Maria took their lunches and walked to the park. After their walk around the park and thanking the Lord for their food, Esther said, "Maria, on Sunday evening Dad called Ruth and me. He's decided that it's time for me to go work in Jason's office so I can learn everything about how things are done there. So today is my last day here."

"Oh Esther, I'm so sad!" exclaimed Maria. "I've enjoyed our times together so much. But I guess 'father knows best,' like the old TV show title says. That was suppose to be an attempt at a joke to make me feel better, but it didn't work."

Ruth spoke up, "We'll all get over our sadness, and we'll see how God can use this change for good. In fact, I was thinking that maybe Jason and Esther could take one co-worker with them to lunch each day as he introduces her to them, like I did with you, Maria. Two Christians working together is probably better than the way we've been doing it here. Do you see what I mean?"

"Yes. And again you're correct my dear big sister. It <u>will</u> be good for Jason and me both, to get our minds off our disappointments and get busy serving God. At least I'll be able to continue living in the same apartment with you, Ruth. And the job will be very much like this one, so I won't complain," agreed Esther.

"I can see what you both mean, and I agree, plus I can see you at church on Sundays, so let's pray while we eat, that God will help us accept this, and that we'll be able to do his will," suggested Maria. They did that and all of them were feeling better about it by the time they walked back to the office building.

At the end of the day, Esther grabbed Maria and they went to Ruth's office. She said, "I have a suggestion. You know the two co-workers who accepted Jesus and will be baptized this week? Each of you could pair up with one of them as you ask another co-worker to accompany you to lunch. That way, you'll have two Christians times two, working together to win the rest of these co-workers to the Lord."

"Thank you, Esther, your idea is very good," agreed Ruth, and Maria nodded enthusiastically. "We'll ask them in the morning to go with us as a foursome to a cafe where we can discuss the idea."

"Plus, we can get together on the weekends sometimes. In addition, Mom wants to have all three of us over for a meal at a time when Jason won't be there," Esther explained.

"That sounds nice. I'll look forward to it," said Maria, and then they all went home.

*****

Julie and Ted got home very close to the same time from their jobs and greeted each other with their normal hugs and kisses. As they worked together to fix supper Julie said, "I just realized something that I'm very thankful for. I don't have to give up my job of teaching so that Pam can come back to the school and teach. Plus, the other teacher who has to move is happy about it because now they can get a head start on beginning a family. God worked this situation out for the best for all three of us!"

"You're right. This will be a happy time for all of you. "Thank you Lord, for this great blessing!" said Ted.

"How was your day at work, Honey?" she asked.

"It was very good. We finished up a repair on a car we started last week, and we were a day early. The people will be glad to get it back early," he replied.

"It is nice you have such a positive job, and I do also. Thank you Lord, for these blessings and for the food we are about to eat. We pray in Jesus name, Amen.

During the meal, Ted asked, "Where would you like to go to celebrate the second anniversary of our wedding?"

"Oh my! I'm so glad you remembered. The time has gone so fast since we moved that I forgot it was coming up soon. How about Ami's Japanese Restaurant? It should be warm enough outside now that we could sit in that beautiful garden," she answered.

"That sounds wonderful to me! The atmosphere and the food are both excellent," he answered.

*****

Tuesday

While Don and Anita ate breakfast, they discussed the pastors' small group meeting they had attended the night before. "That was really good news about the committee finding some property with some very old run down warehouses on it that need to be torn down," Anita mentioned.

"Yes," he replied, "plus, it's in a very centralized area, just on the opposite side of town from our church. It isn't as close to the center of the city as ours, but that's probably a good thing."

Anita continued, "The price sounded reasonable, and on top of that they gave an allowance for having to tear the buildings down."

"That was a great benefit. From the looks of the pictures they showed us, even just tearing them down will improve the looks of the area. Add the landscaped new church and school building, and it will look magnificent. Plus, the worth of their purposes is beyond measure," stated Don.

"That's for sure. I'm looking forward to the baptismal service this evening. I've been thinking that if they would like to, it might be good for Timmy and Mary to attend and sit beside me," suggested Anita.

Don agreed, "Yes, the twins were at the last one and will be there tonight for Cory's baptism. Maybe you could take a little time to explain it to them today."

"That's another good idea. In fact, one of the Bible stories for next week is about Philip and the man from Ethiopia who believed and asked to be baptized. I'll just use it today by switching places, and explain a little more if it does not have enough detail. I'll sit near the back, and if they get antsy, I can take them over to childcare," she said, and he agreed.

*****

By the time everyone arrived for the special Baptismal service, it was almost a full house. Churches 1,2,3, and 4 were all there, and each one had about the same number of new believers to be baptized. Many people had come to hear about the good results the Good News.

Cory nudged his dad and whispered, "Look, there are my classmates from this year and last. I'm glad we all get to be in the same special service." His dad nodded and his mom smiled. He always added so much pleasure to their lives.

The lead pastor opened with prayer, and they sang the same songs as they had a month ago, but added one extra because several of the new believers wanted to refer to it in their testimony. It's message was that since Jesus changed me, he can change you too. It tells the story of a person who had been in a very bad lifestyle, but was saved and changed by Jesus. The people who desired that song had asked some of their old friends to come to the service, and they were praying that they would be saved also.

Churches 1,2, and 3 went through their baptisms first, and then it was time for church 4. Pastor Don was ready with the first person, which was the man Larry and Jane had led to Jesus. They and Ted and Julie listened with grateful tears in their eyes as he told of his miserable failures but that Jesus had made him into a new man who now had a good job, no desire for alcohol or drugs, and he had written and apologized to his wife and children. They understandably were waiting in the other state to see if it lasted. He ended by singing part of that song.

The next people were Cory and his parents and grandparents, and we already know their testimonies. Roy and the twins were elated to get to watch their baptisms.

One of Cory's classmates testified, "When I saw Cory walk into our classroom knowing he had never been able to walk since he was born, I was totally amazed. Then when Cory told our class about how Jesus had healed him and then saved him and his family, I wanted that for me and my family, too. Thank you, Jesus, for all you've done."

The mother of a classmate in Cory's small group said, "Cory and my son have always been good boys, but I could tell a positive difference after Jesus saved them. I'm so glad Jesus saved my son and us, his parents."

That classmate added, "Thank you Jesus for healing Cory and saving him. Thank you, Cory, for having the courage to stand there in front of our whole class and our teacher and the principal and tell us all about how Jesus healed and saved you. I ran with you to that big tree at recess so I could pray to be saved, too. Thank you, Jesus!"

The next people were the ones who had accepted Jesus at the last Baptismal service. Each of their testimonies was connected in some way to a testimony they had heard at that service that had clicked with them in some way. They had listened carefully to the Gospel message and gratefully prayed the prayer with the pastor. Many of them included a statement like, "If you don't know Jesus yet, I hope you will soon!"

Two preteen girls and their families came next. One of the girls said, "I wasn't at the last service, but a girl who was baptized then told me her story at school. She <u>definitely</u> is a changed person, and I'm convinced that only Jesus could make a change like that. Thank you, Jesus for saving me and my family. Please use us to tell others." Candy was smiling her best smile as she listened to that testimony.

The other girl added, "Another girl who has always been very well behaved had befriended that girl, even before she was saved. I could tell she was a good influence, and when she told us her testimony also, I could see that I needed a Savior like that, too. Thank you Jesus, that my parents and I have asked Jesus to be our Savior." Mindy smiled at her humbly, and gave thanks also.

Ted and Julie had done the same thing earlier when they heard the older Jewish woman give her testimony and tell the people she was praying for and witnessing to her family.

The Suehiros had closed their restaurant early again so they could all be there for Yoshi. He gave a summary of what had happened to his cousin, and how that woke him up to his need. He said, "Thank you Dad and Mom for continuing to pray for me until I saw the light. Thank you Jesus for this wonderful salvation! Now I want to live for you."

Julie turned on her recorder so she could catch what the children and families said about their time in the park. One child said, "There was a man who was telling a story to some kids, but it was in Spanish, so I couldn't understand it. When he finished, he took some of the kids with him. Another man told me and some other kids the same story in English. When he was done, I knew why the other man took some kids with him. This man did also, and he helped us understand better and then pray for Jesus to become our Savior. Then he gave us a little book to share with our parents. They understood too, and now we all love Jesus and are going to church and a small group. Thank you Jesus for that man and that he told us the story in English!"

The other children and their parents said similar things, and when Tony listened to the recordings the next morning as he had breakfast with Ted and Julie, he had tears of joy in his eyes. "It's such a privilege to be used by Jesus to bring others into the Kingdom," he said. Of course they agreed.

Maria's co-workers were close to the last ones to be baptized, and their testimonies included a summary of the things they had heard her say when they went to lunch with her. They thanked Jesus for a co-worker who made friends first, and then cared enough to get them interested, and after that, tell them the Gospel and help them to pray. One of them added, "I desire for Jesus to use me to tell others about him now." Maria was filled with joy about them.

During those two testimonies, Jeff, Matt, and the rest of the second shift men had slipped into the back of the sanctuary, after leaving half an hour early from work. Jeff had a big smile, but Matt looked totally bewildered. But then he saw the person in the baptismal water and heard this: "A little over a month ago I heard a story I could not believe about a man who had a heart attack but was healed and then saved. All his co-workers and mine on the other shift believed and they were also saved, but I told them I wasn't ready yet. They didn't give up on me. I know all of them were praying for me. I could see a big difference in the men on my shift that had believed, and I wanted what they had. My wife and I started going to see one of them and his wife to get our questions answered. About two weeks ago we finally understood and believed. Thank you, Jesus, for saving us!"

His wife was the last one to testify and she said, "It was a struggle for both of us, because of the way we were raised, but Jesus didn't give up on us either. He is very patient. It is an important decision and a person needs to be certain, but be sure that you don't wait too long. None of us know how long we're going to live, and there's no second chance after death."

The pastor of church #1 built on that last testimony and then explained what the Gospel and being saved meant. He was careful, clear and emphatic, knowing that there were unbelievers including some more children who came at the request of their friends. Then he led those who wanted salvation in a prayer like those on Sundays. "If you prayed that prayer with me, please tell the people who invited you here and then come up here with those people so we can meet you and rejoice with you. Then we'll give each family or individual if you came by yourself, a little booklet that will explain more about your decision. There's a card in the booklet which you can fill out and give to the pastor of the church you'll hopefully attend this coming Sunday."

There were cheers and praises all over the auditorium as people told the ones who had invited them that they had prayed that prayer. Then they were taken up and introduced to the pastor of the appropriate church. He rejoiced with them and gave each family a little booklet.

Much praise and rejoicing came from the parents of some very young children. Joy, Hope, Timmy and Mary had sat very still and attentively during the baptisms and testimonies. They had heard the Gospel many times, but this time it had been very personal, especially since there were so many children in the audience. This time they realized that Jesus had died for them. When the pastor led in the prayer, their little mouths moved to silently say what he had said. They were able to tell the parent they were sitting beside what they had done and why.

Pastor Don was overjoyed when he saw the happy tears in Anita's eyes as she brought their children up to tell him that they now believed in Jesus as their Savior. He rejoiced with Roy when he brought Joy and Hope to tell him the same thing. He only wished their mother had been able to get off work so she could have been here, also. Oh well, the twins would tell her all about it in the morning. He gave each family a little booklet with a card in it. Maybe they could start a Sunday school time small group for these very young new believers. They would need something like that. He asked the lead pastor about it and he agreed.

*****

Wednesday

Early Wednesday morning, Pam and her Dad went to the local trailer rental place, filled out all the necessary paperwork and paid the rent on a small, one-way trailer which they took to their house and proceeded, with the help of many friends and neighbors to wrap and load all the furniture and the things Pam had been packing since Monday. Then they had a surprise early lunch and sendoff party that her mother had prearranged as a thank you for all Pam had done for her. Her parents really were changed for the better now that Jesus' Spirit lived inside of them! It had been worth it all.

Pam left at noon and drove carefully for the next 8 hours with several stops along the way to stretch and walk, fill up with gas and eat supper. She arrived at Jeff and Karen's home shortly after 8 PM and met Karen in person who took her to see the apartment they had found.

"Oh, I really love it! Thank you Lord. You're so good to me," Pam prayed and then thanked Karen. She met her landlords and was very impressed with them also. She wrote a check for the first and last months rent and repaid Karen for the deposit. A quick look outside revealed that not only was there a parking place around on the side of the building, it was a carport, so there would be no problem of a snow covered vehicle or even a frosty windshield in the winter. That was a bonus blessing!

Karen suggested, "Shall we go get your car and trailer from where we left them at our house? We can leave a note for Jeff to meet us here and meanwhile we can start unloading the light things."

"Very good idea, let's do it," answered Pam.

They had made very good progress by the time Jeff arrived and met Pam in person. As they unloaded the bed, which had been put near the door of the trailer, she told them about the nice party her mother had given for her. After that, she said, "Thank you both again for all your help. I can make the bed and we can finish the rest of the unloading in the morning. Now you both go home so you can have supper and go to bed, too."

"Okay," said Jeff. I'll bring some people from our small group to help with the rest tomorrow. We'll be here after breakfast, about 9 AM."

"That will be wonderful. I brought enough food with me for a couple of days, so I can eat breakfast here," explained Pam.

*****

After supper that day, Ted and Julie went for a walk. It had cooled off, and they went back to that same neighborhood again after practicing the new sign language they had learned. This time there were about ten other people in the yard. It looked like a party. They kept walking and praying, and decided to pass on by. But the dad saw them and called for them to come over, "The BBQ is over, but we're going to make s'mores. Please come join us."

Ted said, "Thank you. That sounds like fun." They enjoyed it and got to meet the people who were having a family reunion. Most of them were from out of state. They were a pretty noisy bunch.

At one point, Julie saw the deaf young woman looking on with longing, and told Ted she felt the go ahead to pray for her. So she went over to her mother and asked, "Could we pray for your daughter? I learned how to sign 'Jesus loves you and he wants to make you be able to hear and talk. May we pray for you?' If she agrees, would you ask her if we can put our hands on her head while we pray?"

Her dad was listening also, and they both nodded. Looking curious and hopeful, they followed Ted and Julie over to where their daughter sat watching the gathering. They got her attention and signed what they had learned. The girl was thoughtful for a moment and then nodded. Her mother got her permission for them to place their hands on her head while they prayed. Suddenly it got very quiet, as all the people stopped what they were doing to watch and listen.

They carefully placed one hand each over her ears, and the others on her head. Ted prayed out loud with Julie agreeing, "Father in heaven, we ask in Jesus name for Jesus to make this young woman be able to hear and talk." Then he said, "In Jesus name, you deaf and dumb spirit come out of her and never return!" He spoke directly to the ears and mouth, "Ears, be opened. Mouth, be able to talk." They kept their hands on her as they felt Jesus power going through them to her. After that, Julie asked her, "Can you hear me?"

"Yes! I can hear you perfectly, and I can talk, too. Wow! Thank you for praying for me."

"You're welcome, but Jesus is the one who healed you. <u>He</u> is the one to thank. We're glad that he was able to use us to pray for you," explained Ted.

Her father asked, "How did you know it was a spirit?"

Ted answered humbly, "Jesus told me, by his Holy Spirit who lives in me. The spirit that kept your daughter from hearing and talking was evil, and Jesus knew it needed to be cast out. Jesus knows everything. He also knows that there are some people here who don't know him as their own personal Savior. May I tell all of you how you can do that?"

They all nodded, and came closer to be able to hear well. Ted told them all about Jesus and the Gospel. He read from Acts 10:36-43. *God sent his Word to the people of Israel, preaching peace by Jesus Christ the Messiah, who is Lord of all. ... God anointed Jesus of Nazareth with the Holy Spirit and with power. He went around doing good, and healing all who were oppressed by the devil, because God was with him. The disciples were witnesses of all the things Jesus did in Judea and Jerusalem. The people in Jerusalem killed Jesus by crucifying him on a cross. But God raised him from the dead on the third day and showed him openly, but only to the witnesses he had chosen beforehand. They ate and drank with Jesus after he rose from the dead. Jesus commanded these witnesses to preach to the people and to testify that Jesus was ordained of God to be the Judge of the living and the dead. All the prophets gave witness about Jesus, that through his name whoever believes in him shall receive forgiveness of their sins."*

Ted went on from there to explain what happens if people don't believe: "Not only would we continue sinning without being forgiven, we would be open to being controlled by evil spirits. Even worse that that, is the fact that we would be lost forever, separated from the God who loved the world so much *that he gave his only Son so that all who believe in him would not perish, but have everlasting Life. For God did not send his Son into the world to condemn the world, but that the world might be saved through him. He who believes in Jesus is not condemned, but he who does not believe is condemned already, because he has not believed in the name of the only begotten Son of God.* Those verses are in John 3:16-18 in the Bible. If you think about it I think you'll realize that you really only have one good option, and that is to believe in Jesus to be your own personal Savior. Do you have any questions?"

Some of the people did, so Ted and Julie answered them, and then asked, "How many of you already have Jesus as your own personal Savior?" he asked. None of them raised their hands.

"How many of you would like to?" he asked. They all raised their hands, so he led them in a prayer of confessing sins, asking forgiveness, stating their belief in Jesus, and asking him to be their own personal Savior.

There was great rejoicing and praise and thanks to God. The young woman who had been deaf and mute, was heard to loudly thank and praise Jesus for making her be able to hear and talk, and for being her Savior.

Ted and Julie handed out little booklets about their new life in Christ and one about the Holy Spirit to each family, since many of them didn't live in Pine City. They encouraged them to find a good church and small group in their own cities. They also gave their phone number if anyone had more questions. Then they invited the ones who did live in Pine City to come to church on Sunday at 2 PM, and gave them the address. They said they would, so Julie said, "We'll be in the entryway to welcome you and you can sit with us if you like. After the service we'll introduce you to Pastor Don and you can give him that card if you would like to be in a small group for new believers."

It was a much different group of people in that yard now as Ted and Julie stayed to listen as they processed what had happened, and answer more questions.

*****

Thursday

When Sherry arrived at the Ross home with the twins, Timmy and Mary ran over and gave them hugs. Timmy exclaimed, "We're all brother and sisters in God's big family, because we all have received Jesus as our personal Savior! And, we all did it at the same time on Tuesday at the baptismal service!"

Hope agreed, "We can all be baptized at the next one."

"Papa will start a small group just for us," said Mary.

"And he will let other young children join it too, so we can all learn how to live for Jesus," added Timmy.

Joy said, "I'm so glad that we're all in God's family now. It's even better than just being friends."

Their mothers stood back and listened with smiles on their faces and tears of joy in their eyes, because their children had all taken that first important step in following Jesus.

*****

At about 9 AM, Pam opened the door for Jeff and Karen to introduce her to Matt, Fiona, and Tony who had all come to help unload the rented trailer. They made short work of it and then stayed for a while to welcome her back to Pine City. Each one told Pam a little of their personal information, so she would not feel overwhelmed on Saturday morning when they would have their small group meeting at the Suehiro's house. After that, Matt and Fiona took Tony back to his apartment, and were able to do half of the Frisbee golf course before going home for lunch and work.

After everybody but Karen left, she went with Pam to check the trailer in at the rental place. Next Karen insisted on helping to unpack a few more things before she needed to leave to go to work. Pam felt really blessed, because the men had placed every piece of furniture just where she had asked them to, and it was already feeling like home.

Shortly after noon, her cell phone rang. It was Julie, asking her if she could stop by her new home and help if there was anything else left to do, and so they could talk about what to tell the children tomorrow.

Julie arrived a little before 5:30 PM, gave Pam a hug, and exclaimed, "How lovely everything looks! What a nice place this will be for you to live! Is there any way I can help you?"

"Not really. Karen helped this morning after she and Jeff and Matt and Fiona and Tony came and unloaded the trailer. My heavenly Father has taken very good care of me through other members of his family. Thank you for coming, though. It's really good to see you again."

"I feel the same. I've been so excited since I learned that you were coming back here to teach in the church school again. And it will be right next door to me. What shall we tell the children?" asked Julie.

"I went to see Beth today, before lunch, and she said it would be best if she brings me to your classroom right after the pledges and songs and opening prayer. She'll explain the whole situation to the class. She'll tell them that it would be best for them to not change back to having me as their teacher again, since I would not know how much they've progressed and learned, and that they would miss you and you would miss them, and that you would have to start all over with learning about a new class. I totally agree with her, and will say that to the class. They'll accept it, and know that it is for the best. She'll let me have a couple minutes to greet them and tell about my parents miracles.

"Then she'll take me next door and introduce me to that class, and I'll spend the rest of the day getting acquainted with them. I was able to bring home their records and pictures today, so I got started learning their names to go with their pictures like you did.

It may be awkward for a little while, but God will help us all. Just look at all he's already done!"

"You're absolutely right, and so is Beth. I worried over nothing. Thank you Lord for taking care of all this. What are you doing for supper?" asked Julie.

"I already ate an early one and I'll study the pictures and names again before I go to bed early," answered Pam.

"Good idea. In that case I would like to invite you to our apartment for supper tomorrow after school. You can follow me right to my home and meet my wonderful husband and let us pamper you after your busy week," suggested Julie.

"Thank you so much! That sounds blissful! I know I'll be exhausted after tomorrow, so I gladly accept," she said.

*****

That afternoon after school, Mindy told Anita, "I've decided the children at the daycare are enough sisters and brothers for me, but I still want a mother at home. I know Dad does not want any more children because of the way my mother died."

Anita replied, "I can understand the way he feels, and it's good that you can also. Jesus, we pray that a new wife for him will also be able to accept that fact."

"Yes, Jesus, please work out all the details according to your will." Then Mindy described some of the fun Saturday and Sunday afternoons her dad and she had had with Lora.

"She sounds like a fun and interesting person to do things with," responded Anita.

"I sure think so, and it looks to me like she and Dad are both enjoying themselves also," stated Mindy.

*****

Friday

Ruth and Maria had decided that they should keep their routine of having lunch together in the lunchroom or park on Fridays and Mondays. So they met there for a time of debriefing, sharing and prayer.

Maria stated, "I'm very thankful that I get to continue working in this office and that we can continue our friendship. How's Esther doing?"

"I have the same opinion about you being here! Esther is extremely adaptable, so she's doing very well. Jason liked her idea of the two of them going with a co-worker to lunch each day until she's met all of them. He still wants to be called Mr. Beckett, and will stay distanced from them after that. She's been writing down their interests as soon as she gets back to work like you did. Esther prays that at least one of them will believe in Jesus, so that the two of them can do what you and I are doing," Ruth responded.

"That sounds good. I'm glad the two new believers in this office are willing to partner with us at lunchtime. My co-worker and I are making some headway with the other one we've gone to lunch with this week. She is starting to listen better and even ask some questions. Every person is so different. I know I can't expect to keep having easy victories like I had that one week, even if that would be nice," stated Maria.

"True, my partner and I are having a similar experience," replied Ruth. "Let's pray about it before we return to work."

*****

After a busy day at school for both of them, Pam followed Julie to her home where she met Ted. They had her sit in the kitchen and watch them work together to fix supper while she told them about how her day had gone.

Julie told Ted as they were eating, "The children were glad to see Miss Green again and especially to hear about the miracles that had happened for her parents. Plus, they were very accepting of the fact that it would be best for everyone to leave things as they were. I was relieved."

"The other class was sorry to lose their teacher, but they were thankful that they would not have to have a substitute, or someone who was as old as their grandparents. When they heard that I had taught here before it sounded even better to them," explained Pam.

"I do enjoy hearing them share their thoughts and prayers every day. They're so candid and open," said Julie.

"In a way I envy the two of you, especially when I hear Julie tell of the fun and interesting things the children do and say, but I know I would never have the patience or the ability to be a teacher," commented Ted.

Everywhere There's a Sunrise, Let's Tell The Good News!

"Well I know I could never do your job either, so it's best to just keep the jobs we have," laughed Julie.

"What is your job, Ted?" asked Pam. He explained it to her and she laughed and agreed with Julie.

*****

***Saturday ***

Aneko went to her small group, and Yoshi went with her, since she had gotten permission from the facilitators to have him join that group. Tomo and Ami were already at theirs since it was meeting at their house today. All things were in readiness. They were looking forward to meeting Pam, after hearing so much about her.

Jeff and Karen came and they helped them put the books in place with name tags on each set. After that, they had time to pray together and visit a little before the members arrived. Karen opened with prayer and the first praise report was: "We thank you, Lord, that Pam arrived safely on Wednesday, and Fiona's suggestion for an apartment was just right! Many of you have already met her, but for those of you who haven't, this is Pam Green sitting next to me. Keep your name tags on during refreshment time and next week, so she'll have a chance to learn a few names."

Next, Julie said, "I praise you, Jesus, that my friend, Pam, will be teaching in the room right next to mine, and that you made so many things work out for the best of so many people in this situation."

Pam added, "Thank you, Lord, for your help and timing and the miracles you performed, and for this small group which has been so supportive while I was gone and since I arrived back."

Tomo changed the subject saying, "We thank and praise you that Yoshi has moved back to Pine City and will be working with us in the restaurant, taking care of the business end of it. His testimony on Tuesday was so special."

Larry agreed with him and then said, "We praise you for all the salvations and blessings in that family."

Tony continued, "Thank you, Jesus that I got to hear the testimonies of the children and their families, because of the caring of friends and the wonders of technology, recording them while I was at work."

Ami added, "We thank you for this small group and the many things we're learning here."

Jane prayed, "Thank you, Father, that the children came again on Wednesday and listened well to the study time and story."

Clara continued, "Thank you, Jesus, for all the people who were saved as a result of the testimonies and gospel message given at the baptismal service."

Roy shared, "The baptismal service was awesome, and resulted in our twins and Pastor Don and Anita's children all asking Jesus to be their own personal Savior along with all the others who prayed that prayer with the pastor!"

Sherry agreed, and prayed, "Thank you for the way Hope and Joy told me all about the service and their prayer."

Then Matt added, "I praise and thank you for saving my co-worker and his wife!"

Ted finished the praise time by telling about their latest four by four ministry time, which started with Larry and Jane on Tuesday last week, and then, "Julie and I did follow-up visits ending on Wednesday of this week with Jesus healing a deaf and mute young woman, and saving her, her parents, and many relatives who were there for a family reunion!"

Everybody joined in with applause and oral praise for all the things people had shared.

Jeff asked if there were any announcements. Tomo and Ami both stood up. Ami started passing out papers, and Tomo explained. "We did what Jeff had mentioned for the names of God, the Father, and Jesus with all the scripture verses typed out. Then we made copies of them and that's what Ami is handing to you."

Karen exclaimed, "These are wonderful! I'm going to put mine on my Bible study desk so I can review it from time to time. Thank you for making copies for each of us to treasure." They smiled and sat down.

Next, Jeff asked, "Who would like to host the next meeting?" Clara and Tony volunteered this time.

"Thank you very much," said Jeff. "Now let's sing 'It Is Good to Sing Thy Praises,' which is based on parts of Psalm 92." Next, they sang "Hallelujah, Let's Praise the Lord," Zephaniah 3:9; and "O Could I Speak the Matchless Worth," John 1:14.

The teaching time began with Jeff saying, "Open your hymnals again to 'It Is Good to Sing Thy Praises,' and see if you can find places where the words and phrases are the same as in

Everywhere There's a Sunrise, Let's Tell The Good News!

Psalm 92 as I read some of the verses. *It is good to give thanks to the* LORD *and to sing praises to your name O most High, to show forth your loving kindness in the morning, and your faithfulness every night, on an instrument of ten strings and on the psaltery, and on the harp. For you* LORD *have made me glad through your work. I will triumph in the works of your hands. O* LORD*, how great are your works! And your thoughts are very deep. ... You* LORD *are most high forever. Your enemies shall perish. All the workers of iniquity shall be scattered, ... but the righteous shall flourish like the palm tree. He shall grow like a cedar in Lebanon. Those that are planted in the house of the* LORD *still bring forth fruit in old age ... to show that the* LORD *is upright. He is my rock and there is no unrighteousness in him.* We praise you for those things, O LORD!

"Our second song has a reference to Zephaniah 3:9, and the last part of that verse talks about people serving the LORD with one consent, or in unity or one accord. Look up Psalm 133:1, ... it says, *Behold, how good and how pleasant it is for brothers to dwell together in unity!*" Find Ephesians 4:3, which basically tells us to endeavor *to keep the unity of the Spirit in the bond of peace.* Next I'll read verses 11-13 to you. *Jesus gave apostles, prophets, evangelists, pastors and teachers, for the perfecting of the saints, for the work of the ministry, for the edifying of the body of Christ, until we all come in the unity of the faith, and of the knowledge of the Son of God, unto a perfect man, to the measure of the stature of the fullness of Christ.* Jesus, please help us to do that!

"Our last song is one of my favorites. Of course I have many favorites, and for me that's a good thing, because I don't have to look very far to find one I can enjoy singing. It's based on John 1:14, which says, *The Word was made flesh, and dwelt among us, and we beheld his glory, the glory as of the only begotten of the Father, full of grace and truth.* That verse, along with verses 1-3 of the same chapter is very useful if you need to explain the incarnation to someone. Romans 1:3,4 states, *God's Son, Jesus Christ our Lord, was made of the seed of David according to the flesh, and declared to be the Son of God with power ... by the resurrection from the dead.* We praise you Jesus.

"Galatians 4:4-6, adds to our understanding. *When the fullness of time came, God sent forth his Son, made of a woman, and under the law, to redeem those who were under the law, that we might receive the adoption of sons, and because we are sons, God has sent forth the Spirit of his Son into our hearts, crying Abba, Father.* Thank you God that we are now your sons and you are our Father. 1 Timothy 3:16b says, *God was manifest in the flesh, justified in the Spirit, seen of angels, preached to the Gentiles, believed on in the world, and received up into glory.* We praise you God for the incarnation, and that Jesus is now back at your right hand in glory.

"I've just shown you another method of personal Bible study. Your homework is to take one of your favorite hymns and look up the scripture reference given under the title in our hymnals. Read that verse or verses and then praise whichever person of the Trinity is spoken about, or pray something appropriate. After that look up the cross-references and do the same thing. If you want to expand it further, choose words from the hymn and look them up in the concordance. As you go, write the references and praises or prayers in your study notebook."

Conversational prayer time began with Julie praying, "Lord, please help Pam to learn all the names of her new students and of the people in this small group. Bless her as she gets settled and starts teaching again."

Pam nodded emphatically and added, "Yes, please, and also bless my parents and help them continue to grow in the Lord."

Jeff continued, "Thank you that they're off to such a good start, and that you will finish what you started."

Jane prayed, "Father, please open the hearts of all the children who come to the Bible Study and Story groups so they'll believe in Jesus as their Savior."

Larry added, "Then have them bring their friends so that they can hear the Gospel."

Karen continued, "Help all the children who are new believers to grow and learn to do your will."

Tony requested, "Please help us as we do our homework, using the new method of personal Bible study."

Ted added, "Father please continue to guide all of us as we go out to do ministry for you."

Ami prayed, "Heavenly Father, thank you for the time of fellowship we'll have now, and please bless these refreshments to the health and nourishment of our bodies and use us in your service."

Tomo and Ami had made a huge, beautiful fruit salad, which they brought out of the refrigerator in a glass bowl that showed off all the pretty colors of the fruit. They did use paper bowls so the clean up would be easier. It was delicious and nutritious and refreshing. The fellowship was uplifting.

Everywhere There's a Sunrise, Let's Tell The Good News!

During refreshments and fellowship, Pam handed thank you cards to everyone in the group to thank them for their prayers and support while she was gone, with extra words of thanks to all the ones who had helped her get moved in, and to Ted and Julie for having her over for supper. She was also thankful for the name tags. Each person took the opportunity to welcome her to the group and tell her a little personal information if they had not already done that during the week.

*****

Matt walked Fiona home from the meeting and commented; "I noticed that you were rather quiet during the meeting today. Is everything okay?"

"Yes, thank you. I was just wishing that I could have been at the baptismal service, and I felt a little left out. I'm so thankful for the job at The Garden Shop though, that I have no reason to complain," she explained.

"I think I understand," responded Matt. "You've missed two of the special services in a row. I got to attend the first one and the last few minutes of the last one, but only because Jeff dragged me over there to surprise me. Maybe you can take some time off so you can go to the next one."

"I would like that. Since I have Christian bosses, they'll probably agree to it," she said and smiled.

"We're both really very blessed to have Christian bosses. And now <u>all</u> my co-workers are believers, too. There's such a feeling of unity and closeness. It was even better this week. It's a wonder I didn't figure it out by myself that our last co-worker had surrendered to Jesus," said Matt.

"I'm so glad he came to Jesus, and his wife too." Then she changed the subject and asked, "When could we take my parents over to see the progress on the house? I haven't seen it either and I'm sure it's progressing rapidly."

"Yes it is! How about tomorrow after the church service?" he responded.

"Perfect. Maybe we can get some idea of how long it will take them to finish it so we can set a date for the wedding. People keep asking me, and I keep saying that we don't know yet," she said.

"I agree, it would be nice to have a date and be able to plan when and where to have our honeymoon," said Matt. "Plus there will probably be some people wanting to give you a wedding shower.'"

"Yes, that's why some of them keep asking about a date. My parents have told me that their present to us will be to help us clean the house when it's finished and later to unpack all our belongings, and get the house set up the way we want it while we're gone on our honeymoon. We will need to make a list of where to place our things so they can do that and be sure to label all the boxes and put them in the right rooms," explained Fiona.

"Wow! That's a wonderful and practical wedding present, my love. May I thank them ahead of time when I see them tomorrow?" he asked.

She answered, "Sure, I think they would appreciate that."

"Walt said that all the furniture is included in their present, so we'll need to get it picked out and ordered so it will be delivered at the right time. I never knew there was so much planning involved with getting married, but it's worth all the time and effort. Besides, we get to do most of it together!" Matt exclaimed.

"I agree. Do you wish to keep the honeymoon a surprise for me?" she asked.

"It's good that you asked. I need to know if you like surprises, or if you would rather be able to look forward to it by knowing ahead of time," he replied.

"I'm glad you're so thoughtful, Honey! To be honest, I do not like surprises. I would rather be able to know where we're going, so I can look forward to it. I'll also be able to plan what the take with me," she answered.

By now they were at her house. They had a quick hug, and said they would see each other tomorrow. Fiona went inside and told her parents about the plan to go see the progress on the house, and Matt hurried home to eat lunch and then meet Ben at the house to work on it some more. Fiona would be very surprised and pleased tomorrow!

*****

Directly after the small group meeting, Pam drove to a couple of her favorite stores to buy the things she had put on her list as she was getting settled in her new home. She refused to call it an apartment, because it really didn't seem like one to her. The windows already had curtains or drapes and she liked them, so she bought a couple pillows for the couch that would match the drapes. She bought a new trashcan for each room in a color that would match anything else she might want to add later.

Then she bought enough groceries to last the coming week, remembering especially to buy things she could put in her lunches that didn't need to be refrigerated. She was so happy to get back into that routine!

When she got home, she put the groceries away first. Then she admired how the new pillows looked on the couch, and set out the trash cans with plastic shopping bags in them for liners. Later she studied pictures and names of students and continued looking at their records, to get an idea of where they were academically.

*****

That hot Saturday afternoon Vern, Lora, and Mindy went to an art museum, where Vern and Lora discussed what they had learned about some of the artists and their styles. Mindy listened with interest and began to see some of what they were talking about as she looked at the pictures.

When they were finished at the museum, they went out to supper at an Italian restaurant.

"This will be a new experience for me," said Mindy. "I don't think I've eaten Italian food before."

"I think you'll like it," Vern replied. "I can explain what the entrees are like so you can decide which one you would like to try. Maybe Lora can help with the ones that aren't familiar to me."

"Certainly. And if neither of us know, we can ask the waiter," she responded.

Mindy studied the menu and Vern and Lora helped with the pronunciation and descriptions. Mindy chose one that sounded good to her and said, "Maybe I can try something else next time. They sure have a lot of choices."

Vern and Lora agreed with her, and all three of them were pleased with what they chose from the menu. During supper they had a chance to discuss many topics and all three of them got better acquainted.

After they took Lora home that evening, Vern asked Mindy, "What do you think about Lora and me going on a date with just the two of us on a Saturday morning while you're doing daycare for the twins and Don and Anita's children?"

"It's a good idea, Dad," she answered. "That way you can talk about things and go places that I might consider boring. But I would still like to do things with the three of us on some of the

Saturday or Sunday afternoons. I've really been enjoying our times with her."

"I'm glad, because I have been also. We can plan to alternate a Saturday morning as a couple with a Saturday or Sunday afternoon as a threesome," he suggested.

"I like that suggestion," Mindy replied. "Thank you for asking me about it, Dad. I like the way we can talk about things together. I know some kids don't have as good a dad as I do."

"Thank you, Mindy. You're a wonderful daughter," he responded.

*****

Chapter 24

Psalms 119:11, *I have hidden your word in my heart, that I might not sin against you.*

The second Sunday in June

Tony and his partner had gone to a different park than the one they had been at the day before, because that one had very few children in it. This time they chose one with a playground. They set up the temporary booth in a conspicuous place near the playground, hoping the children might tire of playing and would like to sit and listen to a story. That idea worked well, and they both had a chance to tell a story. This time no children responded to the invitations, but they realized that there would be days like that.

So they took the booth apart, loaded it in the pick-up and spent some time talking and praying. They decided that the weekends were much better times than week day mornings, because only preschoolers were in the parks on those days. Most of them were too young to listen very well or understand, especially the ones who had no Christian parents or upbringing. Tony rode his bike home, looking forward to the next weekend of ministry. Then he ate lunch and got ready to go to church.

*****

Matt and Ben met at the house after breakfast and worked hard until half an hour before noon, when Matt stopped them and had them pile some of the materials out of the way and sweep the whole floor. When Matt told Ben why, he wanted to laugh, but he refrained, because he realized just in time that people who weren't used to walking around in sawdust with tools, and building materials scattered around could get hurt. So he did an extra careful job with the broom.

He was very thankful for all the things he was learning from Matt, not just about building, but about life in general. He had to admit that it did look very nice after it was cleaned up. Then they went to Matt's apartment and ate big TV dinners for lunch, took showers and got ready to go to church.

*****

Ted and Julie waited in the entryway and welcomed the family and the healed young woman. The family seemed nervous, but was soon put at ease, after sitting down and listening to instructions about how to find the songs in the hymnals. Julie sat between the mother and daughter so they could follow along in her Bible, and Ted sat on the other side of the father so he could share Ted's Bible. They could practice finding verses later, on their own. The daughter sat spellbound through the first short song, and the first two verses of the second song, just listening to the beautiful music and the singing of the people. Then she tried to join in and soon her voice was added to the others singing praise to God.

The songs for today were: "His Name Is Wonderful," Isaiah 9:6; "Break Thou the Bread of Life," Mark 6:41; "Standing On the Promises," Ephesians 6:17; and "Thy Word," Psalm 119:105.

Pam Green was sitting with some of her friends who were surprised to see her, but had given her a rousing welcome after they got over their surprise. She was smiling and singing with delight because she was back home in her own church. She had really missed the church and her friends while she was gone.

Before the singing, Pastor Don had announced, "We have started a new small group for our youngest new believers. There were four of them that we knew of on the evening of the baptismal service. If any of you have 4 or 5-year-old children who have recently accepted Jesus as their Savior they would be welcome to go now and join that group. There's a lady waving her hand at the rear of the sanctuary. You can take your children and follow her to the room in which they're meeting." Several parents took their children and followed the lady, where they left their children in the room and returned to the sanctuary.

Linda L. Linn

Don welcomed all the new believers to the church, and explained the second hymn to them. "Open again to our second song. When Jesus lived on earth, there were two separate times when he performed miracles making more than enough bread and fish to feed thousands of people out of just a few loaves of bread and a few fish. After everyone had eaten their fill, baskets full of leftovers were picked up so they would not be wasted. In several other places in the first four books of the Bible, Jesus calls himself the Bread of Life. Jesus is also called The Word in John 1:1, and when you put those two ideas together, you can see where the author got the idea for verses three and four. Those two verses help us to realize how important the Bible is for our lives.

"Now, please find our third song and listen as I read part of Ephesians 6:17, *take the sword of the Spirit, which is the word of God.* You'll find that thought in verse three of the song. The promises of this song are found in the Bible, which is God's Word. That's why that little booklet you new believers received states that you should read the Bible every day. It is full of guidelines for daily living and promises of God and Jesus that can help you stand firm.

"Now look at our last song, and follow along as I read from Psalm 119:105. *Thy word is a lamp unto my feet, and a light unto my path.* You notice that these are the exact words of that song, and are the reason that song was chosen for today. There are many other songs that have been written using Bible verses also. They are a very good way to begin to memorize verses from the Bible.

"Some of you might ask, 'Why do I need to memorize verses when they're already all written down in the Bible?' That's a very good question, and here is one very good answer. When you're at work or in school, you might want to remember a verse and not have your Bible with you. If you have memorized that verse, it will be with you wherever you are, whenever you need it.

"Now let's pretend that someone asks you where to find a verse that says there is something which is a light for our path. What else will you need to know about that verse?"

One of the former church school students raised his hand, and the pastor called on him. He answered, "You need to know where it's found in the Bible."

Pastor Don said, "Thank you, you're correct. You could then tell the person the name of the book in the Bible, plus the chapter and verse number. Then if you have memorized the verse, you could quote it. It might not be appropriate to sing it to them for some reason, so you would need to learn it both ways. There are many important verses in the Bible which don't have songs written for them, so you'll need to learn them without a song. You can do this by reading the verse and then selecting the first phrase of the verse. Say it over and over until you have it perfectly, and then tack on the next phrase, until you know the whole verse. Always say the reference or name of the book, chapter and verse number at the beginning and at the end of the verse, because it helps you to remember the reference better. It's fun to work with a partner when you're memorizing verses, but it's not necessary. You <u>can</u> do it on your own.

"You can write these verses on little cards which you keep in a special place and review them regularly. If you do <u>not</u> review them, you'll probably forget them unless you have a <u>very</u> good memory. After you've gotten good at doing one verse at a time, you can move on to learning two or more verses that go together like John 3:16-18. Those are good verses to use if you desire to tell someone about God's love, and his plan of salvation. There are other verses you'll need if you want to tell the person more about the Gospel.

"Those little booklets that you were given just after you accepted Jesus, have many verses with their references. That would be a good place to start a memory program of your own. When you know all of those, start choosing others as you read your Bible every day. Pick ones that will help you in some way, so they'll be meaningful to you.

"I've asked some of the students of the second and third grades of our Grace 'n' Faith School to come up here and recite some of the many verses they've memorized. If you write down the references as they say them, you'll have another good list to choose from for your own memory work."

The second graders recited relatively easy single verses, all with references fore and aft. The third graders recited longer portions of scripture, also with references fore and aft. Every single one of both grade levels spoke clearly and with good expression. Julie and Pam both had a hard time not standing up to cheer the students they knew.

Pastor Don said, "Thank you very much, boys and girls. Each one of you did an excellent job! Let's all sing 'Thy Word' again and then you're dismissed."

Ted and Julie took their new sisters and brother up to the pastor and introduced them. The daughter told him the story of her healing and their salvation, so pleased to be able to communicate. She gave all the praise to Jesus, and Don joined right in. Then her parents handed Don the card, and he told them he would call them as soon as possible with the time and place of the first meeting. He did the same for each individual or family that came up to him with cards as a result of the special baptismal service on Tuesday.

*****

Maria met Ted and Julie at the inside shopping mall, where they shared the news of the week, and then continued walking and praying for the people they saw. Maria noticed a young couple that was having a problem understanding and being understood by a clerk in one of the stores. "Ted, will you pray for us as Julie and I go over there and try to help that couple and the clerk?"

"Of course," he replied. "Just motion for me if you need me to come over later." They nodded.

She and Julie went over and listened long enough to figure out what was going on and then Maria offered to translate for all of them. It didn't take long for her to help them understand each other and the problem was solved.

The couple was so appreciative and wanted to know why she would take her time to help strangers. She explained that she and Julie were in the shopping mall today looking for someone they could show Jesus love to, by helping in whatever way somebody might need. That opened the door for them to explain the Gospel to the couple and take turns answering their questions, while Ted listened at a discreet distance and continued to pray.

Before long, each one in the couple made the decision to accept Jesus as Savior. Julie and Maria rejoiced with them, and then Maria explained to them that there was a Spanish church meeting in the same building as her church, but at a different time. Then she gave the couple a little booklet in Spanish, which had the address of the church, the time it met, the name of the pastor and his phone number.

The couple said they would be sure to attend the church next Sunday and give the card to the pastor. They thanked Maria and Julie again, took their purchases and left the mall with big smiles on their faces.

Ted went to rejoin the ladies and they had a quiet time of praise before he told them, "I was able to understand some of the

Spanish words you used as you explained the gospel and prayed with the couple."

"You're making very good progress learning Spanish. Tony will be proud of you," complimented Maria.

*****

Patrick, Glenda, and Riley followed Matt and Fiona over to the house, after Matt had thanked her parents for the wedding gift they planned to give them. Matt enjoyed the looks of surprise and admiration as they got out of the vehicles and saw the progress that had been made in the last three weeks. The roof was on, the outside walls had the sheeting on them, and were ready for the siding, all the windows and doors were in, and the porch and permanent stairs were built, but not painted. Inside the house, all the room walls were up and the electrical and plumbing were finished. They could start insulating and putting up drywall this week.

Matt led the tour and was so glad they had organized the materials and had swept the floor. The house was looking good.

When Fiona had gotten over her surprise enough, she managed to say, "I had no idea they could accomplish so much in three weeks! I'm so pleased."

"They're doing a very good job. The workmanship is excellent. Nothing sloppy anywhere," commented Patrick.

Glenda added, "I'm so happy for you both! This is going to be a wonderful home for you."

"Yes, it surely is. It seems to be going about twice as fast as a normal house would, but I guess that's understandable when I consider that there are two separate crews working seven hours each with no meal break. What a great concept!" exclaimed Patrick.

Riley stated, "I had no idea all of this was going on while I was in college! This is grand."

Matt stood there smiling broadly at all the nice comments, and responded, "Thank you all for your kind words! The work is actually going even faster than I believed possible. It seems that since all the workers have become believers, they're working better together than before."

"Wonderful!" exclaimed Glenda. "I know it can really make a big difference."

Fiona added, "Plus, they know it's a gift from Walt to Matt, so they put forth even more effort. Also, Matt and Ben have worked half days on the weekends."

As they walked through each room, they could tell what it was going to be since they had seen the floor plan. After Patrick and Glenda and Riley went home, Matt asked Fiona if she would like to go with him to see Walt and Betty.

Walt and Betty were very pleased to have Matt and Fiona drop in for a visit, and to hear all Fiona's excitement about the rapid progress that had been made so far on the house. "Thank you, very, very much for this wonderful gift! We are so blessed!" Fiona said with great feeling.

"It is our pleasure, and something we've been wanting to do for a very long time. Seeing your enjoyment makes it even more pleasurable," replied Betty.

"The progress seems much faster than I thought possible. People keep asking if we've set a date for the wedding, and we keep telling them we're not sure yet. Could we estimate a finish date for the house, or is it too soon to do that?" asked Matt.

"Let me do a little figuring, and I'll tell you what I think about it tomorrow when you come to work," answered Walt, smiling with understanding about the question and how gently Matt asked it.

"That will be fine," replied Matt. "How have you been, Betty?"

"Just fine. I really enjoyed the church service today. The songs and the teaching time were extra good. I was amazed at those little children reciting from memory all those Bible verses and where they're found. I guess if they can do it, so can I, especially since it's such an important thing to do!" Betty replied.

Fiona agreed, "They did such a good job of saying the verses with expression. I need to practice saying my memory verses with better expression. They were a good example for me."

"I got the point too, and I started learning my first verse this afternoon," Walt added.

"Good for you, Walt. I'm so proud of the progress both of you're making in this new life," Matt encouraged.

"The small group for new believers has been a great help to us. We're learning so much," said Walt.

"I'm glad. The small groups really _are_ very helpful. I hate to leave so soon, but I promised Mother that I would help her with supper, since she asked one of the new families in the church to come over tonight. We'll see you again soon," Fiona promised.

Everywhere There's a Sunrise, Let's Tell The Good News!

*****

Monday

After studying names and faces and student records again, Pam had a very good night's sleep in her new home. She woke feeling rested and excited about the day ahead. When she arrived at school, she greeted the secretary and Beth. Then she stopped in Julie's room for a hug and a quick prayer together before going into her new classroom.

Following a very good day for both of them and their students, Julie went into Pam's room to ask, "How did your day go, Pam?"

Pam answered, "I had a wonderful day, and so did the children. They're so sweet and helpful. I'm still in awe about how God has worked everything out so I can be back here doing what I love to do and serving God while I do it."

"I'm so glad for you, and I know just how you feel, because I feel the same way," replied Julie. "I'm so thankful that we can know we're in the center of God's will for us. It's such a peaceful feeling."

"That's for sure. I'll see you tomorrow. God bless you," said Pam as she gave Julie a hug.

*****

Walt was smiling when Matt came up to him at the job site, his and Fiona's house, a fact that still amazed him.

"I'm glad you asked me about an estimated finish date, Matt," said Walt. "The progress we've made so far seems so fast. In fact it _is_ faster than usual, and I think it's because we're all believers in unity, and we're happy to be working on something for you. You know how slowly finish work can go on a house though, and in light of that, even though we <u>might</u> be able to finish in three more weeks, it think we better make it four so we can be sure. Then you could set the wedding date for the weekend after that, so you can get the furniture you're ordering delivered and set up during the week."

"Wow!" exclaimed Matt, as he took out a calendar and studied it. "That would mean that Fiona and I could set a date for the third weekend in July. I wonder if she can be ready by then. Her parents are going to help us clean the house and later arrange our belongings in the house while we're off on our honeymoon, as their wedding present to us."

Linda L. Linn

"What a wonderful present from them! Betty and I would like to meet them sometime. Do you think they would like to come to lunch this coming Saturday?" asked Walt. "When Betty learned that Riley was home from college, she insisted that he join us for lunch also, 'We want to get to know the whole family,' she explained. And of course I agree."

"I'm sure they would. I'll ask them and get back to you. Now you better tell me the plan for the second shift, before we get talking and forget," said Matt.

*****

Don and Anita took their children and went to the pastors' small group meeting. After their busy day, it was nice to sit back and relax for a while. There were several things to discuss before singing and teaching time. First was an announcement for the next baptismal service since there were enough new believers for each church to have at least one new believers group. He said that the next baptismal service would be in three weeks.

Next was an update on the property purchase for building the second church. Their offer had been accepted and the closing was set for next week. That gave them some time to arrange for demolition of the old buildings and getting the grounds cleaned up and ready for building.

The lead pastor said, "It is time for us to announce our plans to each congregation, so you may all do that this coming weekend. Also tell them they can donate to the building fund in any amount they feel God directs. Make checks payable to Grace 'n' Faith Church. If possible we will not resort to the usual fund raising tactics. Ask them to pray and ask God what he wants them to give, and then give it." That idea was met with nods and murmurs of approval.

"Another thing you can announce is the need for construction company bosses to make an appointment with me to see the building plans and make a bid if they're interested in helping to build the church and school," he said and gave them the phone number they should call.

"The next thing to think about is that since the building project will take several months to complete, we need to add two more churches immediately and have them meet at 8PM on Saturdays and Sundays. We have two pastors ready to graduate from our training sessions. Ask for volunteers from your congregations who would be willing to move from yours to one of theirs. Have them pray about it and talk to you later in the week. It should not be an impulse move that they might regret later," he emphasized.

"One more thing that we've talked about off and on is a church plant. We've chosen a city in a southern state that needs our kind of church." He then gave the name of the city and the name of the pastor couple that would lead the group. "He is another one who is graduating soon, and will need some time to plan and then select from the people who will volunteer to move there with him. He knows and agrees that he will have to support himself with a job and be a pastor also, because that is the way our church plants will work. They'll be starting a small group in about a month. He will want them to be ready to move there by the first week in October."

He then handed out all this information in a memo so they would not have to remember all the details, and so that everybody would be on the same page, so to speak. Then they did all the normal small group activities, with many praises for the way God was working in the churches, and prayers for his guidance in what he wanted them to do.

*****

Tuesday

Matt was all smiles when he arrived at Fiona's house for their Tuesday date. He asked, "Is your mother home? May I come in? I think we might need her help because I have information that will help us set a date for our wedding."

"Magnificent! Yes to both of your questions," she answered as she ushered him inside and called, "Mother, could you please come into the kitchen? Matt would like to talk to us about a date for our wedding."

"Hello, Matt, it's nice to see you," she greeted as she came in and sat with them at the table. Fiona already had the calendar on the table where they could all see it.

Matt greeted Glenda, and told them everything Walt had said yesterday. "That means the soonest we could have the wedding is the third weekend in July. That would be in about five weeks. Do you think you could be ready by then, Fiona?" asked Matt.

"I'm ready right now!" she surprised him by saying. "But I suppose there are some details that need to be taken care of first, like deciding on decorating ideas, ordering a cake, reserving

Pastor Don to officiate, and before that, telling Connie the date so she and Amelia can give me a bridal shower. She's been asking me off and on. Yes, I think we can be ready by then."

"Excellent! What do you think Glenda?" Matt asked her.

"I agree, we can be ready by then. How about you, Matt?" turning the tables on him.

"I agree with Fiona. I'm ready right now! But I know there are details I need to take care of also, like go buy a new suit and choose the men who will stand up with us. Then there are many things Fiona and I need to do together like order the furniture for our house, setting the delivery date for the week before the wedding, draw up a plan to show where it is to be placed, finish the landscaping plan, decide where we would like to go for our honeymoon and how long we would like to spend, and I don't know what else. But yes, I think we can all be ready by then," finished Matt.

Glenda asked, "Have you decided about how big a wedding you would like to have, Fiona?"

"Well," she hesitated, "I have pondered several different scenarios: 1. Ask Don to cut the teaching short on a Sunday and be married at the end of the service so that the whole congregation and any others could be present; no reception would be possible because of the parking problem, 2. Rent a sanctuary in another church for a Saturday afternoon and announce that everybody is invited to come at that time, and have the reception in their all purpose room, or 3. Have a traditional small Irish style wedding in my parents' home with Pastor Don here, and just as many guests as we can fit in standing up, and have the reception in the backyard with a small wedding cake and apple juice."

Glenda commented, "Those are all good, workable options. I would like to know which one you would like the best for <u>your</u> wedding and for the memories to look back on later and what you would like to tell your children."

Fiona smiled and said, "The choice is easy for me, but I'm not sure what Matt will think about it."

He responded, "This is very easy for me, my dear Fiona. I would like any one of the three. I'm just glad you didn't include eloping and going to a justice of the peace!" They all laughed at his outrageous humor.

Fiona stated, "Then it's settled. I like choice number three the best. Mother, your wedding has always sounded so special and memorable, something you've cherished. I would like to be able to tell our children about our wedding like you've told me about yours."

Glenda's eyes were glistening as she smiled at her beloved daughter. "Thank you, Fiona," she said simply.

"So, what day do you think will work best, Fiona?" asked Matt.

"I was thinking I would like it to be on Saturday afternoon, at 3 PM so that we can attend small group, lunch will be over, and I'll have time to don mother's beautiful wedding gown and be ready for my groom in his brand new suit, but you do not need to wear a tie," she informed him.

"Fantastic!" he exclaimed, appreciating the fact that she remembered how he disliked wearing a tie.

"How many brides maids are you going to have?" asked Glenda.

"Only one, Amelia, and a matron of honor, Connie. I'll tell Connie and Amelia both, tomorrow when Amelia comes in for her short shift. I want to see their faces and tell them both at the same time, so I won't use the phone," Fiona responded.

"Now I know how many groom's men to have," commented Matt. "Jeff can be my best man, and Ben the other one. I'll tell him next Sunday morning so I can see his face, and I can tell Jeff at work today, during break time."

They spent the rest of their date time making other wedding decisions, and calling Anita to ask her to find out from Pastor Don if that time would work for him.

*****

Wednesday

When Amelia got to work that evening, Fiona motioned for her and Connie to come into the break room. "I have news, and a request. We've set a date for the wedding. It will be the third Saturday in July at 3 PM in my parents' home. We're going to have a small traditional Irish wedding and your whole family is invited. We're not sending invitations. My request is that both of you stand up with me."

The looks on their faces were memorable and Fiona was ready with her camera, so she captured them for all time.

"We'd be honored to," said Connie when she was finally able to speak. "Wouldn't we, Amelia?"

All Amelia could do was nod for a moment. Then she said, "Yes, we really would. I'm just so surprised that you would ask me! I'm only seventeen and I thought you would have many other friends you would ask."

Fiona took her hand and said, "Amelia, you've become one of my closest friends, and your mother has always been, so I would like her to be the Matron of Honor, and you the bride's maid."

"What shall we wear?" asked Amelia.

"That's totally up to both of you. In this wedding, I don't want unnecessary money spent on clothes that will never be used again. I get to wear Mother's wedding dress, and Matt is buying a new suit that can be used later. I would like you to choose favorite dresses that you already have. Ernest can come in a suit he already has or in casual clothes, whichever he prefers. Ben can use a suit that he already has, since he's standing up with Matt beside Jeff, who will be his best man. But don't tell him yet. Matt wants to tell him this weekend. The important thing is that our dear friends are with us on that day," explained Fiona.

*****

Thursday

Before they left to go for a fun date, Matt asked Fiona, "Do you think your parents and Riley and you would like to go to lunch this coming Saturday at Walt and Betty's home?" I forgot to ask you on Tuesday with all our wedding planning."

"That sounds lovely. You can ask her right now," answered Fiona as they walked into the kitchen.

"Hi, Glenda," greeted Matt. "My friends, Walt and Betty, would like to meet you and Patrick and Riley. They would like to have your family and me come to lunch on this coming Saturday. Would you be able to do that?"

"Yes, and I know it will be all right with Patrick. We've wanted to meet them ever since their baptisms. I wish I had thought about having them over here, but we can do that later," she replied.

"Wonderful. I'll call Betty right now, and let her know that she can expect all of us at noon for lunch this coming Saturday," said Matt.

After he called, Fiona asked, "Okay, shall we go ahead to that museum we talked about the other day?"

"Yes, let's do," answered Matt. "It's a perfect rainy day activity. See you later, Glenda."

Everywhere There's a Sunrise, Let's Tell The Good News!

*****

    Ted's e-mail had instructed him to practice the melody part for one of the songs they would sing this week. He would be the lead singer for that song, if it sounded good. He was a little nervous about it.

    Larry encouraged him, "You'll do fine. Just pretend you're singing in the shower at home. You've told me that you practice that way sometimes. Or close your eyes and sing it to Jesus, since you are doing it for him anyway."

    "You're right," agreed Ted. "I'm always nervous when I'm in the limelight. I'll take your advice and pretend I'm in the shower singing for Jesus."

    When it was his turn to sing, they only had to go through the song one time. On the second time he sang, it was recorded and turned out very well. Ted was glad his turn had come at the beginning of the music time so he could relax and enjoy the rest of the time.

    He liked the way the director planned for each song to be done a different way so that there was a lot of variety for the people singing as well as for those who listened and sang along. He would use the full orchestra and all the singers, or choose just a few instruments that went well together and only some of the singers. Sometimes he would have the whole choir singing without any instruments. Or he would have a solo, duet, trio, or quartet for all or part of a song, accompanied by the piano. There were many ways he could mix and match that many singers and instrumentalists. And of course, everything they produced was beautiful.

Friday

    When Don got home from work on Friday he looked very glum. After all the extra children had gone home and theirs had gone outside to play he told Anita, "I intercepted a shoplifter today, but he rebelled, tried to escape, got caught, and had to go to Juvenile Hall. I warned him that the security officers would probably catch him if he tried to leave, and that would make it go harder on him, but he would not listen. The hardest part of this job is seeing them make the wrong choices."

    Anita put her hand on his arm and said, "I'm so sorry you have to go through that, Honey. I can imagine how awful you must feel. Father, I ask that you'll soften that boy's heart and still draw him to

Jesus for salvation and a useful life. This gives us a little idea about how you must feel when people make the wrong choices in their lives. Please give Don peace and comfort him."

"Thank you, Dear. You always know just the right words to say to me and to pray. I do feel better. At least we have a weekend coming up now. How would you like to go to the late shift small group we started and visit them this Saturday morning since Mindy is coming to take care of our two children and the twins?"

"I would like that a lot," she answered. Shall we call Jeff and Karen, or just show up?"

"I guess I better call them, although it would be fun to see their surprise. Oh, we'll <u>have</u> to call so we'll know where they're meeting. We can see the rest of the members' surprise though. I'll look forward to it." he replied. Then he called Jeff and got their visit approved.

Saturday

On the Saturday morning that he and Lora were to go on their first date as a couple, Vern had second thoughts about it. He felt like he needed to have his head examined for even considering it. With Mindy along, the conversations flowed easily, but how would it be with just Lora? He had asked her where she would like to go, and she had suggested the Botanical Garden. Well, at least they could talk about the flowers if nothing else. He got his case of nerves under control and went to pick Lora up at her apartment.

"Hi, Lora," he greeted her. "We could not ask for more perfect weather to go to the Botanical garden."

She agreed, "Yes, the forecast said today would be a cooler day. "I'm glad to see that you have a wide brimmed hat. I'm bringing mine also, and I have some sunscreen if we need it."

By this time they were at Vern's car. He opened the door for her, made sure she was seated and then closed it, as he always did when they had threesome activities. They carried on a conversation about this and that on the way. When they got parked at the garden, he went around and opened the door for her. They walked to the gate in a comfortable silence. Once inside the garden, conversation flowed easily about the color, variety, names and the creator of the flowers, plus many other topics.

After a while, they sat down in the shade on a bench and Lora asked, "What's Mindy doing this morning?"

"Something she really enjoys and even gets paid for." Then Vern explained, "Every Saturday morning she does daycare for four active preschoolers. Two of them are identical twin girls who just turned five, and the other two are Don and Anita's children who are now five and four."

"Oh my! That's a lot of responsibility for a twelve-year-old, but Mindy is very mature for her age," commented Lora. "I'm glad she enjoys it."

"She's used to helping Anita with five more children on top of Anita's during the weekday afternoons after school and on school vacations. The twins are only there two mornings a week and on Saturdays," he explained. Mindy has been helping Anita for the past three years, since third grade, and that pays for the mentoring I asked Anita to do for Mindy. She's learned so much and likes going there."

"What a brilliant plan for both of them. That means that Mindy has gotten to watch and help as both of the children have been growing up," observed Lora.

"Yes, she really loves both of them and they love her. I like to see them run up to her for hugs when I drop her off on Saturday mornings," laughed Vern.

"That's wonderful. I'm glad you told me about it. What are some things you enjoy doing when you have free time?" Lora asked.

Vern was silent a few moments as he thought about the question. Then he chuckled as he said, "I just realized that the things we've been doing the last few weekends are all things I enjoy doing. I'm glad you and Mindy got me started doing them again. Thank you, Lora. What do _you_ enjoy doing in your free time?"

"I feel just the same, but I could add cooking and sewing to the list," she responded. "Is Mindy learning to cook at the pastor's home?"

Vern answered, "No, I don't think they have time for that with all those little children around and I pick her up at about 5:30 on my way home. I enjoy cooking also. Maybe we can teach Mindy during some of our Saturday or Sunday afternoon threesome activities."

"I like that idea. We could alternate between your home and mine," she suggested.

He agreed. "Do you like to play tennis or ping pong?" he asked next as they got up again to walk and see more flowers.

"I was never any good at tennis, but I do enjoy ping pong. Does Mindy like it?" she asked.

"No, so that could be something for us to do on a Saturday morning. I have a membership at the recreation center and could bring you as a guest, so we could use their ping pong table and equipment," Vern replied.

"I'll look forward to that, although I'm sure I'll need some practice, since I haven't played in a long time," she responded.

"Same here," he said and looked at his watch. "It's time for me to go pick Mindy up at the pastor's house after I take you home. The time sure went fast!"

"This has been a lovely morning. Thank you very much," Lora said as he left her at her door.

*****

The late shift small group met in the school lunchroom, and they were all grateful for the air conditioning on this hot day. Even though the calendar didn't agree, it felt like summer already, even this early in the morning.

Don and Anita arrived at the same time Jeff and Karen got there. Tony and Clara were surprised and thrilled to see them. All of them made short work of setting out the books on the chairs. After that they had time to pray together and visit before the first members arrived. Each individual or couple who came in showed their own style of surprise and then rushed over to greet and welcome Don and Anita. The group got noisier and more enthusiastic as more people arrived. Jeff told Don that he would have to be the one to settle them all down since he had caused all this fun.

Pretty soon Don stood up and did the honors. He just started talking, and everyone quieted down. He thanked everyone for his or her welcome and greetings. "We've missed this group and are very glad we have this opportunity to visit. Thank you Lord for this blessing. We're very glad for your presence here with us, as we continue this meeting. Who else has a praise or thanksgiving to share?" he asked. "Jeff alerted me to the fact that you still hold applause and oral praise until all have had a chance to share. He and Karen have also kept us updated about the many things that God has been doing in this group, so just go ahead with the praises for this week."

Everywhere There's a Sunrise, Let's Tell The Good News!

Pam began with, "I thank our awesome God again for all he did for me and my parents, and for a wonderful week of teaching. The children in my new class have been very helpful and accepted the change of teachers very well. In addition to all of that, I really like my new home. It is so much better than the apartment building I was living in before."

Julie continued, "Pam and I are both thankful that my class understood and accepted the fact that it was better for everyone that Pam take over the other class. It hasn't been awkward at all for any of us, praise the Lord."

Ted prayed, "Thank you Jesus for helping me with the solo they wanted me to sing for the church or small group music, and for Larry's valuable encouragement. We also thank you for the Spanish couple Julie and her friend got to lead to the Lord on Sunday after church."

Karen said, "Thank you, Jesus, that Don and Anita can be here to visit today."

"Thank you Lord that the children are still coming to the Bible study and story groups on Wednesdays," said Jane.

Tony added, "And I thank you that two children responded to my partners invitation last Sunday afternoon."

"Father, thank you for the good news Afta shared about Hana's parents accepting Jesus," said Tomo.

Ami added, "And that they've found a good church and small group to be active in together."

"Father, thank you that all the new believers small groups are off to a very good start." And then she added, "I thank you that Sherry and Roy were such a help to us during that busy time," Anita prayed,

Sherry added, " Thank you, Jesus, that the payback for that help is so immense! Our twins are learning a lot in daycare two mornings a week. They have something new to tell me about it every time."

"Thank your Father for all the things I'm learning about nursing and evangelism," said Clara.

"Praise you, Lord, that Matt and I have a date set for our wedding!" Fiona exclaimed.

Matt added, "And that sometime later, we'll be able to host this small group in our new home."

Jeff started the applause and oral praises. After that he asked if there were any announcements as he looked expectantly at Fiona, who announced, "Our wedding will be the third Saturday afternoon in July at 3 PM, and we invite all of you to witness our vows at my parents' home. There will be a reception afterwards in the backyard. Please remember that this announcement will take the place of written invitations. We would like your <u>presence</u>, but no <u>presents</u> please. There will be a bridal shower given for me, and all the women will be invited to it, so I don't want double presents from this group. Oops, that would leave Tony out of the gift giving, but we already asked him to help Connie Clay to load and unload all the potted plants and flowers she's going to use to decorate the house and yard. So thank you, Tony, that will be your present to us. If you have any questions, please ask us during refreshment time."

Jeff said, "We all accept your gracious invitation and will be looking forward to your wedding! Now it's time to find out who would like to be the hosts for the next meeting."

Larry looked at Jane and she nodded and said, "We would like all of you to come to our house next Saturday."

"Thank you both. Now let's sing. We'll start with 'Thy Loving Kindness,' Psalm 63:3." Next they sang "Greater Is He That Is In Me," 1 John 4:4; and after that, "Jesus, I My Cross Have Taken" verses 2,3, and 4, Luke 9:23,24.

"Our teaching today encourages us to be ready for persecution or trials when they come, and how to deal with them. We're still very blessed in this country because we don't have very much persecution. I know we're all very thankful about that. A few weeks ago we studied about the armor of God, and it would be a good idea for you to review your notes on that teaching this week.

"Please look up 1 John 4:4. *You are of God, ... and have overcome (the spirit of antichrist), because greater is he that is in you, than he that is in the world.* Victory is assured for us believers, because the Spirit of Jesus is in us. But that does not mean that we'll never have a battle to fight. We know there have been many martyrs through the centuries, and there will be many more. We know for sure that even if we would have to die for Jesus, we would win, because Paul said in Philippians 1:21, 23, 24. *For me to live is Christ, and to die is gain. I am in a dilemma, having a desire to depart and to be with Christ, which is far better. Nevertheless to abide in the flesh is more needful for you.*

"The Bible verses that go with our third song are Luke 9:23,24. *And he said to them all, "If any man will come after me, let him deny himself, and take up his cross daily, and follow me. For whoever will save his life shall lose it, but whoever will lose his life for my sake, the same shall save it.* Now look at the words of the song again. Verse two speaks of being despised or left or hated or shunned. If that were to happen to us, we would need to look at Jesus and remember what they did to him. His disciples in the book of Acts counted it a privilege to suffer for the sake of Jesus. They prayed for more boldness to continue speaking in his name. We would need to do the same. Verse four of the song reminds us that this life is fleeting and we look forward to heaven. That would be a great help for us to remember.

"Look with me at Romans 12:12, 14, 17a, 18, 19, 21. *Rejoice in hope, be patient in tribulation, continue ... in prayer. Bless those who persecute you; bless, and do not curse. Do not repay evil for evil. If it be possible, as much as you can, live peaceably with all men. Dearly beloved, do not avenge yourselves. Rather let God take vengeance, since it belongs to him. Do not be overcome by evil, but overcome evil with good.*

"Next, find and read Matthew 10:5-31 to yourselves. In these verses Jesus told his disciples that they could expect to be persecuted, just as he had been. Part of your homework this week is for you to find and write down what Jesus said to do and/or not do in these situations.

"Now please find 1 Peter 1: 1-9. *Peter, an apostle of Jesus Christ, to the strangers scattered throughout the world.* (Notice that I left out all those place names and inserted 'the world' in their place.) *Elect according to the foreknowledge of God the Father, through sanctification of the Spirit, unto obedience and sprinkling of the Blood of Jesus Christ: Grace to you, and peace be multiplied. Blessed be the God and Father of our Lord Jesus Christ, who according to his abundant mercy has made us be born again to a living hope by the resurrection of Jesus Christ from the dead. To an inheritance incorruptible, and not defiled, and that does not fade away, reserved in heaven for you who are kept by the power of God through faith unto salvation ready to be revealed in the last time. You greatly rejoice in this, even though now for a season, if need be, you are distressed by many trials so that the trial of your faith, which is much more precious than of gold that perishes, even though it is tried with fire, may be found to praise and honor and glory when Jesus Christ appears. You love him, even though you cannot see him, and believing in him, you rejoice with joy unspeakable and full of glory, because you are receiving the goal of your faith, the salvation of your souls.*

"Whenever you're persecuted or are going through any kind of trials, read these verses. Better yet, memorize them and they'll be with you at the time you need them. I won't have you look it up right now but write down James 1: 2-5. Those verses can also help in times of trials.

"The rest of your homework for this week is to look up some more verses that could help you be prepared, stay strong, and/or deal with persecution or trials. Choose at least two of those or from the ones in the teaching today to memorize so you can use them when you need them.

"Father in Heaven, we pray in Jesus name that you will help all of us be prepared to deal with whatever persecution or trials may come our way," he prayed as the beginning of conversational prayer time.

Don added, "Thank you that Jesus said in John 16:33, *Be of good cheer, I have overcome the world,* John 16:33. Please help us remember that with Jesus, we win."

Karen continued, "Please enable us to follow your example, Jesus, and the examples of your followers in the New Testament. Thank you that NOTHING, including persecution can separate us from Jesus love, see Romans 8:34-39."

Tony added, "Thank you that Philippians 4:13 says, we *can do all things through Jesus, who gives us strength*, Philippians 4:13."

"And that 2 Corinthians 12:9 says, your *grace is sufficient for (us), for (your) strength is made perfect in weakness*, 2 Corinthians 12:9," continued Ted.

Larry added, "Thank you that in 2 Timothy 1:7. It says we have the Spirit of power, and love and a sound mind, instead of fear, as I paraphrased 2 Timothy 1:7."

"Help us remember and rely on your promise, Jesus, in Matthew 10:19,20, that *we do not need to worry ahead of time what to say when we might be brought before governors, ... because the Holy Spirit will give us the words we need to say*, Matthew 10:19,20," prayed Fiona.

Jane added, "Thank you, Jesus, for saying in Matthew 5:11,12a, You are *blessed when men shall revile you and persecute you and say all manner of evil against you falsely for my sake. Rejoice, and be exceeding glad, for great is your reward in heaven*, Matthew 5:11,12a."

"Please help us do as Jesus said to in Matthew 5:44, *Love your enemies, bless them that curse you, do good to those that hate you, and pray for those who spitefully use and persecute you*, Matthew 5:44," prayed Tomo.

Pam continued, "Please help us do as it says in Hebrews 10:35, to not *cast away our confidence, because it has a great reward,* Hebrews 10:35."

And Roy added, "Help us remember that Romans 5:3-5 says, *... we glory in tribulations, knowing that tribulations work patience, and patience, experience, and experience, hope. And hope does not make us ashamed, because the love of God is shed abroad in our hearts by the Holy Spirit who is given to us,* Romans 5:3-5."

By this time Jeff was having a hard time holding in his laughter, so he said, "Amen! ... Now that these people have already done half of your homework for the week, and have done an excellent job of it by the way, how many of you got all those references written down?"

Julie was the only one to raise her hand, and with an embarrassed, but teasing smile she said, "It <u>was very helpful</u> to have the references fore and aft. I got to double check them, and be sure I was correct, just like a teacher should. Would you like me to read them aloud so the rest can copy them down?"

He did laugh then, and everybody joined him. Finally he was able to say, "Yes, please do that, Julie." When she had finished, he praised the group, "This is the very best small group! We're so blessed to be the facilitators of such an outstanding group!" They all smiled and thanked him.

Matt stated, "We think you and Karen are excellent facilitators for this group. Thank you both!" Everybody cheered, and they both smiled their appreciation.

Clara gave thanks for the refreshments and invited everyone to enjoy. There was much talk and laughter as they enjoyed their fellowship. Don and Anita were extra glad they had come today. They went home feeling very refreshed.

*****

After small group time, Matt and Fiona went to her home to pick up Patrick, Glenda, and Riley. On the way, Matt and Fiona smiled and laughed as they discussed the fun ending of the serious teaching time in the small group today. "Jeff and Karen do make very good facilitators," commented Fiona. "I'm glad they were willing to be trained and take over for our group. This group <u>is</u> very outstanding, just like he said, and I feel blessed to be a part of it."

"Me too. God has done amazing things for and through its members," agreed Matt.

By this time they were at Fiona's home and Matt volunteered to go to the door to tell them they would wait for them in the pick-up, so they could ride with them. Walt and Betty were having the O'Connors and Matt over for lunch this Saturday. Matt was thrilled to be able to spend time with some of his favorite people.

They all had a pleasant time together and enjoyed Betty's excellent cooking. Fiona had a chance to ask Betty for some of her new recipes for healthier living. Betty was pleased to be able to share them. Later Fiona gave copies to her mother.

*****

The third Sunday in June

Matt had called Ben on Friday evening to tell him he could not work on the house Saturday afternoon, but would like to have Ben come help him on Sunday morning. "I'll supply TV dinners for lunch if you want to bring a change of clothes for church."

When Ben arrived on Sunday morning, Matt told him, "I would like to have you stand up with me, beside my best man Jeff Spencer, at my wedding." Ben's look of surprise was just what Matt had expected it to be.

"Really? You want _me_ to be in your wedding?" he asked.

"Yes, I really do, because you and I have become good friends while we have worked together. Jeff has been a good friend for even longer, so he will be best man. Will you do it?" asked Matt.

"Absolutely! I feel it is an honor. Thank you for asking me," said Ben.

"You're welcome, and thank you for agreeing. We're not going to rent tuxedos. Instead we'll keep it simple. Just wear a suit that you already have. You don't even need to wear a tie since I'm not going to," Matt informed him.

"When and where will this be?" Ben asked.

"Fiona and I are getting married on the third Saturday afternoon in July at 3 PM in her parents' house with a reception in their back yard afterward. I can hardly wait! Fiona is such a special lady," said Matt.

*****

The 2 PM Sunday service started right on time as usual. The songs for today were: "Commit Thy Way Unto the Lord," Psalm

37:5; "'Tis So Sweet to Trust In Jesus," John 14:1; and "Thou Wilt Keep Him In Perfect Peace," Isaiah 26:3. This third song is the one in which Ted was the lead singer. Julie was so proud of him, but he looked shy and embarrassed as he stood beside her, even though not many people knew about it. She told him later at home that he had done an excellent job, and he thanked her. "Glorious Is Thy Name," based on 1 Chronicles 29:9-16, was the last song they sang.

    After the singing, Pastor Don said, "Our teaching time will be <u>very</u> different today. As you know, this church has been growing very rapidly the past several weeks, and so have the other eleven that share this building. The pastors of all twelve churches have been praying <u>a lot</u> during those weeks about what would be the best things to do since we'll run out of room to seat everybody if we do nothing. After much prayer we have reached several conclusions. Therefore the leading pastor of the Grace 'n' Faith Church told all the other pastors to make the following announcements this Sunday.

    "Before I start the announcements, I desire for you to know that God is in control, and if we follow his guidance, *he will work out everything for good because we love God and have been called according to his purpose* as it says in Romans 8:28. This is an exciting time for all 12 Grace 'n' Faith Churches.

    "The first announcement is the decision to build a second church and school like the one we already have, because Pine City is a large enough city that it could use not just one more, but many like this to reach all the people in the city. The pastors and their wives all voted to pursue the idea without delay since all 12 churches are growing rapidly."

    There were nods and murmurs of agreement in the congregation.

    "Please find 1 Chronicles 29:9-16 and follow along as I read it. The context for these verses is the offering that was collected for the building of the temple that David had planned and his son, Solomon, built. The people of Israel had given abundantly. *Then the people rejoiced, because they had offered willingly, with a perfect heart, and King David also rejoiced with great joy. Therefore, David praised the LORD before the entire congregation and said, 'Blessed be the LORD God of Israel, our father, forever and ever. Yours, O LORD, is the greatness and the power and the glory and the victory, and the majesty, because all that is in the heaven and in the earth is yours. Yours is the kingdom, O LORD, and you are exalted as head above all. Both riches and honor come from you, and you reign over all. In your hand is power and might and by your hand you make great, and give strength to all. Now therefore, our God, we thank you and praise your glorious name. But who am I, and what is my people that we should be able to offer so willingly this way? For all things come from you and from your own we have given to you. For we are strangers before you and sojourners as were all our fathers. Our days on the earth are as a shadow. ... O LORD our God, all this offering that we have prepared to build you a house for your holy name comes from your own hand, and is all your own.'*

"With the knowledge of what these verses say, <u>please pray</u>, asking God what he specifically desires for you to do about how much to give to build the second church and school, and then do whatever God tells you to do. Make your checks payable to Grace 'n' Faith Church."

Next was information on purchasing property for building the second church. "We heard really good news about the committee finding some property with some very old run down warehouses on it that need to be torn down. It is in a very centralized area, just on the opposite side of town from our church. The price is reasonable, and on top of that they gave an allowance for having to tear the buildings down. That's a great benefit. From the looks of the pictures they showed us, even just tearing them down will improve the looks of the area. Add the landscaped new church and the school building, and it will look magnificent. Plus, the worth of their purposes is beyond measure," stated Don. "Our offer has been accepted and the closing is set for this coming week. They'll arrange for demolition of the old buildings and getting the grounds cleaned up and ready for building."

Then he read the next announcement, "Construction company bosses in our churches who are interested in helping to build the new church and school, need to make an appointment with the pastor of Grace 'n' Faith Church #1 to see the building plans and make a bid." He gave the pastor's name and phone number they should call.

"The next thing to think about is that since the building project will take several months to complete, we need to add two more churches immediately and have them meet at 8 PM on Saturdays and Sundays. The reason for this is to assure plenty of room for each church to keep growing. It is a proven fact that when there are too few empty seats, people start feeling crowded and growth usually stops. We have two pastors ready to graduate from our training sessions. We're asking for <u>volunteers</u> from each congregation who would be willing to move from the congregation they are in, to one of theirs. If you volunteer for this, you will remain in the small group you're already in until January when all the groups are changed. It would be acceptable if a whole small group volunteers. Pray about it and talk to me later in the week if you wish to volunteer. It should <u>not</u> be an impulse move that you might regret later," he emphasized.

"The last announcement is about a 'church plant' that we've talked about off and on. We've chosen a city in a southern state that needs our kind of church." He then gave the name of the city and the name of the pastor couple that would lead the group. "He is another one who is graduating soon, and he will need some time to plan and then select from the people who will <u>volunteer</u> to move there with him. There will be a planning meeting in which he will explain more about the project. He will be starting a small group in about a month. He will want the group to be ready to move there with him by the first week in October.

"I know this is a lot to take in, so I have a summary of each announcement on a memo to give to each family or single person. Please don't make any decisions right here in this service. Take this paper home and pray about each thing and then listen to the Lord for his guidance. Remember that I work from 8-5, M-F, so make your calls about volunteering when I'll be home. We attend the pastors' small group on Monday evenings, and this Wednesday we'll be starting a new believers small group, for those who returned their cards to me last Sunday, so it would be best to <u>not</u> call on those evenings.

"Now let's sing "Tis So Sweet to Trust In Jesus,' again before we're dismissed to go home and pray about all these announcements." After singing it, Don said, "May the peace of the Lord be with you, and may he guide you in all you do."

The members of the congregation were very quiet and serious as they filed out of the sanctuary and received the memo they were handed at the door. Each one had big decisions to make and took Pastor Don's advice to pray and listen for the Lord to give them his guidance. They all canceled any other plans for the afternoon and evening. Everyone went straight home to pray and listen for what Jesus would tell him or her to do.

*****

Linda L. Linn

Chapter 25

Days in June and July

Psalm 31:3, *For you are my rock and my fortress. Therefore for your name's sake lead me and guide me.*

Psalm 43:3a, *O send out your light and your truth. Let them lead me.*

    It took prayer and waiting to get clear guidance from the Lord about the announcements they had heard on Sunday at church. But when the next Sunday arrived, the people came with their regular offerings, <u>plus</u> an extra check for the building of the new church and school. Many of the checks were large ones and others were just as much as the people could afford to give on their limited incomes.
    Fiona and Matt agreed that this would be the best use of her inheritance money and she joyfully wrote the check to take to church on Sunday. It was another big decision as an engaged couple and they were grateful for their unity.

*****

    The Clays had much prayer and many discussions, including at supper on Sunday evening, and at breakfasts at the beginning of the week. It was simple to decide how much to give to the building project. They had a separate part of their budget where they had been putting extra money in a special savings account to be given to help build a new church and school when the time was right, and this was definitely the right time.
    Ernest said, "It would be easy for us to make the move to attend one of the new 8 PM services. The Saturday one would be the best so we can all continue to get to bed early on Sunday nights for work and school the next day."
    "You're right, Dad," said Amelia. "We need to keep that routine in place so that we can stay healthy."
    Connie continued, "That's for sure. I'm thinking it would be easier to change church times and pastors if our whole small group would move with us. We could work together on what ever challenges might come up."

"I have the same opinion about that point, Mom," Ben replied. Amelia and I can ask our group on Tuesday, and you and Dad can ask your group on Wednesday."

"Since there are sixteen people in each of our groups, that would make at least 32 empty seats for church #4, plus any others who volunteer," figured Ernest.

"Right," said Ben, "and when the new building is finished we would follow that pastor there. We would just be moving early, so to speak. At least we would have some people we know going with us."

Connie agreed, "That <u>would</u> be nice. Besides that, we can also enjoy meeting new people from some of the other churches."

That week, on Wednesday and Thursday mornings, they reported back to the family the decisions of the groups. Both groups would be volunteering. The facilitators would call Pastor Don to tell him they would prefer the Saturday service.

*****

Ted and Julie prayed about the announcements and knew that the building fund would be a very good place to give the extra money that they had been putting aside for a special offering. They felt that they should not volunteer to go to one of the 8 PM services. Ted said, "I think it would be best if we could have a few more months with the stability of the same church and pastor, since we've only lived in Pine City since the end of March."

"Besides that," Julie mentioned, "I'm teaching in the church school and I think it's a very good reason to remain where we are. I'm glad that our small groups will remain together until January."

"I agree. When the new church building is finished, I assume that some more people from church #4 will be volunteering to move to some of the new churches along with the ones who volunteer for the 8 PM services," Ted added.

"Yes. The plan is a good one for church growth and for Pine City. There are so many unbelievers to be reached, and they'll need a church home when they are saved," said Julie. "Another church school will be wonderful also. Children can learn so much more in the church school than in a public school."

*****

The rest of the members of the late shift small group prayed separately, as couples or individuals, and decided not to volunteer to go to the 8 PM services, as did Maria, Ruth and Esther, and the new believers of the last month. But each one of them found some extra money that they could give to the building fund. There were others in church #4 who did volunteer to attend one or the other of the 8 PM services. So they called Pastor Don to inform him.

*****

After praying and discussing with all his co-workers on both shifts, Walt Evans called the pastor of church #1 and set up an appointment to study the blueprints and make a bid to work on one or both of the new buildings.

On the day of his appointment, Walt studied the blueprints carefully and said, "These look very good. Since I attend the church, I know what the finished product looks like, so that's a big help. I must tell you that my crew and I will not be available until my present project is finished. That will be in about three weeks. I haven't made firm plans for my next project."

Then Walt emphasized, "All my workers are believers and we work very well together. With the boss and the foreman, there are ten workers in each shift. We work for hourly wages, I have two crews that could continue working in split shifts or could change back to more normal hours, whichever would be most advantageous for this project."

The pastor told Walt that he would consider his bid and get back to him in a timely manner. In a few days, he called Walt and told him that the Evan's Construction Company and several others from the other churches within the overall church were chosen to work together to do the building.

The next work day, he told all the workers on both shifts and they were elated.

*****

Larry and Jane prayed separately and then together on Sunday afternoon about all the announcements and agreed on an amount they could give above their regular offering for the new buildings. Then Larry mentioned, "Remember when we were talking about the new small group, that I felt maybe God might have some bigger plans in mind for us in our future?"

"Yes, I do remember that. At the time I wondered what it could be, but now I think you might have been right," she answered.

He continued, "The church plant would be a <u>very</u> big plan in my opinion, but we have a very big God! What do you think about volunteering for it? I'm willing if you are."

She replied, "But it seems like we're pretty old to uproot and start over in a new city. Although, Moses and Caleb were 80 years or older when they undertook huge projects. If he wants us to do it, Jesus will help us, like it says in Philippians 4:13. The part of the idea that I like best is the name of the city. Our daughter, Lucy and her family live there, and I would love to be near them. Besides the climate is pretty nice all year round. Neither of those facts is enough to move for, but if we agree that the church plant is something God wishes for us to help with, they would be an added blessing."

"You're right," Larry agreed. "On the other side of the coin are all the things we would miss here after we move. We have a lot of friends here and your new outreach ministry to the children, plus my help with the music ministry. Besides all that, are Pastor Don and the rest of the congregation."

"Very true, and we don't want to make a hasty decision on our own emotions and regret it later," she said.

Larry prayed, "Father in heaven, you know our hearts. You know your will and plan for us. Please reveal it to us in a way that we can recognize and have peace concerning what you want us to do."

"Yes, please keep our own feelings, thoughts and emotions out of the way, so we don't go around in circles trying to decide on our own. Thank you that <u>you</u> are in control," Jane added.

Larry said, "Now let's leave it with the Lord and keep our senses open to his answer as we do what ever chores need to be done around here."

Later in the evening, Pastor Don called and said, "I just wanted you two to know that I was the one who suggested the name of that city for the church plant, because of what you had said, Jane, about the milder winter and the need for a good church there. Do <u>not</u> let these be the only reasons you would volunteer to go there, but I want you both to know that I think you would be valuable assets to the group that does go there. Knowing both of you as well as I do, I know you're already considering the move, and that you have already prayed and discussed it. Continue praying and waiting for God's clear guidance."

Larry responded, "You are correct, and we'll do that. But <u>why</u> do you think we would be valuable assets. We <u>are</u> pretty old already."

He answered, "I've been in small groups with you and have seen how you love Jesus and serve him with all your hearts as you let his Spirit work through you. You have the experience of a lifetime that might be needed in this project. Plus, Jane knows a little bit about the city since she spent a couple months there last winter. I'm NOT trying to talk you into going, because I, especially, and all your friends here would miss you. But we would be willing to let you go if you know that's what Jesus desires you to do."

"Thank you, Pastor, for all your kind words. We're glad you called," said Jane.

"You're welcome. When you have your answer from the Lord, let me know. I'll be praying also. Bye for now, and God bless you," he finished. They returned the blessing, and hung up the phone to go pray some more.

"Well, that sheds some different light on the topic," Larry said after they had prayed again. "But I'm not sure what to think about all of it."

"I agree, but we don't need to decide tonight. Let's get a good night's sleep so you'll be ready to go to work tomorrow," she suggested. He had the same thought, so they left the decision in God's hands.

Just then the phone rang again. This time it was Jeff and Karen. Jeff started with, "I know it's getting late, but I think Jesus wants me to tell you something, and I'm not sure why, so after I say it, please pray about it. Jesus said to tell you to go and he will help you."

"Thank you, Jeff, for listening to Jesus and doing what he tells you to do," Larry responded. "<u>That</u> is just exactly what we needed to hear so we can make a very important and very big decision."

Jane continued, "We'll pray about it some more and let you know more about it later. Both of you have a good evening and may God richly bless you!" They all said good-bye.

Larry and Jane prayed together, "Thank you, Jesus! We will do just as you said." Then they gave a sigh of relief and had a very good night of peaceful sleep.

Since the pastors' small group met on Monday, they waited until Tuesday evening after supper, and called Pastor Don. They told him about Jeff's phone call Sunday night, and their decision to volunteer for the church plant group.

Everywhere There's a Sunrise, Let's Tell The Good News!

*****

  The following Sunday, as part of the teaching time Pastor Don said, "It would be a good idea for you to tell your small group and your other friends in this church if you will be attending one of the new evening services or if you will be volunteering for the church planting group so they can pray with you. Remember that you can continue to stay in your current small group until this coming January. The new evening services will begin next weekend. We all need to keep praying and working together especially during this time of so many changes.
  "Don't let the enemy get a foothold in any manner. We're moving forward to win more people to Jesus, and the enemy will try to thwart what we're doing. Put on the full armor of God every day and remember we <u>are</u> assured of victory in Jesus."
  At the end of the teaching time, he announced that the total amount of the offerings given by all 12 churches last Sunday for the building fund was more than enough to build and furnish the new church and school. The whole congregation erupted into praise and thanksgiving to the great Almighty God they loved and served.

*****

(Church services and small groups continue to meet weekly, but are not documented in the rest of the story.)

*****

  Monday at work, Connie said, "Fiona, our family has decided to attend the new Saturday evening service at church." She then told her about the family's prayers and discussions.
  "I'm glad you told me so I can join you in prayer. Your family will be a good one to help get that new church going. It's such a good idea to have your whole small groups move with you. I hope other small groups will do that along with yours. I <u>will</u> miss seeing you at church, but at least we'll still get to work together."
  Ernest told Patrick that morning also. Amelia and Fiona discussed it on Wednesday at work.
  While he was working with Matt on Saturday, Ben said, "My family and I and both of our small groups will be attending the new Saturday evening service at church starting today. Please keep

us in your prayers. I'll miss seeing you and Fiona sitting together in church. You make such a perfect couple."

Matt responded, "Thank you for the compliment. I'll certainly pray for you and your family and small groups. It's amazing how one decision impacts the lives of so many other people. I'll miss seeing you and your family in church also, but at least you aren't moving to a different state. I hope we can continue to be friends and do things together after this house is finished."

"Me too! Let's plan on that," replied Ben.

During the week, the Clays had told the rest of their friends who also promised to pray for them.

*****

Larry and Jane called Jeff and Karen early on Monday morning to explain how Jeff's message to them from Jesus had helped them make their big, important decision. They said they would tell Ted and Julie on Thursday, and the rest of the small group the coming Saturday.

So, on Thursday of that week, Larry and Jane asked Ted and Julie to stay a while after the music practice session at church and the ladies' visiting time. They told in detail about their prayers and discussions about joining the church-planting group. "Of course we haven't been chosen yet. We have just volunteered and are willing to go. The rest is still up to the Lord, although what Jesus said through Jeff makes me think we'll be chosen," finished Larry.

Ted responded, "Wow! Isn't our God amazing? Since we moved to Pine City we've been privileged to see some of the ways he works. I'm glad _he_ is in control and not humans. However, I'm really going to miss you both when you leave at the end of September. I enjoy carpooling with you, Larry, and singing next to you at the music practice times on Thursdays. They'll have to find another bass to take your place."

"Right, but God will provide just like he always does," replied Larry.

"Oh, Julie, I understand. It's okay to cry," comforted Jane as she went to sit next to her. "We still have a few months and we'll be in the same small group until we leave. After that we'll keep in touch by phone and e-mail."

Julie dried her tears and said, "Thank you, Jane. It just hit me kind of hard, because I've enjoyed our Thursday evening visiting times so much, and they can't continue after you move. I know that God knows what he is doing, but the changes are going to take a lot of getting used to. Don said to pray for you, but I think I'm going to need your prayers as much as you'll need mine!" Then she broke down again. Jane put her arms around her and they both cried together, while their husbands, understanding their women, looked at them lovingly and prayed for them.

They both got control again and then Jane commented, "Church and especially small groups are like a family. When family members move away there's often much sorrow for all of the members. Remember how the Ephesian leaders cried when Paul said they would not see him again? But <u>we</u> will probably get to come back for a visit now and then. I'll pray for you and we can help each other bear our burden of sorrow. We can try to have a phone visit once a week, even on Thursday evenings if it works out. I certainly desire that we continue our friendship in spite of the move."

"I'm glad because you've become a precious friend to me. It will be interesting to hear how you're doing there and how God is using you in the new church plant. From what you've told me, that city really needs a church like ours. I'll accept God's will in this matter and pray for you and the new church," Julie responded.

*****

Beth had asked Julie to stop in the office on the way home one day toward the end of June. She said, "I need someone to revise part of the curriculum and lesson plans for the third grade. We need to update what we teach the students to expect in the public school's fourth grade, and how to go out into that 'mission field.' I chose you, Julie, because of your experience recently in the public school's fourth grade. Would you be willing to do that in time to be used with this year's classes?"

"Certainly," Julie answered.

"Good. Here is a copy of the current curriculum and lesson plans for that topic," said Beth as she handed it to Julie who took it and looked at part of it.

"When is this taught?" asked Julie.

"Not until October unless you think it needs to be sooner," replied Beth. "Keep track of the hours you spend doing this and we'll pay you your hourly wage when you're finished."

"Okay. I'll do my best, and bring it for you to review when it's done," said Julie.

Linda L. Linn

*****

Vern and Lora had several other Saturday morning dates, including playing ping-pong. They found out they were pretty well matched, and both of them got better with practice.

One morning they went to a museum they knew Mindy would consider boring, but both of them enjoyed it.

As they were sitting on a bench to rest, Vern said, "I know Mindy has handled losing her mother better than I did. It was because of your help, Lora. Do you remember what you told her?"

"Yes, I told Mindy about how I had been engaged to my college sweetheart. He was killed in an automobile accident just after we graduated from college. It was two weeks before our wedding would have been. I told her that I had a very hard time getting over that. After about two years, I went to a counselor and it really helped me. The counselor told me about God's sovereignty and that I had two choices. I could continue to grieve and be bitter about losing my fiancé, which would result in unhappiness and an ineffective life. Or I could accept the accident as God's will for him, <u>and</u> for me. Then I could surrender to God's will and let him fill me with his joy and peace, as I would follow his guidance and do what he directed me to do. The result has been wonderful," she explained.

"Thank you for telling me. I would have never guessed that you had come through such sorrow. Every time I see you, you are filled with such joy and peace. I desire that for myself, so I'll take the advice of your counselor and make the right choice," he responded. "Father in heaven, forgive me for wasting time in grief and bitterness. I accept your will about losing my wife in childbirth. I surrender to your will and ask you to fill me with your joy and peace. Make me effective at whatever you guide me to do."

Lora added, "I agree with that prayer and we claim the yes answer in Jesus name, Amen.

*****

Tony and his partner continued reading stories in the park. They had even added some puppets at the beginning and that helped to get the attention of children so they would come over and listen. They were beginning to see some repeat listeners from other weeks at some of the parks.

Some of the children who had accepted Jesus in earlier weeks brought their friends to listen. On those days the groups were bigger, and often the child who had been invited was likely to listen more carefully and would say yes to the invitation. In this way Jesus was using Tony and his partner to help some children and their families become believers.

Ted and Julie had Tony come over for a meal on a rainy Sunday afternoon, and he was able to tell them how things were going in his ministry.

"We're so glad for you, Tony!" Ted exclaimed. "That to so much more important than our walks and practicing Spanish. Julie and I have been practicing Spanish daily and I'm getting pretty good at understanding what is said and can even answer many times. When we go walking with Maria on Sundays, she joins in the fun."

They spent the rest of the meal conversing in Spanish, and Ted only had to ask them to slow down a couple times. After supper and clean up, they visited some more in the living room and prayed together before Tony went home. This time was just one of many times they enjoyed Tony's company on a rainy Saturday or Sunday.

*****

Vern asked Pastor Don to come over to his house one evening while Mindy was doing her homework in her room. He told Don about Lora and their fun times together with each other and with Mindy. Then he told him in detail about his prayer during their last date. "After my wife died, I thought I could never consider marrying again, but Mindy expressed her desire to see me happy again and to have a mother at home. I've prayed a lot about it and I think I have a green light for marriage. I think Mindy will be thrilled with Lora as the possibility," he said.

Don responded, "I'll bet she will. Mindy likes helping Anita with the children, but when she goes home in the evening, the house must feel rather empty."

"It does for me also. I know that Lora and I will have many things to discuss and the only way I can ask her to marry me is if we can have unity in all the important areas. Please pray with me that we'll all do God's will and nobody will get hurt feelings for any reason," Vern requested.

"Of course I will. And I praise God for the healing he's done in your heart," Don responded. "May I share what you've told me with Anita? We have both been praying for you. She'll be delighted, and we can pray for you in unity."

"Please do. I just didn't know when I could get both of you together at a convenient time to listen," he answered.

*****

When Connie got to work one Thursday, she enjoyed telling Fiona about the nice time she and Ernest had enjoyed yesterday morning when they had both taken some time off work. "We went to the art museum and took our time looking at the paintings and beautiful landscape photography. It was very relaxing to be able to sit in front of some of them and study various aspects."

"I remember that museum. Ted and I were sitting in front of a beautiful scenery picture when he proposed to me," said Fiona.

As they were working together later that evening, Fiona commented, "Connie, I've noticed that the cute little blond who comes in to be the cashier for the afternoon and evening looks unhappy most of the time. I know it's not really my business, but I just wanted to alert you to what I've noticed, and offer to pray for you as you talk with her. My job here does not lend itself to talking to the cashier, but yours does."

"Thank you, Fiona, I've noticed that also, but I'll have to admit that I've procrastinated about talking to her. I needed your offer to pray for me to help me get started. I think God has you working here for reasons just like this. He knows that I need someone to nudge me into action and then back me up." responded Connie.

"Let's pray about it this evening as we nurture these plants, okay?" asked Fiona.

"Yes! Father in heaven, first I thank you for Fiona's observant and caring nature. Second, I ask you to forgive me for my procrastination. Please give me the words to say to the cashier and show me the best timing. Help me to be a friend to her," prayed Connie.

Fiona continued, "Please either have her open up to Connie or give Connie a word of knowledge about what's bothering her and what to do about it. Holy Spirit, please draw her to believe in Jesus."

They continued praying off and on through the early evening. During a lull in business Connie went over and chatted with the cashier for a while. It took several weeks of small talk and showing interest, but finally, Connie was able to become a friend in whom the cashier could confide.

Fiona was glad to take over the register so Connie and the cashier could go to supper together and have longer talks, including Connie giving her testimony, explaining the gospel, and answering many questions. After a few more weeks in which Fiona faithfully prayed for them, the cashier became a new believer in Jesus, and the joy of the Lord filled up the void that was making her unhappy.

The evening that Connie shared that victory, Fiona was filled with rejoicing that she could have a part in praying for them both. Connie told her, "I planted, you watered with your prayers, and God gave the harvest. It says something like that in 1 Corinthians."

*****

Jane's Wednesday Bible study and story groups continued to flourish and grow. This week the ones who had accepted Jesus as their Savior each brought a friend. They listened well, because the study and stories were interesting, and Jane did a good job teaching. Also, they all enjoyed the refreshments every week.

This type of ministry takes time and perseverance. Since these children have grown up in families who don't attend church, many of them need a lot of teaching before they can understand their need of a Savior. Each week they would learn more about the Bible, and each week had a gospel presentation and an invitation to accept Jesus as their Savior. Some weeks, Jane would ask one of the new believers to give their testimony. Once in a while, a light would go on and a child would stay after the meeting to pray with Jane. Those were her encouragement to keep going. Many times that child would bring a friend to the next meeting.

She had talked many of her friends into starting their own groups and they all got together on Tuesday afternoons to pray for the children in their Wednesday groups.

One Thursday evening Jane explained all this to Julie who exclaimed, "Praise the Lord! I'm so glad you were courageous enough to start these groups. I'll continue to pray for you and your friends."

"Exactly what we need, since prayer and encouragement to keep going are very helpful," said Jane.

"I enjoy hearing about your groups when we get together on Thursday evenings. Since all my students already are believers, I get my rejoicing times when I hear about the ones who accept

Jesus in your groups. It's like you're planting the seeds, and I'm helping to water them with my prayers. Of course God is the one who causes the reaping," said Julie.

"That's basically what Paul says in 1 Corinthians 3:6-9a," replied Jane. "Listen while I read it. *I have planted, Apollos watered, but God gave the increase. So then neither he who plants, nor he who waters, is anything, but God is the one who gives the increase or harvest. Now he that plants and he that waters are one, and every man shall receive his own reward according to his own labor, for we are laborers together with God.*"

"Thank you for reading that to me, Jane. Sometimes I forget that each part of Jesus body has a different function and that all we need to do is be faithful in doing our part," Julie responded.

"Yes," continued Jane. "It's good to remember that we're not in a contest to see who can win the most souls. If we know we're in the center of God's will we can be at peace."

"Exactly," agreed Julie. Then she held up her embroidery project so Jane could see it. "Look at this other project we're doing together. You did the calligraphy on the material for me and I'm in the process of filling it in with the colored thread. Like you said, it's taking a very long time to do it, but it will be worth it. The work you and I are doing together with these children is even more worthwhile."

*****

Lora had been telling Beth about each time she went with Vern and Mindy and then each date with just Vern. She told Beth that she had prayed after her fiancé's death about whether to stay single or if marriage would still be in God's will for her. She felt he had said at that time, "Marriage would be good, but not for some time yet."

"After Vern prayed for forgiveness and to surrender to God's will during our last date, I realized that I could very easily love that man. I don't know how he feels, or if he could ever marry again, so I need to be careful," she told Beth.

"Yes, you need to guard your heart because of that. I know you've told me that he's a good Christian man, so you're safe on that issue. But you'll need to discuss so many other things if you're going to consider a relationship and possible marriage," Beth cautioned.

Everywhere There's a Sunrise, Let's Tell The Good News!

"You're so right. I still have that book my mother gave me before I got engaged. I'll read it again and be sure to evaluate and discuss everything that's important if we ever even get to that point," promised Lora.

"Be sure you think about the ramifications of a ready made family with an almost teenager, and whether he might want more children. If he does, it would end your job here at the school, and I don't know how you feel about that," said Beth.

"You're right again. I need to be sure about all of those things. Let's pray together," Lora replied.

Beth began, "Father in heaven you've heard all of this conversation and since you are all wise, you know what is the very best thing for Lora to do about Vern and Mindy. Please be in complete control and give Lora your wisdom so she'll know what to do."

Lora continued, "Yes, Father, you know that I desire to do your will. I especially need your guidance in this uncharted area of my life. I only know that I've felt very drawn to Mindy and Vern ever since January when we were all put in the same small group. If you don't want me to continue doing things with them, please show me very soon so that neither they nor I will be hurt if I stop."

"We're in agreement and trust you to do your perfect will in all three lives. We pray in Jesus name, Amen," finished Beth. She gave Lora a hug and a smile and told her to relax now and let God be God.

*****

One afternoon after school, Julie went next door and asked, "Pam, would you like to join Maria, Ted and me in a four by four ministry on Sundays after church?"

She declined saying, "Thank you for asking, but I've already joined two of my other girl friends, and we're going on Saturday afternoons. The ministry is such a wonderful plan. I missed doing it while I was gone."

"Yes, it's a wonderful plan. Ted and I have been finding that the ideas this church has for bringing other people into God's family and for teaching them how to live their new lives, plus caring for all the believers are all great ideas. I'm so thankful that we were able to move here to Pine City and become involved with this church and school," said Julie.

"And I'm just as grateful that I got to come back here so soon!" exclaimed Pam.

"We're both very blessed! Thank you Jesus!" Julie agreed. "I've really enjoyed singing patriotic songs the last couple weeks with the children. The ones they liked best are also my favorites: 'My Country 'Tis of Thee,' 'God of Our Fathers,' 'God Bless America,' and 'America the Beautiful.' It's been enjoyable to teach why we have The Fourth of July as a national holiday. What are your plans for the vacation during the Fourth of July week?"

"I'm going to drive back to my parents' home and spend some time just enjoying their Christian fellowship. They changed so much for the better after accepting Jesus that it's amazing!" exclaimed Pam.

"That is wonderful. If I don't see you again before that, have a great trip," wished Julie.

"Thank you, Julie. I hope you have a nice week also. What are your plans?" Pam asked.

"Wow! A whole week off!" Julie exclaimed. "I think I'll miss my students. But I plan to read, sew, relax, and then clean house with a vengeance. Somehow I've gotten behind and it needs a lot of attention," answered Julie. Then she remembered that she needed to finish up that curriculum revision that Beth had asked her to do, so in her mind she put that in first place so it would be finished when the week was over.

*****

During the week of the Fourth of July, a third grade boy from Julie's class, went on a vacation with his family to a national park where they listened to a park ranger give a talk about fossils. The ranger explained how fossils were made, and how old each one was. At the end of the talk, the ranger asked if there were any questions. The boy raised his hand patiently several times. His dad encouraged him to keep trying, and the ranger finally called on him. "How can you know how old they are?" he asked. The ranger explained to him about carbon dating as if it were an established fact and not just a theory.

Then the boy asked if he could tell what he had learned in his school. The ranger said that he could. First, he sang the fun song about how fossils formed. Then he gave details about what he had learned on the subject of how and when fossils were formed using the facts he had learned in his class at school and from answersingenesis.org. The ranger and other people listened patiently, but most of them looked skeptical, until he mentioned the great flood and Noah's Ark, giving the reference in Genesis 7:17-24. He told them that by reading other verses in Chapter 7 and 8, he had figured out that the water covered the earth for almost one year, so that would have been plenty of time for the dead things to settle to the bottom of the water and be covered by layers of sediment. At this point, several people looked more interested, but others openly scoffed at what the boy was saying. The boy just smiled and finished what he was saying. The ranger thanked the boy for his input and then went on to answer other questions.

When it was over, some interested people stayed and asked the boy and his parents more questions, which they gladly answered. A few of the scoffers hung around in the background, but didn't say anything. Then the boy asked the people some questions like, "What do you believe about the Bible? What do you believe about God's Son, Jesus? Why do you think he had to die on a cross? When they could not, or would not answer, the boy asked them, "Could I tell you what I believe?"

They all nodded and he said the following: "I believe that the Bible is a book that God had many people write to explain the truth about the creation of the world and people. The Bible tells about how most people went against what God said to do, and did what they wanted to instead. They got so bad that God regretted making them and sent the World Wide Flood that killed all but eight of the people on earth. Only the pairs of animals they had taken with them in the ark, and those eight people were left to repopulate the earth.

"After that, for thousands of years God sent prophets and teachers to try to get people to believe in him. He finally sent his only Son, Jesus, but they would not listen to him either. The people schemed to get the Romans to kill him by hanging him on a cross until he died. It was God's plan that his perfect Son, who always did God's will, and never sinned, would die on that cross. In that way he would pay the penalty for all the sins people had committed. But that wasn't the end of Jesus. God raised him from the dead, and he still lives in heaven with God. Anybody who will believe in Jesus and all he did, can be forgiven for all the sins they've committed. They can be sure that they'll spend eternity in heaven. Would any of you like to do that?" he asked as he finished.

The three children in the group that was listening all raised their hands like they would do in school. The boy told them to come with him to another area so he could help them pray. His father and mother took it from there with the rest of the adults and answered their questions. Before long many of them, including a couple of the scoffers, made the same good decision the children had made. Since this family knew they might have an opportunity to witness, they always had some of the same booklets that the pastor gave out at church for new believers. They gave each family of new believers one booklet, and encouraged them to find a Bible believing church and a small group when they returned to their homes.

"Feel free to call us if you have any questions about living for Jesus. Our phone number is in the back of the booklet," the father said.

After their vacation, the boy returned to school and shared his testimony with the class. The class clapped and praised and thanked Jesus that many people were saved because of the boy telling the people the truth about fossils and then sharing the gospel with them.

*****

After church one Sunday, Jeff and Karen asked all four of the Suehiros to come to their house for supper, and showed them the way the outdoor barbecue worked. They all had fun turning the steaks on the grill while trying to keep out of the smoke.

Aneko suggested, "Could we set up a fan to blow the smoke away from the barbecue?"

Karen exclaimed, "What a super idea, I'll run in and get one!" It was much easier to turn the steaks after they set up the fan.

Jeff said, "I wonder why I never thought of that before? Maybe it's because we don't do this very often."

They ate out on the patio when everything was ready and left the fan running to cool them off on this very warm July evening. The food was delicious, and they all enjoyed visiting together.

"Tomo asked, "What did you enjoy about the teaching time today?"

Yoshi responded, "I liked hearing about the fruit of the Spirit in Galatians 5: 22,23 where it says *the fruit of the Spirit is love, joy, peace, patience, gentleness, goodness, faith, meekness and self-control.*"

Karen added, "The verses Pastor Don read from Colossians 3:12-15 went so well with those two verses. *Put on ... mercy, kindness, and humbleness of mind, meekness and patience. Be tolerant of one another and forgive one another ... as Christ forgave you. And above all these things put on love, which binds them all perfectly together. Let the peace of God rule in your hearts, ... and be thankful.* Then verse 17 says *whatever you do in word or deed, do all in the name of the Lord Jesus, giving thanks to God the Father by him.*"

"Those are good verses to help new believers like Yoshi and me to learn about Christian living," said Aneko.

The Suehiros lives had blossomed after joining the small group and God had answered so many of their prayers! They were also thankful that they could be friends with Jeff and Karen.

*****

The morning after her week off, Julie stopped in Beth's office to hand her what she had done so far on the revised part of the curriculum and lesson plans about what the children could expect in the public school's fourth grade. She included ideas for role-playing different scenarios and questions they might want to ask the current fourth graders about their experiences this year. Then she added that they were learning these things not just for being missionaries to the fourth graders, but also to others for the rest of their lives.

One important thing to learn from the fourth graders would be which plans are the most effective in being a missionary in the public schools. She obtained permission to begin collecting that information when the fourth grade children came to her classroom on the next few Wednesdays. Those could then be included in this revision of that part of the curriculum. So she started asking the fourth graders to write about their experiences in fourth grade and also what they considered to be their most effective method of evangelism.

When she had received enough of them, she added the best ideas to the revisions of the curriculum. Beth was very pleased with the way the curriculum and lesson plans had been improved. The time Julie had spent at home working on this project wasn't a chore to her like grading papers had been. It was more like a ministry and it was a joy to her.

The third graders at the Grace 'n' Faith Church School enjoyed having Julie (Mrs. Blake) as their teacher. When they returned from their vacation after The Fourth of July, they were all set to continue learning, and didn't take very long to settle down into the routine again.

But it did take almost that whole week during class meeting and sharing time for everyone to have a chance to tell each other and Kippy about the things they had done while on vacation. When the boy shared about his opportunity to tell all those people the truth about fossils and then witness about Jesus, it took up one whole sharing time. Kippy was a very good listener and was especially interested in what each child had to say.

One of them asked him, "What did you do last week, Kippy?"

"I took a very nice long nap, so that I wouldn't miss all of you so much," he answered. They all clapped and laughed. He was such fun.

*****

On a Friday evening, Maria, Ruth and Esther enjoyed a meal with Anna and William at their house. Jason wasn't there and Anna and William were able to tell Maria how he had dealt with his disappointment after the lunch and questions of that particular Saturday.

"I'm glad to hear that," Maria responded. "His prayer shows that he's growing in the Lord. I think he will be much more able to continue growing because he won't be focusing on courting me. We're so different that it never would have worked out anyway. Besides, I'm pleased to be able to tell you all that I have the same kind of peace that Ruth has about remaining single. I know that I can serve Jesus better this way. God has worked out so many details for the better in my life as a result of the whole situation with Jason. All I can say is, 'Thank you very much, Lord. Please continue to lead me and use me in your service.' I know that he will answer that prayer. Now, let's hear from Esther."

"I knew you would put me in the spotlight," responded Esther. "Okay, here goes. I'm over my infatuation with Tony. He made the best choice for both of us. His joy when he told me about his new ministry was wonderful. Besides, our jobs and the hours we work would always have been a problem, and neither one of us could change jobs. Plus who knows what other obstacles there would have been in our way."

After a moment of silence she continued, "I don't have the peace Ruth and Maria have about remaining single, so I'll continue to pray about that. Jason and I have finished my introductions to all my co-workers in that office building. Now I'll follow Maria's plan and go to lunch with two who have common interests and see what the Lord will do."

"My turn," inserted Ruth. "Maria commented about how the Lord has worked out so many things for the better because of the situation with Jason. Also as a result of that situation, he blessed me with an employee who is a Christian and has become a dear friend. The three of us were able to come up with a plan to become friends and then witness and share the gospel with our co-workers. So far, the progress has been slow, but we'll continue doing it as a ministry, and I know that God will bless our efforts. So far a believing co-worker and I have been going to lunch with another co-worker. We've had some good discussions for a couple weeks but she still has a lot of issues keeping her from believing."

Anna said, "I'm proud of all three of you young ladies. God is at work in your lives and you are all following his leading. Yes, he will bless your efforts, so keep up the good work."

Before they went to their homes they sang the song, "Let Your Love Flow Through Me" as a prayer and a reminder to keep working at their ministries.

*****

It was time for Julie to teach her third graders about evangelism. Each child would prepare and write his own story of how he received Jesus to be his own personal Savior. This took several weeks and included the fourth and fifth graders helping with the writing on Wednesdays. Then he or she would practice it and become at ease with sharing it with one or more other classmates.

They would learn and use many other methods or presentations and then practice on each other to become familiar and comfortable doing it. She emphasized, "It is usually best to make friends with others and show them Jesus love by your actions before you tell them the Good News."

She reminded them again that sometimes they might be ridiculed for what they're doing, just like the disciples were after Jesus went back to heaven.

"Remember to do just what the disciples did in those cases. They thanked God that they could suffer for the sake of Jesus name. Then they asked God for more boldness to continue working for Jesus," she said.

One student asked, "Why would people want to make fun of us, Mrs. Blake?" Julie called on several students to answer that.

"They don't want to change the way they're living," replied a boy.

"Because they don't know how wonderful it is to know Jesus," answered a girl.

"Some people just like to be mean," said another girl.

Julie said, "Those are all correct answers, and that's the reason we need to continue trying to gently convince them that asking Jesus to save them and help them live for him is so much better than the way they're living right now."

Julie called on another student who added, "If we get angry and fight back, we would be just as bad as they are, and they would have a good reason to not listen to us any longer."

"Very true, so we need to be very careful to be humble, gentle and friendly," agreed their teacher.

After all their testimonies were finished, the fourth and fifth graders demonstrated how they were witnessing on the playground at school. Since recesses were so short they had to get right to the point and not have testimonies that were too long. Or they might just "plant seeds" on consecutive days. Sometimes a person would ask to hear more about Jesus because of what he or she had been hearing.

One of the fourth graders said, "The important thing is to pray every morning for Jesus to show us opportunities or tell us when to talk or when to just listen. We don't want to be too pushy and turn kids away."

*****

Roy and Sherry and the twins went to the shopping mall on a Saturday after lunch and nap time for their two by two ministry time. As they walked around in the mall praying for direction, they noticed couple who were arguing about something. They found a child-sized bench where Hope and Joy could look at the picture books they had brought along and still be in view. Then they went to converse with the couple.

When they were able to get past small talk, they even found out what the argument was about. But when they tried to share how Jesus could help them with their problem, neither one wanted to listen. Sherry ended with, "We'll be praying for you and if you would like to talk some more, give us a call at this phone number." She gave them a card with their first names and phone number.

It was a disappointment to them when they never got a call. But they prayed that what they had said would get them thinking and maybe someone else would talk to them, and eventually they might come to the Lord.

*****

Chapter 26

Hebrews 13:4a, *Marriage is honorable...*
Proverbs 18:22, *He who finds a wife, finds a good thing and obtains favor from the Lord.*

Vern talked to Mindy about the possibility of marriage when they got home from one of their fun Sunday afternoon threesome activities. He began, "Some time ago you told me that you wished I would find and marry a wonderful Christian woman so that I could be happy again and you could have a mother. Do you think that maybe Lora could be that woman?"

"Oh yes, Dad! I've been thinking that for several weeks now. Have you asked her?" Mindy asked hopefully.

"Not yet. I wanted to see how you would feel about it before talking with Lora. If it is okay with you, then I'll discuss it with Lora," he explained.

"It's very okay with me!" Mindy exclaimed. "She's smart, fun to be with, caring, and humble."

"Yes she is all of those things and more," he replied with great feeling. "I don't want to put a damper on your excitement, but I need to tell you that there are many things that Lora and I will need to discuss before I can ask her to marry me. You know from our Bible reading times together that a husband and wife need to be in unity about the important issues. If we can't be, then I would not be able to ask her," he said gently.

"I understand, Dad. It's too early for me to be able to celebrate. I'll try to be patient," she replied.

Then they prayed that God would do his will for all three of them.

*****

After Matt and Fiona had chosen the refrigerator, electric range, and dishwasher for the kitchen, they had them scheduled for delivery and installation. They also chose and ordered a washer and a dryer. Then they went shopping for the furniture for their house at several different stores in town. They tested the couches and chairs for comfort and compared prices. They looked at master bedroom, child bedroom and nursery furniture, trying to picture the styles and woods set up in the house.

Then they took pictures and took them to the house on the weekend to see if that would help them to choose. All those empty rooms would look so much better with furniture and people filling them.

While they were shopping one day, Matt inquired, "What are we going to do with those two extra bedrooms until we have children who are old enough to want their own rooms?"

"That's a very good question. Let's pray about it and maybe God will give us some creative ideas," she answered.

Later as they were looking at furniture she asked, "How would you like this furniture for our office?"

He replied, "I like it a lot. The wood is cherry and is finished to perfection. It looks like it's well built and has just the right number of pieces for the way we planned to set up our office. Let's order it. One room is furnished!"

"Hurrah! Now let's go look at dining room furniture. On the way there we can decide how many people we might want to be able to seat. How fancy do we want that room to look and how will it go with the living room since there's no wall between them? Do we need a fancy china cabinet and if so do we want to buy fancy china to fill it?" Fiona asked.

"My wonderful Fiona, you ask many hard questions, but they're good ones that we need to answer. First, how many people? I think no more than eight, since it's hard to visit with more than that at once. So we need a table that will seat eight with eight matching comfortable chairs that can also be used for small group members' seating. Second, how fancy do we want it to be? You get to answer that one," he said with relief.

"I think I know both of us well enough to say that we don't want it to be fancy. I would rather have it be pretty, practical and welcoming. I don't want a fancy china cabinet or fancy china. I would rather have unbreakable, dishwasher-safe dishes. Then if a child or we drop something it won't get broken and maybe cut someone. Everyday dishes can be pretty enough to use for company. The people we invite over are not going to notice a difference anyway," she finished.

"I agree with you. Third, how will it go with the living room? We'll find the right table and chairs and then we'll find a couch and recliners that go well with their colors. Plus, they all need to go well with the drapes you are making," he said.

"You're absolutely correct. I brought a small piece of the material today so we can see how it matches. There, we answered all those questions and here we are in the dining room section." she said. They looked at all the choices with the answers to their questions in mind.

Matt pointed, "Look at that one over there. It has three chairs on each side and one at each end. Let's check the chairs for comfort and see how the table is made."

They went and sat down. "This table has a pretty wood grain Formica top. That would be very good to have since we would not have to worry about spills ruining a wood top. We would not even have to use a tablecloth or place mats, so that would save a lot of time doing laundry and ironing. There's a matching cabinet that also has the same Formica top. It's drawers will hold a lot of things and the top will be useful for times that we would like to serve buffet style meals instead of passing things around, " commented Fiona.

"Right, and the table is well made. The two leaves fit together very well and could be left in all the time so we would not have to change back and forth with table sizes unless we wanted to," he observed. "The chairs are very comfortable and even have rollers on them so they would be easy to move to the living room for small group time."

Fiona took out the piece of drapery material and held it next to the upholstery of the chair next to her and noticed that it didn't go well. But Matt found a display of other choices and they were able to choose one that did match.

"Now let's check the living room furniture and see if we can find a match there," suggested Fiona. They found comfortable recliners and a sofa that went well with the dining room chair upholstery and drapery material. They also chose a coffee table and then an end table to go between the recliners. So they ordered the office suite, the dining room table with chairs, the matching cabinet, the sofa, two recliners, the coffee table and the end table to be delivered after the house was complete.

*****

When Vern and Lora went on their next couple's date each one of them broached what they thought would be an easy issue to discuss and were pleased to find that they agreed with each other. Lora was also alert to a few things her book had mentioned and was able to check them off as "passed" in her mind, so she determined to just enjoy the rest of their time together.

Vern had taken Lora back to the recreation center which had an inside walking track, so that they could get some exercise while they talked. It was a lot cooler than being outside that day. The track even had an uphill and downhill portion so they were able to get their heart rates up and work all their muscles better. They had both read that if you can converse comfortably while exercising then your heart rate is about correct for that exercise. This way, they didn't have to bother with some kind of monitor to tell them when the heart rate was high enough.

After about a half hour of walking they enjoyed playing ping-pong until it was time to take Lora home and go pick up Mindy at the pastor's house.

Vern was able to tell Mindy, "We began to discuss some issues and so far, we agreed with each other. But we still have a lot left to talk about."

"Thank you for telling me, Dad. I think I understand that it will take time. We'll keep praying for God's will to be done and that we can accept it," said Mindy. He nodded and gave her a big hug.

*****

Connie and Amelia gave Fiona a bridal shower at the Clay's house on a Saturday afternoon. It was fun for everybody. Fiona didn't realize that she had so many friends in the church and the city who wanted to come. The house was crowded.

They played several fun games before they watched Fiona open her gifts. She received many gifts and expressed her delight and thanks for each one. Connie's gift was to have Fiona choose potted plants for their new house. Other gifts were bought after consulting the gift registry at Wal-Mart, because Fiona didn't want people to spend extra money at fancier stores. The invitations to the shower had stated that Wal-Mart was the store that had Fiona's gift registry. Also this way they could exchange things that might be the wrong colors. There would be no duplicate gifts, because each time a gift was bought for them it dropped off the list of the gift registry.

The gift registry was a good way to be sure of getting things that were needed, rather than a bunch of candle holders they would never use. Matt and Fiona had spent part of one of their working dates at Wal-Mart looking at items and writing down a list of things they would like to receive as gifts. Then they had that list entered into the gift registry.

The refreshments at the bridal shower were delicious and cool, and everyone enjoyed visiting together. Fiona had given many showers for her friends and that had been fun, but she decided that it was even more fun to be the one receiving a shower. After showing Matt all their nice gifts, he helped her by addressing the thank you notes as she was writing them.

*****

A small group for preteens and young teens had been started on Wednesdays after early dismissal from school. It included many new believers as a result of Mindy and Candy's witnessing at school and the testimonies at the baptismal service of the two other girls who had recently become believers. The meetings were held at the home of a caring homemaker who desired to help these young people learn the things Jesus wanted them to know. Her husband prayed with her for them every Tuesday evening. (Mindy didn't attend, because she was already in a small group, and she didn't want to miss time with Anita and the daycare children.)

They had many interesting discussions and learned a lot about the Bible. They memorized all the names of the books in the Bible so they could find them easily. The lady kept several used Bibles available that she had bought from the church. Once in a while they would play a fun game called a Sword Drill, since the Word of God is called a sword in a Christian's armor. The game was a good way to practice finding scripture references quickly.

The kids also started memorizing scriptures that would help them when they told others about Jesus. The lady had obtained ideas from the church school's principal, Beth, about how to teach the young people to tell the Good News to their friends at school, so she incorporated that into the meetings.

Sometimes one of them would bring a friend with them to a group meeting. Occasionally the testimony of a fellow young person would get through to that one and he or she would also become a believer.

*****

"I think we did very well on our last shopping trip," commented Matt as they drove to the furniture store another day and Fiona agreed.

"Thank you, Lord, for your help finding that furniture. What shall we do with those two empty bedrooms until they're filled with our children?" Matt prayed.

They were silent a while and then Fiona suggested, "If we would get two extra long twin beds for each room, we could have two missionary couples who are here from foreign countries to study at the church's school of evangelism, stay here with us for no charge. We could push the beds together to make king-size beds. One couple could be in each room and it could be part of my ministry to cook meals for them and do their laundry, freeing up their time to study. When our boys or girls get old enough, they could share a room with twin beds if we have two boys or two girls. The other room could still be used for one couple. Or later if a son or daughter wants his or her own room, and a friend to sleep over the friend could use the other bed."

"Thank you for that excellent idea. What about your job at The Garden Shop?" Matt asked.

"Well, they might have to cook their own suppers while I work, because I <u>would</u> like to continue working there until a month before our first child is born," answered Fiona.

"I like talking about our children and I'm looking forward to becoming a father. I'm also glad that you'll be able to stay at home to be a mother and homemaker." After a pause he added, "But even more, I'm anticipating to being married to you and having you all to myself for a while. Do you think we could leave those bedrooms empty for a few months while we enjoy our married life together?" Matt inquired.

"That would be great. I can hardly wait!" Fiona exclaimed. "I totally agree with you! Here we are at the furniture store again. Let's see if we can fill our bedroom first, then the nursery and then those two bedrooms with furniture that will go along with our plans. I'm so glad we have this time to talk, plan, and make decisions."

Matt agreed as they went to the area that had master bedroom furniture, walked around and looked at each idea first before thinking about a choice. Matt spoke first, "What do you think about this set? It is very similar to the cherry wood we chose for the office. I think I'm partial to cherry wood."

"I like it very much also because it's a cheery color and it's beautiful. We can have cheery, cherry wood in our master bedroom and in the office both," she laughed. "We'll take very good care of it and it will last us a lifetime."

He laughed with her and said, "I'm glad you can make these shopping trips so fun!"

"Thank you, Dear. I have one request that might seem strange to you, but here goes. I would like to NOT get the head and foot boards for any of the beds in the house except the baby crib of course," she stated.

"Okay," he paused and then asked, "Please tell me why. I would like to understand, so please explain your reason to me."

It's a purely selfish reason. I've made my bed at home all these years and fought to get the sheets and blankets to go between the head and foot boards, even skinning my knuckles in the process. I'd really rather not continue doing that for the rest of my life," Fiona explained.

"I understand now. Thank you for telling me, my dear! I completely agree that we don't need those nasty things around to hurt my sweet love. Besides it will be that much less that you have to dust," he finished.

She laughed and replied, "I never thought of that. It will save time and effort that way. Thank you for being so understanding my wonderful future husband. You don't know how hard it is for me to keep from hugging you right here in this store. We better take the order information and go look at nursery furniture."

Matt was thinking as they walked, that he really did know how hard that was, but he wisely held his tongue.

"How many children do you think we might have?" she asked as they arrived at the nursery area.

"I would like at least three if the Lord so wills. What do you desire?" Matt asked.

Fiona answered, "I've been thinking about that a lot, and I decided I would like either two or four. Three is an odd number, and there's often an odd person left out of many activities, and they get their feelings hurt. But I guess the number and gender will be up to the good Lord, and we'll be grateful and happy with whatever he gives. The reason I asked is because I think we should get sturdy, washable furniture for the nursery, not some fancy wood that can be easily ruined by accidents with water or other things."

"Good points. We'll look for that kind of furniture for our future babies," he agreed.

They found a nursery ensemble made of a very sturdy plastic that had a light colored wood grain appearance. It was guaranteed to last through at least five babies. Neither of them liked the plain white color that was an option. The room was large enough for a comfortable rocking chair and a daybed that could later be used for a young child that still needed to be close to where his parents were sleeping. They bought an extra dresser that could be used for that child.

Taking the order information with them to the children's bedroom furniture, they found dressers and desks made of that same sturdy plastic in two different wood grain imitations. They would be appropriate for the missionaries also until the children got old enough to be in one or both of the rooms. A tall bureau of five drawers and two desks would fit in each room with the beds being used as twin or king-sized beds. They would choose mattresses, foundations and bed frames at a mattress store on another day.

"Now for the sewing room activity table. We can look in the area where they have tables to fit in some kitchen areas. It needs to be sturdy and washable also. If I get a sewing/cutting board to use on it, the top won't be ruined by the straight pins used for sewing," she finished as they walked to that area.

There were a lot to choose from including round, square, and rectangular. Fiona decided, "I think a rectangular one 3 feet by 5 feet would work best for laying out and cutting out patterns."

"Come look at this one. It has a Formica top and the legs are sturdy and washable," said Matt.

"Yes, I like this one. It has a pretty light colored wood grain for the Formica top," she responded.

Matt agreed, "I like it too. I think we're both partial to wood grain, even if it isn't real wood. It makes good sense to buy things that are sturdy and washable especially when they're going to be used by children."

"Do we have all the furniture we need now for the house?" Fiona asked.

Matt replied, "I think so, because the bookcases, cupboards and drawers are all in the process of being custom built. Oh, I remember one more piece we need to find. You wanted to have a Bible study desk in the sewing room."

Fiona exclaimed, "Right, I'm glad you remembered! Let's get one like those in the children's rooms that will match the activity tabletop. I'll take a picture and see how close we can get to it." So they found one that would work, and then went to order all those pieces and give them the delivery date.

"Furniture shopping has been fun, but I'm glad we're finished except for the beds," remarked Matt.

Fiona agreed, "Me too! It <u>will</u> be enjoyable to see them all in the right places in our beautiful home. I can hardly wait until we're married and living there.

*****

Sunday morning of the next weekend was a fun threesome activity. Lora fixed a picnic breakfast <u>and</u> lunch. Vern drove the three of them to the mountains where they would take a short hike to a beaver pond.

Mindy yawned as they were on their way. "Tell me again why we needed to leave so early. It's still dark out!"

Lora answered, "Beavers are mostly nocturnal animals. If we can get to the beaver pond while it's still pretty dark, then we might have a chance to see the beavers working on their dam or lodge or cutting aspen trees to eat or for their winter food storage."

"Cool! I hope it works. I've never seen a beaver in the wild, only on videos," Mindy replied. "I'm just not used to getting up so early," she giggled. Lora and Vern laughed with her. Then they took turns telling her more about beavers and their lifestyles. Mindy learned a lot before they arrived at the trail head.

They walked quietly along the mountain path to the pond and hid behind some trees to silently and patiently watch for the beavers. Soon they were rewarded. They got to see a large beaver dragging a long branch from an aspen tree down the hillside to the pond. Another beaver was standing on his hind legs gnawing on a small aspen tree on the other side of the pond. The first beaver cut the long branch into three pieces, and then pulled the first piece into the pond. He swam and pulled it with him to the center of the pond where he dove down to the bottom with it. The water was too murky to see how he attached it to the bottom, but he came up without it and proceeded to do the same with the other two pieces. Those would be used for winter food.

Linda L. Linn

Their attention was riveted on the scene before them and they stayed quiet hoping to see more. Once again their patience paid off. They got to see the small aspen tree fall when the other beaver had finished cutting it. It landed with a thud away from where that beaver was. Then he expertly bit off a twig and gnawed the bark off of it for breakfast. The three watching could hardly keep from laughing at how cute it looked to see him clean the bark off that twig.

To top all of those things off, pretty soon mother beaver was seen swimming with her four kits trailing behind her. The other two beavers were also swimming in the water by now. Pretty soon the threesome saw a coyote coming down the hillside. Father beaver saw him too, and slapped his broad, flat tail on the water, making a loud splash. All the beavers disappeared by diving underwater and swimming back to their lodge in the middle of the pond. The coyote continued on down the hill and got a leisurely drink from the pond as if to say, "I would not have hurt you guys. All I wanted was a drink."

Then the three observers could not help laughing out loud and that scared the coyote away. So they sat down on a log near the pond and praised the great creator for his creation and their opportunity to see this part of it first hand.

"This was the best hike I've ever taken. I'm so glad your idea worked, Lora. You're such fun to be with. Now I'm really hungry for that picnic breakfast you brought today."

They looked at the beaver pond again before leaving, but all was quiet. Then they talked about the beavers all the way back to the car, where they got out the picnic and took it to one of the tables. It was warm enough to eat outside. Vern gave thanks and then they enjoyed breakfast.

After breakfast, they drove to another trail head. This time they would be following a trail through a meadow where they were going to see and identify wildflowers. Lora was pretty adept at this activity, because she had gone to the mountains often to see the flowers. She taught Mindy and Vern what details to look for on a flower and its plant, and how to find the flower in the book. It was hard at first but pretty soon they got better at it. On the way back to the car they tried to see how many flower names they could remember to go with the flowers.

Mindy commented, "I enjoyed that hike too. There are so many pretty flowers and I like learning their names."

"I enjoyed both hikes too, and now I'm hungry and looking forward to the picnic lunch you brought, Lora. Thank you for bringing the food and for all your ideas for this fun morning in the mountains!"

"You're welcome. It's fun for me to see both of you enjoying yourselves. After lunch we'll have just enough time to change out of our hiking boots into regular shoes. Since our clothes didn't get dirty we won't need to go to our homes to change clothes before church. I'm glad my plans worked out. I've never seen that much activity at a beaver pond before. We were really blessed today to get to see so much."

*****

Their house was finished, and Matt and Fiona spent a few mornings cleaning up the rest of the construction dust. The workers had done a good job of clearing out the big chunks. Patrick and Glenda came over several evenings and did the other cleaning they had promised to do as part of their wedding gift. Matt and Fiona were both there Thursday morning when the truck arrived with all the furniture they had ordered. The men put everything in the right rooms and in the right places with directions from Matt and Fiona. After the men left, she and he walked through every room admiring how nice everything looked. Then they cleaned the dresser drawers so they were ready to be filled.

Fiona and Glenda spent one morning washing the linen closet, the pantry, and all the cupboards inside and putting shelf paper on all the shelves and even in the drawers. They would be ready for Glenda and her to put the things from Fiona's shower and her "hope chest" in their places next week. Fiona's "hope chest" was really a series of boxes and included not just hand-embroidered linens, but also everything else she would need in the house.

They asked Walt and Betty to come over and see the finished product of their wedding gift the next afternoon, which was Saturday. After a tour of the whole house, Matt and Fiona both hugged and thanked them profusely, talking about how lovely everything was. They planned to have them and Fiona's parents over often for meals so they could visit.

After Matt put up all the curtain rods, Fiona and Glenda spent several mornings washing windows and hanging the curtains and drapes they had made. They looked great! They put the cushions on the couch and even made up the bed in the master bedroom so it would be ready for the night after their honeymoon. The bedspread went very well with the drapes, because Fiona and Glenda had chosen the material and made it. Everything they did helped Fiona grasp the fact that she really <u>was</u> going to get married and the date was approaching quickly.

Patrick and Glenda would unpack their other belongings including their books, and get the rest of the house set up the way they wanted it while Matt and Fiona were on their honeymoon.

*****

On Monday, after their trip to the mountains, Lora noticed all the pictures Julie had up in her school room about beavers so she said, "Julie, there's a beaver pond in the national forest not too far from here where you can see beavers in action. There's also a big field of wildflowers not very far from there. It makes a great half-day outing, but you have to get a very early start to get there while it's still pretty dark. We even made it back in time to go to church."

Julie asked, "Would you please write the directions on how to get there and how to make it work. My husband, Ted, and I would love to be able to see both of those natural wonders. I wish my whole class could go there. We're studying beavers in science and I'm reading an interesting story to the class called 'Flat Tail.' It tells the story of a beaver growing up with his family and finally taking off on his own to start a new beaver dam. They <u>will</u> get to watch a video about beavers sometime soon."

Lora wrote all the directions down and gave them to Julie on Wednesday when she came again to teach health in Julie's room. Julie excitedly told Ted all about it that night.

Ted and Julie invited Larry and Jane to accompany them when they saw them on Thursday. They went together the following Sunday morning and were able to tell it as a praise in the next Saturday small group meeting. Ted read the directions out loud so anybody could copy them down if desired. Matt did copy it all down, because he hoped Fiona and he could plan to go there soon. It sounded just like something Fiona would really enjoy. Of course he would too.

The Monday after the trip, Julie had told the other third grade teachers about the beaver pond and wildflowers. They wanted to go see them also. Julie got permission to send a half page memo with the directions home with each of the third grade students the next day. Possibly, the parents could take their children to see that part of God's creation up close, especially since they were studying beavers in science. The wildflowers would be an added benefit.

*****

    Just as soon as Matt and Fiona's house was finished, all the contractors and their crews started building the church and school. It had taken that long anyway for the city to issue the required permits and for grounds crews to finish cleaning up after the demolition of the old warehouses. Then the land had been leveled and the parking lot areas were graded so that water would drain off them and away from the buildings from rains and melting snow.
    All the building crews were on the same split schedule that Walt and Matt had been using to make the most of the daytime hours. Therefore the progress went almost twice as fast as it would have otherwise. All the workers were excited to be building the new church and school and did their best work since all we do is for Jesus.

*****

    Like all the church families who did daycare for other families that needed it, Don and Anita made a big effort to have special family fun times with their own children when the others went home. As with other things this church did well, it also included several pages in the daycare binder of ideas for parents to use for that purpose.
    Today Don was reading a funny story to Timmy and Mary. He would read a short part of the story and then have one or the other of them run to find their mom and retell it to her. That way Anita could get some housework done along with some good laughs with the children.
    Later that evening Mary shared some of the fun she had had playing with Joy and Hope on Tuesday of that week. They had all been in the bathroom taking turns making faces at themselves in the mirror while the others watched. Pretty soon they were all giggling so much that they couldn't make faces any more. Don and Anita realized that Mary was really going to miss the twins and Timmy when they went to school in January and the small groups changed so that Roy and Sherry would not need Mindy to do daycare on Saturday mornings. Maybe they could arrange some ways for all of them to get together once a week. They'd be sure to talk to Roy and Sherry about it when the time came.

Linda L. Linn

*****

    The week before their next couple's date, Vern asked Lora to write down her viewpoints on a number of topics that he listed for her. "I'll do the same and we can both bring what we have written to breakfast at that new healthy foods restaurant. My reason for doing this is so we can discuss important topics and evaluate whether we're compatible and unified enough to consider marriage."
    Lora had almost gasped in surprise when he said that, but had to admit inwardly she had been considering it. She replied, "This is an excellent idea. I'm glad you thought of it. More people should do this before they become too emotional to think straight or be honest."
    So the next Saturday while they ate a delicious breakfast, each one read the other person's "thesis" in preparation for a conversation about each topic.
    Finances were easy to agree upon since they both liked giving as much as they could over the tithe. He told her he had a savings account for Mindy's college education if she decides she wants to go. Lora said that was an excellent plan. They talked about life insurance, and decided it would be a very good idea, especially if they could find some that was <u>not</u> just term insurance where you have to pay every month but lose everything if you quit paying.
    When they had finished breakfast, they went for a walk in a shady park where they continued the discussion. They had both written that it was important to continue attending Grace 'n' Faith Church and small groups, and that they both adhered to the beliefs of that church. Each one was committed to following Jesus and doing his will. Putting God first in their lives and each other next was essential. They would need to pray about a ministry they could do.
    Every important decision needed to be talked over and prayed about. Both of them agreed that a healthy diet and good exercise were also necessary for a good lifestyle.
    "I notice that we agreed about all those things. Now it's your turn to give me a list of issues that you think we need to discuss. Please take some time right now to compile it and tell me what they are so we can both be ready for our next couple's date," Vern recommended.

"Okay. I'll just use this notebook and write us each a duplicate list while you pray that I'll be able to think of them," she replied. He took that as a cue for him to be quiet, so he did pray. She was able to finish quickly. By then it was time for Vern to take her home and go pick up Mindy. It had been time well spent.

*****

Walt and Betty were almost as excited about Matt and Fiona's upcoming wedding as they had been about their own so many years ago. Walt said, "It's just as good as if Matt really is our own son. The house turned out even better than I had hoped."

Betty agreed, "With the furniture in place, it looks every bit as good as our own home. It's going to be a friendly, welcoming place for them to live and raise a family."

Walt added, "I'm very pleased with the changes Matt and Fiona made to the blueprints and the practical furniture they chose."

"Me too. It was such fun to go to the house and see the furniture they bought as that part of our gift to them. Matt and Fiona are so grateful for all we've done that it just added to the delight of being able to give to them. We've already become like family," said Betty.

*****

It was Saturday of the third weekend in July and it would soon be 3 PM. The time had finally come for Matt and Fiona's Wedding. They were so eager. Matt had packed and brought what he needed to take for their honeymoon, and Fiona's suitcase was ready to load in the pick-up after the reception.

Matt had eaten lunch with Walt and Betty after the small group meeting because they knew he would not eat if they didn't encourage him. Betty stated, "You need to stay healthy and have enough energy to enjoy this happy time, so you must come here for lunch before the wedding."

"Right! Then you'll already be here to get showered and dressed, since you moved all your things to the new house from your apartment and stayed in a motel last night," agreed Walt.

Fiona was so keyed up that she would have skipped lunch except for the same advice about eating from her parents. She had plenty of time and help from her mother to don her wedding dress and arrange her hair after her shower. She made a beautiful bride of course. All her small group and other friends were enchanted when her father walked her down the stairs in the family home accompanied by Irish music played by bagpipes on their stereo.

The living room was decorated to look charming with extra flowering plants that Connie had brought over from the Garden Shop on 'loan' with Tony's help. Connie and Amelia wore pretty dresses of different colors that were the same as two of the flowers they had brought to decorate the room. They were so pleased to be able to stand next to Fiona as she pledged her life to the man she loved. Matt, Jeff, and Ben all looked very nice in their suits and nobody cared that none of them were wearing ties.

Pastor Don officiated the ceremony. Many things were done as per Irish customs. But Matt and Fiona had written their own vows and memorized them, so they could look at each other to say them without having to repeat what the pastor would have said. It was very meaningful. After they exchanged wedding rings Don placed his hands on their heads and prayed a blessing upon their lives together.

Then he said, "I now pronounce you husband and wife. Matt, you may kiss your bride." When he finished, they both felt like they didn't want it to end, but they knew there would be many more to come. Don turned them to face the people standing in the living room and said, "I present to you Matt and Fiona Anderson."

There was a lot of applause plus cheers and praises to the Lord who had brought them together again after that two-year separation, and had made everything work out for their good. Fiona threw her wedding bouquet straight to Clara who caught it with a very surprised look on her face. (Fiona had been praying for several weeks that Clara would find and marry just the right man who could serve with her in the town where she was going to move when she finished her training. It would not be safe for her to minister alone.) After Clara caught the bouquet, the people formed a line to congratulate and give their best wishes to the newlyweds.

The reception was held in the backyard, which had been freshly mowed and had been decorated to look even more attractive with some more flowering potted plants brought over from the Garden Shop by Connie with the help of Tony who would also help take them all back. The weather was perfect for an outdoor reception. The cake was a traditional Irish wedding fruitcake filled with almonds, raisins, cherries and spices.

Everybody enjoyed the cake and apple juice and had time to visit in the shady back yard. Even after the bride and groom had left to go on their honeymoon, people stood around talking or praying for the newlywed couple.

*****

When Clara got back to her apartment, she put the pretty wedding bouquet she had caught into some sugar water to make it last longer. Then she spent some time praying. "Father in heaven, are you trying to tell me something or is this just a coincidence? I've been thinking off and on, that it's not really very safe for a single woman to go out alone to minister and try to win others to you. That booklet about two by two ministries states that very clearly. Please guide me, and if you wish for me to get married, please send me just the right man so we can serve you together. I'll be sure to pray about it in the small group next Saturday also so I can have the group agree with me. I thank you so much for that small group! They've been such a blessing in my life. I pray in Jesus precious name, Amen."

*****

Since all the presents had already been received and thank you cards sent, Matt and Fiona were free to leave for their honeymoon right after the reception was over and they had changed into casual clothes. They had decided and planned together to spend Saturday through Monday night at a quiet hotel in a nice mountain town. They would use it as their base to go sightseeing and hiking. Their meals could either be in the hotel restaurant or in various cafes in the town. The hotel would even pack them a picnic lunch to take with them.

After they arrived and checked in at the hotel, they went for a short walk to get the kinks out after the drive. As they walked, they prayed that Jesus would guide everything they did as a husband and wife and would use their lives in his service. Then they ate a light supper in the hotel restaurant since they weren't very hungry after the cake and apple juice at the reception.

Finally they could be together, alone in their spacious hotel room as husband and wife and didn't need to restrain their emotions any longer. They were free to explore and enjoy what God had planned for them as married people. It was the beginning of many more memorable and wonderful times they would have together.

They slept in the next morning, ate a leisurely breakfast, and then hiked to a waterfall that neither of them had seen before. The picnic lunch packed by the hotel tasted extra good out in the fresh air, while they were looking at the waterfall after their long hike. Being out in God's creation was an excellent way to refresh them after the pressures of the past few weeks of planning, furniture shopping, and even the wedding. At least they were all good stresses.

When they got back to town, they stopped at a grocery store and found things they could take with them for breakfast and lunch the next day. Then they returned to the hotel, swam for a while in the nice pool, returned to their room for showers and to get ready for supper in an interesting looking cafe in town.

It turned out to be the most entertaining place they had ever eaten. The cafe was just getting started and was run by a bunch of teenage girls just out of high school, who tried to outdo each other by giving the best and fastest service they could possibly give. That resulted in several near crashes as they brought the meals to the tables. Luckily no food was spilled. It made for an interesting show and it was hard not to laugh. But the girls were trying so hard to do a good job; it would have spoiled it to laugh at them. The food was tasty and their waitress was friendly and liked to talk.

Fiona took this opportunity to ask, "What do you think about the Messiah, Jesus, and all he did for people?"

She answered, "He's my very best friend and my Savior. Please pray for the rest of the girls in here. I'm the only one here who knows him." Matt and Fiona both promised to do that, and she went back to work.

On the way back to the hotel they prayed for the girls in that cafe that all of them would soon know Jesus as their Savior. When they reached their room, they made all the preparations needed for an early wake-up call so they could go to the beaver pond with the hopes of seeing some of what Ted and Julie had described at the small group meeting. They enjoyed the rest of the evening with each other, and then they went to sleep early.

It was still dark when they left to go to the beaver pond. This beaver pond was in the national forest and had free access. Following Ted's directions, they were very quiet as they walked on the path toward the pond. They hid behind the trees he had mentioned, and were pleased to get to watch many of the same activities as they had been told about at the meeting. This time it was a bobcat that came and caused a beaver to slap the water with his big flat tail to warn the others. They all immediately went underwater to safety and swam to their lodges which all have entrances below the water level. The bobcat certainly didn't want to get wet trying to swim after them. Then Matt and Fiona sat on the log that was close to the pond and got to see a doe and her twin fawns come to the pond for a drink just as it was beginning to get light.

They talked about what they had seen as they walked back down the path to eat their breakfast in the pick-up where it felt a little warmer than being out in the early morning breeze. After that they went to the field of wildflowers with a new book they had bought about the mountain wildflowers and their names. It was so much fun to be able to identify them and learn their names. The creator had made such a great variety of size, shape, and color! It was a great privilege to see all they had seen that morning.

Lunch was enjoyed at a viewpoint of some mountain peaks reflected in the still water of a huge, beautiful, blue lake. Fiona had been busy all morning taking pictures of everything except the beavers. (She didn't want to startle them and not get to watch as long.) They would have some pretty picture memories of their honeymoon when they had prints made of the better shots.

Back in town by about 3 PM, they stopped at the interesting cafe again for a late lunch or early supper dessert, hoping it might not be as busy as it was at supper yesterday. They were right. While their dessert was being prepared, they started telling any of the girls who wanted to listen about their fabulous morning watching the beavers and then seeing and learning about wildflowers. Since many of them weren't busy they sat and listened in nearby chairs.

While Matt was talking, Fiona was praying. When he finished, she shared, "I was just praying, and Jesus told me that one of you girls is worried about a date you have planned for this coming Friday. Jesus said for me to tell you not to go."

One of them gasped and admitted loudly, "That's me! I'm very worried. It's a blind date with an older man. And I don't know anything about him."

Fiona responded, "That could potentially be a very dangerous situation, especially if he takes you to a place where there are no other people around. Is there a way you can cancel that date?"

"Yes, I'll do that as soon as it's my break time. Now would you please tell me more about this Jesus who told you to tell me not to go? I would like to know more about him," said the girl.

"Certainly!" answered Fiona. "Jesus is my very best friend and my Savior. He loves you so much that he wants you to stay safe, and to learn about him." She continued and explained everything they needed to know about Jesus to all the girls, including the cooks who had come to listen when they had heard the girl's loud exclamation.

"You mean the Jesus that the little kids sing about in Sunday School? I thought that was just a story," said one of the girls, but nobody laughed because they could tell she was serious, not just mocking.

Fiona responded, "Jesus is much more than just a story. Like I said, he didn't stay dead after they crucified and buried him. He arose from the grave, and was seen by many of the people who had believed in him. He told them to go and tell everybody about him so they could believe in him also. He wants all of you to believe in him so you can become children of God the Father. He will guide you and help you to tell others about Jesus too. Do you have any other questions?"

Several of them did, and she and Matt answered them and explained how they could become children of God. Then Fiona asked, "How many of you would like to do that?" Almost all of them raised their hands and Fiona led them in a prayer much like Pastor Don would have, but they all prayed out loud.

The girl who was going to cancel her blind date said, "I've never felt so much peace. I'm so glad you told me how dangerous that date could be and then told me about Jesus. I can tell *he* is going to be my best friend too!"

Matt and Fiona congratulated all of them and welcomed them into the family of God. They all praised and thanked God for making them his children.

Fiona asked, "Could I also tell you all some things that I learned about dating as I was growing up, and while I was dating?"

"Yes, please do," several of them answered. So Fiona shared with them about how to keep dating safe, and what to look for in a husband if they wanted to get married, and be especially careful to only date men who believe in and love Jesus. As she finished, she showed them her rings and looked at Matt with all her love showing as she shared that they were on their honeymoon.

"While we were dating, I did the things I just told you about. It was well worth the time and effort!" Fiona exclaimed.

Matt added, "Fiona is everything I could ever hope or pray for as a wife, because she has become the woman God meant for her to be."

The girls congratulated them. Matt and Fiona thanked them and then handed out a little booklet to each new believer with their phone number written in it so they could call if they had any more questions.

Afterward they enjoyed their dessert, and since it was so close to suppertime by then, they ordered different meals than last night and enjoyed watching the girls serving them and the other guests who had come in by then. The waitress from the day before came to talk to them and she was beaming with pleasure and joy about the salvation of all her friends.

Fiona asked her, "What is the church you attend like? Will it have a small group for new believers so these girls will have a way to learn how to live their new lives?"

She replied, "Yes. It's a very good church and if I agree to go with them I think they'll attend the small group. I'm so glad you came back here today and shared that warning from Jesus to my friend and then explained all the things you did to the group, even the cooks came and listened and accepted!"

"We're also very glad we came back here today. May God richly bless all of you," said Matt.

Back in their hotel room, Fiona said, "God is so good. Thank you, Jesus, for using me to speak to that girl and then to all of them. Thank you, Holy Spirit, for drawing all of them to Jesus. Please help them to live for you now."

Matt added, "Keep them all safe and help them take Fiona's good advice about dating. Have them go to that good church and small group so they can grow and learn how to serve you. We pray in Jesus name, Amen."

"This had <u>already</u> been the best honeymoon I can imagine. The salvation of all those girls made it over the top magnificent. I'm really glad we got to talk with them!" Fiona exclaimed.

"I am too. We can now go to our new home tomorrow and get our things settled before we have lunch and go back to our jobs with so many praises to tell our co-workers at break time or as we work," agreed Matt.

*****

On a Monday, Larry stated, "I would like to take my wonderful wife out to supper sometime this week. What day would be best for you and where would you like to go?"

She answered, "Thank you, Honey. What a nice idea! Wednesday would be great, because I'm always a little tired after the children's Bible groups are over. I would like to go to Ami's Japanese Restaurant. It's been a long time since we've been there and their food is always so good tasting. Maybe we can see their grown children too, since they have both moved back home."

"Very good choice, so I'll call and make reservations for 6 PM this Wednesday," replied Larry.

When they got there that Wednesday, Tomo and Ami both came to greet them. Later Aneko served them when their orders were ready. Yoshi came toward the end of the meal and asked them some questions from a survey he was doing for the purpose of improving the restaurant.

They enjoyed their time there very much, and made a point to go to Ami's Japanese Restaurant a couple more times before moving away from Pine City.

*****

Matt and Fiona shared with Pastor Don and Anita that next Saturday afternoon about the girls who were saved in the mountain town where they had been on their honeymoon. Matt asked, "What can be done when people visit other places that don't have a good church and small groups to teach new believers how to live their new lives? It was a blessing that the town we visited had those things to take care of all those girls who accepted Jesus on Monday."

After praising and thanking God, Don replied "I'm happy to be able to tell you that in the case of several or many new believers as a result of a miracle, word of knowledge, or a testimony, a 'missionary' pastor/small group facilitator can quickly be sent out from our church to that city or town. A small group can be started that same week and it can eventually become a church. The 'parents', like you two, would just need to call me from the place where 'it' happened or tell me about it when you get home. If you had been gone longer the telephone call would have been quicker. It's important to get those new believers started learning quickly and be able to answer their questions so they don't become discouraged.

Everywhere There's a Sunrise, Let's Tell The Good News!

"If only one or two people believe in a city or town, their names and phone numbers should be obtained. The 'parent' can keep in touch with them and tell them that as soon as possible, a church plant group will be coming to their city or town to start a church and small groups. The 'parent' would need to disciple them until it got there.

"I praise the Lord with you for the salvation of those precious girls. I also understand that our churches have been remiss in not explaining the way this can work to our congregations so that our vacationing or traveling 'missionaries' will know what to do in either case. I'll call and talk with pastor of church #1 and suggest that all of us tell our congregations and then remind them off and on about how to care for new believers resulting from vacations or traveling places. I'm really glad you came to talk with me about what can be done."

Fiona responded, "Thank you, Pastor Don, for explaining all this to us. I agree with your suggestion. Matt and I had the most wonderful honeymoon, and the fact that all those girls were saved made it even more extraordinary!"

That very Sunday, Pastor Don and all the rest of the Sunday pastors were sure to tell their whole congregations what Don had told Matt and Fiona. The Saturday pastors would do that next Saturday.

*****

After Clara asked for God's guidance in the next small group meeting, several of the members agreed with her prayer and added things like: Help her look only for a believer. Bring her someone who has a heart for evangelism like she does. Enable her to be patient as she waits.

Fiona talked to her at refreshment time. "If you would like to read some books about dating and relationships, I could loan you the ones that helped me so much while I was dating Matt."

Clara said, "That would be very useful." So Fiona brought them to the next meeting.

Clara knew this might take a while, and was willing to be patient and learn what God's perfect will would be for her, so she spent much time in prayer. She also made time in her busy schedule to read and take notes on the books Fiona had loaned to her, so she could get them back to Fiona. She found a lot of important things to be looking for in a possible mate.

After reading the books, Clara started noticing the young men in some of her nursing classes. She was also alert to the ones in the evening evangelism classes at the church.

*****

Days in August and September

The next weekend couple's date for Vern and Lora was in the shopping mall where it was cool and in a place that was relatively quiet. They even found seats that were facing each other. As before, each one read the other's written thoughts. This time it was about the issues Lora had suggested. The first one made both of them laugh because they had written identically about how to handle disagreements.

The second one was about being a mother to Mindy who was almost a teenager. Lora would basically have to ask for all the help she could get since she had never been a mother before. They talked of ways she could get that kind of information from books they could buy. He also told her all of the ideas he could think of that he had been doing. Then he mentioned, "Maybe you could also talk to Anita and see what she would suggest."

"For sure! She's been mentoring Mindy for the past three years and might know her just about as well as you do," agreed Lora. "Besides, all your suggestions are very good."

Her next topic was about whether they would desire to have children. Having no more children was a hard topic to talk about, but he knew they had to discuss it. He had had an operation after his wife died, because he didn't ever want to put any other woman at risk of dying or the pain of childbirth. Being able to have it all written down so she could read it, made it much easier. Amazingly enough she was very understanding and even relieved, because she desired to be able to continue her job as nurse at the church school, and her contract made her promise to not get pregnant during the school year. She had written that information plus the fact that they could plan to have children later, if he and Mindy desired to have more in the family.

"Mindy understands how I feel and has accepted it. She told me the other day that the children at Anita's daycare take the place of brothers and sisters, and that what she desires most is a mom at home," explained Vern.

The next topic was where they would live and how to get rid of all sad memorials, but not get rid of good memories. Lora said, "I sold my engagement ring after that talk with my counselor, and gave the money to the church. It was a good way to break with the disappointment of no wedding. But no doubt you need to keep photographs and things that help you and Mindy remember the joys of your family's time together. Just so that it does not result in bitterness returning to plague you."

Vern agreed and they decided they needed to find a different house or apartment and get a fresh start.

When they had completed all the important issues, they both realized that they had agreed on all of them.

Vern leaned forward in his seat and took both of her small hands in his large ones. "I've enjoyed getting to know you, Lora, and we've done so many fun things together the last few months. I would like that to continue for the rest of my life. Lora, I love you. Will you marry me and be my beloved wife and Mindy's mom?" Vern asked her.

"Yes, Vern! I love you and Mindy both, and I would be honored to become your loving wife and a mom to sweet Mindy," she answered with misty eyes and a joy filled smile.

"Now I'm among the happiest of men! Thank you, Lora. We are in the perfect place for what I would like to do next," Vern said, pulling her to her feet. He took her hand and led her into the nearby jewelry store. "Now, please find an engagement ring you really like and wedding bands to match. I came prepared to buy them today if you would only answer, 'Yes.' And I'm so glad you did!"

"And I'm so glad you asked. I'm overflowing with happiness," she replied. Looking at her watch she asked, "Do we have enough time?"

"Yes, because I alerted Anita to my plans and she'll keep Mindy busy. Then if you have time, I could take you and Mindy out to lunch so she can hear the news and celebrate with us. She'll be delighted," he answered.

"I'm glad to hear that she'll be delighted," Lora said. "I forgot to have us discuss that topic, but I understand now that we didn't need to. What a great idea to go to lunch and share our news with Mindy! This is going to be so fun!"

She chose a simple but elegant engagement ring with a small single diamond in a setting of laurel leaves. The matching wedding bands also had laurel leaves engraved around them.

She commented, "My full name is Laurel. When you wear your wedding ring, it can remind you of me."

"Yes it will. Every time I look at my ring I'll ask God to bless my sweet Laurel," he responded.

They had a joyful time at lunch with Mindy, and she was totally delighted to hear their news! When they finished lunch, they went back and informed Don and Anita. They were thrilled also.

Mindy said to Anita, "I'll still get to come here every afternoon after school because Lora will continue to be the nurse at the school. They said that it's okay for me to continue to come on Saturday mornings to do daycare for Timmy and Mary and the twins. I'm so thankful to God for the way he worked all this out in his perfect will."

"Me too!" Anita exclaimed. "Just like it says in James 1:17a, *Every good and perfect gift comes from God.*"

*****

The last few Saturday afternoons, Jeff had been spending some time with a church friend who was single and wanted to get married. He had said he wanted counsel from Jeff, but what he really wanted was for Jeff to agree with what he wanted to do. After a couple weeks, he confided that he had fallen in love with his secretary.

He said, "The problem is that she's married, and isn't a Christian. I want her to get a divorce and marry me instead. Later I can convince her to become a Christian."

Jeff knew he would have to disagree and confront this man about his sin, but do it meekly and like it says in Galatians 6:1, *Brothers, if a man is caught in a sin, you who are spiritual, restore that one in the spirit of meekness. Consider yourself so that you also will not be tempted.*

"I think there's another problem in this situation. Let's look at these verses in the Bible," suggested Jeff.

He had the man read out loud Matthew 5:27,28,32. *You have heard that was commanded, you shall not commit adultery. But Jesus said that whoever looks at a woman with lust has already committed adultery with her in his heart. Whoever divorces his wife except for the cause of fornication, causes her to commit adultery, and whoever shall marry her that is divorced commits adultery.*

Jeff asked, "What do you think that means for you in this situation?"

"I think it means that I have already sinned in this situation. I'm just glad the woman does not know anything about what I have been thinking or feeling," he confessed, visibly shaken.

Jeff said, "I agree with you about that. What can you do about this problem?"

"First, I thank you for confronting me about it and next, I will pray. Father in heaven, please forgive me for this horrendous sin of adultery in my heart. Cleanse my heart and mind of all these thoughts and keep me focused on only obeying and doing your will from now on and forever. Thank you for forgiving me. I pray in Jesus name, Amen."

Jeff continued the prayer, "Thank you, Lord, for your Word and the Holy Spirit to show people where they're wrong, and for your promise of forgiveness when they repent. Please show my friend what steps to take so the thoughts and feelings will not have a chance of coming back."

"I think my first step on Monday will be to ask for a transfer to another office building so I won't be near that woman. In the future I'll consider only single, Christian women for marriage."

"Those are both good steps. I also suggest that you keep your mind focused on Jesus and pray for his will to be done in this and every area of your life. Remember that the best place to look for a single, Christian woman is in your small group or church," finished Jeff.

The man nodded, shook hands and said he would call off and on to keep himself accountable.

*****

Mindy, Vern and Lora went on some more threesome activities and enjoyed them even more since the engagement. One Saturday afternoon they drove to a nearby city and went to a butterfly pavilion. They were handed a pamphlet with photographs of the butterflies. Mindy was challenged to see and check off as many as she could on the checklist that was on the last page. It was fun, and she appreciated the help she got from Lora and her dad. The plants and flowers were just as beautiful and interesting as the butterflies. Vern bought them a poster with photographs of the butterflies and flowers and they were all labeled. It also showed and described in detail the life cycle of a butterfly.

Another weekend they hiked to the waterfall that Matt and Fiona had seen on one of their first dates after she returned to Pine City. Since it was later in the summer, the waterfall wasn't roaring or splashing them. It was just looking spectacular as many waterfalls do.

Vern commented, "If it's all right with both of you ladies, I would like us to continue these threesome activities after the wedding, at least two times a month if we can, and couples activities the other two times a month. I wasted too much time before and I would like to make up for it. Plus, we can go out to dinner as a family on Thursdays. I desire lots of laughter and happiness for all three of us."

"That sounds very good to me," Lora agreed. "Our motto can be 'The family that prays and plays together, stays together.' I sure have been enjoying our times together."

Mindy nodded vigorously. "It's a super idea, Dad. You're the best!"

"And you're the best too!" exclaimed her dad.

Lora added, "I agree. Both of you *are* the best, and we'll make the best family I can imagine." At school, Beth was delighted to hear about this and the other things Lora had told her.

*****

Three weeks after their honeymoon, Matt and Fiona hosted the small group at their new home. They had announced at the last meeting that everyone who wanted a tour of the house should come 20 minutes early. All of them came and there were expressions of delight about many of the ideas they had incorporated into their home. They especially liked the idea of using the empty bedrooms for the missionaries until they were filled with children.

Small group time was wonderful as usual and for refreshments, as requested by many at the last meeting, they had another Irish wedding fruitcake and apple juice, just like they'd had at the reception.

*****

After the church service one Sunday, a man hurried up to Larry and Jane before they could leave for home. He introduced his wife and children to them. He said, "I wanted you to meet the rest of my family and rejoice with me that we're all back together. As of last Sunday they are all new believers and we're all attending the small group so they can be baptized at the next special baptismal service."

Larry responded, "We're very pleased to meet all of you and delighted to hear that you are all now believers!"

"We're committed to live for Jesus. I thank you both again for caring enough to talk to a broken, worthless sinner and tell him the Good News of how to get real life with Jesus help. It's been worth all the effort," he said sincerely.

Jane replied, "You're very welcome. We're grateful that we could let Jesus work through us. Would you and your family like to come and eat supper at our home next Sunday evening?"

His wife answered, "Oh, yes. We would enjoy that a lot. What can I bring?"

"A tossed salad would go well with the rest of the meal I'm planning. I have several different kinds of salad dressing, so just bring the salad, and be at our home about 6 PM," said Julie as she handed her the address.

*****

Vern and Lora set a date for their wedding with Mindy's help. They chose the Sunday before Labor Day because Lora and Mindy would both have that week off from school. Vern made arrangements to also take that week as a vacation from his job at Happy Smiles for Kids.

During their couples dates on Saturday mornings they started looking at houses and apartments, with the stipulation that Mindy would be able to attend the same school. They also wanted to stay in the wedge for Church #4, since it was very important to Vern and Mindy to continue with Pastor Don and Anita. They found a very nice small house in a quiet neighborhood that fit all their desires. They would be able to pay it off as soon as the other house sold.

The three of them had many discussions about what kind of wedding to have. Vern asked Pastor Don and his family to come over for supper one evening so they could talk about some of the ideas and pick the best ones.

The following is how it turned out.

Their small group's present was to help on the Saturday before the wedding to clean the new house. Then they would move all furniture and belongings to the new residence and get everything put in place.

Since the three had moved out of their other homes during the day before the wedding, the bride stayed with Beth that night, the groom with a friend in the small group, and Mindy stayed with Don and Anita in their guest room.

Pastor Don added the song, "O Perfect Love" and shortened the teaching time just enough so there would be time for their ceremony at the end of the service. He modified the teaching time to include Ephesians 5:21,22,25. *Submit yourselves to one another in the fear of God. Wives, submit yourselves to your husbands as unto the Lord. Husbands, love your wives even as Christ loved the church and gave himself for it.*

Mindy stood up on the other side of her dad, as they became a family. Lora and Mindy had chosen similar style dresses each in their favorite pastel colors. Lora's was lavender, and Mindy's was pink, and they had corsages in matching colors. Vern had a new brown suit. He said later that he looked like a tree trunk between two pretty flowers!

The week before, Don had announced and invited the congregation to, "come prepared to celebrate the wedding of Mr. Vernon Jones and Miss Laurel Nelson, long time members of Grace 'n' Faith Church #4, as they and Mindy become a family. Your presence is requested, but no presents, please. There won't be a reception."

Their honeymoon was in a mountain town not too far from where Matt and Fiona had stayed. Vern and Lora enjoyed their time together as they became very comfortable being married. Mindy stayed with Don and Anita while they were gone. They came back on Thursday to finish setting up their home before Mindy came home on Friday morning. That gave them their first night in the 'new' house by themselves. There was all new furniture in their bedroom, and they had made that room really their own. Vern and Mindy had kept all the important items that would help them remember the way the other family was, but not sorrow and become bitter about it.

When they brought Mindy home on Friday, they all had a three-day weekend of fun living in their 'new' house before returning to their jobs and school.

*****

Everywhere There's a Sunrise, Let's Tell The Good News!

One day at lunch before they both went to work, Matt and Fiona talked about several different topics. Matt started with, "I'm so delighted to be married to you my dear Fiona. It's even better than I ever dreamed it could be. While we were revising the house plans and shopping for furniture we learned how to work together, share our likes and dislikes, be honest about what we desired and now we have a wonderful home that we enjoy because we made it happen together. Unity is a real blessing."

"Thank you. I'm delighted to have you as my husband and I agree with what you said. We even had fun while we were doing all that work. It was good for us, and I know we'll be able to continue to work together on whatever we need to do," Fiona responded.

"Yes, and I've enjoyed these last couple months of having the house all to ourselves. I don't want to seem selfish, but I would like to continue that for a few more months," suggested Matt.

"That's a good idea. I've enjoyed it also and wish for it to continue. The missionaries are all taken care of for now anyway. In January a whole new class will be starting and we could volunteer then to have two couples stay here. They would probably both be here for two years since it takes that long it takes to be able to graduate," said Fiona.

Matt agreed, "I like that plan. We'll have an opportunity to really get to know them if they stay here for two years. Now, here is another topic. Where would you like to go for our nature outing this month? Last month we hiked up to that waterfall to compare it with the springtime flow,"

She replied, "It sure was different with only a small amount of water in the stream, but it was delightful anyway. I liked it both ways and would like to put it on a list to do again next year. This month I would like to drive up to the mountains and see the colorful fall leaves and maybe hike to a different lake or waterfall so we can be outside while it's still warm. We can smell the autumn and hear the leaves crunch under our feet."

"I can almost smell and hear it right now the way you describe it. Yes, let's do that soon before the leaves are all gone. Walt was asking when we're going to have a baby. He says he's looking forward to spoiling it for us. I told him we had agreed to let God decide when that will happen, and I know we'll both be thrilled when it does," finished Matt. Fiona nodded enthusiastically and ended up on his lap for hugs and kisses before they finished their lunch.

Linda L. Linn

*****

Mindy was so pleased and content to be able to continue going after school to help Anita and the daycare children and then go home to <u>both</u> a dad and a mom each evening. Vern was still a wonderful dad, and Lora made an excellent mom. The house did <u>not</u> seem empty any more. Now it was filled with joy and laughter as they learned how to live as a family. Sure, they made some mistakes but the apologies and forgiveness were quick. As the weeks passed they became more and more bonded in family unity and in unity with God.

They looked forward to couples or threesome activities each week, along with going out to dinner together as a family on Thursday evenings. For a while they took turns thinking up some activity they had not done yet, and when they all ran out of ideas they started repeating favorite ones.

*****

Chapter 27

Philippians 1:6, *Being confident of this very thing, that he who began a good work in you will perform it until the day of Jesus Christ.*

Plans for sending the Good News with a church-planting ministry to the city in a southern area by the first week in October were in progress. It was a smaller city and would be an experiment with the house church plan at first until it grew too big for meeting in a house. The small groups would meet in homes as they did in Pine City. For united weekend services they could meet in a large home. When the congregation got too big for a home, they could meet in a park if the weather would permit. For baptismal services they could use private home pools or even public swimming pools.

The pastor and small group leaders would use the same songs and teaching notes as those used in Grace 'n' Faith Church in Pine City. The small groups would function in the same manner as in the church that sent them and continue to do two by two ministries. Other outreaches would be done, such as the Wednesday children's groups, workers who stock shelves being alert to catch and redirect shoplifters and gang members, and have Safe Care

Homes for those children who needed them. The pastor and his congregation would be alert to other needs in the community and try to provide for those needs.

When there were enough members, they could rent a sanctuary from another church for a unified Sunday or Saturday service, whichever day and time would be available. When it looked like the congregation was getting too large for that sanctuary, it would be time to consider other options like, renting a larger sanctuary, dividing into two groups and having two services, or sending a church plant to another city. If the congregation would get close to 275 members, they could call Grace 'n' Faith church for another pastor and divide into two similar churches and keep growing.

All the people would need to cooperate and work together to make this church plant operate the way it was intended to work. (See Philippians 2:1-5 and John 17:20,21.) New believers would need to be taught in small groups, so members would need to volunteer and be trained to be facilitators of new believer small groups. Every person going with the church plant group would need to agree with the plans and be willing to work very hard. It would <u>not</u> be just moving to a different city and getting new jobs. It would be doing everything possible to make the plan a success and see many people brought into the family of God. In essence, it would be a missionary project.

For families with children in the group, women who didn't work outside the home could do daycare using the Grace 'n' Faith preschool curriculum. As the membership of the church grew, and if there were enough children later for Kindergarten through third grades, other women could do daycare and use the Grace 'n' Faith School curriculum for each of those grades. By doing this, no school building needed to be built.

During the planning stages of the church plant, about thirty couples attended a meeting to hear the how, when, where, and why of the project. They all heard the above plans and were able to discuss and ask questions. People could leave the meeting at any time if they felt something would not work for them. By the end of that meeting, they were down to fifteen couples, who set up appointments to interview and be interviewed by the pastor. He would choose the nine couples or families that would accompany him.

Larry and Jane Kelsey were chosen to go with the pastor couple who have been trained in the Grace 'n' Faith evangelism school, along with eight other couples or families, making twenty adults plus children. While they were getting ready to leave they would stay in their regular and new small groups. They could share requests and praises in their first group but without using the names of the people.

Before they moved, Jane and any other women who had Wednesday children's groups found women in Pine City who would take over their groups and met with them and their groups for a couple weeks to help the children get used to the new leaders.

The people who owned houses put them on the market with the stipulation that they could remain in them until they moved at the end of September. Many of the people took trips to the city to find lodging and jobs before moving. Larry and Jane would stay with their daughter until they found a place.

After the move, Larry and Jane sent back reports about their progress, and Jane and Julie talked on the phone and e-mailed each other. Jane started new Bible Study and Story groups on Wednesdays and so did some of the other women.

Ted missed Larry but made other friends in the Music group, which gained a couple new members, because Larry and another singer went with the church plant group.

*****

One Sunday morning Roy and Sherry had Cory and his parents over to their house to have playtime for the three children out in the yard, and so the grownups could visit. They would eat lunch together before going to the church service.

While they were visiting, Sherry commented, "I don't remember if we told you about the Grace 'n' Faith Church School and our plans for the twins and how good the school is."

Cory's mother said, "No you didn't tell us. Please tell us now." Cory, Joy and Hope came over just then to sit and rest and listen. The twins were so excited about school starting in a few months that they could hardly keep quiet.

Sherry and Roy took turns telling them as much as they could remember from the same booklet that Julie had read about the school. "You could pick up one of those booklets from the church office and it will tell you the details we missed," finished Roy.

They did that and quickly registered Cory for third grade. (He and one of his friends would be in Julie Blake's class beginning in January.)

Everywhere There's a Sunrise, Let's Tell The Good News!

When Cory told his friends and the rest of his class, plus his class from the year before about the church school, many of them talked to their parents who were now believers and they found out more information. Part of those children would be third graders in the new school building. Part of them would attend in the old building since many people and children would be moving to the new one, so there would be room for them. Others would stay in the public school and be evangelists there, because two new small groups had been started for them to attend on early release Wednesdays. They were being taught how to tell the Good News the same way the ones in the school were being taught.

Cory's second grade teacher was also now a believer. When Cory told her about the church school and that he would be attending there next year, she asked for one of those booklets at church and applied for a job in second grade. She was hired to teach second grade in the old building to replace one who would be going to the new building.

*****

Days in October and November and December

Patrick, Glenda and Riley all enjoyed the many times they got to eat lunch or supper, play games, or visit in Matt and Fiona's home on a weekend. Plus, there were just as many times they all enjoyed eating and playing games or visiting at the O'Connor residence.

At one of those times in late October, Matt and Fiona had an announcement to make. In about seven months, Matt and Fiona would become parents, Patrick and Glenda would become grandparents, and Riley would be an uncle. They were all so excited and pleased that they couldn't finish eating!

The same thing <u>would</u> have happened when they had Walt and Betty over for a Sunday supper and told them the news, <u>if</u> they had not waited until after dessert.

*****

It was October and therefore time for the third graders to learn how to be fourth graders in the public schools. Julie used the newly revised curriculum and lesson plans at the specified time of the day and got them ready to ask questions of the fourth graders who would come on Wednesday afternoons to answer them. She was able to build excitement instead of stress and worry. The children were looking forward to being Jesus representatives in the public school. This is what they've been training for all these years in the church school.

Pam came into Julie's classroom one evening on the way home and said, "Beth told me you worked on revising the curriculum and I really like the changes you made, especially about building excitement. Other years the children seemed almost scared at times. It's a big responsibility for them to take on at such a young age, but they will be well prepared for it. It really helps to have the fourth graders role play things that happened to them."

"Thank you for sharing that with me. I'm glad to know that the curriculum really is better than it was," responded Julie.

*****

Sherry was talking to Anita while she was there sewing. "I'm so glad the church has an alternative to Halloween for the children, called 'Guess my Bible Character Night.' I like the name and the idea.

"Me too," agreed Anita. "It is good to be able to explain to the children that it's really just the evening before November first which is All Saints Day. The devil has totally eclipsed that holiday with his counterfeit one, and it's completely evil."

"That's for sure! Roy and I avoid taking Joy and Hope into the stores at this time of year because they have so many horrid, scary costumes and decorations out. Anyway, the girls are looking forward to dressing up as Mary and Martha and having the children guess who they are and the Bible story too," replied Sherry.

Anita responded, "Timmy is going as David with a sling, but without stones. Mary will dress like Jesus mother, Mary, and carry a baby doll for baby Jesus. Well, I'll see you later. I hear one of the children calling to me."

She went quickly to the children and one of them asked her, "What could I dress up to be, for 'Guess my Bible Character Night'?" Anita sat with them on the floor and together they brainstormed ideas for the child.

The celebration was held in the church's multipurpose sanctuary with most the chairs stacked out of the way. Even if the night fell on a weekend, the celebration would be held instead of the 6 PM and 8 PM services. The people who would have attended those services chose another church's service time so they would not miss out on a church service. If it was during the week, whatever other activity usually took place in that room was canceled for that evening.

Since it was for all 12 churches, it was usually very crowded. If the character could not be guessed in half a minute, the older children enjoyed acting out their character. Sometimes it was such an obscure one that the child would have to tell the audience who it was. After two hours of fun the children went home carrying a little bag of fruit instead of candy.

*****

Ruth, Esther, Maria, Julie and Pam decided to join a basketball team for women one Friday a month in the multipurpose sanctuary of the church. The teens had mixed teams and used the area two Fridays a month. That left one Friday a month for the men to play basketball. Ted joined a team, and was able to make a couple friends in this way. If the month had a fifth Friday, it was open to anybody who wanted to play basketball. The mixed teams on those days were varied in age and ability. Some Fridays other people would come and watch the others having fun.

There was a square dance once a month on Tuesday. Ted and Julie enjoyed learning how to square dance, and met a lot of other couples. They made many good friends that way, besides getting good exercise. They really liked dancing with Jeff and Karen in their square, and often sat beside them to visit between dances. Sometimes they would sit out a dance just to enjoy watching the other couples so they could see the beautiful square dance dresses worn by the ladies who looked like butterflies gliding over the floor.

*****

Now that they were married, Vern and Lora decided to use some of their Saturday morning couple's time for two by two ministry. They did various things, depending on the weather. The wonderful warm autumn mornings were great for walking hand in hand around their new neighborhood praying for the people in the other homes and often stopping to talk or lend a hand with yard work. Other weekend afternoons, they and Mindy would go as a threesome to minister. They had many opportunities to plant

Gospel seeds as they showed Jesus love by helping out. As the weather cooled too much for those activities, they spent time in the shopping mall or stores, walking together with or without a shopping basket or a cart as they prayed for guidance and opportunities minister to people.

One time they noticed a couple from their neighborhood sitting on a bench in the shopping mall. The couple looked very depressed, so after praying for a while Vern and Lora went over to the bench.

"We met you about a month ago while we were walking around in our neighborhood. As you probably remember, I'm Vern and this is my wife, Lora. We noticed that you both look sad, and we wondered if there is anything we could do to help you," said Vern as he and Lora sat down to face them on the opposite bench.

"Thank you for caring enough to offer," answered the man. "We're at our wits end and as you can see, we are very discouraged. Our only son has gotten in with the wrong crowd and has started drinking and using drugs. He was caught shoplifting in a liquor store today and is now in jail."

"We had no clue! He's been sneaking around for months now, and has kept his activities so well hidden that we had no idea what he was doing until today when we got a phone call from the jail," added his mother.

"This is so sad. We're sorry you have to go through all this hurt and upset," comforted Lora. "Do you have any idea how long he will be in jail?"

"It's only overnight this time and he has a big fine to pay. If it happens again he will end up in Juvenile Hall, which is like a prison for young people," she answered.

"If you would be interested, I know of a small group of young people in our church who have gone through similar things, and who would welcome a chance to help your son if he would be willing to spend time with them. Some of their parents meet at the same time on the same evening and would be happy to have you join them," suggested Vern.

"The young people would tell your son their stories and how Jesus has delivered them from their addictions, and their parents would gladly share with you how Jesus has helped them through the hard times," explained Lora.

"I think they're having a meeting tomorrow evening. If you would like to go with us to church tomorrow, we can introduce you to some of them, and you can find out when and where the meeting will be," said Vern.

"I like that idea. It is sure a lot better than anything else we can think of doing," replied the man.

"Okay, then, we'll pick up both of you and your son at 1:30 PM tomorrow and you can all ride with us to church," stated Lora, and it was settled. The people looked relieved and hopeful.

After several weeks of meetings for them and their son, Jesus delivered him from his addictions, and all three of them accepted Jesus as their Savior. They remained with the groups that had helped them and learned how to help others who might need it.

*****

"Thanksgiving is one of my favorite holidays," Anita commented. "The teaching times about being grateful have been so good this month also. I'm glad we sang songs related to being thankful for two weeks before, and the week after Thanksgiving. My favorites are: 'Now Thank We All Our God,' 'For the Beauty of the Earth,' 'We Thank You Lord,' 'With Grateful Hearts We Say Thank You,' and 'Thanks to God.'"

"I agree, but how can you remember all of those titles?" Don asked her.

"I wrote them down in my notebook and then sang them to the daycare children. Now they like them all too," she answered with a smile.

"You <u>are</u> a wonder! I'm blessed with a very talented, intelligent wife," exclaimed Don.

"Thank you, Honey. You're talented and wonderful too. Just think of all the scripture verses you've memorized. Say Ephesians 5:20 for me," requested, Anita.

"Okay. Ephesians 5:20, *Give thanks always for all things to God the Father in the name of our Lord Jesus Christ,* Ephesians 5:20, " he said and she applauded him.

Just then Timmy and Mary came in the room so Anita asked, "Would you like to hear us sing one of those Thanksgiving songs?"

"Of course. Please do," he replied. They sang "With Grateful Hearts," and they sounded very good.

When they had finished, Timmy said, "Christmas is the next holiday. We'll be hearing lots of songs on the radio about it now that Thanksgiving is over."

"Yes but they have so many about Santa Clause that it must be confusing for kids who haven't been taught about what make-believe is. Too many children in our city don't know the real reason for the season," responded Don.

Mary added, "Jesus is the reason for Christmas. Let's sing some Christmas songs now."

So all four of them sang together: "Joy to the World," "Thou Didst Leave Thy Throne," The Birthday of a King," "Hark the Herald Angels Sing," and "Emmanuel."

*****

One day in early December, during sharing time at school, Kippy asked the children, "Which stories did you like when Mrs. Blake read those long chapter books to you during penmanship time and why?"

One boy answered, "I really enjoyed hearing 'The Good Master' because the boy and his cousin did so many interesting, fun, and dangerous things. He said his cousin was almost as good as a boy. I'm glad she learned how to behave and became a very helpful person in their family."

Another boy said, "I liked 'Caddie Woodlawn' for that same reason."

A girl added, "It was fun listening to all the adventures Flat Tail the beaver had. I got to tell my family about the things we had learned about beavers when we went to see the beaver pond up in the mountains."

"I liked all the stories at both story times because Mrs. Blake reads them with such good expression and makes them so interesting, and I'm glad we get to have two story times each day," shared the girl who had suggested the extra story time.

Another boy said, "The story about Inky, the seeing eye dog, was sad in places and happy in places. We heard it when we were learning about our eyes."

"I liked the story about Helen Keller. It was a true story and we also heard it when we were studying eyes," said a girl.

"I liked all the stories about famous Americans because they're important in United States history. I especially liked the one about Abraham Lincoln," added a boy.

Another boy almost gave a book report. "There was another story about a boy who wanted to go to sea, but was apprenticed instead. I liked 'Carry on Mr. Bowditch' because it was a true story and the boy grew up to become a navigator on a ship and he corrected all the navigation charts. Besides that, he learned many different languages by using New Testaments in English and one in the other language. The reason he did that was to help the captain of the ship converse with people in those countries. He overcame all his problems and became a great man."

A girl added, "I really liked the story about Misty of Chincoteague because I like stories about horses a lot. That story was especially exciting in places, and the brother and sister got along and worked well together."

The next student said, "I'll tell about two stories I liked during regular story time because we got to see the pictures in the books and the stuffed animals Mrs. Blake had made to go with the story. 'Winnie the Pooh' and 'The House at Pooh Corner" were both make-believe. But they were extra fun because all the animals had such different character traits and Mrs. Blake read what each one said in a voice that went very well with that animal and its behavior."

Then Kippy exclaimed, "Wow! You have very good memories. Thank you for sharing that with me."

And the children answered, "You're welcome."

*****

Matt continued to work second shift even after the evening light became shorter, because they were inside the church and school shells by then with lights and later on heat to help them. The church and school were finished by the first week in December. Consequently they could be furnished and arranged, and were able to start services and school classes by the first week in January.

Before that, during the summer, ten more pastors who had been in the school of evangelism for almost two years had been trained to take over congregations of about equal numbers leaving about that same number in each of the other 12 churches. They decided to name them Grace 'n' Faith Church with numbers 1a through 12a. They would have overlapping wedges with the corresponding church number. Volunteers from each corresponding wedge moved to the new church with the new pastor.

Sixteen new teachers with at least two years experience were hired by the first week in December, and they each spent one day observing in the classroom like Julie did before she started teaching. Before that they were given the same memos and new teacher information as Julie had been given, so they could read it beforehand. If they wanted to, they could come at noon with their lunch and ask questions of a teacher in their grade level.

Two new teachers per grade level would teach at the old school in order that two experienced ones could go to the new one to help or answer questions for the other new teachers. At the old school, the experienced teachers who had stayed would do the same for the new ones. With all that good help and training, it wasn't long before all the new teachers were proficient in the church school's method of teaching. Julie and Pam both stayed at the old school. Pam moved over one room and a new teacher took that room so she could be closer to Julie when she needed help.

*****

Ted continued to eat lunch with various co-workers. Many of them were becoming friends so he felt free to share with them about what Jesus had done for him. One of them asked him, "Why is this so important?"

Ted answered, "Because if he had not done all of these things, I would not be able to know that my sins are forgiven and that I'll spend eternity in heaven. Besides, I would not be able to ask Jesus for guidance or help and know he will give it. I have a peace in my life that I did <u>not</u> have before I accepted Jesus as my Savior." At this point Ted told his story of salvation, explained the Gospel, and then asked, "Would you like to ask Jesus to be your Savior?"

His co-worker said, "Yes." So Ted led him in the prayer. Ted's boss had been standing where he could hear and he also joined in the prayer and then came over to tell Ted.

"I'm so thrilled and thankful that both of you now know Jesus as your Savior. I have a little booklet, which tells you more information about what you just did. I invite both of you and your families to come to church with my wife and me this coming Sunday. If you'll fill out the little card and bring it with you, I'll introduce you to my pastor at the end of the service and you can give the little card to him. Then he can answer your questions and get you into a new believers small group."

He handed them the booklets and they all went back to work with smiles on their faces and peace and joy in their hearts. They did come to church and brought their <u>now</u> believing families with them on Sunday. Ted was so pleased! So was Julie. Now Ted had a Christian boss too.

*****

"Would you like to learn how to cook, Mindy?" Vern asked her one evening during supper.
"I'd like that. You're a good cook, so you could teach me," she answered.
"Lora is also a good cook and would like to be in on the fun. She suggested we alternate being your teachers. This way you'll get variety and different recipes."
"This is a great idea, especially now that we are a family," responded Mindy.
"During vacations from school I could also teach you how to sew if you would like to learn," Lora suggested.
"I would like that also. I saw the cute dress and nice shirt that Sherry Foster made for Mary and Timmy. She makes her own clothes and clothes for the twins too, plus shirts for Roy. She did even more before she went back to work so the twins could go to the church school," finished Mindy, looking a little embarrassed for talking so much.
"Don't worry, Mindy. We love to hear you talk. This is part of what families are for," Vern encouraged her.
Lora nodded and said, "Absolutely! Parents like to hear what their children are thinking."
Mindy remembered that Anita had told her something like that at one time also. "Thank you Dad and Mom. You're both the best!" Mindy exclaimed.
"And you're the best too!" Vern and Lora said in unison.

*****

Ernest, Connie, Ben and Amelia were doing fine at the new church time. Their new pastor was a good speaker and was a very caring person. He had taken time to visit with each person or family who had volunteered to go his extra service. They were making new friends, and used their small group times to pray for the needs of the new church.
Don and Anita heard good news about both new evening service times at the pastor's small group meetings on Mondays. The people had settled in and adapted very well. When it came time for them to move to the new building there would be a few

more people to join those two churches, but most of the people would be moving to one of the other ten new churches. All 24 churches would be much smaller in numbers so there would be much opportunity for growth, which is exactly what the plan was.

*****

Fiona's work hours at The Garden Shop changed to 8:30 - 5:00, the first week of November when the person hired for the daytime shift left. And since the store hours changed for the winter months, Amelia's work hours also changed to 3-5. She came to work right from school. Her family got to go home for suppers together after closing the store at five o'clock.

It was a little awkward for Matt and Fiona, married only about four months, to adjust to two different work schedules, but by the first week of December the church and school buildings had been completed, and Walt put Matt in charge of his crew doing a remodel project from 8 to 5, while Walt and his crew did another one in a different building also from 8 to 5. They were all back to regular hours.

When Jeff's hours changed accordingly, Karen was also able to get her hours changed. When the new groups formed in January, the couples all ended up in different evening time small groups. In that way they could meet new people and make new friends. The other people with late hours would join forces with people in the other churches to have Saturday or Sunday morning small groups in the New Year. As a result everybody would be provided for with a small group.

*****

The third week in December on Wednesday, there would be a special service in the sanctuary for the second year evangelism class to graduate and be commissioned and sent out by all the pastors to do their ministries in their own countries or in cities or towns in the USA. It was time to send the trained missionaries to tell the Good News so they could win new believers, start small groups, and develop churches. This time the class included ten pastors for the new churches being started in Pine City's newest church building.

Clara used the announcement time in her small group and said, "I would like to invite this whole small group to attend the special service for the graduation and commissioning of the pastors and missionaries in the evangelism class in the sanctuary on Wednesday evening at 7 PM if you can get off work. I must tell you that I won't be graduating until next December."

Ted and Julie, Jeff and Karen, and Matt and Fiona were happy they could attend. They asked Clara if they could sit with her and she said, "I would be honored."

Many people attended the special graduation service from all fourteen of the current Grace 'n' Faith Churches. By the first week in January there would be twenty-four. Many people were amazed by that fact.

Special music was presented by two of the graduating couples. One wife had written a poem, and her husband had written music for it. They sang it with another couple as an acapella quartet.

(The lyrics are included here, and are actually by Linda L. Linn, so you won't find them in a songbook.)

Everywhere There's a Sunrise

Verse one

Everywhere there's a sunrise,
   Let's tell the Good News!
Work together and be wise.
   Show people what to choose.
So many people need to hear,
   Before it is too late,
How they can have Jesus near,
   And that Heaven is so great.

Chorus

They might be far away,
   Or right next door to you.
Since sunrise still starts each day,
   Please tell them the Good News!

Verse two (see 1 Peter 3:15)

Always be prepared to give
   An answer to all who ask,
The reason you have incentive,

And in such hope can bask.
With humility and meekness,
　Tell them to confess their sin,
Which can cause them great distress,
　Then ask the Savior in.

Chorus

They might be far away,
　Or right next door to you.
Since sunrise still starts each day,
　Please tell them the Good News!

　　After the song, each graduate was given a few minutes to tell the audience about where they would be going and what they would be doing there. The future pastors of the new Grace 'n' Faith Churches used the time to assure the listeners that they would do their best to be as good as the present pastors. They asked for everyone to pray for them.
　　The pastor of church #1 officiated at the service. At the end of it all fourteen pastors placed their hands on at least one of the graduates and their wives if they were married. They prayed as in Acts 13:3 for God to bless each one being commissioned and sent out to do their work for Jesus.

　　　　　　　　　　　*****

　　One day at work, Karen asked her co-worker, "How's it going?"
　　She answered, "It is much the same. It is so sad to think that he might never accept Jesus."
　　"Yes that is very sad," Karen agreed.
　　"I miss the unity we had when we were first married and he had said he was a believer. I really miss the man I thought I had married." she added.
　　Karen responded, "That must be very hard. Jesus, you have heard all we've said and you want his salvation even more than we do. Please help him to do your will, which is to believe in you, like it says in John 6:40. *This is the will of the Father who sent me, that every one who sees the Son and believes on him, may have everlasting life, and I will raise him up at the last day.*"
　　"Yes, Jesus, I agree with that prayer and ask you to help me to continue to be patient and love him with your love. Holy Spirit,

please draw him to Jesus. Use the Good News that he's heard so often to convince him," added her co-worker.

Karen kept praying for her co-worker with the unbelieving husband and kept encouraging her. They both realized that the choice was entirely up to him. God would not force him to believe. If he never did, he would bear the eternal consequences himself. But as long as there was any hope, they would continue to pray, and Karen would continue to help her friend bear the burden as it says in Galatians 6:2. *Bear one another's burdens, and so fulfill the law of Christ.*

*****

Julie said good-bye to her third grade class on the Friday before Christmas vacation. She tried to make it as happy a time as possible so they would have good memories. During sharing time she invited all them to come back and see her whenever they might have a chance after five o'clock and before five twenty of course. She included Kippy by having him say, "Oh, please do come often because I've enjoyed all of you so much."

Then she said, "Remember when you are fourth graders starting the first week in January, some of you will get to come and help out on Wednesdays here in this room, so we'll both get to see you then." Kippy nodded his head and jumped up and down for joy. As they went out the door, all who wanted to, got hugs from Julie (Mrs. Blake).

During her 2 weeks off, Julie studied records and pictures for her new class coming to her classroom the first week in January. But she also made sure to enjoy her time off and get as much sewing and housework done as possible.

She and Ted had some quiet evenings at home those weeks, but many nights they had some friends over for supper or went to supper at someone's house to celebrate the reason for the season.

*****

The last Saturday morning of December was the last meeting of the late shift small group, since all groups ended the last day of December and new ones would begin the first week of January. Don and Anita had been invited and were glad to come. The group met at Jeff and Karen's house and spent a longer time with praises this week than usual. They were all feeling nostalgic and they praised and thanked God for everything they could remember that had happened since their group started last April. It included many more miracles and salvations that had resulted from two by two ministries in the months since June. It was a lot! Tomo and Ami praised God that both his and her parents and their other siblings had all accepted Jesus during the big family reunion they had had at Christmas time.

Their group had stayed smaller since Larry and Jane had moved away the last week in September and everyone still missed them. But the rest of the group had all grown even closer and had developed lasting friendships. During announcement time, Julie showed her completed embroidery of the names of God and Jesus, done in calligraphy. She explained, "I embroidered it after Jane had written the words in calligraphy on the material, so it was a joint project and it's a nice reminder of the times we had spent together. I sent a picture by e-mail to Jane so she could see it also." Many people exclaimed how beautiful it was and Jeff and Karen thanked her for bringing it to show them.

Next they sang songs such as: "Communion Song" Mark 14:22,23; "We Remember You" Luke 22:19b, and "A Communion Hymn for Christmas" 1 Corinthians 11:26. Then they partook together with joy and unity and much thanksgiving as they remembered all Jesus had done for them by coming to earth as a tiny baby, growing up to minister, teaching and healing while he was on earth, willingly dying for all of the world so sinners could be saved, and for rising from the grave, ascending to heaven, where he intercedes for us, and promising to come back and take believers to live with him forever.

Jeff and Karen had trained the Blakes and Suehiros to be small group facilitators during the last part of November and all of December. Tomo and Ami were ready to take over in January with a new late shift small group. Ted and Julie would have a regular evening small group. Conversational prayer time started with the rest of the group laying their hands on both couples to consecrate them for their new positions. That was followed by all the members asking God's blessing on someone else in the group so that each person had a blessing to carry home that day.

Refreshments were delicious as usual, and the people made sure to promise each other that they would call and get together often during the next year even though most of them would be in different small groups. That part seemed a little sad, but they realized it would be good for them to meet new people and make more friends as well as keep the old ones.

*****

Various Days in the Next Year

In January, Clara met a male nursing student who had just transferred to the university from another city because he had learned about Grace 'n' Faith church and their evangelism classes. He had registered for those classes also.

When Clara found out all that information, she was very interested and became very observant when this young man was around. She had finished reading the books she borrowed from Fiona and had made a list of the good qualities to carry with her and mark off as she noticed them. That way she had been able to give the books back to Fiona with a thank you card and still have the information she needed.

Clara and the new student were in the same late shift small group that restarted with mostly new members in January. Clara, Tony, and the Suehiro parents were the only carryovers. Their children Aneko and Yoshi joined them, making seven members from church #4 and the other nine members were from late or swing shifts in some of the other churches.

The small group was an especially good place to observe and get to know more about this young man, and that is exactly what Clara did. As the weeks went by, she liked what she was learning.

She found out that he also was being funded by this church like she was, and was planning to be ready to graduate from the accelerated nurses training and evangelism training by the end of December. Therefore he was taking both the first and second year evangelism courses this year. He was going to be super busy. He said that he didn't know where he was going to minister yet.

*****

After Christmas/New Years vacation, Julie and Kippy met their new class. She knew Cory's story, so she felt blessed to have him in her class. He and one of his best friends were thrilled to be in the same class. Thankfully they were very well behaved and eager to learn all they could, so they could be witnesses next year in fourth grade with a whole new big class of unbelievers to win to Jesus.

All the classes in both church schools were smaller this year even though there had been a waiting list to get into the old school. By next year all the classes would be larger if the churches continued to grow the way they had been during the year before.

This class was looking forward to the new things they would learn in third grade because their second grade teachers had told them about learning cursive handwriting, doing harder arithmetic, and learning how to be missionaries for the fourth grade students in public schools when they finished third grade.

Many of Julie's former students did stop by to visit. She and Kippy took time with each one to ask how they were doing in fourth grade and to encourage them to keep up the good work.

*****

Don and Anita, Roy and Sherry, and the four children got together regularly after the twins and Timmy went to school in January. That way Mary had a chance to enjoy playing with them pretty often although it wasn't once a week as they had preferred. Life was just too busy for it to always work out. At the end of one month, they asked Mindy if she would do daycare again on Saturday mornings at Don and Anita's house so the children could play together while their parents went out to do two by two ministry or go on a date to have a special time together. She was very glad to be able to help them out that way.

On one of the first times the two couples got together, Anita asked, "Do you know how much money the church school subtracts from the tuition for each day that you volunteer?" Sherry shook her head so Anita told her and then asked, "How does that compare with what you make a day at your job?"

Sherry did some quick figuring and exclaimed, "That's more per day than I can make at my job! Besides that, I would get to alternate between Joy and Hope's classrooms and see firsthand how they're doing. I would not need to schedule conferences and take off work to be there on time." After a moment she asked, "Is it very hard to volunteer?"

"I know it would be an hour longer than your present work day, and I don't know from experience, but I've talked to many parents who do it, and they have said it's not hard. The teacher gives you a written plan of what to do each day when you arrive and answers any questions you might have. They're always very appreciative of your help," answered Anita.

"I'll look into it right away. Thank you for the information and for helping me think about it," responded Sherry. (She and Roy decided she should volunteer, so she quit her job and went four days a week to volunteer at the school where she rotated through all four kindergartens. Her one day off each week gave her some uninterrupted time to sew for her family.)

The children ran up to their parents just then laughing and giggling about some joke Timmy had told. They sat down to rest for a while.

Mary said including all the parents, "Thank you all for all this fun." The four parents told her she was welcome. Then she continued, "I like having Hope and Joy play with us."

Joy added, "This is even more fun than school. School is fun, Mary, and you'll get to go there next January."

"If we had been twins too, you would be there with me this year except in a different classroom," commented Timmy. "They don't allow twins to be in the same classroom."

"Can there be boy and girl twins?" Mary asked looking very dubious.

"Yes, but they can't be identical like we are," answered Hope and they all giggled some more.

Timmy continued, "They're like a brother and sister, but they're born on the same day."

Joy complicated it by saying, "I guess they could be born a day apart if one was born near midnight of one day and the other one was born just after midnight so it was the next day."

"Can girl twins or boy twins be born a day apart?" Mary asked next.

"Yes, I guess it would work just the same way," Hope replied and started giggling again.

Then Mary asked, "Do girl twins or boy twins always look so much alike?"

"No," replied Joy. "They're not always identical. They can look like only a sister or a brother. It's called fraternity ... or something like that."

Then even their parents joined in the laughter, and Anita asked, "How do you know so much about twins?"

"My teacher told my class and me a lot about it one day," answered Joy. "Then I told Hope and Timmy."

"Very good," Don encouraged them. "The word is <u>fraternal</u> instead of fraternity, but they're very closely related. You've learned a lot at school already."

*****

Without Clara knowing it, the new student was observing her, and he was very interested and impressed by what he had learned about her. They both kept observing and learning about each other in the classes they had together and in the small group.

Neither of them had much free time but eventually they were able to find some time to visit, like when they walked across campus to classes or during refreshment time at the small group. They used the walking time to discuss their beliefs, dreams and plans, and issues of importance to each one. Since they were in most of the same classes, they did a lot of walking and talking. They both liked what they were learning in the classes and about each other.

*****

After church the last Sunday in March Julie said, "Ted, do you realize we've been going to this church for a whole year?"

"Yes, it's amazing how fast the time has gone and how much we've learned and how much has happened," Ted responded. "We've both agreed and told many of our new friends that it was the best move we could ever have made."

"I'm so glad we moved!" Julie exclaimed. "When I think back about how discouraged we were in that other city, I'm really thankful we had the courage to do what many of our friends there thought was crazy."

"It wasn't crazy at all. We were led by God every step of the way." Consequently Ted sang, "My Father Planned It All." Julie smiled and nodded all the way through the song.

*****

One week near the beginning of April, Matt suggested, "Fiona, I would like us to celebrate a milestone in our lives by going out to lunch at our favorite Italian restaurant this coming Sunday before church."

Everywhere There's a Sunrise, Let's Tell The Good News!

"I'd like that very much," she replied. "But what's the milestone?"

"See if you can figure it out," he encouraged.

"Well, let's see. ... It's been several months since I have had morning sickness," she tried.

"That's a very good reason to celebrate. We'll add that one to the list," he responded.

Next she tried, "In about two months this little one will arrive, and it will be difficult to go out to a restaurant to eat with a baby."

"Another good one to add to the list," he laughed.

"How about, I'm more in love with you every day?" she giggled. He could tell she knew the answer he was looking for and was just having fun. Then she said, "I know! That date marks one year since you knew I was back in Pine City. Plus we had our first date in that restaurant the day after that. This is an excellent milestone to celebrate! I'm so glad you thought of doing this. It's fun to have a romantic husband."

"And it's fun to have you for my wife. I love you more every day too. I'm glad you're not having morning sickness any more, Honey. I know that wasn't very nice for you. We'll both be glad when he or she arrives. You're right and I agree that it's better to keep that part a surprise. It adds suspense to the anticipation."

*****

Chapter 28

Colossians 1:9b,10, ...*We... pray for you that you might be filled with the knowledge of God's will in all wisdom and spiritual understanding, so that you might walk worthy of the Lord, pleasing to all, being fruitful in every good work, and increasing in the knowledge of God.*

Connie told Fiona at work one day, "Ernest, Ben, Amelia and I all like being in the new church. Since it looks so much like the old one, it does not seem much different, except for the pastor and fewer people. It is a little further to drive, but that doesn't matter."

"I'm glad for you. I still miss seeing you at our church services, along with all the other people who moved to the new building. Our church services have fewer people also since many went to be in the new ones. But it's very good to know that all the churches have room to grow," responded Fiona.

"Right, plus I like the fact that we can still discuss the teaching times because all the churches and small groups are on the same page," Connie added and went on to say, "Ben is doing well in the trade school. He did decide to become a contractor, so it will take him a couple more years than it would to just learn one part of building. We're proud of him. He enjoys getting together with Matt when they both have time on Saturday mornings. They either just visit, or he gets his questions answered.

"Amelia is doing well as a senior and hasn't had any dates yet. She is taking your advice and observing young men in her small group and in church. She doesn't even look at the guys in school because most of those boys there are not believers. Besides that, she is praying for God to lead her about whether she should stay single or if he would like her to get married and have a family," Connie told her.

Fiona replied, "It's good to hear about both of them. Amelia told me she got very good grades last year and that she decided not to do college prep."

"Right, and you already know that she's added Monday to her work schedule. She's saving money to help pay her way through trade school. She'll study business so she will be able help us here at The Garden Shop by taking care of the flowering plants and the business part of the Shop. I'm glad she desires to work with us," Connie said with a look of pure satisfaction.

Fiona responded, "That will be wonderful for her and you both. She really has learned a lot about plants. I'm happy she can work here three days a week and still keep her grades up. I've enjoyed working with her. She wasn't very happy when I told her on Monday that this is my last week here. But I told her she can come with Ben on those Saturdays to visit with me so we can keep up our friendship. This little one is really making it hard to bend over and nurture the plants. I've enjoyed working here and I'll miss it. I hope you and I will make times to get together also, so we can still nurture our friendship!"

"Of course! Let's plan on a morning every week, either at your house or mine," suggested Connie.

"I like your great idea! We'll do it. Matt and I decided we won't try to have a garden this year. Besides, I would like this coming month at home to finish some sewing projects and make sure the nursery is ready. Plus I need to do some more research and study about how to care for and nurture infants, toddlers, and little

Everywhere There's a Sunrise, Let's Tell The Good News!

children instead of plants. The booklet the church gives out to expectant mothers is extra good," finished Fiona.

*****

Maria did get to be in a small group with Ted and Julie who were now the facilitators. All of them were happy because it would give them some extra time to be together. When it came time for them to choose partners for two by two ministry times, they continued their three by three ministry team. They decided to continue their walks on Sunday afternoons in the shopping mall, and looked forward to warm weather so they could be out in the parks again. Both were good places to have an opportunity to minister to someone.

Ted was becoming more fluent in Spanish since he studied hard and had so much good practice with Julie and Maria.

Maria told Julie and Ted on one of their walks in the shopping mall on a Sunday after church, "I'm very pleased with the way my life is going. Before you guys moved here I was lonely and had no ministry. Now I have both of you as friends, plus Ruth and Esther. Three of my co-workers are believing friends. Some of the others are friends, but without the close bond believers can have."

Julie responded, "I'm so pleased for you. Are you still at peace about staying single?"

"Yes. I rarely even think about it. I enjoy being free to give as much as I can to the Lord's work, continue working where I can minister to my co-workers, and only have to try to please the Lord," answered Maria.

Ted commented, "Julie and I are very happy with our lives here in Pine City also. We get to see how God is working through people in the church and even through us. This was the best move we could have ever made."

In that case, I think we should celebrate. I would like to invite you to my apartment for supper next Saturday. I'll fix you some authentic Mexican dishes and we'll have sopapillas for dessert. I like to watch Ted enjoy them! Afterward, I have a new Bible board game we can try out," suggested Maria.

"We accept, and we'll be looking forward to supper with you next Saturday!" Julie exclaimed.

*****

Linda L. Linn

Walt and Betty were sitting on the couch studying the Bible together as they often did since they had accepted Jesus. Today they were reading the first chapter of Ephesians. After the first fourteen verses, Walt said, "Let's make a list of all the spiritual blessings we have because we know Jesus and look up a cross reference which goes with each of them."

"Okay. I have my notebook here and a pen, so I'll write them as you find and read them," agreed Betty.

"Number 1 is that we're chosen as it says in verse 4 and a cross reference verse that goes with it, is 2 Thessalonians 2:13b, which says, *God has chosen you to have salvation through sanctification of the Spirit and belief of the truth.*"

"I have those references written down beside the word chosen," Betty said. "I'll just give you a nudge when I'm ready for you to go on."

"Good, number 2 in verse 5 is that we're adopted, and that goes with Romans 8:15b, and it says *we have received the Spirit of adoption, and we can cry Abba Father.*

"Number 3 in verse 6 is that we're accepted, and I don't see a reference to go with it. We can look 'accepted' up later in the big concordance.

"Number 4 in verse 7 is the forgiveness of sins and it goes with Romans 3:24. *We are justified freely by God's grace through the redemption that is in Christ Jesus.*

"Number 5 in verse 11 is that we have an inheritance. This goes with Romans 8:17. *Since we are children, then we are heirs of God and joint heirs with Christ, if we suffer with him so that we may also be glorified with him.*

"Then verses 13b,14a say we *were sealed with the Holy Spirit who is the guarantee of our inheritance,* which goes with 2 Corinthians 1:22 *God has sealed us and given the down payment of the Spirit in our hearts.*"

"We really <u>are</u> very blessed! Thank you, Lord, for all these blessings we've listed and help us to always live *to the praise of (your) glory* as it says at the end of verse 14," Betty prayed.

"And thank you for what we're learning from the other couple we go with to do four by four ministries. It is such a privilege to be able to serve you Jesus. We're so thankful for all you've done for us!" Walt added.

*****

Don and Anita had Jeff and Karen come over for supper one evening and then they all enjoyed playing games with Timmy and Mary before they went to bed. Then the four grown-ups had time to visit.

"How's your new small group going?" Don asked.

Jeff answered, "Very well. Just last night during praise time one couple told about being able to witness to another couple as they walked together in the park. The couple made fun of them at first, but instead of reacting in anger, they were gracious. Pretty soon the couple started asking questions really wanting answers instead of heckling. After about an hour of answering questions and having the gospel explained to them, they both accepted Jesus as their Savior. Another couple was able to counsel and help some parents and their suicidal teenager. All three of them are now believers."

After they all thanked and praised God and gave him the glory, Don said, "That's wonderful. It's much the same with all the small groups in all the churches. Almost every month we have enough people to start a new believers small group and have a special baptismal service. It's a good thing there are two churches in town now, so we have room to grow."

*****

The Suehiros asked Ted and Julie to come to their house for supper on a Sunday after church. They had a nice time getting to know the family better. They also talked about the good things they had learned in the church teaching time that day.

Ami said, "I thought it was very good to be reminded to shun false teachings that are just men's ideas, as it says in Galatians 1:6-9, and Colossians 2:8."

Ted agreed, "You're so right. We need to put everything we hear through the Bible filter and discard anything that does not agree with Scripture."

Later Julie asked, "Aneko, what was it like in the other city where you lived for a while, and do you miss it since you moved back to Pine City?"

She replied, "It was just like most big cities: busy, impersonal and lonely. I tried going to several churches, but they were unfriendly and no help at all. No, I don't miss it in any way. When Dad and Mom tried to tell me about their new faith and the good church they had found, I didn't really want to hear it, but it planted a seed. So after a while it took root and grew. Pretty soon I decided I liked Pine City and wanted to move back here. They told me later that their small group and some friends in it had been praying for Yoshi and me to be saved. We're so glad that God answered their prayers with 'yes,' aren't we Yoshi?"

"That's for sure! There's no comparison to living in that city and coming back here where we both accepted Jesus and he filled us with such peace," he answered. "We both really like working with Dad and Mom in their restaurant and this church is very good. So is the small group we were able to join then, and the new one that Dad and Mom are leading now."

Aneko continued, "We're enjoying being together as a family again and it's even better than it was before since all of us are believers. We get to go out as a four by four group to minister and we're learning a lot."

"I'm in no hurry to get married," Yoshi shared. If God has somebody for me, he will show me when it is the right time. Until then I have a lot to keep learning about my new life in Christ."

Aneko nodded and stated, "Those are my feelings exactly."

Tomo and Ami smiled as they listened to their beloved children who were now also children of God.

Then Ted told them the story about how as believers they had searched for months to find a church like this one and how they had moved to Pine City from another city just so they could be a part of this church. "It was the best thing we could have done. We've learned so much and it's been such a great adventure."

Julie added, "I remember that Anita said that very thing when we talked to them the first Sunday after our move. She said, 'With the Holy Spirit leading the way, it's bound to be an adventure!' It really has been, and probably will continue to be. We consider ourselves very blessed."

"We have also been greatly blessed since we started attending that small group. We've seen several of our prayers answered, especially the one asking God to bring salvation to our dear son and daughter," said Tomo.

"Yes, and God graciously answered our prayer that they would move back to Pine City. We're so delighted with those two answers to our prayers," added Ami.

*****

Jason decided to stay single because he realized he was too set in his ways as a bachelor to get married. He also recognized that he would never understand women well enough to help them be happy. He acknowledged that a relationship with Maria would never have worked because they were too different. He would have made her miserable in the process of figuring that out, if she had said "Yes." Over time he learned that just spending money on a woman would not prove his love. Nothing in life is that easy.

He decided to live more simply, and use more of his money to further God's Kingdom. He did research on the ministries the church had. Then he prayed for them and gave as much money to each of them as he thought God wanted him to. He joined a committee on missions, went faithfully to the meetings and prayed just as faithfully.

One ministry became very treasured to him, since his first name means healer in Greek. It was the one in which young people in the university studying nursing could be funded by the church so that they could accelerate their training and get out into the home or foreign mission fields to help heal people and win them to Jesus. He gave more money and put extra time and effort into praying for that particular ministry. His life was now filled with purpose and joy. He thanked God for all his blessings every day.

He became closer than ever to his parents, William and Anna, and visited them often. He and his mother did a lot of fun cooking together and had his sisters, Ruth and Esther, over to enjoy the meals.

*****

Every week Julie and Jane would spend at least half an hour visiting on the telephone. It was almost as good as being in person and a lot better than e-mail because they could hear each other's voices. They were able to keep up with all the happenings in each city.

Once in a while Larry and Ted would join the visit via speakerphones. On one such visit Ted said, "Larry, I really miss singing beside you. The new bass has a good voice but he's so quiet I can hardly hear him."

Larry replied, "Maybe he's just shy and needs your encouragement to get over it."

"Thanks for the idea. I'll try that this coming Thursday. How's your church doing?" Ted asked.

Larry answered, "It's growing rapidly because the people here are hungry, and because God is doing many miracles here just like he does in Pine City. We have two new believers groups who were just baptized in the public swimming pool. Besides our congregation, there were many onlookers in the crowd. They got to hear the good testimonies and our pastor gave a gospel message to them at the end and an invitation to pray with him for salvation. I haven't heard how many accepted Jesus there, but we're so thrilled to be a part of God's team working to tell his Good News here in this city."

Julie said, "We're delighted to hear about God adding to his church. My former third graders are starting to see the results of their missionary work in the fourth grades of the public schools. They come on Wednesdays and tell me about how it's going. Yesterday a boy told me that the kid he was talking to, told him to shut up or he would knock him down. The boy was gracious and quit talking but smiled at the other kid as he walked away praying for his salvation. Pray for him and all the rest of them. Many times they do come and tell me about their victories and we have a praise session. I'm blessed to have this job!"

Jane commented, "Yes, you really are, and I'm blessed to be able to have Wednesday groups. Children are so much more open than grown-ups. If we can reach them and they accept Jesus, we continue to teach them how to live the Christian life. After that they'll be likely to keep on growing and help bring others to Jesus also."

They closed their visit with conversational prayer, and then Julie said, "I look forward to talking to you next week."

*****

Esther continued to have a very good and profitable ministry with her co-workers in Jason's office. Part of that was due to Jason's prayers for her ministry. He didn't want to be involved personally, but had carried through on his promise to pray faithfully every noon hour while she and her first converted co-worker took one other person with them to eat lunch in the park after a walk, or after walking to a cafe. The office was becoming a much friendlier place to work. Even Maria would have agreed, but she was very happy to stay in Ruth's office where they were having slow but steady success also.

In January Esther was put into a new small group with several other singles along with several couples. Two of the singles were very good looking young men. She used her newly honed observational skills and things she had learned last year to find out as much as she could about them during the small group time. She still desired to be married and patiently prayed that if it would be God's will he would bring just the right man for her into her life. Maybe it would be one of those two. She and Ruth prayed a lot about it. They were happy to still be sharing an apartment.

*****

Clara and the new student continued their discussions and an unusual romance began. Unusual, because neither of them had any money. They thought they'd have to wait, and could not consider marriage until a long time after they would graduate and find good enough jobs in the small city Clara would be. He told her that if he could get a job there, he would move there also.

They decided that if they ever did get to marry, they should not have any children because it would hamper their ministry. All the other issues they discussed were also agreed upon, but it still remained a mystery whether they <u>would</u> get to be married. So they prayed and left it in God's hands. Ultimately <u>he</u> always knows and does what is best.

*****

Julie's former third graders often stayed after 5 PM to visit when they came on a Wednesday to help. One day Julie asked a girl, "How's it going for you in fourth grade this year?"

"It <u>is</u> a lot harder than I thought it might be. The other girls are in little groups of friends that have been together since Kindergarten, so it's very hard to make friends. But this church school requires the public school to register at least two girls and two boys together from Grace 'n' Faith Church School to be in each class. That way we have a two by two ministry and it's not as lonely. My friend and I are trying to befriend loaners who are left out of the groups of friends. It is slow work, but this week we've seen a little bit of progress. I'm glad you taught us to be patient and go slowly and carefully so we don't push them away."

"Good for you. I'm proud of you and I know Jesus will help you and you'll see some victories pretty soon," Julie responded.

Another day a boy commented, "I like trying to be a missionary in the public school. Those fourth grade kids who came on Wednesdays to our class really knew what they were talking about when they said it was hard work. Many times some of the kids make fun of us. They call us those 'Church School Kids,' but I think it's a compliment."

"What a good way to look at something they do to be mean. Keep up the good work. Jesus is helping you and pretty soon you'll be telling me about one of those kids accepting Jesus as his or her Savior," said Julie.

Later in the school year one after another <u>did</u> come to tell her about one and sometimes two or three they were privileged to lead to Jesus for salvation. They were excited and thankful to Jesus because he had been able to use them to bring another kid into God's Kingdom. Julie rejoiced with them and thanked God for putting her in this school so that she could have the joy of teaching the children how to be missionaries, not just in fourth grade, but for all of their lives.

No matter what they said, she always asked, "Would you please write it down in your daily journal and then make me a copy so I can have it. Maybe I can use some of your experience as I teach this year's third graders."

Each one would ask, "Do you really mean that it would help you teach even better, Mrs. Blake?"

"Yes, of course. I got many ideas from last year's fourth graders and used them to teach you," answered Julie. "I'm always looking for better ways to teach."

Some of them would say something like, "Oh, I understand. That's why you're such a good teacher!"

And Julie would reply humbly, "Thank you. My goal is to be a good teacher, with Jesus' help."

*****

"Have you done your homework for the small group yet?" Vern asked Lora.

"No, but thank you for the reminder. I'll get it done right after supper, so it will be ready for the meeting tomorrow evening," she answered. "Please remind me again what we're suppose to do."

Vern responded, "He told us to read Philippians 2:2-8 and to notice what it says about humility, and then find some cross references that add to, or clarify those verses."

"Thank you. It sounds like a good study," Lora said as she finished getting supper on the table.

After supper, Mindy offered, "I'll do the cleanup so you can go work on your homework, Mom."

Vern said, "I'll help you, Mindy. I assume you have yours completed already."

"Yes, I did it the next day and it was interesting," replied Mindy.

"Thank you! You're both the best!" Lora exclaimed as she went to her desk and got to work.

Vern and Mindy responded in unison, "And you're the best too!"

Lora wrote in her notebook: I like verse two very much because it says to *be like minded, having the same love, being of one accord and of one mind.* Verse three is good also, especially this part: *in lowliness of mind let each one esteem others better than themselves.* Verses 5-8 tell us to be like Jesus who humbled himself even to death.

1 Peter 5:5b,6 says to *be subject to one another and be dressed with humility. ... Humble yourselves therefore under the mighty hand of God, that he may exalt you in due time.* Yes, just like he exalted Jesus after he died and rose again. 1 Peter 3:8 says to *be of one mind, have compassion, love as brothers, have pity and be courteous.* Romans 12:10 says to *be kind to one another with brotherly love, in honor preferring one another.* Verse 16 says to *be of the same mind toward one another. Mind not high things, but condescend to men of low estate. Do not be wise in your own conceits.*

When she finished, Lora called Vern and Mindy over, thanked them again, and then complimented them, "Both of you just did for me what these verses were telling us to do. You put the scriptures into action. Father in heaven, please help me to always have these good virtues showing in my life."

Vern added, "I ask the same thing for myself, Father."

"Me too. And I thank you for such good parents who are first-rate examples for me to follow," concluded Mindy.

*****

At one of the special baptismal services there was one testimony after another about how God had done a miracle, which had convinced the person that **he** is real and that he or she needed the salvation God provided. Each one also stated that the salvation **he** gave them was another miracle. One person shared how he had been raised from the dead, and as a consequence, many of the hospital staff and the rest of his whole family had become believers because of what God had done through his believing brother and his wife.

Additional testimonies were about how a person had observed the lifestyle of a believer and wanted that kind of life for himself. Others said how someone had told them the Good News and made it clear enough for them to understand so that they accepted Jesus. Many had requested that the song "How Great Thou Art," would be sung that evening because especially verse three was like their own testimony. The results of the Gospel in all these lives were outstanding, and God got all the glory!

Julie was there that evening and was quickly writing down what each of them said. The notebook she had started in the late shift small group was now full of all the praises and miracles and salvations that she had recorded in it.

Noticing that fact, Ted commented when they got home, "Let's get you a new notebook and put that one on the bookshelf for safekeeping. If we ever get discouraged, all we need to do is read some of the things you've written in it and we'll immediately be lifted up again."

*****

Anita and Mindy were visiting one Wednesday afternoon while the children were napping. Mindy remarked, "It sure is different with all the five-year-old children being gone to kindergarten now."

Anita replied, "You're right about that. I'm thankful that three other families wanted care for their four-year-old children, or I would not have enough to earn the money we need for the church school tuition."

"Oh that's right. This coming January, Mary and all the rest of your day care children will be in Kindergarten also, and you'll be there at the school volunteering as many days as you can to keep the tuition price down. Which means that my time of coming here to help you will be over," Mindy said with a sorrowful look.

"Life is like that. Change is a certainty, but we've been blessed to have these years of working together and can always keep the memories. Besides, we still have the rest of this year, so let's not be sad," suggested Anita.

"Okay. But do you have any ideas of another lady in our church who might need help with daycare or even just with her own children so I can have a place to go after school each day rather than roaming the streets or going to an empty house until Dad and Mom get home?" Mindy asked.

"I know that Fiona and Matt are expecting a baby pretty soon. You might talk to her and see if she's going to do daycare along with taking care of the new one or if she would just like help with that one," answered Anita.

"I'll try that and tell her that I would be available this coming January. In the meantime I'll continue enjoying my time with you and Mary and the daycare children," stated Mindy.

*****

Tony was having Sunday supper with the Suehiros in their home. He said, "I'm really glad you're the leaders of the new late shift small group. You're doing a great job. I'm also really glad Aneko and Yoshi are in this group also. It's been nice to get to know all of you better."

"Thank you for the compliments. We're glad you're in our group also. How's your ministry going with the children in the parks?" Yoshi asked.

Tony answered, "It is much better in the parks now that the weather has warmed up again. Somehow it does not work as well in the shopping mall where it's usually so noisy. But we keep at it, wherever we can, and once in a while a child or two and even their parents will accept Jesus. This is what makes it all worthwhile. How's your four by four ministry going?"

"It seems slow at times to us like it is for you, but if we keep at it and follow what Jesus says to do, we will also see some more people accept Jesus. It won't always be as exciting and profitable as when Jesus healed Denji and saved him and his parents," replied Ami.

Tomo exclaimed, "We have very good news from them! Afta called this morning and said that Hana's parents and her brothers and sisters all accepted Jesus at church this morning. We had a rousing praise time on the telephone."

"How wonderful. I'm so thrilled to hear that, since we've been praying for them so long in the small group. You'll get to share that next Saturday as a praise," Tony responded.

"I've been wanting to tell you, Tony, that your English has improved so much. You don't even have much of an accent any longer," mentioned Ami.

"Thank you. Jesus has helped me along with reading those stories and talking to the children and their parents. Plus, I've been spending some time with Ted and Julie who help me correct my grammar and pronunciation."

Aneko commented, "I've heard that there's a free class called 'English as a Second Language' at the church every Monday and Wednesday and Thursday. But it's in the evening so it would not have worked for you to attend. Anyway, they're having very good attendance and the people of several different languages are learning swiftly. They have many opportunities to practice on each other and the teachers walk around and help them with grammar and pronunciation. Besides that they get a chance to hear the Gospel. They can ask questions and get them answered."

Yoshi added, "That's wonderful. I'm so impressed with this church. That building gets used more than any other building in town. As we drive past it on the way home from working at the restaurant, there are lights on almost every night! And that's not counting all the weekend services."

Tomo explained, "The sanctuary is also used for basketball every Friday, and square dancing once a month on Tuesdays. Other times small groups meet there to learn about water baptism and see the facilities. The evening evangelism classes for missionaries are held in the school lunchroom and in the music room except on Thursdays when it's used to prepare the music for the services and small groups."

*****

In the middle of June, the teacher of the evangelism class contacted Jeff and Karen asking them to talk to Clara and the new student. So they were treated to lunch at the Spencer home.

After lunch as they were visiting in the living room, Jeff said, "The teacher of your evangelism class has noticed how your relationship has grown. He told us about your decision to wait and see if jobs can be obtained in the small city where Clara's parents live before you consider getting married. He contacted many places in that city, and learned that there is a definite need for nurses and there are people there who are looking forward to your arrival after your December graduation."

"We are really glad to hear about that. Perhaps we will be able to get married after we get settled there," said the student. Clara smiled and nodded.

Karen said, "Clara, you remember that Jeff and I are on that committee which funds students like the two of you. The committee has discussed your situation and has agreed that **if** you would rather not have to wait, you could be married as soon as you would like. It's a proven fact that it is cheaper for two married people to live together than for two single people to live separately, and besides that you might be able to do a better job of studying after you get used to being married."

"Are you saying that we could get married and live in one apartment while we're finishing our schooling?" Clara asked.

"Yes," Jeff answered, "and the money that you would save by doing that could be put away and used later to help you get settled in that city where jobs are waiting for you."

"Besides that, we have found a nice one bedroom apartment close to the church and the university that only costs a little more than one studio apartment. It's furnished and would be easy for you to move into after your wedding," continued Karen.

At this point, the student rose from his chair and knelt on one knee in front of Clara. "Clara, I love you so much and would be honored to have you be my wife and partner in working for Jesus for the rest of our lives. Will you please marry me?"

"Yes, I would be delighted to be your wife. It will be a privilege to serve Jesus with you," answered Clara. He stood and helped Clara to her feet for their first hug and kiss. It was better than either of them could have imagined. Then she looked at Karen and seeing the twinkle in her eyes she asked, "I have a feeling you knew we'd like to do this, and already have other plans in mind. Please tell us."

Karen smiled and outlined their ideas, "Indeed we do! The wedding will not take a long time to plan. We are thinking that the weekend before the Fourth of July would not be too soon. Since that will be a vacation week for both of you, it will give you a week to get settled in your new apartment and then take a short honeymoon, which would be our wedding gift to you both. It will be in a mountain town of your choosing for two nights in one of their hotels and whatever you would like to do for the days you are there. Sherry Foster is planning to give you a wedding shower. Fiona said that she and you are the same size, and that she would like to loan you the dress she wore for her wedding. The suit he already has is fine."

Jeff added, "If you would like, we could have the wedding at our home on that Saturday afternoon. I will be the stand-in for your own father since your parents won't be able to be here. We have a nice backyard, which would work for the reception. Your small group has volunteered to use that Saturday morning group time to help you both pack and move all your belongings into the new apartment."

By this time, both Clara and the student were sitting with astonished looks on their faces. Neither of them had never even imagined something like this could happen.

"Since we are trying to not spend much money, you two will be expected to orally invite the people you desire to have come to your wedding." Karen then asked, "What do you think of our ideas?"

Clara replied, "I think we are both overwhelmed and amazed and totally grateful especially to God and to all the people and who have worked together to make all this happen. It will be the most wonderful wedding I could ever have dreamed of, and it's to the most wonderful Christian man! Thank you for planning all of this and telling us about it. Heavenly Father, our provider, we thank you very much for your plans and provisions for our lives. Please help us as we become husband and wife and serve you together."

*****

Pam and Julie ate lunch together once in a while so they could visit. One day Pam asked, "How's the new teacher next to you doing?"

"She's doing very well and likes it here," answered Julie.

"I think it was such a good idea to have two new and two experienced teachers in each school," Pam commented.

"I agree. Everything about this church and school is well planned. Everything they do is high quality and it works. I'm sure that it brings much glory to God," replied Julie.

"You're right about that. I heard them say that is one reason for their existence. The other one is to bring the lost into God's Kingdom."

"It's working! I'm so blessed to be a part of the church and the school both, exclaimed Julie. "Ted and I have decided that instead of having a family of our own by adoption, it's more important for me to continue my ministry here at this school where we prepare children to go out and be missionaries in the public school system and for the rest of their lives."

Pam agreed, "It's wonderful both of you can agree. For that same reason, I have decided to never get married. If I had a husband, I would be obligated to do what would please him. This way I only have to try to please Jesus and he isn't hard to please, because his yoke is easy and his burden is light as it says in Matthew 11:30."

Everywhere There's a Sunrise, Let's Tell The Good News!

*****

    The first church plant experiment went so well that Grace 'n' Faith Church decided to send more of them to other cities. As the churches in Pine City continued to grow and reached about 200 people in the congregation, they would ask for nine couples or families to join a pastor who was ready to graduate and go to another city as missionaries to start a new church. They even started new churches in Pine City, using the same ideas. That way no new church and school buildings needed to be built.
    Each new church carried the Grace 'n' Faith Church name, and they followed the same general plan as the first church plant. They were very successful, because Jesus was right there helping every person do his best to cooperate and work together to win as many people to him as possible. They followed the instructions in Romans 15:5b,6 which says, *Be like-minded toward one another according to Christ Jesus, so that you may with one mind and one mouth glorify God the Father of our Lord Jesus Christ.*

*****

Epilogue

Happenings during the Next Several Years

1 John 4:10,11, *This is love, not that we loved God, but that he loved us and sent his Son to be the payment for our sins. Since God so loved us, we also ought to love one another.*

    Fiona didn't get a whole month to sew and prepare the nursery, because her little one decided to come a week early. Matt drove her carefully to the hospital that Saturday morning and made sure she was settled in a room before he called Patrick and Glenda and then Walt and Betty. They had all told him they wanted to be there at the hospital even if they could not be with Fiona.
    Matt stayed with Fiona all the way through the hours of her labor letting her squeeze his hand with amazing strength through each contraction as he encouraged and prayed for her. The part he disliked the most was all the pain his dear wife had to go through. He was there to see and hear that they had a son and to tell Fiona what a fine job she had done. She was worn out, but

very happy when the doctor laid their son in her arms after they had cleaned him up. After he spent a few minutes with both of them a nurse came to take the baby to the nursery and another came to help Fiona get clean and comfortable so she could rest.

Matt went to tell the grandparents so they could rejoice too. Riley was there by this time and they all went to look through the nursery window at their new son, grandson, or nephew, whose name was John Matthew Anderson in honor of his deceased grandfather and his father. But they would not hang The Third on the end of the name. It was too cumbersome and sounded too sophisticated.

Matt went back to check on his wife who was sleeping peacefully. So he and the family went to the hospital cafeteria to eat the lunch they had skipped while they were waiting. After a couple hours they asked Matt to go check and see if she was up to having visitors. She was awake and glad to visit with each of them for a few minutes before they went home. They would all be back the next day with flowering plants for Fiona and gifts for John.

This happy scenario would be repeated two more times during the next several years. In just one year, Fiona presented another son to Matt and they named him Patrick Walter Anderson in honor of those grandfathers. Less than two years later Fiona became the mother of beautiful twin girls. They named the twins Betty Grace Anderson and Glenda Faith Anderson in honor of their grandmothers and the name of the church. It is interesting to note that Betty was also the name of Matt's deceased mother.

All of the children brought great joy to the Anderson household and to all the grandparents and one uncle. Walt and Betty finally had grandkids they could enjoy and spoil a little bit. They came often, either together or Betty would come while Walt was at work. Both sets of grandparents were a great help with all those little children. Moreover, they all knew it would be unwise to spoil them very much.

Matt and Fiona agreed that these four children were just the right number for their family, and they loved, enjoyed, and nurtured them. They also planned and saved for the time when all of them could attend the Grace 'n' Faith Church School.

*****

Mindy did talk to Fiona who was glad to have her volunteer to come after school starting that coming January to help with their son. It was a big help since there was another little one on the way by then. After a couple months, they started to pay her for the hours she spent there because they wanted to give her an incentive to continue coming. She told them that she would be glad to do it anyway because she enjoyed it. But she put the money into a savings account to help pay for her education after high school even though she didn't know yet what she wanted to be. She and Fiona became good friends. Shortly after their second son was born, Fiona said, "Mindy you're such a wonderful helper! Could we add Saturday mornings to your time? Feel free to say 'no,' if you don't have time."

Mindy answered, "I would love to, Fiona. I enjoy the time I get to spend here with you and your sweet children. Like I told Anita a couple years ago, the children take the place of brothers and sisters for me, and then I get to go home to a wonderful dad and mom and have them all to myself. I really have the best of both worlds." Fiona smiled and nodded.

Vern and Lora were glad Mindy had found another place to be after school. They were used to her being gone on Saturday mornings when she was taking care of Timmy and Mary and Joy and Hope so that that foursome could still have times of fun together on the weekends after they started school. After Mary began Kindergarten they didn't need to do that any longer, so Mindy was available to help Fiona.

*****

Sherry called Fiona one Saturday afternoon a week after she had brought the twins home from the hospital and asked, "Are you feeling up to having a little company? May Hope and Joy and I come over to visit and bring a present?"

"Oh, that would be lovely. I would love to see you all," Fiona responded.

The three of them came in, each carrying as large a box as she could hold onto. They were wrapped in butcher paper that each one had decorated with felt-tip markers. They looked so nice that Fiona would unwrap them carefully to preserve their artwork.

But before she opened the gifts she had to exclaim over how much Joy and Hope had grown. "Wow! I don't think I've seen you two for a while. How old are you now, and how's school going?"

Hope answered, "We're eight years old and are in the third grade. I'm in Mrs. Blake's class and she's such a good teacher. She has a little koala puppet named Kippy. Twice a day we get to share whatever we want to tell him. We realize that he's just make believe but it's such fun to watch him move with her hand inside him and hear her talk for him."

Joy added, "I'm in Miss Green's class and she's a very good teacher also. She has a puppet too, but we only get to share with it once a day. It is fun though. Both of us are learning how to go be missionaries in the fourth grades of the public schools and for the rest of our lives. It will be a privilege but also a big responsibility."

"I hope we can stay quiet enough so that your children will stay asleep for their naps while you open these presents," Sherry said softly.

"They're good sleepers and that's a big blessing. I can hardly wait to see what's in all these boxes. The wrapping paper is very pretty so be patient while I try not to tear it to pieces. I want to save it," explained Fiona. Then she carefully unwrapped each box and folded the paper before opening any of the boxes. The suspense was tantalizing. "Which one should I open first?"

Joy and Hope put the boxes in a line and then pointed to the first one. "Open them in this order," they said.

Fiona opened the first box and gasped. It was full of twin baby clothing, including sleepers, daytime outfits, dresses, booties, even tiny shoes and two delicate dresses for their dedication. Everything was sorted in all the sizes from infant, to things that would fit when they were two years old.

"Ladies! Are you sure you really want to give all this away?"

"We are very sure!" Sherry emphasized. "We've been saving all these things with the hope of being able to bless some wonderful Christian sister who has twin girls. We couldn't be happier that it turned out to be you!"

"These are all precious and priceless, and even more amazing because they're all made by you, Sherry!" Fiona exclaimed as she looked closely at some of the dresses. She made sure to keep them in the well-sorted piles.

Next she opened the second box in the line and found clothing including coats and shoes in sizes that would fit from ages two through four years old. The third box contained clothing, coats and shoes on up to age seven or more years. Fiona sat, surrounded by all these treasures and felt overwhelmed with gratefulness and amazement.

She asked, "Did you know that whenever I had an ultrasound to check on the baby's progress, Matt and I never would let the doctors tell us the sex of the child or if it would be more than one? Therefore we weren't prepared for twins. They were so small I had no clue."

"Yes, a Mindy bird told me, so we hurried to sort these and get them boxed and wrapped to bring them to you," answered Sherry.

"I'm so glad. We've been scrambling this last week to buy enough things to take proper care of them. But our great God just took care of all our needs in spite of our silliness. He provided all we need through the love and generosity of our Christian sisters. Thank you so very, very much!"

"You're very, very welcome," they all said together and all four of them laughed aloud forgetting the sleeping children. Noises and little footsteps alerted them that at least one of them was awake. John came in and hurried to snuggle in his mother's lap. He was feeling shy because he wasn't used to so many people in the room.

Fiona picked up two sleeper sets. "Look, John, these are for your new little sisters. Aren't they pretty?"

He nodded. "Pretty on our twins," he said sleepily.

Pretty soon Matt came in the room holding Faith and Grace in their not matching sleepwear. All they were interested in was an afternoon snack. So Fiona sat in one of the recliners and discreetly fed them under the baby blanket Matt had brought with him. She said, "Matt, let Sherry and her twins show you the fabulous present they brought to us."

Matt held John on his lap and was just as amazed as Fiona had been. "How can we ever thank you enough for all these treasures? I can see there are enough clothes here to keep them well dressed for many years to come."

"Furthermore, if we can take good enough care of them, maybe someday we'll get to bless another Christian sister who has twin girls. All of them are well made, and children grow out of their clothes so quickly. Maybe we'll get to pass on the blessing," suggested Fiona as the little twins finished drinking.

"May we sing a blessing we've been practicing for the twins?" Joy asked. When Fiona smiled and nodded, Sherry, Joy, and Hope sang a beautiful song asking for God's blessing on the precious babies.

Fiona had moist eyes when Matt thanked them and told them how beautiful it sounded, and how meaningful the words were.

"Now, since these two are clean and dry and satisfied, let's try on one of those pretty dresses each. Sherry, will you help me?" Fiona asked.

"Sure. Which one do I have?" Sherry asked and also said, "I'll bet they're going to be as beautiful as their mother when they grow up."

"Thank you, Sherry. The one you're holding is Grace. You'll notice that she has a dimple in her chin, and Faith does not," explained Fiona.

"Just like I have two freckles on my right cheek and Joy has none," commented Hope. "It is good that there's a way to tell them apart."

"Oh! See how pretty they look," exclaimed Joy. Do you have a camera or a video? Dad and Mom took lots of pictures of us and put them in albums. I remember seeing a picture of us in these dresses."

Matt answered, "Yes, the camera is right over there. Who knows how to use it? Good, Sherry, please take pictures of us with all of these treasures. Then we better get them put into the dressers and cupboards before Patrick wakes up and comes out here thinking they're all for him to play with and scatter around." They all laughed quietly this time.

Sherry put Grace back on Fiona's lap and quickly took all the pictures Matt instructed her to take. Just as she finished, two nosy neighbors from across the street and next-door knocked quietly on the door. Matt went to answer it and invited them inside.

"We're sorry to interrupt, but we just couldn't stand the suspense another minute," one of them stated.

And the other one added, "So we just had to come and see what those people brought in those pretty boxes."

Fiona welcomed them, "Oh, do come and see what our dear friends have given us for Grace and Faith!"

"Oh my!" was all they could say. Fiona introduced them to Sherry and Hope and Joy, and then explained why they had done this.

The first neighbor said, "You Christians really DO love each other and show it in amazing ways. We've seen a parade of people bringing covered dishes here all week knowing Fiona would not be up to cooking for her family let alone those two missionary couples who live here too. We'll come back another day when you're not so busy and ask you to explain everything you've tried to tell us all these years."

"We'll be glad to," replied Fiona. "Bring your husbands and families and come after eight o'clock tonight. The children should be sleeping by then." They nodded and said they would, and Matt told them good-bye at the door.

Right after those two left, Sherry and her twins quickly packed all the clothing back in the boxes so they could be moved into the nursery or wherever they would need to be stored until they were used.

As they went through the sewing room to the nursery Sherry noticed that it had been converted to a bedroom for the two boys who were really not old enough yet to be so far from their parents at night. For a wonder, Patrick was still sleeping! Matt had quickly bought another crib and dresser for the nursery.

The sewing machine in its cabinet had been put next to the dining room cabinet and looked fine there. Fiona could use the dining room table to cut out patterns if she ever had the time to do it. The activity table was in the garage for now. Mindy provided some of that time for Fiona to sew while she cared for all four of these delightful children, except for when the twins got hungry. Then she just kept the boys busy.

Before they left, Matt and Fiona thanked Sherry, Joy and Hope again for the lovely gifts and asked them to join them in prayer for the neighbors who would come to visit that evening.

That evening, the neighbors met with them in the living room with most of the dining room chairs rolled in there for extra seating. It was almost as many as a small group meeting. Matt and Fiona explained the Gospel to them again and answered all their questions.

One neighbor said, "We've seen both sets of the children's grandparents, especially the grandmothers, coming to help with the two boys. Now they're coming even more often to help with all four children. Besides that, there are other people who have been helping you even more than before, now that you have twins. And on top of all those people, is that girl who comes almost daily to help you. I know you have said that you're paying her, but she sure is faithful. Ordinary people don't act that way."

Another of the neighbors said, "I for one, am totally convinced that all you say about Jesus is true and your lives and the lives of these other people who come to help you have proven it to me. I would like to believe and live the way you do."

The rest of the visitors agreed and Fiona led them in prayer as they all asked Jesus to be their Savior and fill them with his love so they could show it to others as well.

*****

Linda L. Linn

THE END

Philippians 4:23 *The grace of our Lord Jesus Christ be with you all. Amen.*

****

Addendum: Curriculum

The following is just a short summary of the **curriculum for each grade level.**
Kindergarten: The year begins like preschool with fun and learning how to play and get along together. They will hear many stories, poetry and rhymes. There are a lot of Big Book stories with the teacher pointing to words as she reads to acquaint the children with left to right reading and that there are words on the page. They will learn the alphabet and the sounds of the letters, but nobody will be required to learn to read yet. Some children might on their own, but most children are not physically or mentally ready to read at this age. Their eyes need time to develop to be able to focus on small things like letters and words. They will learn to count to 20 by using hands-on methods, to help with understanding, and use active games that reinforce the learning and keep them moving. They will be taught healthy social and physical habits. They will have a time of resting in the morning and afternoon, since many of them have been doing that at home.
First Grade: The children will continue to hear many stories, poetry and rhymes. They will learn how to print the capital and small letters of the alphabet and be encouraged to keep their work neat and legible. Those whose eyes are ready will start learning to read. Others will continue with Big Books, phonics drills using fun games, and being read to one-on-one by those who are already reading. Since reading and spelling go hand in hand, they will learn how to spell using phonics. But they will memorize the words that cannot be sounded out (sight words). The children will write simple stories that they will read to the parent volunteer, who will help them make corrections. Then they will recopy the stories to put in a little book that they can take home and read to their parents. They will be learning to use correct oral and written grammar, and how important it is to spell correctly when they write anything. In Math, they will be counting to 100, and will learn to

add and subtract those numbers but without carrying or borrowing. They will do simple oral story problems and later in the year those who can read, will work on simple written story problems. They will continue to learn healthy social and physical skills. We follow the public school curriculum for Health, Science, Social Studies, and the History and Geography of Pine City. Art and Music will include many projects that coincide with other learning in the classroom.

Second Grade: The children will continue all those skills, plus everybody will focus on learning to read if they are able to, so that all can read by the end of the year. (There will be some who cannot read even then, and they will not be considered failures, just not ready yet. They will go on with their class to third grade but be given extra help in learning to read, without any stigma attached.) The children will review printing and practice improving their letters. Their short stories will get longer and they will use their new spelling words and correct grammar. They will learn how to write simple friendly letters and thank-you notes. We follow the public school curriculum for Health, Science, Social Studies, and the History and Geography of our state. In Math they will count to 1,000 and add/subtract those numbers learning how to carry and borrow. Those skills will be demonstrated and practiced using hands-on materials that improve understanding. They will learn about geometric shapes and simple fractions by using hands-on materials that enhance understanding. They will learn basic computer skills.

Third Grade: The children will continue all the second grade skills becoming proficient in them and expand their reading to longer books, then chapter books. They will learn and practice writing in cursive, or longhand as it is sometimes called. They will learn to write simple book reports and get up and share them with the class. Later in the year they will learn to write a simple business letter, do short research reports and write short nature essays about animals, plants, and human body parts that include scientific facts that show the design and engineering of the Great Creator, God. They will do these with the individualized help of fourth and fifth grade students who come to help on Wednesday afternoons when they have early release time so _their_ teachers can have meetings. (Our school does not have early release days or teacher's meetings, because our teachers get the training they need and all teacher's meeting topics by way of memos and booklets.) We follow the public school curriculum for Health, Science, Social Studies, and the History and Geography of our country. In Math they will count to 10,000 and add/subtract those numbers with carrying and borrowing. They will learn to multiply and divide, first with smaller numbers with hands-on materials, which will help them understand the concepts involved. They will also learn to add/subtract, multiply/divide fractions in the same way. They will review and learn more computer skills.

Each grade level except Kindergarten will take the school district proficiency tests in the first part of December. The tests help us to explain to parents why a student might need more extra help at the next level to become proficient in some of the skills.

Bible and Christian Living Curriculum

This school uses age appropriate scripture verses especially from Proverbs and the New Testament, plus stories that teach how to live for Jesus, fun action games, drills, memorization, songs, poems, rhymes, and role playing, Some of the materials that will be used are Keys For Kids Devotionals, songs with scriptures by Steve Green and the Hide 'em in Your Heart Gang, songs by Buddy Davis that emphasize that God created the universe, and online materials available from creation.org. and answersingenesis.org, They will hear and read many Bible verses about creation, and numerous stories about plants, animals, and humans that emphasize the variety, intricacies, and ways of living that could not have happened by evolution, but instead had to be designed and engineered by an all knowing, loving, all powerful, Creator.

Kindergarten: They will hear many Bible stories and the Gospel, learn the Golden Rule and be taught to ask themselves: "How do I want others to treat me?" Then they will try to treat others that way. They will get much practice using role playing to act out how to get along with others well, how to share and take turns and follow rules. When problems arise, they will discuss how to solve them and keep them from happening again. They will learn the difference between make believe (including Santa Claus and the Easter Bunny) and reality. They will learn why fairy tales can't be real, and are therefore make believe, and why the Bible is **not** make believe, but is real and true and can be trusted.

First Grade: <u>Continue the above</u> with changes appropriate for this age level, plus: they will start scripture memorization, with and without music, learn to encourage one another, and do conflict resolution, and forgive and be forgiven. They will also memorize simple poems and rhymes that teach valuable Christian living concepts.

Second Grade: <u>Continue the above</u> with changes appropriate for this age level plus: they will start a devotional journal, during a daily time of reading the Bible and write one thing they learned. Then once a week they will get together with a little group to share at least one thing they learned and wrote in their journal with the group. They do not have to share something that is personal though. They will learn about Creation by the Triune God versus evolution, using many verses from Scripture, and many stories from nature to prove it. The scriptures will include Genesis 1:1,21,27; Isaiah 45:7,12,18; and Colossians 1:16,17; this last one will be memorized.

Third Grade: <u>Continue the above</u> with changes appropriate for this age level, plus Evangelism. Each child will prepare and write his own story of how he received Jesus to be his own personal Savior. Then he will practice it and become at ease with sharing it with one or more other classmates. They will practice how to witness using many different methods or presentations by role-playing with each other each other to become familiar and comfortable doing it. They will learn how to believe in Creation by God in spite of the public school focus on evolution and how ignore, but not confront. They will learn what has been and will be taught about evolution in the public schools. They will learn what flaws are in that theory, and why it cannot be true. If asked what they believe about Creation by God, they will be able to explain what it is and why it is true. Scriptures about Creation by God will include the ones for second grade plus: Genesis 14:19,22; Psalm 33:6, 9; 89:12; 148:5; Isaiah 41:20; 42:5; Proverbs 3:19,20; Mark 10:6; Romans 1:20; Romans 8:19-22; 1 Timothy 4:4; Hebrews 4:3; and 2 Peter 3:4; Romans 11:33-36. Many of these will be memorized.

****

List of Characters (in the order they are first mentioned)

Fiona (fair one) O'Connor, is 22 years old, is not yet married and has lived in Pine City all her life. She is a florist who takes care of plants at The Garden Store from 8:30 AM to 5 PM, M-F at the beginning of the story. Later she works there from 12:30 to 8 PM.

Ernest (serious and determined) and Connie (steadfast) Clay are in their early 40's, and have lived in Pine City all their lives. They own and operate The Garden Store (Shop). Ernest works from 8 to 5, and Connie has changing hours Monday - Saturday. Their son, Ben (dim of Benjamin) is 16 and is in high school. Amy (dim of Amelia, industrious) is 15 and just starting high school.

Matthew (gift of God, Matt) Anderson is 24 years old, is not yet married, and has lived in Pine City for all his life. His parents are deceased. He works for Evans Construction Company, M-F, 8 AM to 5 PM at first. Later, he works the second shift there from 1:30 to 9 PM.

Walter (to rule, Walt) and Betty (dim of Elizabeth, God of plenty) Evans, are in their late fifties, and have lived for 20 years in Pine City. They were not able to have children. Walt is the owner and boss of Evans Construction Company and works 8 AM to 5 PM, M-F in the Prologue. Later, he works first shift, from 7 AM to 2PM. Betty is a homemaker.

Patrick (for the saint) and Glenda (holy, good) O'Connor, are in their 40's and have lived in Pine City all their lives. They are the parents of Fiona and Riley, who is 21 and is attending college. Patrick works at the Garden Store from 8 to 5, M-F. Cara (loving) O'Connor lives in another city and is Fiona's great aunt, the sister of her dad's mother, but about 15 years older.

Theodore (Ted) and Julie Blake, both are 24 years old when they move to Pine City. Ted works at Superior Auto Body Shop, and Julie works for a while at Happy Smiles for Kids as a dental office receptionist. They both work M-F from 8 - 5 at first.

Pastor Don and Anita (dim. of Anna, grace) Ross are both in their late 20's and have lived in Pine City for 7 years. Don is the pastor of Grace 'n' Faith Church #4, and also works stocking shelves at the Local Grocery from 8 - 5, M-F. Anita is the pastor's wife and homemaker. She also does day care from 7:30 to 5:30, M-F. Their children are Timmy, who will be 5 years old on May 20, and Mary, who will be 4 on May 24.

Everywhere There's a Sunrise, Let's Tell The Good News!

Maria (Spanish for Mary) Gomez, is 24 years old, and is Julie Blake's former college roommate. She is not married. She has lived in Pine City for 2 years. She works as an accountant at Beckett CPA's, from 8 - 5, M-F. Her boss at the beginning is Mr. Jason Beckett.

Jason (Greek for healer) Beckett is 28 years old and has never been married. He is the boss at the third office of Beckett CPA's.

Jeffery (peaceful, Jeff) and Karen (dim of Katherine, pure) Spencer, are in their 40's and have lived in Pine City for 10 years. They have no children. Jeff works with Matt at Evans Construction Company, M-F, from 2 to 9 PM. Karen works at Subway from 12 to 8 PM, M-F.

Mindy (dim of Amanda, loved) Jones is 12 years old. Her father Vernon (Vern) Jones is in his 30's. He is a pediatric dentist at Happy Smiles for Kids. They've lived in Pine City for 11 years. Both are members of Grace 'n' Faith Church #4. Mindy is an only child whose mother died four years ago. She helps Anita with the day care children after school and during vacations.

Tomo (twin) Suehiro. His twin brother's name is Afta, which means he was born after, and so he is younger than Tomo. His wife is Ami (friend). Both are in their early 50's, and have lived in Pine City for 25 years. They own and operate Ami's Japanese Restaurant from 11 AM to 9 PM, M-F. Their grown children are Aneko (older sister), and Yoshi (quiet/shy). They've both moved away from Pine City and have not yet married.

Clara (bright, clear) Morgan, 22 years old, and has lived in Pine City most of her life. She is not yet married, goes to school for nurses training in the mornings and works at American Furniture Warehouse from 1 to 9 PM, M-F.

Roy (king) and Sherry (from the white meadow) Foster are 25 years old and have lived in Pine City for 7 years. Their identical twin girls, Hope and Joy, will be 5 on May 22. Roy works at Home Depot from 6 AM to 2 PM, M-F and Sherry works at Wal-Mart from 2:30 to 10:30 PM, M-F.

Linda L. Linn

Antonito (praiseworthy, Tony) Valdez is 26, and has lived in Pine City for 9 years. He has never been married and has recently been promoted to be assistant manager at Fiesta Espanola Restaurante from noon to 9 PM, M-F.

Larry (dim of Laurence, a town or laurel tree) and Jane (God has shown favor) Kelsey are in their early 60's and have lived in Pine City for 20 years. Their children are grown and live in other cities. Larry works at Triple A Plumbing and Heating from 8 to 5, M-F. Jane has been a Lamaze trainer and midwife with uncertain hours.

William Beckett, in his mid 50's is the founder and owner of Beckett CPA's. He is the father of Ruth Beckett, his eldest daughter who is 30 years old, has never been married and is the boss at her father's second office, Jason Beckett, who is 28 and is the boss at the third office, and Esther Beckett his youngest daughter who is 26 years old, has never been married and works at her father's second office with Beth in the first parts of the story. William's wife is Anna, who also in her mid 50's. She is a homemaker.

Candy Smith is a girl who is 12 years old. She is in a Safe/Care Home.

Miss Beth Davis is 40, has never been married, and has lived in Pine City 15 years. She is principal of the Grace 'n' Faith Christian School. She also teaches History and Geography.

Miss Pamela (Pam) Green is 26, and has never been married. She lived in Pine City for over 4 years. She taught second grade in public school before teaching third grade in Grace 'n' Faith Church School for a little over two years, and then had to leave for awhile.

Miss Laurel (Lora) Nelson is in her 30's has never been married. She has lived in Pine City for 11 years. She is the school nurse at Grace 'n' Faith Church School and also teaches Health and topics related to it.

Kippy (sleeps a lot) is a koala puppet, belonging to Julie Blake.

Cory is a handicapped seven-year-old boy, who is in a wheelchair at first.

Everywhere There's a Sunrise, Let's Tell The Good News!

Hana (bud, blossom) is Afta Suehiro's wife, and their son is Denji (bequest from ancestors.)

****

Linda L. Linn